CP/M and the Personal Computer
THOMAS A. DWYER · MARGOT CRITCHFIELD

CP/M and the Personal Computer

THOMAS A. DWYER · MARGOT CRITCHFIELD

ADDISON-WESLEY PUBLISHING COMPANY

Reading, Massachusetts · Menlo Park, California
London · Amsterdam · Don Mills, Ontario · Sydney

This book is in the
**Addison-Wesley Microcomputer Books
Popular Series**

SPONSORING EDITOR: Thomas A. Bell
COVER DESIGN: Marshall Henrichs
ILLUSTRATIONS: Margot Critchfield

Library of Congress Cataloging in Publication Data

Dwyer, Thomas A., 1923–
  CP/M and the personal computer.

  (Addison-Wesley microcomputer books popular series)
  Includes bibliographical references and index.
    1. CP/M (Computer program) 2. Microcomputers—
Programming. I. Critchfield, Margot. II. Title.
III. Title: CPM and the personal computer. IV. Title:
CP/M and the personal computer. V. Series.
QA76.6.D89 1983   001.64'25   82-20703
ISBN 0-201-10355-9

Second Printing, August 1983

Preface

Personal and business microcomputers are remarkable machines when you consider that all the odds say they really shouldn't work. For one thing, the performance of a modern micro depends on the precision with which millions of fleeting electrical pulses interact each second, never missing a beat as the seconds build into minutes, hours, or even days. Further, these pulses must mirror the logic of some of the most sophisticated algorithms ever developed by the human mind.

An even less appreciated problem is that the complexity of microcomputers has now reached the point where designers must work 90 percent on faith that *other* designers (say, of LSI chips) knew what they were doing, and these folks must work 90 percent on faith that . . . well, you get the picture. It's a tangled web the microcomputer age has woven for beginners and pros alike.

And yet we know that microcomputers do work—reliably and at imaginative levels that can be a joy to experience. The reason seems to be that we've learned to harness the complexities of micro systems by continually re-packaging their evolving structures as new entities, as deceptively simple building blocks that let newcomers tackle the best computing has to offer right from the start.

This is a book that invites you to master one of the most successful of these new building blocks, something called a *microcomputer disk operating system*. The particular operating system we'll investigate was originally called "Control Program for Microcomputers," but it is now known simply as CP/M.

A disk operating system like CP/M is actually a collection of several high-level building blocks. Each block is an easily accessed computer program that can be used in conjunction with the others to manage the operations of a disk-based microcomputer system. This collection functions something like the sets of tools used by professionals in other fields—say the oscilloscopes, signal generators, and wave form analyzers used by electronic specialists. How these tools are used is pretty much up to the person who uses them. In the case of CP/M, it's in the hands of the microcomputer user/programmer. Our goal is to help you master this challenge by explaining what tools CP/M includes, how they work, and how to apply them to business, professional, and personal computing.

This last goal is supported by a large number of lab exercises interspersed with "how it works" information throughout the book. The

vii

lab exercises give detailed instructions for carrying out useful projects, and they will work on just about any microcomputer that has disk drives and is able to run CP/M. Even if you don't have access to a CP/M machine, running through the labs as "thought exercises" will prove informative and useful.

There are also a number of question/answer sections and *instant quizzes* that reinforce the text. These are designed to support self-study in conjunction with the problems and projects at the ends of chapters. The practice provided by the labs, quizzes, problems and projects, together with the information given on how CP/M really works, are all meant to open the door to what could easily become one of the most fascinating experiences you've yet had with personal computing.

Acknowledgments

We wish to express our sincere thanks to Tom Bell, editor of the Addison-Wesley Microcomputer Books Series, for guiding this project through its many stages, and to Elydia Siegel, Cheryl Wurzbacher, and Marshall Henrichs for their technical and artistic expertise in making its final form so handsome. We are also grateful to Sol Libes, Blaise Liffick, and Helen Schwartz for their careful reviews of the manuscript, and their many valuable suggestions. Particular thanks go to Jerry Sales for the professional viewpoint he contributed to the accounting and spreadsheet sections of Chapter 4, and to Bob Hoffman for the technical insights he shared with us on so many occasions.

Pittsburgh, Pennsylvania   T.A.D.
January 1983   M.C.

Contents

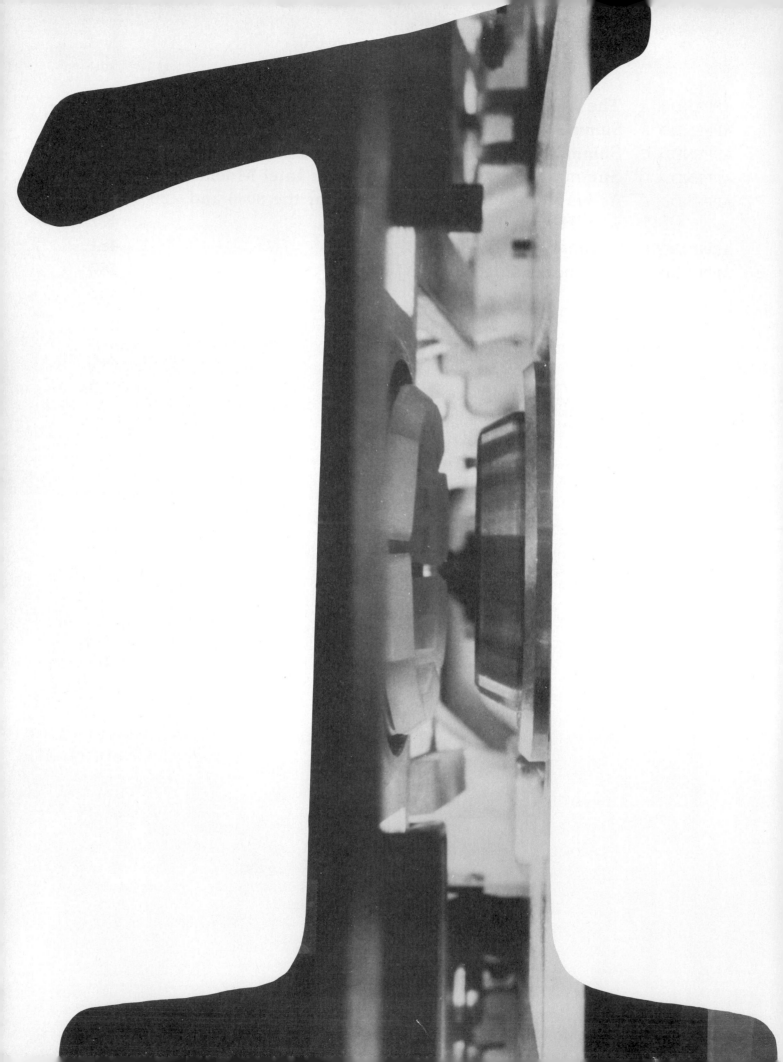

CHAPTER ONE
What Is CP/M?

1.0 Introduction

The goal of this book is to help users of both personal and business microcomputers master one of the most useful (but for beginners one of the most intimidating) features of any modern computer—something called a *disk operating system* (often abbreviated DOS).

The particular disk operating system we'll investigate is called CP/M. These letters originally meant "Control Program for Microcomputers," and that's still a pretty accurate description of what CP/M is. It's a computer program (or to be more accurate, a set of computer programs) that makes it easy to control some of the more advanced features of a modern microcomputer, including the ability to manipulate information stored on magnetic disks.

Disks come in a variety of sizes and formats. We will be concerned mainly with the low-cost "floppy" kind. What these are, and how they are used, will be explained shortly. Suffice it to say that adding disk drives and a disk operating system to a personal microcomputer is guaranteed to increase its power dramatically. The importance of CP/M is that it provides the tools for using this power with a minimum of effort.

There are a variety of features in the CP/M disk operating system, with most of them bearing rather cryptic names. Some are built into CP/M as "permanent" facilities (like the ERA command, which means "erase a disk file"), while some are "transient" programs that are called upon only when there is need to do more complicated jobs (like DDT, which means the "dynamic debugging tool" facility).

The names of the standard CP/M facilities are brief—usually six letters or less. This has resulted in a vocabulary that includes words like ERA, DIR, REN, SAVE, TYPE, STAT, ASM, LOAD, DDT, PIP, ED, SYSGEN, SUBMIT, DUMP, and MOVCPM. Further, each of these names represents a subsystem that has its own additional vocabulary.

The result is a jargon that's pretty confusing on first contact. The strangeness will disappear with repeated use, but in the beginning it helps to keep in mind that this new vocabulary is really a kind of slang. Like most slang, it grew out of usage, and it doesn't have formal roots. As a result, it has elements that are inelegant, illogical, and even inconsistent. Yet, in some strange way, most of the terminology will eventually seem to be OK, more "in your bones" than you would have allowed possible. When that happens you'll know there's no turning back; you've just become—for better or worse—a true CP/Mer.

PHOTO 1-1   This is a CP/M computer system assembled from components made by several manufacturers. The CP/M software is on the outer two tracks of the floppy disk being inserted into the lefthand disk drive (drive A). The rectangular enclosure resting on top of the two disk drives is an S-100 mainframe. This uses a standardized 100-wire system bus into which a large variety of S-100-type circuit boards can be plugged, making it easy to add extra memory, input/output circuits, graphics, or other special features.

1.1 What's CP/M Really Like? The Quick Tour

To get some feel for the role CP/M plays in a typical computing session, let's look over the shoulder of someone using a microcomputer that has CP/M as its disk operating system.

The particular computer we'll show is one of three example computer systems described in greater detail in Section 1.4. It's a mix-and-match component system based on what's called the S-100 bus (more about this later). The system was assembled* from components made by several different manufacturers, and it uses a "customized" version of CP/M supplied by the company that sells the disk components used in the system (Morrow Designs). Actually *all* versions of CP/M are customized, that is, matched to the computer hardware on which they're used. The idea is to hide the features of the hardware in the software, allowing users of different CP/M systems to work as if they were using similar machines.

---

* Assembling customized systems takes some technical know-how. Unless you've had experience with such things, it's best handled in collaboration with a knowledgeable friend or computer dealer. If neither of these is available, it may be better to stick to one of the packaged systems described later on.

Photo 1-1 shows our mix-and-match CP/M system being started up, using a procedure called *booting* (or *cold booting*) CP/M. This procedure varies with machines, but it's always easy to accomplish. In the case of the system shown in the photograph, all the user has to do is turn the power on, insert the floppy disk containing CP/M in the first disk drive (called drive A), and close the door. If, later on, the user wishes to get a fresh start without turning the machine off, another cold boot can be performed by pressing the *reset* button seen at the lower righthand corner of the main computer box.

After booting CP/M, the first thing a user sees on the computer's display screen is a message announcing which version of CP/M has just been loaded into the computer, followed by the two symbols A>. This is called the *system prompt*, and it can be interpreted to mean, "Don't just sit there—tell me [CP/M] what to do." Photo 1-2 shows the user responding by typing DIR and pressing the carriage return key. This causes CP/M to read the directory of "files" stored on the disk in drive A, print their names on the display screen, and then ask, "What next?" by printing the A> prompt again.

The bottom of Photo 1-2 shows the user responding to the second system prompt by typing RALLY(CR), where (CR) means "carriage return" key (the symbols <cr> are also used to represent the carriage return key). This is a command to CP/M to load a program file officially called

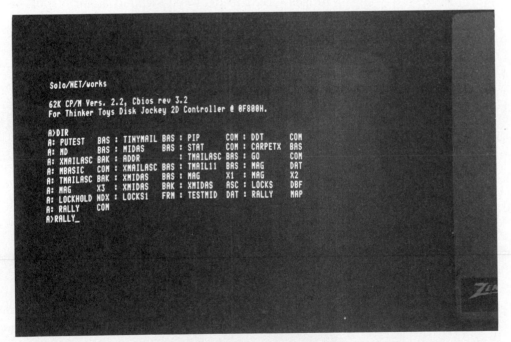

PHOTO 1-2   After the CP/M system is booted, a "sign-on" message appears on the screen of the system console, followed by the CP/M prompt symbols "A>". The console of this machine is a Zenith Z19 terminal which has a video output screen and a full-sized keyboard. The user has responded to the first system prompt by typing DIR, producing the disk directory. The filename RALLY was then typed after the second prompt. When the carriage return or enter key is pressed, CP/M will interpret this as a command to start executing the program stored as the file RALLY.COM.

RALLY.COM from the A disk into memory, and immediately start it running. The extension .COM is added to a file name to indicate that it's a program you can <u>com</u>mand to run simply by typing the first part of the name (up to .COM). The same idea holds for all the other .COM files you see listed in a directory. They've been stored in a form that makes them "self-executing," that is, ready to run as soon as their name is typed after the CP/M system prompt.

In our example, when RALLY(CR) is typed, CP/M temporarily loses control of the computer, and the program RALLY takes over. This happens to be a fun game that we'll tell you more about when we later discuss a computer language called "C". The main point to be noticed here is that CP/M frequently behaves more like a "master of ceremonies" than a "performer," serving mostly to introduce the next act (RALLY, in our example).

What happens next is up to the performer. In the case of RALLY, it responds by telling the user to press any key to get started, after which it runs a clever variation of an electronic road rally game.

We'll leave our quick tour of CP/M here, assuming that the users of the system we've shown are too engrossed in playing RALLY to do much useful work for a while. However, if and when they decide to try a different program, they can return to CP/M with a CONTROL-C (which means pressing the CONTROL and C keys simultaneously). This causes CP/M to do what's called a *warm boot*, returning the user to the

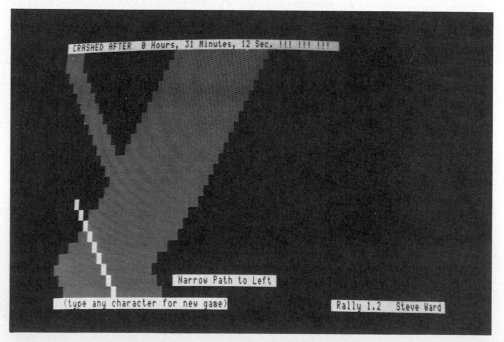

PHOTO 1-3   *This is a snapshot of the screen of a CP/M system on which the game RALLY is being played. The program was written in the BDS C language, discussed in Chapter 5. If the program is stored as a CP/M command file like RALLY.COM, it can be made to run merely by typing RALLY after the CP/M prompt symbol, A>. The program RALLY was written by Steve Ward. The BDS C compiler was written by Leor Zolman.*

CP/M operating system where the A> prompt appears again. This tells the user, "You can now type another command." As before, this command can either tell CP/M to provide one of its built-in services (like DIR), or to run another disk-based command program (like RALLY).

Getting Ready for Longer Sessions with CP/M

We'll be presenting detailed information about the CP/M commands and how to use them in those sections of the book that contain Lab Exercises. The first of these labs is found in Section 1.5. If you're anxious to get some immediate hands-on experience, you can skip to this section and read the intervening sections later on.

To prepare the way for those who'd like a little more background, there are three preparatory sections before the first lab. The first two (Sections 1.2 and 1.3) present general information about the computer hardware usually used with CP/M. The third (Section 1.4) gives specific information about the three example computer systems we'll be using to illustrate the labs, and gives some inside information about what happens when you boot a CP/M system.

1.2 Why CP/M? The Components of a Microcomputer System

As the RALLY example of the previous section showed, CP/M is not something you use by itself. Its real purpose is to help a user work with *other* software on a computer that uses disks for storage. An important (and legitimate) question to ask here is whether all CP/M systems work in the same way. In other words, is CP/M "machine- and application-independent"?

The answer is, "Yes—almost." The "almost" is there because of small variations in start-up procedures (like the one we called "booting the system"). There are also variations in how CP/M application software is distributed (for more information on this subject see Section 4.0). But, in general, the great virtue of CP/M is that it works on a large variety of machines, and with a large variety of software. As a consequence, just about everything you learn to do with it on Computer X applies to Computer Y. To see why this is a truly important development, let's take a look at all the hardware and software options a serious newcomer to microcomputing faces these days.

The physical parts of a computer system—the things you can see and touch—are called *hardware*. The sets of instructions that tell the hardware what to do are called computer programs. Collections of computer programs are also referred to as *software*.

There are two general classes of software: *application software* and *system software*. Application software consists of programs that instruct a computer how to carry out a specific task, say, to do word processing, produce payroll checks, or play a game (like RALLY). Examples of some

FIG. 1-1   Diagram of components available for use in a modern microcomputer system.

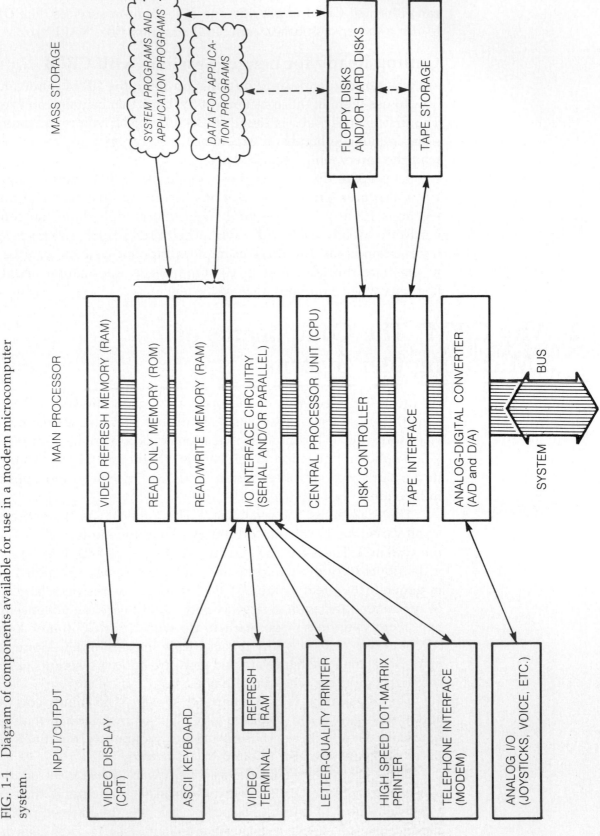

of the application software available for use on CP/M systems will be given in Chapter 4.

System software consists of programs that help a computer user develop application programs, and control how they "interface" with the hardware. The three principal examples of system software we'll discuss in this book are CP/M, MBASIC, and BDS C. MBASIC is a system for developing and running programs written in disk-extended BASIC, while BDS C makes it possible to compile and run programs written in the language "C". MBASIC and C are both discussed in Chapter 5.

The diagram in Fig. 1-1 shows that there can be quite a few hardware components in a modern microcomputer system. It helps to group these components into three categories, which we've labeled *INPUT/OUTPUT*, *MAIN PROCESSOR*, and *MASS STORAGE*.

TECHNICAL NOTE

One of the most common pieces of jargon you'll come across in computer-related writing is the term "ASCII." Although it is frequently pronounced like the word "ask-key," the letters really stand for "American Standard Code for Information Interchange." This is a scheme that was established by a committee of the American National Standards Institute in 1968. They defined 128 binary codes for use in communicating character by character information. The codes can be written as the 7-bit binary numbers from 0000000 to 1111111, as the decimal numbers from 0 to 127, or as the hexadecimal numbers from 00 to 7F. For example, the ASCII code for the letter "A" can be written as 1000001 binary, 65 decimal, or 41 hex. The decimal and hex forms are useful in programming, but the binary form is valuable in hardware design, since it shows which electrical on/off signals should be used to represent each ASCII code. For example, to store the character "A" in one byte of memory, either the 8-bit pattern 01000001 or 11000001 may be used, since in both cases the rightmost seven bits give the correct ASCII code (the first bit can either be ignored or used for what's called "parity error checking"). Similarly, to send the letter "A" to a printer (or receive it from a keyboard), electrical voltages that correspond to the ASCII code bits can be placed on a connecting cable made up of seven *parallel* wires (plus ground). It's also possible to send these codes on a single wire (plus ground) by sending the 7-bit codes in carefully timed sequences. Data transmissions of this kind are called *serial*.

Appendix A shows the 128 ASCII codes in binary, decimal, and hex forms. The codes with values from 0 to 31 decimal are used for control functions (for example, to ring a bell on the terminal or to cause a carriage return). The codes from 32 to 127 decimal are used to represent printable characters, including the decimal digits, upper- and lowercase letters, and special characters or punctuation marks. ASCII codes can be manipulated by computer software. For example, to convert from an ASCII decimal code to its corresponding character in a BASIC program, the CHR$ function is used. The BASIC statement PRINT CHR$ (65); CHR$(7); CHR$(10); CHR$(13) will print the letter "A", ring the bell, and cause a line feed followed by a carriage return. The inverse function in BASIC is called ASC. The BASIC statement PRINT ASC("A"); ASC("B"); ASC("C") will cause the numbers 65, 66, 67 to be printed on the console.

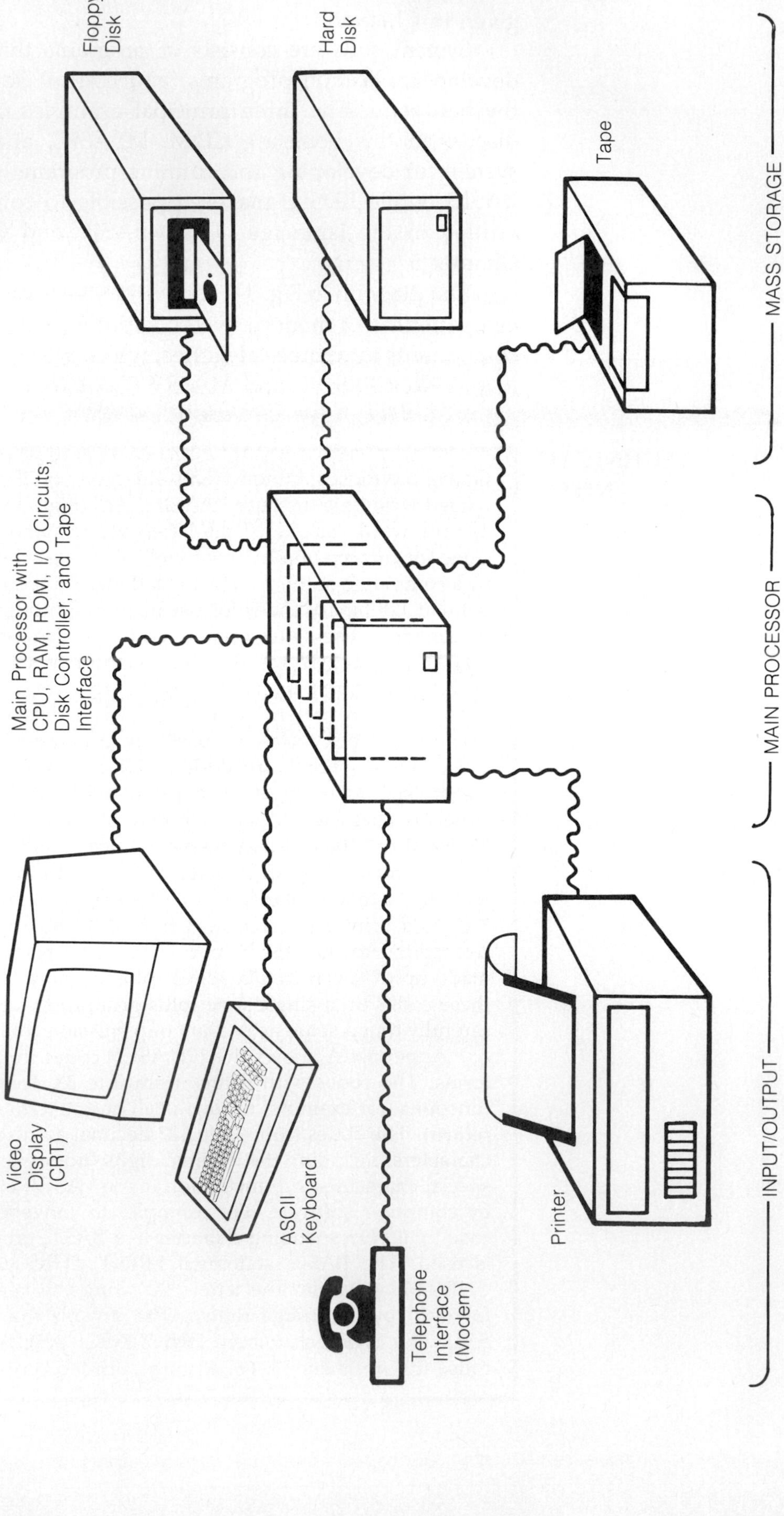

FIG. 1-2   Example of a microcomputer system using some of the components shown in the chart of Fig. 1-1. Other examples are shown in Figs. 1-4 and 1-5.

Not every computer will have all the components shown in the diagram, but even the simplest system will have all the categories represented. Computers assembled from a "mix-and-match" selection of components will usually have the three groups enclosed in physically distinct cabinets, while "packaged" systems may combine components from different categories in the same enclosure. In Section 1.4 we'll describe three specific systems that illustrate these two approaches.

The function of INPUT components is to make it easy for people to feed data and/or programs into the computer. The most common form of input device is called an ASCII keyboard (because the codes it generates conform to the American Standard Code for Information Interchange). OUTPUT components are used for viewing the results of processing the data in printed and graphical form. The two most common output devices are video displays (similar to TV screens) and "hard copy" printers.

One of the least appreciated features of a modern microcomputer is its diversified memory structure. This is where both data and the "intelligence" (programs) that say how to manipulate this data are stored. A few special programs are kept in *read only memory* (ROM) where they are available for immediate use. However, most programs and data are normally stored on a mass storage device such as magnetic *disk*, and they must be copied into the computer's internal *random access memory* (RAM) before they can be worked on by the *central processing unit* (CPU). New or modified data that results from this processing is recorded back on the mass storage device for future use. The storage of both programs and data on disks is organized in logical groupings called *files*, and one of the principal functions of CP/M is to make it easy to manipulate these files.

We'll have more to say about the use of hardware, and terms like *disk, file, RAM, ROM,* and *CPU* in later sections of the book. The main point to be made here is that anyone who buys a system like this has a problem—it's complicated! Each of the components shown is actually a complex piece of electronic (and sometimes mechanical) technology in itself. Getting all of these components to work together in harmony could be an incredibly difficult problem.

Fortunately, a solution to this problem has been developed in recent years. It comes in the form of system software like CP/M which helps the user manage the hardware, write application programs, and keep track of files. In particular, CP/M contains programs to handle input and output, programs to manage the use of disk storage (a very complicated business), an editor program to help users create or modify files, programs to debug other programs, a program to move programs and data from one place to another, programs to translate from assembly to machine language and back again, and so on. CP/M also makes it easy to add other software to your system, including translator programs for languages like BASIC and C, word processors, games, and a host of business applications.

With this many advantages, an obvious question to raise at this point is whether every microcomputer system can use CP/M. The answer is "No." To see which machines can, let's next say something about the various categories of microcomputers available today, and indicate on which hardware configurations CP/M works best.

1.3 Which Computers Can Use CP/M?

Personal and small business computers have come a long way since their introduction in the late 1970s, and there is now a bewildering array of choices facing the microcomputer enthusiast. The question, "Which is the best machine for me?" has almost as many answers as the number of people asking it. But if we assume that the person asking the question wants as much "professional power" per dollar as possible, the choice becomes a lot simpler.

The graph in Fig. 1-3 shows why this is so. It plots the professional power of computers (a phrase we'll explain shortly) against cost. As you'll notice, there are several plateaus in the graph. You'll also see that CP/M can be used when you get to the second plateau, but that its "best use" range corresponds to plateau 3. So the question of whether CP/M is for you is tied in with the question of which plateau you'd like to aim for in selecting (or upgrading) your computer system.

The circled plateau numbers 1, 2, 3, 4, and 5 on the diagram correspond to categories based on real microcomputer systems. Let's discuss these a bit.

Category 1 starts with the new low-cost home computers (e. g., the Sinclair and the VIC-20) at one end, and goes up to the packaged

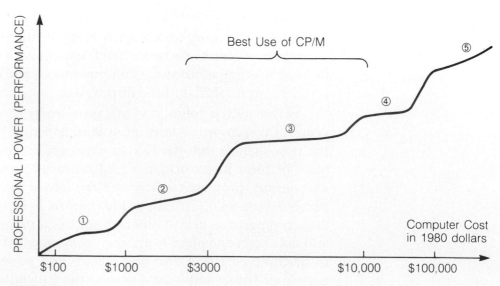

FIG. 1-3 Graph of plateaus in personal computer performance as a function of cost.

machines that sell for approximately $1000 (e. g., the TRS-80 Model III, the Atari 800, the PET, the Apple II, and other entry-level home computer systems that do *not* include disk drives or printers).

Category 2 consists of machines similar to those in category 1, except that disk drives have been added. These drives usually use 5 1/4-inch mini-floppy disks (also called mini-diskettes). Modified versions of CP/M can often be obtained for such systems. In some cases, hardware modifications must also be made to the original computer (e. g., by adding the Microsoft SoftCard to an Apple II with disks). This is an attractive choice for those who already own such machines, but there are some compromises involved. If you're starting from scratch, it's a better idea to seriously consider category 3.

The things that distinguish category 3 are superior input/output facilities, lots of memory, a high-speed CPU, and large-capacity disk

TECHNICAL NOTE

In addition to having disk drives, a computer that is going to use CP/M should have at least 32K bytes (48K to 64K is preferred) of user memory (RAM) which starts at address 0000. The abbreviation K means 1024, so a 64K memory has 65,536 bytes. A byte is equivalent to 8 binary digits, called bits. A good way to evaluate memory size to is know that it takes one byte to store one character of text.

Another requirement for running CP/M is that the computer use an "8080 compatible" microprocessor. CP/M was originally written for use with the Intel Development System which used the 8080 microprocessor. The machine language for the 8080 is compatible with the newer 8085 and Z80 microprocessors, so CP/M will also run on machines that use these processors. To run CP/M on the Apple II (which uses the 6502 microprocessor) special cards containing the Z80 and some extra memory must be used.

There is also a version of CP/M called CP/M-86 written for machines that use the 16-bit 8086 or 8088 microprocessor chips. These chips use 16-bit internal registers, and must be programmed with a machine language instruction set different from that used by the 8080, 8085, and Z80. Externally, the 8086 uses a 16-bit data bus, whereas the 8088 uses the same 8-bit data bus as the original 8080. The IBM Personal Computer uses the 8088, so it can run CP/M-86.

In summary, if your computer uses an 8080, 8085, or Z80 microprocessor chip, the original CP/M can probably be used on your machine. If your computer uses the 8086 or 8088, CP/M-86 can probably be used. The word "probably" was used in both these statements because it's always true that before CP/M can be used on any computer, it first must be adapted ("customized") to the specific disk controller and I/O hardware of the system. The customization is done either by the manufacturer of the complete computer system, by the manufacturer of the disk controller used on the system, or by a software vendor that sells CP/M customized for a specific machine (e. g., the TRS-80 Model II). On machines where RAM memory does not begin at location 0000 (e. g., the TRS-80 Model III), "memory mapping" hardware modifications are also needed before CP/M can be used.

FIG. 1-4 An example of a component microcomputer system based on the S-100 bus. The bus is a set of 100 parallel conductors plated on a printed circuit *mother board.* This board has anywhere from 6 to 22 sockets attached to the bus, each of which can accept a standard S-100 card. There are S-100 cards containing CPUs, RAM,

ROM, multiple I/O circuits, disk controllers, graphics controllers, electronic calendar/clocks, and so on. These should be purchased from companies that adhere to what's called the IEEE-696/S-100 bus standard to insure that they all use the S-100 bus lines in the same way.

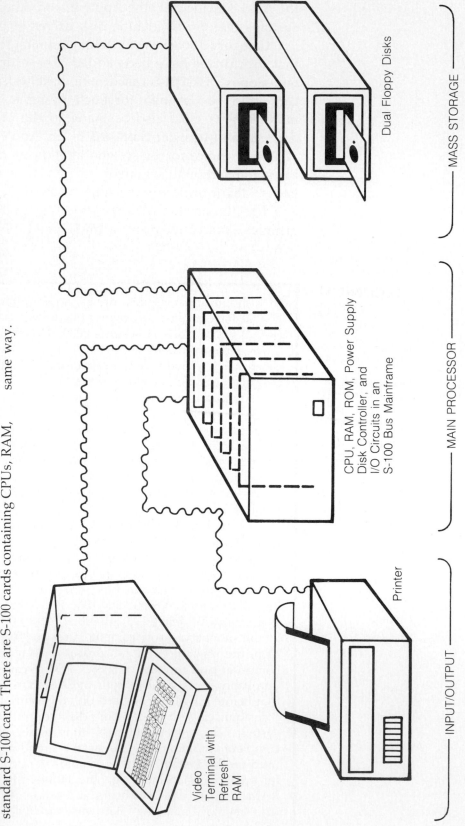

MASS STORAGE

Dual Floppy Disks

MAIN PROCESSOR

CPU, RAM, ROM, Power Supply
Disk Controller, and
I/O Circuits in an
S-100 Bus Mainframe

INPUT/OUTPUT

Video
Terminal with
Refresh
RAM

Printer

PHOTO 1-4   *The Zenith Z89 and Z100 computers (also available from Heathkit Company) have CP/M available for use on a 5 1/4-inch diskette. The Z100 also features five S-100 expansion slots, and high resolution color graphics. The Z100 is shown in the color plates.*

drive systems. Most experienced users of microcomputers consider category 3 as the best goal to shoot for simply because it gives the serious computer user the most capability for the dollar. Moving into category 3 is analogous to upgrading from a consumer oriented hi-fi record player to a customized audio system assembled from top-of-the-line components. In both cases, the cost is higher, but the excellence of the resulting system is well worth it for the serious user.

A good example of a category 3 computer is a customized system based on what are called "S-100 components." These components can be chosen from a wide variety of manufacturers, and we'll give a detailed example of one such choice in the next section. However, it is also possible to buy category 3 systems in the form of complete packages, such as the Ithaca Pascal Development System or the Intecolor 8000 Series Business Color Systems. These Intecolor machines are of particular interest because of their excellent color graphics output capability, and we'll be showing some examples of their use in later sections.

We'll not discuss categories 4, 5, 6, . . . (and on up!) since, by definition, these involve costs anywhere from $20,000 to $2,000,000. These computers are also likely to be multi-user, multi-process systems, so they would require use of disk operating systems more complicated than CP/M (e. g., the UNIX system developed at Bell Laboratory).

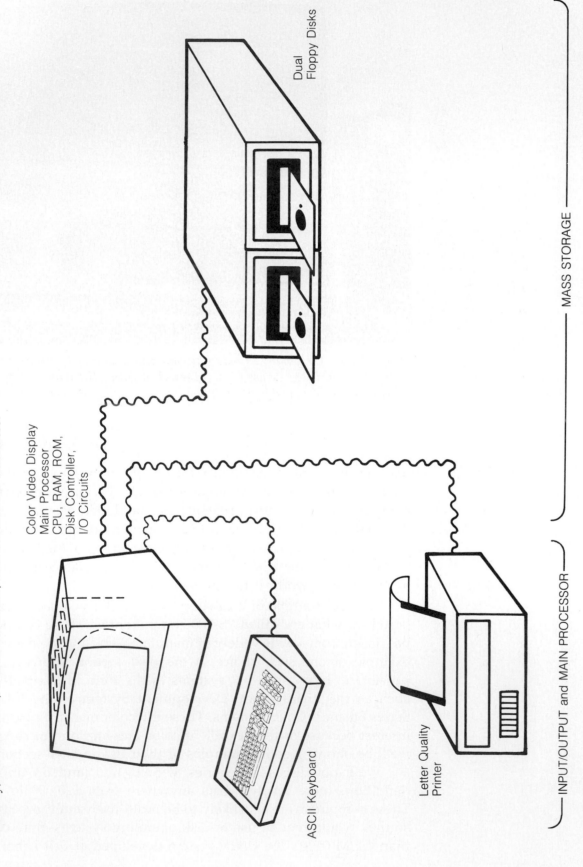

FIG. 1-5 An example of a packaged CP/M system based on the ISC Intecolor 8063 Series microcomputer. The color display unit also contains 64K of user memory, an 8080 CPU, a disk controller, and several I/O interfaces.

PHOTO 1-5   *The Ithaca Intersystems computer uses the S-100 bus, with a Z80 CPU and two 8-inch floppy disk drives. It employs an advanced version of CP/M with a feature called "Cache BIOS." The* cache *is extra RAM memory used as a disk buffer. The most recently used tracks of disk data are stored in this buffer, resulting in very short access times for reading or writing data on these tracks.*

1.4 Getting Ready for the Labs; Cold and Warm Boots; Three Examples of CP/M Computer Systems

The lab exercises in the pages ahead are meant as self-study guides for learning to use the facilities of CP/M. Wherever possible, they also illustrate the use of CP/M to solve a practical problem. For this reason, the labs are presented as complete sessions rather than isolated segments. This sometimes results in repetitions, but we felt it better to err in this direction than clutter up the labs with too many cross-references to material presented in another part of the book.

If you have access to a "CP/M-speaking" machine, we strongly recommend that you run through all the lab exercises "on-line," that is, by doing everything right at the computer console (the keyboard/display unit) of your machine. Even if the computer system you're using differs from those shown here, you'll find that most of the ideas work in a similar manner. If you don't presently have access to a computer that runs CP/M, then try doing the exercises as what scientists used to call "gedanken experiments"—as "thought" exercises in which you think things through in the same sequence that would occur if you were working with the real thing.

The three computer systems we've chosen to illustrate the lab exercises represent three very different approaches to hardware design. But, as will be seen, this makes very little difference in the lab exercises themselves. Except for a few minor variations in startup procedures (explained at the end of this section), machines that run CP/M behave quite similarly from the user's point of view.

This is a very powerful idea, and it's the main reason for putting up with the complexities of CP/M. Any time you're tempted to go back to a simpler way of computer life, just remind yourself that (a) in a few months it will all seem like child's play, and (b) the extra study is a small price to pay for mastering one of the most important developments in the history of microcomputing, namely a software system that allows users of radically different machines to share ideas based on a common experience.

The Three Lab Computers

The computer systems we're using for the labs are shown in the accompanying photographs. The first one (Photo 1-6) is what's sometimes called a *modular*, or *component*, computer. It consists of S-100 type "mainframe" components (memory, central processor, power supply, and enclosure) made by California Computer Systems, disk drives and a disk controller from Morrow Designs Co., a Z19 video terminal made by Zenith Data Systems, and a Diablo Model 630 daisy-wheel printer.

The second computer (Photo 1-7) started out in life as an Apple II, but it has been converted to a CP/M machine by adding extra memory and the Z80 SoftCard sold by Microsoft Company. The third example

PHOTO 1-6   *This is a modular S-100-type system using a Z80 CPU, 64K bytes of RAM, two double-density 8-inch disk drives, and a video CRT (cathode ray tube) console. The two disks can hold over one million bytes of data in single-sided format, and over two million bytes in double-sided format. A large variety of extra features can be added to the system by plugging additional S-100 cards into the mainframe.*

PHOTO 1-7   *The Apple II computer can be converted into a 44K CP/M system with MBASIC by plugging the SoftCard (a circuit board that includes a Z80 microprocessor) into one of its slots. If an additional memory card is also plugged in, the total size of the CP/M system is 56K. There is also a 60K SoftCard with the extra memory "on board."*

PHOTO 1-8   *Professional quality color graphics can be added to CP/M systems by using a high quality color terminal (such as the Intecolor ISC 8001) as the console on any standard CP/M system. A complete, packaged 64K CP/M color system is also available as the model 8063 ISC system shown. It includes two 8-inch double-density floppy disk drives, available in either single- or double-sided format. The CPU, computer memory, and I/O circuits are all inside the console cabinet. A large extended keyboard is used to make it easy to control the special color graphics features. Examples of ISC graphics output are shown in the color plates.*

FIG. 1-6   Relation between CP/M, its general built-in facilities, and specialized subsystem facilities. Many subsystems have sub-subsystems, so this diagram could be extended several levels lower than shown. When you are finished using a subsystem, you usually return to the system level by doing a warm boot (by pressing the CONTROL and C keys). At this point you can use a built-in CP/M facility like DIR, or go back "down" to another subsystem. For example, you could use the CP/M Transient called PIP (explained in Chapter 2) to make safety copies of any files you created while in the previous subsystem (e. g., a letter you just wrote while using a word processor).

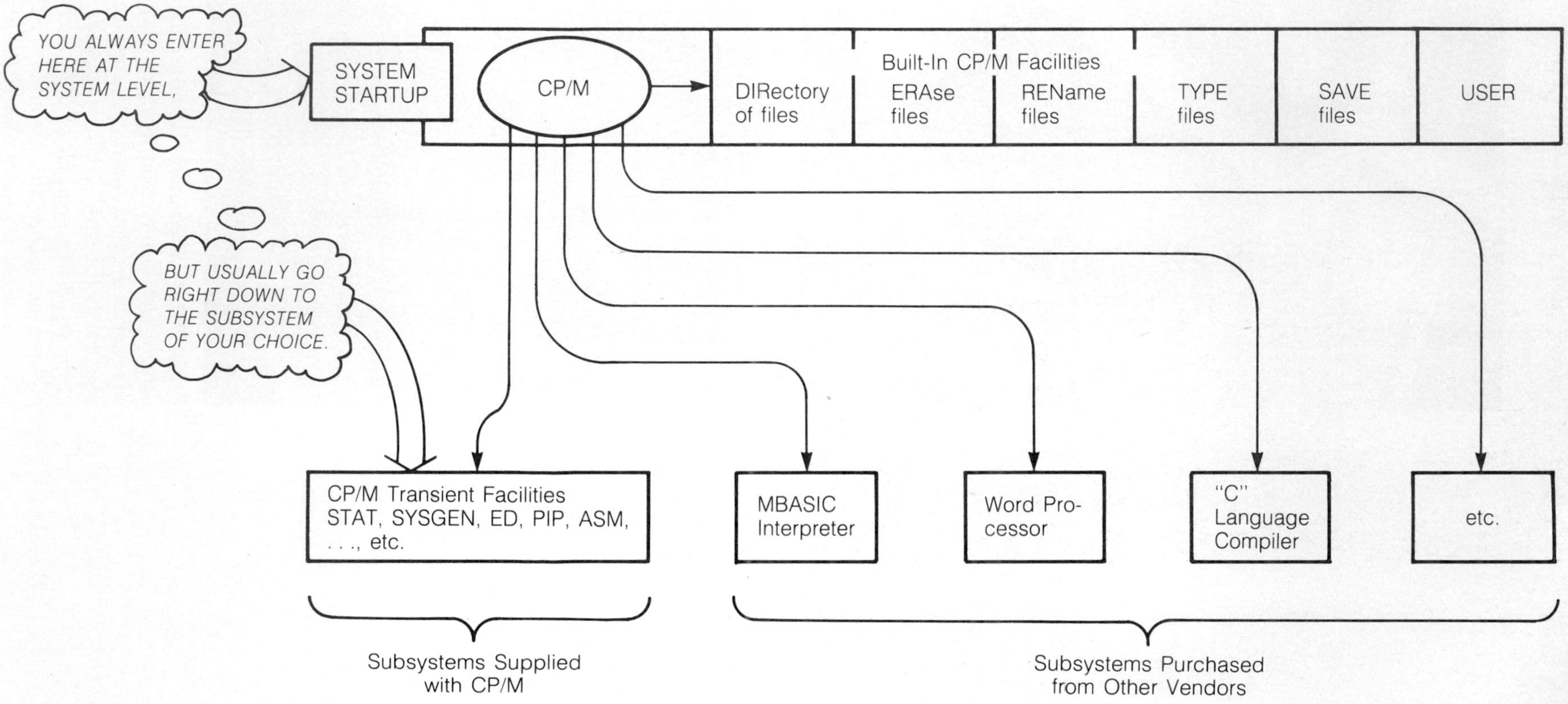

SYSTEM STARTUP

CP/M

Built-In CP/M Facilities

DIRectory of files | ERAse files | REName files | TYPE files | SAVE files | USER

YOU ALWAYS ENTER HERE AT THE SYSTEM LEVEL.

BUT USUALLY GO RIGHT DOWN TO THE SUBSYSTEM OF YOUR CHOICE.

CP/M Transient Facilities STAT, SYSGEN, ED, PIP, ASM, ..., etc.

Subsystems Supplied with CP/M

MBASIC Interpreter | Word Pro-cessor | "C" Language Compiler | etc.

Subsystems Purchased from Other Vendors

18

(Photo 1-8) is a professional-level color computer, the Intecolor 8063 made by Intelligent Systems Corporation (ISC). All three machines are able to use Microsoft Disk-Extended BASIC (also called BASIC-80 and MBASIC), a bonus that comes from the fact that BASIC-80 is one of the many high-level computer languages that "run under CP/M." Later on, we'll show examples of other languages that run under CP/M, including a fascinating newcomer called "C".

The Relation Between CP/M and Other Software

One possible source of confusion that could arise in some of the labs is the fact that CP/M doesn't seem to do much by itself; its main contribution appears to be one of loading and running other software. For example, the most useful part of the first lab will seem to take place when you leave CP/M and use the MBASIC interpreter "under CP/M." The same situation will hold in other labs, particularly when sophisticated application packages such as word processors are (here's that phrase again) "run under CP/M." Before going any further, let's try to clarify the relationship between CP/M and the software that runs under it.

What the word "under" really means is that these software packages are able to call upon CP/M to provide the special routines needed to move data to and from the computer's peripheral devices, particularly those connected with disk operations and console I/O (input/output). This way, software authors don't have to know anything about your specific I/O hardware; instead they write their programs in terms of CP/M specifications, assuming that the details connected with disk and I/O routines will be taken care of inside the CP/M that was tailored to your machine.

The use of these special routines is invisible to the person running the program. In fact, for someone whose main interest is in applications, the principal function of CP/M will seem to be one of selecting and loading application programs from their place of storage on disk. This is why the start-up procedure on a CP/M computer first puts you in contact with CP/M itself, at which time you're said to be working at the *system level*. A number of useful things can be done at the system level, but most of the time you'll want to use CP/M to put you in contact with more specialized "subsystems" (e. g., a BASIC language interpreter or a word processor). The big advantage to this arrangement is that new subsystems can be added any time you wish, and the only change to the operating system you'll notice is that a new name has been added to the directory of subsystems you now have available.

From the point of view of the user, dealing with CP/M is something like dealing with the receptionists and clerks at the entrance level of a business building. They can answer some questions and perform a few "built-in" services, but when there's need for more specialized treatment, they'll more than likely send you to another level. The result is that the number of special services can be almost unlimited. Fig. 1-6 shows how this concept applies to some of the subsystems which run under CP/M.

Question

That sounds like overkill. If all I want to do with my computer is write and run BASIC programs, isn't CP/M a layer of complexity I can do without?

Answer

Yes. As a matter of fact the Microsoft company will be happy to sell you a version of MBASIC called "Standalone BASIC" that works without CP/M. Most lower-priced computers operate in a similar manner: as soon as you turn them on they put you in contact with BASIC and there's no need to deal with an operating system. But keep in mind that removing the system-level layer of "software bureaucracy" has its price. Unlike many other bureaucratic structures, operating systems can be powerful and useful allies, well worth the extra complexity they seem to introduce. This advantage will become clearer in the later lab exercises as additional features of CP/M and the many subsystems it supports are introduced.

Cold and Warm Boots

Now that we have some feel for the role of CP/M as a software system that makes it easy to use all kinds of *other* software, let's address the question of what makes it possible to use CP/M itself. Or to say it another way, how do you start using the software that makes it possible to start using software?

The process of getting CP/M up and running is usually called "booting the CP/M system," and it must be done whenever the computer is first turned on, or when certain difficulties cause the need for a fresh start. The purpose of booting (or, as it is also called, "cold booting") is to copy the CP/M system from disk into the computer's read/write random access memory (RAM), and start it running.

However, there's a problem. When a computer is first turned on, its random access memory has nothing in it—it's a clean slate, or to be more correct, a jumble of nonsense bits caused by the previous removal of power from RAM. This means that the machine has no "intelligence" in the form of either system or application programs. There are undoubtedly plenty of programs on disk, but these can't be used by the CPU until they are first brought into RAM.

Unfortunately, reading software from disk and writing it into RAM is a complicated process. In fact it's a process that itself requires a fairly sophisticated program. The CP/M system includes such a program (called a loader), but when you first turn the computer on, the CP/M loader is also on disk, so it's of no use until it too gets into RAM! We are obviously caught in a kind of chicken-before-the-egg dilemma. Or to use the analogy that motivated the term "bootstrapping," we seem to

be faced with the impossible task of lifting ourselves up by our own bootstraps.

There are two solutions to this dilemma. They both involve sneaking a small *bootstrap program* into memory—one that is just "smart" enough to read the loader program from disk into the lower part of RAM. After this is done, the loader program is told to start executing. What it then does is to read the rest of CP/M from disk into the top of RAM, and start the part called the "console command processor" (CCP) running. Once that's accomplished, we're in business. Our hardware now has CP/M in RAM as its "brains," and from then on we've got a real computer.

The two ways in which the bootstrap program is gotten into the computer are "by hand" and "by ROM." The hand method involves "toggling" the bootstrap in, which means flipping toggle (up–down) switches on the front panel in a sequence that corresponds to the binary form of the bootstrap program. This is a pretty primitive approach, and most modern computers use the ROM form of bootstrap instead. They do this by storing the bootstrap program on a ROM (read only memory) chip which does *not* lose its contents when power is interrupted. The bootstrap program stored on this ROM chip can be accessed by the CPU, and it can be made to start executing by pressing only one or two switches. On many computers the only switch that needs to be pressed is labeled RESET. On the Intecolor computer two buttons are pushed: CPU RESET followed by AUTO. The Zenith/Heathkit (Z89) is booted by typing the letter "B" at the console. On S-100 systems using the Morrow disk controller, merely closing the door on the disk drive causes the bootstrap program to execute. S-100 systems with front panels usually require that you push two switches labeled RESET and RUN. On the Apple II with the autostart ROM, just turning the power on makes the bootstrap loader operate. As you can see, machines differ in this detail, so you'll want to check out the exact "booting" procedure in your computer reference manual. In all cases, you must of course put the CP/M disk in drive A *before* following the bootstrap procedure.

Whatever the technique, we'll refer to this process from now on as *doing a cold boot*, or as *booting the system*. The word "cold" is used because originally it referred to the startup needed on a machine that had been completely turned off. However, a cold boot can be performed any time, and the term is now used to distinguish it from something called a *warm boot*.

We'll explain the technical difference between a cold boot and a warm boot in Chapter 3. Suffice it to say for now that a warm boot is done on a machine that is already up and running, and it's usually accomplished by pressing CONTROL-C (which means press the C on the keyboard while simultaneously holding down the CONTROL key). A warm boot is used to reload *part* of CP/M, giving the user a semi-fresh start. A warm boot works only on a computer that has already been loaded with a cold boot, and which still has the part of CP/M in

RAM called BIOS (which means the Basic Input Output System of CP/M). A warm boot is used to exit a program and return to the system level (also called the *command level*) of CP/M. It's also required every time you change disks.

In summary then, when you first start using a CP/M system you must perform a cold boot. This is accomplished on most computers by turning the power on, inserting the CP/M disk, and pushing one or two buttons. When you finish executing a program, or when you change disks, you should do a warm boot. This is usually accomplished by pressing CONTROL-C (sometimes written as CTRL-C or ^C). The photographs and captions in Lab Exercise 1.5-1 show exactly how this works on our three example systems. The lab also shows that the procedures for using CP/M on different machines are very similar once the system is booted. In fact, the booting procedure is one of the few things that differs from machine to machine; as you'll soon see, it is a small detail in the overall picture of using CP/M.

1.5 What's CP/M Really Like? A Hands-On Lab Tour

We now have all the background we need to get started on some real labs on real machines. The first lab exercise will direct you in the use of two of the "built-in" features of CP/M (DIR and REN), and one of the "transient" features (STAT). It will also show how to use the MBASIC subsystem under CP/M to write and test a short BASIC program. There will be seven steps in the lab:

1. Turning the system on and "booting" CP/M.
2. Using the DIR (directory) feature of CP/M to make sure BASIC is available, and using STAT to see how much disk storage is available.
3. Loading the BASIC subsystem.
4. Creating and running a BASIC program.
5. Saving the BASIC program as a CP/M file.
6. Returning to CP/M, rechecking the directory, and using REN to rename a file.
7. Returning to BASIC and using BASIC's LOAD command to retrieve the BASIC program.

It will turn out that step 1 is the only one that differs from computer to computer, so this step will be given in three parts corresponding to our three sample computer systems. Since all of our systems have the Microsoft version of BASIC (MBASIC), the program we'll use for illustrating step 4 will run equally well on all three machines. The only differences you'll see will be in the appearance of the output on the display screens. The S-100 system has a standard 24-line by 80-column display, while the Apple has 24 lines by 40 columns. The Intecolor has 48 lines and 80 columns, and it's also able to produce its output in glorious color (an example showing how to use the Intecolor for color graphics is given in problem 8 of Section 1.6).

So much for the briefing. Here's the actual lab with the five steps spelled out in detail. The start and finish of this and all the other labs in the book are marked by the two "transfer of momentum" diagrams seen below and on page 30.

| SAFETY NOTE | You shouldn't do this lab using your original CP/M disk. A backup copy should be used instead. If you don't have a backup copy, get a knowledgeable friend to help you make one using the techniques explained in Chapter 2. |

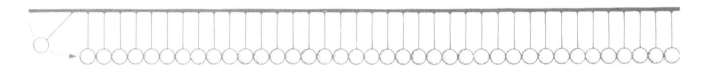

LAB EXERCISE 1.5-1

Writing and Running a BASIC Program under CP/M

Step 1.   Turn the system on, insert the CP/M disk in drive A, and boot the system. (This step is a little different for the Apple II; see the caption for Photo 1-10.)

"Turn the system on" means make sure that all the cables have been properly connected between different parts of the system, that all the power cords are plugged into outlets of the right voltages, and that the appropriate power switches are turned on. Next insert the CP/M disk in drive A. The word *drive* refers to the mechanism used for spinning the disk, and reading or writing information on it. On multi-drive systems, drives are labelled A, B, C, D, etc. Drive A is always used with a disk that contains CP/M, so it's sometimes called the system drive. The photos show which is drive A on our sample systems. In multi-drive systems, it's usually the leftmost or topmost unit.

The terms *disk*, *diskette*, or *floppy disk* refer to the thin black square object you see in the person's hand. There should be a label on it saying something like "AJAX CP/M 48K VERSION 2.2", and the label should face up. (For vertically mounted disk drives the label should face the side on which the drive door is hinged.) In either case, the edge of the disk nearest the read/write slot opening goes in first, which means the label goes in last. Incidentally, the actual floppy disk is a round piece of magnetically coated plastic inside the square jacket, but this jacket is never removed. Floppy disks should be handled very gently. In particular, don't touch the exposed surfaces of the inner magnetic "platter."

PHOTO 1-9   *The S-100 system shown is booted by turning the power on, inserting the CP/M disk in drive A, and closing the drive door. It can later be re-booted by pressing the lighted* reset *button in the lower righthand corner of the mainframe box (seen sitting on top of the two disk drives). Disk drive A is on the left, and disk drive B is on the right.*

PHOTO 1-10   *The Apple II computer is booted in an unorthodox way. Turn the power off, put the CP/M disk in drive A (the top drive in the photograph), close the door, and then turn the power on. If you have an Apple II Plus or an Apple II with autostart ROM, CP/M will then boot automatically. If you have a standard Apple II without autostart ROM, you must also press the RESET key, and then type 6, CONTROL-K, and RETURN.*

PHOTO 1-11 *The ISC computer is booted by turning the power on, inserting the CP/M disk in drive A, pressing the CPU RESET button, and then pressing the AUTO button. Disk drive A is on the left, B is on the right.*

Gently and slowly insert the disk into the drive until you feel a gentle click, after which you should shut the door of the disk drive. (Never insert a disk into a drive unless the red "head activity" light is either off, or only blinking.) It's a good idea to get someone to show you how to do this step. The best rule to follow in dealing with mechanical devices of this sort is, "Don't force anything."

As you know by now, "boot the system" translates into, "Do whatever your system manual says is necessary to get CP/M started." The procedures vary from machine to machine, but they all have the same purpose: to transfer a copy of the CP/M operating system from disk into the computer's memory, and start it running. The exact procedures for booting our three example systems are given in the captions to Photos 1-9, 1-10, and 1-11.

Once CP/M is booted, all control is transferred to the *system console*, that is, to the keyboard/screen control unit of the computer. From then on, the differences between various computers pretty well vanish. In all cases, you'll know the booting procedure has worked if disk drive A makes some clicking noises, followed by the appearance of a message on the output screen of the console. This will be something like "ACME 56K CP/M VERSION 2.2", followed by the CP/M prompting symbols A>.

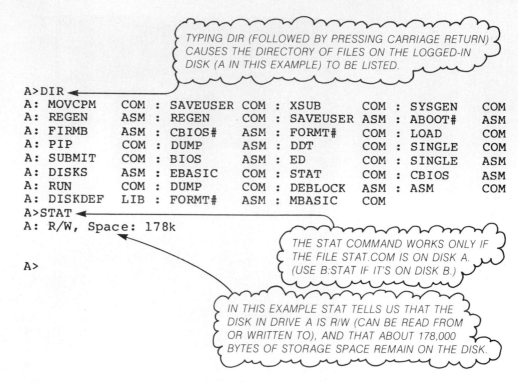

```
A>DIR
A: MOVCPM    COM : SAVEUSER COM : XSUB       COM : SYSGEN   COM
A: REGEN     ASM : REGEN    COM : SAVEUSER ASM : ABOOT#   ASM
A: FIRMB     ASM : CBIOS#   ASM : FORMT#   COM : LOAD     COM
A: PIP       COM : DUMP     ASM : DDT      COM : SINGLE   COM
A: SUBMIT    COM : BIOS     ASM : ED       COM : SINGLE   ASM
A: DISKS     ASM : EBASIC   COM : STAT     COM : CBIOS    ASM
A: RUN       COM : DUMP     COM : DEBLOCK  ASM : ASM      COM
A: DISKDEF   LIB : FORMT#   ASM : MBASIC   COM
A>STAT
A: R/W, Space: 178k

A>
```

FIG. 1-7 Use of the DIR and STAT commands to get information about the files on disk A. The directory shown in this example indicates that the disk has two BASIC interpreter files (called EBASIC.COM and MBASIC.COM). To obtain similar information about the disk in drive B, the commands DIR B: and STAT B: would be used.

Step 2.   Next look at a disk directory to see if there's a BASIC command file on your disk. No matter what system you're using, you do this by typing DIR(CR) after the A> prompting symbols, where (CR) means press the carriage return key (also called the ENTER key). This will cause a directory of files to print as shown in Fig. 1-7.

You'll know that you have BASIC available if there's a file with a name like MBASIC, CBASIC, OBASIC, EBASIC, or just plain BASIC. Our examples will be based on use of Microsoft BASIC which usually has the filename MBASIC.COM. It's also a good idea to give the CP/M transient command STAT A: (or just plain STAT) at this time. As Fig. 1-7 shows, this will tell you how much space is still available on the disk in drive A.

TECHNICAL NOTE

Since CP/M and MBASIC are supplied by different companies, they may initially come on separate disks. We're assuming that someone—perhaps the computer company or store owner who sold you your system—has included MBASIC in the price, and has transferred it to the CP/M system disk. If not, you can buy it separately and transfer it to your CP/M disk by following the procedure explained in Lab Exercise 2.6-2 of Chapter 2.

Step 3.   Load the MBASIC subsystem and start it running. To do this, simply type MBASIC after the A> prompt as follows

A>MBASIC(CR)

The reason this works is that MBASIC is stored as what's called a *command* file. You can spot command files in a directory by the COM shown at the end of their name. For MBASIC, the full file name is MBASIC.COM. This and all the other COM files displayed in the directory work in the same way: you load them *and* start them executing by typing the first part of their name (up to .COM) after the A> prompt. (Note: The directory shows the name as MBASIC   COM, but MBASIC.COM is the proper way to write the full file name.)

Step 4.   Write and run a BASIC program. You'll know you are in the MBASIC subsystem by the opening message, and the MBASIC prompt "Ok". This means it's OK to do anything allowed in BASIC. In other words, you've left the CP/M system level, and are now dealing exclusively with BASIC. If you already know BASIC, you can try writing and running your own program here. If you don't, go ahead and copy the example shown in Fig. 1-8, remembering to press the RETURN or ENTER key at the end of each line. If you make a mistake, press RETURN and retype the entire line. If you spot a mistake in a line already entered, retype the line. To erase a line—say line 120—type 120 (CR).

We'll have a lot more to say about BASIC programs in Chapter 5. You might also want to read the first few chapters of references [1], [2], or [4] listed in Appendix G, and try some of the examples given

PROGRAM NOTE

> The program listed in Fig. 1-8 calculates and prints a depreciation table with all the information needed for filling out income tax forms in which depreciation is based on the tax laws prior to 1981. It uses the "200 percent declining balance method" for the first five years, and then switches over to the straight-line method. Advantage is taken of the initial 20 percent deduction that was allowed on new purchases, so the full 40 percent deduction allowed by law is taken in the first year. This table would be of use even after 1981 (say for someone who purchased a microcomputer for business use in 1980), since it contains a permanent record of the data that needs to be entered in the depreciation schedules over an 8-year period. The 1981 tax law introduced the "accelerated cost recovery system" (ACRS). This provides tables that say what percent depreciation to use each year (e. g., for "5-year class" equipment purchased in 1981 through 1984 the percentages are 15%, 22%, 21%, 21%, and 21%). However, many businesses will continue to calculate their internal *book* depreciation with programs like TAXDEP, even though they must use the ACRS tables to calculate tax-related depreciation.

```
A>MBASIC
BASIC-80 Rev. 5.2
[CP/M Version]
Copyright 1977, 78, 79, 80 (C) by Microsoft
Created: 14-Jul-80
31046 Bytes free
Ok

10 '--------------------------------------------------
20 '       TAXDEP (PROGRAM TO PRINT DEPRECIATION SCHEDULES)
30 '--------------------------------------------------
40 PRINT "TYPE STARTING YEAR, COST (E.G. 1979,980.50)";
50 INPUT Y,C
60 PRINT "***    DEPRECIATION SCHEDULE FOR 8 YEAR LIFE    ***"
70 PRINT "***    20% 1ST YEAR, 200% DBM & SL  ON BALANCE   ***"
80 F=.2*C : B=C-F : V=B : S=0
90 PRINT: PRINT "20% DEDUCTION FOR 1ST YEAR ="; F ;"   BALANCE ="; B
100 PRINT "------------------------------------------"
110 PRINT "YEAR      DEPREC-   SUM PREVI-  BOOK VALUE"
115 PRINT "          IATION    OUS YEARS"
120 PRINT "------------------------------------------"
130 PRINT TAB(29);:PRINT USING "#######.##";C
140 FOR K=Y TO Y+7
150   IF K>Y+4 THEN D=B/3: GOTO 170
160      D=.25*B : B=B-D
170    V=V-D
180    PRINT USING "####";K;:PRINT USING "#######.##   ";D,S,V
190    S=S+D
200 NEXT K
210 END

RUN
TYPE STARTING YEAR, COST (E.G. 1979,980.50)? 1980,3450.95
***    DEPRECIATION SCHEDULE FOR 8 YEAR LIFE    ***
***    20% 1ST YEAR, 200% DBM & SL  ON BALANCE  ***

20% DEDUCTION FOR 1ST YEAR = 690.19    BALANCE = 2760.76
------------------------------------------
YEAR      DEPREC-   SUM PREVI-  BOOK VALUE
          IATION    OUS YEARS
------------------------------------------
                                 3450.95
1980      690.19        0.00     2070.57
1981      517.64      690.19     1552.93
1982      388.23     1207.83     1164.70
1983      291.17     1596.06      873.52
1984      218.38     1887.24      655.14
1985      218.38     2105.62      436.76
1986      218.38     2324.00      218.38
1987      218.38     2542.38        0.00
Ok
SAVE "TAXDEP"
Ok
```

TYPING THE COMMAND MBASIC AFTER A> LOADS THE BASIC-80 INTERPRETER. THE USER CAN THEN ENTER AND RUN A BASIC PROGRAM AS SHOWN BELOW.

TYPING SAVE FOLLOWED BY A FILENAME IN QUOTATION MARKS STORES A COPY OF THE BASIC PROGRAM THAT'S IN MEMORY AS A CP/M DISK FILE. THE EXTENSION .BAS IS AUTOMATICALLY ADDED TO THE FILENAME.

FIG. 1-8 Writing, running, and saving a BASIC program using the MBASIC subsystem.

there as part of this step. If you try more than one program, type NEW (to erase the previous program) before typing in the next one.

Step 5. The final thing you'll usually want to do after writing and testing a BASIC program is to save it as a disk file. This is done in MBASIC by typing

```
A>DIR
A: SAVEUSER COM : XSUB     COM : SYSGEN   COM : REGEN    ASM
A: REGEN    COM : SAVEUSER ASM : ABOOT#   ASM : FIRMB    ASM
A: CBIOS#   ASM : FORMT#   COM : LOAD     COM : PIP      COM
A: DUMP     ASM : DDT      COM : SINGLE   COM : SUBMIT   COM
A: BIOS     ASM : ED       COM : SINGLE   ASM : DISKS    ASM
A: EBASIC   COM : STAT     COM : CBIOS    ASM : RUN      COM
A: DUMP     COM : DEBLOCK  ASM : ASM      COM : DISKDEF  LIB
A: FORMT#   ASM : MBASIC   COM : DBMPROG  BAS : TAXDEP   BAS
A: MOVCPM   COM
```

THE REN COMMAND IS USED HERE TO CHANGE THE NAME OF THE FILE TAXDEP .BAS TO BOOKDEP .BAS

```
A>REN BOOKDEP.BAS=TAXDEP.BAS
```

NOTICE THAT THE ORDER FOR RENAMING IS REN NEWNAME = OLDNAME

```
A>DIR
A: SAVEUSER COM : XSUB     COM : SYSGEN   COM : REGEN    ASM
A: REGEN    COM : SAVEUSER ASM : ABOOT#   ASM : FIRMB    ASM
A: CBIOS#   ASM : FORMT#   COM : LOAD     COM : PIP      COM
A: DUMP     ASM : DDT      COM : SINGLE   COM : SUBMIT   COM
A: BIOS     ASM : ED       COM : SINGLE   ASM : DISKS    ASM
A: EBASIC   COM : STAT     COM : CBIOS    ASM : RUN      COM
A: DUMP     COM : DEBLOCK  ASM : ASM      COM : DISKDEF  LIB
A: FORMT#   ASM : MBASIC   COM : DBMPROG  BAS : BOOKDEP  BAS
A: MOVCPM   COM
A>
```

FIG. 1-9   After returning to CP/M, the DIR command can be used to verify that the SAVE "TAXDEP" command of BASIC has stored the file TAXDEP.BAS on disk. The REN command is then used to change the name of this file to BOOKDEP.BAS, and DIR is again used to verify that the change has taken place in the directory.

SAVE "TAXDEP"(CR)

where TAXDEP is a filename with 8 characters or less that you invent. (The rules for naming MBASIC files are the same as those given in Section 2.3 for naming CP/M files. However, it's a good idea to avoid lowercase letters and the "/" character for the reasons given in Section 5.0.) If you also want a "hard copy" listing of your program on paper, you can now obtain this on the system printer by typing LLIST(CR).

Step 6.   Return to CP/M, check the directory, and try the REN command.

To return to CP/M you must do a warm boot. However MBASIC is one of the few subsystems where you *can't* do this by pressing CON-TROL-C. (MBASIC uses CONTROL-C as a "break" signal.) Instead, you do a warm boot by typing SYSTEM(CR) after which you'll see the CP/M prompt. (Incidentally, you can't use CONTROL-C for disk changes in MBASIC either. Use the RESET command instead.) After typing SYSTEM, you can issue a CP/M command such as DIR. Fig. 1-9 shows what this step looks like.

You'll notice that a new file name has been added to the directory. It's called TAXDEP.BAS, where the .BAS has been automatically added to the filename you invented in step 4. This is to remind you that the file is actually a BASIC program.

The conclusion to be drawn is that even when you work in MBASIC, the management of files is handled by CP/M. As a result, you can use CP/M to manipulate these files—say, to PIP them onto another disk (see Section 2.5), to erase them with ERA, or to rename them with REN. To test the REN feature, type the following:

A>REN BOOKDEP.BAS = TAXDEP.BAS(CR)
A>DIR(CR)

You'll find that the directory now has the name BOOKDEP.BAS instead of TAXDEP.BAS. It's the same file, but CP/M has given it the new name you asked for.

Step 7.   Now go back into MBASIC by typing A>MBASIC. Try typing LIST. You'll find your program is gone. To work on it again, type the MBASIC command LOAD "BOOKDEP". If you now type LIST, you should see the program you saved (and renamed) in steps 5 and 6. If you type RUN, the program should execute as before. If you wish, you can modify the program, and save the new version under the same name (in which case the modified program will replace the earlier version), or under a new name (in which case you'll have both versions saved on disk). When you're ready to call it a day, remove all the disks, and then turn all power switches off.

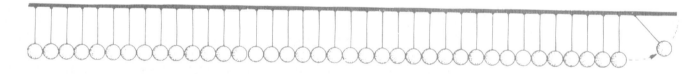

Summary

In this section we've seen that CP/M is a higher level system that lets you do such things as look at a directory of the files on disk, get statistics about the files, rename files, and execute those that have .COM (command) in their name (like MBASIC.COM). You execute COM files by typing the first part of their name. Once the COM file starts executing, CP/M seems to disappear. You then work under the rules of the particular COM file you asked for. In the first lab we worked under the rules of MBASIC (Microsoft BASIC), using *its* syntax in the form of statements like 10 PRINT "TEST PROGRAM", and commands like LOAD, RUN, LIST, SAVE, and so on. Once in MBASIC, you can write new BASIC programs or work with old ones. BASIC programs can usually be spotted in the directory by the .BAS in their names. These *cannot* be executed from CP/M. You must use the MBASIC command to start BASIC running, and then use the LOAD and RUN commands of BASIC to get your

 program into memory and start it executing. Incidentally, the LOAD and SAVE commands of BASIC are *not* the same as the LOAD and SAVE commands of CP/M explained in Chapter 6.

Of course there are many other uses of CP/M that have nothing to do with BASIC. We'll be looking at these in later chapters, starting in Chapter 2 with the use of CP/M to make backup disks of important software.

1.6 Problems and Projects

1. If there's a computer club in your area, see if they have a CP/M user group. Attending user group meetings can be a source of many good ideas. An interesting project would be to tabulate the different kinds of CP/M systems owned by the members of the group. An even more interesting question to ask members would be, "What CP/M system would you get if you had a chance to start over, but with about twice your original budget?"

2. Try the same question (above) on local computer store dealers. Don't be surprised if there's not much information available at those stores that handle only game-type machines. CP/M is associated more with higher-end professional systems.

3. If programming in BASIC is new to you, and you want to learn more about it, here are some short programs to try as part of Lab 1.5-1. The programs are taken from Chapter 2 of the book *BASIC and the Personal Computer* (Reference [1] in Appendix G). Explanations of how the various BASIC statements used in these programs work are also given in this reference. Don't forget to type NEW between programs.

```
10 LET X=695
20 LET Y=37
30 PRINT X*Y
40 END

RUN
 25715
Ok
```

```
10 PRINT (28.45 + 28.45*.15)/3
20 END

RUN
 10.9058
Ok
```

BE SURE TO TYPE NEW (CR) BEFORE ENTERING EACH NEW PROGRAM

```
10 FOR N=1 TO 12
20    PRINT N, N*N, N*N*N
30 NEXT N
40 END
```

```
RUN
 1              1              1
 2              4              8
 3              9              27
 4              16             64
 5              25             125
 6              36             216
 7              49             343
 8              64             512
 9              81             729
10              100            1000
11              121            1331
12              144            1728
Ok
```

```
10  PRINT "DIAMETER","SQUARE INCHES"
20  FOR D = 6 TO 16
30     LET R=D/2
40     PRINT D, 3.1416*R*R
50  NEXT D
60  END
```

```
RUN
DIAMETER        SQUARE INCHES
  6               28.2744
  7               38.4846
  8               50.2656
  9               63.6174
 10               78.54
 11               95.0334
 12               113.098
 13               132.733
 14               153.938
 15               176.715
 16               201.062
Ok
```

```
10  FOR J=1 TO 8
20     PRINT TAB(J);"JACQUELINE"
30  NEXT J
40  END
```

```
RUN
JACQUELINE
 JACQUELINE
  JACQUELINE
   JACQUELINE
    JACQUELINE
     JACQUELINE
      JACQUELINE
       JACQUELINE
Ok
```

```
10  PRINT "WHAT´S YOUR NAME"
20  INPUT N$
30  PRINT "HI ";N$
40  END
```

```
RUN
WHAT'S YOUR NAME
? RUDY
HI RUDY
Ok
RUN
WHAT'S YOUR NAME
? I DON'T KNOW
HI I DON'T KNOW
Ok
```

```
10 LET F=9206
20 LET A=2136
30 LET T=A+F
40 PRINT "          NUMBER              PERCENT"
50 PRINT "FOR.......";F,  F/T*100;"%"
60 PRINT "AGAINST...";A,  A/T*100;"%"
70 PRINT "TOTAL # OF VOTERS = ";T
80 PRINT "THE WINNER IS ";
90 IF A>F THEN PRINT "'AGAINST' BY "; ELSE PRINT "'FOR' BY ";
100 PRINT ABS(A-F);" VOTES."
999 END
```

```
RUN
          NUMBER              PERCENT
FOR....... 9206              81.1674 %
AGAINST... 2136              18.8327 %
TOTAL # OF VOTERS =  11342
THE WINNER IS 'FOR' BY  7070  VOTES.
Ok
10 LET F=1022
RUN
          NUMBER              PERCENT
FOR....... 1022              32.3623 %
AGAINST... 2136              67.6378 %
TOTAL # OF VOTERS =  3158
THE WINNER IS 'AGAINST' BY  1114  VOTES.
Ok
```

4. Write a program similar to TAXDEP (Section 1.5), which prints comparative depreciation schedules based on the Accelerated Cost Recovery System (ACRS). Consult your local IRS office for details about the various options available.

5. Make a study of the special graphics capabilities of your system, and try some experiments in MBASIC to test these out. If you are using a separate 24-line by 80-column CRT terminal (*not* a memory mapped video display as in the Apple), find out what the cursor positioning code sequences are for this terminal. For example, on the Zenith Z19 (or Heathkit H19), the sequence is ESC Y R$ C$. The variables R$ and C$ are the ASCII characters given by CHR$(row + 32) and CHR$(col + 32) where row should be in the range 0 to 23, and col should be in the range 0 to 79. The program at the top of page 34 plots a sine curve using the cursor positioning codes for the Z19.

```
5  ´**********************************************************************
6  ´*     Z19SINE.BAS   (SINE WAVE USING Z19 CURSOR POSITIONING       *
7  ´**********************************************************************
10 GOSUB 100                        ´CLEAR SCREEN AND DRAW AXES
20 XSCALE=6.28/79                   ´SCALE 80 COLUMNS TO 2*PI
30 FOR COL=0 TO 79                  ´DRAW THE GRAPH
40    X=COL*XSCALE
50    Y=INT(11.5-11.5*SIN(X))
60    PRINT CHR$(27);CHR$(89);CHR$(Y+32);CHR$(COL+32);"*";
70 NEXT COL
80 GOTO 10                          ´ONE MORE TIME
100 ´===== SUBROUTINE TO CLEAR SCREEN AND DRAW AXES =====
110 PRINT CHR$(27);CHR$(69)         ´CLEAR SCREEN
115 PRINT CHR$(27);CHR$(70)         ´ENTER GRAPHICS CHARACTER MODE
120 FOR R=0 TO 23                   ´DRAW Y AXIS ON LEFT SIDE OF SCREEN
130    PRINT CHR$(27);CHR$(89);CHR$(R+32);CHR$(32);CHR$(124);
140 NEXT R
150 FOR C=0 TO 79                   ´DRAW X AXIS IN CENTER OF SCREEN
160    PRINT CHR$(27);CHR$(89);CHR$(43);CHR$(C+32);CHR$(97);
170 NEXT C
180 PRINT CHR$(27);CHR$(71)         ´LEAVE GRAPHICS CHARACTER MODE
190 RETURN
```

6. Write a program in MBASIC that produces game-related graphics, for example, a bouncing ball "pong" game, an arrow shot toward a target game, or a "bad guy" chasing a "good guy" in a maze game. An arrow trajectory program is described in references [1] and [2]. There is also a general math function plotting program in [1]. An extensive treatment of 3D and other computer graphics is given in [3]. (Numbered references are found in Appendix G.)

```
100 ´---------------------------------------------------------------------
110 ´   PLTRIPLE   (PROGRAM TO PLOT RED, GREEN, AND BLUE CURVES ON ISC)
120 ´---------------------------------------------------------------------
130 PRINT CHR$(12): ON ERROR GOTO 400
140 PRINT"TYPE 6 DIGITS, EACH FOLLOWED BY ´RETURN´ (E.G., 1 1 1 5 5 5)"
150 FOR I=1 TO 6: INPUT;N(I): NEXT I
160 PRINT: PRINT "YOUR NUMBERS WERE";
170 FOR I=1 TO 6:PRINT N(I);:NEXT I:PRINT" -- OK (Y/N)";: INPUT A$
180    IF LEFT$(A$,1)="N" THEN 140
190 PRINT CHR$(12)
200 FOR I=1 TO 6: D(I)=2^(N(I)+1): NEXT I
210 FOR I=1 TO 3: READ X(I),Y(I): NEXT I
220 DATA 80,100,75,90,85,90
230 ´================= START DO FOREVER LOOP ==================
240 IF X(1) < 0 OR X(1) > 159 OR Y(1) < 0 OR Y(1) > 191 THEN 270
250 PRINT CHR$(17);CHR$(2);CHR$(X(1));CHR$(Y(1));CHR$(255)
260 PRINT INT(X(1));TAB(8);INT(Y(1))
270 IF X(2) < 0 OR X(2) > 159 OR Y(2) < 0 OR Y(2) > 191 THEN 300
280 PRINT CHR$(18);CHR$(2);CHR$(X(2));CHR$(Y(2));CHR$(255)
290 PRINT INT(X(2));TAB(8);INT(Y(2))
300 IF X(3) < 0 OR X(3) > 159 OR Y(3) < 0 OR Y(3) > 191 THEN 330
310 PRINT CHR$(20);CHR$(2);CHR$(X(3));CHR$(Y(3));CHR$(255)
320 PRINT INT(X(3));TAB(8);INT(Y(3))
330 Y(1)=Y(1)-(X(2)-X(1))/D(1)
340 X(1)=X(1)+(Y(2)-Y(1))/D(2)
350 Y(2)=Y(2)-(X(3)-X(2))/D(3)
360 X(2)=X(2)+(Y(3)-Y(2))/D(4)
370 Y(3)=Y(3)-(X(1)-X(3))/D(5)
380 X(3)=X(3)+(Y(1)-Y(3))/D(6)
390 GOTO 240    ´=================================================
400 PRINT CHR$(255);CHR$(18);: ON ERROR GOTO 0: END
```

FIG. 1-10   This is a listing of the color graphics program PLTRIPLE. Samples of the output it produces are shown in the color plates.

7. If you're using an Apple II with the SoftCard CP/M system, there are two versions of BASIC available called MBASIC and GBASIC. Both of these have the following graphics commands: GR, COLOR, PLOT, VLIN, HLIN, and SCRN. In addition, GBASIC (which is available only on systems with 16-sector disks) supports the high resolution graphics commands HGR, HCOLOR, and HPLOT. Experiment with writing graphics programs in BASIC that use these features. There are several short examples of Apple II graphics programs shown in Chapter 4 of the book *A Bit of BASIC* (reference [4]). Many additional examples can be found in *Microcomputer Graphics* (reference [3]). These are all written in Applesoft BASIC, but MBASIC and GBASIC are "supersets" of Applesoft, so conversion should be easy. Part 4 of the SoftCard manual explains which features are different.

8. If you have access to an Intecolor or Compucolor computer, type in the program of Fig. 1-10 and run it. The results can be quite artistic as shown in the color plates. See if you can modify the program so that it will produce similar (although not nearly as spectacular) results on an ordinary console.

CHAPTER TWO
CP/M in Action

2.0 Introduction

The goal of this chapter is to build familiarity with CP/M through use. There will be eight lab exercises that direct you in this use. Taken together, these form a packet of how-to-do-it information on the subject of making duplicate CP/M disks.

The labs also introduce you to files, and show how to use the CP/M commands DIR, STAT, TYPE, and DUMP. You will also see how to use the CP/M *utility programs* FORMAT, SYSGEN, PIP, MOVCPM, and COPY (also called DUP). Finally (and in the long run most importantly), we'll present some technical information on what actually goes on inside a CP/M-based computer by introducing the important ideas of *disk* and *memory maps*.

Note: It is recommended that you read the entire chapter before making any backup disks. Then go back to Section 2.2 and follow the directions for Lab Exercises 2.2-1, 2.4-1, and 2.5-1 in sequence. If your machine differs from our example computers, be sure to use the reference manual that came with your system in conjunction with the labs. Also be aware that some systems may not permit making backup disks; be sure to check this out before buying.

Note on the Note: Examples of some nonstandard approaches to CP/M disk duplication are given in Section 2.6. This section also discusses the procedures required on systems that have only one disk drive.

2.1 Getting Ready to Use Disks; the Need for Backup Copies

We're going to start our look at CP/M in action by using it to do something quite practical: to make extra copies of the original CP/M disk you bought. Let's see why this is important.

Like any complex software product, CP/M has both its virtues and its faults. From a beginner's point of view, the principal fault of CP/M is that it is not as human-oriented as one would like. The "dialogue" a user must hold with CP/M in order to use it effectively can get to be quite cryptic. (In all fairness, however, we should mention that beginners find more advanced operating systems such as UNIX even more mysterious.)

It also turns out that the rules governing this dialogue (what might be called the "syntax" of CP/M) vary with the different parts of the system. For example, the rules for using the editor supplied with CP/M (a program called ED) are different from those that govern use of other parts of the system such as the debugging program (called DDT), or the "peripheral interchange program" (called PIP).

This difficulty will disappear with the familiarity that comes from repeated use, and doing the lab exercises in this book is a good way to get started on gaining this familiarity. For such practice to be most effective, however, you should also plan on trying a few experiments of your own. You'll be amazed at how expert you'll feel (and in fact *be*) after conquering a few challenges that aren't discussed in books.

It's at this point that a book is supposed to say, "Don't be afraid to experiment—you can't hurt anything." Unfortunately that's not quite true. You can't hurt anything with one exception: the original CP/M system (and other software) supplied to you on disk. You can harm this in two ways. First, you can physically alter the disk by doing such things as sitting on it, letting the dog chew on it, leaving it in a hot car, scratching (or even just touching) the exposed surfaces, putting it near magnetic fields (including those around power cords), or exposing it to any of a dozen or so electronic diseases to which the delicate bit patterns on disks can succumb. Secondly, it is possible to accidently "write" (magnetically record) new data on top of the original CP/M programs, and of course this is just as bad as erasing them.

The solution to this twofold potential for disk mayhem is simple: make spare "backup" copies for actual use, keeping the original disk in a secure and magnetically friendly environment. This same advice applies to other valuable software you may purchase on disks, whether it be other system software (like MBASIC), or application software (like the word processor and business packages we'll describe in later chapters). In particular, we recommend that you make at least three backup copies of your important disks, and distribute them as follows:

To Be Placed in Safe Storage

0. Original disk you purchased, stored in location A.
1. Backup copy #1, stored in location B.

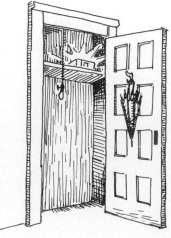

A   B

To Be Used on Your Computer

2. Backup copy #2, used for learning and experimentation.
3. Backup copy #3, used for normal application work.

In the next three lab exercises, we're going to show you how to make such backup copies. The first time you go through these exercises, you'll be asked to follow the instructions pretty much on faith. However, as you'll later see, the steps outlined here are an introduction to several powerful features of CP/M itself.

In particular, we'll use some of the *utility* programs supplied with CP/M for "formatting" disks, and for copying software from one place to another. If you're asking whether this means CP/M can use these programs to copy itself, the answer is yes—and then some. If you're saying, "Hey, that's very clever," you are absolutely right. The ability of CP/M to regenerate itself is, in fact, one of its outstanding features.

We'll save a full discussion of system "regeneration" (using the advanced features of the CP/M utility programs DDT, SAVE, SYSGEN, and MOVCPM) until a later part of the book. However, in this section we'll be able to use SYSGEN to generate an unaltered copy of CP/M, and then use the PIP utility program to copy all the "extra" programs found on CP/M disks. We'll also discuss use of the COPY (also called DUP) utility program supplied with some computers, and then tell you how to use MOVCPM to modify CP/M in case it doesn't use all the memory on your machine. Later on (in Chapter 6) we'll explain how to add new features to the basic input/output section of CP/M (BIOS) to customize it to use new printers, terminals, and other I/O devices.

2.2 Using a Format Program to Initialize Disks

The first fact of life to be faced is that you can't make backup copies on blank disks; before any data can be recorded on them, disks must be *formatted*. This means that some preliminary information must be recorded on the disks to mark the places where programs and data can be stored. It's a bit like marking the sections and rows in a parking lot before letting motorists use it.

The most common "medium" on which CP/M is distributed is the 8-inch *floppy disk* (also called diskette, or simply disk). CP/M has also been released on 5 1/4-inch floppy disks (sometimes called mini-diskettes). Because of their limited storage space, 5 1/4-inch CP/M disks may carry fewer "utility programs" than their 8-inch counterparts, but the essential features of CP/M work the same way for both sizes. Incidentally, disk *drives*—the mechanisms that rotate the disks—are sometimes also called disks for short. Sloppy jargon, but very common. We'll use "floppy disk," "diskette," and "disk" interchangeably when referring to the medium, but use "disk drive" or "drive" for the mechanism.

Floppy disks are thin circular sheets of plastic on which a very fine magnetic coating has been deposited. In order to organize the information recorded on such a disk for easy access, a standard format (sometimes called the IBM 3740 soft-sectored format) is used by CP/M for 8-inch disks. This standard is basically an agreement to record information on 77 concentric circular paths called *tracks*. These tracks are numbered 0 to 76, with track 0 located nearest the outer edge of the disk. It has further been agreed that each track is to be subdivided into 26 arcs called *sectors*. The sectors are numbered from 1 to 26, with the starting point indicated by a small hole punched in the disk.

The term "soft-sectored" means that there is only a single hole to mark the start of a track, and that the starting positions of the sectors within a track are marked by magnetically recording the sector number and some other information at 26 equally spaced positions on each track. This is done with a special formatting program that's supplied with most versions of CP/M. (There are also "hard-sectored" disks on which the sector positions are marked by holes punched near the inner circumference of the disk, but these are not used on CP/M systems.)

Before proceeding with formatting disks for use with CP/M, you should make sure you have a supply of new (or erased) soft-sectored disks on hand. You'll also want to know whether (a) your system uses single- or double-density disks, and (b) whether your system uses single- or double-sided disks.

On single-density disks, 128 bytes of information are recorded in each sector (a byte consists of 8 on–off "bits" of information, and it's usually used to represent a single letter, digit, or special character). On double-density disks, there are usually 256 bytes stored in each sector. In both these cases, there are 26 sectors per track. Another possibility used on some systems is to put 15 double-density sectors of 512 bytes

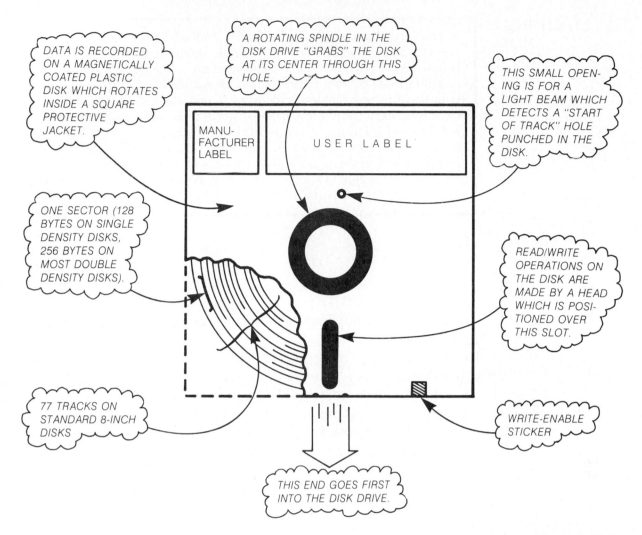

DATA IS RECORDED ON A MAGNETICALLY COATED PLASTIC DISK WHICH ROTATES INSIDE A SQUARE PROTECTIVE JACKET.

A ROTATING SPINDLE IN THE DISK DRIVE "GRABS" THE DISK AT ITS CENTER THROUGH THIS HOLE.

THIS SMALL OPENING IS FOR A LIGHT BEAM WHICH DETECTS A "START OF TRACK" HOLE PUNCHED IN THE DISK.

MANU-FACTURER LABEL

U S E R   L A B E L

ONE SECTOR (128 BYTES ON SINGLE DENSITY DISKS, 256 BYTES ON MOST DOUBLE DENSITY DISKS).

READ/WRITE OPERATIONS ON THE DISK ARE MADE BY A HEAD WHICH IS POSITIONED OVER THIS SLOT.

77 TRACKS ON STANDARD 8-INCH DISKS

WRITE-ENABLE STICKER

THIS END GOES FIRST INTO THE DISK DRIVE.

FIG. 2-1   Physical layout of an 8-inch floppy disk (diskette). Most CP/M software is distributed on 8-inch diskettes recorded in the IBM 3740 single-density format. All 8-inch CP/M systems can read this format, which consists of 26 sectors per track, with 128 bytes of information recorded in each sector. Most computer systems also permit use of double-density disks, but there are no standards for this format. For this reason users of 8-inch systems buy their software on single-density diskettes, and then copy them onto double-density diskettes formatted for their particular machine. At present, there are no standards for 5 1/4-inch disks, so disk exchange between different 5 1/4-inch systems is usually not possible.

on each track, giving the equivalent of 60 single-density sectors. Recording in double-density is a more demanding electronic feat, and not all computer systems can handle it. To help make the process more reliable, most manufacturers sell double-density versions of their disks. These are similar to the single-density versions except that more quality control is exercised in their manufacture.

Double-sided disks are just what the name suggests: they have magnetic coatings on both sides. They can be used only with disk drives specifically designed for double-sided disks. Double-sided disks can be recognized by the manufacturer's number, or by the fact that the single hole used to locate the start of a track is in a slightly different position than on single-density disks.

TECHNICAL NOTE

If you buy a system that uses 8-inch double-density disks (which is a good idea), be sure that it can also handle single-density disks. The reason is that most CP/M software is distributed on single-density disks, so your machine must be able to read single density even though you make all your backup copies in double-density. In fact, the only "universal" format for CP/M software is the single-density 8-inch disk. You can buy some software on 5 1/4-inch disks, but these are specific to one machine, and of no use to users of different hardware. The only way users of 8-inch and 5 1/4-inch systems can share programs is by sending them over wires attached to suitable I/O ports on the two systems. For more information on this subject, see Section 6.5.

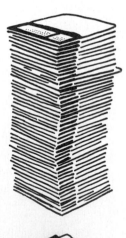

One last but very important thing to know is that many 8-inch disks come from the manufacturer with a *write-protect* notch cut in the square cover. If this notch is left uncovered, a light sensing photo-diode in the disk drive locks out the recording circuits, so you can't format the disk, or copy anything onto it. To get around this, you should therefore place one of the small patches of sticky paper that come with the disks over the notch in each disk you wish to use. This patch should be folded in half so that it sticks on both sides of the disk jacket. A disk on which this notch has been covered is called *write-enabled*. If you later wish to restore it to the write-protected condition (to prevent accidentally writing on it and destroying valuable information), you simply remove the patch. (Warning: the notch on 5 1/4" mini-diskettes is used in exactly the opposite way—covering the notch write-protects the disk.)

With a supply of write-enabled disks prepared, and assuming you followed our advice to read this chapter through at least once if you've never made backups before, you're now ready to do the next lab exercise. It is recommended that the labs be done on a real machine. If this isn't immediately possible, you can still get a lot out of the lab exercises by "walking them through" in your mind.

Notice that the lab exercises are numbered by section and exercise number. For example, Lab Exercise 2.6-3 is the third lab in Section 2.6. The directions for carrying out each lab exercise are given as a sequence of steps that tell you what to do and why. In a few cases, the exact procedures depend on the computer system you're using. When this happens, the step will be broken up into three sub-steps that correspond to the three example machines we introduced in Chapter 1. If you have a different system, you'll want to consult the manuals that came with it and/or experiment a little to develop your own "fourth column" for these steps. Most of the labs in Chapter 2 assume that you have two disk drives. If you don't, first look at Lab 2.6-3 for some information on how to make backups on a one-drive system.

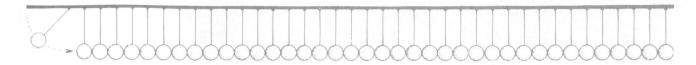

LAB EXERCISE
2.2-1

Formatting Disks

Step 1. Turn the computer on, put the CP/M system disk in drive A, and put a write-enabled disk (one where the write-protect notch is covered if 8-inch, uncovered if 5 1/4-inch) in drive B. Close both drive doors.

Step 2. Boot the CP/M system, following the directions given in step 1 of Lab Exercise 1.1-1. You'll know that the boot has been successful if the red light of disk drive A comes on for a few seconds, and something like the following appears on the console screen:

AJAX 48K CP/M Ver. 2.2 of 4-3-81

Copyright XYZ Corp. . . . etc. . . .

A>

The symbols "A>" are called the *system prompt* or *system readiness symbol*. They tell you that the next "command" you type will be handled by the CP/M system, and that unless you say otherwise, any programs you ask for will be read from the disk in drive A.

Before typing any commands, if your keyboard has either a CAPS LOCK or UC (upper case) button, it would be a good idea to press it into the down position. This will cause all the letters you type to print in uppercase. It's actually all right to use lowercase letters in CP/M commands, since they're translated to uppercase by the system. However, there are times when you want to avoid lowercase (e. g., in MBASIC), so it's a good idea to become familiar with use of the CAPS LOCK key. Notice in particular that it affects only the letter keys A to Z; the SHIFT key must still be used with number or special character keys.

Step 3. To make sure you have a formatting program available, you should next command CP/M to give you a directory of all the files currently on the disk in drive A. Recall that you do this by typing DIR after the system prompt A>, and then pressing the carriage return or RETURN/ENTER button. We've been using the symbol (CR) to mean "press carriage return," but even when it's not shown you should assume that a (CR) is required at the end of most lines you type. You'll recognize the few cases where it's not needed by the fact that something happens before you get a chance to press RETURN.

After using DIR, it's a good idea to see how many kilobytes of storage are still available on the system disk. You do this by typing the

```
A>DIR
A: SAVEUSER COM : XSUB     COM : SYSGEN   COM : REGEN    ASM
A: REGEN    COM : SAVEUSER ASM : ABOOT#   ASM : FIRMB    ASM
A: CBIOS#   ASM : FORMT#   COM : LOAD     COM : DUMP     ASM
A: DDT      COM : SINGLE   COM : SUBMIT   COM : BIOS     ASM
A: PIP      COM : SINGLE   ASM : DISKS    ASM : EBASIC   COM
A: STAT     COM : CBIOS    ASM : RUN      COM : DUMP     COM
A: DEBLOCK  ASM : ASM      COM : DISKDEF  LIB : FORMT#   ASM
A: MBASIC   COM : ED       COM : MOVCPM   COM
A>STAT
A: R/W, Space: 178k


A>
```

FIG. 2-2   Output from DIR and STAT on an S-100 CP/M system that uses the Morrow disk controller.

command STAT. Figs. 2-2, 2-3, and 2-4 show the output produced by these commands on our three lab computers.

Fig. 2-2 shows the directory of program files stored on the CP/M disk supplied with the Morrow Designs disk system used in our S-100 example system. As you might guess, the program we're interested in is called FORMT#.COM. Figs. 2-3 and 2-4 show the directories for the Apple and ISC computers where the formatting program is called FOR-MAT.COM. The period before COM doesn't show in the directory, but it's part of the filename. (There may be some CP/M disks that do not contain a formatter program; check on this before you buy.) Notice how little space is left on the Apple II 5 1/4-inch disk compared to the 8-inch double-density disk systems.

```
A>DIR
A: FORMAT   COM : COPY     COM
A: MBASIC   COM : GBASIC   COM
A: CONFIGIO BAS : PIP      COM
A: STAT     COM : ED       COM
A: ASM      COM : DDT      COM
A: LOAD     COM : RW13     COM
A: APDOS    COM : SUBMIT   COM
A: XSUB     COM : DUMP     ASM
A: DUMP     COM : DOWNLOAD COM
A: CPM56    COM : DBMPROG  BAS
A>STAT
A: R/W, Space: 2k
```

FIG. 2-3   Output from DIR and STAT on the Apple II computer equipped with the MicroSoft card and CP/M.

```
A>DIR
A: MOVCPM   COM : PIP      COM : SUBMIT   COM : XSUB    COM
A: MBASIC   COM : ASM      COM : DDT      COM : LOAD    COM
A: STAT     COM : CBIOS    ASM : DUMP     COM : DUMP    ASM
A: FORMAT   COM : DUP      COM : SYSGEN   COM : CBOOT   ASM
A: NOGAP    COM : REMSIN   BAS : ED       COM : DISKID  COM
A>STAT
A: R/W, Space: 348k
```

FIG. 2-4   Output from DIR and STAT on the ISC 8063 CP/M Color Computer.

The COM in any of these names means that the program is stored as a *command file*, and that you can make it execute simply by typing its name after the CP/M system prompt A>. So you next type FORMAT (or FORMT#), followed by pressing the RETURN/ENTER button.

    A>FORMAT (CR)   or   A>FORMT# (CR)

    or   A>whatever your formatting program is called (CR)

Note: On some systems (e. g., the Osborne I), the format program is included as part of a copy program (usually called COPY.COM).

Step 4.   You should next hear some noises from disk drive A, and the red light on the front of the drive should go on. This indicates that the formatting program is being transferred from the disk in drive A into RAM, and then being told to execute. As soon as this happens, a series of prompting messages will appear on the screen. These vary with systems, but you can get a good idea of how to respond from Figs. 2-5, 2-6, and 2-7.

FIG. 2-5 These are the responses given to the formatter programs on two S-100 systems (Morrow and CompuPro). These programs are more sophisticated than usual, giving the user a choice of four different sector sizes.

TECHNICAL NOTE

The differences between the four options given in Fig. 2-5 are as follows. The first two options both format 26 sectors per track. However the second option sets the disk up for double density, that is, for recording twice as many bytes per inch as the first option. The third and fourth options also use double density, but they record fewer (and longer) sectors per track (15 and 8, respectively). This allows squeezing even more information on a track. For example, with the third option each track holds the equivalent of 60 sectors of single-density format (15 times 512 is the same as 60 times 128), while the fourth option gives the equivalent of 8*1024/128 = 64 single-density sectors per track.

In studying Figs. 2-5–2-7, notice the question that asks you to select the drive containing the disk you wish to format. With a two-disk system you should respond by typing B, which means you want to format the blank disk in drive B. Be sure you do this correctly. If you should accidentally format the CP/M disk in drive A, you're dead! To prevent this, the write-protect notch on the disk in drive A should be uncovered if 8-inch, or covered if 5 1/4-inch. Unfortunately, some disks don't have this notch. In this case, to be doubly safe, you can remove the CP/M system disk from drive A before continuing. If you have only one disk drive, you *must* remove the CP/M disk and replace it with the fresh disk (see Lab 2.6-4).

After the last question asked in the formatting program is answered, the formatter program will go into action, and start marking the "header"

```
A>FORMAT


        APPLE ] [ CP/M
   16 Sector Disk Formatter
     (C) 1980 Microsoft


Format disk in which drive? B:

Insert disk to be formatted in drive B:
Press RETURN to begin

Disk in drive B: will be ERASED
Continue (Y/N)? Y

Formatting...


FORMAT Complete

Format disk in which drive?
```

FIG. 2-6 This is the FORMAT program supplied with the Apple SoftCard CP/M. It can be used with a single drive by answering A: to the first question, and then being *very sure* to replace the system disk with the disk to be formatted. As a double check, the warning message "Disk in drive A: will be ERASED" will be printed on the console.

```
A>FORMAT
 . . . screen clears . . .
ISC Double Density Floppy Disk Formatter for CP/M V1.10

Format or Read Check > F

Device Name > B


Formatting B: Track 03   . . . numbers change . . .

Read Check B :    . . . when finished, cursor returns to the position
                        after Format or Read Check . . .




      . . . Note: this display is simulated.   Screen is 80 columns by 48 lines.
```

===

FIG. 2-7   The FORMAT program on the ISC 8063 computer gives you a choice
of formatting or of checking whether the disk in question may already be
formatted.

information (26 sectors on 77 tracks for standard 8-inch disks). To keep
you informed of what's happening while this takes place, many format
programs print some sort of symbol on the screen for each track they've
finished formatting. For example, the program FORMT# prints an asterisk
for each track, so you'll know it's finished when there are 77 asterisks
across the output screen. The ISC FORMAT prints hexadecimal numbers
showing both the track and sector numbers being formatted.

   Suggestion: Since formatting programs are all different, it would
be good to keep notes on the proper responses for your system for
future use.

Step 5.   When the formatting program is finished, you usually get a
            message asking if you wish to format another disk. If you do,
            first remove the disk from drive B, and carefully place it in a
            box marked "formatted disks." Then put a fresh disk in drive
            B, close the door, type "F" (or whatever is requested) to mean
            "format another disk," and then repeat all the responses given
            in the previous step. When you've finished formatting all the
            blank disks you have (or when you get anxious to move on),
            you can leave the formatting program and return to the CP/M
            system prompt by typing CONTROL-C, or in the case of some
            format programs, by pressing RETURN (*Warning:* Make sure
            the CP/M system disk is in drive A before doing this). You'll
            recall from our earlier discussion that what you are really doing

here is performing a warm boot. You'll know this has worked if you again see the CP/M system prompt symbol A>.

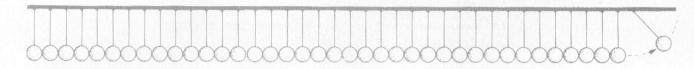

2.3 CP/M Files; Disk and Memory Maps; Using TYPE and DUMP

In this section we're going to take time out from the subject of making backup disks to say something about how CP/M is organized, how it is stored on disk, and how it gets stored in a computer's random access memory (RAM). This will make it a lot easier to understand what's going on when we return to the lab exercises for using SYSGEN, PIP, and MOVCPM to duplicate disks.

Disk Maps and Memory Maps

One of the best ways to explain the organization of CP/M is in terms of the concepts of *disk map* and *memory map.* In general, a map is a symbolic representation of something that's too large (or too complicated) to grasp through direct observation. If this book were called *A Guided Tour of the Dungeons of Liechtenstein,* a map showing how the various passageways and secret chambers of the dungeons interconnect would undoubtedly make it a lot easier to conduct the tour. The concept of map serves the same purpose in computer work, but it goes even further.

In addition to clarifying what goes where and why, disk and memory maps provide a valuable tool for understanding the *dynamic* aspects of a disk operating system—the things that change with time. We'll find that CP/M moves things around quite a bit, continually shifting programs from disk to RAM and back again. The reason it does this is that there are far too many programs to fit in RAM. One of the principal tasks of CP/M is to move things around in a way that makes best use of available RAM space.

The strategy of moving files in and out of RAM might be compared to the way theaters are used. RAM memory is like the theater's stage; it's relatively small, but it's where all the action takes place. Disk storage is like the larger backstage area where the props and scenery for many kinds of performances are kept. They have to be moved on stage before they can become part of the performance. As the analogy suggests, managing this kind of operation calls for two maps (one for RAM and one for disk), together with a set of rules that say how transfers between the two areas are to take place. The map of RAM shows where all the programs go that are "on stage," while the map of disk shows where these programs are stored for use in future performances.

In this section we'll introduce the disk and memory maps used in CP/M in simplified form. Detailed versions of these maps will be given later in the book, along with information about how the two maps are related. Let's start with the simplified version of the disk map.

The Layout of CP/M Disks; CP/M Files

Fig. 2-8 shows the layout of tracks and sectors on a typical 8-inch CP/M disk. We have to hedge and say "typical" because there is some variation in the way different versions of CP/M use disks. The only agreement on a standard is for 8-inch single-density disks, and the disk map of Fig. 2-8 is for this standard.

You'll notice that tracks 0 and 1 of the 8-inch disk are labelled CP/M, or what we prefer calling "CP/M proper." CP/M proper consists of four parts called CCP, BDOS, BIOS, and the cold start loader. Part of track 2 contains a file directory, while the rest of track 2 plus tracks 3 to 76 contain files. As we'll see shortly, some of these files are utility programs used in connection with CP/M proper. We'll use the phrase

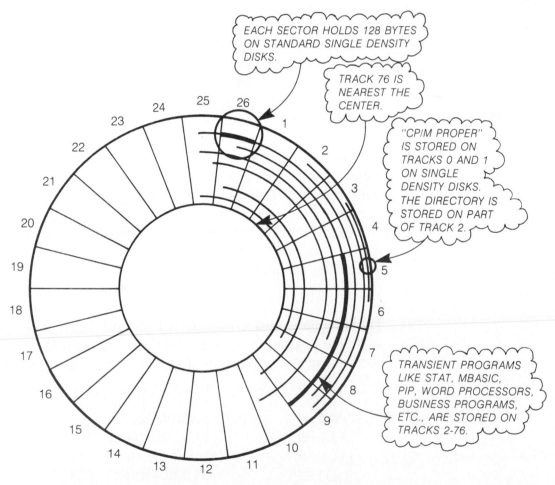

FIG. 2-8 Disk map showing use of the tracks and sectors on a standard 8-inch CP/M disk. The 5 1/4-inch disks used on the Apple II have 35 tracks with either 13 or 16 sectors per track, and 256 bytes per sector. The Apple CP/M system is stored on tracks 0, 1, and 2.

CP/M system to mean the combination of CP/M proper, the file directory, and the standard CP/M utility programs stored on inner tracks.

Too much jargon, you say? You might be right. Let's unravel it a bit by slowing down and going over some of those words in greater detail.

Computer Files

The word *file* is used in computer work to mean a collection of related information. It's the same idea as found in such non-computer uses as "recipe file," "Ipswitch Secret Agent File," "accounts receivable file," or "music I'd like to have on a desert island file." When information is stored on a magnetic disk it is called a disk file, or a computer file, or simply a file. Many of the files on a CP/M disk happen to be computer programs. Since programs can be written in various computer languages, you'll see references to BASIC files, assembly language files, and various forms of machine language files. When a program file serves as a useful tool (usually in conjunction with the operating system proper), it is called a *utility program*. The FORMAT program which we used in Lab Exercise 2.2-1 is an example of a utility program file.

In addition to program files, there are also *data files*. These consist of collections of information used as input to programs, information that is output from programs, or simply information someone has decided to store on disk for future use. Data files can contain numerical information (e. g., the number-pairs used to describe the coordinates of a graphical display), or non-numerical information (e. g., the text entered into a word processing system).

A CP/M disk directory is a catalog of all the files on that disk. It contains information about where they are stored on disk, and how large they are. To make it easy to use the directory, CP/M allows you to refer to files by name (rather than by track/sector positions). The names given to files consist of two parts called the *primary* and *secondary* *names*. The primary name can have up to 8 characters. These can be any of the printable characters except the following:

$$< \quad > \quad , \quad . \quad ; \quad : \quad = \quad ? \quad * \quad [\quad]$$

The secondary name is optional; when used, it can have up to 3 characters. A period is used to separate primary and secondary names. Here are some examples of correctly and incorrectly formed CP/M file names:

Correctly Formed	Incorrectly Formed
SAM	SAM.BASIC
ELIZABET	ELIZABETH
JACK.RIP	JACK:RIP
R2D2.RBT	R2D2 = RBT
GOOGOO.NUT	GOOGOO,NUT
CHARLIE.403	CHARLIE*.403
HOT&COLD.ICE	HOT.COLD.ICE

Instant Quiz

What's wrong with each of the file names in the second column above? (Answers: 1—has more than three characters in the secondary name, 2—has more than eight characters in the primary name, and 4 to 7—all have illegal characters in the primary name.)

The correct examples are all acceptable to CP/M, but not very conventional. You usually try to choose a name that says what the file is—like SORT7.BAS for the seventh version of a sorting program you wrote in BASIC. The secondary names are usually chosen to say what type of file it is, and for this reason they are also called *file types*, or *file extensions*. A number of these file type secondary names have been standardized. Some are automatically assigned by CP/M under appropriate circumstances (e. g., .BAS is added to file names saved while in MBASIC unless another extension is specified by the user). Here are some examples of secondary names associated with language processors.

FILE.ASM	A file that's an assembly language program.
FILE.BAS	A file that's a BASIC language program.
FILE.COB	A file that's a COBOL language program.
FILE.FOR	A file that's a FORTRAN language program.
FILE.MAC	A file that's a macro assembly language program.
FILE.PLM	A file that's a PL/M language program.
FILE.C	A file that's a C language program.

The above examples are of files that contain programs written in languages understood by people (not computers). These are sometimes called *source files* because they contain the original programs from which machine language versions are derived. Machine language programs are produced by running source programs (files) through "translator" programs such as a BASIC compiler, an 8080 assembler, a C compiler, and so on. When the results of this translation are saved on disk, you then have a *machine language* program called an *object file*. There are several kinds of object files, and these are distinguished by secondary names as follows:

Note: If you are a beginner, the following won't make much sense, but we're putting it here for completeness. If you wish, this section can be skipped on a first reading.

FILE.COM	.COM means *command* file. This is a machine language program which can be executed by typing its primary name after the CP/M prompt (e. g., A>FILE). This is also called a *binary file* since it contains the exact binary numbers (both instructions and data) that must be placed in memory for the program FILE to execute.

FILE.HEX   .HEX means a machine language file stored in *Intel Hex Format*. This is a file in which each 8-bit binary number (or instruction) is stored as two ASCII characters. For example, the number 194 would be stored in a COM binary file as 11000010, but for a hex file it would first be broken up into two chunks, "1100" and "0010". If we now interpret these "chunks" as hex numbers, we can write them as "C" and "2" or simply as C2. To store C2 in a HEX file, the computer stores the ASCII codes for C and 2 in two successive bytes. If you check the table of ASCII codes in Appendix A you'll see that this would mean storing C2 as 01000011 and 00110010. *Conclusion:*   There are two ways to store a number like 194:

—In binary form as 11000010

—Or in Hex form as ASCII C = 01000011
  followed by ASCII   2 = 00110010.

Hex files are obviously wasteful of storage, but they can be transmitted, displayed, or saved on any device that can handle ASCII codes. They also disguise control codes as data. For example, a hex file encodes a CONTROL-Z "end of file" signal as the two innocent-looking characters "1" and "A". *Quick Quiz:*   Why 1 and A? (See Appendix A for a clue.) *Note:*   There is a third way to store 194 if you consider it not as a number, but as a string of three characters. In this case the ASCII codes for 1, 9, and 4 are stored in three successive bytes. This is the way 194 would be stored as part of an ASCII (or text) file.

FILE.REL   This is a *relocatable file*, which is a machine language file in binary form produced by a *relocatable assembler* (e. g., the Microsoft M80 assembler). It has to be fed into what's called a *relocating linker* before it can be executed by the computer.

Remember: Trying to understand the above before getting practice in using machine and assembly language could be hazardous to your mental health.

In addition to the above standard secondary file names (also called extensions) used for program files, there are secondary names used for pure text files—things like letters, term papers, or other documents produced by word processing systems. All of these are ASCII files, that is, they are sequences of ASCII character codes that match the text on a one-to-one basis. The names commonly used are:

FILE.DOC   A document file.
FILE.MSG   A message file.

FILE.TXT   A text file.

FILE.BAK   A backup copy file.

FILE.LIB   A library file (see Section 3.4).

FILE.SUB   A submit file (see Section 5.4).

FILE.PRN   A printout file produced by the assembler which shows both source and object code, i. e., an assembly language program before and after being assembled along with the machine addresses used (see Section 6.1).

TECHNICAL NOTE

The Intel hex format was developed in the days of paper tape storage. At that time, the most commonly used paper tape punch and reader were those attached to teletype printers. However these machines could punch only the ASCII 7-bit codes; there was no way, for example, that they could punch an 8-bit binary number like 11111110. So Intel hit on the idea of splitting 8-bit binary codes into two parts, and interpreting each part as a hex number. Thus 11111110 would be interpreted as FE. To store this on paper tape, the ASCII codes for F and E were punched in sequence. When an entire file was punched on tape, it was stored in groupings called records, with each record defined to have the following format:

:NNAAAATTD1D2D3D4. . .DNCC

The colon means start of record, NN is the number of data bytes in the record (called the length of the record) given as two hex digits, AAAA is the hex starting address at which the record is to be stored in memory, TT is a record type (usually 00), D1, D2, D3, D4, etc., up to DN are the hex representations of the data stored in the record, and CC is a pair of check-sum digits (sum of all byte values modulo 255). The end of a file is marked by a record of length 0 (NN = 0). This format is now used by CP/M to store hex files on disk. Several examples showing how to manipulate hex files with PIP, LOAD, and DDT are given in Chapter 6. When either LOAD or DDT is used on a hex file, the file is automatically translated into binary form.

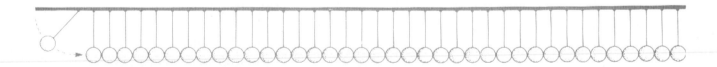

LAB EXERCISE 2.3-1

Using the TYPE and DUMP Commands to Look at Files

Note: This lab is placed here since this is the logical time to show how to examine what's actually stored on the files shown in a directory. However this lab (like all the other exploratory labs) shouldn't be run using your original CP/M disk. If you haven't yet made a backup disk, treat this lab as a reading exercise for now, and return to actually running it after completing the backup process as described in the next two labs.

In this lab we'll use the TYPE and DUMP commands of CP/M. TYPE is used to display files which have been stored as ASCII files.

This includes most source program files (files with secondary names like .ASM or .C), and text files (files with secondary names like .DOC or .PRN). The DUMP command can be used to display *any* file. However its output is in hex form, which is hard to decipher. For this lab, experiment with using TYPE and DUMP to examine a few files just out of curiosity. Here's what to do.

Step 1.   Turn on your computer and boot CP/M.

Step 2.   Use DIR to examine the names of files on your system.

Look for .ASM, .PRN, or .DOC files in particular, since these are ASCII files. (Apple II users will be out of luck here—there aren't any.) Incidentally, .BAS files are *not* stored as ASCII files when created by the SAVE "FILE" command of MBASIC. However, the command SAVE "FILE",A (see section 5.2) does create an ASCII file which can be displayed with the TYPE command.

Step 3.   Take a look at one of the ASCII files (say, BIOS.ASM) by typing it out on your console as follows:

A>TYPE BIOS.ASM (CR)

Note: The file will probably flash by pretty fast on the screen of your computer's output device. To "freeze" the display type a CONTROL-S (hold down the CONTROL key while also typing S). To resume, type any character *except* CONTROL-C (pressing the space bar or another CONTROL-S is a handy way to do this). To interrupt the process and get back to CP/M, do a warm boot by typing CONTROL-C.

Note on the Note: The TYPE command puts the output onto the "console" of your system, usually a video monitor. If your system has a printer, and you want the output to appear on this as well, type a CONTROL-P *before* giving the TYPE command. To turn off this simultaneous print feature, type another CONTROL-P. (Because it turns printing ON, then OFF, then ON, etc., CONTROL-P is called a "print toggle.") Here's an example of how you might proceed:

A>DIR (CR)	(to see the filenames)
A>CONTROL-P (CR)	(to toggle the printer ON)
A>TYPE BIOS.ASM (CR)	(to type the file BIOS on both screen and printer)
CONTROL-S	(to freeze the output)
CONTROL-S	(to continue typing BIOS)
CONTROL-C	(to quit typing and return to CP/M)

This last CONTROL-C does a warm boot which restarts CP/M and *also* turns the CONTROL-P print toggle off.

A>TYPE BIOS.ASM(CR)	(to type the file BIOS on the screen only)

. . . etc. . . .

Step 4.   Repeat the previous steps, using DUMP instead of TYPE, but this time on either ASCII or binary files. The output will be pretty meaningless, so be prepared to hit CONTROL-C to prevent terminal boredom from setting in.

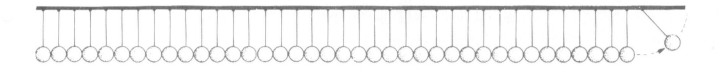

Ambiguous File Names

When you refer to a file by its exact name—say, LUNAR.BAS—that's called an unambiguous file reference. This is because there's no doubt about which file you want; there can be only one file with that name. The CP/M books refer to such a name as an "ufn" which means "unambiguous filename."

Sometimes it's handy to make a single reference to several files that have similar names. This can be done in CP/M by using what are called ambiguous filenames, abbreviated "afn". You do this by using either the ? or * symbols to mean "any character" or "any group of characters," respectively. The ? and * are sometimes called *wildcard* symbols. Here are some examples of afn references:

SORT?.BAS	This refers to all filenames made up of the four characters SORT, followed by any *one* legitimate filename character, followed by .BAS. So it would include names like SORT3.BAS, SORTX.BAS, and SORT/.BAS.
HO???.CO?	This name has four unspecified characters, and it could refer to such filenames as HOHAH.COM, HO.CO, HOHO.COW, HO123.COM, HO/#2.COP, and so on.
LUNAR.*	Here the * means "any secondary name," so this could be a reference to files named LUNAR, LUNAR.C, LUNAR.BAS, LUNAR.COM, LUNAR.ASM, and so on.
C*.*	This means any file name beginning with C. Examples are C.BAS, CHARLIEC.HAN, CAN.CAN, and CRAPS.C.
?A??.*	This means any filename which has between 2 and 4 characters in the primary name with the second one the letter A, and any secondary name. Examples are BA.C, BAD.PRN, and BANK.
*.BAS	This refers to any file with the secondary name BAS. Examples are SORT.BAS, LUNAR.BAS, and X.BAS.

.   This means a file with any primary name and any secondary name, so it's really a reference to *all* the files on a disk.

As an example of using the afn feature, you could use

A>DIR *.BAS

to ask for a directory of all the BASIC files on disk A, or use

A>STAT B:C*.*

to ask for statistics about all the files on the disk in drive B that have names starting with C.

Warning: The afn *B.* does *not* mean all files such that the primary name ends in B. Because of a design bug in CP/M, it is interpreted as *.*, so ERA *B.* will erase *all* your files. Dangerous!

Disk Drive Names

If you have several disk drives (most systems have two drives called A: and B:) you can specify the disk drive as part of the filename by putting A: or B: in front of the filename. Thus,

>DIR B:*.BAS

means "give me a directory of all the BASIC files on the disk in drive B:".

If you leave off the A: or B: it is understood that you want the disk drive that is currently "logged in." What's that mean? Well, when you first boot a system, drive A: is automatically logged in, so a file reference like LUNAR.BAS is taken to be the same as A:LUNAR.BAS. However, you can change the logged-in disk drive from A: to B: at any time by typing B: after the CP/M prompt symbol as follows:

Type   A>B:(CR)
and you'll get   B>

From this point on, CP/M will use B> as its prompt symbol to remind you that the logged-in disk drive is now B:, and that a reference to a file like LUNAR.BAS means the same as B:LUNAR.BAS. If you want to switch back to A: as the logged-in disk drive,

Type   B>A:(CR)
and you'll get   B>

For more about this feature, and the names allowed for disk drives, see the explanation of the command d: in Section 3.3.

Instant Quiz

What is the effect of each of the following commands (assume you just booted the system, and are logged-in to disk drive A)?

```
(1)  A>DIR
(2)  A>DIR A:
(3)  A>DIR *.*
(4)  A>DIR A:*.*
(5)  A>DIR B:
(6)  A>B:
(7)  B>DIR
(8)  B>DIR B:
(9)  B>DIR *.*
(10) B>DIR B:*.*
(11) B>DIR A:
(12) B>A:
```

Answers

(1), (2), (3), and (4) all do the same thing. They give you a directory of all the files on the disk in drive A. Step (5) gives a directory of all the files on the disk in drive B *without* switching the logged-in drive. Step (6) changes the logged-in drive to B. Steps (7), (8), (9), and (10) are equivalent ways of asking for a directory of all the files on the disk in drive B. Step (11) gives a directory of all files on the disk in drive A *without* making A the logged-in drive, while (12) switches the logged-in drive back to A.

Memory Maps

The last bit of theory we should cover before getting on with the lab exercises for backing up a CP/M disk has to do with the question of "what goes where" in the computer's random access memory. This is also called RAM, user memory, main memory, internal memory, and read-write memory. You'll even see it (mis)called "core" memory by oldtimers who remember when such memory was built from tiny doughnut-shaped magnetic cores.

Most microcomputers can have up to 64K "chunks" of main memory storage (64K means 64 * 1024 = 65536). Each chunk holds 8 bits of information called a *byte* of memory. A moderately large BASIC program might occupy 15000 bytes, while an extended BASIC interpreter (which has to be in memory when you run BASIC programs) could take as much as 25000 bytes. And what about CP/M? It, too, has to be in main memory, and a customized version of CP/M can occupy over 8000 bytes (although some of this can be overlapped by your BASIC program). The conclusion is that a serious computer user will want to have at least 48000 bytes of RAM (a "48K system"). If you want to run larger programs, or do word processing (which also uses lots of RAM to hold the text you're processing), then a 56K or 64K system is recommended.

A memory map of RAM is a diagram that shows what goes where in memory. It's usually shown as a vertical "storage bin" with numbers next to each slot of memory that give the *address* of the corresponding

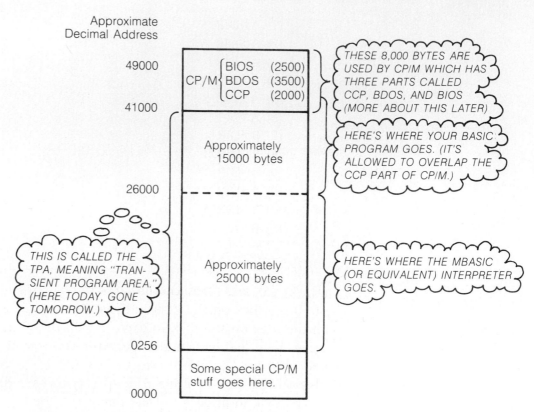

FIG. 2-9 Simplified memory map of a 48K system using CP/M and MBASIC. This diagram doesn't show the CP/M *cold start loader* program. This loader is placed down in the "special stuff" area during a cold boot, but it's immediately overwritten once it loads BIOS, BDOS, and CCP into the top of memory. The memory sizes given for CP/M are for the Morrow system. Other CP/M systems will differ in these numbers.

byte. For a 48K system using CP/M and MBASIC, a simplified memory map is shown in Fig. 2-9.

If you weren't using BASIC, then of course the TPA would have other "stuff" in it (that's why it's called the transient program area). For example, if you were using a word processor written in machine language, you wouldn't need the MBASIC interpreter at all. So the TPA could be used to hold the word processor machine language program plus the text you were working on.

2.4 Using SYSGEN to Duplicate CP/M

We'll return to the subject of the CP/M memory map in Chapter 3, and discuss it in greater detail there. We'll also explain what the three parts of CP/M (called CCP, BDOS, and BIOS) do, and introduce the hexadecimal notation for giving memory addresses. But we don't need this additional information to proceed with the making of backup disks, so let's resume with the labs that show how it's done.

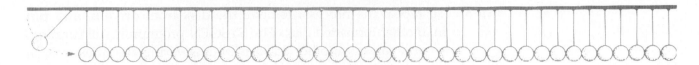

**LAB EXERCISE
2.4-1**

Copying CP/M Proper with SYSGEN

This lab shows how to copy the information on tracks 0 and 1 (what we earlier called CP/M proper) from the disk in drive A to the disk in drive B, using the CP/M program SYSGEN. (The SYSGEN program is not supplied with Apple CP/M; Apple II owners should use COPY/S instead as described in Lab 2.6-2.)

Note: This lab assumes that your original CP/M disk is "configured" for the memory size of your computer. For example, if your computer has 48K of user memory, we assume that your CP/M is configured for 48K. If it isn't, read Section 2.6 before proceeding.

Step 1.   Put the original CP/M disk in drive A, put a formatted disk in drive B, and then boot the system.

Step 2.   Run the command program SYSGEN.COM by typing

    A>SYSGEN (CR)

This will start the program SYSGEN running. The first thing SYSGEN will do is ask for some information. The questions you'll see, with the responses you should give, are shown in Fig. 2-10.

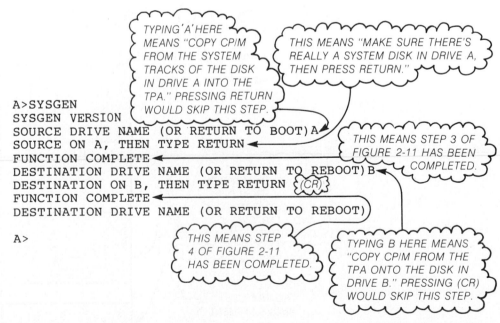

FIG. 2-10   This is the dialogue you'll see when running SYSGEN. The best way to follow what's going on is to compare the notes in the "balloons" of this figure with those of Fig. 2-11.

Step 3. To repeat the process, remove the disk from drive B, and put in another formatted disk. The SYSGEN program is still running, so you can do another backup by answering the questions in step 2 again.

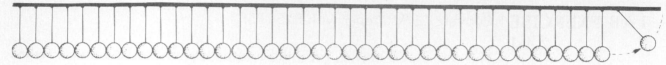

How SYSGEN Works

This is a good place to put our knowledge of disk and memory maps to work, using it to explain how the SYSGEN program works. In step 1, when you boot CP/M, a working copy of CP/M is loaded into the top of RAM, and started running. When you run SYSGEN, the first thing it does is to put a *second* copy of CP/M in RAM, but in the TPA right above SYSGEN. This is a non-working copy being made ready for "export." Then after you answer the questions shown in step 2, SYSGEN (in collaboration with the working copy of CP/M at the top of RAM) transfers the export copy of CP/M from the TPA over onto tracks 0 and 1 of the disk in drive B. In other words CP/M is being used to copy a clone of itself onto your newly formatted disk. Very clever.

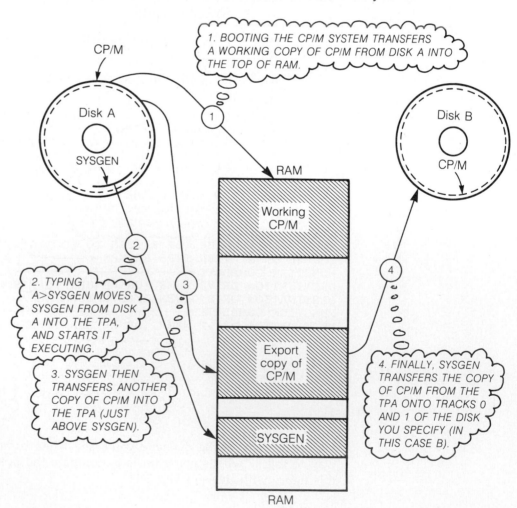

2.5 Using PIP to Complete the Backup

Let's review what we've done so far. In Lab 2.2-1 we formatted a bunch of blank disks. In Lab 2.4-1, we used SYSGEN to copy CP/M onto tracks 0 and 1 of these newly formatted disks. But we still haven't copied the rest of the files (those on tracks 2 to 76) onto our backup disk. If you don't believe this, try using one of your new CP/M backup disks in drive A. You should be able to *boot* it OK, but if you then try to get a directory, you'll get the message "NO FILES". All the CP/M files (like FORMAT, SYSGEN, STAT, etc.) still have to be transferred.

There are two ways to transfer CP/M files from one disk to another. The first uses the PIP utility program supplied with every CP/M disk. The other uses a utility program called COPY (or possibly a name like DUP), but this is *not* found on every CP/M disk. So let's look at PIP first.

The letters PIP mean *peripheral interchange program*. This is a utility program that lets you move copies of files from one place to another. Most of the time it's used to move copies of files from one disk to another, but it can also be used, for example, to move a copy of a file from a disk to a printer, or to another computer by way of a serial port.

The simplest use of PIP is to copy a single file from one disk to another, giving the copy the same name as the original. There are two forms of the PIP command for doing this. The first uses one line as follows.

> A>PIP B: = A:GOODFILE.BAS (CR)
> A>

This means, "Load PIP, and then have it move a copy of the file GOODFILE.BAS from the disk in drive A: onto the disk in drive B:" Notice that the direction is always from right to left (it's similar to the direction of assignments in BASIC statements like LET X = 5). When this move is finished, there will be *two* identical files called GOODFILE.BAS— the original on the disk in drive A:, and the copy on the disk in drive B:. The same command can be given in two steps as follows:

FIG. 2-11   This diagram uses simplified disk and memory maps to show how SYSGEN works. There are four steps in the process: (1) Booting the CP/M system, (2) Running SYSGEN, (3) Using SYSGEN to generate an export copy of CP/M, and (4) Copying the export copy onto the new disk. The balloons on the figure explain what the steps do. Step 3 can be skipped by pressing RETURN when SYSGEN asks for "SOURCE DRIVE NAME", and step 4 can be skipped by pressing RETURN when asked for "DESTINATION DRIVE NAME". One reason you might skip step 3 is that the TPA already contained an export copy of CP/M. Step 4 might be skipped if you wanted to save the export copy of CP/M as a COM file (using the SAVE command) rather than as a bootable system on tracks 0 and 1. Sections 6.6 and 6.7 explain why these two options are of interest.

```
A>PIP (CR)
*B: = A:GOODFILE.BAS (CR)
*
```

Here the first line is used just to bring the PIP program into the TPA and start it running. PIP then lets you know that it's ready for a transfer command by printing "*" as its prompting symbol. This second form is preferred if you're going to use PIP several times in a row, since PIP will need to be loaded only once. You'll keep getting *s asking for further PIP commands until you quit PIP by typing CONTROL-C.

You can also ask PIP to copy a bunch of files by using an ambiguous file name on the right. For example,

A>PIP B: = A:*.BAS (CR)

means "copy all BASIC files (extension .BAS) from the disk in drive A to the disk in drive B". Similarly, PIP B: = A:*.* would mean copy *all* files from A: to B:.

PIP can also be used to make a spare copy of a file on the same disk by using a new name (e. g., PIP XTRA.BAS = OLD.BAS or PIP B:XTRA.BAS = B:OLD.BAS).

We'll cover all the features of PIP (including the "PIP parameters") in Chapter 6. For now, the main thing to know is that PIP B: = A:*.* means "move onto disk B copies of all the files that are on disk A."

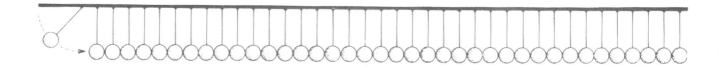

LAB EXERCISE
2.5-1

Transferring Files with PIP

Step 1.   Put the original CP/M disk in drive A, and a formatted disk onto which you copied CP/M (in Lab Exercise 2.4-1) in disk drive B. Boot the system.

Step 2.   Run the PIP.COM command file by typing

A>PIP(CR)

You'll know PIP is working if you eventually see its "prompting symbol" (the asterisk *). This tells you that PIP is waiting for further instructions. For this lab, you should respond as follows:

B: = A:.*(CR)

This means, "Copy onto B all the files listed in the directory of A." *Remember to keep telling yourself that the direction of the file transfer is from right to left.* An example of the output that PIP produces while copying files from A to B is shown in Fig. 2-12.

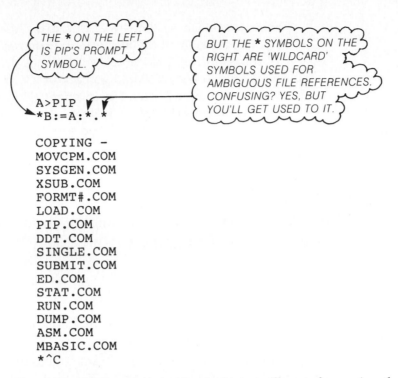

```
A>PIP
*B:=A:*.*

COPYING -
MOVCPM.COM
SYSGEN.COM
XSUB.COM
FORMT#.COM
LOAD.COM
PIP.COM
DDT.COM
SINGLE.COM
SUBMIT.COM
ED.COM
STAT.COM
RUN.COM
DUMP.COM
ASM.COM
MBASIC.COM
*^C
```

FIG. 2-12   This is an example of what you'll see when using the PIP command to copy all possible files from A to B.

Step 3.   When PIP is finished (it will take a while), you'll see its * prompting symbol again. To make another backup copy of the files on the disk in drive A, you can repeat the whole process by replacing the disk in drive B with another newly formatted system disk, and going back to step 1. A faster way is to replace the disk, type CONTROL-C, and then use the Special Trick from page 64 to restart PIP. When you see the * again, type B: = A:*.*(CR) to make another backup.

While you're waiting for this second disk to be copied, it would be a good idea to label the disk you just finished. *Do not write directly on disks.* Write on a separate label that has a sticky backing, and then gently press the label in place next to the manufacturer's label.

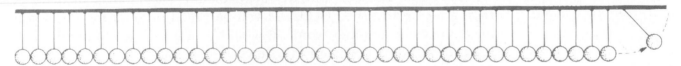

More About Using PIP to Copy Files

• You can combine the two command lines of step 2 into a single line as follows

A>PIP B: = A:*.* (CR)

but when you've finished, this returns you to the system prompt A>, not to the PIP prompt *.

• When you finish "PIPing" files to a disk, it's a good idea to check its directory to see if all the files were transferred. If you used the form of PIP shown in step 2 above and still have its prompt symbol * displayed, you'll have to leave PIP and go back to CP/M where you can ask for a directory. To leave PIP (and most other CP/M programs) do a warm boot by pressing CONTROL-C. You'll then see the A> prompt, at which time you can ask for a directory of the new disk.

```
*(CONTROL-C to return to CP/M)
A>DIR B:(CR)
—directory—
```

If you want to use PIP again, the obvious procedure is to load it into the TPA again by typing

```
A>PIP(CR)
```

Special Trick

If PIP has already been loaded (as in step 2 above), and all you've done since using it is a warm boot followed by DIR (or any other built-in command of CP/M), the PIP program is actually still in the TPA. In this case there's a way to restart PIP *without* reloading provided one of your disks contains a file we'll call GO.COM. If it does, all you'll have to do is type

```
A>GO (CR)   (Or A>B:GO (CR)   if GO.COM is on B)
```

and you'll immediately see the asterisk *. The * tells you that PIP is running again and ready to do more work. The advantage to GO.COM is that (unlike PIP) it takes *zero* space on a disk, and almost zero time to execute.

How do you get the file GO.COM on a disk? It's easy. To put it on the A disk, type

```
A>SAVE 0 GO.COM (CR)
```

To put it on the B disk, type

```
A>SAVE 0 B:GO.COM (CR)
```

Your best bet is to put GO.COM on the master disk in drive A right after step 1. Then GO.COM will be PIPed onto all the disks you make in step 2. In other words, it would be a good idea to modify Lab 2.5-1 to include a new step as follows:

Step 1.5   Add the file GO.COM to your master disk by typing

```
A>SAVE 0 GO.COM
```

This says "save a file of zero length on the disk in drive A and give it the name GO.COM." We'll explain how and why GO works as it does in Section 6.4. For now, think of it as meaning, "Go to the beginning of the TPA and start executing whatever program is found there."

2.6 Relocating CP/M with MOVCPM; COPY and DUP

The previous labs concentrated on making backup copies of the original CP/M system disk that came with your computer. These labs assumed that this disk was customized to work on your specific system, and that it already "knew" about all the features of that system. This will be a correct assumption in most cases since CP/M is usually packaged with computers at the time of sale.

If you obtain CP/M independently, however, then you may need expert help in adapting it to your specific computer. We'll say something about "customizing" CP/M for various kinds of hardware in Chapter 6, but for beginners the only sensible approach is to buy a CP/M guaranteed to work on *your* system. You should not attempt to modify or customize CP/M until you've had a lot of experience.

There's one exception to this rule. If you buy a CP/M designed for a system with limited memory, say 24K, but your computer system has a larger amount of memory, it's usually easy to modify CP/M so that it loads at the top of your expanded memory. That way, you'll be leaving as much room as possible in the TPA for application programs. The next lab shows how to perform this modification with a CP/M utility program called MOVCPM. The process of using MOVCPM to modify CP/M so that it will work at a new location in memory is called *relocation*. Although most people use MOVCPM to relocate the system to a higher place in RAM, it can just as well be used to move CP/M to a lower position. (You might want to do this if there are some special routines you want to protect by putting them at the top of memory, above both the TPA and CP/M.)

One caveat is needed: not all CP/M systems have a MOVCPM utility (Apple II doesn't), and even those that do might not have one that's customized to your system. For more on this subject, see the technical note at the end of this lab. There will also be more about MOVCPM in Sections 6.6 and 6.7.

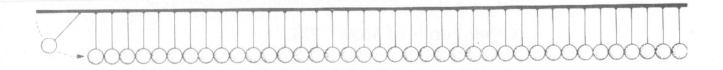

LAB EXERCISE   Using MOVCPM to Relocate CP/M

2.6-1   *Step 1.*   Place your regular CP/M system disk in drive A, and a formatted disk in drive B. Boot the system.

Step 2.   Use the MOVCPM command to put a relocated "export" version of CP/M in the TPA. The exact form of the MOVCPM command depends on where you want to relocate CP/M, and whether you want to save the relocated version on the system tracks of your disk. Our example is based on using an original CP/M system disk of the type distributed with Morrow disk systems. This comes configured for use with 24K of RAM. We'll assume that we want to relocate it for use with 62K of RAM (the maximum allowed for Morrow systems) and save the relocated system. Based on these assumptions, here's the procedure. In step 1, when you place the original 24K Morrow disk in drive A, and boot the system you'll see the following:

> 24K CP/M Vers. 2.2, Cbios rev. 3.1
> For Thinker Toys Disk Jockey 2D Controller @ 0F800H.

For step 2, you should now execute MOVCPM as follows (the spaces shown are important; the 62 means relocate for a 62K RAM; the asterisk * means you'll want to save it):

> A>MOVCPM 62 * (CR)
>
> CONSTRUCTING 62K CP/M Vers. 2.2
> READY FOR "SYSGEN" OR
> "SAVE 44 CPM62.COM"

To actually save the relocated system on your disk, you should next use SYSGEN with the following responses:

> A>SYSGEN(CR)
> SYSGEN VER 2.2
> SOURCE DRIVE NAME (OR RETURN TO SKIP) (Press CR here)
> DESTINATION DRIVE NAME (OR RETURN TO REBOOT)B
>   (Answer B here)
> DESTINATION ON B, THEN TYPE RETURN   (Press CR here)
> FUNCTION COMPLETE
> DESTINATION DRIVE NAME (OR RETURN TO REBOOT)
>   (---etc.---)

The last line can be answered "B" if you wish to make another 62K CP/M system (in which case you should put another formatted disk in drive B:). If not, press carriage return for a warm boot.

Other Forms of MOVCPM

If MOVCPM 62 * is typed without the asterisk (MOVCPM 62), the relocated system will immediately start executing, but it can't be saved. If two asterisks are used, separated by spaces (MOVCPM * *), this means, "Move CP/M as high as possible and get ready for SYSGEN or SAVE." If only MOVCPM(CR) is typed, this is taken to mean, "Move CP/M as high as possible and start executing the relocated system (without a SAVE or SYSGEN)."

Step 3.   Test the relocated CP/M system (62K in our example) you have just made by removing the original disk from drive A, and replacing it with the newly constructed disk from drive B. Do a cold boot, and if everything's working OK, here's what you will see:

62K CP/M Vers. 2.2, Cbios rev 3.1
For Thinker Toys Disk Jockey 2D Controller @ 0F800H.
A>

This disk does not have any files on tracks 2 to 76, so you should next use PIP (Lab 2.5-1) to complete the job. Then you can use this 62K CP/M disk as your master disk, making backup copies as shown in Labs 2.4-1 and 2.5-1.

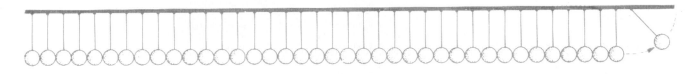

TECHNICAL NOTE ON MOVCPM

If your MOVCPM doesn't work as just described, the problem may be that your copy of MOVCPM wasn't customized for your system. Customization is needed because MOVCPM doesn't use the CP/M on the system tracks of your disk (0 and 1); it carries its own special "relocatable" copy. As supplied by Digital Research, this copy contains a loader and BIOS for a very early CP/M system (the Intel Microcomputer Development System). Customized MOVCPM programs will have had these Intel parts replaced. If your copy of MOVCPM hasn't had such a change, your only recourse is to do the MOVCPM operation in two stages. First you use whatever MOVCPM you have, and then you use DDT to overlay the old Intel loader and BIOS with customized versions for your particular system. The overlaying procedure is a bit tricky, so it won't be explained until Section 6.7. Incidentally, the reason MOVCPM gets into all this trouble is that it isn't too bright. It has the job of modifying a bunch of addresses in the relocated CP/M it generates, but it only knows how to do this for the private copy of CP/M it carries, not for the working copy of your disk. If that private copy is obsolete, then your MOVCPM (which carries a "bit map" showing where to modify its private copy) won't work as advertised. The only solution is to use the two-step process described in Section 6.7.

Using COPY and DUP

Some CP/M disks contain a program called COPY.COM, DUP.COM, or some such name. This program, when executed, allows you to copy an entire disk (from track 0 on up to track 76 for 8-inch disks) in one operation. It is not a standard CP/M utility, so you'll have to read the instructions that come with it to see exactly how it's used. Also be aware that COPY programs usually work only with the specific disk systems for which they were developed. For example, the Apple II CP/M COPY program works only for the 35-track Apple II disks. Even here, there are two versions, one for 13-sector disks, the other for 16-sector disks.

The advantage to COPY programs is that they execute more quickly than PIP, and you get all the tracks copied in one operation. The disadvantage is that they copy disks exactly, placing files in the same sectors as before. PIP, on the other hand, is "smart" enough to rearrange files to use up empty spaces (created perhaps by previous file erasures) in the most efficient manner.

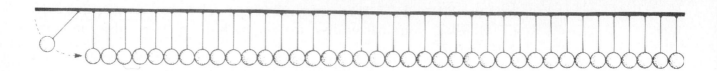

LAB EXERCISE 2.6-2

Using COPY and DUP Programs; COPY/S on the Apple

Step 1.   Check the directory of your system for a program with a name like COPY, DCOPY, DUP, FASTCOPY, etc., stored as a command file. Run the program by typing its name (plus any other required information) after the A> prompt.

Step 2.   Place the disk you want copied (called the *source* or *master*) in drive A, and a *formatted* disk onto which you want to do the copying (called the *destination* or *slave*) in drive B. Here's an example of the prompts and replies used with the Apple II CP/M system COPY program.

> A>COPY B: = A:
>   APPLE] [CP/M
> 16 SECTOR DISK DUPLICATION PROGRAM
>   (C) 1980 MICROSOFT
> INSERT MASTER DISK IN A:
> INSERT SLAVE DISK IN B:
> PRESS RETURN TO BEGIN
> .
> .
> .
>   COPY COMPLETE

Note: This will copy the entire A disk onto the B disk. If you want to copy CP/M only (tracks 0, 1, and 2 on the Apple 5 1/4-inch disk) use the command A>COPY B: = A:/S. You can later use PIP to copy selected files onto the B disk.

Step 3.   Test the copy you just made by placing it in drive A and seeing if the system boots. Also do a DIR to see if all the files you wanted were transferred.

Each COPY program is a little different. Here are two more examples of step 2.

Step 2.1.   Using DUP on the ISC 8063 computer: Place a source disk
containing DUP in drive A, and a *formatted* destination disk
in drive B. Then type

A>DUP A: TO B: (CR)

There are no prompts to answer, so be sure that you do this correctly.
The program DUP must be on the disk in drive A.

Step 2.2. Using COPY on the Godbout CompuPro S-100 computer: This
program gives you a choice of copying the system tracks, the data tracks,
or all the tracks as follows:

A>COPY
CompuPro COPY Utility Version 2.4
Do you want to copy:
     SYSTEM tracks only? (type S)
     DATA tracks only? (type D)
     ALL of the disk? (type A)
     Exit back to System? (type X) D

Source drive? (A,B,C, or D) A
Destination drive? (A,B,C, or D) B

Put source disk on A
Put destination disk on B
then type <RETURN>

Note: For this and other copy programs, the disks on drives A and B
must have the same format. On the other hand, many systems allow
you to PIP files between disks with different formats.

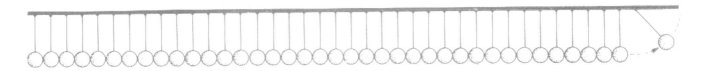

Adding Files to a Disk

The labs up to this point have shown how to backup the CP/M disk
that came with your system, including all the files it contained on tracks
2 through 76 (3 through 34 on the Apple). Some of these files come
with CP/M, but others are really "extras," and its up to whoever sells
you CP/M to decide what these are.

     One of the extra files included on many CP/M disks is a BASIC
interpreter. However, there are also systems where CP/M and BASIC
are supplied on separate disks. In this case, it's convenient to move
BASIC over to your CP/M disk so that it will immediately be available
when you boot the system. The same idea applies to other CP/M software
you buy. Here's how to do this.

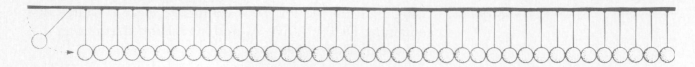

LAB EXERCISE 2.6-3

Adding Files to a Disk

Step 1. Place one of your CP/M backup disks (*not* your original CP/M disk) in drive A, and place the disk with the program(s) you wish to move onto this disk in drive B. Boot the system. If there are any files you *don't* want on the A disk, use ERA to erase them (*Warning:* Never erase files from your original CP/M disk.) For example, to erase the file DOC.BAK, you'd type

> A>ERA A:DOC.BAK (CR)

Step 2. Use PIP to copy either all the files from the disk in B to A, or just selected ones. To copy all the files, type

> A>PIP A:=B:*.*(CR)

To copy selected files (say MBASIC.COM and DEMO.BAS), transfer them one at a time with PIP as follows

> A>PIP(CR)
> *A:=B:MBASIC.COM
> *A:=B:DEMO.BAS

Step 3. Do a warm boot by pressing CONTROL-C, and then check the directory of the disk in drive A

> *(CONTROL-C)
> A>DIR
> --- directory ---

You should now see the files you copied from the disk in drive B added to the files that were originally on the disk in drive A (minus of course any files you may have erased).

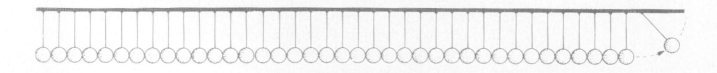

Systems with at least two disk drives are recommended for computer operations that involve the transfer of files from one disk to another, including of course the making of backup disks. However, it *is* possible to handle such transfers on a single disk system provided that you have software that makes the single disk drive sometimes act like the A drive and sometimes like the B drive. You'll also need lots of patience because it will be up to you to alternately insert the source and destination floppy disks into your single drive at the right times.

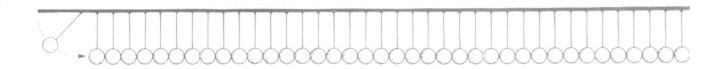

LAB EXERCISE 2.6-4

Copying on Systems with One Disk Drive

There is no standard way to handle single-disk file transfers, so you'll have to read the documentation for your particular system. Two examples of how the process works for the Morrow and Apple II computers are given in steps 1 and 2 below. If you have a different system, it would be a good idea to jot down some notes on the procedure as "step 3" for future reference.

Step 1. When using a single-drive Morrow 2D Discus system to copy files, you pretend that you have two drives called A and B. To copy from "disk A" to "disk B" you do the following:

1a. (Optional) If you're going to copy files onto a new disk, first FORMAT it with the program FORMT#. Type

    A>FORMT# (CR)

but then remove the system disk from A and replace it with a blank (or obsolete) write-enabled disk. Answer the prompt, "SELECT DRIVE" with A, and proceed as in Lab 2.2-1.

1b. Label the source disk (from which you wish to copy files) as "A", and the destination disk as "B".

1c. Put the source disk in your (one and only) drive. We'll assume that this disk contains (among other things) SINGLE, PIP, and SYSGEN.

1d. Run the SINGLE program by typing A>SINGLE S (the S means start).

1e. Now use PIP or SYSGEN as though you really had two drives (A and B), following the prompts you receive for switching disks "A" and "B". The dialogue for steps 1(d) and 1(e) will look something like the following, where it is understood that you insert the proper disks as prompted.

    A>SINGLE S
    Single Installed
    A>PIP B:=A:TEST.DOC
    Insert "B" (CR)

Insert "A" (CR)
Insert "B' (CR)
. . . etc., alternately inserting disks until finished.
A>SINGLE E

This last line means end the SINGLE program.

Step 2. If you have access to an Apple II with CP/M but only one disk drive, you can use the COPY program by answering A for both source and destination drives. The only two options you have are to copy the entire disk, or to copy the system tracks (this is the /S option explained in Lab 2.6-2). The dialogue for copying the entire source disk (what Apple calls the master disk) looks like this:

A>COPY A: = A:
        APPLE] [CP/M
16-SECTOR DISK DUPLICATION PROGRAM
        (C) 1980 MICROSOFT
INSERT MASTER DISK   (Put in the source disk.)
PRESS RETURN TO CONTINUE   (Press CR.)
INSERT SLAVE DISK   (Replace the source disk
                                    with the destination
                                    disk.)

INSERT MASTER DISK   (Replace the destination
                                    disk with the source
                                    disk.)

. . etc. . . .
COPY COMPLETE

Note that the destination disk must be formatted. If it isn't, first run the single-disk version of Apple FORMAT by responding A to the question "Format disk in what drive?", and then being sure to put the blank disk into the drive before pressing carriage return.

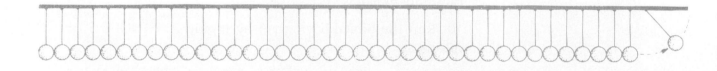

2.7 Problems and Projects

1. Why would anyone ever want to use the DIR command with a single file name as, for example, A>DIR HTEST.COM ? *Hint:* Notice that a DIR of all files does not list the names in alphabetical order.

2. Draw a picture of the memory map for the ISC 64K CP/M system, given the following information: CCP starts at E400 hex, BDOS at EC00 hex,

and BIOS at FA00 hex. How large is each section in hex? In decimal? How large is CP/M in hex? In decimal?

3. Suppose you want to enlarge the BIOS section of the 64K CP/M described in question 2 so that it can have an additional 4096 bytes (decimal) of code. Assuming that the CCP and BDOS don't change in size, draw a new memory map for this "super BIOS" system. Do you think the new system will actually work? Why? Why not? How will application programs know where to find it?

4. Suppose you have a disk with some useful files on it, but PIP is not one of them. Outline an efficient procedure for making multiple copies of this disk *without* using a copy program. It's OK to use the PIP that's on another disk.

5. Suppose your CP/M is up and running but the telephone rings. You leave to answer it, and when you come back you find that another member of the household has been trying a few things, generating lots of error messages. Explain what might have caused each of the error messages shown in the following snapshot of the console screen left behind by your phantom CP/Mer.

```
A>DIRECTORUUY
DIRECTORY?

A>DIR A
NO FILE
A>DIRA:
DIRA:?

A>DIRA:?
DIRA:??

A>DIR C:
Bdos Err On C: Select
A>STATIC
STATIC?

A>STAT
A: R/W, Space: 224k


A>STAT A

File Not Found
A>STAT A:

Bytes Remaining On A: 224k

A>DIR A:
A: PIP      COM : STAT     COM : ED      COM : DDT      COM
A: ASM      COM : MBASIC   COM : FORMAT  COM : DUMP     COM
A: SYSGEN   COM : BASCOM   COM : BASLIB  REL : M80      COM
A: L80      COM : CREF80   COM : CC1     COM : CC2      COM
A: CLINK    COM : C        CCC : DEFF    CRL : DEFF2    CRL
A: BDSCIO   H   : TABSET   COM : TABSET  C   : ROYALTY  BAS
A: LROYALTY BAS : XREF     COM : GO      COM : MYPOEM   TXT
A: MYPOEM   BAK
A>STAT C**

File Not Found
A>STAT C*

File Not Found
A>STAT C*.*
```

```
Recs  Bytes  Ext Acc
   9     2k    1  R/O  A:C.CCC
  94    12k    1  R/O  A:CC1.COM
 118    16k    1  R/O  A:CC2.COM
  33     6k    1  R/O  A:CLINK.COM
  30     4k    1  R/O  A:CREF80.COM
Bytes Remaining On A: 224k

A>STAT CON:=ZENITH:

Invalid Assignment
A>STAT CON:=CRT:


AA>>MMBBAASSIICC

BASIC-80 Rev. 5.2
[CP/M Version]
Copyright 1977, 78, 79, 80 (C) by Microsoft
Created: 14-Jul-80
31046 Bytes free
Ok
DIR
Syntax error
Ok
DIR A:
Syntax error
Ok
FILES
PIP      .COM  STAT    .COM  ED      .COM  DDT      .COM  ASM      .COM
MBASIC   .COM  FORMAT  .COM  DUMP    .COM  SYSGEN   .COM  BASCOM   .COM
BASLIB   .REL  M80     .COM  L80     .COM  CREF80   .COM  CC1      .COM
CC2      .COM  CLINK   .COM  C       .CCC  DEFF     .CRL  DEFF2    .CRL
BDSCIO   .H    TABSET  .COM  TABSET  .C    ROYALTY  .BAS  LROYALTY.BAS
XREF     .COM  GO      .COM  MYPOEM  .TXT  MYPOEM   .BAK
Ok
FILES B:
Type mismatch
Ok
FILES "B:*.*"
PIP      .COM  STAT    .COM  GO      .COM  ED       .COM  MYPOEM   .TXT
Ok
^C
^C
^C
^C
^C
NUTS
Syntax error
Ok
SYSTEM

A>DIR B
NO FILE
A>DIR "B:*.*"
NO FILE
A>DIR B"
NO FILE
A>DIR B:
B: PIP        COM : STAT      COM : GO        COM : ED        COM
B: MYPOEM     TXT
A>
```

6. The following four uses of PIP do exactly the same thing. What is it?
   Which form do you prefer? (Assume the logged disk drive is A.)

   A>PIP B:NEWPROG.BAS = A:NEWPROG.BAS
   A>PIP B:NEWPROG.BAS = NEWPROG.BAS
   A>PIP B: = A:NEWPROG.BAS
   A>PIP B: = NEWPROG.BAS

7. Suppose that NEWPROG.BAS is on the disk in drive A, and you want to save *two* copies of it on the disk in drive B. Show how to use PIP to do this (see Section 6.4 for more information about PIP). Show how to use MBASIC to do the same thing.

8. Sometimes one wants to change the contents of a disk, removing some files, and adding others. Read Section 3.3 to see how the ERA (erase) command works, and then list the set of commands needed so that if the disk in drive A contains PIP, FILE1, FILE2, FILE3, and FILE4, it will be changed to a disk which contains PIP, FILE2, FILE3, FILE5, FILE6, and FILE7, using a disk in drive B: that contains FILE5, FILE6, and FILE7. To see how to automate this process, read about SUBMIT in Sections 5.4 and 5.8.

CHAPTER THREE
CP/M by the Book

3.0 Introduction

When you buy CP/M—either as a separate software product, or as part of a disk or computer system—you usually receive copies of the official CP/M manuals. These come from Digital Research [33], the software company that sells (or licenses others to sell) CP/M. Some computer manufacturers also supply reprints of the same materials bound into a single book.

It's safe to say that beginners have found these manuals confusing. Several less charitable adjectives have also been used. The fact is that if you know how to dig the material out, the Digital Research manuals can be quite valuable. And of course the explanations come right from the "horse's mouth."

Our goal in Chapter 3 is to help you use the CP/M manuals more effectively. We'll do this by identifying which sections in the manuals are advanced, and should therefore be postponed for later study. We'll then go through a whirlwind tour of those features which can be handled with the background provided in Chapters 1 and 2 of this book. To help make the tour more memorable, we'll conclude the chapter by showing how to apply these features in a lab that integrates the use of most of the CP/M commands into a single (albeit slightly contrived) project.

Topics Covered in the Digital Research Manuals

Over the years there have been several revisions of CP/M, with the most important being versions 1.4, 2.0, 2.2, and 3.0. These versions are sometimes called CP/M-80, since they all run on 8080/8085/Z80 micro-processors.* Version 2.2 is undoubtedly the best known of the lot. It has been licensed to hundreds of computer companies, and it's in use by over a million people.

The set of manuals originally supplied by Digital Research for versions 1.4 and 2.0 came in nine sections (labelled I through IX). The Digital Research documentation for version 2.2 consists of a short User Guide plus six technical manuals (labelled I through VI). These six manuals are also supplied as a single bound volume by other companies (e. g., Morrow and CompuPro). The SoftCard CP/M system for the Apple II includes a reprint of the first five of these 2.2 manuals. (The missing

---

* There is also a version of CP/M for the 8086/8088 microprocessors called CP/M-86. For further information on CP/M-86, and the multi-user/multi-tasking version of CP/M called MP/M, see Section 6.8. The additional features of CP/M-80 version 3.0 are also discussed there.

manual is the "CP/M Alteration Guide"; it's not included because Apple SoftCard CP/M does not include the BIOS, MOVCPM, and SYSGEN programs discussed in the Alteration Guide.) The following chart shows what the content of these manuals is, and how it relates to the material in this book.

Topics Related to CP/M

1. **Introductory material, general description of the system, explanation of the CP/M built-in commands ERA, DIR, REN, SAVE, TYPE, and USER, the CP/M transient commands STAT, ASM, LOAD, PIP, ED, SUBMIT, XSUB, DUMP, SYSGEN, and MOVCPM, and the use of control characters for line editing.**

   • In the 1.4/2.0 manuals this is covered in Section I, and part of Section II. However, the USER command is not available in these versions.

   • In the 2.2 manuals this material is all found in Section I, except for SYSGEN and MOVCPM which seem to have been lost in the shuffle (although they reappear in Section VI which refers you to Section I for information on how to use them!).

   • In the present book this material is distributed over Chapters 1, 2, 3, 4, 5 and 6. These chapters also contain material not found in the manuals, including a description of how CP/M works in terms of memory maps, and detailed lab exercises showing how to use the commands.

2. **Information on how to interface the features of CP/M to custom-designed programs.**

   • This is an advanced topic, and it should only be looked at after you have had experience with CP/M and machine language programming. It's covered in Sections VIII and IX of the 1.4/2.0 manual, and Section II of the 2.2 manual.

   • This material is briefly covered in Chapters 4 and 6 of this book. There is also some information in Chapter 5 on how MBASIC interfaces with CP/M.

3. **Information on how to use the ED (editor), ASM (assembler), and DDT (dynamic debugging tool) programs.**

   • This is covered in Sections III, IV, and V of both the 1.4/2.0 and 2.2 manuals.

   • The use of ED is introduced in Chapter 3 of this book, with additional material in Chapters 5 and 6. There is an introduction to machine language programming and the use of ASM and DDT in Chapter 6.

4. **Guide to Altering CP/M.**

   This is also an advanced topic. It's concerned with using MOVCPM and SYSGEN to adapt CP/M to different memory sizes, and modifying the BIOS (or CBIOS) sections of CP/M to make them work with new I/O devices.

   • The 1.4/2.0 manual covers this in Sections VI and VII. The 2.2 manual discusses it in Section VI. Apple II users should note that the SoftCard CP/M system does not supply MOVCPM, SYSGEN, or the "source code" of BIOS, so true user modification of CP/M is not possible on this system.

   • Simple uses of MOVCPM and SYSGEN appear in Chapter 2 of

this book; advanced use is described in Chapter 6. The last two sections of Chapter 6 show how to change or add selected assembly language sections to BIOS, and then install the results as features of your own customized BIOS.

5. **How to Use Other Programs (Such as Word Processors, Business Programs, or Language Processors Like BASIC) "Under CP/M".**

   • This topic is not discussed in the Digital Research CP/M manuals.

   • It is covered in Chapters 4, 5, and 6 of this book. Chapter 4 covers application software, Chapter 5 discusses MBASIC, and Chapter 6 explains machine and assembly language. The programming language C and examples of application programs written in C are also discussed in Chapter 5.

3.1 More about Memory Maps; Binary, Octal, and Hexadecimal Numbers

When you "start up" CP/M by doing a cold boot, what you actually do is move a bunch of machine language code (about 8000 bytes of it for a well-developed CP/M) from the system tracks (0 and 1 for 8-inch disks, 0, 1, and 2 for 5 1/4-inch disks) of the CP/M disk into the main memory (RAM) of your computer. This code is structured as three big blocks called BIOS, BDOS, and CCP. The code is usually loaded into the "top of RAM," that is, into those locations with the highest addresses. In a 48K machine (one which has $48 * 1024 = 49152$ bytes of RAM), after a cold boot the memory map is approximately as shown in Fig. 3-1.

You'll notice that a new feature has been added to this memory map. The memory addresses are given in both decimal and hexadecimal (also called hex) form. The hex form is a bit strange at first, but it has many advantages and is used in computer literature extensively. Let's see how it works.

The four principal notations for representing numbers in computer work are *binary* (base 2), *octal* (base 8), familiar *decimal* (base 10), and *hexadecimal* (base 16). These are four different ways of representing exactly the same numbers. For example, the age of majority (21 years old) can be represented as

10101 in binary	$(1*16 + 0*8 + 1*4 + 0*2 + 1*1 = 21)$
25 in octal	$(2*8 + 5*1 = 21)$
21 in decimal	$(2*10 + 1*1 = 21)$
15 in hex	$(1*16 + 5*1 = 21)$

(*Note:* The fact that the calculations on the right are done in the decimal notation for all these examples can be pretty confusing. If necessary, just put a little subscript beside the numbers to keep track of what base each number is in, that is, 21_{10}, or 10101_2, 15_{16}, etc.)

We'll not discuss octal any further since this isn't used much in microcomputer work. The main skills you'll want are in dealing with hex and binary notation.

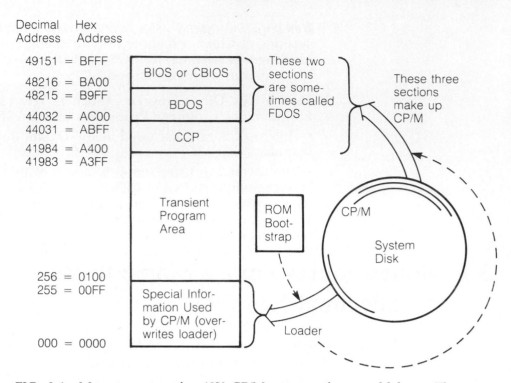

FIG. 3-1   Memory map of a 48K CP/M system after a cold boot. The exact addresses for the CCP, BDOS, and BIOS vary since the BIOS section is usually expanded by the computer company supplying CP/M into what is called a customized BIOS (CBIOS). The system tracks on a CP/M disk contain CP/M and a "cold loader" program. When you do a cold boot, a ROM bootstrap program moves the cold loader into the bottom of RAM. The loader then moves CP/M into the top of RAM and starts it executing. The first thing CP/M does is to overwrite the loader with special information it needs (explained in Section 6.4). The abbreviation CP/M means "Control Program for Microcomputers," CCP means "Console Command Processor," BDOS means "Basic Disk Operating System," BIOS means "Basic Input Output System," and FDOS means "Floppy Disk Operating System."

The trick for translating binary numbers into decimal is to write the powers of 2 as the pattern:

| 256 | 128 | 64 | 32 | 16 | 8 | 4 | 2 | 1 |

Then use the corresponding binary digits as multipliers (line up the binary number in question starting with the rightmost binary digit under the 1). For example, the binary number 11110001 lines up like this:

256	128	64	32	16	8	4	2	1
	1	1	1	1	0	0	0	1

and becomes:

$$128 + 64 + 32 + 16 + 1 = 239_{10}$$

So the binary number 11110001 equals the decimal number 239. For hex numbers write the powers of 16 as this pattern:

| 4096 | 256 | 16 | 1 |

Then use the hex digits as multipliers. Thus, 2014 hex is

$$2*4096 + 0*256 + 1*16 + 4*1 = 8212_{10}$$

One other thing you'll have to know about hex is that it uses 16 different digits (0,1,2,3,4,5,6,7,8,9,A,B,C,D,E,F) with decimal equivalents as follows:

0 = 0	4 = 4	8 = 8	12 = C
1 = 1	5 = 5	9 = 9	13 = D
2 = 2	6 = 6	10 = A	14 = E
3 = 3	7 = 7	11 = B	15 = F

Thus BFFF, the top address in our 48K machine, translates into decimal as $11*4096 + 15*256 + 15*16 + 15*1 = 49151$. An easier way to translate BFFF is to realize that it's one less than C000 (just as you realize a number like 2999 is one less than 3000). Thus BFFF = C000−1 = C*4096−1 = 12*4096−1 = 49151.

The addresses shown in Fig. 3-1 are for a "standard" 48K CP/M system, but many computer manufacturers enlarge the area marked BIOS, resulting in a different set of addresses. For example, the Morrow Design DISCUS-2 system uses the following hex addresses in 48K and 62K systems:

BIOS — From B300 to BFFF in 48K, EB00 to F7FF in 62K
BDOS — From A500 to B2FF in 48K, DD00 to EAFF in 62K
CCP   — From 9D00 to A4FF in 48K, D500 to DCFF in 62K

Instant Quiz

1. Complete the following table:

Binary	Decimal	Hexadecimal
_____	_____	400
_____	_____	FF
_____	_____	1B00
_____	_____	1AFF
_____	16	_____
_____	255	_____
_____	256	_____
_____	4095	_____
_____	4096	_____

2. What are the starting decimal addresses for CCP, BDOS, and BIOS in the Morrow 48K CP/M?
3. How many bytes of main memory does Morrow CP/M take?

Answers

1. The missing decimal numbers are 1024, 255, 6912, and 6911. The missing hex numbers are 10, FF, 100, FFF, and 1000. The next paragraph shows how to obtain the binary equivalents.
2. CCP starts at 40192, BDOS at 42240, and BIOS at 45824.
3. Morrow CP/M takes 8960 bytes of main memory.

Here's a tip on a fast way to go from binary to hexadecimal (and back). Memorize the binary patterns that correspond to the 16 hex digits as follows:

Binary	Hex
0000	0
0001	1
0010	2
0011	3
0100	4
0101	5
0110	6
0111	7
1000	8
1001	9
1010	A
1011	B
1100	C
1101	D
1110	E
1111	F

To convert a hexadecimal number into binary, substitute one of the above four-digit binary patterns for each hex digit. Thus FF is 1111 1111, 400 is 0100 0000 0000, 1B00 is 0001 1011 0000 0000, and so on. 16 decimal is 10 in hex and therefore is 0001 0000 in binary; 256 decimal is 100 in hex and 0001 0000 0000 in binary; and so on. The leading zeros can be dropped, so it's more normal to write 256 as 10000000, etc. To go from binary to hex, reverse the process. Thus, 01000001 is 31 hex, and 10110100 is B4 hex.

Note: To distinguish hex numbers, the letter H is frequently appended. However, books on the Apple II and other 6502 computers put a $ sign in front of hex numbers. In the language C, hex numbers are written with 0X in front; in BASIC they're preceded with &H. Thus you'll see the number B4 hex written as $B4_{16}$, B4H, $B4, 0XB4, and &HB4. Sigh!

3.2 The Organization of CP/M

This section is a continuation of the previous one, with the goal of providing additional information on how CP/M is organized. While such information isn't strictly needed for using CP/M, it can be very helpful in dealing with situations that aren't covered in books. And of course it's the indispensable starting point for anyone inclined to tinker with the innards of CP/M.

So far we've used disk and memory maps as a graphical way of explaining the "what," "where," and even some of the "why" of CP/M. These maps will prove to be more and more useful as you gain experience with their use, but they do have their limitations. Just as a small green rectangle on a map of London can only suggest the jewel of a park awaiting those who go there in person, the cryptically labelled rectangles on a CP/M memory map often find their best use in suggesting the most promising areas for further exploration.

It's at this point that several questions face the newcomer to CP/M. Just how detailed should one's "further exploration" be? And should it be in terms of the "real thing," or should it be more of a vicarious experience, conducted on familiar grounds made possible by metaphor and analogy?

In this section we're going to opt for the analogy approach for a start, and then switch over to a more realistic summary of how all the pieces in the CP/M jigsaw fit together. We'll postpone a discussion of the inner coding of CP/M until Chapter 6, where the necessary background in machine and assembly language programming will have been made available.

CP/M by Analogy

Suppose you've just had the following idea for a new kind of business venture. You've decided to found a company called Ethereal Enterprises, whose sole purpose is to provide other companies with the facilities for doing business. Here's how it works.

Your company starts out by acquiring a large building called the Rotating Action Marketplace. It's a skyscraper with 48 king-sized levels (abbreviated 48K for trademark purposes). In fact there are so many

RAM

rooms on each level that five-digit room numbers are needed—numbers like 47132 near the top, or 00256 near the bottom.

The plan is to rent out most of the building—approximately the first 40 levels—to transient businesses. Since all 40 levels are designed as first-class accommodations, your advertising brochure calls them the Terrific Palatial Accommodations (trademarked of course as TPA).

TPA

So far this looks like little more than a scheme to get into the office leasing business in a big way. But here's the difference. Clients who sign up for space in the TPA are given the right to use the facilities of several built-in service operations which occupy the top eight levels of the building. These services are collectively called the Cooperative Production Melange.

CPM
BIOS

There are three divisions within the coop. The Bionic Services division resides way up on the top levels. It's a kind of super mailroom/telephone-center/shipping & receiving department. Its principal job is to communicate with the outside world, particularly the inhabitants of a place called Peripheral Park. The top floors may seem like an odd place to put Bionic Services, but there is exceptionally good elevator service so this location works out just fine. Besides, if you should ever acquire that new 64K building across the street, you can simply tell all your workers to move into the top floors. This will simplify the move, and more importantly, it will reserve the prime areas of the new building for clients who need lots of space on adjacent floors.

BDOS

Just below the Bionic Services office there's another in-house facility that handles boxed delivery out of state. This operation is needed because you also own a large warehouse in New Jersey, and you intend storing fileboxes belonging to your clients over there when they leave town. The New Jersey warehouse happens to be circular in shape, so everybody calls it the Disk. The Boxed D. O. S. group is in charge of managing the Disk building, and keeping track of where everything stored there is located.

CCP

The heart of your operation is just below BDOS (roughly from levels 40 to 42). It's officially called the executive suite (although it has also been referred to as the Chief Cook and Pooh-Bah area). This is where clients go to submit requests for services, and have them examined, interpreted, and dispatched.

Actually, there are only a half dozen requests that can be handled in the executive area. These are called built-in services. For example, a client can request a directory (DIR) of all the other services, and immediately get a response. Clients can also request that some of their belongings be stored in the New Jersey warehouse (this is called a SAVE request), or ask that these belongings be tagged with the name of the person to whom they belong (a USER request). The CCP group also takes care of putting new labels on things (REName), throwing stuff out (ERAse), and providing complete inventories of what's in storage (TYPE).

DIR
SAVE
USER
REN
ERA
TYPE

That's a lot of work, and one might ask if the executive types found in CCP are up to it. The answer is "No," but like all good executives,

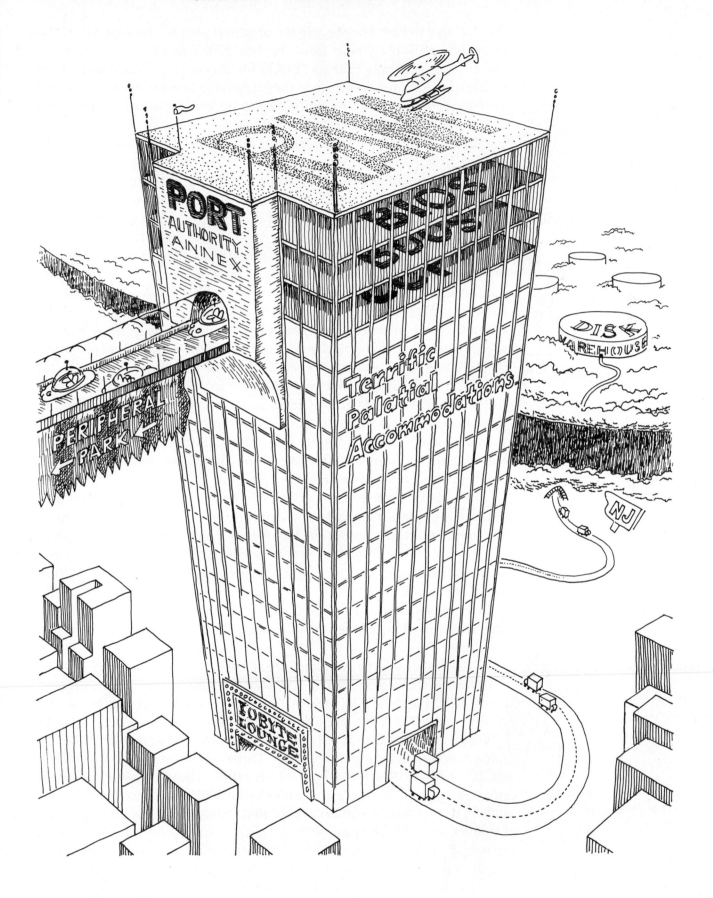

they've learned to use the talents of other people. In particular, they frequently call upon help from the bunch up in BDOS. (Around the office this is smilingly called a "BDOS function call.") This doesn't really overload BDOS, however, since they have also learned to pass the buck. To where? Well there's no place else to go except Bionic Services, and that's where all the real work gets done.

In addition to being the real workhorses, the Bionic Services people are the best trained of the lot. In particular, they know all about the physical layout of the building—where its exits and entrances are and how to best get there. It's for this reason that they are sometimes called **CBIOS**—the Customized Bionic Services group. They are also able to provide clients with a large variety of outside shipping and receiving services, even though only four "standard" names are used inside the building. These are CON, RDR, PUN, and LST (it's rumored that the names were taken from an ancient computer book where they referred to "console," "reader," "punch," and "listing" devices). Up in CBIOS when they get an order to do something involving one of these names— say to send something out by way of CON—they look in a chart called IOBYTE that specifies what "physical" kind of shipping company should be used. For example, the chart might say, "Until further notice, all CON shipments are to go by Cheapest Rail Transport (CRT)." Then the shipping clerk finds out which CRT is currently available (say the Zenith RR), and sends the order on its way. Thus all three names (CON, CRT, and Zenith) end up meaning the same thing, but tenants inside the building need remember only the first one.

In addition to in-house services, clients will undoubtedly want other kinds of support. Your plan for handling such requests is to hire the appropriate outside service on a part-time basis, and give it temporary office space in the TPA. It's even possible that both the outside service and the client who requested it will reside in the TPA at the same time. For example, if the Elite De Paris Restaurant rents space in the TPA, but complains about bugs, you plan on moving the Dynamic Debugging Therapists in right above them, leaving DDT there until they get the job done.

One last thing. In thinking about ease of access to your services, you realize that some clients will want a simple way of finding and using BDOS and CBIOS. So you reserve an area near the street level where rooms 00000 to 00255 have been set aside for special use. For example, rooms 00000, 00001 and 00002 act as a reception area that has information on where to find CBIOS. Three other rooms (numbers 00005, 00006, and 00007) are reserved as an office where more sophisticated clients may go to find out exactly where the BDOS services (the "function calls" we mentioned earlier) are located. Room 00003 is also special. It contains the IOBYTE chart with the latest information on what internal shipping names are currently used with which external carriers. The workers in CBIOS frequently use the information kept there, but clients are also allowed to peek and poke around in it if they wish.

But seriously. . . .

CBIOS

CON
RDR
PUN
LST
IOBYTE

DDT

A Short Technical Description of CP/M

It's been said that all analogies limp, and ours is no exception. It will have served its purpose if it helps make the following more conventional description of CP/M a little more meaningful.

CP/M is a microcomputer disk operating system that resides at the top of user memory (RAM). It is functionally divided into three modules:

1. CCP which means the *console command processor*. All the commands typed at the console after the symbol > are interpreted and sent on their way by the CCP.

2. BDOS which means the *basic disk operating system*. This is actually a misnomer; BDOS contains about 39 functions which handle both disk *and* console I/O management. These functions are used both by CCP and by transient application programs.

3. BIOS which means the *basic input and output system*. The program segments in this section are used by the functions in BDOS to handle the *actual* transfer of data to disks, printers, console keyboard, console screen, and any other physical devices connected to the computer. BIOS must therefore be customized for the computer, console, and other peripherals with which it will be used, whereas CCP and BDOS are machine-independent.

CP/M resides at the top of RAM where it occupies approximately 8K bytes. Its exact location depends on the size of RAM available. In addition, CP/M always uses the first 256 bytes of RAM as a fixed base of operations. For example, the exact location of BDOS is stored in locations 6 and 7 (location 5 has the instruction "jump," while locations 6 and 7 contain the actual address of BDOS). Location 3 contains 8 bits called the IOBYTE. These bits show which physical devices are to be associated with the "logical" devices of BIOS. (The difference between physical and logical devices will be explained in Chapter 5, where we'll say more about the IOBYTE and how to modify it with STAT. Also see Section 3.3.)

Starting at location 256 (which is 0100 HEX), the bytes of RAM are used for what's called the *transient program area* (TPA). It's here that various application and utility programs reside. When a new application program is called for, it overwrites the TPA, destroying the old one—hence the name "transient."

If a transient program needs to store data in RAM, the TPA is also used. This data is usually stored right above the transient program itself. If necessary, application programs and data can overwrite the CCP and in some cases BDOS, but they shouldn't go past BIOS. When a new program (and/or data) are put in the TPA, the old contents of the TPA may first be saved on disk in the form of CP/M *files*.

Now we can tell you what a *warm boot* does. It reloads the CCP and BDOS modules of CP/M just in case these were overwritten by a transient program or its data (which is perfectly normal in many applications). A warm boot also resets some information about the disks that are currently being used, including what are called file allocation bit maps (see Chapter 6). The machine language program for carrying out a warm boot is in BIOS, so this part of CP/M should never be overwritten. If it is, the only way to restart is with a cold boot which reloads *all* of CP/M. Although overwriting BIOS is definitely not recommended, it's quite possible since CP/M resides in *user* memory. This is RAM where you can write anything you want (e. g., with POKE). A few badly placed operations of this sort could mess up BIOS enough to send CP/M into a spin, but a cold boot will always give you a fresh start.

Incidentally, the address of the warm boot section of BIOS is stored in locations 1 and 2. Location 0 contains a jump instruction, so locations 0, 1, 2 hold the instruction "jump to warm boot." Thus an application program can cause a warm boot even if it doesn't know where the warm boot code is stored. It can always get there indirectly, by using the instruction JMP 0000. This is the technique used by programs that allow you to do a warm boot by some other means than pressing CONTROL-C (for example by pressing RETURN in the SYSGEN program, or by typing SYSTEM in MBASIC).

Armed with this picture, let's next look at the commands that are processed by the CCP (called the built-in commands of CP/M), and some of the transient utility programs supplied with CP/M (also called the transient commands of CP/M).

3.3 An Overview of the CP/M Commands

A CP/M command is really a program name. It's typed at the system console (right after the > prompt symbol), along with the name(s) of any file(s) you want the command to work on. For example, typing

    A>ERA B:GLUE

causes the command program ERA to execute. This program then does its job, which in this case is to *erase* the filename GLUE from the directory of the disk in drive B. In this example ERA is called the *command*, while ERA B:GLUE is called a *command line*. It is understood that you must also press carriage return (CR) at the end of a command line. (From now on, we won't show the (CR).)

ERA is one of the seven *built-in commands* of CP/M: ERA, DIR, REN, SAVE, TYPE, d: (where d is a drive name like A, B, C, etc.), and USER. They are called built-in commands because the programs they call upon are located in CP/M proper as part of the module called CCP (console command processor). Since the CCP is already in RAM when you see the A> prompt, the built-in commands can be executed immediately.

In addition to the built-in command programs, CP/M also allows the user to call upon *transient command* programs. These programs are stored as files on disk (somewhere on tracks 2 to 76), so when you call upon them they must first be loaded into the TPA (transient program area) of RAM. This doesn't take very long, so using a transient command works in about the same way as using a built-in command. For example, to use the STAT transient command on the file B:GLUE you would type the command line

    A>STAT B:GLUE

This gives you statistics on how much space GLUE is taking up on disk B.

There are nine transient command programs supplied with CP/M 2.2: STAT, ASM, LOAD, DDT, PIP, ED, SUBMIT, XSUB, and DUMP. In addition, there are a variety of transient command programs available from other suppliers, and from CP/M user groups. All it takes to make one of these commands available is to buy a disk that contains the program you want as a file of type .COM (command file). For example, to make the command MBASIC available, you would buy the program called "Microsoft BASIC for CP/M" on a disk of the proper size for your system (for example, on an 8-inch single-density disk using the standard soft-sectored format described in Chapter 2). This disk contains the file MBASIC.COM. To copy this file (and any other files the disk contains) onto your normal system disk in drive A, you would put the Microsoft disk in drive B and then give the command

    >PIP A:=B:*.*

Chapter 5 shows how to use the MBASIC command. Chapters 4 and 6 give additional examples of application programs that can be stored as command files on your system disk.

Control Characters

When you type a command line you're "talking" to the CCP. This processor is set up to *trap* certain control characters, that is, not accept them as part of the command line, but to use them as a signal to do something else—usually to correct a typing error. Some of these same control characters are trapped and used in a similar manner by other programs (for example, the ED program described in the next section). The principal control characters used in CP/M 2.2 this way are the following:

CONTROL-H

(Also called BACKSPACE and shown as <-- on the Apple and ISC keyboards.) This moves the cursor back one position, erasing whatever was previously typed there. The cursor is a symbol on your console screen (usually the underline _ or a solid rectangle) that shows where the next character will be printed.

CONTROL-X

This cancels the current line, erases it from the screen, and moves the cursor back to the beginning of the line.

CONTROL-U

This cancels the current line. The effect is similar to control-X, except that the cancelled line is not erased, and the cursor moves to the beginning of the next line.

CONTROL-P

If you have a printer connected as your LST (listing) device, this causes output to appear on both the console screen *and* the printer. Output to the printer continues until you type another control-P, a control-C, or execute a transient program that doesn't recognize this code (e. g., MBASIC).

DELETE (RUBOUT)

This is not a control character, but it can be used to delete previous characters typed at the console. However the deleted characters are not erased from the console screen—in fact they are printed again in reverse order. For example, if you type ERA GRUE, press delete three times (to delete RUE), and then type LUE, you'll see this

        A>ERA GRUEEURLUE

To double check on what this looks like to CP/M, type control-R ("retype") instead of (CR). In our example, this will display ERA GLUE on the next line. If that's what you want, *then* type (CR).

CONTROL-R

This retypes the current line with all deleted characters removed as shown in the above example.

The use of other control characters is discussed in Section 3.4. Here's a summary of all the CP/M recognized control codes, followed by their ASCII codes in decimal and hex form (03H means 03 hexadecimal).

Name	Meaning	ASCII Decimal	Hex
^C	Warm boot.	3	03H
^E	Start new line.	5	05H
^H	Backspace and delete.	8	08H
^I	Tab 8 columns.	9	09H
^J	Line feed.	10	0AH
^L	Represents (LF) (CR) in ED.	12	0CH
^M	Carriage return.	13	0DH
^P	Printer on/off	16	10H
^R	Retype current line.	18	12H
^S	Stop display (any character except ^C to restart).	19	13H

Name	Meaning	ASCII Decimal	Hex
^U	Delete line; start on new line.	21	15H
^X	Delete line and erase from screen.	24	18H
^Z	End of string or of console input.	26	1AH
DELETE	Delete and echo last character.	127	7FH

The CP/M Built-In Commands

In the following, ufn means "unambiguous file name" (like B:GLUE.POT), and afn means "ambiguous file name" (like B:?LUE.*). Also recall that when you do not use a disk drive designator like B: in a filename, the system assumes you mean the file on the disk that's currently logged-in. If the prompt says A>, the logged-in disk is on drive A, and the file name is assumed to be A:filename. The logged-in disk can be changed by typing A>B: (or A>C: or A>D:). When you do this, you're actually giving the first of the following seven built-in commands of CP/M. Each of these commands is typed after the system prompt symbol > and made to execute by pressing (CR).

●   d:

This command changes the logged-in disk to d: (the colon is part of all device names in CP/M), where d is a letter from A to P representing one of the 16 allowable disk drives. Example:

    A>B:
    B>

The number of disk drives that can be referenced is usually the number you can see sitting next to the computer, but not always. For example, some hard-disk systems permit assigning different disk drive names to different areas on the one hard disk. The ISC 8063 Color Computer allows you to refer to the same drive in more than one way depending on whether you want it to be treated as single or double density. The letters A, B, C, and D refer to the four double-density drives normally allowed on this system, but E and F refer to the A and B drives used in single-density mode. Thus to copy the file TEST.BAS from a single-density disk inserted in the usual B drive onto a double-density disk inserted in the A drive, you would type

    A>PIP TEST.BAS=F:TEST.BAS

Similarly, you would use DIR F: to get a directory of the files on the single-density disk which was placed in drive B.

●   ERA afn

This command erases the file(s) with name(s) afn. Examples:

A>ERA GLUE.POT	erases the file GLUE.POT from the disk in drive A:
A>ERA B:*.BAK	erases all backup files (files with secondary name BAK) from the disk in drive B:
A>ERA WS????.*	erases all files that have primary names with 6 characters or less beginning with WS

Warning: Using ? or * usually means erase a lot of files—be sure that's what you want! Incidentally, ERA doesn't erase the actual contents of the file. Rather, it erases the file reference from the directory, freeing up the space used by that file for use by new files. This means that it's sometimes possible to retrieve an erased file, but a special "disk fix" utility program (not supplied with CP/M) is required (see Section 4.0).

● DIR afn

This command lists the names of all the file(s) with name(s) afn on the console output device. Examples:

A>DIR	lists names of all files on the disk that's in the logged-in drive (A: in this example).
A>DIR *.*	same as DIR.
A>DIR A:	lists names of all files on the disk in drive A:.
A>DIR ????????.*	same as DIR. (This is silly, but it's interesting to ask why it's the same as DIR.)
A>DIR B:	lists names of all files on the disk in drive B:.
A>DIR B:C*.*	lists names of all files on the disk in drive B: which have primary names beginning with the letter C.
A>DIR *.BAS	lists names of all files on the disk in drive A: which have the secondary name BAS (all BASIC files).
A>DIR ???.*	lists names of all files on the disk in drive A: that have primary names using 3 or fewer characters.
A>DIR ?S*.*	lists names of all files on the disk in drive A: that have primary names in which the second letter is S.

● REN ufn2 = ufn1

This is the rename command. The file ufn1 has its name changed to ufn2. Notice that the renaming process goes from right to left. Tell yourself it means REN newname = oldname.

Example:

     A>REN STICKY.COM = GLUE

This changes the name of the file GLUE to STICKY.COM. The old name GLUE will be overwritten in the directory of the disk in drive A: by the name STICKY.COM.

Note: The change of name can be made only in the directory of one disk. Thus REN B:INSECTS = B:BUGS is permissible, but REN B:INSECTS = A:BUGS is not. If you want to put a file on other disks under different names, use PIP. You must also use PIP if you want two copies of the same file under different names on the same disk.

Example: Suppose you have a file called VALUABLE.COM on the disk in drive A:, and want a spare copy for experimental purposes. The command

A>PIP SPARE.COM = VALUABLE.COM

will put a second copy on the disk in drive A: while

A>PIP B:SPARE.COM = VALUABLE.COM

will put a similar copy on the disk in drive B:. In both cases the name of the new file will be SPARE.COM but the contents will be the same as that of the file VALUABLE.COM.

● SAVE n ufn

(This command is included here for completeness; it's used mostly in advanced work as described in Chapter 6.) SAVE takes whatever is in the first n *pages* of the TPA (where n is a decimal number from 1 to 255) and saves it on disk with the name ufn. A page is defined to be a block of memory 256 bytes long. Page 0 starts at decimal address 0, page 1 starts at 256, page 2 at 512, and so on. Page boundaries are easier to spot in hexadecimal notation than in decimal. In hex, the page number of any address is given by the fourth and third most significant digits in the hex representation of that address (the two digits on the left). For example, 0100H is the address of the zeroeth byte in page 01 (which is also the start of the TPA), 0A82H is an address near the middle of page 0A (which is page 10 in decimal), and 2BFFH is at the end of page 2B (which is 43 in decimal).

To use the SAVE command, the program you want to save must be in the TPA, and you must know the minimum number of pages it occupies. For example, if you know that a program occupies locations 0100H to 0A82H, you can save it as PROG3.XX on the logged-in disk with the command

A>SAVE 10 PROG3.XX

We used the decimal number 10 since the last location 0A82H is in page 0AH which is 10 decimal. The question of how to get this program into the TPA in the first place, and how to know what locations it occupies is more complicated. We'll return to this subject in Chapter 6. For now it's worth noting that the use of SAVE in CP/M is usually connected with use of the SYSGEN, DDT, and MOVCPM transient command programs, and that this can get tricky. It is *not* the same as the SAVE "file" command in BASIC which is much simpler to use.

- **TYPE ufn**

This command lists the contents of ufn on the console output device. It should only be used with an ASCII disk file, that is, a disk file containing information in the form of a sequence of ASCII character codes. For example, if the file POEM.TXT has been created and saved on disk with the editor program ED (see Section 3.4), it can be listed on the console screen with

    A>TYPE POEM.TXT

Assembly language programs can also be listed this way. For example, you can see the assembly language form of BIOS by typing

    A>TYPE BIOS.ASM

Control-S is used to interrupt such listings; pressing any other character except control-C resumes the listing. Also recall that the listing can be typed on both the console and printer if control-P is first typed as follows:

    A>^P
    A>TYPE BIOS.ASM

- **USER n**

This command is available in CP/M versions 2.0 and later. It can be used to distinguish between the files of 16 different users of the same disk. If a user types A>USER n where n is an integer from 0 to 15, then all that user's files will be invisibly labelled with the number n. For example if a husband, wife, and child all wish to use the same CP/M disk, they can agree to always issue the commands USER 1, USER 2 or USER 3, respectively, after booting the system. Then even if they all happen to use the same file names, there won't be any conflict—the user numbers will be used to store these files on different parts of the disk. If the USER command is not given, the default condition upon a cold boot is to assign all files to USER 0. To check on how many different users have files on the logged-in disk, the command STAT USER: can be given.

The CP/M Transient Commands

The transient commands are usually more complicated to use, involving subsystems that take a while to learn. We'll give a brief introduction to two of them here (STAT and DUMP), followed by a reference to later sections of the book that explain the others (PIP, DDT, ASM, LOAD, ED, SUBMIT, XSUB). There will be additional information about STAT in Section 5.3. The SYSGEN and MOVCPM transient commands were already discussed in Sections 2.4 and 2.6.

```
A>STAT
A: R/W, Space: 224k


A>STAT A:

Bytes Remaining On A: 224k

A>STAT B:

Bytes Remaining On B: 100k

A>STAT
A: R/W, Space: 224k
B: R/W, Space: 100k


A>STAT D*.*

   Recs  Bytes  Ext Acc
    38    6k     1  R/W A:DDT.COM
    61    8k     1  R/W A:DEFF.CRL
    44    6k     1  R/W A:DEFF2.CRL
     4    2k     1  R/W A:DUMP.COM
Bytes Remaining On A: 224k

A>STAT D*.* $R/O

DDT.COM set to R/O
DUMP.COM set to R/O
DEFF.CRL set to R/O
DEFF2.CRL set to R/O
A>
   STAT D*.* $S

  Size  Recs  Bytes  Ext Acc
   38    38    6k     1  R/O A:DDT.COM
   61    61    8k     1  R/O A:DEFF.CRL
   44    44    6k     1  R/O A:DEFF2.CRL
    4     4    2k     1  R/O A:DUMP.COM
Bytes Remaining On A: 224k

A>STAT A:DSK:

     A: Drive Characteristics
  3888: 128 Byte Record Capacity
   486: Kilobyte Drive  Capacity
   128: 32  Byte Directory Entries
   128: Checked   Directory Entries
   128: Records/ Extent
    16: Records/ Block
    52: Sectors/ Track
     2: Reserved Tracks


A>
```

THE COMMAND STAT (CR) GIVES SLIGHTLY DIFFERENT RESULTS BEFORE AND AFTER DRIVE B HAS BEEN ACCESSED.

THE $R/O OPTION IS USED HERE TO GIVE "READ ONLY" STATUS TO ALL FILES WITH NAMES BEGINNING WITH "D".

THE 'SIZE' STATISTIC IS THE SAME AS 'RECS' (NUMBER OF RECORDS) FOR SEQUENTIAL FILES. ITS MAIN USE IS TO SHOW HOW MUCH SPACE HAS BEEN RESERVED FOR RANDOM ACCESS FILES.

FIG. 3-2 This shows the STAT command being used in a number of ways to give statistics about files and about the disks on the system.

● STAT or STAT "command line"

This command can be used for several purposes. Its simplest use is to give statistical information about disk file storage. There are several forms of the command used for this purpose as follows:

> A>STAT or A>STAT d:

where d is a drive name like A, B, C, or D. This form displays statistics on how many bytes of storage remain on disks as shown in Fig. 3-2. Two related forms of STAT are the following:

> A>STAT afn or A>STAT d:afn
> A>STAT afn $S or A>STAT d:afn $S

These all give statistics on the files that satisfy the afn. To get statistics on all the files on a disk, use *.* for afn. The $S adds the "size" statistic to the display as shown in Fig. 3-3. This is the same as the number of records except for random access files (see Section 5.2).

A>STAT afn $R/W   A>STAT afn $R/O

These commands make the named files read/write or read/only, respectively. To change all the files on disk d to R/O, use STAT d: = R/O, where d is A, B, C, or D.

A>STAT afn $SYS   A>STAT afn $DIR

The first form gives the named files system status, which simply means they don't show in the directory; the second form removes this status. SYS files are still available for copying with PIP. They can be worked on like any other file if they have R/W status.

```
A>STAT VAL:

Temp R/O Disk: d:=R/O
Set Indicator: d:filename.typ $R/O $R/W $SYS $DIR
Disk Status  : DSK: d:DSK:
User Status  : USR:
Iobyte Assign:
CON: = TTY: CRT: BAT: UC1:
RDR: = TTY: PTR: UR1: UR2:
PUN: = TTY: PTP: UP1: UP2:
LST: = TTY: CRT: LPT: UL1:
A>
```

```
A>STAT DEV:
CON: is TTY:
RDR: is TTY:
PUN: is TTY:
LST: is LPT:

A>
```

THE OUTPUT FROM THIS COMMAND DEPENDS ON THE IOBYTE. BY STUDYING FIG. 5-7, YOU CAN TELL THAT ON THIS SYSTEM THE IOBYTE CONTAINS 80 HEX.

FIG. 3-3 The STAT VAL: and STAT DEV: commands produce a summary of valid I/O device assignments and actual device assignments respectively. The second display can be used to indirectly give the current value of the IOBYTE (to do this, compare the assignments shown by STAT DEV: with those listed in the IOBYTE table given in Fig. 5-7).

A>STAT d:DSK: A>STAT DSK: A>STAT USER:

These give statistics on the named disk, all disks, and user numbers respectively.

A>STAT VAL: A>STAT DEV:

The first of these (VAL:) shows all the possible physical to logical device assignments, while the second (DEV:) shows which assignments the IOBYTE has made on your system. What does this mean? The next few paragraphs plus Section 5.3 tell you something about the mysterious subject of "device assignments."

Redefining I/O Devices with STAT

One of the most intriguing uses of STAT is to let a user redefine which physical I/O devices on his or her computer are to be associated by CP/M with its "in-house" (called *logical*) I/O device names. For example, CP/M always expects to find a logical I/O device called console (CON:) on the system. However, you are allowed to have up to four physical devices connected to your computer for possible use as the console. Only one can be used at a given time, so whenever CP/M is booted it "chooses" which one by consulting a little table called the IOBYTE. To change the contents of this table, you use STAT in the form

STAT logical device = physical device

There are four logical device names you can use in this command. They are called CON:, RDR:, PUN:, and LST:. For example,

A>STAT CON:=TTY:

means "make the console be the physical device TTY." It's true that there are hundreds of physical devices available, but CP/M has provision for only four physical device names for each logical device. The names are rather ancient, but you *must* use one of them, substituting in your own mind the *real* name.

For the console, the allowable physical names are TTY:, CRT:, BAT:, and UC1: (which mean "teletype-like device," "cathode ray tube device," "batch I/O device," and "special user console device #1"). Inside CP/M (in BIOS to be exact), each of these names is associated with something called a "driver program." Driver programs talk to the outside world by way of actual *port* addresses on your computer, that is, by way of specific locations in the I/O circuitry of the machine.*

For example, suppose your system is set up so that the TTY: driver program uses port #1, and the CRT: driver program uses port #2. Let's

---

* Apple II users should note that a port address is *not* the same as a slot number—that would be far too easy! The Apple slot numbers are just that— numbers used to label plug-in slots on the Apple chassis. They have no obvious relation to actual computer addresses. Re-routing I/O on an Apple fitted with the SoftCard CP/M system is better governed by faith than logic.

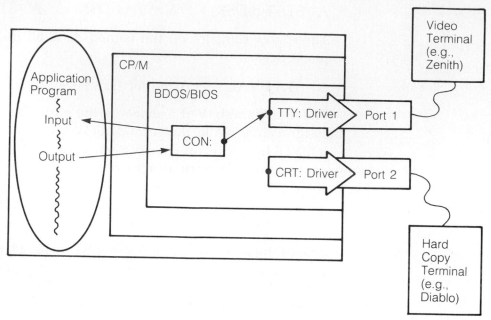

FIG. 3-4 This is a simplified diagram of a CP/M system where the CON: (console) logical device is connected to the TTY: driver/port. This port is shown with a video terminal connected to it, so the user would use the video terminal for console input and output.

also suppose that your system normally uses the physical device connected to port #1 as the logical device CON: (console). This physical device might actually be a teletype, but it could just as well be a video terminal—it's up to you. In either case you would say that the *default* console device on your system is the TTY:. So even if the brand new video terminal sitting on your desk was made by Zenith you'll have to let CP/M call it TTY: whenever you plug it into port #1.

Let's now suppose that you buy a printing (or "hard-copy") terminal, and that you connect it to the CRT: port of your system (in our example this was port #2). Fig. 3-4 shows what this arrangement looks like.

To make the printing terminal become the console, you can switch CON: from its default TTY: driver/port connection to the CRT: driver/port connection as follows:

A>STAT CON: = CRT:

This means "from now on, all console operations are to be handled by the physical device connected to the CRT: driver/port." It may sound crazy to refer to your printing terminal as a "CRT:", but all you really mean is that you have physically connected it to the port that your BIOS uses with the CRT: driver program. The above STAT command will therefore assign the printing terminal as your console. In other words, the switch in the diagram now looks like what is shown in Fig. 3-5.

We'll return to this subject in the next chapter and elaborate on all the device switch possibilities. We'll also show how to reassign physical devices from BASIC without using STAT.

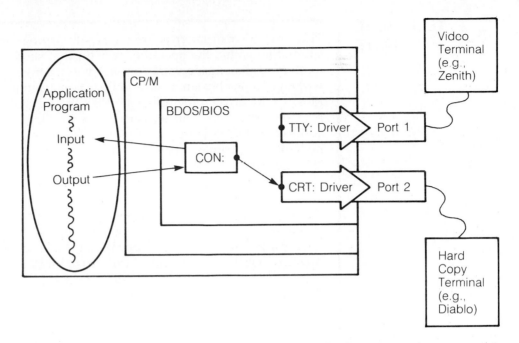

FIG. 3-5 This diagram shows the change in BIOS after giving the command

A>STAT CON: = CRT:

The CON: logical device is now connected to the CRT: driver/port. This port happens to have a hard-copy terminal connected to it, so now the user can do console input and output through the hard copy terminal. You can see that the names TTY: and CRT: (which CP/M calls physical device names) don't have to correspond to the kinds of hardware usually associated with these names.

- ## DUMP afn

    This command is similar to TYPE, except that the contents of the file are displayed in hexadecimal form, 16 bytes per line. The first entry on each line is the relative address of the first data byte on that line, where the first line is given an arbitrary starting address of 0000. Examples of the output produced by DUMP are given in Lab 2.3-1 and in Lab 3.5-1.

- ## PIP, ASM, LOAD, ED, SUBMIT, XSUB, DDT

    These commands are more complicated to use, so they are explained in separate sections of this and other chapters as follows:

PIP	Sections 2.5 and 6.5
ED	Sections 3.4 and 5.4.
ASM, LOAD	Sections 6.1, 6.2, 6.3, and 6.4.
SUBMIT, XSUB	Section 5.4.
DDT	Sections 6.5, 6.6 and 6.7 (also see below).

    The programs ASM (Assembler) and DDT (Dynamic Debugging Tool) are usually used in conjunction with 8080 machine language programming. However, there is one command in DDT worth mentioning now since it combines some of the features of TYPE and DUMP. It is

The term *driver* or *driver program* refers to a program segment (usually a subroutine within the operating system) that sends data from a memory location to the outside world, or vice versa. Driver programs are usually written in assembly language and then translated into machine language. Most CP/M driver programs use 8080/Z80 IN and OUT instructions to read or write data from specific I/O ports. Both the 8080 and Z80 can address up to 256 I/O ports. The port addresses are usually determined by hardware settings. They can range from 00 to FF hex, i. e., from 0 to 255 decimal.

Here's a simple output driver program written in 8080 assembly language. It starts by looking at port 3 to determine the *status* of the output circuitry. We're assuming that port 3 is part of this output circuitry, and that if its first bit is 0 (zero) the circuit status is "not ready." In this case the program stays in a wait loop. When the bit changes to 1, the output circuitry (usually the part called the transmitter holding register) is ready, so one character of data is moved from the C register to the A register of the 8080, and then sent out port 1.

```
OUTPUT:  IN      03          ;Get status byte from port 3
         ANI     01          ;Check the first bit
         JZ      OUTPUT      ;If it's zero go to OUTPUT
         MOV     A,C         ;Else move character into A
         OUT     01          ;And send it out port 1
         RET                 ;Return to calling program
```

To send a stream of n characters out port 1, the main program would call this driver subroutine n times. If you've never seen 8080 code before, you'll understand this example better after reading Chapter 6. Examples of slightly more complicated output drivers which also do "handshaking" with a printer are shown at the end of Chapter 6.

called the *display* command of DDT. It shows both the hex and (where possible) the ASCII representations of the characters in a file. For example, suppose you have created a file called POEM by using a word processor that inserts control characters in the text. If you try to use TYPE on this file, the control characters may drive your printer crazy. Instead, use

        A>DDT POEM

DDT will then show its prompt symbol (-) after which you type D (meaning "display") to see 192 bytes of memory in hex form, and *where possible* the equivalent ASCII printable characters. When there is no equivalent ASCII printable character (e. g., a control character) a period (.) is displayed. To see the next 192 bytes, type another D. To skip over part of the file and start the display at the address s, type Ds. To display from byte s to f, type Ds,f where s and f are hex addresses.

An example of the output produced by the display feature of DDT is shown in Section 3.5 (Super Lab). You'll notice there that the 192 bytes are displayed as 12 lines of 16 bytes each, and that each line also shows the starting address of its 16 bytes on the left side. Incidentally, if DDT was on one disk (say in drive B), but POEM was on another (say in drive A), you could type

    A>B:DDT A:POEM

or

    A>B:DDT POEM

and then type D to obtain the display.

There will be a great deal more said about DDT in Chapter 6 where we will find that D is just one of its twelve subcommands (D, A, F, G, I, L, M, R, S, T, U, X). Lab Exercise 3.5-1 will briefly illustrate three of these: D (display), F (fill), and S (set). Fill and Set are used to modify selected bytes of memory. Fill inserts a given byte of data in all the locations of a block of memory you specify, while Set allows you to change individual bytes of memory. For example, by using the Set command on location 3 (−S0003), you can change the IOBYTE. The reason for doing this will be explained in Section 5.3, where we'll also address the question of what values one might want to put in the IOBYTE.

3.4 An Introduction to ED

ED.COM is the name of a program supplied with CP/M for use as a *text editor*. It's a program that lets you enter, modify, and save on disk anything that can be expressed as text, that is, with letters, numbers, and other printable symbols. ED can therefore be used to enter and edit poems, contracts, letters, term papers—and of course computer programs. The ED program is stored as a COM disk file, so it's classified as a transient command. To give the ED command, you type ED followed by the name of the text file you wish to edit. For example, if you wish to edit a text file called MYPOEM.TXT you type

    A>ED MYPOEM.TXT

Notice that you cannot type A>ED. The reason is that the ED command must do two things: (1) bring the program ED.COM from disk into the TPA and start it executing, and (2) *open* the disk file MYPOEM.TXT. Opening the file means "connecting" it to the ED program so that ED can perform both *read* and *write* operations on the file MYPOEM.TXT.

As soon as these two things happen (it takes only a few seconds), ED prints an asterisk (*) as its prompting symbol. This is a signal that it is now waiting for you to type one of the two dozen or so (sub)commands available in ED. A complete list of these commands is given at the end of this section. Before going through this list, it will help if we first introduce some of the basic ED commands by way of an example.

When ED is first used, there are two possibilities: the text file you wish to work on is brand new (and therefore it is not in the directory), or the text file already exists and you wish to modify it through changes, additions, or deletions. To show the difference, we'll break our example up into two sections called "Day 1" and "Day 2". Additional techniques will be shown in sessions called "Day 3", and "Day 4".

Day 1

We'll assume that on Day 1 you wish to create a brand new text file called MYPOEM.TXT. To do this, turn on the computer, boot CP/M, and then type the command

A>ED MYPOEM.TXT.

Of course you can't really *edit* a non-existent file, so what this really means is that you want to create the file. However, in the world of computing the word "edit" includes both creating a new file (by *inserting* text into an initially empty file), and later modifying it (by deleting old text and/or inserting new text). The system will know that this is a new file by checking the directory. It will tell you if the name MYPOEM.TXT is not already in the directory by printing the message NEW FILE. Then it will print an asterisk (*) which is the ED *command prompt*. Whenever you see * in ED, you know that it is expecting you to type a command (*not* text). At this point the console screen will look like the following:

A>ED MYPOEM.TXT (CR)
NEW FILE
   : *__

In CP/M versions 2.0 and 2.2, space for a five-digit *line number* and a *colon* (:) will be inserted at the beginning of each line. If you don't want these line numbers, the first command you should give is -V (which means turn off line numbering). However, line numbering is handy to have, so you'll usually want to leave it on. In case you have turned line numbering off with -V, you can turn it back on again with the command V. Incidentally, the letter V was chosen to mean "verify all line numbers." The command 0V means "verify (type) how much space is left in the text buffer" (explained below).

Note: In version 1.4, the above works in exactly the opposite way. The ED program starts out with line numbering off, so you have to type V to turn it on.

So far, we have a poem with nothing to it. Assuming that we're not interested in starting a new fad called "null poetry," the next thing to do is to put some text into this empty file. The command for doing this is the letter i (or if you are using upper case, I), which means "insert text into the file." The source of this text is understood to be whatever is typed at the console keyboard. So you type i, press carriage return, and begin typing your poem. Each time you want to start a new line, you must press carriage return. Here's what you'll see on the screen after typing in two lines of text. The symbol __ shows where the cursor will be on your console screen after doing this.

```
A>ED MYPOEM.TXT
NEW FILE
  : *i (CR)
 1: Roses are red (CR)
 2:      Electrons are blue (CR)
 3: __
```

The symbol (CR) means press the carriage return key (sometimes called the enter key). When you do this at the end of a line of text, nothing will show on the screen, but ED will insert both a carriage return *and* a line feed into your text file. You don't actually type the line feed (LF), but ED always adds it. Why? Because while (CR) causes the cursor to move to the extreme *left*, (LF) is needed to get you down to the next line. The lines of text are stored in memory, one character per byte, as follows:

Memory

R	82
o	111
s	115
e	101
s	115
	32
a	97
r	114
e	101
	32
r	114
e	101
d	100
(CR)	13
(LF)	10
	32
	32
	32
E	69
l	108
e	101
.	.
.	.
.	.
l	108
u	117
e	101
(CR)	13
(LF)	10

This part of memory is called the ED *text buffer*.

The column showing memory locations contains the decimal values of the ASCII codes corresponding to each character. The equivalent hex and binary values, and further information about ASCII codes are given in Appendix A. Note that the decimal code for a space is 32—it's a genuine ASCII character. The binary values are what are actually stored in memory, but the decimal and hex equivalents are easier to use in writing about these codes. The part of memory used by ED to hold this text is called a *text buffer*.

Another thing to note about our example is that both upper- and lowercase letters were used. If you want to have all letters *stored* using only the ASCII uppercase codes (no matter how they were typed in), first give the command U, which means, "Translate lower to *upper* case before storing in the buffer." If you want all the letters stored exactly as typed in, use the command -U to mean, "Don't translate to upper case." When you first call upon ED, the -U command is taken as the default (normal) condition. However, there is an undocumented (and quite confusing) "feature" of ED where typing *capital* I for insertion turns uppercase translation on. Moral: Use small i for insertion if you want lowercase preserved, and forget about -U.

Suppose you next type in a few more lines, but then have to leave for an appointment. You can save what you have just typed by copying the contents of the text buffer onto disk under the filename MYPOEM.TXT. To do this, *first leave the insert mode* by typing Control-Z (often written as ^Z, which means press the CONTROL and Z keys simultaneously).

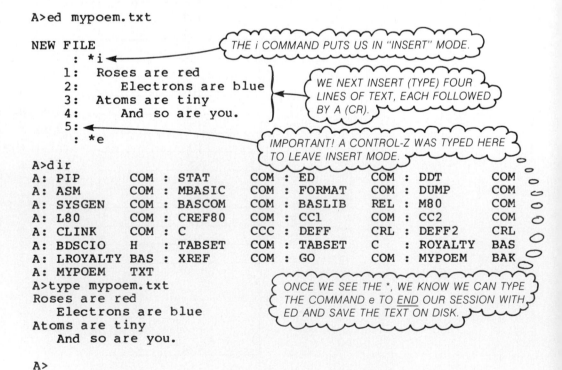

```
A>ed mypoem.txt

NEW FILE                          THE i COMMAND PUTS US IN "INSERT" MODE.
     : *i
   1:   Roses are red
   2:       Electrons are blue       WE NEXT INSERT (TYPE) FOUR
   3:   Atoms are tiny               LINES OF TEXT, EACH FOLLOWED
   4:       And so are you.          BY A (CR).
   5:
     : *e                           IMPORTANT! A CONTROL-Z WAS TYPED HERE
                                    TO LEAVE INSERT MODE.
A>dir
A: PIP       COM : STAT    COM : ED      COM : DDT     COM
A: ASM       COM : MBASIC  COM : FORMAT  COM : DUMP    COM
A: SYSGEN    COM : BASCOM  COM : BASLIB  REL : M80     COM
A: L80       COM : CREF80  COM : CC1     COM : CC2     COM
A: CLINK     COM : C       CCC : DEFF    CRL : DEFF2   CRL
A: BDSCIO    H   : TABSET  COM : TABSET  C   : ROYALTY BAS
A: LROYALTY  BAS : XREF    COM : GO      COM : MYPOEM  BAK
A: MYPOEM    TXT
A>type mypoem.txt                   ONCE WE SEE THE *, WE KNOW WE CAN TYPE
Roses are red                       THE COMMAND e TO END OUR SESSION WITH
    Electrons are blue              ED AND SAVE THE TEXT ON DISK.
Atoms are tiny
    And so are you.

A>
```

FIG. 3-6   This is a sample of a complete Day 1 session with ED, followed by the use of DIR, and TYPE to double-check on what was done.

This takes you back to the asterisk (*) command level of ED. The normal way to then end the editing session *and* copy the text buffer's contents from memory out on disk is to type the E (End) command. Fig. 3-6 shows what the whole Day 1 session will look like after you do this. It also shows use of the DIR and TYPE built-in commands to double-check on the name and contents of the file you just saved.

Note: If you want to leave ED and *not* save the contents of the buffer on disk, type Q (for Quit) instead of E. If you want to save the latest version of MYPOEM.TXT on disk, and then return to ED to continue editing it, type H (Head). If you want to "scratch" the editing you've just done and return to ED for a fresh start, type O (return to Original situation).

The directory shows that the disk in drive A now contains a new file called MYPOEM.TXT. Since this is a file of ASCII characters, the CP/M built-in command TYPE can be used to double-check the contents of this file (there is a similar command called T which can be used to type the text buffer contents while still in ED, but this doesn't verify what's been saved on disk).

Instant Quiz

1. How can you store a second copy of MYPOEM.TXT on the disk in drive B?
2. Suppose you want MYPOEM.TXT saved on the disk in drive B, but *not* on the disk in drive A,
   (a) Describe three ways of doing this.
   (b) Under what circumstances might this be a good procedure?
3. There are two common mistakes made by first-time users of ED. What do you think they are?

Answers

1. Use PIP as follows:

   A>PIP B: = A:MYPOEM.TXT

2. (a) You could first use PIP as above to copy the file onto B, and then use A>ERA A:MYPOEM.TXT to erase it from A. A simpler method is start out ED in the following way:

   A>ED B:MYPOEM.TXT

   This works if you are creating a new file, or editing an old file already stored on the disk in drive B. If you want to edit a file already on A, but store the edited version on B, the following "two disk" form of the ED command line is allowed:

   A>ED MYPOEM.TXT B:

   When you finish this editing session (by typing E or H), the

new version is stored on B as B:MYPOEM.TXT, while the original
file stays on A as A:MYPOEM.BAK.
(b) You might do this if the disk in drive A is loaded with system
programs, and you therefore prefer using a fresh, formatted disk
in B exclusively for saving text files.

3. Forgetting to type CONTROL-Z when they want to leave insert
   mode and give a command, and then forgetting to type i (or I)
   to get back into insert mode so more text can be entered.

Day 2

In this session we'll use ED to make some changes in MYPOEM, and
to add some new lines. The session is started the same way as on Day
1 by typing A>ED MYPOEM.TXT. However, even though MYPOEM.TXT
is now a genuine text file, this command does not actually bring it into
memory. To move text from a disk file into the memory text buffer
(where ED can work on it), the command nA (or na) must be used,
where n is a positive integer. This means "append" (add) n lines of
text from the disk file MYPOEM.TXT (which is termed the *source* file)
to the ED text buffer. If you type 100A, 100 lines are appended. If you
type 1A or just A, only 1 line is appended. These commands must all
be typed after the * symbol of ED, e. g., *100A (CR).

The A command can be used several times in an editing session.
To keep track of what's already been appended, a pointer called SP
(source file pointer) is used. It starts out pointing at the first line of the
source file. In our example, this would be the first line of MYPOEM.TXT.
If you then type 2A, two lines are appended to the buffer, and SP is
changed to 3. So the next time A is used, text is transferred from
MYPOEM starting at line 3.

Similarly, the system keeps track of where it can next append text
to the memory buffer by using a pointer called MP (memory pointer).
MP starts out as zero, and it's increased by n each time the command
nA is given. MP is decreased by n each time n lines are removed from
the buffer by the command nW. Thus it always points at the *last* line
of text still in the buffer.

The user of ED doesn't have to know anything about SP or MP. If
you don't know how many lines of text are on the source file, you can
either take a guess on the high side (say, 500A), or you can use #A
which means "all possible lines." Actually, the # is equivalent to saying
65535A, which is the maximum number of lines permitted. Another
shorthand allowed is 0A which means "append enough lines to fill the
buffer half way."

Question

Each time you do an Append, text is added to the buffer right *after* the
text that was previously added. This could be bad for two reasons: the

available space for the buffer might be exceeded, and/or if there's a hardware or power failure, everything in the buffer (including all the changes you may have just made) will be lost. Is there a way to (1) regularly empty out the buffer, and (2) save its contents on a disk file?

The answer to (1) is yes, by using the W (Write) command. To empty the complete buffer, type #W after the * command prompt. To empty the top half of the buffer (and then shift all the remaining lines up to the top), type 0W. To empty the top n lines, type nW. The answer to (2) is that W stores what's removed from the buffer on a temporary file called MYPOEM.$$$. However this file won't be written onto disk until it exceeds a certain size. To force a disk save (for safety), use the H command (H is like E except it takes you back into ED again). Then use *nAnWnA to bring lines n + 1 to 2n into the buffer for further work.

Command	Contents of Text Buffer after Giving This Command	Files Used	Contents of Files after Giving This Command
A>ED MYPOEM.TXT	Empty.	MYPOEM.TXT	On Day 1: Empty. On Day 2: Text saved from the previous editing session.
: *300A	Up to 300 lines of text from MYPOEM.TXT.	MYPOEM.TXT	Unchanged.

(Note: The above step is skipped on Day 1 since there is nothing in the file MYPOEM.TXT.)

: *I	Whatever was appended in the previous step plus whatever is inserted here by typing at the console.	None.	

(Note: Various editing commands to modify the contents of the text buffer usually go here. Also, additional insert and append commands may be used.)

: *#W	Emptied out.	MYPOEM.$$$	Any previous contents plus whatever was in the text buffer—maybe!
: *I	Whatever new text is typed at the console.	None.	

(Note: Various editing commands and/or additional A and I commands can go here.)

: *E	Unchanged.	MYPOEM.$$$	Previous contents, plus buffer contents, plus any lines of MYPOEM.TXT that were not appended to the buffer.
		MYPOEM.BAK	Copy of MYPOEM.TXT.
		MYPOEM.TXT	Copy of MYPOEM.$$$.
		MYPOEM.$$$	Erased.

FIG. 3-7   Diagram Showing How Files Are Used in a Typical Session with ED.

Alternately, you can use the command mNstring to load the buffer until the m-th occurrence of the designated string is found.

When you finally end the editing session with the E (or H) command, four things happen. (1) Any remaining text in the buffer is moved to MYPOEM.$$$, (2) Any remaining lines on the source file (that is, lines of MYPOEM.TXT that were never appended to the buffer) are tacked onto the end of MYPOEM.$$$, (3) Then a simple—but quite neat—trick is performed by ED. It deletes any previous backup file (e. g., MYPOEM.BAK) from the directory, and *renames* the "old" source file MYPOEM.TXT as the new backup file MYPOEM.BAK. (4) Finally ED

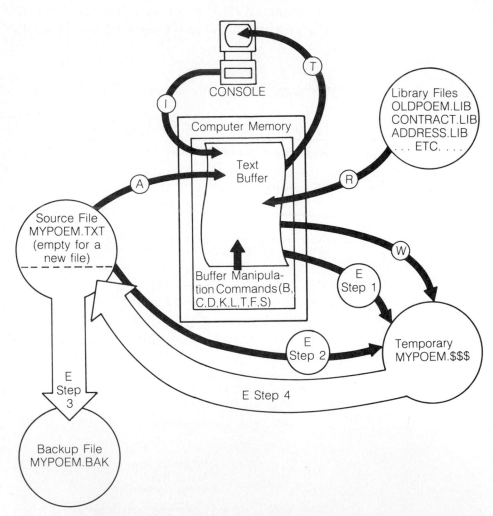

FIG. 3-8   The A, E, I, R, T, and W commands move data between disk files and the text buffer of ED (heavy lines). The E command does four things in the order shown as "step 1," "step 2," etc. Steps 3 and 4 don't have heavy lines because they don't actually move data. They use the trick of simply renaming the appropriate files—MYPOEM.TXT as MYPOEM.BAK, and then MYPOEM.$$$ as MYPOEM.TXT. Library files are text source files (previously created using ED) which can be inserted anywhere in the buffer using the R command. Not shown on the diagram are the H (head) command which manipulates files in the same ways as E, and the Q (quit) and O (original) commands which don't do anything with files at all. The command nT types n lines from the buffer onto the console as explained in Fig. 3-11.

renames the temporary file MYPOEM.$$$ as the "new" source file MYPOEM.TXT, and it erases the name MYPOEM.$$$. So now there are two files: MYPOEM.BAK (BAK means "backup") which is a safety copy of the source file you had before starting the current editing session, and a new source file MYPOEM.TXT which is the original source file plus or minus whatever changes were made in the current editing session. Fig. 3-7 summarizes the way files are used in a typical editing session, and Fig. 3-8 gives a pictorial view of what the A, I, W, and E commands actually do.

Keep in mind that you can use either lower- or uppercase letters for all the ED commands. The only time you have to be careful is with the *insert* command where I forces uppercase translation, while i turns it off. Also keep in mind that the most important command to give when you're finished with an editing session is E (since this will save all your work on disk). Be sure you see the * symbol before typing E. If you don't, type CONTROL-Z first.

A graphical summary of how the various file saving and retrieving commands of ED function is given in Fig. 3-8. Although not shown on this figure, the H command functions in the same way as E. The only difference is that H then takes you back into ED, whereas E takes you back to CP/M.

Fig. 3-8 shows that there is also a special R command for reading "library text" files from disk and inserting them into the buffer. Library files are simply text files you have previously created using ED, and then saved with the secondary name .LIB. The command *R OLDPOEM means copy the contents of the file OLDPOEM.LIB into the text buffer right after something called the *character pointer* (CP). This is normally at the end of the text last inserted. If you want OLDPOEM placed at a different position in the buffer, you must first move the CP to that position. So let's next look at the ED commands which can be used to manipulate the CP.

The Character Pointer

The character pointer (CP) is an imaginary marker that indicates the position in the text where the next insertion, deletion, or search will start. ED contains several commands that move the CP around the text buffer, allowing you to invisibly "mark" the spot where you wish to begin insertions, deletions or searches.

The position of the CP doesn't show up on the console screen, so if you move it around very much it's easy to get lost. This is one of ED's biggest drawbacks; it's not a very visual editor. The best way around this problem is to stay away from character position dependent commands as much as possible, and to think more in terms of *lines* and *strings* of text within lines.

To illustrate the difference, we'll go through the Day 2 example using two CP dependent commands: C (move the CP), and D (delete characters on one side of the CP). Then we'll do another session called "day 3" where we'll use the command S (substitute string) and a command of the form "5:T" which means, "Go to line 5 and type it." It's the Day 3 approach that we'll recommend for most editing, but this will be appreciated more if we first do Day 2.

To start Day 2, we'll append all of the previous text to the buffer and then type it on the console screen to make sure of what's there. Here's how to do this:

```
A>ED MYPOEM.TXT
   : * #A      (Append all of MYPOEM to the buffer.)

   0: * #T     (Type out all of the buffer.)

   1: ●Roses are red
   2:      Electrons are blue
   3:  Atoms are tiny
   4:      And so are you
   1: *_
```

In this example, the two commands #A and #T could have been typed on the same line as: *#A#T. In general, a whole string of ED commands can be typed on one line—a nice feature once you get used to it. This is called entering a *command string* or *command line*.

After giving the append command, the CP is at the beginning of the buffer—just *before* the first character. We have shown its position by a heavy dot ●. Suppose now that we want to delete the word "tiny," and insert "brilliant" in its place. To do this using the D command, we must first move the CP in front of tiny. Then we'll delete "tiny," and insert "brilliant."

```
1: *2L           (This moves the CP down two lines to line 3.)
3: *10C          (This moves the CP over 10 character positions in
                     front of "tiny".)
3: *4D           (Delete the four characters of "tiny".)
3: *i            (Go into text insert mode, lower case.)
3: brilliant^z   (Insert the new word, leave insert mode.)
 : *0TT          (A weird but very handy command which types
                     the current line without moving the CP.)
3: Atoms are brilliant
 : *E            (End the edit session, save new text on disk.)
```

When using the command nL, it's helpful to think in terms of what ED calls the *current line* or CL. This is defined as the line that contains the CP. When we started, CL was 1. The first command 2L moved it down two lines, making the CL = 3. In general, the command nL puts the CP at the beginning of the line which is n lines from where you started. The command 0L simply moves the CP to the beginning of the current line. Fig. 3-9 shows the complete Day 2 session as it would appear on the console.

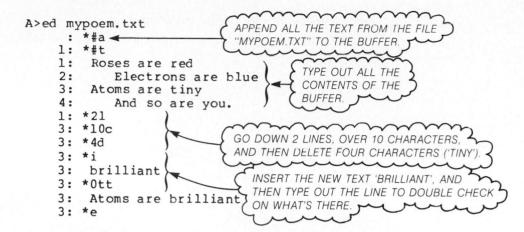

```
A>ed mypoem.txt
        :  *#a
      1:  *#t
      1:   Roses are red
      2:        Electrons are blue
      3:   Atoms are tiny
      4:        And so are you.
      1:  *2l
      3:  *10c
      3:  *4d
      3:  *i
      3:   brilliant
      3:  *0tt
      3:   Atoms are brilliant
      3:  *e
```

APPEND ALL THE TEXT FROM THE FILE "MYPOEM.TXT" TO THE BUFFER.

TYPE OUT ALL THE CONTENTS OF THE BUFFER.

GO DOWN 2 LINES, OVER 10 CHARACTERS, AND THEN DELETE FOUR CHARACTERS ('TINY').

INSERT THE NEW TEXT 'BRILLIANT', AND THEN TYPE OUT THE LINE TO DOUBLE CHECK ON WHAT'S THERE.

FIG. 3-9   This is the Day 2 session in which the editing work started on Day 1 is continued. The #a command is needed to append the previously created text to the buffer.

For anyone who has used a modern word processor, this must seem pretty messy. And it usually is. But cheer up—there are some recent additions to ED that improve it a lot. (We'll also show you how a good visual editor works as part of a word processor in Chapter 4.)

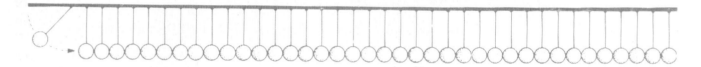

LAB EXERCISE 3.4-1   Creating and Modifying a Text File with ED

Go back to the beginning of this section and actually do all of Day 1 and Day 2 on a CP/M computer. When finished, be sure to use the E command to save your work for the next lab.

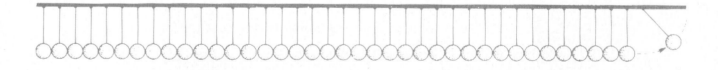

Day 3

We'll continue with the poem written on Day 2, this time changing the word "brilliant" to "sparkling," by using the *substitution* command:

nSxxxx^Zyyyyy^Z(CR)

This means substitute n times, replacing (if possible) the next n occurrences of the text "xxxx" with the text "yyyyy". The substitution process starts at the CP and moves forward through the text buffer. Fig. 3-10 shows how to use this command to change "brilliant" to "sparkling." It also illustrates use of the command   5:   which means, "Go to the beginning of line 5," i. e., put the CP at the start of line 5.

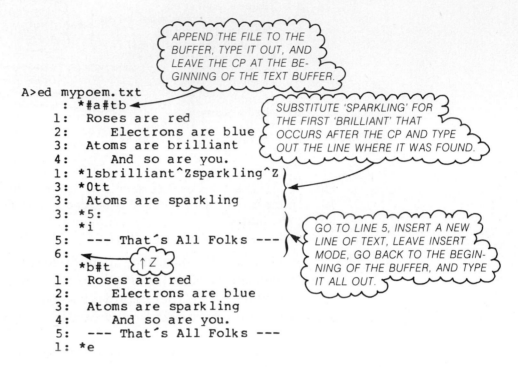

```
A>ed mypoem.txt
   : *#a#tb
  1:   Roses are red
  2:        Electrons are blue
  3:  Atoms are brilliant
  4:        And so are you.
  1: *1sbrilliant^Zsparkling^Z
  3: *0tt
  3:  Atoms are sparkling
  3: *5:
   : *i
  5:   --- That's All Folks ---
  6:
   : *b#t
  1:   Roses are red
  2:        Electrons are blue
  3:  Atoms are sparkling
  4:        And so are you.
  5:   --- That's All Folks ---
  1: *e
```

FIG. 3-10   This is an example showing how to use the ED substitution command.

We'll return to the use of the substitute and line manipulation commands in our final example (Day 4), but let's first summarize the commands that either move the CP (like nC), or do something with respect to the position of the CP (like nD). We'll use the symbol +/− to mean "plus or minus" in these commands. To get plus, type + or nothing; to get minus, type − . Thus to move the CP forward 30 characters, type 30C or +30C. To move backwards, type −30C.

B	Move CP to beginning of the text buffer.
−B	Move CP to the end of the text buffer.
+/−nC	Move CP forward/backwards n characters.
+/−nD	Delete n characters after/before the CP.
+/−nK	Kill (delete) n lines of text after/before the current line. Also delete all characters after/before the CP in the current line.
+/−nL	If n=0, move the CP to the beginning of the current line. If n<>0, move the CP to the beginning of the line which is n lines after/before the current line.

FIG. 3-11   CP Related Commands of ED

+/−nT   If n=0, type from the beginning of the current line up
             to the CP.
             If n>0, type from the CP to the beginning of the nth
             line after the current line.
             If n<0, type from the beginning of the nth line before
             the current line up to the CP.

+/−n   Shorthand for +/−nLT. Thus 0 means 0L1T, which
             means move CP to the beginning of the current line
             and type it.

Note 1:   It's OK to put several of these commands on a single line. For
example you could use the command line:

    1: *4L10C5D

to mean "go down four lines, go over ten characters, and then delete
five characters."

Note 2:   If you make a mistake when typing such a string of commands,
you can use the BACKSPACE key (sometimes shown as a ← back arrow
key) on your console keyboard to delete single characters, or CONTROL-
X to delete the entire line. The DELETE key (also called the RUBOUT
key) can be used to erase characters, but it echoes the deleted characters
on the console.

Note 3:   You can also use the BACKSPACE (or ←) key and CONTROL-
X to correct mistakes while inserting text. In many situations this is the
best approach to editing, provided you carefully proofread each new
line you insert *before* pressing (CR). Incidentally, tabs can be inserted
in text with CONTROL-I, and CONTROL-E can be used to start a new
line on the screen *without* inserting (CR)(LF) in text. (This is how you
enter a long line on a small screen like the Apple II without pressing
RETURN.)

Note 4:   The command string B#T is a convenient way to type out the
contents of the buffer. It leaves the CP at the beginning of the buffer.
The command string B#T-B types out the contents of the buffer and
leaves the CP at the end of the buffer.

Note 5:   The command 0K (where 0 is a zero) deletes all characters in
front of (to the left of) the CP in the current line.

Note 6:   Two handy commands for typing the current line are 0 and
0TT. The first form is shorthand for 0L1T, so it moves (and leaves) the
CP at the beginning of the line. The second form is often preferred,
since 0TT = 0T1T which doesn't disturb the CP at all. It means type
what's to the left of the CP on the current line followed by what's to
the right of the CP. On the other hand, the 0 command is useful in
combination with F (find) and S (substitute). For example, to find, *verify*,
and change a suffix (say "ing" to "ed"), do this:

: *Fing (CR)
: *0 (CR)

If the 0 shows that the "ing" found is the one you want to change, then change it to "ed" with

: *Sing^Zed (CR)

Otherwise, do another

: *Fing (CR)
: *0 (CR)
. . . etc. . . .

Note 7: The command B#T is a fast way to type out the entire buffer. However, if you want to examine the buffer more slowly, with a chance to edit any bad lines that show up, just use the command B. Then press the carriage return or enter key each time you want to see a new line. This allows you to step through the buffer at your own pace, making any desired changes as you go. To step through a long text one page at a time, use *B0P to see the first "page" (23 lines), followed by using *P to see each additional page.

Instant Quiz

Suppose you use ED to create a new file as follows:

: *i
1: First, be prompt. (CR)
2: Second, be good. (CR)
3: Third, be gone. (CR)
4: ^Z
: *(command)
: *B#T-B

1. If the command is 1K, what is typed out?
2. If the command is 0K, what is typed out?
3. If the command is −1K, what is typed out?
4. If the command is −2K, what is typed out?
5. Suppose you have inserted about 200 lines of text into ED, and saved it with H or E. How can you bring just lines 51 to 60 back into the text buffer for editing?
6. How can you bring lines 90 to the end into the buffer?

Answers

1. 1: First, be prompt.   2. 1: First, be prompt.
   2: Second, be good.   2: Second, be good.
   3: Third, be gone.   3: Third, be gone.
   : *   : *

```
3. 1:  First, be prompt.       4. 1:  First, be prompt.
   2:  Second, be good.           :  *
    :  *
5. *50A50W10A                  6. *H
                                 *89A#W#A
```

The Find, Substitute, and Juxtapose Commands

The *find* command, nFstring^Z, finds the nth occurrence of a string of text, and leaves the CP right *after* that string. The end of the string is marked by ^Z in the command. Thus the two commands

: *B
: *2Fare^Z

mean (1) move the CP to the beginning of the buffer, and (2) now go forward until the second occurrence of the string "are" is found, leaving the CP right after it.

The *substitute* command, nSold^Znew^Z, finds the string "old" and substitutes the string "new" for it. It does this n times, starting at the CP. Here's how to substitute "nuts" for "fooey" n times starting at the beginning of the buffer. The CP will be left right after the last substitution of "nuts."

: *B
: *4Sfooey^Znuts^Z

Juxtaposition means "insert between" two strings after throwing out what was already there. The form is nJstart^Znew^Zend^Z. For example:

: *B
: *Jfourscore^Z days ^Zago^Z

means delete what was formerly between "fourscore" and "ago," and then insert "days" between them. nJ is supposed to mean repeat J n times, but it has a bug which causes some very strange results. If you want to repeat the J command for n different parts of the text, use the macro command with J instead (see below).

The Macro Command

The *macro* command has the form "nM command string." This means, "Execute all the commands in the command string (from left to right) n times." For example,

B5MFnuts^Z0TT

means, "Reset the CP to the beginning of the buffer, then find (if possible) the next five occurrences of the string 'nuts', each time typing the line in which it was found." This is quite different from

B5Fnuts^Z0TT

In the following, n means a positive *or* negative integer, while m means a positive integer. In the F, S, and J commands, CONTROL-L should be used to represent the (CR) (LF) pair.

mA	Append m lines to the buffer.
B	Move the CP to the beginning of the buffer.
−B	Move the CP to the end of the buffer.
nC	Move the CP n characters.
nD	Delete n characters, starting at the CP.
E	End the edit session, save and rename files.
mFtext(CR)	Find the mth occurrence of 'text' in the buffer and put the CP after it.
H	Do an E and restart ED with the same filename.
I . . . ˆZ	Insert text into the buffer. That is, go into insert mode to
(i . . . ˆZ)	insert text; leave by typing ˆZ.
mJtext1ˆZnewˆZtext2(CR)	Juxtapose 'new'. That is, remove everything between 'text1' and 'text2' and insert 'new' in its place, leaving the CP at the end of 'new'.
nK	Kill n lines after/before the current line plus characters after/before the CP.
nL	Move the CP to the beginning of a line n lines after/before the CP.
mMstring	Repeat a macro (string of commands) m times.
mNtext	Search the entire source file for the mth occurrence of 'text' appending new lines to the buffer as needed.
O	Scratch the results of editing and restart.
nP	Print (and move the CP) n pages; then print one more page (page = 23 lines); 0P means print 1 page.
Q	Quit edit, don't save any work.
Rfilename	Read a library file and insert a copy in the buffer after the CP.
mStext1ˆZtext2(CR)	Substitute 'text2' for 'text1' up to m times, leaving the CP at the last occurrence of 'text2'.
nT	Type n lines (see Fig. 3-13 for details).
U	Turn upper case translation on (−U to turn off).
V	Turn line numbering on (−V to turn off, 0V to print the number of bytes left in the buffer).
mW	Write m lines of the buffer to the temporary file and shift the remaining lines to the top of the buffer.
mX	Part of block move; transfers the next m lines from the buffer to a temporary file; you retrieve them with R; use nK to delete the old block; use 0X to retrieve *and* delete lines from the temporary file.
mZ	Sleep. Suspend the actions of ED for m time units.
n	Move the CP n lines and type the last one.
m:	Go to line m.
m:string	Go to line m and do a string of commands.
string:m	Do a string of commands, from the CL up to line number m.
m::pstring	Do a string of commands, from line m to line p.

FIG. 3-12   ED Commands in Alphabetical Order.

which means "find the fifth occurrence of 'nuts' and type the line that contained it." You can use #M to mean, "Repeat up to 65,535 times," or just plain M to mean, "Repeat as often as possible." *Important:* Use ˆZ to terminate all strings in a macro (including null strings). Example: Suppose you want to change all references of the form "(c.f. T. Bell, 1968)" in a text to "(see references)". Here's the command to use:

MJ(ˆZsee referencesˆZ)ˆZ(CR)

Instant Quiz

1. Could you use the nS command to make the above substitution?
2. Could you use nJ or #J instead of MJ?

Answers

1. No, because the string for which we wish to substitute can have many different values, for example, ''(c.f. T. Bell, 1968),'' ''(c.f. A. Einstein, 1940),'' ''(OP. CIT.),'' and so on.
2. No, because nJ doesn't work as you would assume (or as described in the CP/M manuals). Use MJ for multiple juxtapositions and MF for multiple finds, but nS for multiple substitutions.

Fig. 3-12 summarizes the commands of ED. Fig. 3-13 shows a more extensive example of their use (Day 4). The best way to become adept at using ED is through practice. One suggestion: during this practice, every once in awhile give the command *B#T which means, ''Go to the beginning of the text buffer and type everything out.'' Study this output to see what your most recent commands have done to the buffer text. To return the CP to the line where you were before giving this command—say, line 23—give the command 23: (you could also foresee this by making the first command B#T23:).

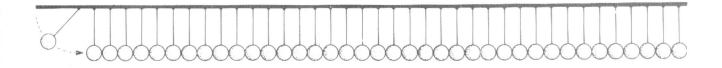

LAB EXERCISE 3.4-2   Using ED's Find, Substitute, Juxtapose, and ''go to'' Commands

Day 4

Follow the instructions of Day 3 to make changes in the POEM.TXT file (the file you wrote in Lab Exercise 3.4-1). Then use the ED Substitute, Find, Juxtapose, and n: (go to line n) commands to further modify MYPOEM.TXT. Fig. 3-13 shows a sample solution to this lab. By examining the buffer text each time it is typed (using B#T), you can get a feel for what the various commands or command strings do.

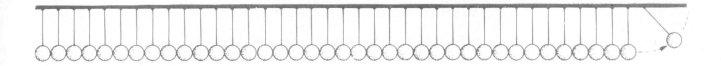

```
A>ed mypoem.txt
  : *#a#t
1:   Roses are red
2:       Electrons are blue
3:   Atoms are sparkling
4:       And so are you.
5:   --- That's All Folks ---
1: *fred^Z0t
1:   Roses are red*i,^Z0t

1:   Roses are red,*2:i
2:       as they should be.
3:
3: *fblue^Z0t
3:       Electrons are blue*i,^Zt

3: *0t
3:       Electrons are blue,*b#t
1:   Roses are red,
2:       as they should be.
3:       Electrons are blue,
4:   Atoms are sparkling
5:       And so are you.
6:   --- That's All Folks ---
1: *3:3d0t
3: *t
3:       Electrons are blue,
3: *4:i
4:       and live in the sea.
5:
5: *b#t
1:   Roses are red,
2:       as they should be.
3:   Electrons are blue,
4:       and live in the sea.
5:   Atoms are sparkling
6:       And so are you.
7:   --- That's All Folks ---
1: *fling^Z0t
5:   Atoms are sparkling*i,^Z0t

5:   Atoms are sparkling,*6:i
6:       in the dark air.
7:
7: *b#t
1:   Roses are red,
2:       as they should be.
3:   Electrons are blue,
4:       and live in the sea.
5:   Atoms are sparkling,
6:       in the dark air.
7:       And so are you.
8:   --- That's All Folks ---
1: *7:3dfyou^Z0t
7:   And so are you*i,^Z0t

7:   And so are you,*8:i
8:       dance, don't despair.

9:
9: *b#t
```

FIND "RED", TYPE THE LINE UP TO THE CP (THUS SHOWING ITS POSITION). INSERT "," AND AGAIN TYPE THE LINE UP TO THE POSITION OF THE CP.

GO TO LINE 2 AND INSERT SOME TEXT.

↑Z AFTER A CARRIAGE RETURN DOES NOT PRINT.

FIND "BLUE", TYPE THE LINE UP TO THE CP. INSERT "," AND TRY TO TYPE THE LINE. SINCE THE CP WAS AT THE END OF THE LINE, t DIDN'T WORK, BUT Øt DID. TYPE ALL THE TEXT TO SEE WHAT THE NEW LINE NUMBERS ARE.

GO TO LINE 3, DELETE THE FIRST THREE CHARACTERS (SPACES IN THIS CASE), PRINT THE LINE UP TO THE CP (WHOOPS, I MEANT t THIS TIME).

↑Z

FIND "LING" (WHICH IS PART OF "SPARKLING") AND TYPE UP TO THE CP. INSERT "," AND TYPE UP TO THE CP AGAIN.

↑Z

GO TO LINE 7, DELETE THE FIRST THREE CHARACTERS, FIND "YOU" AND TYPE UP TO THE CP POSITION.

↑Z

FIG. 3-13   This is a sample solution to Lab Exercise 3.4-2.

```
1:    Roses are red,
2:       as they should be.
3:    Electrons are blue,
4:       and live in the sea.
5:    Atoms are sparkling,
6:       in the dark air.
7:    And so are you,.
8:       dance, don't despair.
9:    --- That's All Folks ---
1:  *8:ki
8:       dance and beware.
9:
9:  *slive^Zswim^Z
```

GO TO LINE 8, KILL THE LINE AND INSERT SOME TEXT.

↑Z

```
BREAK "#" AT ^Z
9:  *b#t
1:    Roses are red,
2:       as they should be.
3:    Electrons are blue,
4:       and live in the sea.
5:    Atoms are sparkling,
6:       in the dark air.
7:    And so are you,.
8:       dance and beware.
9:    --- That's All Folks ---
1:  *slive^Zswim^Z
4:  *b#t
1:    Roses are red,
2:       as they should be.
3:    Electrons are blue,
4:       and swim in the sea.
5:    Atoms are sparkling,
6:       in the dark air.
7:    And so are you,.
8:       dance and beware.
9:    --- That's All Folks ---
1:  *4sare^Zsing^Zb#t
1:    Roses sing red,
2:       as they should be.
3:    Electrons sing blue,
4:       and swim in the sea.
5:    Atoms sing sparkling,
6:       in the dark air.
7:    And so sing you,.
8:       dance and beware.
9:    --- That's All Folks ---
1:  *mjsing ^Zghostly^Z,^Z
```

THIS COMMAND FAILED BECAUSE THE CP WAS BELOW THE POSITION OF "LIVE" AND THE SUBSTITUTE COMMAND ONLY SEARCHES FORWARD.

THIS MESSAGE JUST MEANS THAT ED REACHED THE END OF THE TEXT WHILE SEARCHING. TO SEE IF THE COMMAND WAS ACCOMPLISHED, MOVE THE CP AND PRINT OUT THE WHOLE TEXT.

NOW THE COMMAND WILL WORK.

SUBSTITUTE "SING" FOR "ARE" FOUR TIMES, AND MOVE THE CP TO THE BEGINNING OF THE BUFFER AND TYPE OUT EVERYTHING.

HERE IS AN EXAMPLE OF A MACRO COMMAND—MEANING "DO AS OFTEN AS POSSIBLE THE FOLLOWING: JUXTAPOSE (PLACE BETWEEN) 'SING' AND ',' THE TEXT 'GHOSTLY' (AND DELETE WHATEVER WAS THERE BEFORE)."

```
BREAK "#" AT ^Z
7:  *b#t
1:    Roses sing ghostly,
2:       as they should be.
3:    Electrons sing ghostly,
4:       and swim in the sea.
5:    Atoms sing ghostly,
6:       in the dark air.
7:    And so sing ghostly,.
8:       dance and beware.
9:    --- That's All Folks ---
1:  *e
```

FIG. 3-13 (*continued*)

3.5 A Hands-On Review of DIR, ERA, REN, SAVE, TYPE, DUMP, STAT, PIP, ED, and DDT

The best way to make the rather dull litany of CP/M commands covered in this chapter come alive is to use them. In this section we'll show a sample interactive session in which ten of the CP/M commands (five built-in, and five transient) are used. Of course not all of these commands are of equal importance. In fact, most application-oriented users will find little use for SAVE, DUMP, and DDT. If you have a good word processor (of the type described in Chapter 4), you can also do without ED. But it's still a good idea to use each of the CP/M commands a few times, if for no other reason than to remove the mystery that surrounds the unknown.

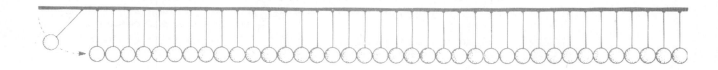

LAB EXERCISE 3.5-1

(Super Lab)

Everything You Wanted to Know about CP/M in One Sitting

There are only two major steps for this Lab, but there can be as many sub-steps as you wish in the form of experiments and variations of your own. So "think creative."

Step 1. Boot the CP/M system, being sure to use one of your backup disks. If you have a two-drive system, put a second backup disk in drive B. Then go ahead and use the ten CP/M commands (listed in the heading of this section) by imitating the interaction shown in Fig. 3-14.

```
A>
```

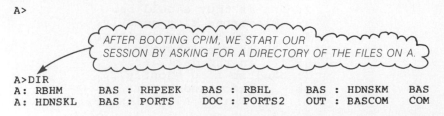

```
A>DIR
A: RBHM      BAS : RHPEEK    BAS : RBHL     BAS : HDNSKM    BAS
A: HDNSKL    BAS : PORTS     DOC : PORTS2   OUT : BASCOM    COM
```

FIG. 3-14   This is a sample interaction with CP/M where five built-in and five transient commands have been used. There are of course many other variations in the use of these commands possible.

```
A: GO         COM : STAT     COM : PIP       COM : BASLIB   REL
A: M80        COM : L80      COM : CREF80    COM : LIB      COM
A: RANTEST    BAS : RANTEST  REL : RANTEST   COM : RANTEST  ASC
A: F80        COM : ED       COM : DDT       COM : ASM      COM
A: FORMT#     COM : SYSGEN   COM : DUMP      COM : MBASIC   COM
A: HBIOS32    ASM : LOAD     COM : SUBMIT    COM : XSUB     COM
A: MOVCPM     COM : FIX      BAS : SINGLE    COM : SINGLE   $$$
A: PORTS          : MYPOEM   BAK
A>STAT
A: R/W, Space: 102k
B: R/W, Space: 36k

A>
```

OUR A DISK HAS LOTS OF FILES, SO WE USE STAT TO SEE HOW MUCH SPACE IS LEFT. WE FIND THAT THE DISK IN A HAS READ/WRITE STATUS, WITH ABOUT 102,000 BYTES OF STORAGE SPACE LEFT.

STAT IS USED HERE TO GET MORE DETAILED INFORMATION ABOUT THE BASIC FILES ON A (EXTENSION .BAS).

```
A>STAT *.BAS

  Recs  Bytes  Ext Acc
     3     2k    1 R/W A:FIX.BAS
   124    16k    1 R/W A:HDNSKL.BAS
   150    20k    2 R/W A:HDNSKM.BAS
     3     2k    1 R/W A:RANTEST.BAS
   110    14k    1 R/W A:RBHL.BAS
   134    18k    2 R/W A:RBHM.BAS
     1     2k    1 R/W A:RHPEEK.BAS
Bytes Remaining On A: 102k

A>DIR B:*.BAS
NO FILE
A>
```

ALSO CHECK THE DISK IN THE B DRIVE FOR BASIC FILES. WE FIND THAT THERE AREN'T ANY. SO LET'S DO A DIRECTORY OF B AND SEE WHAT'S THERE.

```
A>DIR B:
B: GTC30        : GTC10        : GO        COM : GTC13
B: GTC12        : GTC16        : GTC14         : GTC35
B: GTCD         : GTC11       ~: GTC25         : GTC10     BAK
B: GTC15        : GTC33        : GTC34         : GTC20
B: GTC26        : GTC21        : GTC22         : GTC0
B: SBC0         : GTC31        : GTC24         : GTC36
B: GTC23        : GTC27        : GTC32         : GTC11     BAK
B: GTC0    BAK : GTC21   BAK : GTC15   BAK : GTC27     BAK
B: GTC22   BAK : GTC16   BAK : GTC20   BAK : GTC23     BAK
B: GTC25   BAK : GTC12   BAK : GTC14   BAK : GTC24     BAK
B: GTC26   BAK
A>STAT B:

Bytes Remaining On B: 36k

A>
```

THE DISK IN THE B DRIVE IS EVEN MORE CROWDED. THERE'S ONLY ENOUGH SPACE FOR 36,000 MORE BYTES.

WE EXAMINE THE NAMES OF THE BACKUP FILES (EXTENSION .BAK).

```
A>DIR B:*.BAK
B: GTC10   BAK : GTC11   BAK : GTC0    BAK : GTC21     BAK
B: GTC15   BAK : GTC27   BAK : GTC22   BAK : GTC16     BAK
B: GTC20   BAK : GTC23   BAK : GTC25   BAK : GTC12     BAK
B: GTC14   BAK : GTC24   BAK : GTC26   BAK
A>
```

FIG. 3-14   (continued)

```
A>ERA B:*.BAK
A>STAT B:*.BAK

File Not Found
A>
```

WE DECIDE THEY'RE NOT NEEDED ANYMORE, SO WE ERASE ALL OF THEM, AND THEN DOUBLE CHECK ON WHAT'S LEFT.

```
A>DIR B:
B: GTC30        : GTC10        : GO      COM : GTC13
B: GTC12        : GTC16        : GTC14       : GTC35
B: GTCD         : GTC11        : GTC25       : GTC15
B: GTC33        : GTC34        : GTC20       : GTC26
B: GTC21        : GTC22        : GTC0        : SBC0
B: GTC31        : GTC24        : GTC36       : GTC23
B: GTC27        : GTC32
A>STAT B:

Bytes Remaining On B: 200k

A>
```

ERASING THE BACKUP FILES INCREASED THE SPACE AVAILABLE FROM 36K TO 200K.

```
ED TEST
```

NEXT LET'S USE ED TO CREATE A TEST FILE.

```
NEW FILE
   : *I
   1:   THIS IS A TEST FILE BEING CREATED WITH THE CP/M
   2:   EDITOR PROGRAM (ED).  IT WILL CONSIST OF ASCII
   3:   CHARACTERS TYPED IN AT THE CONSOLE, AND SAVED AS
   4:   THE FILE 'TEST'.
   : *E
```

↑Z WAS PRESSED HERE.

```
A>DIR T*.*
A: TEST       BAK : TEST
A>STAT TEST.*

Recs  Bytes  Ext Acc
  2     2k     1 R/W A:TEST
  0     0k     1 R/W A:TEST.BAK
Bytes Remaining On A: 100k

A>TYPE TEST
THIS IS A TEST FILE BEING CREATED WITH THE CP/M
EDITOR PROGRAM (ED).  IT WILL CONSIST OF ASCII
CHARACTERS TYPED IN AT THE CONSOLE, AND SAVED AS
THE FILE 'TEST'.
A>DUMP TEST

0000 54 48 49 53 20 49 53 20 41 20 54 45 53 54 20 46
0010 49 4C 45 20 42 45 49 4E 47 20 43 52 45 41 54 45
0020 44 20 57 49 54 48 20 54 48 45 20 43 50 2F 4D 0D
0030 0A 45 44 49 54 4F 52 20 50 52 4F 47 52 41 4D 20
0040 28 45 44 29 2E 20 20 49 54 20 57 49 4C 4C 20 43
0050 4F 4E 53 49 53 54 20 4F 46 20 41 53 43 49 49 0D
0060 0A 43 48 41 52 41 43 54 45 52 53 20 54 59 50 45
0070 44 20 49 4E 20 41 54 20 54 48 45 20 43 4F 4E 53
0080 4F 4C 45 2C 20 41 4E 44 20 53 41 56 45 44 20 41
0090 53 0D 0A 54 48 45 20 46 49 4C 45 20 27 54 45 53
```

MAKE SURE TEST GOT INTO THE CP/M DIRECTORY. FIND IT WAS SAVED ALONG WITH A BACKUP FILE.

BUT RIGHT NOW THE BACKUP IS EMPTY. STUDY FIG. 3-8 TO SEE WHY.

LET'S LOOK AT TEST WITH THE TYPE COMMAND.

AND THEN DISPLAY IT IN HEX WITH DUMP. SEE IF YOU CAN SPOT THE FOUR LINES BY THE (CR)(LF) PAIRS (HEX 0D, 0A).

FIG. 3-14   (*continued*)

```
00A0 54 27 2E 1A 1A 1A 1A 1A 1A 1A 1A 1A 1A 1A 1A 1A
00B0 1A 1A 1A 1A 1A 1A 1A 1A 1A 1A 1A 1A 1A 1A 1A 1A
00C0 1A 1A 1A 1A 1A 1A 1A 1A 1A 1A 1A 1A 1A 1A 1A 1A
00D0 1A 1A 1A 1A 1A 1A 1A 1A 1A 1A 1A 1A 1A 1A 1A 1A
00E0 1A 1A 1A 1A 1A 1A 1A 1A 1A 1A 1A 1A 1A 1A 1A 1A
00F0 1A 1A 1A 1A 1A 1A 1A 1A 1A 1A 1A 1A 1A 1A 1A 1A
```

CP/M PUTS THE ↑Z "END OF FILE" CHARACTER IN ALL UNUSED BYTES.

```
A>
```

```
A>DDT TEST
DDT VERS 2.0
NEXT  PC
0200 0100
-D
```

NEXT WE EXAMINE THE FILE TEST BY USING THE D COMMAND OF DDT.

```
0100 54 48 49 53 20 49 53 20 41 20 54 45 53 54 20 46  THIS IS A TEST F
0110 49 4C 45 20 42 45 49 4E 47 20 43 52 45 41 54 45  ILE BEING CREATE
0120 44 20 57 49 54 48 20 54 48 45 20 43 50 2F 4D 0D  D WITH THE CP/M.
0130 0A 45 44 49 54 4F 52 20 50 52 4F 47 52 41 4D 20  .EDITOR PROGRAM
0140 28 45 44 29 2E 20 20 49 54 20 57 49 4C 4C 20 43  (ED).  IT WILL C
0150 4F 4E 53 49 53 54 20 4F 46 20 41 53 43 49 49 0D  ONSIST OF ASCII.
0160 0A 43 48 41 52 41 43 54 45 52 53 20 54 59 50 45  .CHARACTERS TYPE
0170 44 20 49 4E 20 41 54 20 54 48 45 20 43 4F 4E 53  D IN AT THE CONS
0180 4F 4C 45 2C 20 41 4E 44 20 53 41 56 45 44 20 41  OLE, AND SAVED A
0190 53 0D 0A 54 48 45 20 46 49 4C 45 20 27 54 45 53  S..THE FILE ´TES
01A0 54 27 2E 1A 1A 1A 1A 1A 1A 1A 1A 1A 1A 1A 1A 1A  T´..............
01B0 1A 1A 1A 1A 1A 1A 1A 1A 1A 1A 1A 1A 1A 1A 1A 1A  ................
-^C
```

THE TWO PERIODS AFTER CP/M, ASCII, AND AS CORRESPOND TO 0D AND 0A, THE NON-PRINTING CODES FOR (CR) AND (LF).

```
A>PIP A:SPARE=A:TEST
```

LET'S MAKE A SPARE COPY OF TEST FOR FURTHER EXPERIMENTATION.

AND MAKE SURE IT'S IN THE DIRECTORY.

```
A>DIR S*.*
A: STAT     COM : SYSGEN   COM : SUBMIT   COM : SINGLE    COM
A: SINGLE   $$$ : SPARE
A>
```

```
A>DDT SPARE
DDT VERS 2.0
NEXT  PC
0200 0100
-D
```

NOW WE'LL USE DDT ON SPARE.

FIRST DISPLAY IT.

```
0100 54 48 49 53 20 49 53 20 41 20 54 45 53 54 20 46  THIS IS A TEST F
0110 49 4C 45 20 42 45 49 4E 47 20 43 52 45 41 54 45  ILE BEING CREATE
0120 44 20 57 49 54 48 20 54 48 45 20 43 50 2F 4D 0D  D WITH THE CP/M.
0130 0A 45 44 49 54 4F 52 20 50 52 4F 47 52 41 4D 20  .EDITOR PROGRAM
0140 28 45 44 29 2E 20 20 49 54 20 57 49 4C 4C 20 43  (ED).  IT WILL C
0150 4F 4E 53 49 53 54 20 4F 46 20 41 53 43 49 49 0D  ONSIST OF ASCII.
0160 0A 43 48 41 52 41 43 54 45 52 53 20 54 59 50 45  .CHARACTERS TYPE
0170 44 20 49 4E 20 41 54 20 54 48 45 20 43 4F 4E 53  D IN AT THE CONS
0180 4F 4C 45 2C 20 41 4E 44 20 53 41 56 45 44 20 41  OLE, AND SAVED A
0190 53 0D 0A 54 48 45 20 46 49 4C 45 20 27 54 45 53  S..THE FILE ´TES
01A0 54 27 2E 1A 1A 1A 1A 1A 1A 1A 1A 1A 1A 1A 1A 1A  T´..............
01B0 1A 1A 1A 1A 1A 1A 1A 1A 1A 1A 1A 1A 1A 1A 1A 1A  ................
```

FIG. 3-14   *(continued)*

```
-S0100
0100 54 55          NEXT WE'LL USE S TO SET FOUR OF
0101 48 49          THE BYTES TO SLIGHTLY HIGHER VALUES.
0102 49 4A
0103 53 54                                        A SIMPLE 'CAESAR'
0104 20 .                                              CIPHER!
-D0100,0120
0100 55 49 4A 54 20 49 53 20 41 20 54 45 53 54 20 46  UIJT IS A TEST F
0110 49 4C 45 20 42 45 49 4E 47 20 43 52 45 41 54 45  ILE BEING CREATE
0120 44 D
-F0140,015F,41          NOW WE'LL BE MORE RADICAL, AND FILL MEMORY
-D                      WITH A'S (HEX CODE 41) FROM LOCATION 140H TO 15FH.
0121 20 57 49 54 48 20 54 48 45 20 43 50 2F 4D 0D  WITH THE CP/M.
0130 0A 45 44 49 54 4F 52 20 50 52 4F 47 52 41 4D 20  .EDITOR PROGRAM
0140 41 41 41 41 41 41 41 41 41 41 41 41 41 41 41 41  AAAAAAAAAAAAAAAA
0150 41 41 41 41 41 41 41 41 41 41 41 41 41 41 41 41  AAAAAAAAAAAAAAAA
0160 0A 43 48 41 52 41 43 54 45 52 53 20 54 59 50 45  .CHARACTERS TYPE
0170 44 20 49 4E 20 41 54 20 54 48 45 20 43 4F 4E 53  D IN AT THE CONS
0180 4F 4C 45 2C 20 41 4E 44 20 53 41 56 45 44 20 41  OLE, AND SAVED A
0190 53 0D 0A 54 48 45 20 46 49 4C 45 20 27 54 45 53  S..THE FILE 'TES
01A0 54 27 2E 1A 1A 1A 1A 1A 1A 1A 1A 1A 1A 1A 1A 1A  T'..............
01B0 1A 1A 1A 1A 1A 1A 1A 1A 1A 1A 1A 1A 1A 1A 1A 1A  ................
01C0 1A 1A 1A 1A 1A 1A 1A 1A 1A 1A 1A 1A 1A 1A 1A 1A  ................
01D0 1A 1A 1A 1A 1A 1A 1A 1A 1A 1A 1A 1A 1A 1A 1A 1A  ................
-^C
```

THE ABOVE, MESSED UP VERSION IS ONLY IN THE TPA, SO LET'S SAVE IT FOR POSTERITY.

IT WORKED, BUT NOTICE THAT ONE OF THE (CR) CODES WAS OVERWRITTEN BY AN A.

```
A>SAVE 1 MESSEDUP
A>DIR M*.*
A: M80       COM : MBASIC   COM : MOVCPM   COM : MYPOEM   BAK
A: MESSEDUP
A>
```

THERE IT IS.

```
A>TYPE MESSEDUP
UIJT IS A TEST FILE BEING CREATED WITH THE CP/M
EDITOR PROGRAM AAAAAAAAAAAAAAAAAAAAAAAAAAAAAAAAAA
                                          CHARACTERS TYPED IN AT THE CONSO
THE FILE 'TEST'.
A>DUMP MESSEDUP
```

TRY TO TYPE IT.

WHAT HAPPENED HERE?

```
0000 55 49 4A 54 20 49 53 20 41 20 54 45 53 54 20 46
0010 49 4C 45 20 42 45 49 4E 47 20 43 52 45 41 54 45
0020 44 20 57 49 54 48 20 54 48 45 20 43 50 2F 4D 0D
0030 0A 45 44 49 54 4F 52 20 50 52 4F 47 52 41 4D 20
0040 41 41 41 41 41 41 41 41 41 41 41 41 41 41 41 41
0050 41 41 41 41 41 41 41 41 41 41 41 41 41 41 41 41
0060 0A 43 48 41 52 41 43 54 45 52 53 20 54 59 50 45
0070 44 20 49 4E 20 41 54 20 54 48 45 20 43 4F 4E 53
0080 4F 4C 45 2C 20 41 4E 44 20 53 41 56 45 44 20 41
0090 53 0D 0A 54 48 45 20 46 49 4C 45 20 27 54 45 53
00A0 54 27 2E 1A 1A 1A 1A 1A 1A 1A 1A 1A 1A 1A 1A 1A
00B0 1A 1A 1A 1A 1A 1A 1A 1A 1A 1A 1A 1A 1A 1A 1A 1A
00C0 1A 1A 1A 1A 1A 1A 1A 1A 1A 1A 1A 1A 1A 1A 1A 1A
00D0 1A 1A 1A 1A 1A 1A 1A 1A 1A 1A 1A 1A 1A 1A 1A 1A
00E0 1A 1A 1A 1A 1A 1A 1A 1A 1A 1A 1A 1A 1A 1A 1A 1A
00F0 1A 1A 1A 1A 1A 1A 1A 1A 1A 1A 1A 1A 1A 1A 1A 1A
```

AHA! HERE'S THE VILLAIN. THIS 41 USED TO BE A 0D—(CR).

```
A>REN MONSTER=MESSEDUP
A>DIR M*.*
A: M80       COM : MBASIC   COM : MOVCPM   COM : MYPOEM   BAK
A: MONSTER
```

GIVE OUR FILE A MORE SUITABLE NAME.

FIG. 3-14 (continued)

```
A>DDT MONSTER
DDT VERS 2.0
NEXT  PC
0200 0100
-D
0100 55 49 4A 54 20 49 53 20 41 20 54 45 53 54 20 46  UIJT IS A TEST F
0110 49 4C 45 20 42 45 49 4E 47 20 43 52 45 41 54 45  ILE BEING CREATE
0120 44 20 57 49 54 48 20 54 48 45 20 43 50 2F 4D 0D  D WITH THE CP/M.
0130 0A 45 44 49 54 4F 52 20 50 52 4F 47 52 41 4D 20  .EDITOR PROGRAM
0140 41 41 41 41 41 41 41 41 41 41 41 41 41 41 41 41  AAAAAAAAAAAAAAAA
0150 41 41 41 41 41 41 41 41 41 41 41 41 41 41 41 41  AAAAAAAAAAAAAAAA
0160 0A 43 48 41 52 41 43 54 45 52 53 20 54 59 50 45  .CHARACTERS TYPE
0170 44 20 49 4E 20 41 54 20 54 48 45 20 43 4F 4E 53  D IN AT THE CONS
0180 4F 4C 45 2C 20 41 4E 44 20 53 41 56 45 44 20 41  OLE, AND SAVED A
0190 53 0D 0A 54 48 45 20 46 49 4C 45 20 27 54 45 53  S..THE FILE 'TES
01A0 54 27 2E 1A 1A 1A 1A 1A 1A 1A 1A 1A 1A 1A 1A 1A  T'..............
01B0 1A 1A 1A 1A 1A 1A 1A 1A 1A 1A 1A 1A 1A 1A 1A 1A  ................
-^C
```

AND PROVE THAT YOU CAN USE DDT TO DISPLAY EVEN A MONSTER.

```
A>DIR TEST.*
A: TEST      BAK : TEST
A>ERA TEST.*
A>ERA MONSTER
A>ERA SPARE.*
A>
```

TIME TO GO HOME, SO WE ERASE ALL THE EVIDENCE.

FIG. 3-14   (*continued*)

Step 2. Create your own interaction with CP/M, trying variations on the previous step. If you have a printer, use the CONTROL-P option to save your experiments on paper. However be aware that any time you do a warm boot, the CONTROL-P toggle will be turned off. When this happens, type another CONTROL-P after the A> prompt and press (CR). If a second A> then appears on the printer, you'll know the print toggle is back on.

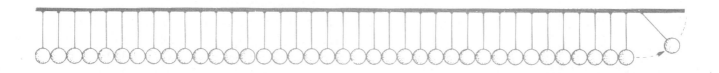

3.6 Problems and Projects

1. Develop a metaphor or analogy to help explain the structure of CP/M to a friend who wants some insight into what's going on behind the "CP/M scene." If it works out well, consider submitting it as an article to one of the popular computing magazines.

2. If you (or a friend) have a CP/M system different from those discussed in this book, make a detailed memory map showing where the CCP, BDOS, and BIOS for this system reside in RAM. Also check out whether

the system has a MOVCPM which works as advertised. How can you be sure?

3. If you're using the Apple II SoftCard system, there is no MOVCPM program. What two size options do you have for the use of RAM on an Apple CP/M machine? If you're ambitious, try to construct a memory map for each of these options, using the information on page 2-6 of the SoftCard manual. (*Warning:* This could drive you bananas. There are actually two maps, depending on whether the 6502 or Z80 micro-processors are being referenced. The reason is that Apple CP/M is a case of patches on patches on patches. The best advice to Apple CP/Mers is, "Enjoy—but don't try to change too much.")

4. Prepare a pocket-sized reference card that summarizes the most important features of CP/M. Leave room for adding the other information that will be presented in later chapters. If pocket-sized is too restrictive, make it pocketbook-sized.

5. The program ED was originally developed for use on hard-copy terminals (like the Teletype). What features would you like to see added to ED on the assumption that it would be used on a video-type console? Would these features still work on a hard-copy console? If not, why not? Does this suggest some even fancier editor features that wouldn't work on video consoles? What kind of radically new kind of console device would be needed? Describe the features in detail, assuming that you could find a "venture capitalist" to take care of engineering and production matters. In short, how about designing a "new and improved" replacement for the console, one of the most crucial machine/person elements in a personal computer system.

6. Based on what you've seen so far, describe some new CP/M command programs that you think would be useful. Could any of these be incorporated as extensions of present CP/M programs (e. g., PIP)? Put another way, what are some of the things you'd really like to do on your CP/M system that currently seem impossible? For some good ideas, see the columns called "The CP/M Bus" by Anthony Skjellum which appeared in volume 2 of *Microsystems* [11].

7. Here's part of a session with ED. Finish it on paper by writing down what you think would be displayed on the console screen after the last B#T command. How can you find out if you were right?

```
A>ed HACKER
  : *#a#t
  1:    PERSONAL COMPUTERS
  2:         The technical characteristics of today's personal computers
  3: are actually superior to those of the large laboratory computers
  4: of the 1960's.  Personal microcomputers operate with internal
  5: speeds measured in billionths of seconds.  They have sophisti-
  6: cated interface capabilities, they can be programmed in high-
  7: level computer languages, and best of all they are affordable
  8: by individuals.  As a result there is a growing personal
  9: computer movement, involving people from all walks of life
 10: who find computer pioneering both exciting and reqwarding.*b
  1: *#scomput^Zhappy hack^Z
```

```
BREAK "#" AT k
   10: *b#t
    1:   PERSONAL COMPUTERS
    2:         The technic
    3:   are actually sup
    4:   of the 1960's.
    5:   speeds measure
    6:   cated interfa
    7:   level happy
    8:   by individu
    9:   happy hack
   10:   who find
```

CHAPTER FOUR
Professional CP/M Software; Word Processing; Executive and Business Computing

4.0 Introduction

One of the most compelling arguments made for using CP/M is that it can open the door to a large variety of other software—everything from business applications usable by just about anyone, to exotic new programming languages guaranteed to gladden the heart of even the hardest-to-please computer programmer.

In the "early days" of CP/M (up to around 1980), this argument was more hope than fact. In recent years, however, the promise of lots of CP/M software has been turning into reality. As of this writing, there are several thousand application programs available for use under CP/M, with new offerings appearing almost weekly. While the quality and price of this software varies greatly, the number of jewels in the pack is definitely on the upswing.

In this and the next chapter, we'll take a look at five of the major categories into which such CP/M software falls, and show how some representative "packages" in each category work. These packages range in price from under $50 to over $2,000, but those in the top dollar brackets aren't necessarily the best. In fact, there is also a large body of "free" software (the current handling charge is about $8 per disk) available through user groups such as CPMUG (CP/M User's Group) and SIG/M (Special Interest Group/Microcomputers). To find out more about what they have, you can write to them at the addresses given in references [8] and [9] of Appendix G. There are also specialized groups such as the BDS C User's Group [10]. Subscribing to their newsletter is a good way to keep in touch.

The principal fly in the ointment of CP/M software availability comes from the fact that the only standard distribution format is the 8-inch single-density disk. If you have a system that can read such disks, you're all set. If not, you'll have to first check on whether your particular format (e. g., Apple II, Zenith, Northstar, etc.) is available for each package in which you're interested. You'll also have to be concerned with whether the software has been "copy protected" to prevent you from making backup copies (see Section 4.5).

Another item you'll want to check on is whether the software you purchase can easily be adapted to a wide variety of consoles and printers.

This is essential for programs that do "fancy I/O" in the form of (1) screen-oriented editing (this is editing in which the cursor can be freely moved about the screen, or where selected portions of the screen can be erased), and (2) fancy printing (this is printing that includes such features as boldface, underlining, subscripts, micro-justification, and so on). Since different consoles and printers require different codes for initiating these special actions, the software should include an "install" program that lets you easily change these codes for your present or future peripherals. An example of a good installation program is the one furnished with the MINCE/StarEdit Editor Programs (see Section 4.1). The CP/M application programs from MicroPro [19], Sorcim [30], and Ashton-Tate [29] also have good installation utilities.

Some CP/M software is sold "custom-installed" for the one console/ printer you specify. This is usually not a desirable arrangement since the software will be useless if you later buy a different console or printer. Trying to get the supplier to "re-install" it can get to be a hassle, cause added expense, and become a waste of your valuable time. It's better to insist on software that has a user-accessible installation program, and to check that it will work for both the present and future hardware you expect to own. End of caveat.

Here are the five categories of CP/M software we'll examine. The first four will be discussed in this chapter, while category 5 will be the subject of Chapter 5. An additional category of "other" is listed to give some idea of the variety of other packages now available.

1. Word Processing Systems. (Section 4.1) These include interactive text editors, "pretty print" output programs, spelling correction programs, and programs that link the word processor to other systems (e. g., to a mailing-list/letter-writing program).
2. Business Accounting Systems. (Section 4.2) The traditional packages here are general ledger, accounts receivable, accounts payable, payroll, and inventory.
3. Data Base Management Systems. (Section 4.3) These are general programs used to store and retrieve information, so they can often be used in conjunction with the other categories.
4. Electronic Spreadsheet/Plotting/Prediction Packages. (Section 4.4) These programs allow the user to build a table of related data, and instantly see the results of changing selected entries.
5. System Software. (Chapter 5) This category includes other operating systems, computer programming languages, and utilities such as "disk-fix" programs, disassemblers, copy programs, and so on. (Some excellent utilities are available from CPMUG and SIG/M, e. g., Ward Christensen's disk utility DU-V75 on CPMUG volume 68, and DUU on volume 78.)
6. Other. (Not discussed in this book.) This category is open-ended, of course. At present it consists of such things as games (e. g., "Adventure"), special purpose applications (e. g., property management, third-party billing systems, diet/nutrition analysis, graphics display, investment analysis, statistical analysis), and general purpose utility programs.

With this much variety, and with the high cost of most software, it pays to read reviews, consult other users, and in general to shop around before buying. You can easily end up putting more money into software than hardware, so cautious evaluation makes sense.

4.1 Word Processing Systems

A writer's dream is to take his or her thoughts and turn them into nice, neat, publishable typescript in one easy step. That dream is closer to being a reality today than ever before with computers, especially microcomputers equipped with word processing software systems.

In this section we will examine several word processing systems. All of them run on general purpose microcomputers. Each of them addresses the problems of designing word processing software in a slightly different way. MINCE [12] (also sold under the name StarEdit [18]) takes care of input or *text editing*, while its companion system Scribble [12] takes care of the output or *formatted printing* stage. The WordStar [19] word processor integrates these two phases into a single program. Both MINCE and WordStar run on a large variety of conventional hardware. Our third example, ISC's WPS80 [23], is an example of an integrated word processing system designed around one particular computer with special function keys and a color display.

In order to appreciate these different approaches to achieving the writer's dream, let's consider briefly some of the problems involved in the design of the two parts of a word processor: text editing and formatted output. Since voice input with reliable instant transcription is still in the future (at least as far as practical, low-cost word processing is concerned), we'll assume that the first step in this process is still *typing*.

Word processing systems have introduced a variety of features to reduce the drudgery of typing in and correcting text. For example, typing is made a lot simpler by the "fill" or "word wrap" feature. This means that no manual carriage return is required at the end of each line. Instead, the word processor moves the overhanging word to the next line while the user types merrily on. In addition, the typist can usually choose between a "ragged" right margin or a straight (justified) one.

The basic tools for making corrections are *deletion* and *insertion*. Deletions can be made instantaneously via special commands or keys. Characters, words, lines, or whole blocks of text can quickly be erased, leaving no gaps. Inserting new text is usually accomplished by positioning the cursor at the chosen point in the text and just typing—the paragraph will rearrange itself to accommodate the new text. When gaps are created (through deletion), or lines get too big (through insertion), the paragraph can usually be reformed with a single command. No more cut and paste! (or retyping whole pages). In general, text is displayed on the screen of the terminal to look as much as possible like the final printed page.

Once the final, edited version of the text is saved on disk, a "hardcopy" paper printout can be produced. Special commands embedded in the text file can make the printer underline, type boldface, number pages, and much more. For extremely high quality printout, your machine-readable file on disk can sometimes be sent off to a professional photo-typesetter—provided you can find one that takes your particular disk size and format.

As you might guess, there is more than one way to design a word processor with the above and other convenient features. To illustrate some of the approaches taken, let's turn our attention to the three specific systems mentioned earlier (WordStar, MINCE/Scribble, and WPS80).

WordStar

The basic WordStar system consists of a program called WS.COM, together with several "overlay" files. These handle both the text input and printed output stages of word processing, allowing the user to request either option from one starting menu of commands. Additional programs (at additional cost) can be used with this word processor to print form letters (Mailmerge), check spelling (SpellStar), or to do data manipulation. Three such data manipulation programs (DataStar, SuperSort, and CalcStar) are discussed later in this chapter.

WordStar is designed to be adaptable to many of the standard terminals and printers. It comes with an installation program which puts the user through a dialog to collect information about his or her configuration of hardware (the installation program is terminal-independent). It uses the answers to these questions to make the necessary modifications to WordStar. Only a rather knowledgeable user will be able to answer some of these questions, so WordStar buyers may prefer to have their dealer do this installation procedure for them. Still, it is very nice indeed to have such a program available, as dealers may come and go and you never know when you'll want to update your system in the future.

WordStar is a system which has been in use for several years now. It appears to be nearly foolproof—we have not had any crashes with version 2.1 that were not attributable to a hardware problem. (The newer version 3.0 is a more ambitious package, and our experience with all its nuances is more limited.)

In the editing process, keystrokes are stored as part of the text, unless they are control characters (or are preceded by control characters, i. e., ^C, ^KS*) in which case they become *commands*. No special keys beyond those found on a standard ASCII keyboard are needed. The commands (there are quite a few) are displayed in an abbreviated form

---

* The convention ^ will be used in this section to indicate that the control key is to be pressed simultaneously with the letter key. <. . .> will be used to indicate pressing other "special" keys on the keyboard, i. e., <cr> for carriage return or enter, <esc> for escape, <del> for delete, etc.

in a number of menus. The user is prompted for *everything*, starting with the filename for storing the text input (or the file to be edited). The menus are supplemented by prompting dialogues at appropriate points. Most menus and some prompts can be suppressed by typing the command sequences more quickly. For more experienced users, the screen can be made even less cluttered by supressing the main editing menu with a special command (^JH2). In general, WordStar leaves nothing to the user's imagination; one is never lost. The command menus are not complete explanations, however, and reading the manual is necessary. (Some people claim to have learned most of the system by experimentation and reading the menus, but the manual is really needed for intelligent use of the system.)

The design of the commands and prompts is such that it's difficult to make "fatal" errors. For instance, in order to end the editing session you must choose to save the work of that session *or* to abandon it. If you choose to abandon, a message inquires whether you really want to do so. In other words, saving a file is not separated in concept or design from ending the session, so it's difficult to lose a file accidentally. Saving and immediately restarting the editing session from the same point is made into one convenient procedure. A backup file is kept and automatically updated from the second "save" onward. For example, after the first time you save TFILE1, your directory looks like this:

. . .

. . .

A:TFILE1

After the second save (and all further saves) your directory looks like this:

. . .

. . .

A:TFILE1   BAK : TFILE1

TFILE1 is the version you just saved, while TFILE.BAK is the prior version. This is similar to the system used by ED, and valuable if you want to "take back" a certain change you made and saved.

Another example of user-friendliness in WordStar is the fact that a command sequence, for example, ^KQ, is taken to mean the same as its near variations: ^K^Q, ^k^q, ^kq, etc.—so both heavy- and light-fingered typists are accommodated.

It is perfectly possible to just start typing, and learn the commands as you go along: think up things you want to do and then look in the manual to see if they are possible (they usually are). The following lab will, in part, try to describe this kind of experience in a way that can be imitated directly if you have the software at hand, or experienced vicariously if you don't. (Note: Besides the User's Manual, a self-teaching text, "The WordStar Training Guide" is now supplied with WordStar. It is more user-oriented than the User's Manual.)

TECHNICAL
NOTE

Automatic File and Disk Buffering in WordStar

Saving your text file is done with a simple command in WordStar (^KD (save and end session) or ^KS (save and restart session)). The procedure for starting an editing session by bringing an old file into memory or giving a new file name to be used is handled with equally simple commands (N for non-document or D for document). The behind-the-scenes process is a bit more complicated, especially with large text files (those larger than the amount of RAM buffer memory available). Since all this is done automatically, most users need not be concerned with the details. For those who are curious, or wonder how WordStar compares with ED or other word processors in its handling of files, here is a more detailed explanation of what is happening.

Suppose you are working on a file called TEXT1. During an editing session, parts of your text file are brought into a buffer area of RAM memory in reasonable sized "chunks" (WordStar doesn't say what these are). As you work your way forward in the file, additional chunks are brought in until the RAM buffer is filled. If you move forward still more, then the beginning of the file (the "top") is stored as a temporary file on the same disk with the name TEXT1.$$$. (You can actually see this file appear if you use ^KF to turn the file directory display option on.) Conversely, if you move the cursor back through the text far enough, text from the temporary file will be reloaded into RAM. In this case, text from the bottom of the RAM buffer will be sent to another temporary file called EDBACKUP.$$$. The manual suggests that to save disk space, you can avoid creating this extra file by using ^KS (save and restart) as an alternate technique for moving the cursor far back to the beginning of a large file. (On a 62K CP/M system, this technique becomes useful with files equal to about 14 double-spaced pages of manuscript.) Fig. 4-1 shows how these files relate to each other.

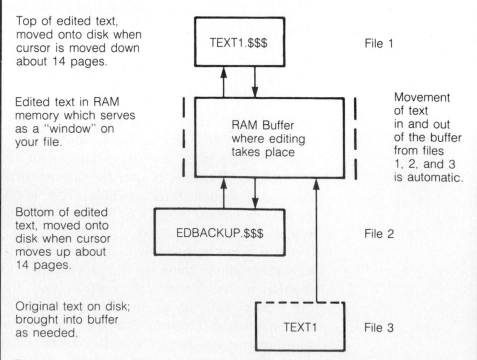

Top of edited text, moved onto disk when cursor is moved down about 14 pages.

TEXT1.$$$ File 1

Edited text in RAM memory which serves as a "window" on your file.

RAM Buffer where editing takes place

Movement of text in and out of the buffer from files 1, 2, and 3 is automatic.

Bottom of edited text, moved onto disk when cursor moves up about 14 pages.

EDBACKUP.$$$ File 2

Original text on disk; brought into buffer as needed.

TEXT1   File 3

Fig. 4-1   Diagram of the movement of text between the text buffer in memory and disk files during the editing process in WordStar.

All movement of text in and out of files is automatic, although you may be aware of it during editing by the noise of disk activity and a message asking you to "WAIT" briefly. When you use ^KD or ^KS to save the file you are editing, all the above segments are consolidated into one temporary file called TEXT1.$$$, which is now the newest updated version. The following steps take place:

I. File 1 + Buffer + File 2 + Unused File 3 ⟶ TEXT1.$$$
   (At this point you have three versions of your file: TEXT1.$$$, TEXT1.BAK, and TEXT1.)

II. TEXT1.BAK is erased.

III. TEXT1 ⟶ TEXT1.BAK

IV. TEXT1.$$$ ⟶ TEXT1

When your text file disk is getting full, and you save a large file, you may get a warning message saying that step II had to be done before step I. This is a good time to "clean up" your disk, or start a new one. As you can see, the designers of WordStar have done a good job of safety-engineering the disk file-saving process.

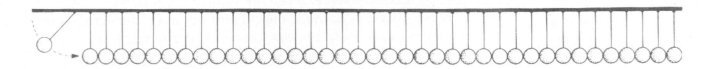

LAB EXERCISE 4.1-1

WordStar in Action

Although there are many options available for onscreen formatting of text (margins, tab stops, etc.) and many possible printer commands, WordStar starts off with a reasonable set of default values for all of these. This means that you can start by knowing very little, and gradually take over more and more control. (It reminds one a lot of BASIC in this regard.)

Step 1. Boot your system. We'll assume that the disk in drive A contains the WordStar programs and that someone has installed WordStar for your system. We'll also assume that you'll save your text files on a separate disk in drive B. This will provide more room for files, and (as we'll show later) making safety backup copies can be done more methodically. To save files on the disk in drive B, you simply put the prefix B: in front of any filename you type to WordStar (e. g., B:TEXT1). If you have only one disk drive, save your file on the same disk as WordStar by using the filename TEXT1.

Enter the WordStar word processing environment by typing WS <cr> (the name of the installed WordStar file is WS.COM, whereas the uninstalled version is WSU.COM). After the copyright message, the "editing-no-file" menu will appear as seen in Photo 4-1.

PHOTO 4-1   *The "editing no file" menu of WordStar.*

Type the command D, meaning "create a document file." A prompting message will request a filename. Type B:WSTEST <cr> (or WSTEST if you have only one drive). After some disk activity, the message "NEW FILE" and the "main" menu will appear, along with a "status line" at the top and a "ruler line" just below the menu, as shown in Photo 4-2.

Step 2.   Type in just what you see in Photo 4-2. Space normally, use <tab> and <caps lock> normally, but *don't* use <cr> except at the end of the heading PERSONAL COMPUTERS. There you press <cr> twice. If you see you have misspelled something, press <delete> to move the cursor back over the incorrect text (erasing as it backs up, one character at a time). If the error is too far back when you discover it, leave it alone for now.

What you have just done is create a text file in memory, using the default values of WordStar for tab stops (every 5 characters) and margins (1 and 65). WordStar decided when a new line should start, and "wrapped" the word that didn't fit in the last line to the next line. (The term "wrap"

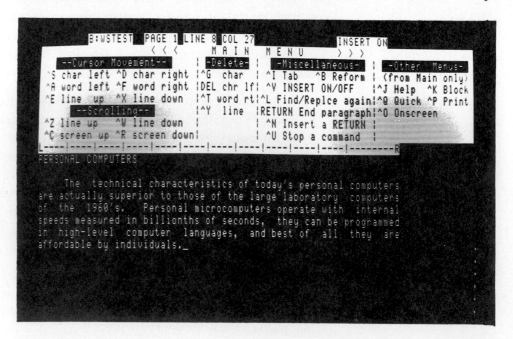

PHOTO 4-2   *The "main" menu of WordStar with some text inserted.*

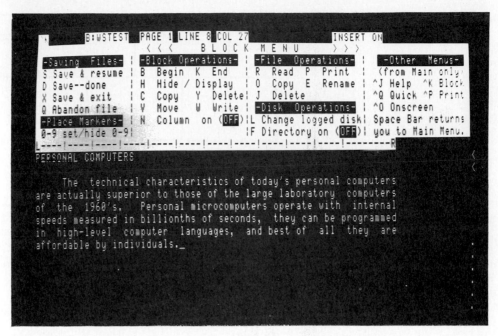

PHOTO 4-3   *The WordStar "block" menu.*

is used to indicate that the end of one line "wraps around" to the beginning of the next, something like the stripes on a barber pole. "Word wrap" means that if a word can't fit on one line, it is not split, but wrapped around to the next one. Also notice that WordStar inserts extra spaces in a line to create a straight right margin. This is called "filling" the line and that kind of margin is called a "justified" right margin.)

Before going any further, type ˆK. The "block" menu (a better name would be the file saving menu) will appear as shown in Photo 4-3. ˆK is a "prefix" to which you must add a letter from this menu to make a command sequence. For our lab, type S.

In the jargon of WordStar, you have used ˆKS to save a copy of WSTEST on disk and reenter the document editing mode. (Ignore the message about the cursor for now.)

Step 3.   Try out the cursor control commands. They are arranged "keypad style" on the left side of the keyboard following the pattern shown in Fig. 4-2. You can learn these commands by looking at the menu and trying them out.

Cursor movement takes place only within the text you have already typed in—it's impossible to move the cursor outside this text. Next try positioning the cursor and deleting some things using ˆG (delete one character at the cursor position), DELETE (delete one character to the left of the cursor position), ˆT (delete one word—all characters in a word to the right of the cursor), and ˆY (delete the entire line where the cursor is positioned). Now try correcting any spelling errors. How? By deleting the bad text and then replacing whatever you erased by typing in the new text (first moving the cursor if required). When finished, type ˆKS. Incidentally, while moving the cursor around, notice how the "status"

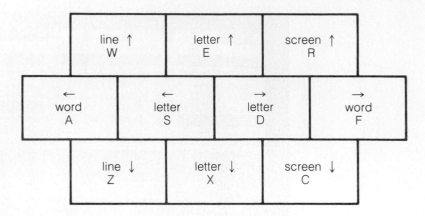

FIG. 4-2   In WordStar, to move the cursor, you hold down the control key and simultaneously press one of these keys. That is, the cursor movement commands are: ^W, ^E, ^R, ^A, ^S, ^D, ^F, ^Z, ^X, and ^C.

line at the top of the screen displays the current row and column position of the cursor.

Step 4.   Experiment with turning INSERT off.

4a. Position the cursor at the end of the text. (Use the cursor control commands as before.) Type enough asterisks to *almost* fill in the last line, *type a space,* then type in more asterisks.

4b. Position the cursor after the end of the word "individuals." Type ^V. Notice that the "INSERT ON" message disappears

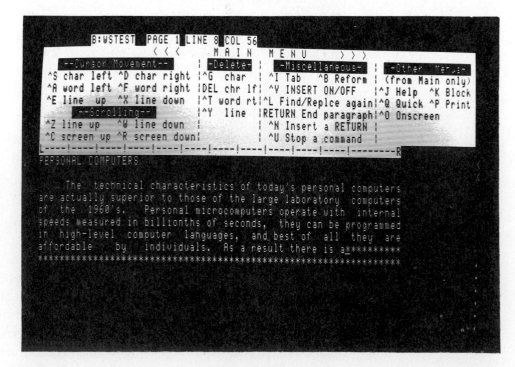

PHOTO 4-4   *After typing in asterisks and repositioning the cursor, insert mode was turned off with ^V.*

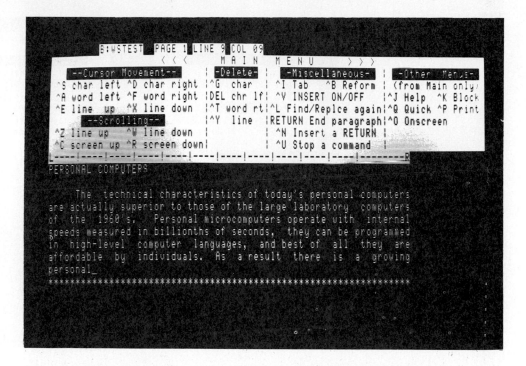

PHOTO 4-5   Overstrike mode was used here to replace asterisks with text.

from the status line. Now type the text you see in the series of "snapshots," labeled Photos 4-4, 4-5, 4-6.

Now type ^V again (the "INSERT ON" message will pop back on). The process just illustrated can be termed typing in "overstrike" or "insert off" *mode*. (A mode is just a situation where familiar keys are made to have a different effect.) The asterisks in the cursor's starting

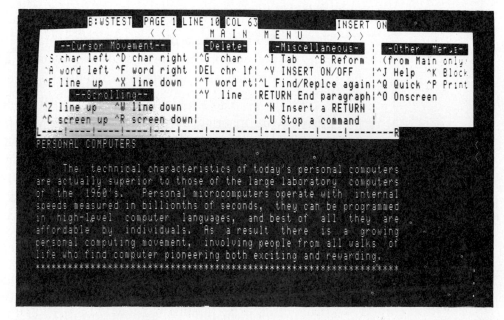

PHOTO 4-6   More text was entered here in overstrike mode. Then insert mode was turned back on with ^V.

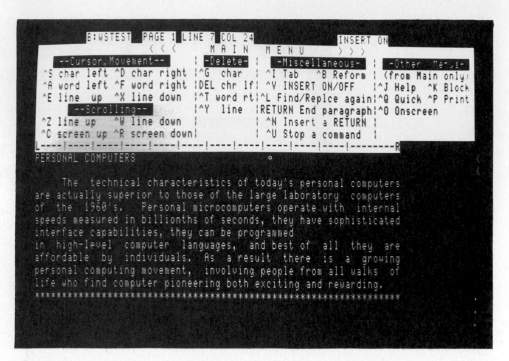

```
 B:WSTEST  PAGE 1 LINE 7 COL 24              INSERT ON
              < < <        M A I N   M E N U   > > >
    --Cursor Movement--      | -Delete- |   -Miscellaneous-   |   -Other Menus-
^S char left ^D char right |^G  char  | ^I Tab    ^B Reform | (from Main only)
^A word left ^F word right |DEL chr lf| ^V INSERT ON/OFF    |^J Help  ^K Block
^E line  up  ^X line down  |^T word rt|^L Find/Replce again|^Q Quick ^P Print
       --Scrolling--       |^Y  line  |RETURN End paragraph|^O Onscreen
^Z line up   ^W line down  |          | ^N Insert a RETURN  |
^C screen up ^R screen down|          | ^U Stop a command   |
L----!----!----!----!----!----!----!----!----!----!----!--------R
PERSONAL COMPUTERS                          o

     The  technical characteristics of today's personal computers
are actually superior to those of the large laboratory  computers
of  the  1960's.   Personal microcomputers operate with  internal
speeds measured in billionths of seconds, they have sophisticated
interface capabilities, they can be programmed
in  high-level  computer  languages,  and best of  all  they  are
affordable  by  individuals.  As a result  there  is  a  growing
personal computing movement,  involving people from all walks  of
life who find computer pioneering both exciting and rewarding.
**************************************************************
```

PHOTO 4-7   *New text is inserted after "billionths of seconds,".*

line were overstruck. But whenever typing moved to the next line, the subsequent line(s) weren't lost; they were simply moved down. If you reposition the cursor with overstrike mode still on, however, the typing you do will cause previous characters on that line to be overstruck or replaced. This is an example of a word processor design decision. WordStar puts you in "insert mode" as the normal mode, but lets you change to "overstrike mode" if you wish. Some users like to turn on overstrike mode to make corrections, instead of deleting and inserting—that's up to you.

Step 5.   Try inserting a phrase and reformatting the paragraph. Position the cursor on line 4 after the comma and type: "They have sophisticated interface capabilities", as shown in Photo 4-7.

Photo 4-7 also shows that the text on the rest of the line where the phrase was inserted is moved over, but the paragraph itself is not completely reformatted. To finish the job, position the cursor at the beginning of the paragraph, and type the reformat command, ^B. During this reformatting process, WordStar will pause and ask you if you want a word to be divided at the end of a line. This is the "hyphen-help" feature. For this lab, just type ^B again whenever this message occurs and the word will be wrapped to the next line. The result should be as seen in Photo 4-8.

Step 6.   Onscreen formatting. Now that you have some text to fool around with, let's look at some of the other options you have for formatting the text you input. Type ^O. The menu of onscreen formatting commands will be displayed. Now type J. This will turn the right justification feature off, resulting in ragged right margins from now on in the editing session. To see what this

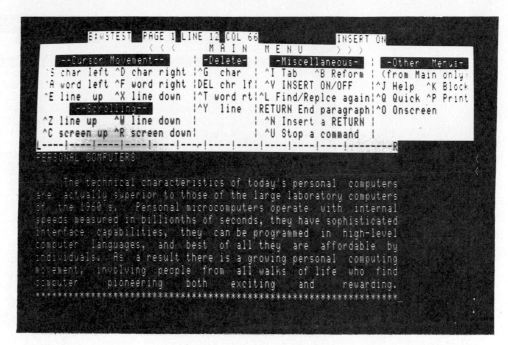

PHOTO 4-8   *Result of using ^B to reformat a paragraph.*

looks like, simply reformat the paragraph by positioning the cursor at the beginning and typing ^B. The result should look like that in Photo 4-9. Type ^O again to view the menu. You can see that the justification feature is now turned off. Press <space> to go back to the main menu.

Now position the cursor on the line with the title and type ^OC. Presto, it's centered. Talk about fun!

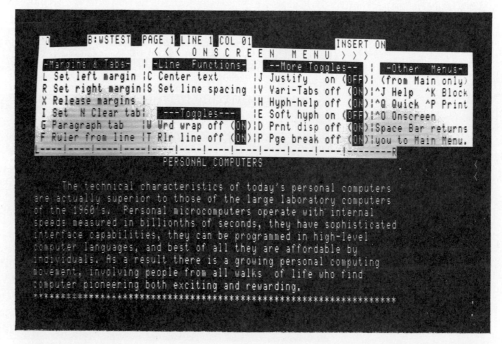

PHOTO 4-9   *Reformatted paragraph after turning justify OFF and using ^B again.*

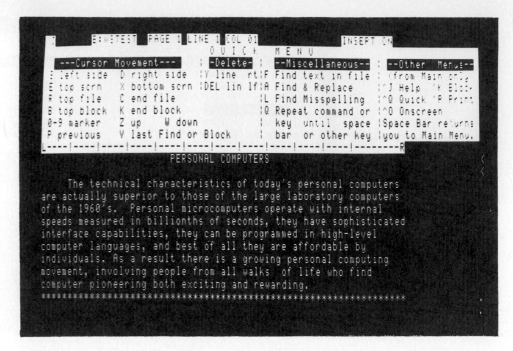

PHOTO 4-10   *The ^Q menu which includes the Find and Replace command.*

Step 7.   Finding and replacing. WordStar allows you to look through your file for a specified string of characters. You can just find this string, or find and replace it with another string of characters. To see how this is done, let's look at the "quick" menu by typing ^Q. This menu, shown in Photo 4-10, contains additional cursor moving commands and erasing commands as well as ^QF (find) and ^QA (find and replace). To get the second one, type A.

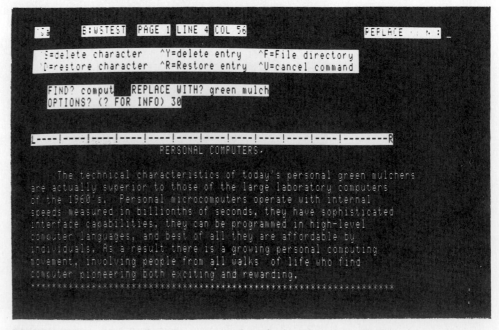

PHOTO 4-11   *Using the ^QA command to find and replace 30 limes.*

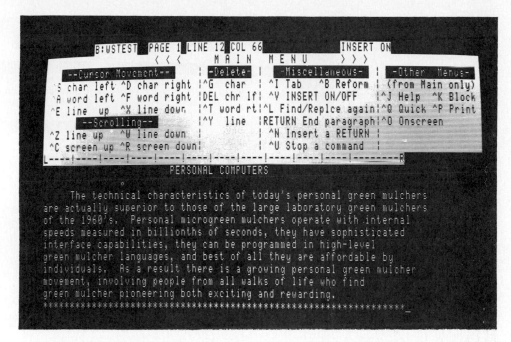

PHOTO 4-12   Result of replacing "comput" with "green mulch".

Since this is a complex command, you will first see the dialogue of Photo 4-11 asking (1) what string you want to find, (2) what string you want to substitute for it, and (3) what options you wish to use. You ordinarily would study the manual before using the ^QA command. In case you get confused, this command (and all others) can be aborted by typing ^U. For this demonstration, find the string "comput" and replace it with the string "green mulch," and choose the option of doing this 30 times, as shown in Photo 4-11.

During this process you will be asked to type Y for yes or N for no for each replacement. Type Y each time. When no more of the specified strings are found, an error message is printed. This is no problem since it is easily recovered from by typing the escape key (as the message suggests). The result should be as seen in Photo 4-12.

At this point, you should reformat the paragraph by moving the cursor to the first line, and then typing ^B.

Step 8.   Using the print control characters. Suppose we decide that the word "individuals" in line 7 should be underlined, and the words "exciting" and "rewarding" in the last lines would look better in boldface type. To do this, first position the cursor at the "i" in "individuals," then type ^P. This will cause the print menu to appear.

Now type S. Typing ^PS causes a ^S to be inserted in the text. It will appear on the screen but will not be printed out on the printer. Now move the cursor to the period just beyond "s" in "individuals" and type ^PS again. During printing, the first ^S will cause the printer underlining feature to "turn on." The second ^S will cause it to "turn off." Now move the cursor to the "e" in "exciting" and type ^PB. ^B will be inserted in the text and will "turn on" the boldface print feature.

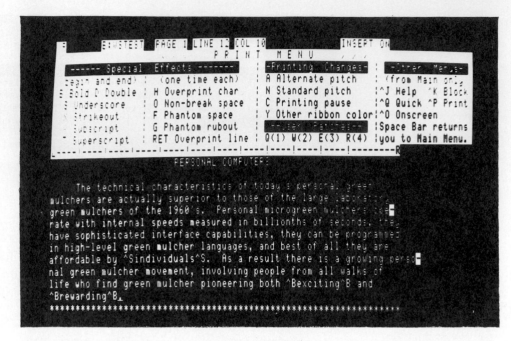

PHOTO 4-13   *The ^S and ^B print control characters are inserted in the text to turn underline and boldface on or off during printing.*

Move the cursor to the space after "exciting" and type ^PB again. Now type ^PB while the cursor is positioned before and after "rewarding." The result should look like what is shown in Photo 4-13.

Step 9.   Printing out your file. Suppose you are finished editing and wish to see what your file looks like. First, end the editing session by typing ^KD. This will save the latest version, make a backup out of the previous version, and return you to the

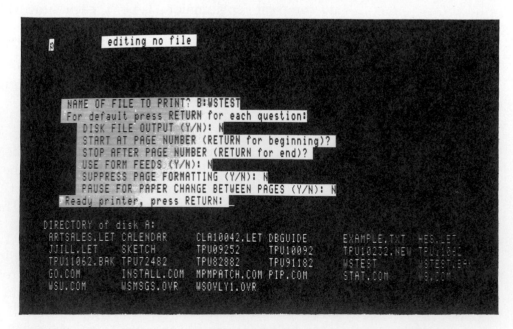

PHOTO 4-14   *Dialogue produced by the P (print) command of WordStar.*

PERSONAL COMPUTERS

The technical characteristics of today's personal green
mulchers are actually superior to those of the large laboratory
green mulchers of the 1960's. Personal microgreen mulchers operate with internal speeds measured in billionths of seconds, they
have sophisticated interface capabilities, they can be programmed
in high-level green mulcher languages, and best of all they are
affordable by <u>individuals</u>. As a result there is a growing personal green mulching movement, involving people from all walks of
life who find green mulcher pioneering both **exciting** and
rewarding.
****

FIG. 4-3 WordStar's print function printed out the "Personal Computers"
paragraph, following the print control commands shown embedded in the text.

"editing-no-file" menu. Then the P command can be used from
this menu to start the print dialogue. This will produce the
series of questions shown in Photo 4-14.

If you simply press RETURN in response to each question, you will
get the normal, or default values. These will be fine for now. You can
see there are a lot of options available and a look in the manual is
necessary to understand them. The result of printing out the final,
reformatted version is shown in Fig. 4-3. (Recall that we used ^OJ in
step 6 to select a ragged right margin.)

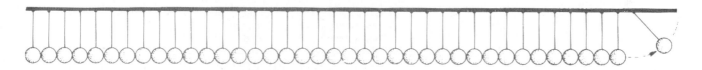

Fig. 4-4, on pages 146 and 147, shows in brief the commands used
most often in WordStar. This summary is organized by function rather
than by screen display menu.

FIG. 4-4   Summary of WordStar Commands.

In this summary, the most often used commands are grouped by function. (The menus of commands shown on the screen by WordStar are grouped according to prefix letter, and they show the complete editing command set.) The conventions used here are: the ˆ to indicate that the control key is to be pressed simultaneously with another key, and <...> to indicate that a special key is to be pressed (e.g., <cr> for return, <esc> for escape, <del> for delete, <space> for space bar, etc.) <cr> is assumed after some commands; in practice this is made clear by prompts.

Note on command "prefixes": the following commands require another letter to create a command. They each have a menu display of these letters. Pressing <space> cancels a prefix and makes the menu disappear.

ˆJ	the "help" menu (capsule reference information)
ˆK	the "block" menu (handling blocks of text, saving files)
ˆQ	the "quick" menu (additional cursor, delete commands, also find and replace)
ˆP	the "print" menu (commands to insert control characters in the text for various print functions)
ˆO	the "onscreen" menu (margins, tabs, linespacing and other page formatting commands)

0.   Preliminary commands: (from the "editing-no-files" menu)

WS<cr>	run the WordStar program
WS filename<cr>	run the WordStar program, edit the named document file
D filename<cr>	edit a document (natural language text)
N filename<cr>	edit a program
	(d and n load a file in the text buffer, start editing mode (with different default conditions)
P filename<cr>	print a file
X	exit from WordStar to CP/M

1.   Cursor movement: (from the "main" menu)

ˆS	move cursor left one character
ˆD	move cursor right one character
ˆA	move cursor left one word
ˆF	move cursor right one word
ˆE	move cursor up one line
ˆX	move cursor down one line

2.   Scrolling the screen: (from the "main" and ˆQ menus)

ˆZ	shift the screen down one line of text
ˆW	shift the screen up one line of text
ˆC	shift the screen down one (almost) screenful
ˆR	shift the screen up one (almost) screenful
ˆQC	move to the end of the file
ˆQR	move to the beginning of the file

3.   Deleting: (mostly from the "main" menu)

<delete>	erase one character to the left of the cursor
ˆG	erase one character at the cursor
ˆT	erase one word forward from the cursor
ˆY	erase the whole line where the cursor is positioned
ˆQY	erase from the cursor position to the end of the line
ˆKY	erase a marked block of text (see below)

4.   Other text entering commands: (mostly from the "main" menu)

ˆU <esc>	cancel a command
ˆV	turn overstrike mode on/off
ˆN	insert <cr> at the cursor position, a blank line
ˆQQ	repeat the following command or key until interrupted

5.   Onscreen formatting

ˆB	reformat a paragraph (insert hyphens on request)
ˆOC	center the line where cursor is positioned
ˆOL n	set left margin at column n
ˆOR n	set right margin at column n
ˆOS n	set linespacing, single, double, etc.
ˆOG	set hanging indentation to a tab
ˆOJ	turn justification mode on/off
ˆOW	turn word wrap mode on/off

6. Handling blocks of text:

^KB	mark the beginning of a block
^KK	mark the end of a block (turn it to reverse video)
^KV	move the marked block to the cursor position
^KC	copy the marked block at the cursor position
^KY	erase the marked block
^KN	turn column mode on/off (allow marking and moving of rectangles within text)

7. Searching and replacing strings:

^QA string string	find and replace a string with another string
^QF string	find a string
^L	repeat the last find or replace command

8. Merging files:

^KW filename	write a marked block to the named file
^KR filename	insert (read) the named file at the cursor position

9. Special features:

^JH n	set 'help level', (turn off some or all menus)
(no display)	'soft' <cr> automatically inserted during wordwrap, moved during reformatting
(–, reverse video)	'soft' hyphen inserted at user command during paragraph reformatting (does not show during printing, after further reformatting)
————P	automatic page break display
^OR 255	maximum right margin is 255 columns, screen displays by scrolling horizontally

10. Ending an editing session:

^KS	save changes and restart editing session
^KD	save changes and end editing session
^KQ	quit editing without saving
^KX	save, end editing session, exit to CP/M

11. Print formatting

^PS	during printing, turn underscore on/off
^PB	during printing, turn boldface on/off
^PT	during printing, turn superscript on/off
^PV	during printing, turn subscript on/off
^PH	backspace once during printing (allows overstrike)
^PC	stop printing

(Note: the following dot commands always begin in column one and occupy one line each.)

.mt n	set margin at top of page to n lines
.mb n	set margin at bottom of page to n lines
.he text	specify a heading for the top of the page
.fo text	specify a footing for the bottom of the page
.op	omit the default page number (at center bottom)
.pn n	start page numbering at n
. .	comment line, ignore (also .ig)
.cw n	set character width
.lh n	set line height
.uj n	set microjustification on/off (n = 1, 0)
.sr n	set subscript roll
.pa	start a new page (supersedes auto. page break)

TECHNICAL NOTE

A Procedure for Using CP/M to Make Backup Disks of Text Files Produced with a Word Processor

When you edit a file, most word processors save the old version as a BAK file, along with the new updated version. In our examples, both of these files were saved on the text-only disk in drive B. Common sense dictates that, in addition, the updated version be copied onto a second text-only disk. This acts as a physically separate backup which protects against mechanical or magnetic degradation of your "working" text file disk. For very important documents, a third backup disk is often made and kept in a different location for even better protection. These backup copies should be updated frequently, and a systematic procedure should be invented by the user for doing this.

Making such backups usually requires changing disks and using PIP, so you must exit from the word processor and return to CP/M. This is done in WordStar by using the X command from the first menu. After changing disks, a warm boot is needed before CP/M will allow you to write on the new disk (see Section 6.4 for the reason). Then, using the PIP program, or a copy of PIP already in the TPA, you can copy the newest versions of one or more files onto the new backup disk.

Here's one example of such a file backup procedure. It is the one that was used to protect the manuscript of this book as it went through its many revisions.

The manuscript resided on four 8-inch double-density floppy disks and four corresponding backup disks. For instance, Chapters 1 and 2 were on disk #501, and its backup was on #502. Chapters 3 and 4 were on #503, with backup on #504, and so on. Now suppose some changes or additions were required in files residing on disk #501 (Chapters 1 and 2). Here's the procedure followed for using WordStar to make the changes on #501, and then using PIP to backup #501 onto #502.

1. Insert a "system" disk in drive A, that is, a disk containing CP/M, WordStar, and PIP. Insert the primary text disk (#501) in drive B. Boot the system, load WordStar, and proceed to use it as desired to edit any of the files on disk #501 (which is in drive B).

2. After making the changes, and saving them back on the B disk with ^KD (by using a filename like B:GTC41), exit from WordStar by typing X to the first menu.

3. Run PIP by typing A>PIP <cr>.

4. Remove the system disk from drive A. Replace it with disk #502. Close the drive door and do a warm boot (press ^C).

5. Type DIR. Type DIR B:. This is to check that the disks you think you have are really there.

6. Run PIP. Since there is no copy of PIP on the text file disks, you can't do this with A>PIP. However PIP is still in the TPA from step 3, so it can be restarted by typing A>GO, provided GO.COM is on disk #502. (If it isn't, first type A>SAVE 0 GO.COM as explained in Section 6.4.)

7. You can now use any PIP command you wish. Related groups of files can be copied with one PIP command if the filenames have been carefully chosen. For example, names like GTC23, GTC11, GTC10, etc., can all be backed up from #501 to #502 as follows:

```
*A: = B:GTC*
COPYING -
GTC23
GTC11
GTC10
. . . etc. . . .
```

Note that using B:GTC* instead of B:GTC*.* avoids copying .BAK files (which is usually what you want).

8. If a third backup copy is desired, repeat steps 4–7, using the third disk in the A drive in step 4. When finished, store all disks in a dust-free enclosure.

MINCE/Scribble

And now for something different. A word processor with features that will delight computerists even more than typists. Make no mistake—this is a really good word processor, but it's definitely a system that favors the person who wants to be challenged.

Our description will be in two parts (MINCE, the editor, and Scribble, a related printout producer) and both will be brief. If this system sounds like your cup of tea, by all means contact the supplier/authors at Mark of the Unicorn [12]. MINCE is also available under the name StarEdit from SuperSoft at [18]. A new (and presumably improved) version called "The FinalWord (TM)" is also available from [12].

MINCE

MINCE is patterned after a larger editor developed at MIT called EMACS. In fact the name MINCE is a (recursive?) acronym for "MINCE Is Not Complete EMACS." MINCE was written in the language C (discussed in Sections 5.6 and 5.7), and since you are given most of the original C "source programs" when you buy MINCE, there is the intriguing possibility that if you get expert enough at programming in C, you could modify MINCE. However that's not necessary—it's extremely flexible as supplied.

MINCE consists of several files. The principal one is called MINCE.COM (or SE.COM). There is also an installation program called CONFIG.COM which allows the user to select from a large variety of terminals. There are several "lesson" files to work with (along with the tutorials given in the manual) before launching on your own experiments. *Warning:* MINCE does not keep automatic backup files, so the user must remember to do this.

MINCE has a basic similarity to WordStar: commands are all special characters or escape sequences, while normal keystrokes are always stored as part of the text. There the similarity ends. MINCE commands are all named differently, MINCE has major features that are not included in WordStar, and MINCE's onscreen result does not necessarily correspond to the final printout (as does WordStar's).

MINCE commands come in four "styles" as shown in Fig. 4-5. There are control characters (for example, ^D means delete one character at the cursor position); there are escape sequences (for example, <esc>D means delete one word forward from the cursor position); there are commands prefixed by ^X (for example, ^X^C means exit to CP/M); and there are escape sequences combined with control characters (for example, <esc>^K means kill a whole line).

FIG. 4-5 Summary of MINCE Commands.

In this summary, the most often used commands are grouped by function (rather than style). The conventions used here are: the ^ to indicate that the control key is to be pressed simultaneously with another key, and <...> to indicate that a special key is to be pressed (e.g., <cr> for return, <esc> for escape, <del> for delete, <space> for space bar, etc. <cr> is assumed after some commands; this is clear in the context of use.

0. Preliminary commands:

MINCE<cr>   run the MINCE program, start edit mode
MINCE filename<cr>   run MINCE, load named file into main text buffer, start edit mode

1. Cursor movement:

^P   move cursor to previous line
^N   move cursor to next line
^F   move cursor forward one character
<esc>F   move cursor forward one word
^B   move cursor back one character
<esc>B   move cursor back one word
^A   move cursor to beginning of line
<esc>A   move cursor to beginning of sentence
^E   move cursor to end of line
<esc>E   move cursor to end of sentence
<esc><   move cursor to beginning of file
<esc>>   move cursor to end of file

2. Scrolling the screen:

^V   view next screenful (with some overlap)
<esc>V   view previous screenful (with some overlap)
^L   redisplay screen

3. Deleting:

<delete>   erase one character to the left of the cursor
^D   erase one character at the cursor
^K   erase one line forward from the cursor*
<esc><del>   erase one word leftward from the cursor*
<esc>D   erase one word forward from the cursor*
<esc>K   erase one sentence forward from the cursor*

4. Other editing commands:

^G   cancel prefix (<esc>, ^X, ^S, ^R)
^XM modename   select normal, fill, or page modes
^U n   repeat the following command n times
^O   insert <cr> at cursor position, a blank line
^T   transpose two characters to the left of the cursor
^X=   "Where am I?" causes position of point and marker (in number of characters
                              from beginning of file) to be displayed

5. Onscreen formatting:

^X<tab>   set tab at cursor position
^XF   set fill column (right margin) at cursor position
^X.   set indent column (left margin) at cursor position
^\   delete indentation
<esc>Q   reformat or fill paragraph
<esc>S   center the line where cursor is positioned

6. Handling blocks of text:

^@   set a marker at the cursor position
^X^X   exchange cursor and marker (so you can see them)
<esc>H   mark whole paragraph where cursor is positioned
^W   erase ('wipe') marked block of text*
^Y   retrieve ('yank') marked block at cursor position*
<esc>W   erase marked block and immediately 'yank'*
<esc>^W   prepare to add next erased text to kill buffer*

7. Searching and replacing strings:

^S string   forward search
^R string   reverse search

---

*These commands use the kill buffer to store deleted text.

8. Merging files:

(use block moving commands together with multiple buffers, see also Scribble @ Include [. . .] command)

9. Special features:

ˆXˆB	list all the active text buffers
ˆXB buffername	switch to another buffer or create a new buffer
ˆXK	kill the current buffer
ˆXˆF filename	find the named file in a buffer, or create a new buffer and read the named file into it
ˆX2	make the screen into two windows
ˆX1	return screen to one window
ˆXˆ	enlarge window where cursor is positioned
ˆXO	switch cursor to other window
ˆXˆZ	scroll back other window one screenful
ˆXˆV	scroll forward other window one screenful

10. Ending an editing session:

ˆXˆC	quit the editor, abandon unsaved contents of buffers
ˆXˆW<cr> or ˆXˆS	write the contents of the buffer to the last mentioned filename
ˆXˆW filename	write contents of buffer to the named file
ˆXˆR filename	read the named file into the buffer

11. Print formatting: (see Scribble summary.)

Having this much variety in command formats could be confusing on first contact, but the apparent difficulty disappears with time. A more serious consideration is MINCE's Spartan approach to user feedback. There are no onscreen menus of commands, and less "what's going on" information is displayed on the screen. It's up to you to study the manual or use a summary of commands like the one just given. It's difficult to learn MINCE by just fiddling around with it. You *can* get lost. (MINCE actually has a command that means "Where am I?"). You can also lose part of your file with the unwary use of the command to end a session.

The good news about all this is that you have more control over what's going on. MINCE compares to WordStar something like a sports car manual shift compares to an automatic transmission. The manual is the choice of most pros, but it takes extra training, and there can be more lurching than driving in the beginning.

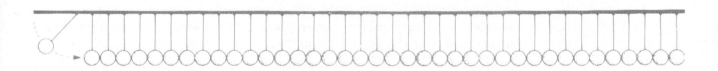

MINI-LAB
4.1-2

MINCE in Action

Step 1. After booting CP/M, load MINCE with the command A>MINCE<cr> (or A>SE for StarEdit). You will *not* be prompted for a filename, although you may use one at this point (A>MINCE TEST.MIN, for instance). If you don't give

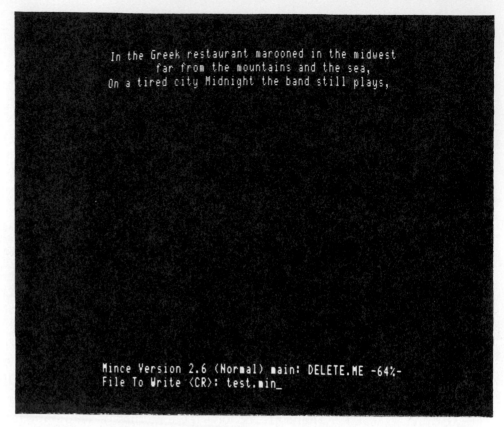

In the Greek restaurant marooned in the midwest
            far from the mountains and the sea,
On a tired city Midnight the band still plays,

Mince Version 2.6 (Normal) main: DELETE.ME -64%-
File To Write <CR>: test.min_

PHOTO 4-15   *MINCE screen display when text is first entered.*

one, the standard filename DELETE.ME will be associated with the main text buffer in memory.

Step 2.   At this point you can start typing in text and using all the commands, but the screen does not tell you this directly. The next-to-last line of the screen, called the "mode line" does give some information as seen in Photo 4-15.

What the terse message of the mode line signifies is actually pretty exciting: (1) The screen is now a window on the main text buffer. (You can create more text buffers if you wish, and divide the screen into two windows to view two buffers at the same time); (2) You are in "normal" editing mode. (If you want word wrapping, you must request "fill" mode); (3) The filename currently associated with the contents of the main buffer is DELETE.ME; (4) The "point" (the place where changes will occur, that is, the cursor position) is some percent forward through the contents of the buffer; (5) No changes have been made in this buffer since the last save command (otherwise an asterisk (*) would appear in the mode line).

The line below the mode line (the bottom line of the screen) is called the "echo line." It will be used intermittently for echoing commands, displaying prompting messages and error messages. (The prompt for the filename of step 4 below is shown in the echo line of Photo 4-15.) There is no ruler displaying tabs and margins.

Step 3.   Type in the text as shown. Try the cursor moves and delete commands as listed in the summary.

Step 4.   In order to save the contents of the buffer, you must remember to type ^X^S or ^X^W before you exit to CP/M. This can be done at any time and is not associated with ending the session. When you do this the asterisk in the mode line disappears. To end the session, you type ^X^C. You will be asked if you wish to "Abandon Modified Buffer(s)?" if some text or changes have been typed in and not previously saved. If you type "y" they will be lost; "n" cancels the command. Try typing ^X^W TEST.MIN. Notice that you are still in MINCE editing mode when this command is completed. Nothing has changed, except that the asterisk in the mode line has disappeared and the filename now associated with the main buffer is TEST.MIN. At this point you can add more text, make changes, read a new file into the main buffer, or end the session (with ^X^C).

Step 5.   Multiple text buffers and the option of turning the screen into a dual display are what make MINCE unusual. These features greatly facilitate the "cut and paste" that often occurs in the construction of both programs and English prose.

For example, suppose we wish to use some notes and a quotation to support a statement in an essay, and suppose (lucky for us) both the rough draft of the essay and the notes and quotation exist as ASCII files. (To actually do this exercise, you'll have to first create the two ASCII files.)

5a. Read the file containing the essay into the main buffer by typing ^X^R, followed by the filename of your choice (B:PHEN2.MSS in this example) after the prompting message. If there is anything not yet saved in the buffer, MINCE will ask if we want to lose it. (Clobber Modified Buffer?) Type "y". The first page of the essay file is now loaded into the main buffer.

5b. Create a second buffer by typing ^XB and giving the buffer a name, say, SECOND. The "point" (cursor) is now located in the new buffer (which is empty), and the mode line gives information about it. If we now use the command ^X^R, and give the filename B:IHDE1.NQ, the notes and quotation this file contains will be read into the second buffer.

5c. Now let's split the screen into two windows so we can see both buffers at once. The command ^X2 requests that the screen be turned into a two-window display. At first this will just show two copies of the current buffer, SECOND, where the "point" is located. But if we ask for the other buffer (^XB, MAIN), the contents of the main buffer will appear in the top window while the note file will remain visible in the second window. The mode line will now contain information on whichever buffer

```
@Chapter(The Relevance of Philosophical Phenomenology to the Present Study)
@Begin[Verbatim]
@MajorHeading(This Paragraph Will Be Printed Out Verbatim)
     @B(The history of phenomenology) reveals a number of goals or
motivations, certain of which are of interest for this study.
Phenomenology arose in the late 19th century at least partly in
response to the splitting off of the natural sciences from
philosophy.  Some philosophers reacted to the split by giving
science the job of searching for empirical truth and philosophy
the task of uncovering logical or formal truth, that is, of
developing a theory of meaning.
------------------------------------------------------------------------r
Ihde, Don.  "A Phenomenology of Man-Machine Relations".  In Feinberg, W. and
Henry Rosemont, Jr, @U(Work, Technology, and Education).  (Urbana: University
of Illinois Press, 1975).

transparency --    (Man-machine) =========) World     sensory-extension-reductn.
translucency --    Man =====) (machine) =====) World transformational
opacity --         Man =========) (machine-World)    technosphere

"There is ... an inverse ration within the transformational factor between what
is first starkly apparent and what later beomces intuitive and taken for granted
in the successful use of the machine.  That is, the more adept the machine user
Mince Version 2.6 (Normal) main: B:PHEN2.MSS -0%-
Switch to Buffer <CR>: main
```

*PHOTO 4-16   This is a MINCE editing screen display showing two windows displaying
two text buffers. Blocks of text can be moved from one buffer to another in MINCE.*

the cursor is pointing to. That is, if we switch to the other
window (^XO) the cursor will move to where the point is located
in the other buffer, and the mode line will change to show
information about that buffer. Photo 4-16 shows the dual window
appearance of the screen after giving this sequence of commands.

With this arrangement, it becomes possible to compare notes and
draft text while composing at the console. You could then mark out the
quotation that you want and copy it from the SECOND buffer to the
MAIN buffer which holds the draft essay. (A similar operation can be
done in WordStar, but it is not as automated, and of course, you cannot
see two files on one screen.)

Rather than go on with the marking and moving of a block of text,
we'll end this mini-lab exercise here. Type ^X^C. Since no changes were
made, no question about "abandoning modified buffers" appears.

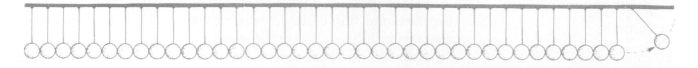

MINCE keeps track of a good deal of information for each text
buffer. Each buffer not only has its own contents, but a mode, a position
of the point (cursor), and a marker position (useful in moving or deleting
lots of text at once). There is also a special buffer for holding deleted
text, and another buffer for holding search/replace strings.

The number and/or size of text buffers depends on the size of a disk file called the "swap" file (MINCE.SWP). This is created on disk during installation of MINCE and can be any convenient size (64K is usually recommended). What the swap file does, briefly, is to allow the use of a private text buffer-to-disk I/O arrangement by MINCE. Remember that when WordStar ran out of room in RAM memory for its single text buffer, it created temporary files on disk to hold the extra text. WordStar did this by using regular CP/M disk I/O, and you could see the temporary files pop up in the directory. MINCE does essentially the same sort of thing, but it has a variable number of text buffers to look after (as well as other, smaller, buffers). So the design decision was made to use one large "swap" file on disk to manage the various buffer/disk file transfers, and wait until a save command is given before creating regular CP/M text files. This arrangement makes the multiple-file, multiple-buffer system workable, and it can speed up disk access times.

Scribble

Scribble consists of a group of programs including SCRIBBLE.COM, CRAYON.COM, PENCIL.COM, and SCONFIG.COM. Scribble will take as input any ASCII file, however rough, and attempt to generate neat, reformatted copy. Its formatting commands allow still more possibilities. Scribble generates an intermediate file (to which it gives the old filename plus .FIN) which is printed out by the Crayon program to get the final formatted effect. Scribble can also send its results directly to the printer, if that's preferred. Pencil is a program which simply prints any ASCII file without formatting it, but making use of the information in Scribble's configuration program. A large number of printers, from "plain vanilla" (as they put it) to fancy microspace, microfeed, bidirectional models are accommodated.

To use Scribble, the user inserts function-like commands in the text. These always start with an "at" sign (@). (If you want to print an "at" sign, you must type it as @@ for MINCE/Scribble.) These commands can appear anywhere in the text and can be strung together (some can also be nested). In general Scribble commands have the form:

@Command[. . .text. . .]

(You can choose to use (. . .), [. . .], {. . .}, or other convenient pairs of delimiters to enclose text which is to be affected by the command.)

There are three classes of commands: *environments, inline environments,* and *directives.*

1. Environments are general patterns or templates for the layout of text which take care of a number of formatting problems all at once: margins, linespacing, identation style, and numbering of paragraphs for example. Each environment has a preset list of values which you can, of course, change. Example:

@Quotation[. . .text of a quotation. . .]

The quotation environment single-spaces and widens the margins while printing the text.

Environment commands can also be given in a second form as follows:

@Begin[Quotation]
. . . text . . .
. . . text . . .
. . . text . . .
@End[Quotation]

This command set is so complete that it even includes directions that are more easily carried out at typing/editing time on a modern CRT terminal, i. e., @Flushleft[. . .], @Blankspace[n lines]. Scribble's assumption seems to be that it can make no assumptions about what shape the text file is in, or how good the editing terminal is. Scribble is designed so that it is possible to do all formatting *after* the editing stage. For completeness, there is also an environment @Verbatim[. . .] which will print text "as is."

2. Inline environments take care of character-oriented printing tasks like underscore, boldface, sub- and superscript.

3. Directives take care of a variety of printing and organizing tasks that don't fit in the above classes. Some of these take a number of values as arguments which can then vary the results. Some of the more interesting of these are:

@Include[file.MSS]

This allows you to merge other files with the file being printed or sent to a disk file.

@Index[. . .item to be indexed. . .]

Here Scribble will construct an index and print it (or file it) at the end of the formatted file.

@Chapter[. . .text of chapter heading. . .]

This command not only prints out a correctly numbered chapter heading according to a preset style, but also adds the entry to a table of contents. There are also three levels of sectioning within chapters available. A summary of Scribble commands is given in Fig. 4-6.

Fig. 4-7 shows a file prepared for formatting by Scribble. It shows a sampler of Scribble commands as they appear in the file produced by MINCE. Fig. 4-8 shows the same file as it is printed out by Scribble and Crayon. The Scribble manual contains a number of samples like this.

Taken together, MINCE/Scribble enable a user to tackle tasks not easily undertaken with other word processors. And yet, given the typical microcomputer system running CP/M, some users might opt for a simpler word processor life. Why is this?

The text editing and formatted printing tasks are distributed quite differently between MINCE and Scribble as compared to the editing and

FIG. 4-6 Summary of Scribble Commands

In this summary, the most often used commands are grouped by type. Scribble commands can be inserted in the text file, or Scribble's default environments will be used.

11.0 Preliminary commands:

scribble filename.ext	finds named file, creates formatted .FIN file to be printed by crayon
scribble filename.ext -p	sends formatted output to printer
scribble filename -c	finds filename.MSS, sends formatted output to console
crayon filename	finds filename.FIN, prints it
pencil filename	finds filename, prints it

11.1 Environments

@Address[. . .]	for letters, left justified, single-spaced, starts at center
@Center[. . .]	centers each line of text within [ ]
@Display[. . .]	left and right margins indented, linespacing 'as is'
@Enumerate[. . .]	numbered, indented paragraphs, wrapped
@Flushleft[. . .]	left justified, not wrapped
@Flushright[ ]	right justified, not wrapped
@Quotation[. . .]	left and right margins inset, single-spaced
@Text[. . .]	wrapped, indented paragraphs (this is the default environment)
@Undent[. . .]	hanging paragraphs, wrapped
@Verbatim[. . .]	reproduces document exactly
@Verse[. . .]	each line indented, wrapped if necessary and indented a bit more, extra <cr> are ignored

11.2 In-line Environments

@+[. . .]	Superscript
@−[. . .]	Subscript
@B[. . .]	Boldface
@I[. . .]	Italics
@U[. . .]	Underscore

11.3 Directives

@Begin[. . .]	takes an environment name, opens the environment
@End[. . .]	takes an environment name, closes the environment
@Blankspace[n lines]	inserts n blank lines in document
@Foot[. . .]	takes a footnote, inserts at bottom of current page, or two other styles
@Include[. . .]	takes a filename, finds and inserts it in document, CON: argument will take input from the console
@Index[. . .]	takes a string, creates an index entry with the page number
@Newpage	starts a new page
@Pagefooting[ ]	defines a footing in several parts, takes variables, can be for odd or even pages
@Pageheading[ ]	defines a heading (as above)
@Style[. . .]	takes parameters that affect environments
@Chapter[. . .]	takes a title, numbers it, creates a table of contents entry with page number
@Section[. . .]	takes a title, numbers it (1.1), creates a table of contents entry with page number
@Subsection[ ]	takes a title, numbers it (1.1.1), creates a table of contents entry with page number
@Paragraph[ ]	takes a title, numbers it (1.1.1.1), creates a table of contents entry with page number

printing modes of WordStar. In MINCE/Scribble, it is anticipated that much of the formatting will *not* take place during on-screen editing—that it will be delayed until printing. Thus, what you see on the screen while using MINCE may be quite different from what you get on the printed paper after using Scribble. WordStar, on the other hand, makes a real attempt, within the limits of an ordinary CRT terminal display, to give the user editing and formatting commands that will produce a screen image that looks very much like the final printed document.

This is a major difference in design philosophy between the two systems. And there's a reason for it. If you think about it, the design

```
A>TYPE B:PHEN2.MSS
@Chapter(The Relevance of Philosophical Phenomenology to the Present Study)
@Begin[Verbatim]
@MajorHeading{This Paragraph Will Be Printed Out Verbatim}
        @B(The history of phenomenology) reveals a number of
goals or motivations, certain of which are of interest for this
study. Phenomenology arose in the late 19th century at least
partly in response to the splitting off of the natural sciences
from philosophy.  Some philosophers reacted to the split by
giving science the job of searching for empirical truth and
philosophy the task of uncovering logical or formal truth, that
is, of developing a theory of meaning.
@End[Verbatim]
@Heading{This Paragraph Will Be Printed Out Default Style}
        Phenomenologists were more @U(militant).  Edmund
@INDEX(Edmund Husserl)Husserl proposed "to reformulate the
foundations of science itself." This was to be done by "starting
with the human subject and his consciousness" @Foot{Von Breda.
@U(Husserliana). (The Hague, Netherlands: Martinus Nijhoff,
1965.)} and attempting to build a theoretic science that might
serve as a root science for all the special sciences."
@Begin[Verse]
@SubHeading{This Paragraph Will Be Printed Out As Verse}
        In order to get from the raw experience of the individual
to a basis for empirical truth a new philosophic method (actually
a series of methods) were proposed by scholars we now label
phenomenologists.
@End[Verse]
This Paragraph Will Be Printed Out As a Hanging Paragraph
@Begin{Undent}
        Quite naturally, many of the examples of this method
tended to deal with classes of experience which were uniquely
human: emotions, perception, self-awareness.
@End{Undent}
@Begin[Quotation]
        Also of interest for the present study is the historical
emphasis of phenomenology on the importance of technology in the
history of ideas.
@End[Quotation]
@Begin[Flushright]
        Concern of phenomenology with technology continues to the
present day, giving rise to some interesting recent studies which
may provide background and direction for the present study.  For
example, Dr. Don Ihde has written extensively on the role of
@End[Flushright]

A>
```

FIG. 4-7   This sampler of Scribble commands was printed out using the TYPE command of CP/M. This is possible because PHEN2.MSS is an ASCII file.

of a word processor always makes some assumptions about the hardware that will be used. The MINCE/Scribble division of labor makes sense if your editing terminal cannot really be made to look like your final printout—as with, for example, multiple font printers or typesetting systems. The WordStar division of labor makes good sense when your CRT terminal *can* come close to looking like your printer—as with many of the microcomputer systems in use today.

The human engineering of interactive systems must concern itself with these complex relationships of hardware, software, and human needs, but they are not easy to plan for. A small-scale example of such a relationship is the assignment of the much used cursor move commands. Cursor moves tend to be used repeatedly, especially the shorter moves (forward and back one character, or forward and back one word). It turns out that from the user's point of view, the escape key is less satisfactory for repeated use than the control key. You must press the escape key for every repeated command, whereas you can "park your

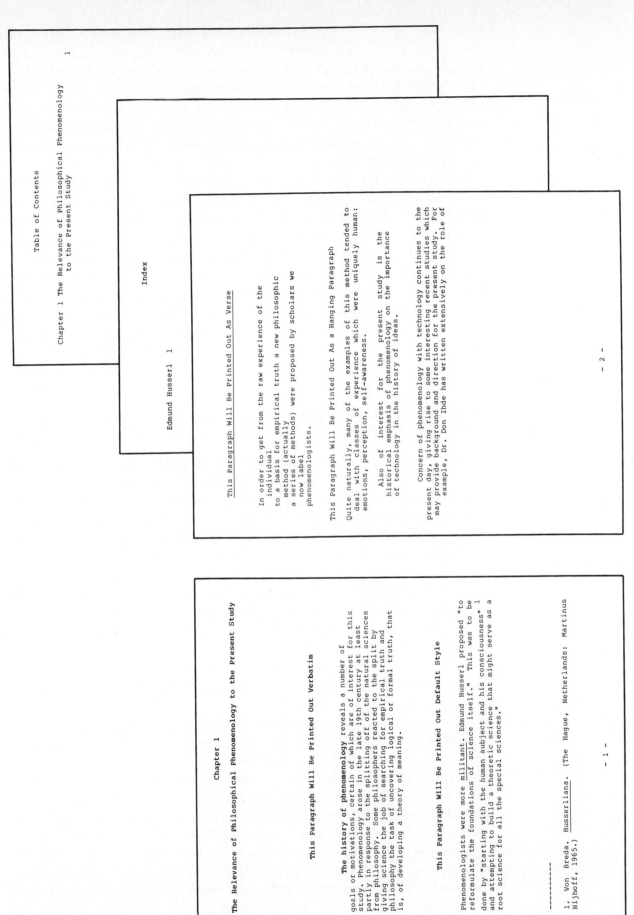

FIG. 4-8 This is the final result. PHEN2.MSS was translated into PHEN2.FIN by Scribble and then printed out by Crayon.

159

pinkie" (as one reviewer puts it) on the control key while repeating. This design decision affects others. For example, when the small cursor moves are made easy, there is less need for a variety of different cursor move commands (i. e., forward and back by sentences and paragraphs). The use of escape sequences makes more sense for commands that are not repeated very often.

Of course, the fact that MINCE and Scribble come with much of the C source code opens up the possibility of changing many of these design decisions. This is flexibility on a different level than just user-friendliness. As both users and hardware become more sophisticated, the "C" advantage could become one of considerable significance. It should also be noted that the authors of MINCE and the BDS-C compiler (see Section 5.6) have won consistent praise for their willingness to help users and answer questions, often at a level well beyond that which the low cost of their software would lead one to expect. (Conversely, some of the highest priced software is from companies who never answer questions.) All in all, MINCE and BDS-C rate a AAA + rating as a unique contribution to "author-friendly" software.

WPS80: A Colorful Word Processing System for the ISC Computer Line

If you happen to own a desktop microcomputer from the Intelligent Systems Corp. with its eight-color display and fancy keyboard, then you can run a word processing system called WPS80. This program, which runs either under CP/M or as a free-standing software package, is tailored to ISC hardware components and thus needs no installation or configuration program. (When the WPS80 manual talks about installation, they mean plugging the machine in.)

This is a full-featured word processing system roughly comparable in its capability to WordStar and MINCE/Scribble, but again, everything is accomplished in a somewhat different manner. WPS80 also has some unique features of its own.

WPS80 commands are largely conveyed by pressing special keys that are distinct from those of the regular keyboard. The position of these keys is shown in Fig. 4-9.

Cursor movement and the print features underline, boldface, super- and subscript are obtained by pressing special keys on a multicolored keypad to the left of the regular keyboard. This keypad does double duty since it has its own shift key labeled "command." Deletions are made by pressing one of another group of keys at the upper right. Most other editing functions (searching and replacing strings, moving blocks of text for "cut" and "paste," merging files, saving) are obtained by using a row of 16 keys across the top of the keyboard. The use of special keys goes as far as having a special <auto> key to boot CP/M and using the two keys <down arrow> and <attn break> together to cancel word processing commands. A control key is present but it's normally not used for word processing. The regular keyboard itself is heavily "annotated" on the sides of the keys with indications of the control character

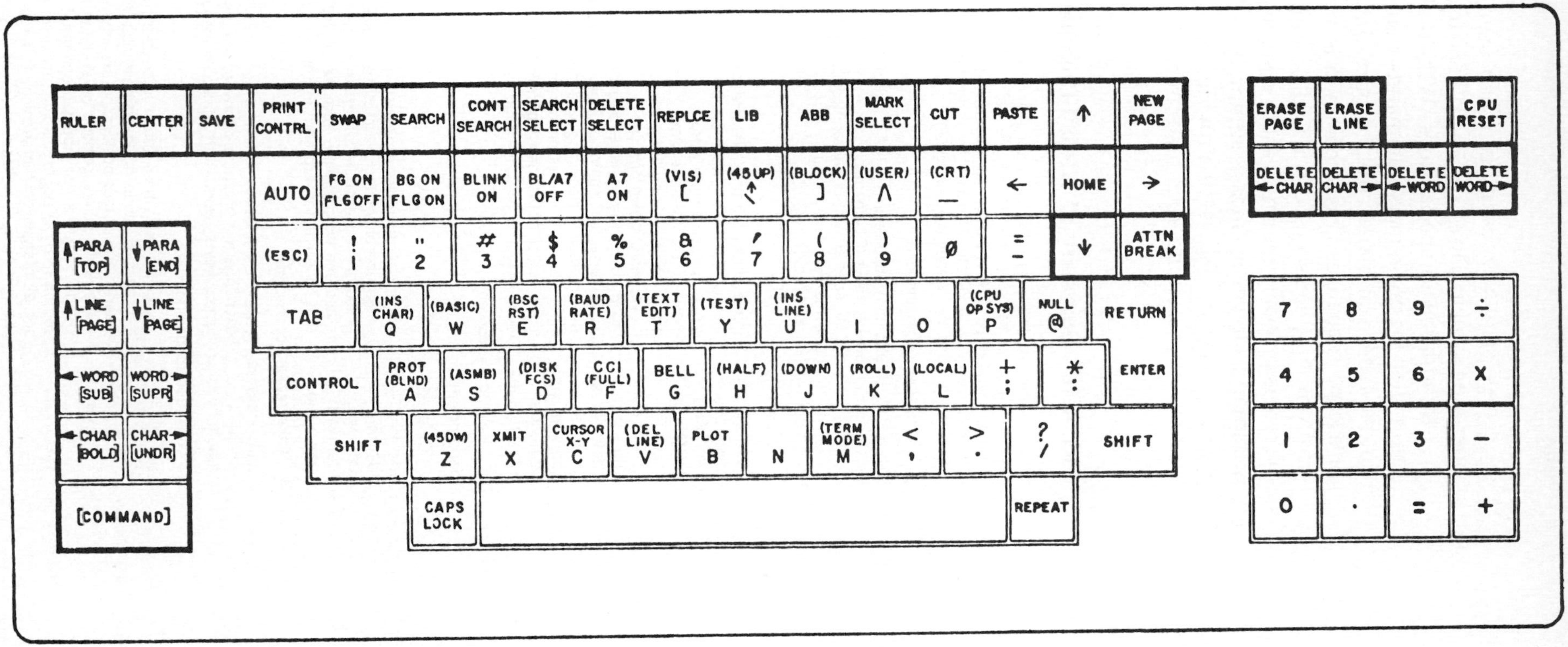

FIG. 4-9 Special keys are used for word processing commands on the ISC line of computers using WPS80.

or escape sequence meanings when used by other software or the ISC operating system. However, the WPS80 user may ignore these notations.

In addition to special keys, WPS80 also makes use of single-letter commands for preliminary commands from a menu (similar to WordStar), double-letter commands from a print-time menu, and a small number of escape sequences. These commands are associated with menus and/ or prompting messages. As a result, of all word processors, the WPS80 system is probably the one least in need of a "cheat card" type command summary. However, such a summary is handy when first learning to use any system. Fig. 4-10 provides a capsule portrait of the WPS80 system by presenting such a summary.

FIG. 4-10　Summary of WPS80 Commands.

In this summary, the most often used commands are grouped by function (rather than style). The conventions used here are: the ˆ to indicate that the control key is to be pressed simultaneously with another key, and <...> to indicate that a special key is to be pressed (e.g., <cr> for return, <esc> for escape, <del> for delete, <space> for space bar, etc. <cr> is assumed after some commands, this is made clear by prompting messages.)

0.　Preliminary commands:

E	edit (old) document
C	create (new) document
I	display special WPS80 index of documents
P	go to the print time menu
Q	quit and return to CP/M

1.　Cursor Movement:

<left char>	move cursor left one character
<right char>	move cursor right one character
<left word>	move cursor left one word
<right word>	move cursor right one word
<up line>	move cursor up one line
<down line>	move cursor down one line
<up para>	move cursor to beginning of paragraph
<down para>	move cursor to beginning of next paragraph
<top doc>	move cursor to beginning of document
<bottom doc>	move cursor to end of document
<up page>	move cursor to last newpage symbol
<down page>	move cursor to next newpage symbol

2.　Scrolling the screen:

(none given)

3.　Deleting:

<del lchr>	erase one character to the left of the cursor
<del rchr>	erase one character at the cursor position
<del lwrd>	erase one word to the left of the cursor
<del rwrd>	erase one word forward from the cursor position
<erase line>	erase the line forward from the cursor position

4.　Other editing commands:

<attn><break>	cancel a command
<swap>	exchange two characters forward of cursor position
<repeat>x	repeat key x, works with some command keys

5.　Onscreen formatting:

<center>	center the line where cursor is positioned
<ruler>	turn on ruler mode (to insert new tabs, margins)
T	insert tab at cursor position on skeleton ruler
<space>	erase tab at cursor position on skeleton ruler
W	insert wrap point (for indented paragraph) on skeleton ruler
L	set left margin, single spacing, at cursor pos.
D	set left margin, double spacing, at cursor pos.
J	set right margin, justified, at cursor position

R	set right margin, ragged, at cursor position
\<shift\>n	store current ruler in ruler buffer n (n = 1. . .9)
\<cr\>	turn off ruler mode, insert new ruler in text file
\<ruler\>n	retrieve ruler in ruler buffer n (1 becomes default)
\<new page\>	insert page break at cursor position
\<esc\>P	set page markers throughout whole document

6. Handling blocks of text:

\<mark select\>	turn mark mode on/off, move cursor to mark region
\<del select\>	erase marked block of text
\<cut\>	erase and save marked block in a paste buffer
\<paste\>	retrieve contents of a paste buffer at cursor pos.
\<replace\>	retrieve contents of a paste buffer to marked block

7. Searching and replacing strings:

\<search\> string	forward search for string
\<cont search\>	repeat forward search for previous string
\<search select\>	forward search and mark string found

8. Merging files:

\<esc\>G filename	insert named file at cursor position
(see also 9)	

9. Special features:

\<abbrev\> string	search an abbreviation file for corresponding string
\<esc\>A filename	switch to named abbreviation file (ABBREV is default)
\<lib\> string	search a library file for corresponding paragraph
\<esc\>L filename	switch to named library file (LIB is default)
\<esc\>\<paste\> x	switch to numbered paste buffer x (36 available, 0 is default)
MG filename	at print time, merge data from selected records of a selection file to marked
selectcharacter	variables within a printing file, i.e., form letters.

10. Ending an editing session:

\<save\>	save and end editing session
\<esc\>K	quit editing without saving

11. Print formatting:

\<sub\>	turn on/off subscript feature
\<supr\>	turn on/off superscript feature
\<bold\>	turn on/off boldface
\<undr\>	turn on/off underscore
\<print contrl\>	turn on/off print control mode, for entering headings, footings

(Note: commands below are examples from the print time menu.)

FP n	first page number
TM n	top margin
BM n	bottom margin
PI n	pitch or characters per inch

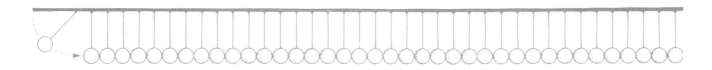

MINI-LAB WPS80 in Action
4.1-3

Step 1.   To start using the ISC computer, turn the power on, insert the appropriate disks, initialize the graphics display by pressing \<CPU reset\>, and then boot CP/M by pressing \<auto\>. When the A\> prompt appears, type WPS80\<cr\>. The main menu of WPS80 will then appear.

Step 2.   Type C to create a new file and type in a filename in response to the prompting message. This filename can be longer than a

CP/M filename and can contain spaces. WPS80 keeps its own directory, using both a filename and an index number n (the file shows up in the regular CP/M file directory as WPSn.DOC and eventually also WPSn.BAK, where n is the index number written as three digits). You are now in editing mode and can start typing in text and using commands. The text will appear on the screen between two multicolored rulers which will move apart vertically to accommodate text as it is entered. Below the lower ruler are two lines of information: the filename and the disk space left. The color plates show examples of WPS80 screen displays.

Step 3. Type in some text of your own. Experiment with the <undr>, <bold>, <sub>, and <supr> keys. These cause the underline, boldface, subscript, and superscript features to be activated at print time. On the screen, different colors are used to show the same features in a unique use of the machine's 8-color capability.

Step 4. Now experiment with changing tabs and margins. The ruler scale at the top controls onscreen and print time formatting from the beginning of the document up to the point where you insert a new ruler. The bottom ruler, referred to as the "skeleton ruler" is used for visual reference, and for creating new rulers.

To create a new ruler, you press <ruler> which places you in "ruler creation" mode. The cursor will move to the left margin position on the skeleton ruler. You can now move the cursor along the skeleton ruler with cursor movement commands, and type in T to make new tabs, <space> to erase old tabs, or set margins and linespacing as described in the command summary. When you are finished, type <cr>. The new ruler will be inserted in the text at the old cursor position, and you will be returned to editing mode. You can now type in more text, but formatted by the new ruler.

Different rulers can be inserted in the text to vary the format of a document. Rulers can also be saved in a series of special ruler buffers, numbered 1 through 9. The ruler stored in buffer 1 is the one that appears at the beginning of each new file. To reinsert this "default" ruler (#1) after text which used a different ruler, type <ruler>, 1, <cr>. More text can now be typed in with the original format. When finished, you save all of your work by pressing the special key labeled, you guessed it, <save>.

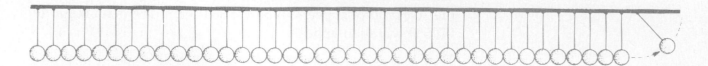

More about WPS80

As you can see, this word processor has its own way of accomplishing the same basic tasks as the other two systems. It also has some unusual features not offered by the others: abbreviation files, library files, and selection files. These are specially formatted files that the user must create according to strict specifications. Once they are created, however, they can make routine typing even easier.

Abbreviation files consist of pairs of data. The first is a two-letter abbreviation, the second is any text, except double curly brackets like {{ or }}, the chosen delimiters for all these special files. The pairs are referred to as a "field" and the format looks like this:

{{AB}}text for field 1{{bc}}text for field 2 . . . etc. . . .

The end of the abbreviation file is signaled by {{}} (an empty or "null" abbreviation). Once you have created at least one abbreviation file, and given it the default name ABBREV, when you are editing another file you can make use of your abbreviations simply by pressing <abbrev> and typing the two-letter abbreviation. WPS80 will automatically look for the file ABBREV, search it, and insert the corresponding text at the cursor position. Neat! If you want more than one abbreviation file, just create and name the ones you want. To obtain a differently named abbreviation file during an editing session, type <esc>A and you will be prompted for the abbreviation filename to be used.

Library files work much the same way, except that the field names can be strings of up to thirteen letters, instead of just two, and the text for each field can be a paragraph (no actual limits were mentioned in the manual). The format looks like this:

{{field name 1}}paragraph of text for field 1{{ . . . etc. . . .

ending with {{}}. During editing, you press <lib> and are prompted for a paragraph name. The associated text will be inserted at the cursor position. The file searched is called LIBRARY, or you can specify a differently named file by pressing <esc>L and then providing the new filename.

Selection files come into play at print time. They allow the merging of selected records of multiple fields of data, such as are needed to construct form letters. Each record contains the data needed for one letter such as a company name, several lines of an address, person's name to be written to, and so on. Each record also contains, as the last field, a selection code. This is used at print time to select only those records suitable for a particular form letter. This arrangement is similar to that of the MailMerge program provided as an "extra" with WordStar, whereas with WPS80 it comes as part of the package.

Other features worth noting: This system *does* keep backup files and automatically updates them. In fact, if you delete a WPS80 file, it automatically keeps the latest version as a backup file which must be deleted separately. If you take a look at the command summary, you

will notice that WPS80's print time routine takes care of some of the
tasks which are done in WordStar and MINCE/Scribble by print commands
stored within the text file. This may seem strange, but it proves once
again that there is more than one way to design any function in a word
processor. In general, WPS80 seems thoughtfully designed for the production typist who does lots of routine typing, as well as the writer
engaged in original manuscript or report creation.

4.2 Computer-Based Accounting Systems

The Big Five: General Ledger, Accounts Receivable, Accounts Payable, Payroll, and Inventory

Business accounting and record keeping are among the best-known
"bread and butter" applications for computers—and the ones that affect
our lives most pervasively. Microcomputer software vendors have been
quick to realize this. They have been busy developing systems designed
to serve the general needs of business microcomputer users (and to
interest those who would like to become microcomputer users). Ready-
made software is already starting to appear in various "flavors" for
doctors, lawyers, dentists, real estate management, and so on. Companies
are also springing up which offer customized microcomputer software
tailored to the needs of the more affluent microcomputer user. The extra
cost of such software is often a good investment, but general "packaged"
software is a fairly adaptable alternative for many users.

Microcomputer business systems can cost from as little as $250 for
a packaged, single application to more then $20,000 for a customized,
multi-application system. In any case, you want to be sure that you are
getting what you paid for. Packaged software costs less because, although
a lot of time is required to develop it, mass production is very simple
(some say, too simple, giving rise to a piracy problem). The consumer
must be willing to accept the decisions made by the designers of packaged
software, however. One might compare it to buying a ready-built home
versus hiring an architect to custom design a house just for you. You
may pay a lot more for a custom-designed home, but the hope is that
the final product will be a lot closer to what *you* want. However, just
as you end up making compromises due to cost concerns or other specific
problems when having a custom-designed home constructed, you may
have to compromise somewhat in the capabilities of your custom software,
if you decide to go that route. So packaged business systems are definitely
worth considering.

One aspect to consider as you weigh the advantages and disadvantages of the different packages available is whether they have the
ability to function together by sharing data, that is as an "integrated"
system. To demonstrate what integrated versus non-integrated functioning
means, let's look at a summary description of the functions performed

by the "big five" accounting packages discussed in this section. You'll see that the functions are quite similar to the calculator-and-paper versions traditionally used in business.

1. *General Ledger.* The general ledger keeps track of transactions that affect your assets, liabilities, equity, revenues, and expenses. The general ledger is the source of information in the preparation of a business' financial statements. All businesses should have a general ledger.

2. *Accounts Payable.* All businesses have to keep track of what bills they have to pay. This may be as simple as a file folder or as complicated as a subsidiary ledger showing invoice number, due date, and discount date.

3. *Payroll.* Any business that has employees has to be concerned about payroll taxes and maintaining the required payroll tax records. Quarterly 941 tax returns must be filed and annual W-2 forms have to be provided employees. Additionally, wages subject to federal and state unemployment taxes have to be tracked in order to help determine amounts owed on tax form 940.

4. *Accounts Receivable.* Any business that bills its customers for products or services has to keep track of amounts which are owed to it. Businesses with accounts receivable usually want a way to monitor amounts outstanding so that statements can be sent at appropriate intervals and as a way to identify potential problem accounts before they become excessively overdue.

5. *Inventory.* Any business that purchases goods which it eventually resells (perhaps after performing some fabrication) needs to be able to keep track of its inventory. In a retail or wholesale environment, an inventory system usually needs to keep track of how much of each specific inventory item is on hand, how much of each item is being sold, how much each costs, etc. In a manufacturing environment, an inventory system needs to keep track of the information above, but it also needs information on the costs of raw materials and accumulated additional costs as the raw materials are transformed to new products through the manufacturing process.

In examining the reports related to these areas, you will notice that the specific items which are monitored in the accounts payable, payroll, accounts receivable, and inventory systems are also summary captions on the general ledger. This is where the transfer of data between application packages can be of use. Instead of having to maintain separate special purpose journals to feed the general ledger, some packages have the ability to create special transfer files which carry out the functions of these special purpose journals. These files can eliminate the need for creating certain journal entries each month, thus freeing time for more interesting and useful tasks.

Some other factors to keep in mind when looking at business software are: (1) development and installation time, (2) ease of use, (3) flexibility, and (4) dealer support and stability. Packaged software can be installed and debugged in a relatively short time (usually less than one month), and there is no real development time involved.

As far as ease of use is concerned, software is the result of some programmer's conception of how to perform the ongoing functions of your business. If the designer's ideas are close to your reality, the resulting software may fit right into your operations. Otherwise, you may find yourself forced to adapt to the software's limitations. Some software may assume a high level of technical knowledge; some may be designed for use by novices.

Flexibility means the ability of the software to adapt to substantial changes in the conduct of your business. Change is typical of business. Some examples of changes that might occur are: (1) the introduction of a new product line, (2) beginning minor fabrication operations, (3) starting a mail-order operation, (4) rearranging the method you use to pay your bills to take advantage of all discounts, (5) taking out a loan with a bank, (6) implementing a detailed budgeting system, (7) changing from a weekly payroll to a semimonthly payroll, and (8) changes in tax law which affect withholding rates for payroll tax purposes. The key question is, when you want to make these changes, what will it cost for your software to accommodate them? One programmer may put withholding tax rates in the program itself while another may establish a separate file for withholding tax rates. It would be much simpler to update a separate file than to attempt to find the program code and rewrite the program itself.

Software vendors have "grown like Topsy" because the only cost of getting into the business is obtaining the requisite skills. Ask around to find out what kind of reputation your potential software vendors have for quality support. You can ask for names of other customers who are using their products and contact them for references. The failure rate for these new businesses is also high. You will want to satisfy yourself that your software vendor will still be around to provide service when you need it in the future.

The Peachtree Big Five

This family of application packages exemplifies an integrated system. It is sold by Peachtree Software [28], and consists of five programs. Let's look at each one of these in turn, first showing the typical functions of each application and then looking at Peachtree's solution to computerizing them.

General Ledger

The general ledger is the source of information used in the preparation of a business' financial statements. It keeps track of transactions and updates assets, liabilities, equity, revenues, and expenses through a system of double-entry bookkeeping. Each individual asset, liability, equity, revenue, and expense category is assigned a unique account number, and activity related to that item can be posted to its account.

A good general ledger accounting system is one which can process routine transactions quickly, and accurately post transactions to the proper general ledger accounts. It should allow for sufficient detail such that an analysis of general ledger accounts can easily explain the information summarized therein. This is usually done with special purpose journals. Each page of a journal is given a numerical reference so that a "trail" is provided. Thus, when the totals are posted to the general ledger, the reader can determine the source of the transactions by checking the numerical reference. Examples of special purpose journals include the following:

1. Cash Receipts. This is a listing of cash receipts that shows what the cash was received for. This is done via the coding of the cash receipts to the appropriate general ledger accounts.
2. Voucher Register. This is a listing of the vendor invoices received that shows what asset or expense account should be charged.
3. Cash Disbursements. This is a listing of each check written that shows what general ledger accounts should be affected.
4. Sales Journal. This is a listing of invoices issued to your customers that shows what asset and revenue accounts should be affected.
5. Payroll Journal. This journal summarizes information from employees' paychecks and indicates the amount to affect your cash, liability, and expense accounts.
6. General Journal. This journal contains all other journal entries. Typical entries would be for correction of errors, accrual of amortization and depreciation expenses, valuation of accounts receivable and inventory, and accrual of income taxes.

Peachtree's General Ledger

The Peachtree General Ledger system (especially when integrated with the other systems described later) has most of the characteristics of a good general ledger system. The summary transfers from the other systems can function as special purpose journals described above. If you do not purchase the other applications, Peachtree still provides for up to nine different journals, including one for standard journal entries that are made each month. Other functions it can perform with ease include:

1. Preparation of monthly trial balances of transactions to determine whether the general ledger as a whole is still in balance. (In double-entry bookkeeping, debits must always equal credits.)
2. Analysis of activity in specific general ledger accounts.
3. Creation and summarization of monthly journals.
4. Generation of financial statements quickly and accurately.
5. Comparison of financial statement accounts with prior year balances and/or budget balances.
6. Preparation of departmental financial statements with comparison to prior year balances and/or budgeted balances.
7. Creation of fixed asset depreciation schedules and loan amortization schedules.

```
                          PEACHTREE/5 SOFTWARE
                            GENERAL LEDGER
                     COPYRIGHT 1981 PEACHTREE SOFTWARE
                          PROGRAM SELECTION MENU
                     ------------------------------------

        YOU MAY SELECT ANY OF THE FOLLOWING PROGRAMS:

                     DA      SET TODAY'S DATE - CURRENTLY  4/13/82
                     MF      MASTER FILE MAINTENANCE
                     ML      MASTER FILE LIST
                     ET      ENTER TRANSACTIONS
                     DT      DELETE TRANSACTIONS
                     AT      ACCOUNTING TRANSFER
                     QA      QUERY ACCOUNT STATUS
                     RP      FINANCIAL REPORTING (SUBMENU)
                     EP      END OF PERIOD PROCESSING
                     SI      SYSTEM INITIALIZATION
                     FX      DATA FILE RECOVERY
                     END     END GENERAL LEDGER SYSTEM

        WHICH PROGRAM DO YOU WISH TO SELECT? RP
```

PHOTO 4-17   Peachtree's General Ledger has a main menu of functions which appears when the program is run.

The main menu display of Peachtree's general ledger system is shown in Photo 4-17. Each item listed there represents a separate sub-program which is loaded and executed upon typing the two-letter selection code. One other menu is used by the general ledger. This is the financial reporting submenu which appears when you type the code RP while viewing the main menu. This submenu lists the various reports which can be generated by the general ledger system.

To give you an idea what the reports generated by the general ledger system look like, some sample reports are shown below. These are derived from the sample data supplied with the programs. Fig. 4-11

```
                          PEACHTREE/5 SOFTWARE
                            GENERAL LEDGER
                     COPYRIGHT 1981 PEACHTREE SOFTWARE
                          PROGRAM SELECTION MENU
                     ------------------------------------

        YOU MAY SELECT ANY OF THE FOLLOWING REPORTS:

                     TB      TRIAL BALANCE
                     BA      BALANCE SHEET
                     IN      INCOME STATEMENT
                     DI      DEPARTMENT INCOME STATEMENT
                     TR      TRANSACTION REGISTER
                     DS      DEPRECIATION/AMORTIZATION SCHEDULES
                     ME      RETURN TO MAIN MENU

        WHICH PROGRAM DO YOU WISH TO SELECT? ME
```

PHOTO 4-18   The General Ledger submenu of reports.

```
RUN DATE  4/13/82        HOWELL ENTERPRISES, INC.           PAGE   1
                             GENERAL LEDGER
                          TRANSACTION REGISTER            BATCH:  10

ACCOUNT BATCH         DESCRIPTION          REF   SC   DATE      AMOUNT
=====================================================================


 102      10   SALE - JAMES WILSON        6342   1  4/5/81      765.00
 102      10   SALE - BAKER HARDWARE      7940   1  4/5/81    1,256.80
                                                              2,021.80   *


 111      10   JOHN MOODY - ON ACCOUNT     501   3  4/5/81      625.00-
 111      10   S. W. WELLS & SONS - PYMT   502   3  4/5/81      582.40-
 111      10   DANIEL B. JOHNSON - PYMT    503   3  4/5/81    3,640.98-
                                                              4,848.38-  *

30101     10   SALE - JAMES WILSON        6342   3  4/5/81      765.00-

30102     10   SALE - BAKER HARDWARE      7940   3  4/5/81    1,256.80-


--------------------------------------------------------------------
                 TOTAL TRANSACTIONS LISTED  =         7
                 TOTAL DEBITS       =         2,021.80
                 TOTAL CREDITS      =         6,870.18-
                                             ===============
                 DIFFERENCE         =         4,848.38-


          *** END OF TRANSACTION REGISTER ***
```

FIG. 4-11   Example of a transaction register.

```
RUN DATE   4/13/82        HOWELL ENTERPRISES, INC.           PAGE   1
                              GENERAL LEDGER
                           QUERY ACCOUNT STATUS

ACCOUNT        DESCRIPTION         REF  SC  DATE  CURRENT AMT   YTD BALANCE
--------------------------------------------------------------------------

 102      CASH OPERATING        [TYPE 2  DETAIL ACCOUNT]        24,633.01
          JOHN MOODY             501 1 4/5/8      625.00
          S.W. WELLS & SONS      502 1 4/5/8      582.40
          DANIEL B. 503          503 1 4/5/8    3,640.98
          SALE - JAMES WILSON   6342 1 4/5/8      765.00
          SALE - BAKER HARDWARE 7940 1 4/5/8    1,256.80
          SALE - REYNOLDS & BAXTER 823 1 4/9/8    215.60
          SALE - P. J. YOUNG      96 1 4/9/8      635.00
          SALE - C. D. JAMES & CO. 643 1 4/9/8  2,678.90
          ALLEN & JONES          866 1 4/9/8    1,565.00
          HARWICK ASSOC.        1554 1 4/9/8      625.42
          HAYES REALTY - APRIL RENT 745 2 4/14/   800.00-
          SOUTHERN BELL - APRIL  746 2 4/14/      628.30-
          HENDRIX & SMITH - CPA  747 2 4/14/      100.00-
          MUTUAL STATE INSURANCE 748 2 4/14/      100.00-
          GEORIGA POWER          749 2 4/14/       57.60-
          GEORGIA GAS LIGHT      750 2 4/14/       93.46-
          MARY'S OFFICE SUPPLY   751 2 4/14/       53.20-
          DEPT 1 SALARIES 4/15/81 752-757 2 4/14/ 2,600.00-
          DEPT 2 SALARIES 4/15/81 758-762 2 4/14/ 2,200.00-
          ADMIN SALARIES 4/15/81 763-764 2 4/14/   900.00-
          SALE - JOHN MOODY      873 1 4/21/      675.00
          MISC. SALES            871 1 4/21/      354.00
          TAXES PAYABLE - PAYROLL 766 2 4/15/    1,578.00-
          TAXES PAYABLE - PAYROLL 767 2 4/15/      355.00-
          CHECK # 100           1234 3 12/24        5.00-
          CHECK # 100           1234 3 12/24        0.00
          CHECK # 100           1234 3 12/24        0.00
          CHECK # 102           1235 3 12/24       35.00-
          TEST TRANSACTION  # 3 1236 3 12/24       55.00
          TEST TRANSACTION #4   1236 3 12/24       65.00-
          CASH                       A 12/31   331,944.88-
          NET PAY(CASH)              P 12/31     5,014.96-
          PAYMENTS                   R 12/31   530,317.02
                                              197,460.72 *   222,093.73 *


          *** END OF QUERY ACCOUNT STATUS ***
```

FIG. 4-12   Account status report.

```
RUN DATE  4/13/82                                                    PAGE  1

                            HOWELL ENTERPRISES, INC.
                               GENERAL LEDGER
                                BALANCE SHEET
                               AS OF  4/ 9/81

                    ** THIS MONTH THIS YEAR **        ** THIS MONTH LAST YEAR **
  ========================================================================

                                        ASSETS

CURRENT ASSETS
  101  CASH                    222,552.88                  14,670.10
  111  ACCOUNTS RECEIVABLE      50,309.66                  22,331.80
  121  PREPAID EXPENSES            941.10                     310.00
  131  INVENTORY                25,020.99                  18,495.33
                             ------------                ------------
       TOTAL CURRENT ASSETS              298,824.63                  55,807.23

FIXED ASSETS
  171  FURNITURE & EQUIPMENT     4,962.87                   2,445.00
  172  ACCUMULATED DEPRECIATION  1,236.00-                    150.00-
  180  DEPOSITS                    750.00                     575.00
                             ------------                ------------
       TOTAL FIXED ASSETS                  4,476.87                   2,870.00
                                        ------------                ------------
       TOTAL ASSETS                      303,301.50                  58,677.23
                                        ============                ============

                               LIABILITIES & CAPITAL

CURRENT LIABILITIES
  201  ACCOUNTS PAYABLE        124,303.01                  13,205.40
  210  TAXES PAYABLE            15,893.75                   1,190.11
                             ------------                ------------
       TOTAL CURRENT LIABILITIES        140,196.76                  14,395.51

LONG TERM LIABILITIES
  251  NOTE PAYABLE-BANK         1,400.00-                  2,600.00
                             ------------                ------------
       TOTAL LONG TERM LIAB               1,400.00-                  2,600.00
                                        ------------                ------------
       TOTAL LIABILITIES                 138,796.76                  16,995.51

CAPITAL
  291  COMMON STOCK             45,000.00                  30,000.00
  296  RETAINED EARNINGS        18,773.26                   9,000.00
  297  CURRENT EARNINGS        100,731.48                   2,681.72
                             ------------                ------------
       TOTAL CAPITAL                     164,504.74                  41,681.72
                                        ------------                ------------
       TOTAL LIAB. & CAPITAL             303,301.50                  58,677.23
                                        ============                ============
```

FIG. 4-13   A comparative balance sheet.

RUN DATE 4/13/82   PAGE 1

HOWELL ENTERPRISES, INC.
GENERAL LEDGER
INCOME STATEMENT
FOR PERIOD ENDED 4/ 9/81

RATIO: INCOME	THIS YEAR THIS MONTH	RATIO	THIS YEAR 1 MONTH	RATIO	BUDGET 1 MONTH	LAST YEAR THIS MONTH	LAST YEAR 1 MONTH
INCOME							
301 SALES	471,516.35	88.7	582,560.81	91.2	34,266.67	19,446.49	81,228.88
311 SERVICE	60,175.61	11.3	62,188.61	9.7	2,425.00	1,470.00	7,861.21
321 RETURNS & ALLOWANCES	325.20-	0.1-	5,825.20-	0.9-	491.67-	212.50-	1,119.31-
NET SALES	531,366.76	100.0	638,924.22	100.0	36,200.00	20,703.99	87,970.78
COST OF GOODS SOLD							
411 COST OF SALES	417,554.04	78.6	459,292.08	71.9	16,391.67	7,823.00	37,083.60
421 FREIGHT	3,832.47	0.7	8,344.47	1.3	716.67	748.10	3,129.94
431 OTHER COST OF SALES	0.00	0.0	11,756.52	1.8	3,833.33	248.10	1,129.94
GROSS PROFIT	109,980.25	20.7	159,531.15	25.0	15,258.33	11,884.79	46,627.30
501 SALARIES	12,159.87	2.3	34,359.87	5.4	4,941.67	4,800.00	19,200.00
509 PAYROLL TAXES	0.00	0.0	1,000.00	0.2	366.67	1,210.00	4,840.00
511 RENT	2,800.00	0.5	5,800.00	0.9	850.00	800.00	3,200.00
512 OFFICE EXPENSES	53.20	0.0	830.32	0.1	200.00	162.18	568.08
513 TELEPHONE	733.30	0.1	2,823.30	0.4	158.33	686.08	2,919.02
514 UTILITIES	151.06	0.0	751.06	0.1	191.67	157.77	645.77
521 ADVERTISING	970.00	0.2	4,970.00	0.8	1,033.33	450.00	2,350.00
522 INSURANCE	1,300.00	0.2	1,800.00	0.3	50.00	100.00	400.00
523 PROFESSIONAL FEES	175.00	0.0	675.00	0.1	108.33	100.00	400.00
531 DEPRECIATION	150.00	0.0	910.80	0.1	141.67	150.00	600.00
532 INTEREST EXPENSE	200.00	0.0	414.00	0.1	16.67	82.00	328.00
533 MISC. EXPENSES	905.00	0.2	915.32	0.1	33.33	5.12	18.50
555 TEST ACCOUNT	50.00	0.0	50.00	0.0	10.00	0.00	0.00
TOTAL EXPENSES	19,647.43	3.7	55,299.67	8.7	8,101.67	8,703.07	35,469.37
INCOME BEFORE INCOME TAXE	90,332.82	17.0	104,231.48	16.3	7,156.67	3,181.72	11,157.93
650 INCOME TAXES	0.00	0.0	3,500.00	0.5	0.00	500.00	2,000.00
NET INCOME	90,332.82	17.0	100,731.48	15.8	7,156.67	2,681.72	9,157.93

FIG. 4-14 A comparative income statement.

RUN DATE 4/13/82

PAGE 2

HOWELL ENTERPRISES, INC.
GENERAL LEDGER
INCOME STATEMENT
FOR PERIOD ENDED 4/ 9/81

*** SUBSIDIARY SCHEDULE ***

RATIO: INCOME	THIS MONTH	THIS RATIO	THIS YEAR 1 MONTH	RATIO	BUDGET 1 MONTH	LAST MONTH THIS MONTH	LAST YEAR 1 MONTH
301 SALES							
30101 SALES - DEPT 1	464,897.65	87.5	520,533.65	81.5	17,341.67	10,550.00	41,985.95
30102 SALES - DEPT 2	6,264.70	1.2	55,957.96	8.8	16,925.00	8,636.39	35,238.67
30104 SALES - OTHER	354.00	0.1	6,069.20	0.9	0.00	260.10	4,004.26
	471,516.35	88.7	582,560.81	91.2	34,266.67	19,446.49	81,228.88
311 SERVICE							
31101 SERVICE - DEPT 1	60,140.61	11.3	61,030.61	9.6	1,166.67	870.00	4,496.21
31102 SERVICE - DEPT 2	35.00	0.0	1,158.00	0.2	1,258.33	600.00	3,365.00
	60,175.61	11.3	62,188.61	9.7	2,425.00	1,470.00	7,861.21
321 RETURNS & ALLOWANCES							
32101 RET & ALLOWANCES - DEPT 1	325.20-	0.1-	2,825.20-	0.4-	233.33-	125.00-	713.10-
32102 RET & ALLOWANCES - DEPT 2	0.00	0.0	3,000.00-	0.5-	258.33-	87.50-	406.21-
	325.20-	0.1-	5,825.20-	0.9-	491.67-	212.50-	1,119.31-
411 COST OF SALES							
41101 COSTS OF SALES-PURCHASES	366,070.10	68.9	390,792.14	61.2	8,333.33	4,500.00	21,410.00
41102 COST OF SALES-PURCHASES	51,483.94	9.7	68,499.94	10.7	8,058.33	3,323.00	15,673.60
	417,554.04	78.6	459,292.08	71.9	16,391.67	7,823.00	37,083.60
421 FREIGHT							
42101 FREIGHT - DEPT 1	1,342.36	0.3	3,954.36	0.6	383.33	402.10	1,702.20
42102 FREIGHT - DEPT 2	2,490.11	0.5	4,390.11	0.7	333.33	346.00	1,427.74
	3,832.47	0.7	8,344.47	1.3	716.67	748.10	3,129.94
431 OTHER COST OF SALES							
43101 COST OF SALES-OTHER	0.00	0.0	5,306.96	0.8	1,666.67	152.10	702.20
43102 COST OF SALES-OTHER	0.00	0.0	6,449.56	1.0	2,166.67	96.00	427.74
	0.00	0.0	11,756.52	1.8	3,833.33	248.10	1,129.94
501 SALARIES							
50101 SALARIES - DEPT 1	5,670.00	1.1	15,470.00	2.4	1,666.67	2,100.00	8,400.00
50102 SALARIES - DEPT 2	5,589.87	1.1	13,989.87	2.2	2,441.67	1,800.00	7,200.00
50104 SALARIES	900.00	0.2	4,900.00	0.8	833.33	900.00	3,600.00
	12,159.87	2.3	34,359.87	5.4	4,941.67	4,800.00	19,200.00

FIG. 4-15 Subsidiary income by departments.

shows a transaction register for batch #10. (Transactions are entered in sessions which are given sequentially numbered batch numbers.) This report shows all the accounts affected by the transactions in batch #10. You will note that, in this case, debits and credits are not equal. Peachtree gives the option of having transactions which do not balance *or* requiring that transactions be balanced before processing is concluded.

In order to make account analysis easier, Peachtree provides a "Query Account Status" report, which is shown in Fig. 4-12. Note that the report shows the beginning account balance, activity for the month, and the ending account balance. In this way you can easily review the accounts for items which are incorrectly coded.

Peachtree summarizes general ledger account data to prepare comparative financial statements. Fig. 4-13 shows a comparative balance sheet. Note that a subsidiary schedule of the accounts summarized in the balance sheet is available as an option.

Fig. 4-14 shows a comparative income statement. A subsidiary schedule of the departmental components summarized in the income statement is available as an option and is included in Fig. 4-15.

Accounts Payable

All businesses have to keep track of what bills they have to pay. A good accounts payable system is one which helps a business actively manage its accounts payable to its best advantage and provides other useful information about its relationships with its vendors. The system should also facilitate the posting of all costs related to the vendor invoices processed to the appropriate general ledger accounts.

Peachtree's Accounts Payable

Peachtree's accounts payable program carries out most of the functions desired in an accounts payable system. Examples:

1. Maintaining a listing of aged open accounts payable which indicates how long the open invoices have been outstanding.
2. Sorting the listing of open accounts payable by due date, or date of expiring discount. This "cash requirements" report can tell the owner how much cash is required by which date to pay which bills to take advantage of all available discounts.
3. Check preparation with appropriate cross-referencing to the invoice actually being paid.
4. Developing a summary entry for posting for the general ledger.

Photo 4-19 shows the main menu display of the accounts payable program. Just as in the general ledger program, each item listed represents a separate subprogram which is loaded and run when you type the two-letter code.

The other menu produced by the accounts payable program is the submenu displaying the options for report generation. This menu lists the various reports which can be generated by the Peachtree accounts payable system.

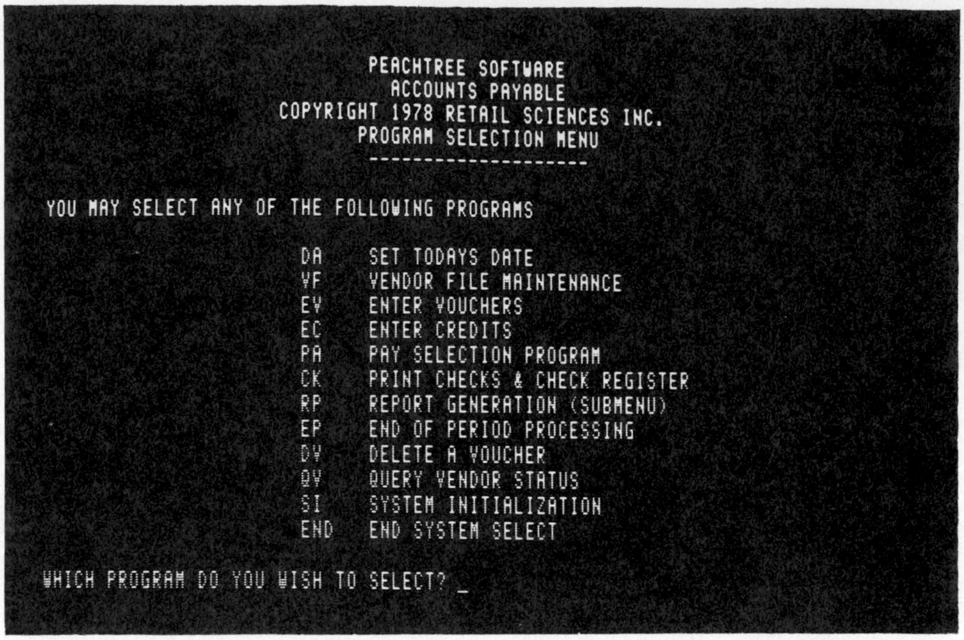

PHOTO 4-19   *The Accounts Payable main menu.*

The accounts payable system allows the production of several reports. Fig. 4-16 shows the transaction register. It lists the general ledger account distribution for each invoice and check entered into the system. The cash requirements report shown in Fig. 4-17 sorts the invoices by payment due date (or by discount-to-be-taken date) and shows cumulatively how much cash is needed each day to pay the bills which are due at that time. The aged payables report in Fig. 4-18 summarizes the amounts owed to the various vendors sorted by days outstanding in order to help monitor the vendors to whom you have decided to postpone payments.

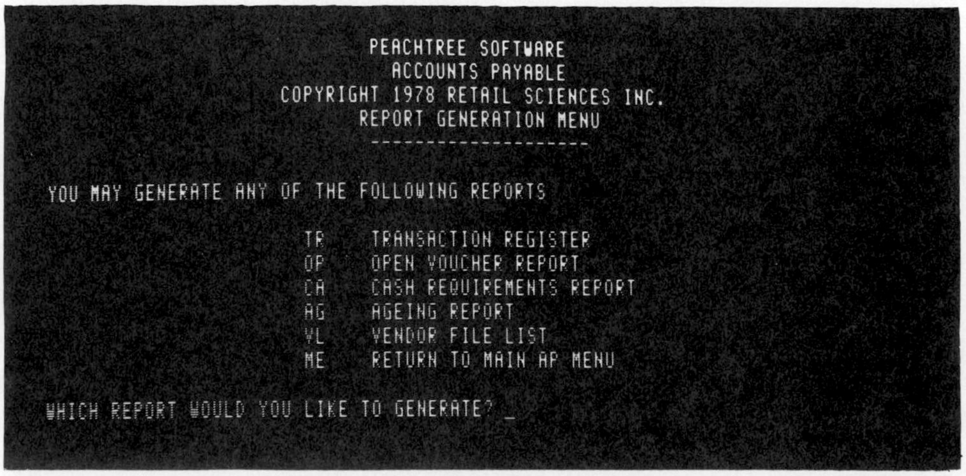

PHOTO 4-20   *The Accounts Payable submenu of reports.*

```
                    TAYLOR OFFICE EQUIPMENT
                       ACCOUNTS PAYABLE
                     TRANSACTION REGISTER
                          12/25/81                            PAGE  1

                       TRANSACTION LIST
```

VENDOR	INVOICE NUMBER	INVOICE DATE	DEBIT ACCT.	DISTRIBUTION AMOUNT	CREDIT ENTERED VOUCHERS	DEBIT PAYMENTS	CREDIT DISCOUNTS TAKEN	CREDIT CASH
ACEOFF	12345		17100	$655.00	$655.00			
	CK. NO. 1	12/31/81				$655.00	$19.55	$635.35
ALLEN	INV#00016	07/05/80	41101	$4,000.00				
			42101	$25.12	$4,025.12			
	INV#00022	07/10/80	41102	$4,950.00				
			42102	$58.76	$5,058.76			
	CREDIT ON ABOVE	07/10/80		-$50.00	-$50.00			
	INV#00034	07/11/80	41101	$7,525.50				
			41102	$6,475.25				
			42101	$189.11				
			42102	$188.34	$14,378.20			
	INV#00056	07/14/80	41102	$3,028.14				
			42102	$548.45	$3,576.59			
	98765	12/15/81	41101	$3,920.00				
			42101	$80.00	$4,000.00			
			41101	-$2,000.00	-$2,000.00			
	CK. NO. 2	12/31/81				$3,008.76	$100.18	$2,908.58
ATLMAG			52100	$350.00	$350.00			
BANKAM		07/07/80	53300	$900.00	$900.00			
COX PR	AUTO VOUCHER		51100	$2,000.00	$2,000.00			
EVANS	0001258	06/16/80	41101	$10,000.00	$10,000.00			
	PRE-PAID VOUCHER	06/16/80				$10,000.00	$200.00	$9,800.00
	0001264	06/20/80	41102	$5,000.00	$5,000.00			
	0001287	06/31/80	41101	$2,005.36				
			41102	$2,005.36				
			42101	$213.01				
			42102	$213.00	$4,436.73			
	45321	12/01/81	41101	$125.00	$125.00			
			20100	-$111.00	-$111.00			
	CK. NO. 3	12/31/81				$14.00	$3.00	$11.00
FRTWAY	WB#3879629	07/08/80	42101	$140.59	$140.59			

FIG. 4-16 Transaction register for accounts payable.

TAYLOR OFFICE EQUIPMENT
ACCOUNTS PAYABLE
CASH REQUIREMENTS
12/25/81

PAGE 1

** DATA SORTED BY DUE DATE

PAY DATE	VENDOR	INVOICE NUMBER	INV. DATE	AMOUNT	DISCOUNT	NET	DAILY TOTAL	REQ. TO DATE
05/01/80	ROYAL		04/01/80	$900.00	$0.00	$900.00	$900.00	$900.00
06/21/80	JOUR-C		05/21/80	$100.00	$0.00	$100.00	$100.00	$1,000.00
07/02/80	EVANS	0001258	07/02/80	$0.00	-$200.00	$200.00	$200.00	$1,200.00
07/15/80	ATLMAG	0001287	06/31/80	$350.00	$0.00	$350.00		
	EVANS			$4,436.73	$88.73	$4,348.00		
	NOSDA	AUTO VOUCHER		$75.00	$0.00	$75.00		
	M BANK	AUTO VOUCHER		$3,000.00	$60.00	$2,940.00		
	GASALE		07/15/80	$2,108.59	$0.00	$2,108.59	$9,821.59	$11,021.59
07/20/80	EVANS	0001264	06/20/80	$5,000.00	$100.00	$4,900.00	$4,900.00	$15,921.59
07/21/80	IBM	AUTO VOUCHER		$120.00	$0.00	$120.00		
	GAINC		07/15/80	$4,250.73	$0.00	$4,250.73		
	JOUR-C		06/21/80	$400.00	$0.00	$400.00	$4,770.73	$20,692.32
07/25/80	SOBELL	AUTO VOUCHER		$105.00	$0.00	$105.00	$105.00	$20,797.32
07/31/80	HARLEN	AUTO VOUCHER		$1,200.00	$24.00	$1,176.00		
	BANKAM	AUTO VOUCHER		$900.00	$0.00	$900.00		
	COX PR	AUTO VOUCHER	07/07/80	$2,000.00	$40.00	$1,960.00	$4,036.00	$24,833.32
08/02/80	SDI	B# 3384	07/02/80	$14,793.58	$295.87	$14,497.71	$14,497.71	$39,331.03
08/03/80	KELLY	AB 0088	07/03/80	$4,000.00	$80.00	$3,920.00	$3,920.00	$43,251.03
08/05/80	ALLEN	INV#00016	07/05/80	$4,025.12	$80.50	$3,944.62	$3,944.62	$47,195.65
08/07/80	KELLY	AB 0203	07/07/80	$8,095.33	$161.91	$7,933.42		
	SDI	B# 3496	07/07/80	$2,831.95	$56.64	$2,775.31	$10,708.73	$57,904.38
08/08/80	FRTWAY	WB#38795629	07/08/80	$140.59	$0.00	$140.59	$140.59	$58,044.97
08/09/80	KELLY	AB 0214	07/09/80	$7,000.00	$140.00	$6,860.00	$6,860.00	$64,904.97
08/11/80	ALLEN	INV#00034	07/11/80	$14,378.20	$287.56	$14,090.64	$14,090.64	$78,995.61
08/13/80	KELLY	AB 0346	07/13/80	$6,066.50	$121.33	$5,945.17	$5,945.17	$84,940.78
08/14/80	ALLEN	INV#00056	07/14/80	$3,576.59	$71.53	$3,505.06		
	SDI	B# 3738	07/14/80	$7,503.64	$150.07	$7,353.57	$10,858.63	$95,799.41
04/30/81	ROYAL	32568	04/02/81	$309.00	$15.45	$293.55	$293.55	$96,092.96

FIG. 4-17 Cash requirement report.

TAYLOR OFFICE EQUIPMENT
ACCOUNTS PAYABLE
AGED PAYABLES
12/25/81

PAGE   1

AGEING DATE: 12/31/81

VENDOR	CURRENT	1 TO 30	31 TO 60	61 TO 90	OVER 90	CREDITS	TOTAL NET DUE
ALLEN	$4,000.00	$0.00	$0.00	$0.00	$21,979.91	$0.00	$25,979.91
ATLMAG	$0.00	$0.00	$0.00	$0.00	$350.00	$0.00	$350.00
BANKAM	$0.00	$0.00	$0.00	$0.00	$900.00	$0.00	$900.00
COX PR	$2,000.00	$0.00	$0.00	$0.00	$2,000.00	$0.00	$4,000.00
EVANS	$0.00	$0.00	$0.00	$0.00	$9,436.73	$0.00	$9,436.73
FRTWAY	$0.00	$0.00	$0.00	$0.00	$140.59	$0.00	$140.59
GAINC	$0.00	$0.00	$0.00	$0.00	$4,250.73	$0.00	$4,250.73
GAPOWR	$1,000.00	$0.00	$0.00	$0.00	$0.00	$0.00	$1,000.00
GASALE	$0.00	$0.00	$0.00	$0.00	$2,108.59	$0.00	$2,108.59
HARLEN	$1,200.00	$0.00	$0.00	$0.00	$1,200.00	$0.00	$2,400.00
IBM	$120.00	$0.00	$0.00	$0.00	$120.00	$0.00	$240.00
JOUR-C	$0.00	$0.00	$0.00	$0.00	$500.00	$0.00	$500.00
KELLY	$0.00	$0.00	$0.00	$0.00	$25,161.83	$0.00	$25,161.83
M BANK	$3,000.00	$0.00	$0.00	$0.00	$3,000.00	$0.00	$6,000.00
MARSH	$1,000.00	$0.00	$0.00	$0.00	$0.00	$0.00	$1,000.00
NOSDA	$75.00	$0.00	$0.00	$0.00	$75.00	$0.00	$150.00
ROYAL	$0.00	$0.00	$0.00	$0.00	$1,209.00	$0.00	$1,209.00
SDI	$0.00	$0.00	$0.00	$0.00	$25,129.17	$0.00	$25,129.17
SOBELL	$105.00	$0.00	$0.00	$0.00	$105.00	$0.00	$210.00
XEROX	$250.00	$0.00	$0.00	$0.00	$0.00	$0.00	$250.00
TOTAL=	$12,750.00	$0.00	$0.00	$0.00	$97,666.55	$0.00	$110,416.55

TOTAL VENDORS LISTED = 20

FIG. 4-18 Aged payables report.

Payroll

Any business that has more than one employee has to be concerned about payroll taxes and maintaining the required payroll tax records. A good payroll system is one that facilitates the preparation of paychecks, maintains the appropriate historical employee payroll data, aids in the preparation of required payroll tax returns, and makes the transfer of summary payroll information to the general ledger easy.

Peachtree's Payroll

Peachtree's payroll system is helpful in the following areas:

1. Maintenance of employee master file data.
2. Maintenance of payroll tax withholding information.
3. Extension of wages and calculation of deductions and net pay.
4. Preparation of actual paychecks and payroll journals.
5. Maintenance of employee earnings records.
6. Preparation of quarterly reports to taxing authorities.
7. Preparation of annual W-2 and 1099 tax forms.
8. Developing a summary entry for posting to the general ledger.

The main menu display of the payroll is shown in Photo 4-21. Two-letter commands invoke the subprograms which carry out the payroll system.

Shown in Figs. 4-19 and 4-20 are sample reports from the payroll system. The payroll register is Fig. 4-19. It summarizes the account distribution of the individual paychecks. The monthly summary report,

```
RUN "PR MENU"

                        PEACHTREE SOFTWARE
                         PAYROLL SYSTEM
                 COPYRIGHT 1978 RETAIL SCIENCES, INC.
                       PROGRAM SELECTION MENU
                       --------------------
  YOU MAY SELECT ANY OF THE FOLLOWING PROGRAMS

             DA     SET TODAYS DATE
             NP     NEW PAY PERIOD INITIALIZATION
             CP     CALCULATE PAYROLL
             PR     PRINT PAYROLL REGISTER
             CK     PRINT PAY CHECKS
             EM     END OF MONTH PROCESSING AND REPORT
             EQ     END OF QUARTER PROCESSING AND 941-A REPORT
             EY     END OF YEAR PROCESSING AND W-2 PRINTING
             EF     EMPLOYEE FILE MAINTENANCE & INQUIRY
             EL     EMPLOYEE FILE LIST
             TX     TAX FILE MAINTENANCE
             SI     SYSTEM INITIALIZATION
             END    END SYSTEM SELECT

  WHICH PROGRAM DO YOU WISH TO SELECT? _
```

PHOTO 4-21   *The Payroll main menu.*

```
                                   TAYLOR OFFICE EQUIPMENT              PAGE   1
                                        PAYROLL SYSTEM
                                       PAYROLL REGISTER
                                          01/14/82

101MPT    PRESTON T. MILLS              TYPE=S    RATE= 760.000

                        ---HOURS---   --EARNINGS-   --------DEDUCTIONS--------   ---TOTALS---
    CHECK NUMBER:   101  REG= 0.000    REG= 760.00   FIC=  46.59   INS= 12.50   EARN= 760.00
    CHECK AMOUNT:   582.12 OT = 0.000  OT =   0.00   FED=  96.77   MI1=  1.50   DEDU= 177.88
                        OH = 0.000    OH =   0.00    STA=  20.52   MI2=  0.00
                                      COM=   0.00    CIT=   0.00
                                      MIS=   0.00


101SSC    SUSAN S. CARMELL             TYPE=S    RATE= 350.000

                        ---HOURS---   --EARNINGS-   --------DEDUCTIONS--------   ---TOTALS---
    CHECK NUMBER:   102  REG= 0.000    REG= 350.00   FIC=  21.45   INS=  4.00   EARN= 350.00
    CHECK AMOUNT:   273.13 OT = 0.000  OT =   0.00   FED=  43.25   MI1=  1.50   DEDU=  76.87
                        OH = 0.000    OH =   0.00    STA=   6.67   MI2=  0.00
                                      COM=   0.00    CIT=   0.00
                                      MIS=   0.00


    *** TOTALS - DEPARTMENT 101

                        ---EARNINGS---   ----------DEDUCTIONS----------   ----TOTALS-----
    TOTAL CHECKS (NET):  855.25  REG 1,110.00  FIC    68.04  INS   16.50  EARN  1,110.00
                                 OT      0.00  FED   140.02  MI1    3.00  DEDU    254.75
                                 OH      0.00  STA    27.19  MI2    0.00
                                 COM     0.00  CIT     0.00
                                 MIS     0.00
```

FIG. 4-19   The Payroll register.

```
                                   TAYLOR OFFICE EQUIPMENT
                                        PAYROLL SYSTEM
                                        END OF MONTH
                                          01/14/82

                                       MONTHLY SUMMARY


           TOTAL ACTIVE EMPLOYEES =  10         TOTAL INACTIVE EMPLOYEES =  1

           TOTAL CURRENT: REGULAR HOURS =  1200
                          OVERTIME HOURS=  0
                          OTHER HOURS   =  0
                                          ----
                          TOTAL HOURS   =  1200

                                       MONTH          QUARTER          YEAR
           EARNINGS  -REGULAR     :  $5,131.90      $5,131.90      $5,131.90
                     -OVERTIME    :    $127.97        $127.97        $127.97
                     -OTHER       :      $0.00          $0.00          $0.00
                     -COMMISSIONS :  $1,200.00      $1,200.00      $1,200.00
                     -MISC.       :      $0.00          $0.00          $0.00
           DEDUCTIONS -FICA       :    $390.85        $390.85        $390.85
                     -FEDERAL     :    $723.00        $723.00        $723.00
                     -STATE       :    $154.06        $154.06        $154.06
                     -LOCAL       :      $0.00          $0.00          $0.00
                     -INSURANCE   :    $145.50        $145.50        $145.50
                     -MISC. #1    :      $9.00          $9.00          $9.00
                     -MISC. #2    :     $22.50         $22.50         $22.50
```

FIG. 4-20   Payroll monthly summary.

Fig. 4-20, summarizes payroll information for the month, quarter, and year-to-date.

Accounts Receivable

Accounts receivable represent amounts your customers owe you for services rendered or for products sold to them. Any business that bills its customers needs to be able to keep track of the amounts owed to them. A good accounts receivable system is one that facilitates the accurate preparation of invoices, can generate customer statements (and possibly dunning notices), helps management keep track of outstanding accounts receivable to identify invoices that become excessively overdue, maintains cumulative sales totals for each customer, and makes the transfer of summary accounts receivable and sales information to the general ledger easy.

Peachtree's Accounts Receivable

Peachtree performs most required accounts receivable functions well. Examples of its capabilities include:

1. Maintaining customer master files with appropriate relevant data such as billing address, shipping address phone number, credit limit, sales terms, etc.
2. Invoice generation. Using the customer master file, the billing address, shipping address, and sales terms can be automatically entered. The software will extend and total the invoices when you provide the appropriate quantity, unit price, tax, and other required information.
3. Entering the invoices on the sales journal and accounts receivable subsidiary ledger.

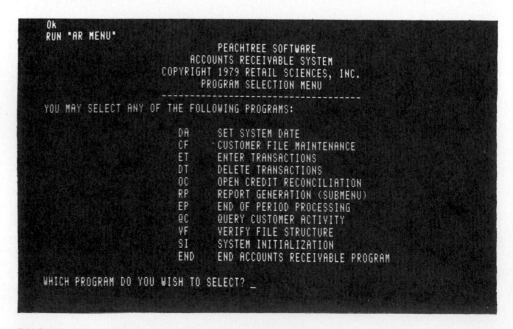

PHOTO 4-22   The Accounts Receivable main menu.

PHOTO 4-23   *The Accounts Receivable submenu of reports.*

4. Customer statement generation.
5. Application of cash receipts to the accounts receivable subsidiary ledger and creation of a cash receipts journal.
6. Generation of an aged accounts receivable trial balance.
7. Developing a summary entry for posting to the general ledger.

Shown in Photo 4-22 is the main menu screen. As before, the two letter commands call up the subprograms which support the accounts receivable system.

The other menu is the report generation submenu, shown above in Photo 4-23.

Sample reports from the accounts receivable system are shown below. The Transaction Register in Fig. 4-21 shows the account distribution of the month's transactions. The Query Customer Activity report in Fig. 4-22 provides details regarding open items as well as historical information regarding your customers. The Detailed Ageing Report in Fig. 4-23 shows how long each unpaid invoice has been oustanding.

Inventory

Any business that purchases goods which it eventually resells needs to keep track of its inventory. In a retail or wholesale business, the owner would want a system to keep track of how much of each specific item is on hand, how much of each specific item is being sold, how much each specific item costs, etc. In a manufacturing business, the owner would need to know the information described above but would also require a system to track the costs of raw materials and accumulate additional costs as the raw materials are transformed in the production process. Each manufacturing operation has its own unique system of accumulating material, labor, and overhead. Such unique applications are beyond the scope of most packaged software, including Peachtree's.

TAYLOR OFFICE EQUIPMENT
ACCOUNTS RECEIVABLE
TRANSACTIONS REPORT
02/28/81

PAGE 1

ID INVOICE	DATE	SALES	FREIGHT	TAXES	SER. CH	MISC. DB	PAYMENTS	CREDITS	RETURNS	DISCOUNT	MISC. CR	AMOUNT
ALLEN												
812	4/ 4/80	104.00								2.08		101.92
812	4/16/80						75.00					-75.00
884	4/28/80	127.00	6.35							2.54		130.81
		231.00	6.35	0.00	0.00	0.00	75.00	0.00	0.00	4.62	0.00	157.73
COX												
	BAL FWD											870.55
1257	6/19/80	1146.37										1146.37
1269	6/23/80	1250.95										1250.95
1288	6/30/80				49.02							49.02
	BAL FWD 870.55	2397.32	0.00	0.00	49.02	0.00	0.00	0.00	0.00	0.00	0.00	3316.89
EVANS												
1030	5/10/80	42.49										42.49
1030	5/15/80						21.02					-21.02
1066	5/22/80	27.50										27.50
1245	6/15/80	22.76										22.76
		92.75	0.00	0.00	0.00	0.00	21.02	0.00	0.00	0.00	0.00	71.73
HARLEN												
1198	5/30/80	180.00										180.00
1198	6/15/80						180.00					-180.00
1260	6/20/80	36.39										36.39
1398	6/30/80	180.00										180.00
1398	7/14/80						180.00					-180.00
		396.39	0.00	0.00	0.00	0.00	360.00	0.00	0.00	0.00	0.00	36.39
JOHNDE												
1230	6/10/80	36.70										36.70
1230	6/11/80						56.83					-56.83
1263	6/21/80	36.75										36.75
1275	6/25/80	102.98										102.98
		176.43	0.00	0.00	0.00	0.00	56.83	0.00	0.00	0.00	0.00	119.60
KELLY												
0	BAL FWD											75.12
1239	7/ 1/80						1750.00					-1750.00
	6/13/80	1335.95		80.16								1416.11
1278	6/26/80	750.00										750.00
1278	6/28/80								38.50			-38.50
1286	6/30/80				33.04							33.04
1427	7/ 9/80	96.95										96.95
	BAL FWD 75.12	2182.90	0.00	80.16	33.04	0.00	1750.00	0.00	38.50	0.00	0.00	582.72

FIG. 4-21 The Accounts Receivable transaction register.

```
                    TAYLOR OFFICE EQUIPMENT              PAGE   1
                      ACCOUNTS RECEIVABLE
                    QUERY CUSTOMER ACTIVITY
                         02/02/81


LENOX                                       DATE LAST DB:    7/ 7/80
                        TYPE      :  BAL FWD  AMT LAST DB :    886.66
LENOX MAMAGEMENT SERVICE CUR. BAL. :  2263.30 YTD SALES   :   2157.39
3400 PEACHTREE RD, NE    BAL. FWD. :   148.64 DATE LAST CR:    7/ 7/80
ATLANTA, GA. 30326       AUTO. BILL:     0.00 AMT LAST CR :     17.73
(404)237-2323            TAX RATE  :   4.000% YTD PAYMENTS:     42.73

INVOICE    CODE     DATE    TERMS OR REF.    DEBITS      CREDITS     BALANCE
-------  --------  -------- --------------  ----------  ----------  ----------
   1215  SALE      6/ 5/80  2-10-NET 30       1250.12        0.00     1398.76
   1215  CREDIT    6/ 5/80  NET 30               0.00       25.00     1373.76
   1289  SERV. CH  6/30/80  NET 30              20.61        0.00     1394.37
   1421  SALE      7/ 7/80  2-10-NET 30        886.66       17.73     2263.30


ROYAL                                       DATE LAST DB:   6/14/80
                        TYPE      :  REGULAR  AMT LAST DB :    365.25
ROYAL IMPORTERS, LTD.    CUR. BAL. :   401.62 YTD SALES   :    401.62
344 AIRPORT IND. PARK    BAL. FWD. :     0.00 DATE LAST CR:    1/14/79
COLLEGE PARK, GA. 30337  AUTO. BILL:     0.00 AMT LAST CR :      0.00
(404)763-3333            TAX RATE  :   3.000% YTD PAYMENTS:      0.00

INVOICE    CODE     DATE    TERMS OR REF.    DEBITS      CREDITS     BALANCE
-------  --------  -------- --------------  ----------  ----------  ----------
   1084  SALE      5/28/80  NET 30              36.37        0.00       36.37
   1242  SALE      6/14/80  NET 30             365.25        0.00      401.62


EVANS                                       DATE LAST DB:   6/15/80
                        TYPE      :  REGULAR  AMT LAST DB :     22.76
EVANS OFFICE SUPPLY      CUR. BAL. :    71.73 YTD SALES   :     92.75
2550 PIEDMONT RD. NE     BAL. FWD. :     0.00 DATE LAST CR:    5/15/80
ATLANTA, GA. 30324       AUTO. BILL:     0.00 AMT LAST CR :     21.02
(404)262-8888            TAX RATE  :   4.000% YTD PAYMENTS:     21.02

INVOICE    CODE     DATE    TERMS OR REF.    DEBITS      CREDITS     BALANCE
-------  --------  -------- --------------  ----------  ----------  ----------
   1030  SALE      5/10/80  NET 30              42.49        0.00       42.49
   1030  PAYMENT   5/15/80  CHECK 3711           0.00       21.02       21.47
   1066  SALE      5/22/80  NET 30              27.50        0.00       48.97
   1245  SALE      6/15/80  NET 30              22.76        0.00       71.73

            *** END OF QUERY CUSTOMER ACTIVITY ***
```

FIG. 4-22 Customer activity report.

Peachtree's Inventory

In general, a good inventory system is one that gives the business better control over its merchandise, allows it to lower its overall investment in inventory, and also improves customer service and response. Peachtree's system can help in the following ways:

1. Maintaining the detailed perpetual inventory records, complete with sales and cost data for each inventory item. This provides the basis for analyzing the relative profitability of a business' various products.

TAYLOR OFFICE EQUIPMENT
ACCOUNTS RECEIVABLE
DETAILED AGEING REPORT
07/30/80

PAGE 1

ACCOUNT	CUSTOMER NAME	PHONE	INVOICE	DUE DATE	CURRENT	1-30	31-60	OVER 60	TOTAL	OPEN CR
ALLEN	ALLEN & COMPANY	(404)255-9999	812	5/ 4/80				26.92		
			884	5/28/80				130.81		
					0.00	0.00	0.00	157.73	157.73	0.00
COX	COX PROPERTIES, INC.	(404)394-6666	----	6/30/80					3316.89	
EVANS	EVANS OFFICE SUPPLY	(404)262-8888	1030	6/ 9/80			21.47			
			1066	6/21/80			27.50			
			1245	7/15/80		22.76				
					0.00	22.76	48.97	0.00	71.73	0.00
HARLEN	HARLEN INSURANCE AGENCY	(404)238-1212	1260	7/20/80		36.39				
					0.00	36.39	0.00	0.00	36.39	0.00
JOHNDE	JOHNSON DELIVERY SERVICE	(404)262-2555	1230	7/10/80		36.75				
			1263	7/21/80		102.98				
			1275	7/25/80						-20.13
					0.00	139.73	0.00	0.00	139.73	-20.13
KELLY	KELLY SUPPLY COMPANY	(404)634-1555	----	7/ 9/80					582.72	
LENOX	LENOX MAMAGEMENT SERVICE	(404)237-2323	----	7/ 7/80					2263.30	
MARSH	MARSHALL, ALLEN & BOOSE	(404)634-6666	----	6/30/80					162.58	
MCMILL	MCMILLAN & ASSOCIATES	(404)233-7777	0	7/ 6/80	90.00					
			1218	6/29/80		33.49				
			1219	7/ 6/80		39.95				
			1236	7/12/80			90.00			
			1395	7/30/80						-90.00
					90.00	73.44	90.00	0.00	253.44	-90.00
ROYAL	ROYAL IMPORTERS, LTD.	(404)763-3333	1084	6/27/80		365.25				
			1242	7/14/80			36.37			
					0.00	365.25	36.37	0.00	401.62	0.00
SDI	SOUTHERN DIST., INC.	(404)633-5555	1206	6/17/80			159.95			
			1251	7/17/80		38.95				
			1271	7/23/80	39.98					
			1292	7/30/80						-150.00
					39.98	38.95	159.95	0.00	238.88	-150.00

FIG. 4-23 Detailed aging report.

```
                    PEACHTREE/5 SOFTWARE
                    INVENTORY MANAGEMENT
              COPYRIGHT 1980, RETAIL SCIENCES, INC.
                    PROGRAM SELECTION MENU
          ---------------------------------------------

YOU MAY SELECT ANY OF THE FOLLOWING PROGRAMS:

          DA       SET TODAYS DATE - CURRENTLY  3/ 1/82
          MF       INVENTORY MASTER FILE MAINTENANCE
          ET       ENTER INVENTORY TRANSACTIONS
          RP       REPORT GENERATION (SUBMENU)
          PH       PHYSICAL INVENTORY WORKSHEET
          IP       INVENTORY PRICE LIST
          EP       END OF PERIOD PROCESSING
          SI       SYSTEM INITIALIZATION
          FX       INVENTORY FILE FIX
          END      END INVENTORY SYSTEM

WHICH PROGRAM DO YOU WISH TO SELECT? RP
```

PHOTO 4-24   *The Inventory main menu.*

2. The system indicates the quantities available so that the sales department can immediately determine whether sufficient quantities are available to fill the available orders.
3. The system identifies those items which need to be reordered so that the purchasing department can order the items sufficiently in advance to avoid an out-of-stock situation.
4. Physical inventory count sheets can be generated which can be used to compare the actual quantities on hand with the recorded quantities shown in the perpetual inventory records.
5. Price lists, with multi-level pricing, can be generated for the use of salespeople when quoting prices to their customers.

```
                    PEACHTREE/5 SOFTWARE
                    INVENTORY MANAGEMENT
              COPYRIGHT 1980, RETAIL SCIENCES, INC.
                    PROGRAM SELECTION MENU
          ---------------------------------------------

YOU MAY SELECT ANY OF THE FOLLOWING REPORTS:

          DT       DETAIL INVENTORY REPORT
          DS       DEPARTMENTAL SUMMARY REPORT
          ST       INVENTORY STATUS REPORT
          OR       REORDER REPORT
          PD       PERIOD-TO-DATE REPORT
          YD       YEAR-TO-DATE REPORT
          ME       RETURN TO THE MAIN MENU

WHICH PROGRAM DO YOU WISH TO SELECT? ME
```

PHOTO 4-25   *The Inventory submenu of reports.*

Shown in Photo 4-24 is the main menu screen. As before, the two-letter commands invoke the subprograms which support the inventory system.

The other menu is the report generation submenu shown in Photo 4-25.

Sample reports from the inventory system are shown below. the Departmental Summary in Fig. 4-24 summarizes inventory value, year-to-date sales, cost of sales, and gross profit (margin) by department. Fig. 4-25 includes the Inventory Status Report which summarizes inventory activity for each inventory item for the month. The Reorder Report in Fig. 4-26 lists those items which should be reordered based on data maintained in the master file. The Year-to-Date Report in Fig. 4-27 provides information regarding sales, cost of sales, gross profit (margin), and average selling price for each inventory item.

Using the Peachtree "Big Five"

In order to begin using the General Ledger or any of the other applications packages described above, you must not only install the packages on your hardware (or have it done for you) but you must also learn enough about the software to initialize data files for it to use. The manuals provided with this software are helpful in this area. Demonstration data files are provided with the programs so that you can teach yourself the system before creating your own data files. A first step in teaching yourself to use a package is to run it with the demonstration data and then try to add some new data to the files. Since the Peachtree (and other) systems are undergoing constant changes, we will not present a lab exercise for this section.

Interested readers should write to reference [28] for information about the latest products in the Peachtree line.

General Caveat

It should be repeated here that, prior to purchasing any packaged software, you should determine what specific requirements you will have for the specific system. For example, some versions of payroll systems allow for only two miscellaneous deductions in calculating net payroll. If your company needs more deductions, you will obviously have a problem. You should also spend time considering data file capacity. Will the system be able to accommodate the number of inventory items which your company is likely to have in the next few years? Similarly, you should carefully study the reports generated by the software you are considering. Are you happy with the formats and report headings? Is there other information you would like on the reports? Are there other reports you would like to have that are not included? Do *not* assume that because you want a certain report that purchasing business software will mean that you are able to get it.

HOWELL ENTERPRISES, INC.
INVENTORY MANAGEMENT
DEPARTMENTAL SUMMARY

DEPT	CURRENT INVENTORY VALUE	% TOTAL INVENTORY VALUE	YTD SALES AMOUNT	YTD SALES % TOTAL	COST OF SALES YTD AMOUNT	COST OF SALES % TOTAL	YTD MARGIN AMOUNT	% TOTAL MARGIN
APP	13,701.98	28.56	87,337.77	20.91	44,364.21	24.19	42,973.56	18.35
BDR	2,924.86	6.10	26,054.51	6.24	13,859.48	7.56	12,195.03	5.21
DNR	18,495.00	38.55	221,986.25	53.16	78,990.00	43.08	142,996.25	61.05
LVR	12,113.00	25.25	79,626.26	19.07	45,241.00	24.67	34,385.26	14.68
MIS	740.50	1.54	2,592.45	0.62	910.50	0.50	1,681.95	0.72
TOTALS	47,975.34		417,597.24		183,365.19		234,232.05	

*** END OF DEPARTMENTAL SUMMARY ***

FIG. 4-24 Departmental summary of inventory.

HOWELL ENTERPRISES, INC.
INVENTORY MANAGEMENT
INVENTORY STATUS REPORT

DEPARTMENT APP

ITEM NUMBER	DESCRIPTION	BEGINNING BALANCE	SALES	RETURNS	RECEIPTS	ADJMTS.	CURRENT BALANCE	CURRENT AVG. COST	TOTAL VALUATION
APP-10000STO	STOVE, ELECTRIC	14.00	2.00	0.00	0.00	0.00	12.00	344.760	4137.12
APP-10010REF	REFRIG, 22 CU. FT.	6.00	0.00	1.00	0.00	0.00	7.00	456.810	3197.67
APP-10030OVE	OVEN, MICROWAVE	8.00	2.00	0.00	0.00	0.00	6.00	496.250	2977.50
APP-10040DIS	DISHWASHER	8.00	4.00	0.00	0.00	0.00	4.00	267.860	1071.44
APP-10040TRA	TRASH COMPACTER	10.00	0.00	1.00	0.00	0.00	11.00	210.750	2318.25
DEPARTMENT APP TOTALS	NUMBER OF ITEMS = 5						40.00	342.55	13,701.98

FIG. 4-25 Inventory status report.

RUN DATE 3/ 9/81

HOWELL ENTERPRISES, INC.
INVENTORY MANAGEMENT
ITEMS BELOW MINIMUM LEVEL

PAGE 1

VENDOR	VENDOR ITEM #	YOUR ITEM ID	P C	DESCRIPTION	BALANCE	REORDER LEVEL	WEEKS BELOW R/O LEVEL	REORDER QUANTITY	DATE ORDERED	FIRST TIME?
BASSET	EAM510	DNR-10010MOB	D	MOBILE SERVER	1.00	2.00	23	2.00	-------	
BROYHL	752DN	DNR-10040OVA	D	OVAL TABLE	2.00	4.00	23	2.00	-------	
BROYHL	772DN	DNR-10050PED	D	PEDESTAL TABLE	4.00	4.00	23	4.00	-------	
DREW	798062	LVR-10000SOF	L	SOFA	10.00	12.00	23	12.00	-------	
DREW	798064	LVR-10020CHA	L	CHAIR	12.00	18.00	23	18.00	-------	
DREW	798065	LVR-10030OTT	L	OTTOMAN	10.00	10.00	23	10.00	-------	
FRIGID	RMP-2398	APP-10010REF	A	REFRIG, 22 CU. FT.	7.00	8.00	23	6.00	-------	
FRIGID	OMP-5782	APP-10030OVE	A	OVEN, MICROWAVE	6.00	6.00	23	6.00	-------	
FRIGID	DMP-6742	APP-10040DIS	A	DISHWASHER	4.00	8.00	23	8.00	-------	
HICKRY	H8120	DNR-10070CAN	D	CANE BACK CHAIR	10.00	12.00	23	12.00	-------	
SEALY	S80658	BDR-10020TWI	B	TWIN SET	1.00	1.00	23	2.00	-------	
SEALY	S80636	BDR-10070QUE	B	QUEEN SET	3.00	4.00	23	4.00	-------	
SEALY	S80605	BDR-10090EX-	B	EX-LONG TWIN SET	1.00	1.00	23	1.00	-------	
SINGER	S0667TB	LVR-10040END	L	END TABLE	3.00	6.00	23	6.00	-------	

TOTAL ITEMS BELOW REORDER LEVEL = 14

*** END OF REORDER REPORT ***

FIG. 4-26 Reordering report.

RUN DATE 3/ 9/81

HOWELL ENTERPRISES, INC.
INVENTORY MANAGEMENT
YEAR-TO-DATE REPORT

PAGE 1

DEPARTMENT APP

ITEM ID	P C	DESCRIPTION	NET SALES UNITS	NET SALES AMOUNT	COST OF GOODS SOLD AMOUNT	% SALES	MARGIN AMOUNT	% SALES	AVERAGE SELLING PRICE
APP-10000STO	A	STOVE, ELECTRIC	26.00	17,699.00	8,963.76	50.65	8,735.24	49.35	680.73
APP-10010REF	A	REFRIG, 22 CU. FT.	23.00	20,031.54	10,506.63	52.45	9,524.91	47.55	870.94
APP-10030OVE	A	OVEN, MICROWAVE	20.00	17,333.20	9,925.00	57.26	7,408.20	42.74	866.66
APP-10040DIS	A	DISHWASHER	37.00	21,049.27	9,910.82	47.08	11,138.45	52.92	568.90
APP-10040TRA	A	TRASH COMPACTER	24.00	11,224.76	5,058.00	45.06	6,166.76	54.94	467.70
DEPARTMENT APP TOTALS				87,337.77	44,364.21	50.80	42,973.56	49.20	

FIG. 4-27 Year-to-date inventory report.

4.3 Data Base Management Systems

It's not too far from the truth to describe computers (and the programs they utilize) as data-crunching machines. Scientific programs crunch numerical data, word processor and information-retrieval programs crunch textual data, and business programs crunch a mixed diet. True enough, there are some programs that are exceptions to this pattern (e. g., prime number generators) but, by and large, when it comes to computer programs and computer data, it's hard to imagine one without the other.

Sometime in the early 1970s, alert application programmers began to notice the shadow of a frightening consequence to this one-on-one relationship between programs and data. As the number of application programs grew, so did the total volume of data they needed for sustenance. The "big five" accounting programs just discussed in Section 4.2 are a good case in point. General ledger, accounts receivable, accounts payable, payroll, and inventory all work on data—lots of it. And in traditional systems, each of these programs maintains its *own* collection of data— its so-called "data base." Some of the better accounting systems attempt to share this data by sending summary results from one subsystem to another, but this actually results in *more* data being generated, not less.

The idea behind data base management systems (DBMS) is to reverse this trend by consolidating data, allowing related applications to share in the use of one "super" data base. The theory is that such an arrangement will be more efficient, and allow for better control of who uses which data for what.

The reasoning is similar to that voiced by a university library system which decrees, "no more departmental libraries—from now on, there will be one central facility, and everyone who deals with data must go there." The catch to both DBMS and centralized libraries is that new inefficiencies can easily creep in. There will be added expense because of the extra "management functions" that must be created; there will be conflicting requests for resources; and the talent of departmental knowledge about the best data to acquire will give way to compromising central decisions. Access times are also likely to increase, and in the event of a shut-down at the central facility, everyone will be out of business.

On the plus side, a centralized data bank with good management is in a better position to solve the problem of updating data that's shared by many users. An airline reservations system is an example of an application where such coordination is crucial. The data one travel agent uses in promising a seat reservation had better reflect the latest reservations made by *all* the agents (and all the programs) using that system. The cost of such coordination is high, but most people agree that it's worth it.

When it comes to data base management systems for microcomputers, many programs that go under that name aren't quite what they claim. They are really information storage/retrieval programs that do about the same thing as the BASIC program FILEBOXM discussed in Sections 5.2

and 5.8. This is OK—in fact such programs are quite valuable—but be warned that many advertising claims about microcomputer DBM systems need to be taken with a grain of salt. It's usually more accurate to think of such programs as forming *part* of a complete DBMS, a kernel upon which a full-blown system might eventually be built.

The Cavalcade of Stars, Part II

An example of an honestly advertised and well-designed DBMS kernel is DataStar. This is a product of MicroPro International, the company that sells the WordStar and CalcStar programs also discussed in this chapter. DataStar is described by its seller as "an easy to learn, yet professionally powerful, comprehensive data entry, retrieval, and update system for microcomputer systems." This appears to be a reasonable description, and there seem to be enough "hooks to the future" in the system to suggest that it might eventually become part of a more complete DBMS for microcomputers.

To see what DataStar and similar programs attempt to do, let's consider how a DBMS might be organized. In general, there are three functions that are desirable in a DBMS: (1) data collection/storage, (2) data retrieval/maintenance, and (3) data application/report generation. The DataStar program handles parts (1) and (2), leaving part (3) to the future (or to the user). To illustrate what these three functions entail, let's use a simple example to compare a manual data system to one that uses DataStar.

Suppose that you are an avid reader of personal computing magazines, and have built up a collection of several hundred back issues. The problem is that each issue could contain a dozen or so articles of value, but when you finally get around to wanting to use the information, it's not likely that you'll remember which issue of which journal to consult. Here's how a small data base collection/storage (function 1) and retrieval/maintenance (function 2) system could be put together to solve this problem. The column on the left describes a manual system; the column on the right shows the comparable DataStar function.

Function 1—Data Collection/Storage

1(a)　Design a standard "master data" collection form, and have a few hundred of these run off at your local print shop. Specify the maximum number of characters per entry with dashes. This form will insure that you or your assistants will collect consistent data for all journals.

1(a)　Run the form generation program (supplied with DataStar) by typing A>FORMGEN. Use it to design a standard "master data" collection form on the screen of your console. Specify the maximum number of characters per entry with dashes. Save the form as the file JNL for later use by you or your assistants.

Here is an example of such a form:

JNL (Data Collection Form for Journal Articles)

Record #0532
TITLE (50 MAX):MIKBUG AND THE TRS-80 _____
AUTHOR (12 MAX):R. LABENSKI ____
REFERENCE (12 MAX):IA JUN78 149
SUBJECT(10):ASSEMBLERS __   SYSTEM(10):MC6800 __
LANGUAGE(10):BASIC _____

1(b)   Go through your journals, and fill out one sheet for each article of interest. File these sheets in the same order that you happen to create them. For each data sheet, also fill out an index card containing the record number, and one key item of your choice (e. g., SYSTEM). File the cards in alphanumeric order and mark the file box "Index by SYSTEM keys."

1(b)   Run the DataStar program

A>DATASTAR JNL

Select the A (add new item) mode, and type in the data. DataStar will add this record (and all others you enter) to a master file called JNL.DTA. It will also create an index file sorted in order for any *one* item (or concatenation of items) you designate as "key", e. g., MC6800 (SYSTEM), or MC6800ASSEMBLER (SYSTEM + SUBJECT). This file will be called JNL.NDX.

1(b+)   If you wish, create additional index files, sorted in order for other key items (e. g., SUBJECT or LANGUAGE).

1(b+)   DataStar can only maintain *one* index file. However, the SuperSort program discussed at the end of this section can be used to create index files for subsets of JNL.DTA.

Function 2—Data Retrieval/Maintenance

2(a)   You can retrieve data manually in one of three ways. The first is to flip through the stack of master data sheets, using the same sequence in which they were created. The second is to flip through the card index in the same order (alphanumeric by key) as it was stored. The third is to "jump" into the card index near the place where you suspect a key item is stored (e.g., into the middle for MBASIC,

2(a)   With DataStar, you can display the records on your console or printer in three ways. The D command retrieves the records in same order as stored in the original master data file. Using the I command displays the records in the sorted order of the index file. The K command displays the first record it finds that matches the key item you specify. DataStar can also modify these commands to

or near the end for XBASIC), repeating the process until you find the desired key item.

show only those items that match a given "mask" you specify (e. g., the mask MC68****** would select MC6800, MC6809, and MC68000, but not ML6800).

2(b) For manual file maintenance you would do such things as deleting records (by marking them VOID), and changing records to correct errors or update the information they contain. There would also be a need for periodic housekeeping at which time voided records would be thrown out, and the latest stack of index cards would be moved from their "I'll get around to filing these tomorrow" pile to their correctly ordered position in the card index file.

2(b) DataStar allows several kinds of file maintenance, including deletion of records, editing of records, and a general "clean-up" process (^EF). This latter command takes care of reclaiming the space used by records that have been marked "deleted," and the re-sorting of index files that were originally kept in order by use of a linked list technique (see the technical note following Mini-Lab 4.3-1).

Function 3—Data Application/Report Generation

DataStar version 1.1 does not support this function (which is why its authors do not call it a DBMS). There are some microcomputer software systems which include part of this function, but there are limits on the number of files that can be simultaneously accessed.

In general, the purpose of function 3 is to complete the following scheme for a DBM system.

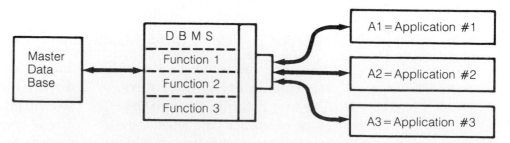

Functions 1 and 2 are used by all the applications to create, retrieve, and maintain that part of the data base which relates to their usage. Function 3 would be used in different ways by different applications to select, and work with subsets of the data that correspond to the information they need. For example, three related applications that could use the files JNL, JNL.DTA, and JNL.NDX can be described in terms of three users, Bob, Ted, and Alice, as follows:

A1. Bob is a computer hobbyist/student who wants to use the information in the data base for projects required in the courses he is taking at night school. His primary interest is in retrieving subject-related information.

A2. Ted wants to publish and sell computer application guides, one for each of the more popular personal computers. His main interest is in filtering out information for specific makes of hardware.

A3. Alice is the acquisitions editor for the Eve Osbite Publishing Company, and she needs information on the most productive authors in various computer-related fields. Her interest is in correlating names with subject areas, and frequency of publication.

It can be seen that what each of these users really wants is a program that will produce a customized report, organized in terms of their special viewpoints (application, machine, and author respectively). Assuming that all three users are able to access the same data (perhaps because they all work for the MaGoo-Mountain Conglomerate), then using a common DBMS in which function #3 is available for producing these customized reports would seem to make sense. Of course if *one* person wears all three hats, and that person can affort his/her own DBMS, then there's no doubt about it—a DBMS is the way to go.

Note that the alternative to a DBMS is to write the programs and maintain the data for three separate systems. In this case, the overall system design is less complex, but it may contain redundant data and programs organized as follows:

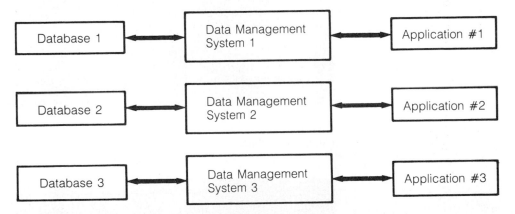

If this diagram looks familiar, that's because it describes the situation used in many traditional systems (e. g., separate payroll, general ledger, accounts receivable, and accounts payable systems).

Is the conventional approach inferior to a DBMS? *It all depends.* The DBMS approach is a lot slicker, but it has problems of its own. The redundancy and "overkill" of the traditional method could (like the design of turn of the century architecture) mean a sturdiness and robustness well worth the redundant costs. It's an area where both enthusiasm and caution are legitimate hats to try on before making a choice.

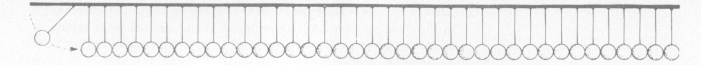

MINI-LAB   Using the DataStar System

4.3-1   *Step 1.*   Locate a dealer who is willing to demonstrate DataStar on a
                         CP/M system similar to the one you own (or hope to own).

Step 2.   Use the FORMGEN program to design a data-collection form.
             Then create a small data base, following the instructions in the
             DataStar manual. For sample data, you could use the index of
             articles in the December 1981 issue of *Byte*, entering the data
             contained there in the format described in the example given

```
ADD MODE                                 current form=JNL
CURSOR:        ^A=prev field      ^S=left char      ^D=right char      ^F=next field
               ^T=first field     ^L=last field
FIELD EDIT: ^G=delete char        ^V=insert hole    ^C=copy from previous record
OTHER:         ^Z=restore screen  ^U=print form     ^O=print data      ^J=help on/off
END/EXIT:      ^B=end entry       ^E=exit current mode
-----------------------------------------------------------------------------------
RECORD # 0007
TITLE (50 MAX.): To err is human (automated correction)_____
AUTHOR (12 MAX.): McGregor, R.
REFERENCE (12 MAX.): 5:3 Mar80___
SUBJECT (10): ASSEMBLER_   SYSTEM (10): _____   LANGUAGE (10): _____
```

*PHOTO 4-26   This is the form seen on the screen in the A (append data) mode of the
DataStar program.*

```
  SCAN MODE (I)                          current form=JNL
  CURSOR:        ^A=prev field      ^S=left char      ^D=right char      F=next field
                 ^T=first field     ^L=last field
  FIELD EDIT: ^G=delete char        ^V=insert hole
  OTHER:         ^Z=restore screen  ^U=print form     ^O=print data      ^J=help on/off
  END/EXIT:      ^B=end entry       ^N=next record    ^P=prev record     ^E=exit mode
  -----------------------------------------------------------------------------------
  RECORD # 0004
  TITLE (50 MAX.): Some example plots_____
  AUTHOR (12 MAX.): Dameron, D._
  REFERENCE (12 MAX.): 5:2 Feb80___
  SUBJECT (10): ART_____   SYSTEM (10): CROMEMCO__   LANGUAGE (10): BASIC_____
```

PHOTO 4-27   This photograph shows the retrieval of data using the DataStar I command.

earlier in this section. Photos 4-26 and 4-27 show some of the interactions you can expect to see on the screen.

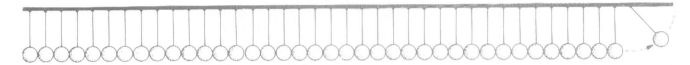

TECHNICAL NOTE

Data Structures Used in a DBMS

Most microcomputer data base management systems organize their data as tables that reflect the structure of direct (also called random) access files. The program FILEBOXM of Section 5.2 illustrates this structure with a table that has two columns, one for a keyword, and the other for information related to that keyword. In addition, every row in such a table is associated with a number that corresponds to a file *record number*.

The advertising for some DBM systems calls such a table-like organization of data a "relational data base," but that's not necessarily correct. To be called a relational data base, a system must also accommodate "normalization" procedures for rearranging the master table of data into specialized tables. An article explaining why normalization procedures are used appeared in *BYTE*, November 1981. It was called "Fundamentals of Relational Data Organization," and was written by J. Neely and S. Stewart.

A DBMS also includes index files (like JNL.NDX) which, when used in conjunction with master data files (like JNL.DTA), function like the indices in a book. The book is the master file, with each of its pages corresponding to one record. Page numbers act as "pointers" which make it easy to find the records.

To find information in a book, a user could just flip through the pages in sequence. However, it's a lot more efficient to first go to the index where an ordering scheme of some sort has been used to make locating key words easy. When the desired index entry is found, it will have one or more pointers (page numbers) that pinpoint the location of the desired data. In a computer index file, the pointers are usually record numbers that tell the system where to go to directly ("randomly") retrieve the needed data from the master file.

Two of the ways one can organize an index file are as a *sorted list*, and as a *sorted tree*. Indices to books use the sorted list approach so that users can easily find an entry with an "eyeball" version of binary search. However, adding new items to a sorted index takes a fair amount of work since everything has to be shifted down to make room for inserting the new item in its proper place. For this reason, an alternate approach using a set of pointers called *links* is sometimes used (e. g., in DataStar). The links indicate the "before and after" positions of the new item. The problem here is that eventually you generate links to links to links, etc., and the index becomes very inefficient.

Tree structures also use links, but they have a much simpler rule for adding new items: start at the top of the tree and work down until an empty slot is found, proceeding left if the new item is "less than" an item already stored in the tree, and proceeding right otherwise. For example, to add the key item FORTRAN to the following tree, you would start at the top box (called the root node of the tree), go left (FORTRAN < MBASIC), go right (FORTRAN > C), and then store FORTRAN in empty node #2.

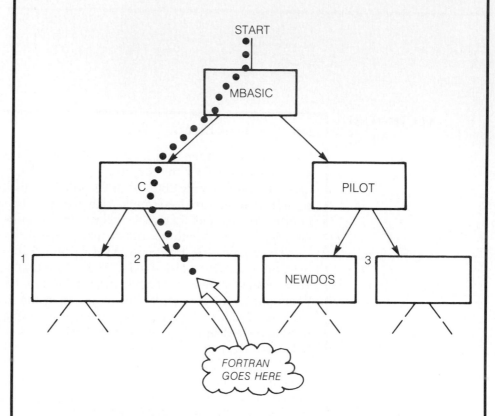

The structure produced by this procedure is called a *binary tree* since there are two branches coming out of each node. It works very well as long as the tree stays more or less balanced on the left and right. There is a slightly more complicated tree structure that guarantees such balance. It is called the B tree (B for balanced), and it allows more than two branches per node. An improvement of the B tree called the B+ tree is used in many commercial systems, including dBASE II (see Lab 4.3-2).

Once a tree has been created, it can then be used as an index to a data file as seen in the following example.

1 SMITH/*GRAPHICS* FOR EVERYONE . . .
2 JONES/HOW TO USE THE *APPLE* . . .
3 MEYERS/LOW COST *GRAPHICS* . . .
4 BAKER/*BASIC* IN THE HOME . . .
5 OSBURN/USING *CP/M* AT WORK . . .
6 OBRIEN/WHERE TO BUY AN *APPLE* . . .
7 ZILCH/LOW COST *MODEMS* . . .
8 ADAMS/THERE'S AN *APPLE* IN YOUR . . .
9 MURRAY/PROGRAMMING IN *APL* . . .
10 FOX/WHY *BASIC* IS SUPERIOR . . .
11 PETERS/USING *XBASIC* FOR FUN . . .

EXAMPLE OF A DATA FILE JNL.DTA WITH ONE *KEY* WORD DESIGNATED FOR EACH RECORD.

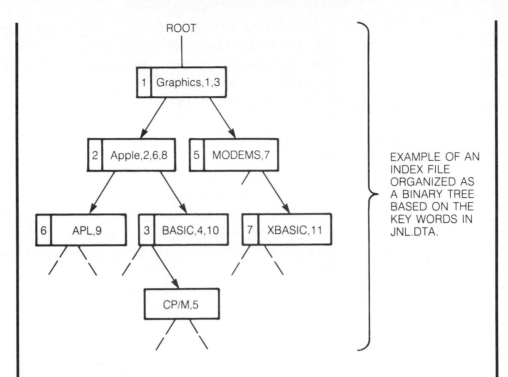

EXAMPLE OF AN INDEX FILE ORGANIZED AS A BINARY TREE BASED ON THE KEY WORDS IN JNL.DTA.

As an example of use of such an index, consider the problem of retrieving all data records that contain the key word *BASIC*. This would be done by starting at the top (root) of the tree, and using the "LEFT IF<", "RIGHT IF >" rule until a match for BASIC was found. The node where this match occurred would show that records 4 and 10 are the ones to be retrieved. This retrieval could then be easily done with two random-access "GET" statements of the kind shown in Section 5.2. Note that just as there can be several indices in a book (for example, by subject, author, and math symbols), there can also be several indices for a data file. The data collection form JNL which we showed earlier had provision for designating three key items (called SUBJECT, SYSTEM, and LANGUAGE), so it would make sense to generate three index files for this data base. DataStar can't do this, but the MBASIC program discussed in project 5 of Section 5.8 can, using ordinary arrays to represent the three index trees. For more on this and related topics, the book by Knuth [13] is recommended. Program examples are available from [22].

Instant Quiz

Draw a picture of the tree index needed for finding *authors* in the JNL.DTA file just shown.

Star III—The SuperSort Utility

SuperSort is a general sorting "utility," that is, a program which can be used to put the records of files into ascending or descending order, using any sorting key (or combination of keys) specified by the user. It is a product of MicroPro International, and it has been designed so that it can also be used in conjunction with their DataStar program. In particular, the .DTA data files created in DataStar can be resorted on new keys. They can also be "pruned" by using the SELECT/EXCLUDE feature of SuperSort to create subsets of the original .DTA file. SuperSort can then be used to produce an .NDX (index) file for each of the new subset files.

SuperSort is general enough to be used on files produced by most other systems, including data files produced by MBASIC, BASIC-E, CBASIC, FORTRAN, and COBOL programs. In fact it can be used to convert the files produced by one system to files with the format required by a different system. It is also possible to link the sorting part of SuperSort (called SORSUB) to your own application program, using it as a private subroutine that your application program can call upon as needed.

The sorting algorithm used in SuperSort is called *Heapsort*. This is explained in Knuth [13] in Section 5.2.3 where it is noted that this is one of the few algorithms with a guaranteed performance, no matter how the original data is distributed. For medium-sized files (up to about 1000 records) the Shell sort algorithm used in Sections 5.5 and 5.7 of this book is usually superior. However as the number of records gets larger (SuperSort can handle files with up to 65,536 records), the performance of heapsort will be superior to that of Shell sort. This fact, plus the ability of SuperSort to sort and merge up to 32 distinct files into one very large master file, puts it in the class of contemporary professional software, with capabilities that exceed those of the sorting utilities found on many larger machines. The fact that products like SuperSort have succeeded in bringing such performance to low cost personal microcomputers is a real tribute to their authors.

Note: If sorting algorithms are new to you, references [1] and [4] discuss the bubble sort, selection sort, counting sort, indexed sort, Shell sort, and quick sort algorithms. All of the algorithms are illustrated with BASIC programs. Bubble sort and Shell sort are also illustrated in this book with programs in MBASIC, C, and 8080 assembly language. Consult the index under *Bubble* and *Shell* for the exact page numbers.

The dBASE II System

The dBASE II system is sold by the Ashton-Tate Software Company [29]. It is billed as a relational database management system. It contains a very large repertory of commands, including some that actually constitute a small programming language. This feature can be used to partially automate the process of data management, but learning to use the language is not easy for non-programmers.

For users who don't wish to learn this language, dBASE II can also be used as a flexible data entry/retrieval system. The following lab illustrates such a use of dBASE II to build a database called LOCKS. The idea is

**TECHNICAL
NOTE**

Installing DataStar

DataStar needs to be configured for the terminal used by your system. This is easy to do with the INSTALL program supplied, provided *your* terminal is on the list of those "supported." If it's not, the manual tells you to use DDT to "patch" both DATASTAR.COM and FORMGEN.COM. Don't try this until you've mastered Chapter 6 of this book. Then you'll understand the following example of how we did the "patching" for a Zenith Z19 (or Heathkit H19) terminal, using the listing of the program segment USER as shown in Appendix B of the DataStar manual as a guide. Our example assumes DDT is on the disk in drive B, while DATASTAR.COM and FORMGEN.COM are on the disk in drive A. Fig. 4-28 shows how to patch and save FORMGEN.COM. The same procedure is used for DATASTAR.COM except that you start with

A>B:DDT DATASTAR.COM

and end with

A>SAVE 94 DATASTAR.COM

The data used in the patching is derived from the Z19 manual. For example, the 2 bytes 1B and 45 are placed in USER locations 0243 and 0244 because (1) they represent <esc>E which is the code for a Z19 clear screen command, and (2) the USER program expects to find this code in locations 0243 and 0244, with the number of bytes used by the command stored in location 0242.

```
A>B:DDT FORMGEN.COM
DDT VERS 2.0
NEXT PC
8000 0100
 −S0242
0242 01 02
0243 1A 1B
0244 00 45
0245 00 .
 −S024F
024F 3D 59
0250 00 .
 −S0270
0270 00 02
0271 00 1B
0272 00 4B
0273 00 .
 −S0287
0287 00 02
0288 00 1B
0289 00 70
028A 00 .
 −S028E
028E 00 02
028F 00 1B
0290 00 71
0291 00 .
 −^C
A>SAVE 127 FORMGEN.COM
A>FORMGEN
```

FIG. 4-28   Using DDT to patch FORMGEN.COM.

to keep records showing which persons are issued keys to various rooms in a large office or institutional complex. The assumptions are that (1) each key carries a unique serial number, (2) one person may be issued several keys, (3) a key may open more than one room, (4) holders of keys are charged a deposit which is refunded when the key is returned, (5) each key has a 3-letter status code such as ACT (in active use), RTN (returned), or LST (reported lost). An example of a report that one could request would be the name of the active holder of a given key along with a list of all past holders of that key.

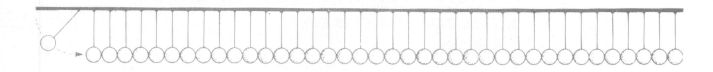

LAB EXERCISE 4.3-2

Using dBASE II

Step 1. Boot your system with the disk containing the dBASE II *system* files in the A disk drive. In this lab, the *data* files we'll create (e. g., LOCKS) will also be saved on the A disk, although normally it would be better to save data files on the disk in the B drive (e. g., by using the name B:LOCKS).

Step 2. Look at the directory for A. There should be twelve files with DBASE as part of their names. The file containing the dBASE II master program is called DBASE.COM. To run it, type

A>DBASE<cr>

Note: The symbols A> are printed by CP/M. You type DBASE and <cr> (which means press carriage return). dBASE II commands can be in upper or lower case letters.

The dBASE II program will ask you to type the date. You may skip this by typing <cr> or you may type the date, e. g., 10/28/82<cr>. dBASE II will print a dot followed by a space as its prompting symbol. The dot means "type a dBASE command."

*** dBASE II   Ver. 2.3C   22 FEB 82

Step 3. Since this is a new application, the first step is to define the *structure* of the database by using the command CREATE. A database is a *file* made up of a collection of *records*. The data in each record is organized as a set of *fields*. The size, type, and number of these fields determines the *structure* of the file. Structures are created by typing

CREATE<cr>

dBASE II will respond with the prompt ENTER FILENAME:. We are going to create a database with a filename of LOCKS, so respond to this request as follows:

ENTER FILENAME: LOCKS<cr>

(or B:LOCKS<cr> if you're using a two-disk system)

If this filename has been used before, you will see the message DESTROY EXISTING FILE? (Y/N). If you don't mind erasing the existing file, type y. Otherwise, type n, and use a different filename.

We're now ready to define the structure of our file. Suppose that we've decided that LOCKS will have six fields in each record. The dBASE II program will prompt for information about these fields as follows:

ENTER RECORD STRUCTURE AS FOLLOWS:
FIELD   NAME, TYPE, WIDTH, DECIMAL PLACES
001

Where

NAME	=	The name you assign to the field. This can be up to 10 characters long. It must start with a letter, and may contain other letters, numbers, and colons. Correct: ACCOUNT:5, ACCT5, ACCT:RCV:5 Wrong: ACCOUNT 5, 5:ACCOUNT, ACCT#5
TYPE	=	C for character data, N for numerical data.
WIDTH	=	The largest possible number of characters you will use for a character field. The maximum width allowed is 254.
DECIMAL PLACES.		If the field type is N, you must specify the *total* number of positions (including the decimal point) required, and (if you want them), the number of digits after the decimal. For example, for integers up to 999999 type 6, but for numbers up to 9999.99 type 7,2.

The number 001 is prompting you to input information for the first field. To create our six fields respond in the following way to six successive prompts:

001 SERIAL:NUM,C,10<cr>
002 ROOMS,C,20<cr>
003 HOLDER,C,20<cr>
004 DATE,C,8<cr>
005 DEPOSIT,N,5,2<cr>
006 STATUS,C,3<cr>
007 <cr>

Step 4.   The <cr> in field #7 indicates to dBASE that we are finished describing our fields. dBASE responds with:

INPUT DATA NOW?

To start entering some records, type y. You'll then be prompted for data with colons showing the width of each field as follows:

```
RECORD #00001
SERIAL:NUM   :              :
ROOMS        :                      :
HOLDER       :                      :
DATE         :         :
DEPOSIT      :       :
STATUS       :    :
```

Step 5.   The above structure (or "skeleton") of a record will be displayed in reverse video mode. For a start, enter data for record #00001 by typing the following data in the corresponding fields.

```
D58693<cr>
AL331,AL332<cr>
SMITH, GEORGE<cr>
10/15/82<cr>
5.50<cr>
ACT<cr>
```

Either <backspace> or <delete> may be used to correct errors. (You can also use editing commands similar to those of WordStar as described in the dBASE II manual.) If a field is filled, a warning beep is heard and the cursor moves to the beginning of the next field. At the last <cr> (or beep), a skeleton for record #00002 will be displayed. Type in similar data you invent for records 2, 3, and 4. Note that SERIAL:NUM is the only entry that must be unique to each record, so it's OK to use repetitions in other fields.

Step 6.   When prompted for record #00005 respond by typing <cr>. This will indicate to dBASE that you are finished inputting new records, and it will again display the . prompt symbol. To see your database type:

```
. USE LOCKS<cr>
. LIST<cr>
```

The command USE LOCKS tells dBASE to close all previously opened files and then open LOCKS, while LIST means display all data on the console.

Step 7.   Additional records can be added to the file at any time with the APPEND command. Respond to the dot prompt by typing

```
. APPEND<cr>
```

The dBASE system will respond by displaying a skeleton for record #00005. Note that APPEND and most other commands refer to the file which is currently in use, that is, *open*. If a file hasn't been opened, you'll be prompted for a filename.

Type in data for record #00005 using the same structure as in step 5. Suggestion: Use the name SMITH, GEORGE again, but for a different serial number. When prompted for record #00006 simply type <cr>. This will exit APPEND mode and return you to the dBASE II command mode.

Step 8. To change data that was previously entered, you can use the EDIT command. For example, suppose the key corresponding to record #3 has been turned in. To change the DEPOSIT field in the 3rd record to 0, and the status to RTN, first type

. EDIT 3<cr>

This will bring the 3rd record onto the screen. Type <cr> until you get to the DEPOSIT field (this will leave existing fields intact). Type 0 <cr> as the new entry for this field. Press <cr> to get to the STATUS field, and type RTN <cr> (recall that RTN means key returned). Finally, type CONTROL-W to save the changes and return to the command mode.

Note: You can also do full-screen editing by using some of the same control characters discussed in Section 4.1 under WordStar. Editing is normally in "overstrike" mode, but CONTROL-V switches to insert mode.

Step 9. When using a database, it is often convenient to have the records sorted according to one of the fields. We are going to sort our database on the HOLDER field. Type the following:

. USE LOCKS<cr>
. SORT ON HOLDER TO TEMP<cr>

This will cause the system to sort the database on the field HOLDER and write the sorted database to the file called TEMP. We can check the file TEMP to see that everything is correct by typing:

. USE TEMP<cr>
. LIST<cr>

If this looks OK and it is the only file we want, we can copy TEMP back onto the file LOCKS and double check the results with:

. COPY TO LOCKS<cr>
00005 RECORDS COPIED
. USE LOCKS<cr>
. LIST<cr>

This should show that LOCKS is now the file sorted in alphabetical order according to the field HOLDER. To get rid of the TEMP file, you can use DELETE FILE TEMP. As an exercise, next make TEMP a file sorted according to SERIAL:NUM. Note that you should not sort a database to itself. This is a precautionary measure since a power surge at the wrong time could destroy the entire database.

```
. SET PRINT ON
. SET EJECT OFF
. USE LOCKS
. LIST STRUCTURE
STRUCTURE FOR FILE:   LOCKS.DBF
NUMBER OF RECORDS:    00006
DATE OF LAST UPDATE: 00/00/00
PRIMARY USE DATABASE
FLD        NAME      TYPE WIDTH    DEC
001     SERIAL:NUM    C   010
002     ROOMS         C   020
003     HOLDER        C   020
004     DATE          C   008
005     DEPOSIT       N   005      002
006     STATUS        C   003
** TOTAL **               00067
. LIST
00001  G34567     AL344,AL345,AL351   SMITH, GEORGE       10/2/83    0.00 LST
00002  H45678     AL922,AL923         JOHNSON, MARIE      4/1/79     0.00 RTN
00003  X29631     AL110,AL111         BROWN, LORRAINE     9/1/82     0.00 LST
00004  F23456     AL123,AL124         SMITH, ALVA         10/18/83   4.25 ACT
00005  D58693     AL331,AL332         SMITH, P. GEORGE    10/15/83   5.50 ACT
00006  E12345     AL234,235           JONES, RALPH        10/16/83   6.50 ACT
. DISPLAY FOR HOLDER = 'SMITH' .AND. DEPOSIT > 0
00004  F23456     AL123,AL124         SMITH, ALVA         10/18/83   4.25 ACT
00005  D58693     AL331,AL332         SMITH, P. GEORGE    10/15/83   5.50 ACT
. SORT ON DEPOSIT TO TEMP
SORT COMPLETE
. USE TEMP
. LIST
00001  G34567     AL344,AL345,AL351   SMITH, GEORGE       10/2/83    0.00 LST
00002  H45678     AL922,AL923         JOHNSON, MARIE      4/1/79     0.00 RTN
00003  X29631     AL110,AL111         BROWN, LORRAINE     9/1/82     0.00 LST
00004  F23456     AL123,AL124         SMITH, ALVA         10/18/83   4.25 ACT
00005  D58693     AL331,AL332         SMITH, P. GEORGE    10/15/83   5.50 ACT
00006  E12345     AL234,235           JONES, RALPH        10/16/83   6.50 ACT
. COPY TO LOCKS
00006 RECORDS COPIED
. USE LOCKS
. INDEX ON HOLDER TO LOCKHOLD
00006 RECORDS INDEXED
. USE LOCKS INDEX LOCKHOLD
. LIST
00003  X29631     AL110,AL111         BROWN, LORRAINE     9/1/82     0.00 LST
00002  H45678     AL922,AL923         JOHNSON, MARIE      4/1/79     0.00 RTN
00006  E12345     AL234,235           JONES, RALPH        10/16/83   6.50 ACT
00004  F23456     AL123,AL124         SMITH, ALVA         10/18/83   4.25 ACT
00001  G34567     AL344,AL345,AL351   SMITH, GEORGE       10/2/83    0.00 LST
00005  D58693     AL331,AL332         SMITH, P. GEORGE    10/15/83   5.50 ACT
. FIND SMITH
. DISPLAY
00004  F23456     AL123,AL124         SMITH, ALVA         10/18/83   4.25 ACT
. DELETE RECORD 1
00001 DELETION(S)
. LIST
00003  X29631     AL110,AL111         BROWN, LORRAINE     9/1/82     0.00 LST
00002  H45678     AL922,AL923         JOHNSON, MARIE      4/1/79     0.00 RTN
00006  E12345     AL234,235           JONES, RALPH        10/16/83   6.50 ACT
00004  F23456     AL123,AL124         SMITH, ALVA         10/18/83   4.25 ACT
00001 *G34567     AL344,AL345,AL351   SMITH, GEORGE       10/2/83    0.00 LST
00005  D58693     AL331,AL332         SMITH, P. GEORGE    10/15/83   5.50 ACT
.


. RECALL RECORD 1
00001 RECALL(S)
. LIST
00003  X29631     AL110,AL111         BROWN, LORRAINE     9/1/82     0.00 LST
00002  H45678     AL922,AL923         JOHNSON, MARIE      4/1/79     0.00 RTN
00006  E12345     AL234,235           JONES, RALPH        10/16/83   6.50 ACT
00004  F23456     AL123,AL124         SMITH, ALVA         10/18/83   4.25 ACT
00001  G34567     AL344,AL345,AL351   SMITH, GEORGE       10/2/83    0.00 LST
00005  D58693     AL331,AL332         SMITH, P. GEORGE    10/15/83   5.50 ACT
. DELETE RECORD 3
00001 DELETION(S)
. PACK
PACK COMPLETE, 00005 RECORDS COPIED
```

FIG. 4-29   This is an example showing how some of the dBASE II commands discussed in steps 9 through 12 of this lab are used. The interaction was captured on a printer by using the dBASE command .SET PRINT ON.

```
. LIST
00002   H45678      AL922,AL923           JOHNSON, MARIE        4/1/79     0.00 RTN
00005   E12345      AL234,235             JONES, RALPH          10/16/83   6.50 ACT
00003   F23456      AL123,AL124           SMITH, ALVA           10/18/83   4.25 ACT
00001   G34567      AL344,AL345,AL351     SMITH, GEORGE         10/2/83    0.00 LST
00004   D58693      AL331,AL332           SMITH, P. GEORGE      10/15/83   5.50 ACT
. REPORT
ENTER REPORT FORM NAME: LOCKS2
ENTER OPTIONS, M=LEFT MARGIN, L=LINES/PAGE, W=PAGE WIDTH M=3
PAGE HEADING? (Y/N) Y
ENTER PAGE HEADING: %%%%%%%%%%  Lock Access  %%%%%%%%%%
DOUBLE SPACE REPORT? (Y/N) n
ARE TOTALS REQUIRED? (Y/N) y
SUBTOTALS IN REPORT? (Y/N) n
COL     WIDTH,CONTENTS
001     10,SERIAL:NUM
ENTER HEADING: Serial #
002     20,ROOMS
ENTER HEADING: Rooms Accessed
003     20,HOLDER
ENTER HEADING: Name of Holder
004     8,DATE
ENTER HEADING: Date
005     7,DEPOSIT
ENTER HEADING: Deposit
ARE TOTALS REQUIRED? (Y/N) y
006     6,STATUS
ENTER HEADING: Status
007


    PAGE NO. 00001


                        %%%%%%%%%%  Lock Access  %%%%%%%%%%

    Serial #       Rooms Accessed       Name of Holder      Date    Deposit Status

    H45678      AL922,AL923           JOHNSON, MARIE        4/1/79     0.00 RTN
    E12345      AL234,235             JONES, RALPH          10/16/83   6.50 ACT
    F23456      AL123,AL124           SMITH, ALVA           10/18/83   4.25 ACT
    G34567      AL344,AL345,AL351     SMITH, GEORGE         10/2/83    0.00 LST
    D58693      AL331,AL332           SMITH, P. GEORGE      10/15/83   5.50 ACT
    ** TOTAL **
                                                                     16.25

. QUIT
*** END RUN     dBASE II      ***
```

FIG. 4-29   (*continued*)

Step 10.   There are times when we want to find certain records in a database. This can be done with the LOCATE command. For example, to find George Smith's records, type the following:

. LOCATE FOR HOLDER = 'SMITH'<cr>

dBASE II will print the number of the first record containing SMITH in the HOLDER field. To see this record, type

. DISPLAY<cr>

You can combine these commands by using DISPLAY FOR HOLDER = 'SMITH'. You can also use the logical connectives .AND., .OR., and .NOT., and relational operators as, for example,

. DISPLAY FOR HOLDER = 'SMITH' .AND. DEPOSIT > 0

The symbol $ can be used to mean "substring of." For example, to find records for all people with TOOLE as *part* of their name, use

. DISPLAY FOR 'TOOLE' $ HOLDER

**TECHNICAL
NOTE**

The LOCATE command works by sequentially searching through the data in the .DBF file. However dBASE also allows you to create index (.NDX) files that "point to" data in the .DBF file. For example, you could create the file LOCKHOLD.NDX as an index based on the HOLDER field of LOCKS.DBF as follows,

```
. USE LOCKS<cr>
. INDEX ON HOLDER TO LOCKHOLD<cr>
. USE LOCKS INDEX LOCKHOLD<cr>
. LIST<cr>
```

The second USE command opens both LOCKS and LOCKHOLD. From then on, commands will make use of this index file wherever appropriate. For example, both LOCKS and LOCKHOLD will be updated during an APPEND.

Index files are structured as B+ trees, which are generalizations of the binary trees discussed at the end of Lab 4.3-1. The command for locating data with index files is FIND, used as follows:

```
. USE LOCKS INDEX LOCKHOLD<cr>
. FIND SMITH<cr>
```

(Note that quotation marks are not used around SMITH.) For very large files, FIND is considerably faster than LOCATE.

Step 11.   The DELETE command. Suppose we want to delete record #3. Type the following:

```
. USE LOCKS<cr>
. DELETE RECORD 3<cr>
. LIST<cr>
```

You'll now see an asterisk attached to record #3. This indicates that it has been marked as deleted. We can still recall this record if we decide that we have made an error. This can be done with the command RECALL RECORD 3. At some point, however, we may want to permanently remove records marked with * from the database. This can be done with the command PACK. This removes all records previously marked for deletion by an asterisk, and "packs" the remaining records together into a smaller database.

Step 12.   The REPORT command can be used to retrieve parts of databases and display them in a "prettied up" format. There are two stages involved in using REPORT. The first time it is used with a particular file (e. g., LOCKS), the user will be prompted for margins, column widths, and headings to be used when printing out information from LOCKS.DBF. This information will be stored as a file with the extension .FRM. See Fig. 4-29 for an example of the dialogue that takes place during the first stage. (Note that the <cr> after ENTER OPTIONS . . . indicates that we will use the default values. The other responses are as shown.) Once the report format .FRM file has been defined for a particular database, you can use the command REPORT in some of its other variations. One of these is to include an expression which searches for and includes only records fulfilling a conditional expression. At these times, the format stored in the format file can be re-used, so you don't have to go through the first stage again.

Step 13.   When you're ready to quit a session and leave dBASE II, use the command QUIT. This will return you to CP/M. Type DIR to examine your new files. Notice that all dBASE II files created by dBASE II have the extension .DBF. You can single out these filenames by typing:

>   A>DIR "*.DBF"<cr>
>   LOCKS   DBF : TEMP   DBF

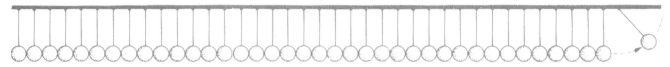

Additional Features

This lab has only touched on the basic capabilities of dBASE II. The system has many other features, including a private programming language (dBASE calls it a command language). It's also possible to store collections of commonly used commands as .CMD (command) files. These files are actually computer programs, so writing and testing them takes programming know-how.

One important use of .CMD files is to produce "turnkey" dBASE systems. For example, one could write a .CMD file that makes a dBASE application look like a simple menu-driven system to an untrained user.

Fig. 4-30 shows an example of such a .CMD file, while Photo 4-28 shows the interaction it produces when used by a non-technical operator.

```
***********************************************************
*        KEYMENU.CMD (DATABASE SYSTEM FOR KEY CONTROL)    *
***********************************************************

TYPE THE LETTER FOR THE COMMAND YOU WISH:

    H   = RETRIEVE RECORDS BY NAME OF HOLDER
    K   = RETRIEVE RECORDS BY KEY NUMBER
    A   = ADD NEW RECORDS
    C   = CHANGE EXISTING RECORDS
    P   = PRINT SUMMARY OF ALL RECORDS
    L   = LIST ALL RECORDS ON CONSOLE
    Q   = QUIT

>>>>>>>  TYPE H,K,A,C,L,P, OR Q WHEN READY  <<<<<<<
WAITING H
TYPE LAST NAME OF HOLDER ($$ TO RETURN TO MENU):SMITH
00001  G34567      AL344,AL345,AL351    SMITH, GEORGE        10/2/83    3.00 LST

00003  F23456      AL123,AL124          SMITH, ALVA          10/18/83   4.25 ACT

00004  D58693      AL331,AL332          SMITH, P. GEORGE     10/15/83   5.50 ACT

TYPE LAST NAME OF HOLDER ($$ TO RETURN TO MENU):_
```

PHOTO 4-28   *Screen display produced by KEYMENU.CMD.*

```
A>TYPE KEYMENU.CMD
SET TALK OFF
USE LOCKS
ERASE
STORE ´ ´ TO CHOICE
DO WHILE !(CHOICE) <> ´Q´
?´***********************************************************´
?´*         KEYMENU.CMD (DATABASE SYSTEM FOR KEY CONTROL)        *´
?´***********************************************************´
?
?´TYPE THE LETTER FOR THE COMMAND YOU WISH:´
?
?´   H   = RETRIEVE RECORDS BY NAME OF HOLDER´
?´   K   = RETRIEVE RECORDS BY KEY NUMBER´
?´   A   = ADD NEW RECORDS´
?´   C   = CHANGE EXISTING RECORDS´
?´   P   = PRINT SUMMARY OF ALL RECORDS´
?´   L   = LIST ALL RECORDS ON CONSOLE´
?´   Q   = QUIT´
?
?´>>>>>>>  TYPE H,K,A,C,L,P, OR Q WHEN READY  <<<<<<<´
WAIT TO CHOICE
  IF CHOICE=´H´ .OR. CHOICE=´h´
    DO KHLDR
  ELSE
    IF CHOICE=´K´ .OR. CHOICE=´k´
      DO KNUM
    ELSE
      IF CHOICE=´A´ .OR. CHOICE=´a´
        DO KADD
      ELSE
        IF CHOICE=´C´ .OR. CHOICE=´c´
          DO KCHANGE
        ELSE
          IF !(CHOICE) = ´L´
            DO KLIST
          ELSE
            IF CHOICE=´P´ .OR. CHOICE=´p´
              DO KPRINT
            ELSE
              IF !(CHOICE)=´Q´
                @ 21,0 SAY ´>>>>> PROGRAM QUITTING <<<<<´
                @ 22,0 SAY ´PRESS ANY KEY TO RETURN TO DBASE´
                WAIT TO DUMMY
              ENDIF
            ENDIF
          ENDIF
        ENDIF
      ENDIF
    ENDIF
  ENDIF
ERASE
ENDDO

A>
```

FIG. 4-30 This figure shows the dBASE command file KEYMENU.CMD. To use it, the command

> A>DBASE KEYMENU

is used from CP/M, or the command

> .DO KEYMENU

is given from dBASE. The result is to produce a menu from which the user selects a simple one-letter command. Depending on which letter is typed, one of the auxiliary command files is executed. These are shown in the listing as KHLDR, KNUM, KADD, KCHANGE, KLIST, and KPRINT. Command files are usually created with the non-document mode of a word processor, but they can also be created with the dBASE Command .MODIFY COMMAND KEYMENU. Incidentally, tests for upper- and lowercase such as IF CHOICE = 'H' .OR. CHOICE = 'h' can be abbreviated as IF !(CHOICE) = 'H'.

210

```
A>TYPE KHLDR.CMD
STORE ´ ´ TO HLDR
DO WHILE HLDR <> ´$$´
   ACCEPT ´TYPE LAST NAME OF HOLDER ($$ TO RETURN TO MENU)´ TO HLDR
   DISPLAY FOR HOLDER=HLDR
ENDDO
RETURN




A>TYPE KNUM.CMD
STORE ´ ´ TO HLDR
DO WHILE HLDR <> ´$$´
      ACCEPT ´TYPE KEY NUMBER OF HOLDER ($$ TO QUIT)´ TO HLDR
      DISPLAY FOR SERIAL:NUM = HLDR
ENDDO
RETURN




A>TYPE KADD.CMD
ERASE
? ´*** YOU HAVE CHOSEN TO ADD RECORDS ***´
?
? ´ TYPE THE DATA YOU WISH TO ADD FOR EACH FIELD´
? ´ TYPE  <CR>  TO LEAVE THE FIELD BLANK´
?
? ´ TYPE  <CR> IN FIELD  SERIAL:NUM  TO STOP ADDING NEW RECORDS´
?
? ´_____´
? ´ PRESS ANY KEY WHEN YOU ARE READY TO APPEND´
WAIT
APPEND
RETURN




A>TYPE KCHANGE.CMD
ERASE
?
? ´*** YOU HAVE CHOSEN TO CHANGE A RECORD ***´
?
STORE ´ ´ TO DONE
DO WHILE DONE <> ´$$´
   ?´  TYPE <CR> UNTIL YOU ARRIVE AT THE FIELD TO BE CHANGED´
   ?´  THEN TYPE THE NEW FIELD ENTRY´
   ?´  USE <CR> TO MOVE  TO  OTHER FIELDS TO BE CHANGED.´
   ?´  TYPE CTL-W TO SAVE CHANGES, CTL-Q TO ABANDON CHANGES´
   ?
   ACCEPT ´TYPE SERIAL NUMBER OF KEY ´ TO SNUM
   LOCATE FOR SERIAL:NUM = SNUM
   STORE # TO NUM
   EDIT NUM
   @ 18,0 SAY ´TYPE <CR> TO MAKE MORE CHANGES, $$ TO RETURN TO MENU´
   ACCEPT TO DONE
ENDDO
RETURN




A>TYPE KLIST.CMD
USE LOCKS
STORE 1 TO FLAG
DO WHILE .NOT. EOF .AND. FLAG=1
     ERASE
     DISPLAY NEXT 10
     IF .NOT. EOF
          ?´TYPE <CR> TO SEE NEXT 10 RECORDS,´
          ?´TYPE $$ TO RETURN TO MENU´
          ACCEPT TO HLDR
     ENDIF
     IF HLDR = ´$$´
          STORE 0 TO FLAG
     ENDIF
ENDDO
```

FIG. 4-30 (*continued*)

```
      IF FLAG = 1
            ?´*** THERE ARE NO MORE RECORDS! ***´
            ?´PRESS ANY KEY TO RETURN TO MENU´
            WAIT TO DUMMY
      ENDIF
      RETURN


A>TYPE KPRINT.CMD
ERASE
? ´TYPE  O  TO PRINT THE FILE IN ORIGINAL ORDER´
? ´TYPE  H  TO PRINT THE FILE SORTED BY NAME OF HOLDER´
? ´TYPE  K  TO PRINT THE FILE SORTED BY KEY NUMBER´
WAIT TO ANS
IF !(ANS) = ´H´
      ?´ STAND BY WHILE FILE IS SORTED BY NAME OF HOLDER´
      SORT ON HOLDER TO TEMP
      USE TEMP
ELSE
      IF !(ANS) = ´K´
            ? ´STAND BY WHILE FILE IS SORTED BY KEY NUMBER´
            SORT ON SERIAL:NUM TO TEMP
            USE TEMP
      ENDIF
ENDIF
ERASE
? ´ADJUST PRINTER PAPER TO TOP OF FORM--THEN TYPE <CR>´
WAIT
SET PRINT ON
REPORT FORM KFORM.FRM
SET PRINT OFF
USE LOCKS
RETURN


A>TYPE KFORM.FRM
M=3
Y
********** LOCKS ACCESS **********
N
Y
N
10,SERIAL:NUM
SERIAL #
20,ROOMS
ROOMS ACCESSED
20,HOLDER
NAME OF HOLDER
8,DATE
DATE
7,DEPOSIT
DEPOSIT
Y
6,STATUS
STATUS
```

FIG. 4-30   (continued)

4.4 Electronic Spreadsheets

VisiCalc and Sons—An Old Idea in Micro Clothing

The electronic spreadsheet is one of the most popular applications ever developed for microcomputers. It harnesses the power of the microcomputer to automate many of the time-consuming computational tasks previously done with paper, pencils, and a calculator. It does this by providing an instantly changeable, easily scanned, and machine storable version of the familiar "worksheet" or "spreadsheet" used in business or personal money planning. Words and numbers are taken as input and displayed on a rectangular grid. Each location of the worksheet grid has a unique horizontal and vertical coordinate. The user can store text, numbers, formulas, or special mathematical functions in each such location (also called a *cell*). Movement of the worksheet cursor from one location to another is easy, requiring only simple keystrokes. The console screen acts as a window through which you observe and manipulate the worksheet. Even though the size of this window is limited by the number of characters your console screen can display, most electronic spreadsheet programs provide a large worksheet, usually with at least 50 columns (of variable width) and 250 rows. Needless to say, you can fit a lot of information on a worksheet that size.

In most businesses (and even at home) there are certain worksheets that regularly are prepared weekly, monthly, quarterly, or annually. The form of the worksheets doesn't change, only the specific data for the point in time at which the data is being viewed. The power of the electronic spreadsheet is that you can also define *relationships* between the cells. When the data in one cell is changed, all cells related to the changed data are instantly updated. Here are some simple examples of worksheet applications that could easily benefit from the use of an electronic spreadsheet program:

1. Price Lists. Many businesses issue price lists to their customers. However, in our age of high inflation, these lists may quickly go out of date. While one can update these lists using a word processing program, someone needs to calculate and input the changed prices to the word processor. An electronic spreadsheet program can make a percentage increase in all the prices at once. Also, some electronic spreadsheet programs produce files that are easily merged with text files during word processing. Thus, once the required changes are made, it is a simple matter to integrate the updated worksheet into the other text (e. g., into a management report).

2. Standard Cost Worksheets. Many manufacturing companies maintain standard cost records for their inventory items. These standard costs are calculated based on material, labor, and overhead factors. Obviously, these factors can change over time with vendors raising prices and labor contracts being renegotiated. An electronic spreadsheet program can easily update these worksheets as the new data becomes available.

3. Cash Flow Projection. Almost everyone has to monitor their available cash. We juggle the timing of the payment of our bills either to maximize our investment income or to keep our creditors at bay (or both!). With an electronic spreadsheet program a model can easily be developed which can help you determine how much cash you have available (or need) to pay your bills at any point in time. If you want to see the

effect of "juggling" your bill payments, it can be as simple as pressing a few keys.

4. Combining Worksheets. Certain businesses may own other businesses or may operate in various locations. In order to see how the business as a whole is performing, combined worksheets can be easily prepared with most electronic spreadsheet programs.

5. Another major use of electronic spreadsheet programs is to do "what if . . ." analysis. Almost all business decisions depend on a series of assumptions. While the assumptions underlying a certain decision seem reasonable, as a responsible decision maker you may want to test the impact of those assumptions. For example:

    a. The new budget assumes that the revenues will increase by 10 percent, but costs will increase by only 6 percent. What would be the impact on net income if costs increased by 9 percent instead?

    b. You are considering borrowing money to buy a new piece of machinery that will increase your productive capacity. What impact would a 3 percent increase in the prime rate have on the feasibility of the project?

    c. You are considering opening an office in a new territory. The income projections would normally indicate that you should move ahead. In order to be conservative, you might want to know what the impact of a slower sales growth rate assumption would be. Electronic spreadsheets allow you to experiment with as many of these assumptions as you wish.

The actual types of analysis that can be performed under an electronic spreadsheet program are limited only by your imagination and the functions that have been built into the electronic spreadsheet program. While these functions will vary from program to program, a typical list might be the following: simple arithmetic, maximum, minimum, counting data items, sums of rows or columns, averages, square roots, absolute value, logarithm (base 10), natural logarithm, net present value, Pi, trigonometric functions, logical operators, and regression.

The earliest on the market, and still most widely known, electronic spreadsheet program is VisiCalc. VisiCalc (and its "extended family" of programs—VisiPlot, VisiTrend, etc.) run on the Apple II and III computers. VisiCalc in its latest revision includes most of the above features and offers a 63-column by 254-row worksheet. The main problem with VisiCalc was its "one machine" limitation (it does not run under CP/M). Luckily, free enterprise has been at work and there are a number of imitators (or if you prefer, competitive improvers) now available for CP/M systems. To see what a session with a CP/M electronic spreadsheet is like, we'll look at one of the best known of these, SuperCalc Version 1.0 by SORCIM [30].

Note: In the following discussion, the convention <key name> will be used to signify pressing a key, whenever it might be confused with the text. ^A will mean press the control key simultaneously while typing A.

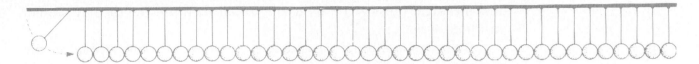

**LAB EXERCISE
4.4-1**

A Consolidating Worksheet Using SuperCalc

We'll assume that you have already installed SuperCalc on your system (tailoring it to your specific console), and have backed up this version onto one or more disks, and that you are using one of your backups for your first experiment, not the original disk.

Step 1. Boot CP/M with SuperCalc present on the disk in drive A. Another disk for storing files resulting from SuperCalc's work can be used in drive B. Type SC<cr>. An informational display will appear on your screen and you will have a choice of calling up some "help" information or going directly to the SuperCalc worksheet display.

Press <?> to see the help message. This message summarizes certain prefix keystrokes and describes the cursor movement keys. You can see similar messages while using SuperCalc by pressing a special key (on the Z19 terminal this is the red key) or by pressing <?>. After reading

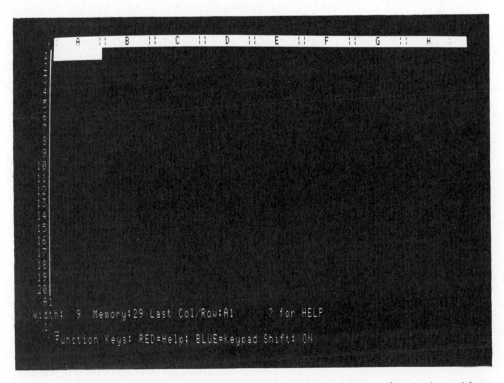

PHOTO 4-29   The SuperCalc worksheet screen at the beginning of a session with no data yet typed in, or read from a file.

this message, press <cr> to go on. You'll then see the display shown in Photo 4-29.

Columns A through H and rows 1 through 20 are visible on the screen. The cell at coordinate A1 is highlighted (math readers should note that what SuperCalc calls "coordinate A1" is really the *pair* (A,1) of coordinates.) This is the "active coordinate" where the "worksheet cursor" is located. This cell is usually the location or destination of any data that we are working with. The cursor can be moved to any coordinate on the worksheet by using the cursor movement keys. Some terminals have arrow keys which can move the cursor, but you can also use ^D, ^S, ^E, and ^X where ^D moves the cursor right one coordinate, ^S moves it left one coordinate, ^E moves it up one row, and ^X moves it down one row.

Note: There are actually two cursors on the screen: the large worksheet cursor and the "mini-cursor" on the edit line. The latter will be explained in step 5.

Step 2.   Experiment with worksheet cursor movement by using control keys or arrow keys. Note that when you move to the right past column H, the screen "scrolls" right one column (column I appears while column A disappears). Also note that when you "scroll" down past row 20, row 21 appears and row 1 disappears. If you continue scrolling, you'll find that the worksheet actually has 63 columns and 254 rows.

The 80-character by 24-row screen display found on most consoles acts as a "window" on the actual 63 by 254 worksheet. Each column of the worksheet has a default width of 9 characters (although this can be changed with the /F command). Thus the window can display only 8 columns at a time. It displays only 20 rows, allowing room for labels at the top, and 3 entry/prompt lines at the bottom.

You may be asking yourself, "Isn't there a faster way to move the cursor?" Indeed there is! The program authors have a "go to" command which accomplishes just that. Type <=>. The prompt line now reads "Enter cell to jump to". Type Z28<cr>. You will note that coordinate Z28 has now scrolled to the top left of your screen. The <=> command is a good way to move around your worksheet quickly. Type <=> A1 to return to coordinate A1.

Step 3.   Notice the three lines of information at the bottom of your screen. The top line is the active coordinate and worksheet cursor "status line." SuperCalc uses this line to give you information about certain functions. The first character (^, V, <, or >) indicates the direction the cursor will move when you hit <cr>. Next the address of the active coordinate is shown, and finally, the contents of the active cell (if any) is displayed. The second line is the prompt line, or "secondary status line." It displays the column width of the active coordinate, the available memory, and indicates the last filled cell of your current application. Since we have not started our model, this indicator shows A1. The bottom line is the entry line. It displays a 1> at the left margin, meaning, "Start typing at position 1." This line allows you to communicate with the SuperCalc program. It acts as a scratchpad where you type data, commands, or responses to prompt messages. It also allows you to check and edit the data or commands you have typed before committing them to the worksheet by pressing <cr>.

Step 4.   In order to become familiar with the SuperCalc commands, press </>, the command prefix. You will see the list of letters:

B,C,D,E,F,G,I,L,M,O,P,Q,R,S,T,U,W,Z,?

These letters represent the various SuperCalc commands. Type <?> to look at the "help" display which gives brief descriptions of these commands. The command "help" display is shown in Photo 4-30.

The SuperCalc manual has a detailed explanation of how to use each of the these commands which you would ordinarily study before

```
        SuperCalc Commands :

B(lank)------>Removes contents of cells.
C(opy)------->Copies contents of cells.
D(elete)----->Deletes entire row or column.
E(dit)------->Allows editing the contents of a cell.
F(ormat)----->Change display format of cells, rows,
                  or entire worksheet.
G(lobal)----->Change global display or calculation options.
I(nsert)----->Create new row or column.
L(oad)------->Read worksheet (or portion) from disk.
M(ove)------->Swap rows or columns.
O(utput)----->Display contents or values of cells on printer,
                  console or disk.
P(rotect)---->Prevent future alteration of cells.
Q(uit)------->Exit SuprCalc.
R(eplicate)->Reproduce partial rows or columns.
S(ave)------->Write worksheet to disk.
T(itle)------>Lock first rows or columns against scrolling.
U(nprotect)->Allow alteration of protected cells.
W(indow)----->Split or unsplit the screen display.
Z(ap)-------->Clear worksheet and all settings.
-

      Function Keys: RED=Help; BLUE=Keypad Shift: ON
```

PHOTO 4-30   *This is the command "help display" of SuperCalc. There are similar displays for most of the other modes of SuperCalc.*

using the worksheet. Our lab will not use all the commands or built-in functions of SuperCalc shown on this list, but you can get some idea of SuperCalc's capabilities from it. To return to the worksheet display, press <backspace><backspace>.

Step 5. We are now ready to start building our worksheet. This will be a combining worksheet which summarizes the revenues, expenses, and net income for Octopus, Inc. and Subsidiaries for January, 1982. Octopus has five subsidiaries in different lines of business. This worksheet will combine the results for the subsidiaries with those of the corporate office to derive consolidated totals.

Move the cursor to C1 and type the following: "Octopus,<cr>. The " is required because this is the way SuperCalc identifies the data as text, instead of numbers or formulas. Enter two more lines of text by placing "Inc. in C2, and "Consolidated in C3.

You may wonder what to do if you make a typing error. If you have not yet pressed <cr> you can move the "mini-cursor" on the edit line back and forth with the cursor motion keys. You move the "mini-cursor" to the position you want to correct and then type normally. The corrected version replaces the previous text automatically. Cursor motion keys for up can be used to insert a space, and for down to delete a space. When you are done, press <cr> and the corrected data will be entered in the cell at which the main cursor was located.

Previously entered data can be corrected by overwriting a cell with new data. A fancier approach is to move the cursor to the cell you wish to correct, and then type the command /E<cr>. This puts you in edit mode, and prompts: From? Enter Cell. Press <cr> and you'll see the contents of the current cell on the edit line. You can now use the mini-cursor to make corrections as above.

Step 6. You will notice that the text is left justified. While this may be OK for our categories later on, the column heading would probably look better if it were right justified. We can adjust this easily with the format command. Type /FR3<cr>. This means format row 3. You will see the following choices:

I,G,E,$,R,L,TR,TL,*,D

These represent the format choices available, namely,

I	= Integer	L	= Left justify (values)
G	= General	TR	= Text right justify
E	= Exponential	TL	= Text left justify
$	= Dollars and cents	*	= Graphic format
R	= Right justify (values)	D	= Default

Since we want to have our text right justified, type TR<cr>. Repeat the right justification process for rows 1 and 2.

You will now see that, while the status line shows that the contents of C3 are "Consolidated," several letters are cut off in the worksheet display. This is because our column is not wide enough. In order to change the column width from the default value of 9, use the following command sequence: /FG13<cr>. This means "format on a global basis" the column width to 13 characters. (You can also adjust the column width of individual columns if you want to.)

Step 7. We're now ready to add more information to our spreadsheet. Using Fig. 4-31 as a guide, input the text shown for rows one, two and three, using cursor movement keys, typing in the text, and using commands to edit where necessary. Notice that rows one, two, and three have right justified text.

Step 8. Move the cursor to D1. You will see that column D reads "Minnow Marketing, Inc." The other four subsidiaries are also incorporated and should have "Inc." in their titles. Instead of entering text in each of these coordinates, we can use the replicate command to duplicate this text in the required locations. Type /R and you will see the following message: "From?(Enter Range)". Type D3<cr> and you will see the following message:

To?(Enter Range), then Return; or "," for Options

Type E3:H3<cr> and instantly the "Inc." appears in cells E3 through H3. Pretty neat, don't you think?

Step 9. Now enter the text as shown in Fig. 4-31 for the A column. At this point we have the outlines of our worksheet. To make it easier to understand, we may want to put some lines (and double lines) to show the groupings more clearly. Go to C9 and type the following: '-<cr>. The ' is the designation for repeating text. What the command does is repeat the text entered, which in this case is a - symbol, giving us a dashed line.

As you look at the screen, you may wonder why the line extends all the way across the screen when you typed this command into cell C9. In fact, much of the text in column A appears to go beyond the end of the column. The reason for this is that the authors of SuperCalc provided the feature that text entered in one cell can extend beyond that cell, provided that the adjacent cell is blank, which in this case it is. This is actually a great convenience because the user doesn't have to figure out how much text can be typed into a column with its related column width.

Now that you know how to draw a line with repeating text, draw lines at rows 18, 21, and 25 and a double line at row 27 (Hint: use <=> for double lines).

	A	B	C	D	E	F	G	H	I
			Octopus, Inc., Consolidated	Minnow Marketing Inc.	Goldfish Coins	Flounder Finance	Marlin Brands	Jonah Interiors	Octopus Corporate Office
4	REVENUES								
5	Merchandise Revenues			100000	55000		1250000		
6	Professional Fees					500000		750000	179500
7	Interest Income				.				
8	Other Income			5000	500	10000	25000	1500	30000
9				-------	-------	-------	-------	-------	-------
10	Total Revenues								
11									
12	EXPENSES								
13	Cost Of Goods Sold			20000	30000		750000	450000	
14	Selling Expenses			5000	3000	10000	50000	35000	
15	General and Admini-			15000	7000	35000	75000	50000	750000
16	strative Expenses								
17	Interest Expenses			3000	1500	400000	15000	10000	
18				-------	-------	-------	-------	-------	-------
19	Total Expenses								
20									
21									
22	Pretax Income								
23									
24	Income Taxes @ 46 %								
25									
26	Net Income			-------	-------	-------	-------	-------	-------
27				=======	=======	=======	=======	=======	=======
28									
29									
30									

FIG. 4-31 SuperCalc printout of the partially completed worksheet after doing steps 1 to 12 of this lab.

Step 10.   Move the cursor to I1. You will see that our lines move far beyond column I. The reason for this is that all cells in the rows which have the repeating text, except for the cells in column A, are blank. In order to stop the lines in column I, move the cursor to J9 and type "<cr>. This inserts blank text into location J9, halting the repeating feature. Adjust the lines in rows 18, 21, 25, and 27, using the same technique. Then move the cursor back to A1.

Step 11.   Well, our worksheet has started to take shape. We now have our companies and revenue and expense categories entered. We are almost ready to enter data. Wouldn't it be easier to do this if we could keep the column headings and revenue and expense labels on the screen as we entered data? The SuperCalc authors thought of this and have supplied a "title lock" command. Move the cursor to C4 and type /T. You will see the following message:

H(oriz.), V(ert.), B(oth), or C(lear)?

This offers the choice of locking the horizontal and/or vertical titles to the left and above the cursor. Type B for both. Move the cursor around the worksheet to see if the titles remain as you scroll. Very nice.

Step 12.   Now enter the numeric data in the cells as shown in Fig. 4-31. Note that you do *not* use <"> to begin numeric data or formulas.

Step 13.   Obviously, we want totals for revenues, expenses, etc. Instead of using a calculator, we can use SuperCalc to provide our totals. Use the <=> goto command to move the cursor to A1 to obtain a good overview of the worksheet, and then move the cursor to D10 and type SUM(D5:D8)<cr>. This command asks that the total of the values in cells D5 through D8 be calculated and the result displayed at cell D10. Notice that the total instantly appears at the worksheet cursor location even though the status line shows that the contents of that location has really become a formula. We can now replicate this formula to the other columns. Type /R and you will see a familiar prompt:

From?(Enter Range)

Type D10<cr>, and you will see the next prompt:

To?(Enter Range), then Return; or "," for Options

Type E10:I10 followed by a *comma*, and you will see another prompt:

N(o Adjust.), A(sk for Adjust.), V(alues)

These choices ask whether you want your function to be copied *exactly* as entered in cell D10, or whether you want the function to use other values which are in the same *relative* location for the cells into which you copy the formula. Since we want column E totals to be comprised of E values, column F of F values, and so on, type A and you will see the prompt:

Adjust D5?

Type Y for yes and you will see the prompt:

Adjust D8?

Type Y again and you will see the totals for columns E through I instantly appear. Now that's fast!!

If the comma had not been typed after E10:I10 in response to the R command, SuperCalc would have assumed that all calculations were to be relative. Thus a short cut for the preceding responses would have been to type E10:I10<cr>.

Our example produced sums of columns of numbers. Sums of rows can be produced in a similar manner. For example, to add up the merchandise revenues in row 10, goto C10 and type SUM(D10:I10). This calculates the sum of the amounts in row 10 for columns D through I, and places the result in C10.

Now that we have learned to use the SUM function with the replicate command, use SuperCalc to calculate the expense totals in row 19 and the consolidated totals in column C. When you are done your worksheet should look like Fig. 4-32.

Step 14.   In order to calculate pretax income, we subtract the expense totals (row 19) from the revenue totals (row 10). To do this, at cell D22 type D10-D19. Then replicate this formula across the line, making adjustments for the relative locations. Pretax income totals should appear in columns E through J.

You may be wondering why the consolidated total changes as you add values to the columns to the right. The reason is that SuperCalc starts calculating at the top left and proceeds across the worksheet column by column or row by row (you can choose which way you prefer). Since the consolidated total was calculated *before* the totals for the subsidiaries, SuperCalc uses the values it has available, some of which were zero at that time. In order to force a recalculation, type <!> and the correct consolidated total will appear.

Step 15.   Income taxes are calculated as 46 percent of pretax income. Type .46*D22 into location D24. (*, /, +, and - mean mutliply, divide, add, and subtract.) Then replicate this formula from column E through column I. Net income is the result of pretax income less income taxes. Type D22-D24 into location D26. Then replicate this formula from column E through column I. Recalculate consolidated totals by typing <!>; then move the cursor to A1, using the "go to" command.

	A	B	C Octopus, Inc. Consolidated	D Minnow Marketing Inc.	E Goldfish Coins Inc.	F Flounder Finance Inc.	G Marlin Brands Inc.	H Jonah Interiors Inc.	I Octopus Corporate Office
1									
2									
3									
4	REVENUES								
5	Merchandise Revenues		1305000	100000	55000		1250000		
6	Professional Fees		850000			500000		750000	179500
7	Interest Income		679500	5000	500	10000	25000	1500	30000
8	Other Income		72000						
9									
10	Total Revenues		2906500	105000	55500	510000	1275000	751500	209500
11									
12	EXPENSES								
13	Cost Of Goods Sold		1250000	20000	30000		750000	450000	
14	Selling Expenses		103000	5000	3000	10000	50000	35000	
15	General and Admini-		932000	15000	7000	35000	75000	50000	750000
16	strative Expenses								
17	Interest Expenses		429500	3000	1500	400000	15000	10000	
18									
19	Total Expenses		2714500	43000	41500	445000	890000	545000	750000
20									
21									
22	Pretax Income		0						
23									
24	Income Taxes @ 46 %		0						
25									
26	Net Income		0						
27									
28									
29									
30									

FIG. 4-32 SuperCalc printout of the worksheet with all but three values completed.

Step 16.   Congratulations! You have just completed your first combining worksheet. In order to "pretty it up" a little, you may want to head up the worksheet with an appropriate title. How can we do this when we already have data in row one? The SuperCalc authors thoughtfully provided the insert (and delete) commands. Type /I and you will see the following prompt:

> R(ow), C(olumn)?

Type R and the next prompt asks for the row number where you want to insert the new row. Type 1<cr> and you will see a new line appear. Repeat this process until there are four blank rows above the column headings. Then type the text shown at the top of Fig. 4-33.

Incidentally, when you insert or delete lines, the "names" of the rows or columns beyond the insertion/deletion point are automatically changed. SuperCalc then re-indexes all previous data and formulas for the new names. Thus its calculations still provide you with correct results relative to the new row/column names.

Step 17.   We are now ready to obtain a "hard copy" of our worksheet. In order to print our worksheet we need to know the coordinates where we want to start and stop our printing. Our worksheet starts at location A1 and ends at location I31. However, when we print out the worksheet, we probably won't want the co-ordinate references along the border to show up. We can suppress these with the command /GB, which switches the border references off (and on). Next type the command /O, for output. The message

> D(isplay) or C(ontents) report?

will appear. Supposing you type D, the message "Enter Range" will appear, at which point you should type A1:I31. After you type P for printer, your report will be printed out. It should look like Fig. 4-33.

In case you want to study the formulas used to produce this report or explain it to someone else, you can print the formulas using the C(ontents) option mentioned above. This will produce a list of the worksheet contents, including text and formulas. You can also produce a hard copy display of the formulas in place with all the other values in the worksheet. This is done by using the command /GF to switch the formulas on before printing using the D(isplay) option. In this case you would very likely want to have the coordinates on the borders switched on, too (using/GB). Such a worksheet would look very much like the screen display. The formula display for our worksheet is shown in Fig. 4-34.

Step 18.   Now that we have our worksheet completed we should save it for future reference (or in case changes need to be made later). In order to save a worksheet, type /S. The prompting message on page 227 will appear:

Octopus Inc. and Subsidiaries
Consolidated Income Statement
As of January 31,1982

	Octopus, Inc., Consolidated	Minnow Marketing Inc.	Goldfish Coins Inc.	Flounder Finance Inc.	Marlin Brands Inc.	Jonah Interiors Inc.	Octopus Corporate Office
REVENUES							
Merchandise Revenues	1305000		55000		1250000		
Professional Fees	850000	100000				750000	
Interest Income	679500			500000			179500
Other Income	72000	5000	500	10000	25000	1500	30000
Total Revenues	2906500	105000	55500	510000	1275000	751500	209500
EXPENSES							
Cost Of Goods Sold	1250000	20000	30000		750000	450000	
Selling Expenses	103000	5000	3000	10000	50000	35000	
General and Admini-strative Expenses	932000	15000	7000	35000	75000	50000	750000
Interest Expenses	429500	3000	1500	400000	15000	10000	
Total Expenses	2714500	43000	41500	445000	890000	545000	750000
Pretax Income	192000	62000	14000	65000	385000	206500	-540500
Income Taxes @ 46 %	88320	28520	6440	29900	177100	94990	-248630
Net Income	103680	33480	7560	35100	207900	111510	-291870

FIG. 4-33   SuperCalc printout of a consolidated worksheet, with coordinates turned off.

Octopus Inc. and Subsidiaries
Consolidated Income Statement
As of January 31,1982

	A	B	C	D	E	F	G	H	I
			Octopus, Inc., Consolidated	Minnow Marketing Inc.	Goldfish Coins Inc.	Flounder Finance Inc.	Marlin Brands Inc.	Jonah Interiors Inc.	Octopus Corporate Office
8	REVENUES								
9	Merchandise Revenues		SUM(D9:I9)	55000	30000		1250000		
10	Professional Fees		SUM(D10:I10)	100000				750000	
11	Interest Income		SUM(D11:I11)			500000			179500
12	Other Income		SUM(D12:I12)	5000	500	10000	25000	1500	30000
14	Total Revenues		SUM(D14:I14)	SUM(D9:D12)	SUM(E9:E12)	SUM(F9:F12)	SUM(G9:G12)	SUM(H9:H12)	SUM(I9:I12)
16	EXPENSES								
17	Cost Of Goods Sold		SUM(D17:I17)	20000	30000		750000	450000	
18	Selling Expenses		SUM(D18:I18)	5000	3000	10000	50000	35000	
19	General and Admini-strative Expenses		SUM(D19:I19)	15000	7000	35000	75000	50000	750000
21	Interest Expenses		SUM(D21:I21)	3000	1500	400000	15000	10000	
23	Total Expenses		SUM(D23:I23)	SUM(D17:D21)	SUM(E17:E21)	SUM(F17:F21)	SUM(G17:G21)	SUM(H17:H21)	SUM(I17:I21)
26	Pretax Income		SUM(D26:I26)	+D14-D23	+E14-E23	+F14-F23	+G14-G23	+H14-H23	+I14-I23
28	Income Taxes @ 46 %		SUM(D28:I28)	.46*D26	.46*E26	.46*F26	.46*G26	.46*H26	.46*I26
30	Net Income		SUM(D30:I30)	+D26-D28	+E26-E28	+F26-F28	+G26-G28	+H26-H28	+I26-I28

FIG. 4-34 SuperCalc printout of a consolidated worksheet, with the option of displaying both the coordinates and the formulas.

Enter filename (or <RETURN> for directory)

Since this is a new file, we can assign it a filename. Type B:OCTOPUS1<cr>. The next prompt will read:

A(ll) or V(alues)

This allows you the choice of saving the worksheet with or without the formulas. Type A<cr>. Your worksheet is now saved on the disk in drive B under the filename OCTOPUS1.

Step 19.   Now to show the real power of SuperCalc in preparing recurring worksheets, we will use the worksheet we created to develop a master worksheet for use in future months. This master worksheet will contain the formulas but no numerical data. Next month when this worksheet is needed, all you need to do is load the master worksheet, enter your data for the month, and SuperCalc will automatically consolidate the new data and print your reports. This is, of course, quite a timesaver.

In order to create the master worksheet we will use the "blank" command to erase the numerical data for January. Before we do this, we will want to protect our labels and formulas to make sure we don't accidently erase them and then need to reenter the data. This is done with the protect command. Type /P and you will see the prompt "Enter Range". Type A5:C31<cr> and you will have protected all of your category labels as well as your consolidated total formulas. Use the protect command to protect the other formulas, column headings, and the report title.

To use the "blank" command, type /B and you will be prompted for a range of coordinates. Since we have safely protected all the items we want to save (we hope), type A1:I31<cr>. Your worksheet should now look like Fig. 4-35, ready for the next month's data. Save this worksheet under the filename OCTOPUSM (for Octopus Master) using the commands described previously.

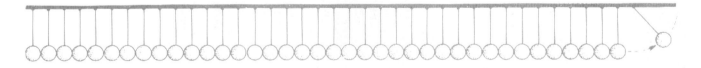

Other Electronic Worksheets. Are the "High-Priced Spreads" Worth It?

A large variety of spreadsheet programs with a large variety of price tags are now available, with features that may be inferior or superior to those we've discussed. The granddaddy of all spreadsheets was first developed by Personal Software (now VisiCorp) under the name VisiCalc (which is why the many similar programs developed since are sometimes

	A	B	C	D	E	F	G	H	I
1	=	=	=	= || Octopus Inc. and Subsidiaries || =	= || = || = || = || =
2					Consolidated Income Statement				
3									
4									
5			Octopus,	Minnow	Goldfish	Flounder	Marlin	Jonah	Octopus
6			Inc.,	Marketing	Coins	Finance	Brands	Interiors	Corporate
7			Consolidated	Inc.	Inc.	Inc.	Inc.	Inc.	Office
8	REVENUES								
9	Merchandise Revenues		SUM(D9:I9)						
10	Professional Fees		SUM(D10:I10)						
11	Interest Income		SUM(D11:I11)						
12	Other Income		SUM(D12:I12)						
13									
14	Total Revenues		SUM(D14:I14)	SUM(D9:D12)	SUM(E9:E12)	SUM(F9:F12)	SUM(G9:G12)	SUM(H9:H12)	SUM(I9:I12)
15									
16	EXPENSES								
17	Cost Of Goods Sold		SUM(D17:I17)						
18	Selling Expenses		SUM(D18:I18)						
19	General and Admini-		SUM(D19:I19)						
20	strative Expenses								
21	Interest Expenses		SUM(D21:I21)						
22									
23	Total Expenses		SUM(D23:I23)						
24									
25									
26	Pretax Income		SUM(D26:I26)	+D14-D23	+E14-E23	+F14-F23	+G14-G23	+H14-H23	+I14-I23
27									
28	Income Taxes @ 46 %		SUM(D28:I28)	.46*D26	.46*E26	.46*F26	.46*G26	.46*H26	.46*I26
29									
30	Net Income		SUM(D30:I30)	+D26-D28	+E26-E28	+F26-F28	+G26-G28	+H26-H28	+I26-I28
31									
32									
33									
34									

FIG. 4-35 SuperCalc printout of master worksheet with only formulas and labels in place.

called visi-clones). Each of the spreadsheet programs now available has its own unique set of advantages and disadvantages. You should carefully consider what you want the electronic spreadsheet to do and find a program that can perform those functions. Do not assume that any electronic spreadsheet program can do anything you want it to!

Although the SuperCalc program illustrated in the lab of this section is similar to VisiCalc, it has several additional features. For example, it produces files that can be easily used with CP/M word processing systems. It can also display worksheets showing all the formulas used and with the border coordinate references displayed. SuperCalc also has many useful "help" menus which provide clues to the meaning of the commands. This minimizes the need to refer to the manual. The column width of individual columns can vary; it is not "locked" into one "global" column width. The "protect" and "unprotect" commands make it easier to create master worksheets. Another convenience is that when typing text, the contents of one cell can extend beyond the cell if no data is entered in the adjacent cells. SuperCalc also has some automatic features that make it easy to work with, such as advancing to the next occupied cell (in a predetermined direction) by pressing <cr>. When printing reports which are wider than the printer width, SuperCalc automatically segments the worksheet and prints it, one section at a time, instead of interleaving lines. Finally, the manual provided by SORCIM is easy to use and provides a good step-by-step tutorial.

Another popular electronic spreadsheet program available for CP/M systems is CalcStar. CalcStar, like WordStar (the word processing system from MicroPro discussed in Section 4.1) has the option of keeping a menu of command clues on display at the top of the screen. It produces files which can be merged with files during word processing. CalcStar, moreover, has regression functions, password protection, and it can center text. It has an automatic forms mode, which helps with the completion of standard worksheets (like detailed fixed asset records and standard cost worksheets). It has a very helpful additional "help" menu. When printing reports, it provides you the opportunity to title the reports when executing the print command instead of inserting the title in the body of the worksheet itself. Like SuperCalc, CalcStar will automatically segment reports which are wider than the printer width. In addition, commands can be inserted which can segment the worksheet into separate pages when the report is being printed.

Memory Space

One problem which is common to all electronic spreadsheet programs is that very large worksheets can quickly use up available RAM working memory. Some spreadsheet programs "bomb out" when you run out of RAM, so data can be lost. For this reason, it makes good sense to save your worksheet at various times as you are working with it. In this way, if the program does fail, you have not lost all the work prepared so far.

Another thing you should consider when purchasing an electronic spreadsheet program is whether the program is "smart enough" to adapt to extra RAM memory you may install. On CP/M systems, most spreadsheet programs will automatically adjust to use all the memory available up to the 64K "address space" limitation of Z80/8080-type processors. To use more memory than this, special bank switching features are needed, but these are usually *not* standard. Whether or not these limitations will apply to future spreadsheets, especially those developed for 16-bit microcomputers with extended memory capabilities remains to be seen. In any case, it will always remain true that the "proof is in the pudding," so direct experience or the reading of good reviews and books that describe these products will still be the best bet for prospective buyers.

4.5 Problems and Projects

1. Research the pros and cons of various word processors. One way to do this is to consult the December (or sometimes January) issues of the personal computing magazines to find references to the software reviews they carry each year. Also look into books on word processing [14] and talk to people who own various brands. The object of this project is to identify the best word processor(s) for your needs. You'll also want to find out something about the service you can expect from the companies you select. A $400 word processor disk costs less than $10 to manufacture, so you have a right to expect vendor support. If and when you get it, the extra $390 is money well spent.

2. There are a number of software packages that have been "copy-protected," that is, technical schemes have been used to prevent users from making backup copies. For example, the standard sector formatting scheme used on a particular disk may be deliberately scrambled, so that normal CP/M disk reading programs (e. g., PIP) won't work. The first few tracks are formatted normally so that an "unscrambling" algorithm can be first read into RAM, but after that *it* reads the rest of the disk. Investigate the pros and cons of such methods so that you can formulate your own personal policy with respect to purchasing such software. A "pro" opinion was given by Chris Morgan in the editorial pages of the May 1981 issue of *Byte* [16]. A "con" opinion was given by Jerry Pournelle in the January 1982 issue of *Byte* [16]. One question he raised was how the software copyright issue compares with the book copyright issue, e. g., why it would or would not be a good idea to copy-protect books from photocopying by, for example, printing in light blue ink? By making purchasers sign an agreement of culpability in the event of copying? By using extra fragile paper that could dissolve in the heat of a copying machine?

3. Now that you have been suitably aroused by the copy-protect issue, put yourself in the shoes of a seller of software. How would you handle this problem? (For a unique answer, developed by one vendor, see the first page of the BDS C Compiler manual [20].) If you decide pro, what new unbeatable protection scheme would you come up with? Would it compromise the stability of your software? Alienate potential customers?

If nothing else, answering this question may bring out some of the devious ingenuity you never knew you had.

4. Investigate the availability and usefulness of "disk-repair" utility programs. For a start, send $8 to the CPMUG [8] and order volume number 78. See if you can master the program DDU using an expendable backup disk for your experiments. If you get good at this, consider writing an article and/or short book on the subject. An article by Alan Miller that described a commercial disk-fix program, called BADLIM appeared on page 94 of the June 1982 issue of *Interface Age* [15]. BADLIM can't retrieve lost files, but it marks bad sectors on the disk to prevent errors.

5. Design a small DBMS with the idea that you might eventually write the final program in MBASIC or in C. The projects at the end of Chapter 5 will give you some ideas on implementation, but for now concentrate on what you'd like the interaction with the user to look like. For further information, write to reference [22].

6. Repeat project 5 for a home-brew electronic spreadsheet program.

7. Repeat project 5 for your own simplified word processor.

8. Repeat project 5 for a home financial/tax report system. Preliminary ideas can be found in [2]. A sample solution is available from [22].

CHAPTER FIVE
CP/M Meets BASIC; Programming in C

5.0 Introduction

In this chapter we're going to continue with the subject of using commercial software packages that run under CP/M, putting an emphasis on two of the language processors from category 5 (system software). As before, by "commercial" we'll mean software that is sold (or licensed) by a company whose principal business is the development, maintenance, and continued support of that software.

The first software package we'll discuss is sold or licensed for resale by Microsoft Company of Bellevue, WA. They have a number of products, but the one we'll be concentrating on is an *interpreter* for an extended version of the BASIC language. Like other CP/M compatible software, this interpreter is supplied as a COM (command) file, either on the same disk that contains CP/M, or on a separate disk (in which case you may want to PIP it over to your working CP/M disk). The name of the Microsoft BASIC interpreter file is MBASIC.COM. (If graphics features have been added, it is sometimes called GBASIC.COM). Microsoft also sells a BASIC compiler called BASCOM.COM; this will be discussed in Section 5.5.

MBASIC is a large file (over 24K) and it should be viewed as a major software system in its own right. Its purpose is to help people write their own programs in the language BASIC or, to be technically correct, in the language BASIC-80, also known as disk-extended Microsoft BASIC.

Actually, MBASIC does a lot more than most people realize. It provides what some professionals call a "programming environment." There are four aspects to this environment:

1. It allows you to use the vocabulary and syntax of disk-extended Microsoft BASIC to write computer programs.
2. It allows you to delete or replace individual lines of a program or modify parts of these lines by using a built-in line editor. There are also facilities for renumbering lines and for deleting groups of lines.
3. When you type RUN, it translates your program into machine language instructions on a line-by-line basis, executing each line as soon as it is translated. In the jargon of computer science, this is called "interpreting" the source program (the one you wrote). There are both advantages and disadvantages to using an interpreter. These will be discussed in Section 5.5 where we compare use of the MBASIC interpreter to the BASCOM compiler.

4. It allows you to ask that the program you've just written (and possibly edited) be printed at the console or on a listing device (the commands for doing this are LIST and LLIST, respectively). Even more importantly, it allows you to store a copy of this program on disk for later use (with the command SAVE "filename"). There are also MBASIC commands for deleting files (KILL), displaying the directory (FILES), updating file information when changing disks (RESET), changing filenames (NAME), and returning to CP/M (SYSTEM).

All this is done conveniently without your having to shift back and forth between communicating with CP/M and communicating with MBASIC. You can probably guess, however, that for some of these features (particularly number 4), the MBASIC environment gets the job done by calling upon parts of CP/M.

In this chapter we will look briefly at the vocabulary and syntax of BASIC-80, the disk-extended BASIC language used in the MBASIC environment (Section 5.1). Then we'll discuss a useful file-manipulating BASIC program (Section 5.2). In Sections 5.3 and 5.4 we'll unveil a few surprises, showing how someone who knows CP/M can make use of a few tricks beyond those normally associated with BASIC programming.

TECHNICAL NOTE ON MBASIC OPTIONS UNDER CP/M

Before reading this chapter, you should review Lab Exercise 1.5-1. As noted there, MBASIC is a COM file, so you cause it to execute by typing MBASIC after the A> prompt (if it's on another disk—say B—you'd type A>B:MBASIC). However, there are additional options that can be added to the MBASIC command line as follows:

1. A>MBASIC TAXDEP

This means load and run MBASIC, and then have MBASIC load and run the program TAXDEP.BAS.

2. A>MBASIC /F:4

This means load and run MBASIC, and allocate enough RAM for handling up to 4 data files. If the /F: option is omitted, a default of /F:3 is used. Use of data files is illustrated in Section 5.2.

3. A>MBASIC /M:36864

This means set a limit of 36864 decimal as the highest location that can be used by MBASIC (and any BASIC program you use with it). The memory between 36864 and the start of CP/M (which we assume to be higher than this) is thus protected for other use—say to hold machine language programs (see Chapter 6) or to serve as video output RAM. The memory location in this option can be given in hex by using the form &H9000. If /M: is omitted, all of memory up to BDOS will be used by CP/M. (This is because MBASIC doesn't use the CCP, so it allows you to overwrite it.)

These options can be combined on a single line, as for example,

A>MBASIC PROG4/F:4/M:&H9000

You can now see why you should not use the / character in filenames even though CP/M allows it.

It will turn out that these tricks work for other applications as well. However, they're a bit easier to understand in the context of BASIC programming. Section 5.5 will discuss the relation between BASIC and machine language, and show how to use the BASCOM compiler to translate a BASIC-80 program into a machine language .COM file. Finally (Sections 5.6 and 5.7) we'll introduce you to the computer language C, one of the most interesting newcomers on the programming scene.

5.1 BASIC in a Nutshell

BASIC and extended BASIC are classified as high-level programming languages. That means they're designed so that ideas can be expressed in a form more like the way humans think about problem solving and less like the way computers actually carry out instructions. This human orientation is not always immediately apparent to a first-time user of the language, but many BASIC statements and commands do in fact mean something like the English words they resemble.

The purpose of this section is to briefly explain the most common BASIC statements and commands and give an example of their use in a moderately simple BASIC program. It will not make you into an instant BASIC programmer, but it should give you a pretty good "reading knowledge" of BASIC.

Programming as Data Manipulation

The way computer programs actually do their work, when you boil it all down, is to place certain values in the computer's memory and keep track of them so that they can be changed in precise ways. In programmer lingo this is referred to as "creating and manipulating data structures."

What is a data structure? It's a collection of data that has been organized (structured) in a way that facilitates use of the data. Many kinds of data structures have been developed by computer scientists, but the bottom line is that they are all "high-level" ways of describing the relationships between numbers and/or character strings that have been stored in the computer's memory. The places where they've been stored are called *program variables* since the program can vary (change, manipulate) the contents of these memory locations.

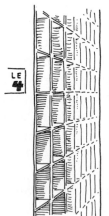

It's helpful to think of the part of the computer's memory where data is located as a very large warehouse with thousands of "bins" in which numbers or strings of characters can be stored. Each bin has a label called a *variable name,* and your program must use this label whenever it wants to reference the bin's contents. The numbers or strings you put into these memory locations are called the "contents" or the "value" of the variable. Whenever you assign a new value to a variable, the old value is destroyed.

Data structures are a way of referring to certain sets of these variables. Just as a warehouse foreman might want to refer to all the storage bins containing "purple widgets" with a single name (like "AISLE P3"), so a programmer might want a simple way to talk about all the memory locations that contain numbers taken from one column in an accountant's journal. This can be done in BASIC with the data structure called an *array*. There are other structures besides arrays (e. g., stacks, linked lists, trees), but in all cases, they are just new ways of talking about the ordinary memory locations used by BASIC.

There are four methods that BASIC uses to get numbers and strings of characters (words, for instance) into the ordinary memory locations of your computer. These correspond to four kinds of BASIC statements that use certain *keywords* as follows: (1) the LET statement assigns a value to a single variable, (2) the READ and DATA statements work together to assign a series of values to variables, (3) the INPUT statement allows a person interacting with the program to type in one or more values which are then assigned to variables, and (4) the FOR statement stores values in special variables to be used as counters that control the number of times some instructions are repeated.

It's easier to understand these statements when they're part of a whole program, so we will start by presenting a program that uses a good selection of these (and other) BASIC keywords and commands. Then we will explain the program in detail on a line-by-line basis.

Program Example 1, ZODIAC

This is a data processing program, but not of the usual business kind. Try to imagine the following situation: You've invited some friends who don't know each other very well to a party, and you think that a computer activity will make a nice ice-breaker. This program will ask each guest in turn for his or her name, month of birth, and day of birth. It will then look up the person's birth sign. After everyone is finished, it will print out a handy list of names and birth signs. Fig. 5-1 shows what the interaction between the person and the machine will look like on the terminal when the program is running.

Now let's look at the BASIC program that was used to make this interaction take place. This is the list of instructions, each one done in turn, that caused the computer to act as it did. Each instruction starts with a line number (chosen by the programmer), and it's written in the form of something called a BASIC *statement*. BASIC statements start with *key words* (like PRINT) and can contain *variable names* (like X), operators (like +, −, *, and /), and constants (like 5, or "JANE"), all put together according to a set of rules called the *syntax* of BASIC.

Before describing how this program works, let's first scan through it and make a list of all the variable names that were used, noting what their values mean in the context of this program.

Reading the meaning of the variable, and then looking at the line number(s) where a value was assigned to it should give you some clue as to what's going on. Take your time, and go over this list carefully. It's the key to understanding the following explanations of what each BASIC statement does. The explanations are in the same order as the lines of the program listing shown in Fig. 5-2.

```
RUN
HOW MANY PEOPLE ARE AT THIS PARTY (TYPE 1-100)? 3
WHAT IS YOUR NAME? ARCHIE
WHAT MONTH WERE YOU BORN IN (TYPE 1-12)? 4
WHAT DAY OF THE MONTH (TYPE 1-31)? 27
HMMMM.... AH YES.  ARCHIE, YOUR SUN SIGN IS TAURUS
NEXT PERSON, PLEASE
WHAT IS YOUR NAME? MELISSA
WHAT MONTH WERE YOU BORN IN (TYPE 1-12)? 7
WHAT DAY OF THE MONTH (TYPE 1-31)? 12
HMMMM.... AH YES.  MELISSA, YOUR SUN SIGN IS CANCER
NEXT PERSON, PLEASE
WHAT IS YOUR NAME? HARRY O.
WHAT MONTH WERE YOU BORN IN (TYPE 1-12)? 11
WHAT DAY OF THE MONTH (TYPE 1-31)? 23
HMMMM.... AH YES.  HARRY O., YOUR SUN SIGN IS SAGITTARIUS
NEXT PERSON, PLEASE
OOPS, SORRY, ALL DONE -- NOW LET'S SEE . . .
THERE ARE  3  PEOPLE AT THIS PARTY, AND
THEIR NAMES AND SIGNS ARE:
ARCHIE          TAURUS
MELISSA         CANCER
HARRY O.        SAGITTARIUS
END OF REPORT
Ok
```

FIG. 5-1   This is a run of the program ZODIAC in which the user answered 3 to the first question. This number was stored in the variable X, and then used in a FOR loop to control how often the remaining questions were asked.

Variable Name	Meaning or Purpose	How BASIC Stores Data There	In Which Line?
X	number of persons	INPUT	40
I	counts from 1 to X	FOR	50,250
PNAME$	person's name	LET,INPUT	60,90
MONTH	month of birth	LET,INPUT	60,110
DAY	day of birth	LET,INPUT	60,130
SIGN$	person's sign	LET,READ	70,150
M1	starting month	LET,READ	70,150
D1	starting day	LET,READ	70,150
M2	ending month	LET,READ	70,150
D2	ending day	LET,READ	70,150
J	counts from 1 to 12	FOR	140
P$( )	array of persons' names	LET	180
Z$( )	array of zodiac signs	LET	180

Line 10   is a remark statement, meant for humans to read. The computer ignores it and goes immediately to the next higher numbered statement. This orderly movement in the execution of the instructions is the way BASIC transfers control from one statement

```
LIST
10   REM    ZODIAC   (EXAMPLE OF LET, INPUT, READ)
20   DIM P$(100),Z$(100)
30   PRINT"HOW MANY PEOPLE ARE AT THIS PARTY (TYPE 1-100)";
40   INPUT X
50   FOR I = 1 TO X
60      LET MONTH=0: LET DAY=0: LET PNAME$=""
70      LET SIGN$="": LET M1=0: LET D1=0: LET M2=0: LET D2=0
80      PRINT"WHAT IS YOUR NAME";
90      INPUT PNAME$
100     PRINT"WHAT MONTH WERE YOU BORN IN (TYPE 1-12)";
110     INPUT MONTH
120     PRINT"WHAT DAY OF THE MONTH (TYPE 1-31)";
130     INPUT DAY
140     FOR J = 1 TO 12
150        READ SIGN$, M1, D1, M2, D2
160        IF MONTH=M1 AND DAY>=D1 OR MONTH=M2 AND DAY<=D2 THEN RESTORE:GOTO 180
170     NEXT J
180     LET P$(I) = PNAME$: LET Z$(I) = SIGN$
190     PRINT"HMMMM.... AH YES.  "P$(I)", YOUR SUN SIGN IS "Z$(I)
200     PRINT"NEXT PERSON, PLEASE"
210  NEXT I
220  PRINT"OOPS, SORRY, ALL DONE -- NOW LET'S SEE . . ."
230  PRINT"THERE ARE "X" PEOPLE AT THIS PARTY, AND"
240  PRINT"THEIR NAMES AND SIGNS ARE:"
250  FOR I = 1 TO X
260     PRINT P$(I),Z$(I)
270  NEXT I
280  PRINT"END OF REPORT"
290  DATA "ARIES",3,21,4,19
300  DATA "TAURUS",4,20,5,20
310  DATA "GEMINI",5,21,6,21
320  DATA "CANCER",6,22,7,22
330  DATA "LEO",7,23,8,22
340  DATA "VIRGO",8,23,9,22
350  DATA "LIBRA",9,23,10,23
360  DATA "SCORPIO",10,24,11,21
370  DATA "SAGITTARIUS",11,22,12,21
380  DATA "CAPRICORN",12,22,1,19
390  DATA "AQUARIUS",1,20,2,18
400  DATA "PISCES",2,19,3,20
410  END
Ok
```

FIG. 5-2   This is a listing of the program ZODIAC. The best way to study it is in conjunction with the line-by-line explanations given in the text.

to another—what's called the "flow of control." The normal flow of control is the same sequence as the line numbers, but this can be changed by the statements themselves (as in line 50 below).

Line 20   is a dimension statement. Variable names with numbers in parentheses after them, for example P$(8), are called *subscripted variables*. A set of such variables, like P$(1), P$(2), . . . P$(100) is an example of the data structure called an *array*. Arrays usually hold data that are related in some way, using one name (but different numbers in parentheses) for different values. It's necessary to reserve space ahead of time for arrays and this dimension statement requests space in memory for up to 100 items in each array.

Line 30   is a print statement. Anything between quotation marks will be printed out just as you type it in.

Line 40   is an input statement. It prints out a question mark and then stops, waiting for the person to respond. When the person types a number and a carriage return, the input statement assigns that value to the variable mentioned in the statement (X, in this case).

Line 50   is a "FOR" statement which, together with a "NEXT" statement in line 210 creates a loop in the flow of control of the program. Notice that lines 60 to 200 are indented. These lines are called the "body of the loop." They will be repeated X times. (The indentations are there just to help humans read the program.) What this "FOR-NEXT loop" does is the following: (1) store a 1 in the variable I, (2) check if the value of I is greater than the value of X, (3a) if not, execute lines 60 to 200; add 1 to the value of I; go back to step 2, (3b) if yes (I is greater than X), transfer control to line 220.

Lines 60   and 70 contain eight assignment statements separated by colons (:). Here the equal sign is used to mean "assign" or "store" the value in the variable. These variables will have their values changed later in the program. Lines 60 and 70 provide them with "initial" or starting values. The double quotation marks mean a "null" string—a string with no characters in it. Variable names used for strings require a dollar sign ($) at the end of the name. In BASIC-80 you are allowed to have several statements on a line, as long as you separate them with colons.

Lines 80   to 130 work similarly to lines 30 and 40. The input statements 90, 110, and 130 store new values in PNAME$, MONTH, and DAY, destroying the old values from line 60.

Lines 140   to 170 are another FOR loop, like lines 50–210. Since this loop is part of the body of the previously described FOR loop, it is said to be "nested" in the other loop. Lines 150 and 160 are the body of this loop. They *may* be repeated as many as 12 times—depending on the decision that is made in line 160 (explained below).

Line 150   is a read statement. It requires that there be some values present in the program in the form of data statements, so READ and DATA go together. Data statements are not executed in turn like other statements. They are there to supply the data needed by read statements. Whenever a value is read from data into a variable, the value is considered "used up"—the next time a variable is read it will be assigned the first "unused" value in the data statement.

Line 160   is the most complex statement in the program, so we'll spend a little time on it. An IF statement makes the program "decide" between one or more alternatives depending on the value of a variable. The alternatives are BASIC statements (or groups of statements). The way this happens is as follows: Appearing just after the IF key word is an expression called the "condition." It's a mathematical-logical statement about some variables, numbers, or strings, and it is always either true or false. If this condition is true, the statement appearing after the THEN key word is executed. If, on the other hand, it's false, that statement is ignored by the computer, and the program continues. In line 160, the condition is long and complicated looking, but it's really just imitating what a person would do when looking at the data and comparing it with the person's input values for month and day of birth. If this compound condition is false, line 170 is

executed, J has 1 added to it, and control is passed to line 140. Line 150 will now read the *next* five data values and line 160 will be executed with these new values. This process will be repeated for all 12 groups of data values—if necessary—but only while the condition is false, that is, until the condition becomes true. This will happen in this example when the data value read into SIGN$ is the person's birth sign, at which time the statements of line 160 after the THEN will be executed. The first of these is RESTORE. This renews all the data so it can be used again (for the next person). It works by resetting a *pointer* back to the beginning of the data. This pointer is used by READ when it needs the next piece of data. The second statement after THEN is GOTO 220 which transfers control out of the loop.

Line 170   is the NEXT statement that works with the FOR statement of line 140. It marks the end of the body of the loop.

Line 180   contains two assignment statements. Because we use the variable I to specify which variable of the P$ array and Z$ array we want to use to store the value of PNAME$ (the person's name) and SIGN$ (the birth sign that was just picked out by the IF statement), P$(1) and Z$(1) will hold the first person's name and sign, P$(2) and Z$(2) will hold the second person's, and so forth.

Line 190   is a print statement that prints both numbers and strings of characters. The values stored in P$(1) and Z$(1) will be printed out first, together with the characters between quotation marks. P$(2) and Z$(2) will be printed next, and so on. In other words, because the program calls these variables P$(I) and Z$(I), the actual variable names (and therefore memory locations) used will depend on the value of I.

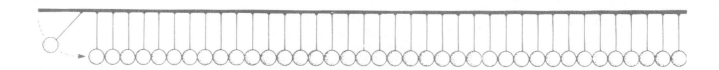

LAB EXERCISE 5.1-1   ZODIAC: A Simple Data Processing Program

The best way to gain familiarity with BASIC is to use it, even if this means imitating and running someone else's program. Do this with the program ZODIAC.

Step 1.   Boot a CP/M disk containing MBASIC and then type A>MBASIC. Enter the program of Fig. 5-2, save it with SAVE "ZODIAC," and then try running it.

Step 2.   If bugs show up, try adding trace statements such as

55 PRINT "LINE 55";SIGN$; M1; D1; M2; D2

to see what values the variables had at line 55. When you have the program running correctly, try modifying and/or extending it. Some ideas on what to try are given in the Problems and Projects section at the end of this chapter.

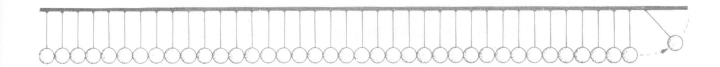

Additional Features of MBASIC

The next section presents an example of a more advanced program using the features of disk-extended BASIC. There are also two references to books on Microsoft BASIC given there, and these will be helpful for those who wish to learn more about the capabilities of BASIC-80. There is a summary of BASIC-80 in Appendix B. For a more complete summary, the book *A Pocket-Guide to Microsoft BASIC* is recommended [31]. This also contains a variety of programs explained on a line-by-line basis.

5.2 Using Random Access Files in MBASIC

Let's review what we've learned so far. To enter the MBASIC programming environment on a CP/M system, all you have to do is type MBASIC after the A> system prompt. (We're assuming that the file MBASIC.COM is stored on the disk in the A drive. If it's on the disk in the B drive, type B:MBASIC after the prompt.) What this does, of course, is load the COM file MBASIC and start it executing.

We've also seen that once in the MBASIC environment, your best bet is to push all the CP/M manuals to the rear of the desk, and bring your books on BASIC front and center. The rules of BASIC are what count at this point; in fact the CP/M commands are no longer available. Of course there *are* interconnections between CP/M and MBASIC, but most of these take place behind the scenes. We'll tell you how to take advantage of some of the CP/M-BASIC connections in the sections ahead, but for the lab exercise of this section we'll continue to concentrate on using MBASIC as though it were a "stand-alone" system. In particular, we'll concentrate on writing a program that uses the random access file capabilities of the language to build an elementary information retrieval system. (Sequential files are discussed in [31].) All of the file manipulation will appear to be done by BASIC; CP/M's role will be invisible (or as some books say "transparent") to the programmer.

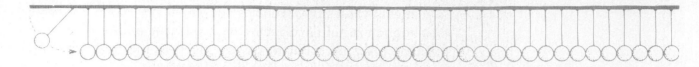

LAB EXERCISE 5.2-1

FILEBOXM: An Information Retrieval Program Using Disk-Extended BASIC

Step 0. The hands-on part of this lab doesn't start until step 1. The reason for prefacing it with a step 0 is to point out that the design of programs of even moderate complexity should not be done "on-line." There should always be a zeroth step that basically says, "Turn off the computer, and do some careful planning with good old-fashioned paper and pencil." In particular, it's a good idea to prepare written notes in four areas:

1. The idea. Write up a clear statement of the idea behind the program: what it's going to do, and why or how it will be useful.

2. Program output. Show an imagined RUN of the program, paying particular attention to exactly what you want to appear on the console output screen (and/or on the computer system's printer).

3. High-level design. Here's where you describe the organization of the program, the variables and data structures that will be used, and the algorithm (possibly expressed as a flowchart) it will follow. A good technique at this stage is to write a skeletal version of the program by describing it as a number of "chunks" called *program modules.* Another good technique is to express the idea behind each of these modules with REMark statements that have line numbers corresponding to their actual position in the final program.

4. Coding the program. This is where you finally write the BASIC statements that do what the high-level design says should be done. If bugs show up (and they will), your program modularization should make it a lot easier to redo this step, possibly on-line.

TECHNICAL NOTE

The paper-and-pencil design techniques suggested here are commonsense applications of the principal ideas behind *structured program design.* This is a phrase that has appeared in recent years to help emphasize the obvious (but often ignored) fact that programs should be planned, not just written. By recommending that planning be done before typing any BASIC code into the computer, we're really recommending that programmers should wear two hats: those of architect and craftsman.

The four design stages described here direct attention to the architect role, and the four documents that result can be thought of as architectural blueprints for the program. It's when you finally enter and test BASIC code that you switch hats and become a craftsman, making the changes and fixes that get the program to do what the blueprints say it should do. This is a helpful analogy, suggesting as it does that the ideal situation is one where architects and craftsmen talk to each other a great deal.

Incidentally, you'll also see the phrase "structured programming" used in this connection. This is really a more specialized term that refers to the use of a programming language (BASIC in our case) in a disciplined way that adheres to the high-level design. Structured programming is what happens when the coding of step 4 follows the design of step 3 with great care.

The programming language used in step 4 can be helpful in this area, and this is why recent extensions to BASIC (for example the IF . . . THEN . . . ELSE . . . statement, or the WHILE loop) have been added. It's also why programmers have been advised to avoid haphazard use of the GOTO statement. The programming language "C" is an example of one of the more modern languages that are considered to be better tools for structured programming. This is true to some extent, but languages themselves are not a cure-all. Sloppy programs can be written in the fanciest of languages and, conversely, clearly structured programs can be written in the simplest languages. The clarity and style of a program are very much in the hands of the programmer, and the creation of good programs will always be as much of an art as a science. More on this subject, and numerous examples of applying the four-stage design process to BASIC programming, can be found in reference [2] of Appendix G.

Here's a condensed version of the four design stages for the program FILEBOXM. It's based on the design of the program FILEBOX as explained in Section 4.3 of reference [2]. This reference also goes into detail on the way random file statements work in BASIC-80.

1. The idea is to write a program that acts like an electronic file box. Each record in the file is to contain a key word, data related to that key word, and a "usage number" showing how often the data has been retrieved.
2. A sample run of the program is shown in Fig. 5-3.
3. The high-level design is described in reference [2] in terms of a manual card filing system. (If the use of data files is completely new to you, it would be good to read this first.) This analogy is the basis of the following remark-statement form of the design. Each remark statement defines a program module for later expansion into BASIC code. Incidentally, remark statements can be written in BASIC-80 using either the key word REM or the apostrophe (').

10'	EXPLAIN PROGRAM; GET FILE NAME FROM USER
201'	IF FILE IS NEW, INITIALIZE ALL THE RECORDS (100 IN THIS EXAMPLE)
301'	FIELD THE DISK I/O BUFFER; GET RECORD # FROM USER
401'	RETRIEVE RECORD FROM DISK AND DISPLAY IT
501'	ASK USER WHAT TO DO WITH RECORD, BRANCH TO APPROP. ROUTINE
601'	ROUTINE FOR EDITING A RECORD
701'	EXIT ROUTINE (ASK USER WHETHER TO QUIT, PRINT, OR RESUME)
801'	PRINT ROUTINE
901'	QUIT ROUTINE

RUN

```
THIS PROGRAM ALLOWS YOU TO SAVE AND/OR RETRIEVE PAIRS
OF DATA OF THE FORM (KEY, INFORMATION).  EXAMPLES:
KEY? SAUERBRATEN   INFO? OLD HEIDELBERG, 555-1234
KEY? ACE BONDS      INFO? SAFE DEP BOX 24, MARGINAL TRUST CO.

NAME OF DATA FILE? TEMP
>>> WARNING:  DO NOT EXIT THIS PROGRAM BY PRESSING CTRL-C <<<
THIS IS A NEW FILE.   STAND BY FOR INITIALIZATION.
---------------------------------------------------------------
RECORD # (0 = EXIT)? 5
RECORD # 5 IS BLANK
DO YOU WISH TO --
     CHANGE (C),  DELETE (D),  OR  RESUME (R) --? C
TYPE NEW DATA FOR RECORD # 5
KEY:    AAA
INFO:   TOWING SERVICE AT 555-7389
---------------------------------------------------------------
RECORD # (0 = EXIT)? 101
ONLY 100 RECORDS AVAILABLE
---------------------------------------------------------------
RECORD # (0 = EXIT)? 45
RECORD # 45 IS BLANK
DO YOU WISH TO --
     CHANGE (C),  DELETE (D),  OR  RESUME (R) --? C
TYPE NEW DATA FOR RECORD # 45
KEY:    BYTE
INFO:   ISSUES TO `79 IN BASEMENT; REST IN DEN ON SHELF
---------------------------------------------------------------
RECORD # (0 = EXIT)? 1
RECORD # 1 IS BLANK
DO YOU WISH TO --
     CHANGE (C),  DELETE (D),  OR  RESUME (R) --? R
---------------------------------------------------------------
RECORD # (0 = EXIT)? 5
DATA FOR RECORD # 5
KEY:    AAA
INFO:   TOWING SERVICE AT 555-7389
THIS RECORD HAS BEEN ACCESSED 1 TIME(S)
DO YOU WISH TO --
     CHANGE (C),  DELETE (D),  OR  RESUME (R) --? 5
DO YOU WISH TO --
     CHANGE (C),  DELETE (D),  OR  RESUME (R) --? R
---------------------------------------------------------------
RECORD # (0 = EXIT)? 5
DATA FOR RECORD # 5
KEY:    AAA
INFO:   TOWING SERVICE AT 555-7389
THIS RECORD HAS BEEN ACCESSED 2 TIME(S)
DO YOU WISH TO --
     CHANGE (C),  DELETE (D),  OR  RESUME (R) --? R
---------------------------------------------------------------
RECORD # (0 = EXIT)? 0
DO YOU WISH TO --
QUIT THE PROGRAM (Q),  PRINT THE KEYS (P), OR RESUME (R) --? Q
END OF PROGRAM:  ALL FILES ARE CLOSED.
Ok
```

FIG. 5-3 This is a run of the program FILEBOXM. It uses a random access file, so the user can ask for data records in any order. The record numbers do not have to be requested in sequence as would be the case if a sequential file were used.

Before expanding each of these modules into BASIC code, it's a good idea to make up a list of the variables that will be used, and to make a diagram of the layout of the records. For our example, there is one file, and each record will adhere to the following layout:

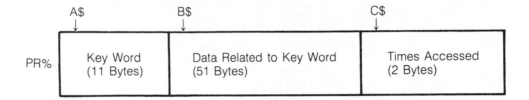

We're using A$, B$, and C$ as *pointers* to the record fields where key word, data, and times accessed are stored. The layout diagram shows that we're allocating 64 bytes per record, 11 for the keyword, 51 for the data, and 2 for the number of times accessed. These last two bytes will hold a binary representation of an integer number, *not* ASCII character codes.

Here's a list of all the variables used in the program. A percent sign (e. g., PR%) means that the variable will be of type integer (from −32768 to 32767), while a dollar sign (e. g., F$) means that the variable (or pointer) will refer to a string, that is, to a sequence of ASCII characters.

A$	Pointer to position in record buffer where key is stored.
B$	Pointer to position in record buffer where data is stored.
C$	Pointer to position in record buffer where C% is stored.
C%	Number of times record is accessed.
F$	String holding the data file name.
I$	String to input data information.
K$	String to input key name.
KN%	Key number for record (same as PR% in this program).
PR%	Physical record number.
R$	User's response to question.
T$	Temporary pointer for initializing record.

4. The BASIC-80 code for the program is shown in Fig. 5-4. If you've never used random files in BASIC before, it would be good to read up on the following key words in Appendix B: OPEN, CLOSE, FIELD, GET, PUT, LSET, MKI$, CVI, and LOF. (If you've used files in an earlier version of BASIC-80, note that in versions 5.0 and higher the OPEN statement can specify a record length as its last parameter. There is usually no need to distinguish between logical and physical records. However, be careful of the LOF function; it always gives you the number of 128-byte records in the file.)

Step 1. It's now time to gather up the planning documents from step 0 and head for the computer. Turn on the machine, boot CP/M, do a DIR to double check which files are on the disk,

```
10  '*************************************************************************
20  '*          FILEBOXM    (SAVES AND RETRIEVES DATA USING DISKS)          *
30  '*          REFERENCE: 'STRUCTURED PROGRAM DESIGN WITH TRS-80 BASIC'    *
40  '*                      MCGRAW HILL PUBLISHING COMPANY, NYC, NY         *
50  '*************************************************************************
110 ' CLEAR 500        NEEDED ONLY FOR VERSIONS OF MBASIC EARLIER THAN 5.0
115 PRINT CHR$(27); CHR$(69)     'CLEAR SCREEN OF Z-19 TERMINAL
120 ON ERROR GOTO 990
125 PRINT "THIS PROGRAM ALLOWS YOU TO SAVE AND/OR RETRIEVE PAIRS"
130 PRINT "OF DATA OF THE FORM (KEY, INFORMATION).  EXAMPLES:"
135 PRINT "KEY? SAUERBRATEN  INFO? OLD HEIDELBERG, 555-1234"
140 PRINT "KEY? ACE BONDS    INFO? SAFE DEP BOX 24, MARGINAL TRUST CO."
145 PRINT: PRINT "NAME OF DATA FILE";: INPUT F$
150 IF F$="" THEN 920
155 IF LEN(F$)>8 OR ASC(F$)<5 OR ASC(F$)>90 THEN PRINT"BAD NAME": GOTO 145
160 PRINT ">>> WARNING:  DO NOT EXIT THIS PROGRAM BY PRESSING CTRL-C <<<"
165 OPEN "R", 1, F$, 64
170 IF LOF(1)>0 THEN PRINT"NOTE:  THIS IS AN OLD FILE.": GOTO 310
175   PRINT "THIS IS A NEW FILE.  STAND BY FOR INITIALIZATION."
200 '-----------------------------------------------------------------------
201 '        IF FILE IS NEW, INITIALIZE ALL THE RECORDS
202 '-----------------------------------------------------------------------
210 C% = 0
215 FIELD 1, 62 AS T$, 2 AS C$
220 LSET T$ = " ": LSET C$ = MKI$(C%)
225 FOR PR% = 1 TO 100
230   PUT 1, PR%
235 NEXT PR%
300 '-----------------------------------------------------------------------
301 '        FIELD THE DISK I/O BUFFER; GET RECORD # FROM USER
302 '-----------------------------------------------------------------------
310 FIELD 1, 11 AS A$, 51 AS B$, 2 AS C$
315 PRINT "-----------------------------------------------------------------"
320 PRINT "RECORD # (0 = EXIT)";: INPUT KN%
325 IF KN% = 0 THEN 710
330 PR% = KN%          'LATER VERSION DISTINGUISHES BETWEEN KN% AND PR%
335 IF PR%>100 THEN PRINT "ONLY 100 RECORDS AVAILABLE": GOTO 315
400 '-----------------------------------------------------------------------
401 '        RETRIEVE RECORD FROM DISK AND DISPLAY IT
402 '-----------------------------------------------------------------------
410 GET 1, PR%
415 C% = CVI(C$)
420 IF C%=0 THEN PRINT "RECORD #" KN% "IS BLANK": GOTO 510
425 PRINT "DATA FOR RECORD #"KN%
430 PRINT "KEY:      "A$
435 PRINT "INFO:     "B$
440 PRINT "THIS RECORD HAS BEEN ACCESSED"C%"TIME(S)": C%=C%+1
445 LSET C$ = MKI$(C%)
450 PUT 1, PR%              'UPDATED # OF ACCESSES PUT ON RECORD
500 '-----------------------------------------------------------------------
501 '        ASK USER WHAT TO DO WITH RECORD; BRANCH TO APPROP. ROUTINE
502 '-----------------------------------------------------------------------
510 PRINT"DO YOU WISH TO --"
515 PRINT"     CHANGE (C),  DELETE (D),  OR  RESUME (R) --";
520 R$ = "": INPUT R$
525 IF R$ = "" OR R$ = "R" THEN 315
530 IF R$ = "C" THEN 610
535 IF R$ = "D" THEN LSET A$ = " ": LSET B$ = " ": C% = 0: GOTO 625
540 GOTO 510
600 '-----------------------------------------------------------------------
601 '        ROUTINE FOR EDITING A RECORD
602 '-----------------------------------------------------------------------
610 C% = 1: PRINT "TYPE NEW DATA FOR RECORD #"PR%
615 PRINT "KEY:    ";: LINE INPUT K$: LSET A$ = K$
620 PRINT "INFO:   ";: LINE INPUT I$: LSET B$ = I$
625 LSET C$ = MKI$(C%)
630 PUT 1, PR%
635 GOTO 315
700 '-----------------------------------------------------------------------
701 '        EXIT ROUTINE (ASK USER WHETHER TO QUIT, PRINT, OR RESUME)
702 '-----------------------------------------------------------------------
710 PRINT "DO YOU WISH TO --"
715 PRINT "QUIT THE PROGRAM (Q),  PRINT THE KEYS (P), OR RESUME (R) --";
720 R$ = "": INPUT R$
```

FIG. 5-4 This is a listing of FILEBOXM. Notice the technique of using new blocks of numbers for each distinct routine, and using 3 lines (like 500, 501, 502) to label each block.

```
725 IF R$ = "" OR R$ = "R" THEN 315
730 IF R$ = "Q" THEN 910
735 IF R$ = "P" THEN 810
740 GOTO 710               'DON'T KNOW WHAT YOU SAID
800 '-----------------------------------------------------------------
801 '       PRINT ROUTINE
802 '-----------------------------------------------------------------
810 PRINT "PRINT ROUTINE MISSING AT PRESENT": GOTO 710
900 '-----------------------------------------------------------------
901 '       QUIT ROUTINE
902 '-----------------------------------------------------------------
910 CLOSE
920 PRINT "END OF PROGRAM:  ALL FILES ARE CLOSED. ": END
990 PRINT "ERROR DETECTED IN PROGRAM"
995 ON ERROR GOTO 0
1000 '----------------------------------------------------------------
1001 '  THIS BLOCK IS RESERVED FOR A SUBROUTINE THAT ALLOWS THE USER
1002 '  TO ENTER A KEY WORD INSTEAD OF A RECORD NUMBER WHEN REQUESTING
1003 '  INFORMATION ON FILE.   THE SUBROUTINE WILL THEN CONVERT THE KEY
1004 '  WORD TO THE CORRECT RECORD NUMBER, USING EITHER A HASH CODING
1005 '  TECHNIQUE OR A B-TREE INDEX STRUCTURE.    FOR MORE INFORMATION
1006 '  ABOUT THESE SUBJECTS SEE THE REFERENCES IN SECTION 5.8
1999 '----------------------------------------------------------------
2000 '----------------------------------------------------------------
2001 '  THIS BLOCK IS RESERVED FOR A SUBROUTINE THAT COMPLEMENTS SUB-
2002 '  ROUTINE 1000.   ITS PURPOSE IS TO EITHER DO THE HASHING REQUIR-
2003 '  ED WHEN STORING A NEW RECORD, OR TO CREATE THE B-TREE STRUCTURE.
2999 '----------------------------------------------------------------
```

FIG. 5-4   (*continued*)

and then enter the BASIC programming environment by typing MBASIC.

Step 2. Type in the program shown in Fig. 5-4. It is not necessary to type in remark (') statements at this time (we were careful to never branch to one of these). If you make an error but don't spot it until after you've entered the line, just retype the entire line. (A more flexible technique for making corrections is to use the EDIT command as explained in the MBASIC manual, but it will take some practice to learn all its features.)

Step 3. Proofread the program on the console screen by typing LIST. This will cause the program to flash by too fast to read, but you can halt the listing by pressing Control-S. To resume the listing, press the space bar. To abandon the listing before it gets to the last line, press Control-C. Another technique is to list just one section of the program at a time. For example, you could first type LIST 1-200, then LIST 200-300, then LIST 300-400, and so on. Other useful forms of the LIST command are LIST -900 and LIST 500- which mean "list up to 900" and "list from 500 on" respectively.

Step 4. Save the program by typing

SAVE "FILEBOXM"

If you have a system with two disk drives (and have a formatted disk in drive B), you can immediately save a backup copy by also typing

SAVE "B:FILEBOXM"

Notice that when MBASIC is used under CP/M it follows the same rules for naming files as CP/M proper. This is no accident; it's because MBASIC calls upon CP/M for its disk and console I/O operations. Also note that we didn't call the file FILE-BOXM.BAS even though that's a good idea. The reason is that the .BAS extension is automatically added by MBASIC. You'll see this when you look at the directory in the next step.

Step 5. Make sure the program was properly saved by looking at the directory. You *could* do this by returning to CP/M and using DIR, but there's a simpler way. While still in BASIC you can see directories for the A and/or B disks by typing

FILES   and/or   FILES ''B:*.*''

You're still in BASIC after doing this, so you can immediately do another LIST and perhaps make some more changes. However, any new changes you make won't be stored on disk unless you use the SAVE command again. If your second save uses the same filename (e. g., SAVE ''FILEBOXM''), then the latest version of the program will be written ''on top of'' the previous version. This will erase the old version, so if for any reason you don't want to lose it (for example, you want to have one version with remarks and another without them), you'll have to use two different file names.

This same restriction applies when you want to save a file in both its normal ''compressed form'' and in what's called its ''ASCII form.'' The compressed form (also called the ''tokenized'' form) uses special codes (called tokens) to represent key words like PRINT, THEN, GOTO, and so on, whereas the ASCII form stores all the letters and symbols exactly as you typed them. For example, it would save PRINT as ''P'', ''R'', ''I'', ''N'', and ''T'' instead of as a single numeric ''token'' code. BASIC files are always saved in compressed form unless you say otherwise. You force the ASCII form by adding ,A after the last quote mark in a SAVE command. For example, to save FILEBOXM as an ASCII file, you type

SAVE ''FILEBOXM'',A

or

SAVE ''B:FILEBOXM'',A

If you want *both* compressed and ASCII forms of the same file, you must use two different names in two separate SAVE commands as for example

SAVE ''FILEBOXM''

and

SAVE ''FBOXMASC'',A

Question:

Which form is best?

Answer:

Normally, the compressed form is best because it saves storage space and a little processing time. However, the ASCII form is needed whenever you want to MERGE a BASIC disk file with another BASIC program that's already in memory. The ASCII form is also needed if you want to run the program through a compiler like BASCOM, or work on it with an editor like ED, or with a word processor like StarEdit, WordStar, or MINCE. The form of a file can always be changed by loading it into memory with LOAD "filename", and then doing a new SAVE in the desired form.

Step 6. Test the program by typing RUN. Use the sample run shown in step 0 to see how to respond to the questions it asks (for this test, answer TEMP to the question NAME OF DATA FILE?).

If the program stops with an error message, it will usually tell you which line was at fault. The most likely problem is a typing error. When the program stops because of an error, MBASIC may put you in EDIT mode to allow you to make changes. In this case, type L to see the offending line, and then use the appropriate EDIT commands. If you don't know these, press RETURN instead, and then use LIST to inspect the offending lines, making any changes needed by retyping the lines in question. When you've got the program running OK, be sure to repeat the SAVE command (as explained in step 4) so that you'll have the corrected version on disk.

Step 7. Once you've got the program running correctly and saved, it's a good idea to get a hard copy on your printer (assuming you have one). Do this by turning on the printer and typing LLIST. When this is finished, if you want to quit it's not necessary to return to CP/M. Just remove the disks, and turn off the power. However, in this lab it will be instructive to return to CP/M and see how it can be used to work with the files that were just created. To return to CP/M from MBASIC type SYSTEM. This causes a warm boot, so the next thing you should see is the system prompt A>.

Step 8. Now that you're back in CP/M, take a look at your directory by typing DIR. You will see that our session with BASIC added two new files to the disk: FILEBOXM.BAS (which was produced by the SAVE command in BASIC), and TEMP (which was produced by the OPEN statement when the program FILEBOXM was run).

Question:

Can we look at these files by using the TYPE command of CP/M?

Answer:

No, because these are not 100% ASCII files. Some of the bytes of information they contain have been stored with codes that must be interpreted as binary numbers, not as ASCII printing or control codes (the ASCII codes are given in Appendix B. The codes that correspond to printable characters have decimal equivalents in the range 32 to 127; control codes go from 0 to 31).

There are two exceptions to the above answer. If you have saved a BASIC program as an ASCII file by using

    SAVE "filename",A

then you *can* look at it with the TYPE command. You can also use TYPE if you have saved data as a *sequential* data file. These files are always saved as a "stream" of ASCII characters (that's because a sequential file is treated as though it were really a printer-like device). For examples of how to use sequential files, see *BASIC and the Personal Computer*, Addison-Wesley, Reading, MA 01867 [1]. Also see the program MLDEC of Section 6.3 and the program SEQINDEX from [22].

In our example, we can't use TYPE because our program used a *random access* data file (the one we called TEMP). Random files are saved as "partial" ASCII files. The text information in them (like "SAUER-BRATEN" and "OLD HEIDELBERG" in our example) is saved as a sequence of ASCII characters, but numerical information (like "number of times accessed") is stored in the form of binary numbers.

To look at a partial ASCII file, you can use the DDT display command. Do this by typing

    A>DDT TEMP
    –D

You'll then see the file displayed in a somewhat strange format. There will be 16 characters on a line, but they'll be shown in hexadecimal form on the left and, *where possible*, in ASCII form on the right. Whenever the hex code does not correspond to a printable character, DDT will print a period (.) to let you know something is there, but that it's not one of the ASCII codes between 32 and 127. Fig. 5-5 shows what the first 12 lines of TEMP look like when the Display command of DDT is used. To see another 12 lines, you would type another D. To leave DDT, you should do a warm boot by typing Control-C.

Step 9.   Another thing you can do before shutting down is to erase files, or rename them. For example,

```
A>DIR
A: PIP        COM : STAT     COM : GO        COM : ED        COM
A: MBASIC     COM : MYPOEM   TXT : FILEBOXM BAS : TEMP
A>
A>DDT TEMP
DDT VERS 2.0
NEXT  PC
1A00 0100
-D
0100 20 20 20 20 20 20 20 20 20 20 20 20 20 20 20 20
0110 20 20 20 20 20 20 20 20 20 20 20 20 20 20 20 20
0120 20 20 20 20 20 20 20 20 20 20 20 20 20 20 20 20
0130 20 20 20 20 20 20 20 20 20 20 20 20 20 20 00 00             ..
0140 20 20 20 20 20 20 20 20 20 20 20 20 20 20 20 20
0150 20 20 20 20 20 20 20 20 20 20 20 20 20 20 20 20
0160 20 20 20 20 20 20 20 20 20 20 20 20 20 20 20 20
0170 20 20 20 20 20 20 20 20 20 20 20 20 20 20 00 00             ..
0180 20 20 20 20 20 20 20 20 20 20 20 20 20 20 20 20
0190 20 20 20 20 20 20 20 20 20 20 20 20 20 20 20 20
01A0 20 20 20 20 20 20 20 20 20 20 20 20 20 20 20 20
01B0 20 20 20 20 20 20 20 20 20 20 20 20 20 20 00 00             ..
-D
01C0 20 20 20 20 20 20 20 20 20 20 20 20 20 20 20 20
01D0 20 20 20 20 20 20 20 20 20 20 20 20 20 20 20 20
01E0 20 20 20 20 20 20 20 20 20 20 20 20 20 20 20 20
01F0 20 20 20 20 20 20 20 20 20 20 20 20 20 20 00 00            ..
0200 41 41 41 20 20 20 20 20 20 20 20 54 4F 57 49 4E  AAA        TOWIN
0210 47 20 53 45 52 56 49 43 45 20 41 54 20 35 35 35  G SERVICE AT 555
0220 2D 37 33 38 39 20 20 20 20 20 20 20 20 20 20 20  -7389
0230 20 20 20 20 20 20 20 20 20 20 20 20 20 20 03 00             ..
0240 20 20 20 20 20 20 20 20 20 20 20 20 20 20 20 20
0250 20 20 20 20 20 20 20 20 20 20 20 20 20 20 20 20
0260 20 20 20 20 20 20 20 20 20 20 20 20 20 20 20 20
0270 20 20 20 20 20 20 20 20 20 20 20 20 20 20 00 00             ..
-
```

FIG. 5-5   After saving and running FILEBOXM, the directory shows two new files: FILEBOXM.BAS, and TEMP. One way to examine the random access file TEMP is to use the D command of DDT. Each period (.) shown on the right corresponds to a byte in the file that does not represent an ASCII character. These appear when random access files contain numbers encoded as binary numbers that do not fall in the range 32 to 127 decimal. The reason that the records of the file contain lots of 20 hex codes is that we initialized the records with blanks (ASCII 32 decimal, 20 hex). You can spot the end of each record since we initialized the last two bytes as zeros. These are stored as the binary numbers zero, *not* as the ASCII codes for zero. Also notice that the last two bytes of the fifth record are 03 00, showing that this record was accessed three times.

A>ERA TEMP

will get rid of the practice data file (a good idea), while

A>REN FBM.BAS=FILEBOXM.BAS

will give the BASIC program the shorter name FBM.BAS. Both of these changes can also be made on the B disk by using B: in front of file names.

Step 10.   Remove all the disks, and then turn off the computer. Now go through the steps for starting up the system at a later time and using the programs you just wrote again. Here's what to do.

10a.   Turn on the computer, insert the proper disks, boot CP/M, and check the directory. If you have a printer, it would be a good idea to type ^P (CR) before typing DIR. That way you'll get a "hard" copy of the directory on paper.

10b.   Next type MBASIC after the A> prompt. When you see the sign-on message from MBASIC, load the program FILEBOXM by typing

LOAD "FILEBOXM"

Now run (and use) the program by typing RUN.

Note: A quick way to give all three of these commands (MBASIC, LOAD, and RUN) is to type

A>MBASIC FILEBOXM

10c.   You are now back at step 6, and can proceed to make changes or use CP/M as described in steps 6 through 10.

Warning: When running FILEBOXM, one name you should *not* use in answering "NAME OF DATA FILE?" is FILEBOXM. Why?

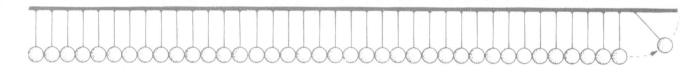

5.3 Logical and Physical Devices; STAT and the IOBYTE

We're going to leave our discussion of BASIC for awhile and set the scene for doing some "undocumented" things with it when we return. We'll start by taking a closer look at how the STAT transient command can be used to assign physical device drivers to logical device names. The basic idea is shown in the following diagram (repeated here from Section 3.3) where the command

STAT CON: = CRT:

has been used to connect a "software switch" from the CON: logical device to the CRT: physical device. The result is that all console I/O will be directed to whatever terminal is connected to the CRT: (port #2 in our example). If, later on, the command STAT CON: = TTY: is given, console I/O will be routed to the terminal connected to the TTY: (port #1 in our example).

What we're going to do in this section is to present a more complete diagram showing how CBIOS can use four sets of software switches to direct I/O to all kinds of other peripheral devices—a very neat feature

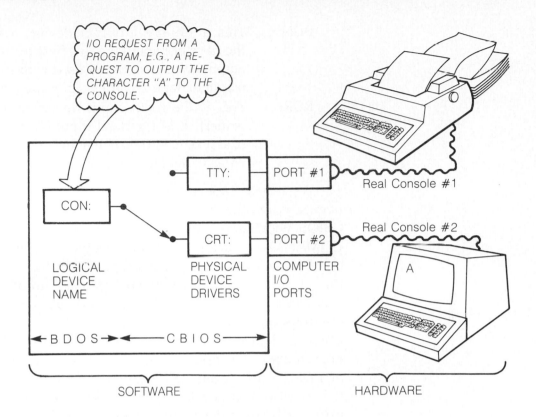

indeed. We'll also explain the function of a memory location called the IOBYTE. Once we know how it works, we'll be able to explain why switches can be changed not only by using the CP/M command STAT, but also by POKEing the right numbers into the IOBYTE with BASIC. This same information will apply to using DDT or assembly language (explained in Chapter 6) to modify the way CBIOS initializes its device assignments.

Devices That Aren't Devices

Let's get started by admitting that this can be one of the most confusing areas of CP/M. The ideas involved are both clever and useful, but the terminology used is enough to drive a saint to programming—or worse.

The root of the problem is that CP/M does all its I/O in terms of "make-believe" peripherals called *logical devices*. There are four of these, abbreviated as follows (the colon is part of each name).

CON: This is the *console* I/O device. It's the work horse of the make-believe peripheral stable. All CP/M input (like you typing DIR) and output (like CP/M typing NO FILE) are done in terms of this device. Most other software uses it too (for example, MBASIC uses it for all PRINT and INPUT statements).

LST: This is the *listing* output device, and it's also used a lot—at least if you have a printer. It's where output goes when you use words like LPRINT or LLIST in MBASIC, or when you use the Control-P "print toggle" in CP/M.

PUN: This is the *punch* output device, a word left over from the days of paper tape. It's best to think of it as a general output device that can be used with such things as printers, magnetic tape recorders, graphics displays, and so on.

RDR: This is the *reader* input device (originally a paper tape reader). It is a general input device that can be thought of as a keyboard, a digital joystick, a magnetic tape reader, an X-Y digitizer, and so on.

We called these make-believe devices because they're really just names. When the "front end" of CP/M uses them for I/O it expects that CBIOS will figure out what *real* devices are to be used. For output, CP/M sends characters to one of the logical output devices (CON:, LST:, or PUN:) with the implied message, "You figure out what to do with this—I can't be bothered with such details." In other words, CP/M isn't concerned with whether a character is displayed by shooting a beam of electrons on a CRT screen, or by whacking a daisy wheel against a ribbon and paper. It leaves that up to CBIOS (and the computer owner's pocketbook). For input, it uses one of the logical input devices (CON: or RDR:) with the implied message, "Give me a character—and don't tell me how you got it." Again, selection of the actual input device is up to each computer system as determined by CBIOS.

So how does the dirty work connected with I/O actually get done? CP/M says that's up to the "physical devices." What this *really* means is that it's up to software routines called physical device *drivers*, and that someone had better make sure that these routines address hardware connections called *ports* into which real-world I/O devices have been plugged. It's for this reason that we're going to use the term *physical device port drivers* (PDPD for short), instead of CP/M's term "physical device." Our term is longer, but it reminds you of all that's involved.

Here's a summary of the names CP/M uses for what it calls physical devices (and which we'll make part of the PDPD names):

LPT: Line printer listing device; output only.
UL1:   User defined listing device; output only.
PTP: Paper tape punch; output only.
UP1:   User defined punch #1; output only.
UP2:   User defined punch #2; output only.
PTR: Paper tape reader; input only.
UR1:   User defined reader #1; input only.
UR2:   User defined reader #2; input only.
TTY: Teletype-like console device; input/output.
CRT: Cathode ray tube console device; input/output.
UC1:   User defined console; input/output.
BAT: Batch mode console; input/output. This is not a separate device, but a combination of a reader and a listing device.

As this list shows, twelve physical device names have been defined for CP/M. What it doesn't show is that there are four kinds of port driver programs (for handling *output, input, in status,* and *out status*). This suggests that there could be 48 different PDPDs. However, of the twelve physical drivers, only six do input (TTY:, CRT:, UC1:, PTR:, UR1:, and UR2:), eight do output (LTP:, UL1:, PTP:, UP1:, UP2:, TTY:, CRT:, and UC1:), six check "in status" (TTY:, CRT:, UC1:, PTR:, UR1:, and UR2:), and four can check "out status" (TTY:, CRT:, LPT:, and UL1:). So at most there can be 24 physical device/port driver combinations (PDPDs).

TECHNICAL NOTE

> An example of an output driver was shown in the technical note at the end of Section 3.3. An input driver works in about the same way except that an IN instruction is used instead of the OUT instruction. The code for "in status" and "out status" drivers is even simpler. It's similar to the first two lines of the output driver shown in Section 3.3, followed by a return to the calling program with the code FF to mean "ready," and 00 to mean "not ready." The reason for having separate status drivers is to allow programs which want to do I/O, first check the status of the I/O peripherals. If the peripheral is not ready (for example, it might be a printer busy doing a carriage return), the computer can go off and do a little useful work for the next fraction of a second, and then come back and check status again. Examples of input, output, and status drivers are given in Chapter 6.

Confused? Welcome to the club. But hang in there, a diagram is on the way. Fig. 5-6 tries to clarify the situation by showing all the PDPDs that correspond to these options. It also gives some idea of the six-step process that takes place any time you input or output data to a terminal device on a CP/M system.

Before tracing these six steps, we should warn you that while most versions of CBIOS have all the "switches" needed for getting from step (1) on the left to one of the PDPD boxes in step (5) on the right, many of the PDPD boxes won't contain actual driver routines. Instead they'll contain jumps to other driver routines. It's like going to a hotel that advertises a dozen fancy restaurants, and then finding out that they all use the same kitchen. Some day they may install separate kitchens, but for the present they have more maitre d's than chefs. It's the same with CP/M. A well-written CBIOS will have place holders for all 24 PDPD routines, but in practice most of them will be jumps to one of the 4 or 5 PDPD boxes that contain actual driver code. For the majority of users this is fine. Three PDPDs for your console (to handle output, input, and "in status"), plus a PDPD for your printer (to handle hardcopy output) are adequate for most systems.

Some idea of the way in which an I/O request proceeds through CP/M can be had by tracing the request from left to right in the order of the circled numbers shown in Fig. 5-6. When a program is ready to do I/O—for example, to output a character to the console screen as would be the case in a word processor program that was read to print the letter "A"—here's what happens:

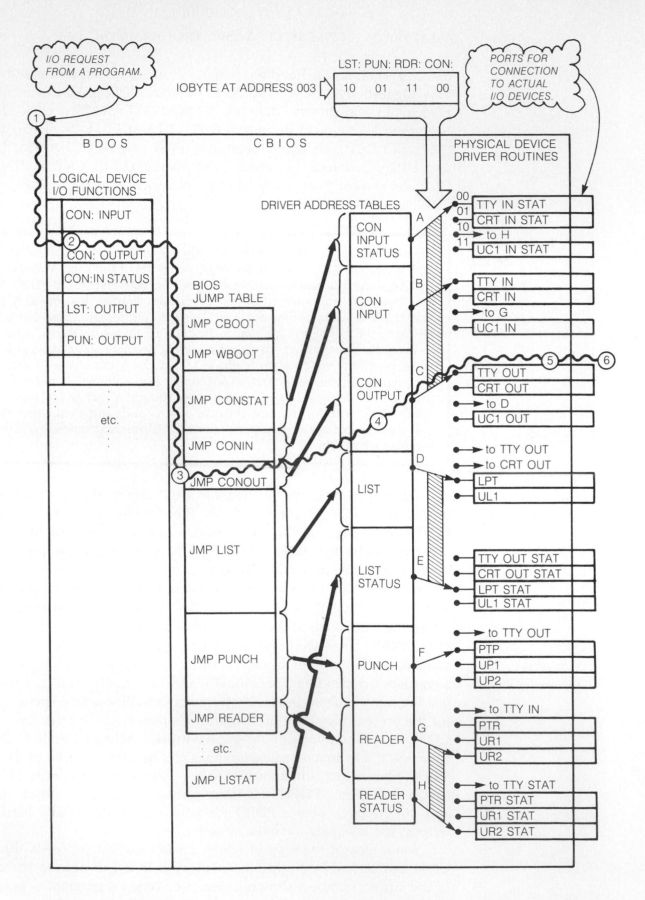

FIG. 5-6 Diagram showing how an I/O request is routed from a program running under CP/M to an actual I/O device via BDOS and CBIOS. Programs don't *have* to do I/O in this manner (they can take a short cut directly to the port driver, for example), but such programs are no longer machine independent.

1. The program puts the character to be output ("A") in a specified machine location (the E register), and then it does a "BDOS function call" of the proper kind. In this case it would be a call for function number 2 (console output).

2. When BDOS "hears" this call, it sends the request to a reserved location at the beginning of BIOS—to the fifth position in what's called the BIOS jump table. The ordering of this table is inviolable, so that when BDOS goes to the fifth position it *always* finds information related to the console output driver, no matter what the system.

3. And what's at this fifth position? Nothing more than a jump instruction, usually written as JMP CONOUT. This is a jump to a location further up in BIOS where there is something called the CONOUT address table.

4. To use this address table, CBIOS looks in something called the IOBYTE. It then applies the information it finds there to selecting one of the four entries stored in the CONOUT address table. This is the software equivalent to selecting a position for the CONOUT switch (labeled C in Fig. 5-6). In our example, the "CON" part of the IOBYTE holds the bits 00, so switch C goes to the top position.

5. The output data (remember the "A"?) is then sent to the PDPD selected by switch C—in our example to the box labelled TTY OUT.

6. The output character is finally shipped out the port used by TTY OUT so that it can show up on whatever real device happens to be connected there. How about that.

More about the IOBYTE

The "switches" which determine the path from step (4) to (5) are really software routines that select the addresses of the desired PDPDs. They do this by decoding a pair of bits from the IOBYTE (which is at location 0003 in all CP/M systems). The IOBYTE has four *pairs* of bits used to select the positions of the LST:, PUN:, RDR:, and CON: switches, respectively. In Fig. 5-6 the IOBYTE contained the bit pattern 10011100. Suppose instead it had the following pattern:

$$\text{IOBYTE} = \quad \underbrace{1 \quad 0}_{\text{LST:}} \quad \underbrace{1 \quad 1}_{\text{PUN:}} \quad \underbrace{0 \quad 0}_{\text{RDR:}} \quad \underbrace{0 \quad 1}_{\text{CON:}}$$

The two low order (rightmost) bits shown here indicate that the CON switch position is now 01. By agreement (see Fig. 5-7), this is the CRT: position. To say this more correctly, 01 is a code that means "move all three of the CON: switches (labelled A, B, C) to CRT: drivers". So if we zoom in on the C switch, for example, here's what we'll see:

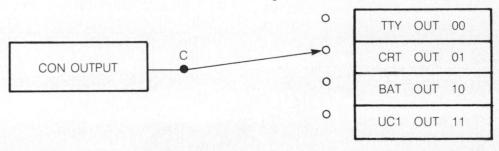

In general, setting the two low-order bits of the IOBYTE to 01 is equivalent to saying "from now on all CON: operations will be routed through CRT: drivers". Of course actual output and input will take place on whatever real terminal device happens to be connected to the CRT: driver ports. The other pairs of bits are used in a similar manner to determine the settings of switches D-E (LST:), F(PUN:), and G-H (RDR:).

Question:

How does a console "switch code" like 00 or 01 get into the low order bits of IOBYTE in the first place?

Answer:

The "normal" (called *default*) position of all the switches is set during a cold boot by an INIT (initialization) routine in CBIOS. This reads an 8-bit number (chosen by the person who wrote CBIOS) into IOBYTE. This number can be changed by using the techniques shown in Chapter 6 for modifying CBIOS.

Question:

Suppose the CON: bits are initialized to something else—say to 10. How can I change them to 01?

Answer:

If you know that 01 is the code for CRT: the easiest way to make the change while working in CP/M is to type

    A>STAT CON:=CRT:

This changes the switches for *all three* CON: drivers. You can see this on the diagram where you'll notice that the switch lines coming out of CON STATUS, CON INPUT, and CON OUTPUT are linked together (they function like what electronics people call a "ganged" switch).

You can make the same change from within BASIC by typing

    POKE 3, B

where B is an 8-bit binary number with the desired switch positions in it. To determine B, you have to decide on all 8 bits. You do this by consulting the following table:

Two-bit Binary Pattern	Bit 7 Bit 6 LST:=	Bit 5 Bit 4 PUN:=	Bit 3 Bit 2 RDR:=	Bit 1 Bit 0 CON:=
00	TTY:	TTY:	TTY:	TTY:
01	CRT:	PTP:	PTR:	CRT:
10	LPT:	UP1:	UR1:	BAT:
11	UL1:	UP2:	UR2:	UC1:

FIG. 5-7 IOBYTE Table.

Plates 1 and 2. The photograph above shows a modular CP/M system of the type used to run some of the examples in this book. It consists of a letter-quality printer, a video terminal for the console, an S-100 mainframe, and two eight-inch floppy disk drives. On the left is a typical set of S-100 circuit boards (CPU, memory, and disk controller) plugged into the S-100 motherboard. The wide ribbon cable connects the disk controller to the disk drives. The smaller cable is used for I/O to the console and printer.

Plate 3. Modular S-100 systems (on the left) are suitable for business, professional, and home use. This system belongs to CPA Jerry Sales who consulted on the business sections of this book.

Plates 4 and 5. The ISC 8063 (above) is a professional CP/M system available in packaged form, with all the components integrated by one manufacturer. It has an extended keyboard (see Section 4.1), and a large screen which can display 48 lines of text, full color graphics, or any combination of these.

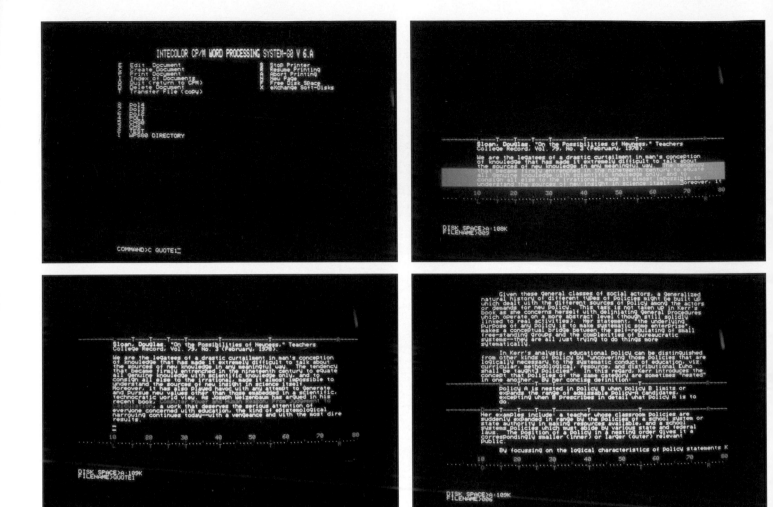

Plates 6, 7, 8, and 9 show how the use of color enhances the screen displays of the WPS-80 word processor. Plate 6 (upper left) is the main menu of WPS-80, used to select word processing functions. Plate 7 (upper right) shows a block of marked text (displayed in white on blue) ready for "cut and paste." Plate 8 (lower left) shows color used to distinguish text that will print either underlined or bold-face. Plate 9 (lower right) shows material in which one section has wider margins, achieved by inserting a new color-coded ruler into the text.

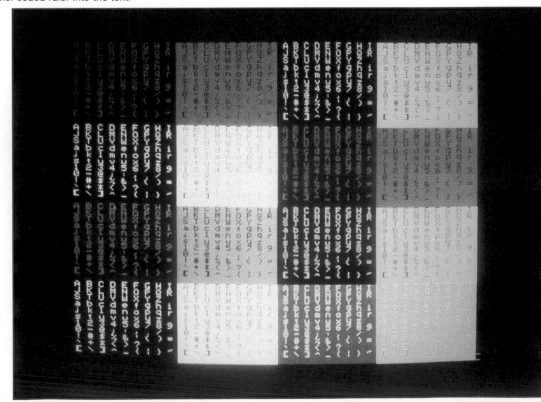

Plate 10 shows a sampler of some of the possible ISC foreground (character) and background color combinations. These are useful for distinguishing different functions of text in word processing or other applications.

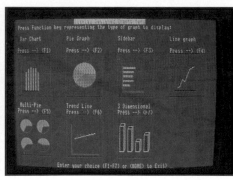

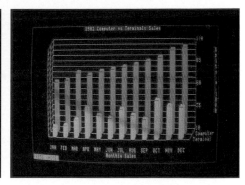

Plates 11, 12, and 13 show examples of output produced by the Zenith Z100 computer. This is a packaged machine that also allows modular expansion via five S-100 slots. The displays illustrate the potential of color graphics in business applications.

Plates 14, 15, 16, and 17 are all examples of the output produced by the program PLTRIPLE on the ISC 8063 computer (see Section 1.6). The differences are produced by the selection of different input parameters, and by the length of time the program is run. The numbers on Plate 16 (lower left) were produced by inserting statements to print the coordinates of the points being plotted (e.g., PRINT X(1);Y(1) etc.).

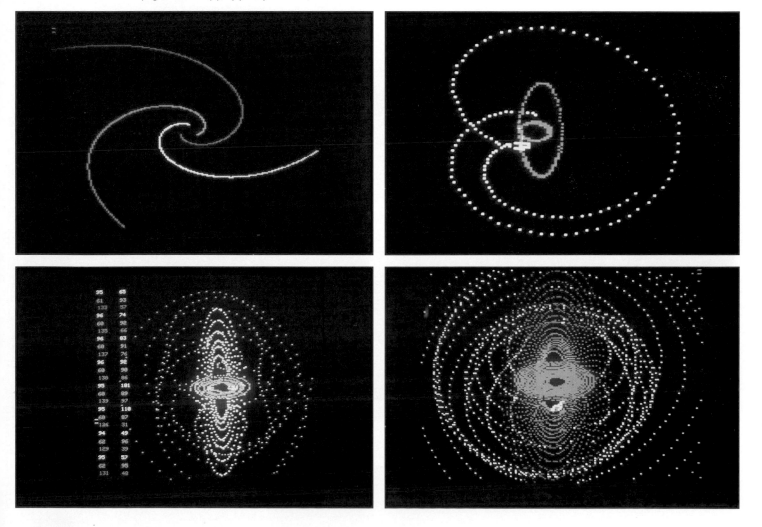

Plates 18 and 19 show the ISC 8063 in a nonbusiness setting. It is being used here to develop a set of experimental illustrations for use in an anthology of poetry. The advent of personal microcomputers has extended the application of computers beyond science, engineering, and business. There are now many professional uses related to the arts and humanities.

Plates 20, 21, and 22 (below) show three of the medium-cost personal computers that can run CP/M: the Apple II (left), the Kaypro II portable (middle), and the Televideo TS802H (right).

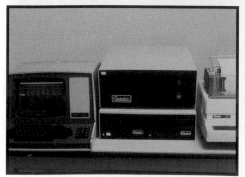

Plates 23, 24, and 25 (above) are photographs of more advanced CP/M systems. The CompuPro (left) features a dual processor CPU board, so that it can run CP/M-80 or CP/M-86. The Ithaca Intersystems machine (center) features a full front panel, and a very sophisticated "cache" BIOS. The Morrow Decision I (right) can support hard disk drives of up to 26 megabyte capacity each. All three machines use the S-100 bus.

Suppose, for example, you want the following assignments

    LST: = UL1: (bits 7 & 6 = 11)
    PUN: = PTP: (bits 5 & 4 = 01)
    RDR: = PTR: (bits 3 & 2 = 01)
    CON: = TTY: (bits 1 & 0 = 00)

Then the IOBYTE should be loaded with the binary number

    B = 11010100

The POKE statement of BASIC needs B in decimal or hex form which is

    128 + 64 + 16 + 4 = 212 decimal   or   D4 hex

Thus, to make the four assignments of logical drivers shown above, use

    POKE 3,212   or   POKE 3,&HD4

either as a direct or indirect statement when programming in BASIC.

Question:

Suppose I want to change just the last two bits (CON:) to 00. Can I do this without knowing what the first 6 bits are?

Answer:

Yes. You can do this "from BASIC" (i.e., while running BASIC) by executing the statement

    POKE 3, PEEK(3) AND 252 OR 0

This takes whatever's already in the IOBYTE (PEEK(3)), "masks out" the first 6 bits (AND 252), inserts the desired bits 00 into the rightmost two positions (OR 0), and then puts the result back into the IOBYTE (POKE 3). To insert a different pair of bits into the rightmost position (say 11), just change the OR part of this statement (for example, you'd use OR 3 to insert the bits 11).

More on STAT; Examining and Modifying the IOBYTE

It's useful to have the table of figure 5-7 in front of you when making new PDPD assignments. You can ask CP/M to display a simplified form of the table by typing

    A>STAT VAL:

This shows all the possible assignments, but it doesn't tell you which ones have been made on your system. To see what these are (and therefore indirectly see what's in the IOBYTE), type

    A>STAT DEV:

To change the device assignments (that is, to change the PDPD switches) use the form

STAT logical device = physical device

For example, to switch the CON: back to TTY:, type

A>STAT CON: = TTY:

To change several PDPD switches,you can use this form several times in succession, or you can put all the assignments (separated by commas) on one line, as for example,

A>STAT LST:=LPT:,PUN:=PTP:, RDR:=PTR:,CON:=TTY:

Since the IOBYTE is always at location 3, you can also take a look at it while in BASIC by using PEEK as follows:

PRINT PEEK(3)
212 (BASIC printed this.)

The 212 is a decimal number so you'll have to convert it back to binary to see what the actual bit pattern is. The pattern can be modified in BASIC by using AND and OR operations as illustrated earlier.

Another way to inspect and/or change the IOBYTE is to use the DDT *set* command S. This requires that you work with the contents of the IOBYTE in hex notation. For example, if the IOBYTE contains 11010100 (D4 hex), and you want to change it to 10000000 (80 hex), here's how you'd do this with DDT.

```
A>DDT
-S0003
0003    D4    80    (CR)
0004    C3    ^C
A>
```

In this example you first type S0003 to mean "set the contents of location 0003". The computer responds by typing the current contents of that location (D4). To change the contents, you type the 80 and (CR). The computer then prints the next address and its contents. To leave DDT, type ^C. The DDT commands are explained further in Section 6.5. On some systems this technique won't work since the warm boot caused by the ^C resets the IOBYTE back to its initial value.

Warning: Once you change the IOBYTE, the *new* assignments are in force. Suppose, for example, you do the following:

```
A>DDT
-S0003
0003    D4    81    (CR)
```

This changes the IOBYTE to 10000001, so all CON: (console) functions will now be routed to the CRT: device (01). If your system happens to use the same driver for TTY: and CRT: (remember our one-kitchen, multi-entrance restaurant example?), you'll never know the difference. However, if the CRT: driver (01) is different from the TTY: driver (00), then you'll have to switch chairs, sitting down in front of whatever device is connected to the CRT: port to continue this dialogue.

Question:

Suppose I have two separate drivers (and ports) for TTY: and CRT:, but I'm still saving up the money to buy a terminal for the CRT: port. In other words, right now there's nothing there. What will happen?

Answer:

Changing the IOBYTE to 81 hex (or any other number where the last two bits of the binary form are 01) will "hang" your system since there's now no way to talk to it (there's no console). The only way out is to do a cold boot, at which time the IOBYTE will be initialized back to its original values, and your standard console will come alive again.

Question:

There seem to be three ways to change the IOBYTE: using STAT or DDT from CP/M, and using POKE from BASIC. Is that it?

Answer:

No. The IOBYTE can also be changed from assembly language programs by using one of the BDOS calls described in Section 6.1, or simply by using the appropriate machine language instruction to load location 3. Similar techniques can be used in programs written in other languages (e. g., "C").

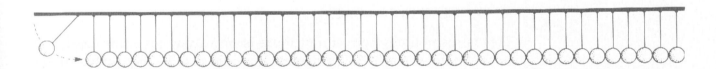

LAB EXERCISE 5.3-1   Using the IOBYTE to Make BASIC PRINT Statements Act Like LPRINT Statements

Step 0. First some background. Let's assume that you have a CP/M system with both a console and a printer. We'll also assume that the printer is connected to a port/driver that has been assigned as the LST: device. (Use STAT DEV: to check on this.) We won't have to know which physical device has been assigned to LST: since our program will be careful to preserve the initial LST: assignment made by your system.

Here's the problem. When using MBASIC, all normal output is to the console. Thus if you run a program with PRINT statements, the output from these statements will show up on the console screen (or paper if it's a hard copy terminal). The same situation will hold when you use the LIST command. It will produce a program listing right on the console.

This is usually a good arrangement since most systems use a high-speed video terminal for the console. In addition to the speed, these devices operate quietly, and of course they don't consume gobs of expensive paper. So for most work, printing and listing to the console is the way to go. However, there are times when you want to save the output on paper, and it's then that you'd like output to go to the printer. Microsoft BASIC tells you that the way to do this is change all the PRINT statements to LPRINT when you're ready to use the printer. Another approach is to write two versions of the program, one using PRINT and the other using LPRINT.

This is OK for short programs, but for longer ones there's a better solution. It's to let your BASIC program change the IOBYTE so that output is directed to the LST: device when hard copy is desired, but directed back to the console when that's preferred.

One way to force normal console output to a printer is to assign the BAT: (batch) physical device as the CON: logical device. The reason this works is that the BAT: physical device is something of a fraud. It's really shorthand for saying that console input should be done via whatever PDPD is currently switched to the RDR:, and console output should be done via whatever PDPD is currently switched to the LST: device. It's this last switch we're interested in since the LST: logical device usually has the line printer associated with it.

If you check Fig. 5-7 you'll see that the way to assign BAT: as the CON: is to make the rightmost two bits of the IOBYTE = 10. We could make this switch from CP/M by typing

A>STAT CON:=BAT:

This is theoretically correct, but there is no way to give this command in the middle of a BASIC program. It would also be impossible to use STAT to switch output from the BAT: line printer back to the console from BASIC.

The solution is to use POKE 3,B where B is a decimal number we're going to let BASIC calculate. How? Well, first note that you can switch from the CON: video screen to the BAT: printer with

POKE 3, xxxxx10

where xxxxx means the same bits that were in IOBYTE to begin with (we don't want to mess up any other device assignments). The trick to

```
10 ´****************************************************
11 ´*      IOBYTE   (POKES THE IOBYTE TO SWITCH OUTPUT)      *
12 ´****************************************************
20 PRINT "MAKE SURE PRINTER IS READY -- OK";:INPUT A$
30 PRINT "THIS OUTPUT SHOULD APPEAR ON THE CON: DEVICE"
40 IOBYTE=PEEK(3): TEMP=IOBYTE AND 252 OR 2
50 POKE 3, TEMP
60 PRINT "THIS OUTPUT SHOULD APPEAR ON THE LST: DEVICE"
70 POKE 3, IOBYTE
80 PRINT "NOW THE OUTPUT SHOULD BE BACK ON THE CON: DEVICE"
Ok

RUN

MAKE SURE PRINTER IS READY -- OK? YEP

THIS OUTPUT SHOULD APPEAR ON THE CON: DEVICE
```

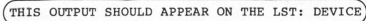
```
THIS OUTPUT SHOULD APPEAR ON THE LST: DEVICE

NOW THE OUTPUT SHOULD BE BACK ON THE CON: DEVICE

Ok
```

FIG. 5-8 Listing of the program IOBYTE which uses POKE to assign BAT: as the CON: device. This makes PRINT statements produce their output on the LST: device.

using the correct bits for xxxxxx (without ever knowing what they are) is to execute three statements based on the AND . . . OR technique we showed earlier

    10 IOBYTE = PEEK(3)
    20 TEMP = IOBYTE AND 252 OR 2
    30 POKE 3, TEMP

The second line is the clever one. It takes the bit pattern 11111100 (which is 252 in decimal), and does a logical AND with it and the bit pattern in IOBYTE. This preserves the first 6 bits, but changes the last two to 00. The resulting pattern is then logically OR'ed with the pattern 00000010. This leaves the first 6 bits alone, but changes the last two to 10 (decimal 2). And that's the pattern which assigns BAT: to CON:. Now for the lab.

Step 1.   Turn the computer on, boot CP/M, load MBASIC, and test the preceding theory. If you need help, try the procedure listed in Fig. 5-8.

When this program is run, you'll see the messages of lines 10, 20, and 30 on the console screen. Then line 60 will print on your listing device (which we assume to be your printer). Line 70 restores the IOBYTE to normal, so line 80 prints its message back on the console.

Step 2.   Now write and run a BASIC program that allows the user to specify on which device the output should appear. For a test, have the program print a table of squares and cubes. Then apply the idea to the program TAXDEP shown in Lab Exercise 1.5-1. Here's an example of how to code the first part of this step.

```
10  '**********************************************************
11  '* BASWITCH (USER CAN SEND PRINT OUTPUT TO CON: OR LST:) *
12  '**********************************************************
20  IOBYTE=PEEK(3): TEMP=IOBYTE AND 252 OR 2
30  PRINT "DO YOU WANT OUTPUT ON C)ON: OR L)ST:";:INPUT D$
40  IF D$="C" THEN 70
50  IF D$="L" THEN POKE 3,TEMP: GOTO 70
60  GOTO 30
70  PRINT "<<<<<<< TABLE OF SQUARES AND CUBES >>>>>>>"
80  FOR I= 1 TO 10
90     PRINT I, I*I, I*I*I
100 NEXT I
110 POKE 3, IOBYTE
120 GOTO 30
Ok


RUN
DO YOU WANT OUTPUT ON C)ON: OR L)ST:? C
<<<<<<< TABLE OF SQUARES AND CUBES >>>>>>>
 1              1              1
 2              4              8
 3              9              27
 4              16             64
 5              25             125
 6              36             216
 7              49             343
 8              64             512
 9              81             729
 10             100            1000
DO YOU WANT OUTPUT ON C)ON: OR L)ST:? L
<<<<<<< TABLE OF SQUARES AND CUBES >>>>>>>
 1              1              1
 2              4              8
 3              9              27
 4              16             64
 5              25             125
 6              36             216
 7              49             343
 8              64             512
 9              81             729
 10             100            1000
DO YOU WANT OUTPUT ON C)ON: OR L)ST:? ^C
Break in 30
Ok
```

THIS OUTPUT WILL APPEAR ON THE CON: DEVICE.

THIS WILL APPEAR ON THE LST: DEVICE.

THIS WILL PRINT BACK ON THE CON: DEVICE.

FIG. 5-9 The program BASWITCH illustrates a technique that allows the user to specify whether BASIC PRINT statements are to produce output on the CON: or LST: devices. In this example, the output is a simple table of numbers, but the same idea would work for any output produced by PRINT statement.

Warning: Some versions of CP/M do not use the IOBYTE, while other versions do not use all of it. For example, the CompuPro G&G system does not allow you to make CON:=BAT:, so the techniques explained in this section won't work. However, there are other ways to capture console output on a printer. These require a knowledge of machine language programming. Details are available from [22].

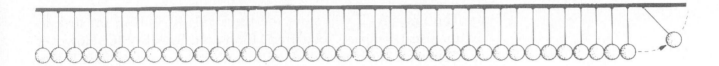

5.4 Using ED on BASIC Files; SUBMIT and XSUB

In this section we'll describe some additional techniques for using the facilities of CP/M in conjunction with BASIC. It should be kept in mind that the same techniques can be used with other programming languages—BASIC is being used simply because it is more familiar to most microcomputer programmers.

The first facility we'll use with BASIC is the CP/M editor ED. If you have a more general editor (of the type described in Section 4.1), the same ideas will apply. Here's a lab that explains how (and why) you'd use ED on a BASIC program. (If you'd like additional information on this subject, there's a good article by Dick Lutz called "Stripping with CP/M's ED" in the July 1981 issue of *Interface Age*. [15])

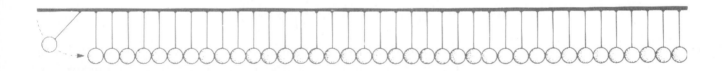

LAB EXERCISE 5.4-1   Using ED to Change PRINT Statements to LPRINT; Removing Remark Statements

The problem we're going to attack is that of making *global* changes in a BASIC program. The built-in editor of MBASIC allows you to make changes in individual lines of a program, but these changes are local. They apply only to the line being worked on, so the process must be repeated for each line in which similar changes are desired. This would not be very efficient if, for example, you wished to change all PRINT statements to LPRINT statements, or if you wanted to remove all remarks (REM or ') from a program. Here's how to make such global changes using the S, F, and J commands of ED.

Step 1.   Load the MBASIC system, and type in a program similar to that shown at the beginning of Fig. 5-10. Pay particular attention to the note in lines 15 and 16 of the program, making sure you use the apostrophe (') symbol for comments as shown.

Step 2. Now save the program, but in two forms as follows:

> SAVE "TESTPROG"
> SAVE "TESTPROG.ASC",A

The first SAVE will store the file TESTPROG.BAS on disk in the usual compact "tokenized" form used by MBASIC. However ED won't be able to work on it since it's not a pure ASCII file. The second SAVE command solves this problem by storing the same program on disk with the ,A (ASCII) option. We chose a different extension (.ASC) to remind ourselves of this, but any name could have been used. In fact if you had typed SAVE "TESTPROG",A the ASCII file would have been saved as TEST-PROG.BAS, overwriting the tokenized version.

Step 3. Now use ED on the ASCII file (we'll assume the name TEST-PROG.ASC was used). You do this by leaving MBASIC, and running ED as follows

> SYSTEM (CR)
> A>ED TESTPROG.ASC (CR)
>   :*#A#T (CR)

This will append all of the BASIC program TESTPROG.ASC to the buffer, and type it out at the console.

Step 4. Next use ED's substitute command to change all occurrences of PRINT to LPRINT as follows:

> *#SPRINT^ZLPRINT^Z (CR)

You can check that this step worked by typing B#T. This will type out the revised file, and leave the CP at the beginning of the buffer, ready for the next step.

Step 5. Our next job will be to get rid of all the remark (') statements. However this will have to be done in three stages.
5a.   First use the macro juxtaposition command to change all comments to null (empty) strings, and double check what happened as follows:

> *MJ'^Z^Z^L^Z (CR)
> *B#T (CR)

Recall that ^L is ED's way of indicating the (CR) (LF) at the end of a line.
5b.   Use the macro find command to locate lines that do *not* have BASIC code in them, back up to the beginning of each of these lines (−1L), and kill the whole line (1K). The way to find such lines is to realize that they all contain the pattern SPACE, ', (CR) (LF), whereas remarks in lines containing BASIC code don't have the SPACE before the ' (we wrote them that

way). Recalling that ˆL means (CR) (LF) to ED, the command to use is

*MF 'ˆL'ˆZ – 1L1K (CR)

Be sure to type a space between the F and ' in this command.
5c.   Return the CP to the beginning of the buffer and do another typing check with B#T. Then get rid of the remaining apostrophe (') symbols, by substituting an empty string for each of them.

*#S'ˆZˆZ (CR)

Step 6.   Do one more B#T to make sure that everything is as expected, and then save the modified file by using the *E command.

Step 7.   Return to MBASIC, load the modified file, list it, and run it to make sure it performs as expected. Fig. 5-10, below and on page 268, summarizes all of the preceding steps by showing an actual session that followed the procedure described here.

```
Ok

10 ´TESTPROG  (CONTAINS ´ REMARKS AND USES PRINT)
15 ´ NOTE: REMARKS ON LINES THAT CONTAIN  BASIC STATEMENTS
16 ´ MUST PUT THE ´ SYMBOL IMMEDIATELY AFTER THE STATEMENT
20 PRINT "TABLE OF SQUARES AND CUBES"´        PRINT HEADING
30 FOR I=1 TO 5´                              TABLE WILL HAVE 5 ENTRIES
40    PRINT I,I*I,I*I*I´                      OUTPUT IS TO CONSOLE
50 NEXT I
60 PRINT "* END OF PROGRAM *"´                END OF TESTPROG
Ok
SAVE "TESTPROG"          SAVE AS THE TOKENIZED FILE TESTPROG.BAS.
Ok
SAVE "TESTPROG.ASC",A    SAVE AS THE ADDITIONAL
Ok                       ASCII FILE TESTPROG.ASC
SYSTEM                   FOR USE WITH ED.

A>ED TESTPROG.ASC
   : *#A#T
   1:   10 ´TESTPROG  (CONTAINS ´ REMARKS AND USES PRINT)
   2:   15 ´ NOTE: REMARKS ON LINES THAT CONTAIN  BASIC STATEMENTS
   3:   16 ´ MUST PUT THE ´ SYMBOL IMMEDIATELY AFTER THE STATEMENT
   4:   20 PRINT "TABLE OF SQUARES AND CUBES"´        PRINT HEADING
   5:   30 FOR I=1 TO 5´                              TABLE WILL HAVE 5 ENTRIES
   6:   40    PRINT I,I*I,I*I*I´                      OUTPUT IS TO CONSOLE
   7:   50 NEXT I
   8:   60 PRINT "* END OF PROGRAM *"´                END OF TESTPROG
   1: *#SPRINT^ZLPRINT^Z      SUBSTITUTE "LPRINT" FOR ALL
                              OCCURRENCES OF "PRINT".
BREAK "#" AT T
   8: *B#T
   1:   10 ´TESTPROG  (CONTAINS ´ REMARKS AND USES LPRINT)
   2:   15 ´ NOTE: REMARKS ON LINES THAT CONTAIN  BASIC STATEMENTS
   3:   16 ´ MUST PUT THE ´ SYMBOL IMMEDIATELY AFTER THE STATEMENT
   4:   20 LPRINT "TABLE OF SQUARES AND CUBES"´       LPRINT HEADING
   5:   30 FOR I=1 TO 5´                              TABLE WILL HAVE 5 ENTRIES
   6:   40    LPRINT I,I*I,I*I*I´                     OUTPUT IS TO CONSOLE
   7:   50 NEXT I
   8:   60 LPRINT "* END OF PROGRAM *"´               END OF TESTPROG
   1: *MJ´ˆZ^Z^L^Z

BREAK "#" AT ^Z        JUXTAPOSE AN EMPTY STRING
   8: *B#T             BETWEEN ALL OCCURRENCES OF
   1:   10 ´           ' AND (CR)(LF).
   2:   15 ´
   3:   16 ´
```

FIG. 5-10   This is an on-line session showing use of ED to make global changes in a BASIC program which had first been stored as the ASCII file TESTPROG.ASC.

```
4:   20 LPRINT "TABLE OF SQUARES AND CUBES"´
5:   30 FOR I=1 TO 5´
6:   40    LPRINT I,I*I,I*I*I´
7:   50 NEXT I
8:   60 LPRINT "* END OF PROGRAM *"´
1: *MF ´^L^Z-1L1K
```

FIND ALL LINES CONTAINING "SPACE ´ (CR)(LF)" AND KILL THEM.

```
BREAK "#" AT ^Z
  1: *B#T
  1:   20 LPRINT "TABLE OF SQUARES AND CUBES"´
  2:   30 FOR I=1 TO 5´
  3:   40    LPRINT I,I*I,I*I*I´
  4:   50 NEXT I
  5:   60 LPRINT "* END OF PROGRAM *"´
  1: *#S´^Z^Z
```

SUBSTITUTE AN EMPTY STRING FOR ALL OCCURRENCES OF ´

```
BREAK "#" AT ^Z
  5: *B#T
  1:   20 LPRINT "TABLE OF SQUARES AND CUBES"
  2:   30 FOR I=1 TO 5
  3:   40    LPRINT I,I*I,I*I*I
  4:   50 NEXT I
  5:   60 LPRINT "* END OF PROGRAM *"
  1: *E
```

SAVE THE MODIFIED PROGRAM UNDER THE STARTING FILE NAME.

THEN GO BACK INTO BASIC TO LOAD AND TEST IT.

```
A>MBASIC
BASIC-80 Rev. 5.2
[CP/M Version]
Copyright 1977, 78, 79, 80 (C) by Microsoft
Created: 14-Jul-80
31046 Bytes free
Ok
LOAD "TESTPROG.ASC"
Ok
LIST
20 LPRINT "TABLE OF SQUARES AND CUBES"
30 FOR I=1 TO 5
40    LPRINT I,I*I,I*I*I
50 NEXT I
60 LPRINT "* END OF PROGRAM *"
Ok
RUN
TABLE OF SQUARES AND CUBES
1              1           1
2              4           8
3              9          27
4             16          64
5             25         125
* END OF PROGRAM *
Ok
```

THIS OUTPUT WILL BE ON THE LST: DEVICE SINCE LPRINT HAS BEEN SUBSTITUTED FOR PRINT.

FIG. 5-10   (*continued*)

Using SUBMIT and XSUB

The idea for the SUBMIT command comes from the "old days" of computing when people often prepared programs off-line (usually on punched cards), and then submitted their "deck" (usually called a *job*) to an operator. The jobs were literally piled up as a "batch" of such card decks, waiting their turn to be run through the card reader of the computer.

CP/M has an analogous facility for submitting a "batch" of jobs, where each job is a CP/M command together with whatever programs it references. The facility is called the SUBMIT transient command. The steps for using SUBMIT (and a related facility called XSUB) are best explained by example as shown in the following lab.

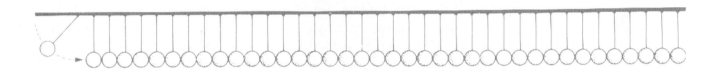

**LAB EXERCISE
5.4-2**

Using SUBMIT and XSUB

The goal of this lab is to prepare a special .SUB file which, when used with the SUBMIT command, will make the computer seem to be run by an operator who submits successive "jobs" in the given sequence.

Step 1.   The first thing to do is prepare a list of the jobs you want done by the computer. These jobs may be any of the tasks expressible as the built-in or transient commands that run on your CP/M system. This includes any programs stored as .COM files *provided the programs automatically return to CP/M at their completion, or you are there to press ^C.*

Here are examples of four such jobs:

Job 1. DIR A: (Display a directory of A.)
Job 2. ERA A:*.BAK   (Erase all backup files on A.)
Job 3. A:MYSTRING   (Run a small ML program stored on A as
                          MYSTRING.COM.)
Job 4. PIP B:=A:*.BAS   (PIP all the BASIC files from A onto B.)

Instant Quiz

Question:

Could one of these jobs be the command MBASIC or the command MBASIC TESTPROG?

Answer:

Yes and no. Both jobs could be started as part of a "batch stream," but neither of these commands returns to CP/M upon completion. The first one loads BASIC-80, and then just sits there waiting for you to do something in BASIC. The second one loads BASIC, runs the program TESTPROG.BAS, and *then* waits for you to do something in BASIC.

Question:

Is there any way to force the second form to return to CP/M so a new job can be run?

Answer:

Yes. Make sure the last line in TESTPROG is 65000 SYSTEM. This will cause a warm boot, and return to CP/M. If SUBMIT is still running, the next .SUB file command will then be given.

Question:

But suppose TESTPROG contains INPUT statements and no one is at the console to answer them?

Answer:

This won't work. You'll have to change your INPUT statements to READ and DATA statements (just like in the days of batch mode computing).

Step 2. Next go into ED, and create a file that has the extension SUB (for example, AUTO1.SUB). This file should contain the CP/M commands you want executed typed in the order you desire. Here are some examples:

Example 1

```
ED AUTO1.SUB
NEW FILE
       : *I
       1:  DIR A: (CR)
       2:  STAT A: (CR)
       3:  ^Z
       : *E
```

Example 2

```
ED AUTO2.SUB
NEW FILE
       : *I
       1:  DIR A:*.BAS (CR)
```

```
2:  MBASIC TESTPROG (CR)
3:  STAT A:*.BAS
4:  ^Z
 : *E
```

Example 3

```
ED AUTO3.SUB
NEW FILE
    : *I
    1: DIR A:*.BAS
    2: MBASIC $1
    3: STAT A:*.BAS
    4: ^Z
     : *E
```

Notice that example 2 and example 3 are almost the same. The difference is that example 2 names the BASIC program you want run in job 2 as TESTPROG, while example 3 uses the symbols $1 instead. These symbols act as a place holder, and indicate that the actual program name will be supplied when the SUBMIT command is used. (As we'll see shortly, for example 2 the command would be SUBMIT, while for example 3 the command would be SUBMIT TESTPROG.BAS.) *In both cases* it is important that the BASIC program used contain the line 65000 SYSTEM, and contain no INPUT statements (unless someone will be at the console to respond to them).

Step 3.   Use DIR to make sure your new files (e. g., AUTO1.SUB) are there. Use TYPE to double check their contents.

Step 4.   If you're using example 2 or example 3 above, make sure that an appropriate BASIC program is on file. For this lab, create one as follows:

```
A>MBASIC

10 PRINT "TESTPROG FOR USE WITH SUBMIT"
20 FOR I=1 TO 5:PRINT I,I*I,I*I*I: NEXT I
30 PRINT "AND NOW IT'S BACK TO CP/M FOR THE
NEXT JOB"
65000 SYSTEM
SAVE "TESTPROG"
SYSTEM
```

Step 5.   You can now test any of these .SUB files by using the SUBMIT command with them as follows (all the files shown should be on the disk in the A drive):

```
For example 1,   A>SUBMIT AUTO1
For example 2,   A>SUBMIT AUTO2
For example 3,   A>SUBMIT AUTO3 TESTPROG.BAS
```

In the first two examples, SUBMIT is typed followed by the name of the .SUB file to be used. In example 3, SUBMIT is typed with two "parameters." The first (AUTO3) is the name of the .SUB file, while the second (TESTPROG.BAS) is the name of the file to be substituted for the place holder $1. There can be several place holders (written as $1, $2, $3, and so on), in which case there would have to be corresponding parameters supplied with the SUBMIT command.

Step 6.   For users with a two-disk system, there's an optional technique you can try. It's a way of creating a special disk that will automatically execute a submit file any time it is booted. The trick is to get the desired .SUB file on the special disk in the form of a system created file called $$$.SUB. If CP/M finds such a file when it first boots, it immediately uses the SUBMIT command with it—you don't have to do anything.

To put such a $$$.SUB file on your special disk, do the following:

6a.   Create the .SUB file of your choice with ED on the disk in drive A as in step 2 above. Let's suppose it's called AUTO1.SUB. We'll also assume that the program SUBMIT.COM is on the disk drive A.

6b.   Place the special disk on which you want an "auto boot" version of AUTO1.SUB stored as $$$.SUB in drive B. Then type

```
A>B:
B>A:SUBMIT A:AUTO1
B>DIR
```

The submit file won't actually execute, but the directory of B: should now show a file $$$.SUB.

6c.   Remove the disk from drive B, and place it in drive A (after removing the original A disk of course!). If you now boot your system, you should see the commands of AUTO1 automatically executed without any intervention on your part.

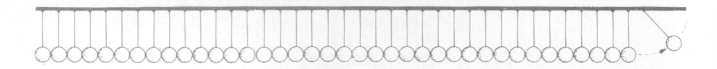

Using XSUB

A number of CP/M commands require that the user type some input once the command program starts executing. For example, when the command "DDT ufn" is executed, it prints the prompt symbol " − ", after which it waits for you to give it one of its subcommands (such as

D for Display, or L for disassemble, or G for "go to"). You can supply these subcommands ahead of time by including them in the .SUB file right after the DDT command. To let CP/M know you want this special feature activated, the command XSUB must be given as the first line of the .SUB file. The XSUB feature will remain activated until "turned off" by the next cold boot.

Here's an example of such a SUBMIT file being created in ED. Lines 3, 4, and 5 are subcommands that will be given to DDT. The command G0 was used to exit DDT. The CP/M manuals say that the two character sequence ^C could be used here, but due to a bug in SUBMIT.COM this doesn't work. (See *Dr. Dobb's Journal* [7], May 1982, page 12 for further details.)

```
ED AUTO5.SUB
NEW FILE
   : *I
  1:  XSUB
  2:  DDT CONCAT.COM
  3:  D0100
  4:  L0100
  5:  G0
  6:  STAT
  7:  ^Z
   : *E
```

In this example, line 2 will cause DDT to execute, and also load the file CONCAT.COM into the TPA. Then lines 3, 4, and 5 will be interpreted as commands which someone typed in at the console, telling DDT to first display CONCAT.COM starting at line 0100, second to disassemble the same lines, and third to "go to line 0" (which causes a warm boot and terminates DDT). Finally line 6 causes the STAT command to be executed.

To use the file AUTO5, you simply type SUBMIT AUTO5 and sit back and watch. Fig. 5-11 shows what happens.

Notice that the XSUB command must always be the first line of a .SUB file; it's never used by itself. It also has limitations, working only with programs like DDT, PIP and ED that do their input via BDOS function #10 (explained in Section 6.1). In particular, XSUB can't be used to provide input to BASIC programs.

5.5 BASIC Meets Machine Language; Using the BAS-COM Compiler

When programs are written using the MBASIC subsystem, they can be executed by simply typing the command RUN. What actually happens when you do this is that MBASIC *interprets* the BASIC-80 program that's currently in memory. The word "interpret" refers to the process of

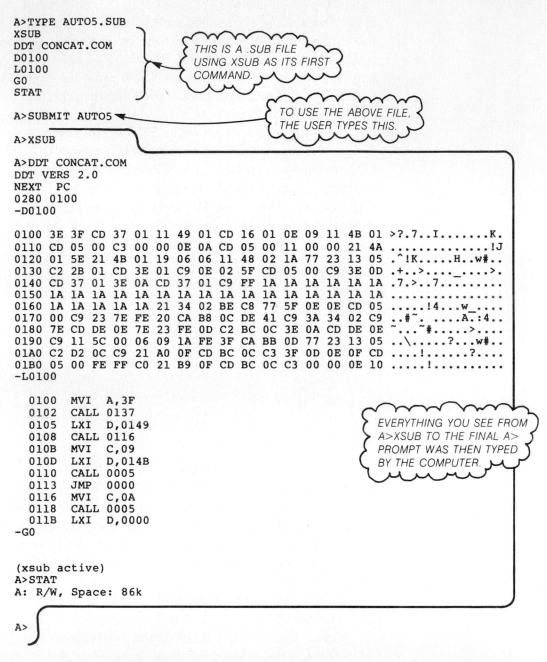

```
A>TYPE AUTO5.SUB
XSUB
DDT CONCAT.COM
D0100
L0100
G0
STAT

A>SUBMIT AUTO5

A>XSUB

A>DDT CONCAT.COM
DDT VERS 2.0
NEXT  PC
0280 0100
-D0100

0100 3E 3F CD 37 01 11 49 01 CD 16 01 0E 09 11 4B 01  >?.7..I.......K.
0110 CD 05 00 C3 00 00 0E 0A CD 05 00 11 00 00 21 4A  ..............!J
0120 01 5E 21 4B 01 19 06 06 11 48 02 1A 77 23 13 05  .^!K.....H..w#..
0130 C2 2B 01 CD 3E 01 C9 0E 02 5F CD 05 00 C9 3E 0D  .+..>...._....>.
0140 CD 37 01 3E 0A CD 37 01 C9 FF 1A 1A 1A 1A 1A 1A  .7.>..7.........
0150 1A 1A 1A 1A 1A 1A 1A 1A 1A 1A 1A 1A 1A 1A 1A 1A  ................
0160 1A 1A 1A 1A 1A 21 34 02 BE C8 77 5F 0E 0E CD 05  .....!4...w_....
0170 00 C9 23 7E FE 20 CA B8 0C DE 41 C9 3A 34 02 C9  ..#~.. ....A.:4..
0180 7E CD DE 0E 7E 23 FE 0D C2 BC 0C 3E 0A CD DE 0E  ~...~#.....>....
0190 C9 11 5C 00 06 09 1A FE 3F CA BB 0D 77 23 13 05  ..\.....?...w#..
01A0 C2 D2 0C C9 21 A0 0F CD BC 0C C3 3F 0D 0E 0F CD  ....!......?....
01B0 05 00 FE FF C0 21 B9 0F CD BC 0C C3 00 00 0E 10  .....!..........
-L0100

  0100   MVI   A,3F
  0102   CALL  0137
  0105   LXI   D,0149
  0108   CALL  0116
  010B   MVI   C,09
  010D   LXI   D,014B
  0110   CALL  0005
  0113   JMP   0000
  0116   MVI   C,0A
  0118   CALL  0005
  011B   LXI   D,0000
-G0


(xsub active)
A>STAT
A: R/W, Space: 86k

A>
```

THIS IS A .SUB FILE USING XSUB AS ITS FIRST COMMAND.

TO USE THE ABOVE FILE, THE USER TYPES THIS.

EVERYTHING YOU SEE FROM A>XSUB TO THE FINAL A> PROMPT WAS THEN TYPED BY THE COMPUTER.

FIG. 5-11 This is an example showing how to create and use a .SUB file that contains the XSUB command as its first line. Once XSUB has been used, the only way to deactivate it is with a cold boot.

translating each line of BASIC into machine language, and then executing it. This is done for each statement every time it is encountered, so in a loop like

FOR I = 1 TO 100: PRINT I*I: NEXT I

the statement PRINT I*I gets translated 100 times. As a result, more of the computer's time is spent in translating than in computing.

For many programs, this isn't such a bad situation since the programs run in a matter of seconds, translation and all. And with a BASIC interpreter, there's a big bonus: the user can stop the program anytime with a CONTROL-C, examine variables with a direct mode (no line number) PRINT statement, make changes, and then be off and running again with a simple CONT (continue), GOTO, or RUN. In general, interpreters are very user-friendly, saving *your* time rather than the computer's.

However in some applications (e. g., sorting large data bases, or displaying animated graphics), higher execution speeds are needed. One solution is to have your computer translate the entire program into machine language, and then to use this translation for actual program execution. A system program for doing such a one-time translation is called a *compiler*. An example of a compiler for BASIC-80 is the system program called BASCOM.COM. It's also sold by Microsoft, usually as part of a package that includes a macro assembler for Z80/8080 codes, and several other utility programs.

A second solution to the problem of gaining speed in a BASIC-80 program is to "hand-code" portions of it into machine language, and then employ the USRn or CALL feature of the MBASIC interpreter to call upon this machine language code. Section 6.3 contains an example showing how the USRn function works. A third option is to write the entire program in machine language with the help of a system program called an *assembler*. The last two approaches require that you know something about *machine language* and *assembly language* programming. These topics will be covered in the next chapter, so we won't discuss them any further here.

In this section we'll concentrate on the first solution, showing how to use the BASCOM compiler to translate BASIC-80 programs into machine language .COM files. As you'll see, the overall process is somewhat tedious, but the resulting run times are very impressive. More importantly, you don't have to know anything about machine language to use BASCOM.

In particular, the next lab will show how to develop a fast sorting program, first using MBASIC to write and test the program, and then using BASCOM to compile the tested program into machine language. The word "develop" is used to get across the idea that several stages (and software tools) will be required to go from the starting idea to the final machine language program.

To be specific, we'll start by using the MBASIC programming environment to write, debug, and interactively test our sorting program in BASIC-80. Then we'll switch over to using the BASCOM environment to *compile*, *link*, and *run* a machine language version of the same BASIC-80 program. As we'll see, these last three steps will require use of three new software tools: BASCOM (the compiler), L80 (the library/linker/loader), and BRUN (the so-called "run-time module"). Our lab will be based on using version 5.3 of all three programs. (The earlier versions

5.1 and 5.2 are not recommended since they produce extremely large machine-language files. Versions 5.2 and 5.3 cost around $400. The update from 5.2 to 5.3 costs about $100.)

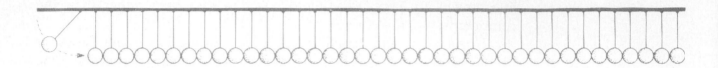

LAB EXERCISE 5.5-1   Using MBASIC and BASCOM to Develop and Compile a Shell Sort Program

Step 0.   The problem we'll attack is that of sorting a large array of integers. The solution we'll show can easily be generalized to the problem of sorting a large array of *string records*, where the sorting can be done on any field within the record. The basic algorithm used will be the Shell sort described on page 85 of Knuth [13]. Knuth formulates this algorithm as a simple but effective extension of the *insertion* sort described on page 81 of the same reference. Both the insertion sort and an extension to a generalized sort of string records are explained in *A Bit of BASIC* [4].

Step 1.   First make sure you have a CP/M disk onto which you have PIPed the files MBASIC.COM, BASCOM.COM, L80.COM, and BRUN.COM. After studying references [13] and [4] above, go into MBASIC to write and test a Shell sort program that can sort up to 500 integers. If you don't have the time or inclination to do this on your own right now, copy the program shown in Fig. 5-12.

Step 2.   Save the preceding program as both a regular file and as an ASCII file as follows:

    SAVE "SHELL"
    SAVE "SHELLASC",A

The ASCII version will be needed in step 4 when we compile this program.

Step 3.   Test the program SHELL in MBASIC by typing RUN, and answering *500* to the first question (number of integers to be sorted). The program will then prompt you to get a stopwatch ready, and press RETURN. The sorting then starts. When it finishes, you're prompted to stop the timing, after which the sorted list is printed. On a computer using a 4 MHz Z80, the sorting time will be around 55 seconds (*not* including printing).

```
10 '******************************************************
11 '* SHELL SORT (REF: D. KNUTH, VOL. 3, PG. 85, SHELL/INSERT) *
12 '******************************************************
20 DEFINT A-Z: DIM R(500)
30 INPUT "HOW MANY INTEGERS TO BE SORTED (MAX=500)";N
40 IF N<1 OR N>500 THEN 30
50 FOR I=1 TO N: R(I)=INT(256*RND):NEXT I: PRINT
60 PRINT ">>>>>    THE UNSORTED INTEGERS ARE    <<<<<"
70 FOR I=1 TO N: PRINT R(I),:NEXT I: PRINT
80 INPUT "SET STOP WATCH & PRESS ENTER TO BEGIN SORT--READY";D$
100 '
110 IF N=1 THEN 210
115 G=N
120 G=INT(G/2)
125 FOR J=G+1 TO N
130    I=J-G: T=R(J)
135    IF I<=0 THEN 160
140      IF T>=R(I) THEN 160
145        R(I+G)=R(I)
150        I=I-G
155        GOTO 135
160    R(I+G)=T
165 NEXT J
170 IF G>1 THEN 120
200 '
210 PRINT "STOP TIMING -- THE SORT IS FINISHED"
220 PRINT "========================================================="
230 PRINT "THE SORTED INTEGERS ARE:"
240 FOR I=1 TO N: PRINT R(I),: NEXT I: PRINT: PRINT "*** END ***"
250 END
Ok
Ok
LOAD "SHELL"
Ok
RUN
HOW MANY INTEGERS TO BE SORTED (MAX=500)? 22

>>>>>    THE UNSORTED INTEGERS ARE    <<<<<
  62            78            79            131           14
  201           127           93            252           230
  186           1             248           0             244
  10            229           169           141           209
  232           219
SET STOP WATCH & PRESS ENTER TO BEGIN SORT--READY? Y
STOP TIMING -- THE SORT IS FINISHED
=========================================================
THE SORTED INTEGERS ARE:
  0             1             10            14            62
  78            79            93            127           131
  141           169           186           201           209
  219           229           230           232           244
  248           252
*** END ***
Ok
```

FIG. 5-12   This is a Shell sort program written in BASIC-80. It is considerably faster than "n-squared" sorts such as bubble sort. The program is an extension of the INSERT sort program shown in reference [4]. The main difference is that a variable G (called the "gap") is used in SHELL (instead of the number 1 used in INSERT) for deciding which pairs of data are to be compared.

Step 4.   Assuming that your disk contains the file BASCOM.COM, you should next compile the ASCII version of the program (called SHELLASC.BAS) by typing the following:

A>BASCOM SHELLASC, SHELLASC = SHELLASC

In this command, the actual names of the three files being referred to are SHELLASC.REL, SHELLASC.PRN and SHEL-

LASC.BAS, in that order. The commnand tells BASCOM to use the last file name (SHELLASC.BAS) as the *source* program, and to generate two new files. The first (SHELLASC.REL) is called the *object* file, and it consists of the program translated into relocatable machine code. The second (SHELLASC.PRN) is called a *listing* file, and it contains a combination BASIC/Assembly Language "printer" listing that's useful for studying how the program was compiled. We've used the same primary name for all three files, but you can choose different names for the first two if you wish. Unclear, you say? Yes, but go ahead and type it in as shown anyway. (Further information on the various options allowed in this command can be found in Chapter 6 of the "Compiler User's Manual" supplied with BASCOM.)

Step 5. Type DIR to check that in addition to SHELLASC.BAS, you now have two new files as a result of step 4 (SHELLASC.REL and SHELLASC.PRN). The second file is exclusively for *your* information, so it can be erased if your disk gets too crowded.

Step 6. Assuming you also have the linker program L80 on your disk, you next use it to link in any other .REL files your program may use, and then to create a machine language command file. You do this as follows:

> A>L80
> *SHELLASC, SHELLASC/N/E

> (wait until several lines of
> messages appear here)

> A>DIR

The /N switch causes a .COM file with the *name* SHELLASC.COM to be created, while the /E switch saves this file on disk, and returns you to CP/M. When the linking is finished, the directory should show the final file we've all been waiting for

> SHELLASC.COM

However, this file won't execute unless there is also a second file available called BRUN.COM. It's the combination of these two that make up the final executable machine language program.

Step 7. Assuming your disk has the files BRUN.COM and SHEL-LASC.COM, you are now ready to run (and time) the compiled version of Shell sort. You do this by typing

> A>SHELLASC

You don't have to load BRUN; this will be done automatically. When the program executes, answer *500* for the number of integers you want sorted, and get your watch set. Then press return to start the sort. On a Z80 running at 4 MHz, we timed the sort (again not counting any printing) at about one-half a second.

Conclusion: For this program (which was slightly biased in favor of the compiler because it used all integer variables), SHELLASC.COM executes about 100 times faster than SHELLASC.BAS runs under MBASIC. Clearly, if you need speed, compilation is the way to go.

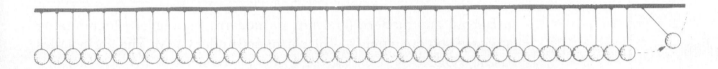

Epilogue—What Does BASCOM Do?

The BASCOM.COM compiler together with L80.COM and BRUN.COM, were used in the preceding lab to translate the original BASIC-80 program SHELLASC.BAS into the executable machine language program SHEL- LASC.COM. What's the difference between these two programs? The file SHELLASC.PRN helps answer that question by showing each of the original BASIC-80 statements, followed by its translation into 8080 assembly language code (see Chapter 6 for definitions of these terms). A portion of the file SHELLASC.PRN is shown in Fig. 5-13. The total .PRN listing is about six pages long. However this size is a little deceptive,

```
         **  0135'         INX     H
         **  0136'         JMP     I00011
         **  0139'I00012:
0139 0400        130    I=J-G: T=R(J)
         **  0139'L00130: LHLD    G%
         **  013C'         XCHG
         **  013D'         LHLD    J%
         **  0140'         MOV     A,L
         **  0141'         SUB     E
         **  0142'         MOV     L,A
         **  0143'         MOV     A,H
         **  0144'         SBB     D
         **  0145'         MOV     H,A
         **  0146'         SHLD    I%
         **  0149'         LHLD    J%
         **  014C'         DAD     H
         **  014D'         LXI     D,R%
         **  0150'         DAD     D
         **  0151'         MOV     E,M
         **  0152'         INX     H
         **  0153'         MOV     D,M
         **  0154'         XCHG
         **  0155'         SHLD    T%
0158 0404        135    IF I<=0 THEN 160
         **  0158'L00135: LHLD    I%
         **  015B'         MOV     A,H
```

FIG. 5-13   This is a small part of the file SHELLASC.PRN. It shows the 8080 assembly language code (which is very close to 8080 machine language) produced by compiling the two BASIC statements I = J − G and T = R(J). The meaning of the various 8080 instructions used here is given in Appendix D.

since there are a lot of calls to routines supplied by BRUN. In other words, the actual machine language program is a lot longer than the .PRN file suggests (about 18,500 bytes for our example; 2,500 for SHEL-LASC.COM, and 16,000 for BRUN).

5.6 Programming in C; Using C Compilers Under CP/M

Just about any modern (and not so modern) high-level programming language you can name is available for use under CP/M. The list includes Pascal, FORTRAN, COBOL, PL/I, several versions of BASIC, FORTH, Ada, and an interesting newcomer called C.

The C language was first developed at Bell Laboratories in the mid 1970s by Dennis Ritchie. It has roots in two earlier languages called BCPL and B. C was originally developed for use on the DEC PDP-11 computer, where it ran under a disk operating system called UNIX. As a matter of fact, UNIX and the PDP-11 C compiler are written in C (think about that one for a while).

There are now several good C compilers written in 8080 machine code for use under CP/M. The principal one we'll discuss here is the BDS C compiler written by Leor Zolman [20]. The BDS C compiler translates C into 8080 code directly, and it costs around $150. There are also compilers that produce intermediate assembly language which you then feed to an assembler like ASM. An example is the Supersoft C compiler [18].

Before explaining how to use the BDS C compiler, let's first take a look at a small program written in C. You'll probably find it to be somewhat cryptic, at least if you're used to BASIC. But as always, familiarity will help smooth out that problem.

Our sample program is a simple one, and it should be understood that it doesn't begin to show the real power of C. For that, we recommend study of some of the longer C programs supplied on the BDS disk. These reveal, among other things, that C is one of the few high-level languages that also allow you to control machine-level details. It's been characterized as a "low-level language with high-level constructs"—as an elegant machine-level language that's much easier to use than a real machine language of the type we'll be discussing in Chapter 6.

How to Create and Execute a BDS C Program

We'll start our look at C by writing a simple demonstration program called CDEMO1.C. Then we'll show how to compile and execute it, using the BDS C compiler to translate CDEMO1.C into the machine language file CDEMO1.COM. The procedures for compilation will be different with other compilers of course. We've chosen the BDS system because it is fast, reliable, and extremely well supported by its author and user group [10].

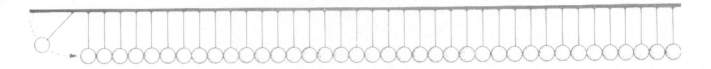

LAB EXERCISE 5.6-1

Writing, Compiling, and Executing a C Program with the BDS C Compiler

Step 0. The program one writes in C is called the source program, and it must be created as an ASCII file which has .C as the secondary file name. This can be done with the non-document mode of a word processor like WordStar, with the free text editor available from [10], or with the CP/M editor program ED. Fig. 5-14 shows such a program typed out after having been created in ED. The line numbers are supplied by ED; they are *not* part of the C program. After finishing with ED, a directory will show that a new file called CDEMO1.C has been created (the name we gave it when we entered ED).

We'll get back to this program shortly, and explain what each line means. For now, let's assume that it works (it does!), and concentrate on the business of getting it compiled and executed.

Step 1. Boot a system disk that contains ED, as well as the system programs supplied by BD Software. The system programs supplied with version 1.45 of BDS C are called CC1.COM, CC2.COM, CLINK.COM, CLIB.COM, C.CCC, BDSCIO.H, DEFF.CRL, and DEFF2.CRL. Next use ED to Create the program CDEMO1.C as given in Fig. 5-14, ending with the E command to save it on disk as the file CDEMO1.C. Use DIR to verify that the file has been saved. You can also use the CP/M command TYPE to inspect the contents of this (or any other) C file.

Step 2. Compile the C program by typing

    A>CC1 CDEMO1.C

This executes the file CC1.COM which is part I of the BDS C compiler (called the "parser"). As you can see in Fig. 5-14, after CC1 does its job, it prints a message about something called "elbowroom", and immediately goes into part II. This refers to what's sometimes called a second "pass" of the compiler (there are actually more than two passes, but the user need not be concerned about this). A separate file called CC2.COM is used for part II. However this file is loaded and executed automatically without any need for intervention on your part. When finished, part II prints a message about how much memory was left (e. g., "32K to spare"), and then returns you to CP/M.

Step 3.   Do another directory. You'll now see the results of the compilation as a new file called CDEMO1.CRL. The extension CRL means "C relocatable" file.

Step 4.   The next thing to do is to use the linker program CLINK.COM on the .CRL file by typing

A>CLINK CDEMO1.CRL   or simply   A>CLINK CDEMO1

The linker program adds whatever standard library functions your program calls on (e. g., printf), and then translates the .CRL code into 8080 machine language code. When the linker

```
B>ed cdemol.c
    : *#a#t
    1:  /* cdemol.c        This is our first demo program in C     */
    2:  /*                 Anything typed between asterisk-slash    */
    3:  /*                 pairs like this is a remark (comment)    */
    4:
    5:  main()
    6:  {
    7:      int num,square,cube;   /*declare all variables as type integer*/
    8:      printf("Table of squares and cubes\n");
    9:      printf("------------------------\n");
   10:      num=1;
   11:      while (num<=10)  {
   12:          square=num*num;
   13:          cube=square*num;
   14:          printf("For %2d, square & cube are: %6d%6d\n",num,square,cube);
   15:          num=num+1;
   16:      }
   17:      putchar('\n');
   18:      printf(".......... END OF PROGRAM ..........\n");
   19:  }
    1: *e

B>dir cdemol.*
B: CDEMO1    BAK : CDEMO1    C
B>ccl cdemol.c
BD Software C Compiler vl.45   (part I)
  38K elbowroom
BD Software C Compiler vl.45 (part II)
  32K to spare
B>dir cdemol.*
B: CDEMO1    BAK : CDEMO1    C    : CDEMO1    CRL
B>clink cdemol.crl
BD Software C Linker   vl.45
Linkage complete
  44K left over
B>dir cdemol.*
B: CDEMO1    BAK : CDEMO1    C    : CDEMO1    CRL : CDEMO1    COM
B>cdemol
Table of squares and cubes
------------------------
For  1, square & cube are:      1     1
For  2, square & cube are:      4     8
For  3, square & cube are:      9    27
For  4, square & cube are:     16    64
For  5, square & cube are:     25   125
For  6, square & cube are:     36   216
For  7, square & cube are:     49   343
For  8, square & cube are:     64   512
For  9, square & cube are:     81   729
For 10, square & cube are:    100  1000

.......... END OF PROGRAM ..........
```

FIG. 5-14   This figure shows how a C program (written with the use of ED) is compiled and executed using the BDS system.

finishes, do another directory, at which time you should see the 8080 version in the form of a third file called CDEMO1.COM.

Step 5.   CDEMO1.COM is a genuine CP/M machine-language command file, so it can be executed by typing its name as follows:

> A>CDEMO1

The output from this execution will appear on the console as shown at the bottom of Fig. 5-14.

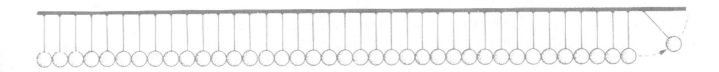

How the Program CDEMO1.C Works

Here's a line by line description of the features of C used in the program CDEMO1.C shown in Fig. 5-14. The line numbers we'll refer to are those supplied by ED; remember that C programs do not contain any line numbers of their own (the way BASIC programs do).

Lines 1, 2, and 3 are called comment statements. They are used for the same purpose as remark (or ') statements in BASIC. However each comment must be enclosed by the symbols /* and */ on the left and right, respectively. Notice that comments can also be placed on the same line as a regular C statement as illustrated in line 7. Comments are for people only, so they are not made part of the compiled program.

In general, a C program is made up of several smaller parts called *functions.* Our example has only one such function, and it's called main(). Every C program must have a main function. This is where execution starts, so some writers refer to it as the "main program." Line 5 is where our main program starts. You *must* use the name main() as shown, and the parentheses are always required. In some programs, certain "arguments" must be placed inside the parentheses. For this example, none are required, so two "empty" parentheses are used.

Lines 6 and 19 use the symbols { and } to show the beginning and end of the main program; they are always required. Another thing you'll notice if you skim down the program is that main() is composed of a sequence of statements, and that each statement must be terminated by a semicolon (;).

Line 7 is where the *type* of the variables that our main program will be using is declared. Statement 7 says that three variables *num, square,* and *cube* will be used in this program, and that they will all be of type *int* (integer). C allows additional types as follows: *float* (floating point), *char* (character), *short* (short integer), *long* (long integer), *unsigned* (unsigned integer), and *double* (double-precision floating point number). However, the C compilers for microcomputers do not usually support all of these types. We'll therefore limit our examples to use of type *int* and *char*.

The rules for naming variables and functions in BDS C are summarized in Appendix C. As noted there, names must begin with a letter or underscore, be 1 to 8 characters long, and use no special characters except the underscore (_).

Lines 8, 9, and 18 illustrate statements that use one of C's standard I/O functions, namely *printf*. This means "print with format", and it's similar to PRINT USING in BASIC. The general form is

printf("control string", argument1, argument2, . . .)

The words control string, argument1, argument2, . . . etc. refer to what are called the *arguments* of printf. The control string argument explains the *format* of the output (including text messages to be used), while argument1, argument2, etc., refer to the expressions (in some cases functions) that determine what *values* are to be printed. The symbols \n mean send the "new line" character, that is, output a character that eventually causes the system to do a (LF) and (CR). On most systems, "newline" is sent as a (LF), and the system later adds the (CR). Lines 8 and 9 do not have argument1, argument2, etc., because they are used solely to print the messages shown.

Line 14 has three arguments in addition to the control string, namely the variables *num, square,* and *cube*. Therefore, three placeholder codes which show where and how these three arguments are to be printed have been included in the control string of line 14. The codes are the following:

%2d is a placeholder for *num*
%6d is a placeholder for *square*
%6d is a placeholder for *cube*

In each of these codes, the % means "here comes a placeholder", while the d means "convert" the argument to *decimal* notation. The numbers 2, 6, and 6 say how many columns are to be used in the output for each of the variables. The output will be right-justified in these columns. To get left justification, you would use a minus sign, e. g., % − 6d. There are several other "convert" symbols (d, o, x, u, c, s, e, f, and g). We'll explain these as needed in later examples, and in Appendix C.

Line 10 is an assignment statement that stores the number 1 in the variable *num*. Incidentally, the symbol = is always used for assignments in C, whereas the symbols = = are used to mean "equal to" (as in "if(x = = 5)". . .etc.). Also note that upper- and lowercase letters can be used in C names, but that they have different meanings. Thus num and NUM are considered to be different variables. Your best bet is not to mix upper- and lowercase for variables. We'll stick to lowercase, as do most books on C, reserving uppercase for "symbolic constants" as explained in Section 5.7.

Lines 11 to 16 make up a *while* loop. The body of the loop is indicated by the curly brackets on lines 11 and 16. It consists of the four statements 12, 13, 14, and 15. These four statements are to be repeatedly executed "while (num< = 10)", that is, until num becomes greater than 10. Since num starts out as 1, and since it's incremented by 1 in line 15, the body of the loop will be executed exactly 10 times, producing the table of squares and cubes seen at the bottom of Fig. 5-14. The asterisk (*) in the assignment statements of lines 12 and 13 means multiply (as it does in most other languages).

Line 17 shows use of putchar(n), another one of the standard I/O functions. This sends exactly one character to the output device. In our case it will output the newline character \n. This is treated as a single character that causes the cursor to go to a new line. It's equivalent to using putchar(10) on most systems, where 10 is the ASCII code for line feed. In either case, the result is to create a blank line in the output just before the final message printed by line 18. For printable characters (like A), the argument of putchar can be either the character or its ASCII code, e. g., either putchar('A') or putchar(65). Notice that single quotes are used around character arguments (double quotes are reserved for strings).

The program CDEMO1.C could have been written in several other ways, of course. In particular, the *while* statement of line 11 could be replaced by a different kind of "loop control" statement. For example, the C *for* statement could be used as follows:

for(num = 1; num< = 10; num = num + 1) {body of the loop}

This statement is *not* like the FOR statement in BASIC. It's actually a compact way of expressing the *while* loop structure. It does exactly the same things as the following separate statements:

num = 1;
while(num< = 10)
{body of the loop; num = num + 1;}

Another simplification allowed in C is to use num + + (or + +num) instead of num = num + 1, and to use num − − (or − −num) instead of num = num − 1. An even more general form that can be used is e1 op = e2, which means e1 = (e1)op(e2), where op = +, −, *, or %.

In the program cdemo1.c, the body of the loop consisted of three statements (lines 12, 13, and 14 of Fig. 5-14). Here's what the new loop looks like when using the for statement.

```
for (num = 1; num< = 10; num + +){
        square = num*num;
        cube = square*num;
        printf("For%2d,square & cube are:%6d%6d\n",num,
        square, cube);
        }
```

The curly brackets show the three statements being controlled by the for statement.

Another change we can make in this program is to rewrite the loop as a user-defined function. User-defined functions are constructed very much like the main() function except that the user must give the function a name (e. g., sq_cube). There are also times when it is necessary to include one or more *arguments* in the parentheses after the function name. For example, we might write the function as sq_cube(n) to indicate that we want a table of squares and cubes for n numbers rather than 10. In this case, we'll have to declare the type of this variable inside the function, as well as the type of the other "private" variables it uses.

```
B>type cdemo2.c
/* cdemo2.c          This is a variation on the program cdemol.c
   It illustrates use of user-written functions and user input */

main()
{
    int num;      /*There will be only one varialbe in main*/
    printf("How many integers to be squared and cubed?");
    scanf("%d",&num);      /*This is like INPUT NUM in BASIC*/
    printf("\nTable of squares and cubes\n");
    printf("-------------------------\n");
    sq_cube(num);          /*Here's where the user function is called*/
    putchar('\n');
    printf(".......... END OF PROGRAM ..........\n");
}

/*----------------------------------------------------------------*/
sq_cube(n)        /*This is a user-written function*/
int n;            /*Function arguments must be declared before
                    defining the function and its variables      */
{
int x, square, cube;
for(x=1;x<=n;x++){
    square=x*x;
    cube=x*square;
    printf("For %2d, square and cube are: %6d%6d\n",x,square,cube);
    }
}
B>cdemo2
How many integers to be squared and cubed?13

Table of squares and cubes
-------------------------
For  1, square and cube are:     1     1
For  2, square and cube are:     4     8
For  3, square and cube are:     9    27
For  4, square and cube are:    16    64
For  5, square and cube are:    25   125
For  6, square and cube are:    36   216
For  7, square and cube are:    49   343
For  8, square and cube are:    64   512
For  9, square and cube are:    81   729
For 10, square and cube are:   100  1000
For 11, square and cube are:   121  1331
For 12, square and cube are:   144  1728
For 13, square and cube are:   169  2197

.......... END OF PROGRAM ..........
```

FIG. 5-15 The program cdemo2.c is a generalization of cdemol.c which allows the user to specify how many numbers are to be squared and cubed. It also "farms out" the calculation and printing work to a user-defined function called sq_cube(n).

The value of n will be supplied to sq_cube(n) by main() when it *calls* upon the function. The function is called upon in main by using the function, either within a larger statement, or simply by typing the one-word statement:

sq_cube(num);

The variable num is the name that main() uses for the number of squares and cubes it wants; num is then "passed" to the actual function sq_cube where it becomes a private copy of that number called n. A listing and run of a revised program using all these ideas is shown in Fig. 5-15 as cdemo2.c. Notice that cdemo2.c uses another new feature, the standard input function scanf. This is something like the reverse of printf. It's used here to allow the user to specify how many numbers are to be squared and cubed. The main() function then passes this information on to sq_cube(n) where it actually gets used.

We'll show more examples of the use of user-written functions in the next section. They are an important part of C programming, allowing one to modularize large programs into small chunks that are essentially independent of each other. This can be done in BASIC with subroutines, but more care is needed since the variables in BASIC are all "global," that is, available for use (including possible modification) by all parts of the program.

In C, most variables are "local," that is, private to each function. If you want global variables (and sometimes it's essential), you must declare them outside of any function, and *ahead of* (before) the place where they'll be used. This is usually before main() as will be illustrated in the program datasys.c of Section 5.7. However before moving on, it would be a good idea to get some experience with user-written functions by doing the next lab.

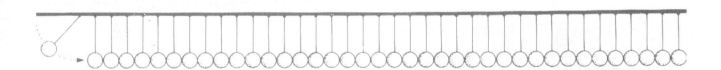

LAB EXERCISE 5.6-2

cdemo2.c: Adding Your Own Functions to a C Program

Step 1. Use ED to enter the program of Fig. 5-15, saving it as the file cdemo2.c.

Step 2. Compile the program by repeating steps 2, 3, and 4, of Lab 5.6-1.

Step 3. Run the program as in step 5 of Lab 5.6-1. Note that you'll have to enter a value for the number of integers to be squared. Experiment with 5, 10, 15, 20, etc. What is the largest value the program will accept before it "bombs out," that is, starts giving incorrect answers? Why does this happen? (Hint: the largest signed integer that can be stored is two bytes long. This is $(2^16-1)/2 = 65,535/2 = 32,767)$.

Step 4. Modify the program so that it won't accept a value of num that's too large. For an idea on how to do this, see the program cshell2.c in Section 5.7.

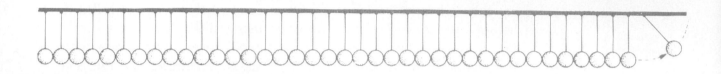

5.7 C in a Nutshell

In this section we'll follow the approach of Section 5.1, using three moderately simple C programs to illustrate additional features of the language. As before, our goal will be to help you develop a reading knowledge of C, and indicate some things to try next if you decide that you'd like to do some serious C programming on your own. The features of C covered in this section are a subset of those given in the book *The C Programming Language* by Kernighan and Ritchie [21]. This reference and [24] should be consulted if you decide to work extensively with the language.

We'll divide our coverage into two parts. In part A, a Shell sort program similar to the one shown earlier in BASIC will be used to illustrate the features of C that are most often used in numerical algorithms. In part B, we'll take a look at two C programs that manipulate string data. A summary of all the features of C is given in Appendix C.

Part A: Using C in a Numerical Sorting Program

Once you get past the idea that every C program is organized around a function called main(), the features used to write an ordinary program in C are similar to those used in most other high-level languages. Our first example will show how most of these features work in a sorting program called cshell2.c. This program is similar to the BASIC-80 program SHELL.BAS discussed in Section 5.5.

How cshell2.c Works

The structure of cshell2.c (Fig. 5-16) will be easier to follow if you notice that it consists of some preliminary lines, a main program, and a user-written program called *showntel*. In general, all C programs are made up of similar "chunks" called *definitions*. There are four kinds of definitions allowed, but only one (the *main* function) is required. The definitions that can be used in a C program are as follows:

1. A mandatory *main* function (lines 3–42 in cshell2.c).
2. A set of user-written functions which can be called upon by the main or other functions as needed (lines 44–59 of cshell2.c).
3. Special information that is *external* to the functions. This takes the form of *#define* and/or *#include* "control-lines" for use by the compiler (line 2 of cshell2.c).
4. Definitions of *external variables*, that is, variables which are available for use by more than one function (not used in cshell2.c).

The use of external variables—also called global variables—is an exceptional thing in C programs (which is just the reverse of BASIC where *all* variables are global). There aren't any global variables in cshell2.c since all the variables are defined inside of functions. For this reason, they are called *internal variables*. They are also called *auto* variables because they automatically appear and disappear at the start and exit of a function. You can think of internal as meaning "private," and external as meaning "public." External variables will be illustrated in the program datasys.c of Lab 5.7-3.

Note: Although C permits both internal and external variables, the only kind of functions it allows are external. In other words, you can't define one function inside another for private use. All the functions you write in a C program are public; any function may be used by any other function.

Instant Quiz

1. Will the following C program (silly.c) work?
2. What will it do?
3. What won't it do?
4. Is the program a good idea?

```
main()         /*silly.c*/
{
printf("Humpty\n");
myfunction();
printf("***END***\n");
}
myfunction()
{
printf("Dumpty\n");
main();
}
```

Answers

1. Yes it will work. Both main and myfunction are external functions, so it's OK for them to call each other.

2. It will print the sequence:

> Humpty
>
> Dumpty
>
> Humpty
>
> Dumpty
>
> . . . etc. . . . until something called the *stack* overflows.

3. It will never print ***END***.

4. It's probably a terrible idea. However, it illustrates the fact that C has been deliberately designed as a very permissive language. Unlike "strict" languages such as Pascal, it would much rather let you do silly things than take away your freedom to try them.

Meanwhile, Back at cshell2.c

Fig. 5-16 shows a listing and run of our Shell sort program. It contains a main program and one user-written function called showntel.

In studying the run of cshell2.c, notice that it does five things:

1. It asks you how many integers you'd like to see sorted.

2. It fills an array called r[] with a random sequence of that many integers.

3. It prints the (unsorted) contents of r[].

4. It sorts the integers in r[].

5. It prints the (now sorted) contents of r[].

```
 1:  /* cshell2.c (Shell Sort of Integers.  Ref: D.Knuth, v3, pg. 85) */
 2:  #define EVER ;;
 3:  main() {
 4:  int r[801];
 5:  int n,i,j,gap,temp;
 6:  char dummy;
 7:  srand(0);
 8:  /* putchar(27);putchar(´E´);       Optional  Z19 clear screen */
 9:  do {
10:          printf("How many integers to be sorted (max=800)? ");
11:          scanf("%d",&n);
12:  } while(n<1 || n>800);
13:
14:  for(i=1; i<=n; i++)
15:          r[i]=rand();
16:
17:  printf(">>> The unsorted integers are <<<\n");
18:  showntel(n,r);
19:
20:  printf("Set stopwatch & press enter to begin sort -- Ready? ");
21:  dummy=getchar();
22:
23:  gap=n/2;
24:  while(gap>0) {
25:          for(j=gap+1; j<=n; j++) {
26:                  i=j-gap; temp=r[j];
27:                  while (i>0)
28:                          if (temp>=r[i])
29:                                  break;
30:                          else { r[i+gap]=r[i];
31:                                 i=i-gap;
32:                          }
33:                  r[i+gap]=temp;
34:          }
35:          gap=gap/2;
36:  }
```

FIG. 5-16   This is a listing and run of cshell2.c.

```
37:
38:   printf("Stop timing -- sort is finished\n");
39:   printf(">>> The sorted integers are <<<\n");
40:   showntel(n,r);
41:   printf("\n.......END OF SHELL SORT PROGRAM.......\n");
42:   }
43:   /* ----- Function to display array, 9 columns per line ----- */
44:
45:   showntel(m,data)                        /* The routine showntel is written      */
46:   int m,data[];                           /* in a clumsy manner to illustrate     */
47:   {                                       /* use of the goto in C.  Here's a much */
48:   int i,k;                                /* cleaner version courtesy of L. Zolman*/
49:   i=0;                                    /*                                      */
50:   for(EVER){                              /* {                                    */
51:           for (k=1;k<=9;k++){             /*   int i ;                            */
52:           i++;                            /*   for(i=1;i<=m;i++){                  */
53:           if (i>m) goto quit;            /*     if((i-1)%9==0)                    */
54:           printf("%7d",data[i]);/*          putchar('\n');                   */
55:           }                               /*     printf("%7d",data[i]);           */
56:           printf("\n");                   /*   }                                  */
57:   }                                       /* }                                    */
58:   quit: printf("\n");
59:   return;
60:   }


A>cshell2
Wait a few seconds, and type a CR:
How many integers to be sorted (max=800)? 80
>>> The unsorted integers are <<<
    26873   20978    9189   18379    3990    7981   15962   31924   31080
    29393   26019   19271    5775   11551   23102   13436   26873   20722
     8677   17355    1686    3117    6490   12980   25704   18640    4513
     8771   17798    2828    5913   12082   24164   15560   31121   29474
    26181   19595    6423   12847   25694   18620    4473    8947   17894
     2764    5529   11058   22116   11720   23185   13346   26693   20874
     8981   17963    3414    6829   13658   27316   21864   11217   22179
    11590   23181   13594   27189   21610   10453   20907    9046   18093
     3418    7093   14186   28372   23720   14417   29091   25158
Set stopwatch & press enter to begin sort -- Ready?
Stop timing -- sort is finished
>>> The sorted integers are <<<
     1686    2764    2828    3117    3414    3418    3990    4473    4513
     5529    5775    5913    6423    6490    6829    7093    7981    8677
     8771    8947    8981    9046    9189   10453   11058   11217   11551
    11590   11720   12082   12847   12980   13346   13436   13594   13658
    14186   14417   15560   15962   17355   17798   17894   17963   18093
    18379   18620   18640   19271   19595   20722   20874   20907   20978
    21610   21864   22116   22179   23102   23181   23185   23720   24164
    25158   25694   25704   26019   26181   26693   26873   26873   27189
    27316   28372   29091   29393   29474   31080   31121   31924

.......END OF SHELL SORT PROGRAM.......
```

FIG. 5-16   (*continued*)

Since steps 3 and 5 do the same thing, we put them in a common function called showntel. As you can see, this function has two arguments: the *number* of integers stored in the array, and the *name* of the array. Why just the name? The reason is that the name of an array in C is also a pointer to the block of memory where the actual contents of the array are stored. Thus the declaration

    int r[801];

means two things: (1) the compiler is to set aside space for 801 integer variables (usually 2 bytes each) with the names r[0], r[1], r[2], . . ., r[800], and (2) r is a *pointer constant*, that is, a name which stands for the *address* of r[0]. Another way of stating (2) is to write r = &r[0], where & means "address of." Here's how you can picture the array declared by int r[801].

Memory Address   *Memory Contents*

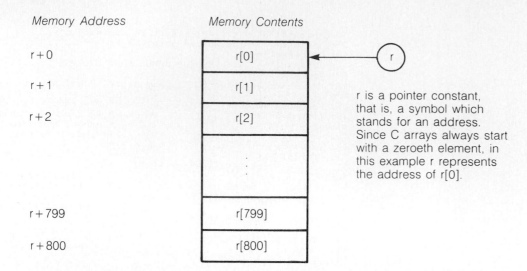

r + 0   r[0]

r + 1   r[1]

r + 2   r[2]

r + 799   r[799]

r + 800   r[800]

r is a pointer constant, that is, a symbol which stands for an address. Since C arrays always start with a zeroeth element, in this example r represents the address of r[0].

Thus the notation r means *pointer* to (address of) r[0], whereas the notations r[0], r[1], r[2], etc. mean the *contents* of successive elements in the array. The notation r+i means the address of the ith element, r[i]. In our example the elements are integers which occupy two bytes each, but C knows this and calculates addresses accordingly. To find the contents at a given address, C also uses the notation *address. Thus *(r+i) means the same thing as r[i], where * is called the *indirection* operator.

Note: Our program stores data in r[1] to r[800] to make it similar to a BASIC program. However, most C programmers would use r[0] to r[799].

Another pointer-related idea shows up in the input statement scanf("%d",&n). The notation &n means *address of n*. The reason this notation *must* be used in scanf is that we have to tell the compiler *where* (at what address) to store the number input by the user. This idea holds in BASIC too, but you are never aware of it; BASIC INPUT statements automatically use the "address of" operator with input variables.

To become familiar with these ideas, try writing, compiling, and running cshell2.c. Use the next lab as a guide to the steps to take.

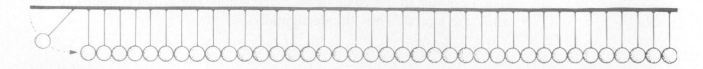

LAB EXERCISE 5.7-1

Writing a Shell Sort Program in C

Step 1. Enter the program cshell2.c shown in Fig. 5-16, using ED or a word processor. Study the program as you enter it, asking yourself what each statement or group of statements does.

Step 2.   Compile and link the program.

Step 3.   Run the program for values of N = 25, 50, 100, 200, 400, and 800. Make a chart of the time it takes to carry out the sorting for each value (do *not* include the time for the printing done by showntel).

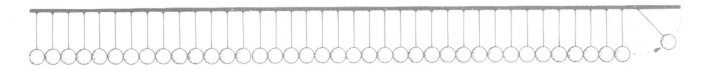

Instant Quiz

Using Appendix C and/or the BDS C manual, determine what the following lines do in cshell2.c.

1. Lines 2 and 49.
2. Lines 7 and 15.
3. Lines 18 and 40.
4. Lines 23 through 36.

Answers

1. Line 2 defines the symbolic name EVER to be the same as two semicolons. Thus the compiler reads line 49 as for(;;). This is interpreted as for("no starting value"; "no stopping conditions"; "no increment") so for(EVER) becomes an infinite loop. We get out of it by using the if . . . goto of line 52. A much better approach is shown in the comment section of showntel.

2. srand(0) initializes the random number generator to a value that depends on how long you take to respond with <cr>, while rand() supplies a new random integer (from 0 to 32,767) each time it's called.

3. Lines 18 and 40 cause the user-written function showntel() to be executed. Notice that even though r[801] was declared as an array of 801 integers, you pass the *name* of the array (r) as a function argument. This is because you only want to tell the function *where* the array is. In C you *don't* pass a copy of an array to a function— just a pointer to it. In this way the array is made *common* to both main() and showntel(), so they can both read it or modify it.

4. Lines 23 through 36 implement the Shell sort algorithm in a slightly different way than shown in Section 5.5.

Statements in C

The program cshell2.c used seven of the dozen different kinds of statements available in C. Here's a summary of all the statement types that can be used in C programs. Wherever you see the word "statement," it may be replaced by *compound statement*, that is, a block of statements surrounded by curly brackets {. . .}. All statements end with a semicolon (;) but you do not put a semicolon after the right bracket of a compound statement.

The simplest kind of statement is an expression followed by a semicolon.

Examples:

```
k+ +;
getchar();
x=15;
```

Note that C considers an assignment (like x=15) to be an expression.

More complicated statements are constructed with various key words as follows:

1. if (expression) statement

Example:

```
if (x= =0) printf("No data available\n");
```

2. if (expression) statement else statement

Example:

```
if ((n%20)= =19) {
    printf("Press any key to continue /n");
    getchar();
}
else {
    printf("%3d",array[n]);
    n+ +;
}
```

Note: n%20 means "the remainder after dividing n by 20".

3. while (expression) statement

Example:

```
k=0;
    while (k <= 99){
    array[k]=100*k+k;
    k+ +;
}
```

4. do statement while (expression)

Example:

```
do{
    printf("how many numbers to be sorted (max=800)?");
    scanf("%d",&n);
    putchar ('\n');
}while (n < 0 || n > 800);
```

5. switch (expression) statement

(See example in 7.)

6. case constant-expression : statement

(See example in 7.)

7. default : statement

Example:

switch, case, and default are usually combined as follows:

```
switch (c) {
    case 'a' :
    case 'A' : r=append(r,lim); break;
    case 'q' :
    case 'Q' : break;
    default  : printf("** Illegal Command **");
    }
```

8. break;

Note: break causes an early exit from the body of switch, for, while, or do statements.

Example:

    (see example in 7.)

9. continue;

Note: continue causes a skip to the next iteration in a for, while, or do loop.

Example:

```
for (i=0; i<99; i++){
```

```
        if (array[i] < 0) continue; /* skip to next i */
        array[i] = i + 100;
    }
```

10. return; or return (expression);

Example:
```
    square(n)
    int n;
    {
        return (n*n);
    }
```

11. goto identifier;

Example:

```
    start:
    puts(CLEARS);
```
— — — —
```
    if (x < 200) goto start;
```

Part B: Manipulating String Data in C

Fig. 5-17 shows a small demonstration program called strdem.c that allows you to enter a string, and then see it printed. It also shows how C stores strings in an *array of characters*, placing one character in each byte of the array. To mark the end of a string, C uses the ASCII null character 00 (written as '\0') which is the same as binary zero. (Note that this is *not* the same as the ASCII code for the digit zero which is 48 decimal).

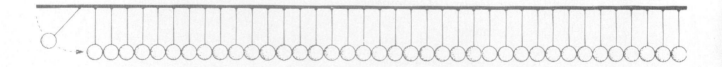

LAB EXERCISE 5.7-2

Using Strings in C: strdem.c

Step 1. Enter strdem.c with ED, then compile and link it.

Step 2. Experiment with using strdem, making sure you understand the printout of ASCII codes used to represent the strings you typed, and how they were stored in memory.

```
B>type strdem.c
/* strdem.c    (demo of use of strings in C) */
main()
{
int k,ln;
char str[129];
printf("Type a string (128 characters max):\n");
scanf("%s",str);
ln=len(str);
printf("\n>>> Length of your string is %3d\n",ln);
printf("The string you typed was:\n\n%s\n\n",str);
printf("The ASCII decimal (hex) codes stored in str[] were \n");
for(k=0;k<ln;k++)
      printf("Character #%-3d = %4d (%2x hex)\n",k,str[k],str[k]);
printf("Terminating code at position %3d was %3d\n",ln,str[ln]);
}
/*------------------------------------------------------------*/
len(s)    /* Function to return length of string s */
char s[];
{
   int i;
   for(i=0; s[i] != '\0'; i++)
      ;
   return(i);
}
/*Note:  The library function strlen(s) could have been used
instead of len(s).  Other useful BDS C string library functions
are  strcpy(s1,s2) which copies the null terminated string at
s1 to location s2,  strcat(s1,s2) which concatenates s2 at the
end of s1,  strcmp(s1,s2) which returns a value >0 if s1>s2,
=0 if s1=0, <0 if s1<s2,  and atoi(s) which is like VAL(N$)*/

B>strdem
Type a string (128 characters max):
All is well

>>> Length of your string is  11
The string you typed was:

All is well

The ASCII decimal (hex) codes stored in str[] were
Character #0   =   65 (41 hex)
Character #1   =  108 (6C hex)
Character #2   =  108 (6C hex)
Character #3   =   32 (20 hex)
Character #4   =  105 (69 hex)
Character #5   =  115 (73 hex)
Character #6   =   32 (20 hex)
Character #7   =  119 (77 hex)
Character #8   =  101 (65 hex)
Character #9   =  108 (6C hex)
Character #10  =  108 (6C hex)
Terminating code at position  11 was    0
```

FIG. 5-17 The program strdem.c illustrates the data structure used by C for storing ASCII strings. *Important Note:* The identifier str in the statement scanf("%s", str); is a *pointer* since it is the name of an array. It is taken to be the same as &str[0] or &str.

Step 3. Modify strdem.c so that it uses the standard library function strlen instead of len.

Step 4. See if you can modify strdem.c further so that it allows input of two strings, and then prints their concatenation. Compare

the results with the machine language program CONCAT of
Chapter 6.

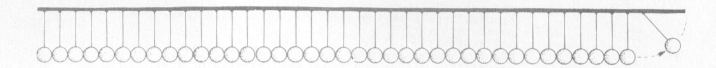

Defining and Using String Arrays in C

Handling arrays of strings in C is a lot more difficult than in MBASIC.
The technique is to set up an array of *pointers* to a large common *string
space*. You also have to use an *allocation* function to parcel out this string
space. We won't explain all the details, but if you study the program
in the next lab you'll get some idea of what's involved.

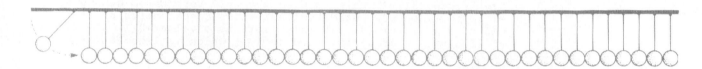

LAB EXERCISE   Advanced String Manipulation in C: datasys.c
5.7-3   *Step 1.*   Study Fig. 5-18 and the accompanying photographs of a run.
Enter and compile this program, and then execute it.

```
 1: /* datasys.c  (Micro data collection system in C)   */
 2: #define EOF -1
 3: #define RLIM 100
 4: #define MAXCHR 132
 5: #define EVER ;;
 6: #define ALLOSIZE 1000
 7: #define INTOREV "\033p"
 8: #define OUTAREV "\033q"
 9: #define CLEARS "\033E"
10:
11: int nr;    /* next record number */
12: char *rcdptr[RLIM];  /* external array of ptrs */
13: char *alloptr,allobuf[ALLOSIZE];
14: main(){
15: char c;
16: nr=0; alloptr=&allobuf;
17: start:
18: puts(CLEARS);
19: puts(INTOREV);
20: putchar(10);
21: printf("*** DATASYS.C  Micro Data Collection System ***\n");
22: puts(OUTAREV);
23: do{
24:     printf("\nA)ppend, D)isplay, L)oad, S)ave, or Q)uit?");
25:     c=getchar();
26:     putchar('\n');
27:     switch(c){
28:        case 'a':                          /* NOTE: The cases which */
29:        case 'A': nr=append(nr,RLIM); break;   /* test for lower case   */
30:        case 'd':                          /* letters can be elimin-*/
31:        case 'D': display(nr); break;          /* ated by using         */
```

FIG. 5-18   This is a listing of the string data-collection program datasys.c.

```
32:            case ´l´:                              /* c=toupper(getchar())  */
33:            case ´L´: load(); break;               /* in line 25            */
34:            case ´s´:
35:            case ´S´: save(); break;
36:            case ´q´:
37:            case ´Q´: break;
38:            default : printf("*** Illegal command ***");
39:        }
40:        printf("\n>>> You have exited from %c) mode. <<<",toupper(c));
41:
42:    }while(c!=´q´ && c!=´Q´);
43:
44: printf("\nProgram is about to terminate -- O.K. (Y/N)?");
45: if((c=getchar()) != ´Y´ && c != ´y´) goto start;
46: else printf("\n*** END OF PROGRAM ***\n");
47: }
48:
49: append(r,lim)
50: int r,lim;
51: {
52: int len;
53: char *p,*alloc(),buf[MAXCHR];
54: putchar(´\n´);
55: puts(CLEARS);
56: puts(INTOREV);
57: printf("\n    Append Mode (To exit this mode press RETURN   \n");
58: puts(OUTAREV);
59: for(EVER){
60:        printf("\n>>>>> Type data for record #%3d:\n",r);
61:        len=stringin(buf,MAXCHR);
62:        if(len==0) return(r);
63:        else if(r>=lim){printf(">>> Max rcd # reached\n");return(r);}
64:        else if((p=alloc(++len))==0)
65:           {printf("Out of str space\n");return(r);}
66:        else{
67:           strcpy(p,buf);
68:           rcdptr[r++]=p;
69:           }
70:        }
71: }
72:
73: stringin(inbuf,maxc)
74: char inbuf[];
75: int maxc;
76: {
77: int c,i;
78: for(i=0; i<maxc && (c=getchar()) != ´\n´ && c!=EOF; ++i)
79:        inbuf[i]=c;
80: inbuf[i]=´\0´; return(i);
81: }
82:
83: char *alloc(n)      /* fcn to return ptr to string space for n chrs */
84: int n;
85: {
86: if(alloptr+n <= allobuf+ALLOSIZE){
87:        alloptr +=n;
88:        return(alloptr-n);
89:        }
90: else return(0);
91: }
92:
93: free(p) /*Function to reclaim string space; not used in this example*/
94: char *p;
95: {
96: if(p>=allobuf && p<allobuf+ALLOSIZE)
97:        alloptr=p;
98: }
99:
100: display(r)
101: int r;
102: {
103: putchar(´\n´);
104: int i;
105: puts(CLEARS);
106: puts(INTOREV);
107: printf("   DISPLAY MODE.  All Records on File Will be Shown   \n");
108: puts(OUTAREV);
109: for(i=0;i<r;i++){
110:     printf("%s\n",rcdptr[i]);
111:     if((i%20) == 19) {printf(".....Press any key to see more.....\n");
112:                     getchar();}
113:     }
```

FIG. 5-18   *(continued on next page)*

```
114: printf("\n:::    Total # of Records Displayed was%3d    :::\n",r);
115: }
116:
117: save(r)
118: int r;{
119: printf("S)ave not available yet.");
120: }
121:
122: load(){
123: printf("L)oad is not available yet.");
124: }
```

FIG. 5-18   (*continued*)

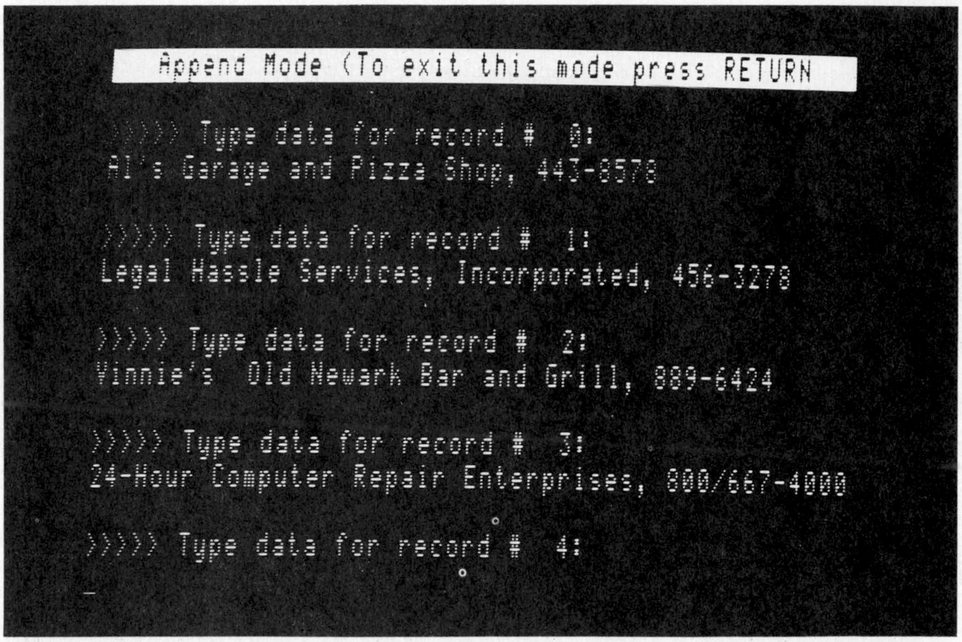

PHOTOS 5-1 and 5-2   *These show parts of a sample run of the program datasys.c. The reverse video titles are made by using the function puts(INTOREV) to send the proper string of codes to the console. For a Z19 terminal, INTOREV is defined as "\033p", that is, as escape (octal 33) followed by p. A similar definition is used for OUTAREV. These definitions would have to be changed for other terminals.*

Step 2. Design your own data collection system as an extension of datasys.c, using ideas that you glean from other books on C. This is *not* an easy task, so expect a need for lots of outside study. See Fig. 5-19 of Section 5.8 for a comparable program in BASIC.

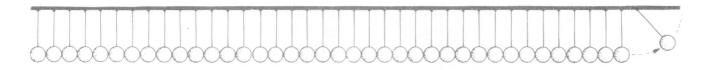

Instant Quiz

1. To what use might datasys.c be put?
2. How does datasys.c store the string data input by a user?

Answers

1. The program datasys.c could serve as a starting point for a data base system of the type discussed in Section 4.3. Of course it's only a start, but the essential data structures have been illustrated.

2. The best way to explain the data storage scheme used by datasys.c is to draw pictures of memory for some specific data. For example, you might show the two records MARY and BILL stored in allobuf[] as follows:

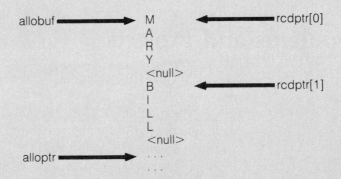

The identifier **allobuf** is a *pointer constant*. It's a symbolic way of representing the starting address of the string space allocated by declaring the character array allobuf[1000]. The declaration "char *alloptr" makes alloptr a *pointer variable*. It's used to hold the address of the next free byte of string space. The contents of rcdptr[] are pointers that show the start of each record in allobuf. Given this picture for a start, try your hand at tracing how the functions append(), stringin(), and alloc() actually use this data structure.

Rally Revisited

The program rally.com shown in Section 1.1 is the compiled version of rally.c which is available from the BDS C user's group [10]. If you obtain this program, you'll notice that it has the statement

    #include "bdscio.h"

at the beginning. This causes the *header* file bdscio.h to be inserted at the beginning of the program. This file contains a number of #define statements plus some special functions that are essential to the operation of rally. However the file bdscio.h as supplied with BDS C will probably not work with your system since it needs to know special things about your console and the I/O (or memory mapped) ports it uses. You should therefore expect that you'll have to ask around to get some help in modifying bdscio.h before being able to use it with rally.c. Then you'll have to re-compile rally.c with the new header file included.

There's More?

Our coverage of C has been a rapid one, and there's obviously a lot more to the language than meets the eye. Three suggestions: (1) forge ahead and read Chapter 6 on machine language, and then re-read this section; (2) check out and study references [21] and [24]; (3) then try studying some of the very long C programs you can get "for free" from the C user's group [10], or when you buy the BDS C compiler disk. We think you'll find that C will look a lot less obscure after you complete these three apprenticeships.

5.8 Problems and Projects

1. Are the file names PROG/M or test.BAS legal in MBASIC? Are they a good idea? Why or why not? How about PROG"3" as a filename?

2. The program ZODIAC (Section 5.1) requires that you input the number of people using the program. You may wish to leave this number open-ended. Modify ZODIAC so that it uses a special string (e. g., $$) to mean "end of data input". Also consider adding a graphics feature to ZODIAC so that it prints a small symbolic representation· of each person's sign.

3. Learn to use the built-in EDIT command of MBASIC by studying Appendix B. Can line numbers be modified with this command? Can they be modified in other ways? (Hint: Read up on the RENUM command of MBASIC. Also consider how ED might be used.)

4. Suppose you have splurged on two printers for your system: a high speed dot-matrix printer and a "correspondence quality" daisy-wheel printer. Write a BASIC subroutine that allows the user to direct output from PRINT statements to the console screen, to the dot-matrix printer, or to the daisy-wheel printer. Assume that the dot-matrix printer is

connected as the UL1: physical device, and the daisy-wheel as the LPT: physical device.

5. Fig. 5-19 shows a simplified program (called TINYMAIL) for entering, saving, and printing mailing list records. List the features you would like to see in the EDIT module at line 615. Also consider having the program maintain a file of cities and states for various ZIP codes. When data is entered, the ZIP code should be requested before city and state. If it is on file, the city and state should then be entered automatically. If it's not, the user will type in city and state, but this information will then be added to the ZIP file. For one solution to this problem, write to reference [22].

6. Modify the TINYMAIL program so that the file of names and addresses can be much bigger than the 100 record buffer B$(,) used in the program. In this case, the buffer will hold data that can be thought of as a "window" on the file. There should be commands for moving the "window" up or down in the file, which means that the program should be able to automatically re-load the buffer in order to make the latest records available for inspection, editing, or printing. For some ideas, see the description of how WordStar manages files given in Fig. 4-1.

7. Further improve MAILIST by adding commands to edit records, that is, to change current records, or to delete current records. In the second case, the deleted record space should be made available for future use. One technique for doing this is to organize the file as a linked list. For further information on this subject, see the program EDIT1000 in reference [2]. A simpler approach is to mark deleted records with a special symbol (say 00000 for ZIP) while they're in the buffer, and then *not* save them on the disk file.

8. Extend the program FILEBOXM so that the user can specify the KEY item (instead of record number) when requesting to see a previously entered record. One technique for doing this is called *hash coding* (discussed in reference [2]). Another is to create a binary search tree from the keys. An advanced book on this and other searching/sorting algorithms is volume 3 of Knuth [13]; also see Section 4.3 and problem 5 of Section 4.5.

9. Write a BASIC subroutine that enables the LST: device (e. g., a printer) to capture the entire dialogue that would normally be seen on the CON: screen. For example, during a run of FILEBOXM, the printer should capture the responses of the user to INPUT requests, as well as output produced by PRINT statements, or messages to or from BASIC. In other words, the printer should show everything you see in Fig. 5-3. (Assume your printer does *not* have a keyboard. If it does, then it's really a console, and there's a simpler solution to this problem. What is it?)

10. Rewrite the SHELL sort program shown in Section 5.5 so that it sorts string arrays, using any column you designate as the sorting key. A solution to this problem based on the insertion sort algorithm is found in reference [4].

```
10 ´**********************************************
15 ´*    TINYMAIL V1.5  (SIMPLIFIED MAIL PROGRAM)   *
20 ´**********************************************
25 PRINT "TINY MAIL RUNNING .............."
30 DEFINT B-R: DIM B$(100,4), A(100): S=0: N=1
35 INPUT ">>> FILE NAME"; F$: IF LEN(F$)>8 THEN 35
40 OPEN "R",1,F$,96: FF=LOF(1): L$=STRING$(37,"-")
45 FIELD 1, 33 AS B1$,33 AS B2$,21 AS B3$,5 AS B4$
46 FIELD 1, 92 AS DUMMY$, 4 AS B5$
50 IF FF=0 THEN PRINT"--- EMPTY FILE ---":GOTO 205
100 ´-----------------------------------------------
105 ´      ROUTINE TO READ AND DISPLAY THE FILE F$
110 ´-----------------------------------------------
115 PRINT "FILE DATA IS BEING LOADED AND ECHOED"
120 PRINT: GET 1,N
125 B$(N,1)=B1$:B$(N,2)=B2$:B$(N,3)=B3$:B$(N,4)=B4$
130 IF LEFT$(B1$,1)="0" THEN 205
135    A(N)=CVS(B5$): S=S+A(N)
140    PRINT ">>> RCD #";N;TAB(35);"AMT.= $";A(N)
145    PRINT TAB(10);B1$: PRINT TAB(10);B2$
147    PRINT TAB(10);B3$;TAB(40);B4$
150    N=N+1: GOTO 120
200 ´
205 CLOSE 1: PRINT: PRINT"TOTAL AMT.= $";S: PRINT
210 PRINT L$:PRINT TAB(11);"COMMAND   MENU":PRINT L$
215 INPUT "A)DD DATA, E)DIT, P)RINT, OR Q)UIT";D$
217 PRINT: PRINT
220 IF D$="A" THEN GOTO 315
225 IF D$="E" THEN GOTO 615
230 IF D$="P" THEN GOTO 415
235 IF D$="Q" THEN GOTO 515
240 PRINT "TYPE A, E, P, OR Q": GOTO 215
300 ´-----------------------------------------------
305 ´      ROUTINE TO INPUT DATA FROM USER
310 ´-----------------------------------------------
315 PRINT"* ADDING NEW DATA   (TYPE 0 TO EXIT)  *"
320 IF N>99 THEN 512
325    LINE INPUT "   NAME: ";N$: IF N$="0" THEN 347
330    LINE INPUT "ADDRESS: ";A$: IF A$="0" THEN 347
335    LINE INPUT "CITY ST: ";C$: IF C$="0" THEN 347
340    LINE INPUT "    ZIP: ";Z$: IF Z$="0" THEN 347
341    INPUT"AMT. RCVD";A(N): IF A(N)=0 THEN 347
342    B$(N,1)=N$: B$(N,2)=A$: B$(N,3)=C$: B$(N,4)=Z$
345    PRINT: N=N+1: GOTO 320
347    B$(N,1)="0": GOTO 210
400 ´-----------------------------------------------
405 ´      ROUTINE TO PRINT MAIL LIST ON PRINTER
410 ´-----------------------------------------------
415 IF N<=1 THEN PRINT"NO DATA IN MEMORY": GOTO 215
420 S=0: FOR I=1 TO N-1: LPRINT L$
430        LPRINT " ";B$(I,1): LPRINT " ";B$(I,2)
432        LPRINT " ";B$(I,3);TAB(32);B$(I,4);
433        LPRINT TAB(39)">AMT = $"A(I):S=S+A(I)
435      NEXT I: LPRINT STRING$(37,"="): LPRINT
440 LPRINT TAB(32)"SUM OF AMTS = $"S:LPRINT:GOTO 210
500 ´-----------------------------------------------
505 ´      ROUTINE TO QUIT AND/OR SAVE DATA
510 ´-----------------------------------------------
512 PRINT "BUFFER SIZE EXCEEDED":B$(N,1)="@"
515 PRINT"QUITTING--DATA WILL BE SAVED ON FILE ";F$
520 INPUT"O.K. TO SAVE (Y/N)";D$:IF D$="N" GOTO 560
525 IF N<=1 THEN PRINT "NO DATA TO SAVE": GOTO 555
530 OPEN "R",1,F$,96
535 FOR K=1 TO N
540    LSET B1$=B$(K,1): LSET B2$=B$(K,2)
542    LSET B3$=B$(K,3): LSET B4$=B$(K,4)
543    LSET B5$=MKS$(A(K))
545    PUT 1,K
550 NEXT K
555 CLOSE:PRINT"**DONE** TO USE AGAIN, TYPE RUN":END
560 INPUT"PROGRAM ENDING WITHOUT SAVE - OK (Y/N)";D$
565 IF D$="Y" THEN GOTO 555 ELSE GOTO 210
600 ´-----------------------------------------------
615 PRINT "EDIT MODULE NOT WRITTEN YET": GOTO 215
```

FIG. 5-19 Listing of the program TINYMAIL.BAS.

11. Write and test a SUBMIT file that, when stored on the disk in drive
    B under the name FIX.SUB, automatically solves problem 8 of Section
    2.7. Fig. 5-20 shows one solution—can you come up with a better one?
    (Assume that the disk in drive A contains PIP and SUBMIT.)

12. Rewrite TINYMAIL in C, using the ideas from Lab 5.7-3 and the
    description of the BDS file functions found in the BDS manual, Appendix
    C, and reference [24].

```
A>DIR A:
A: SUBMIT   COM : PIP      COM : STAT     COM : FILE2
A: FILE3        : FILE1        : FILE4
A>DIR B:
B: FILE5        : FILE6        : FILE7        : FIX       SUB
A>TYPE B:FIX.SUB
PIP A:=B:*.*
ERA A:FILE1
ERA A:FILE4
ERA A:FIX.SUB

A>SUBMIT B:FIX

A>PIP A:=B:*.*

COPYING -
FILE5
FILE6
FILE7
FIX.SUB

A>ERA A:FILE1
A>ERA A:FILE4
A>ERA A:FIX.SUB
A>DIR A:
A: SUBMIT   COM : PIP      COM : STAT     COM : FILE2
A: FILE3        : FILE5        : FILE6        : FILE7
A>DIR B:
B: FILE5        : FILE6        : FILE7        : FIX       SUB
A>
```

FIG. 5-20 A submit file for deleting and adding selected files.

CHAPTER SIX
Inside Files; Assembly Language Programming; Modifying CP/M

6.0 Introduction

Now for the bad news. Although most software advertised as being CP/M compatible is exactly that, every once in a while you can run into a CP/M application program that doesn't "quite" work on your machine. Matters don't get any better when after a few frenzied phone calls the expert at the other end of the line tells you, "Oh, yes, that is a problem, but it's easy to fix. Just use DDT to patch some code I'll give you into the file GARGONZO.LA4, re-SAVE it, and you should be all set. Of course, what you really want to do is modify BIOS, re-assemble it, and do a new SYSGEN. I can give you a rough idea of what to look for. Got a pencil?"

Pencil? Our expert might as well have said "crowbar" for all the good his allegedly simple fix is going to do you. Unless you've had previous experience with machine and assembly language programming, his instructions aren't likely to make much sense. What's worse, innocent sounding words like "patch" and "assemble" imply that you know not only what to do but how to go about doing it. You should also have an understanding of why the changes are being made. Without this, it will be very difficult to follow such instructions, no matter how carefully worded.

In this chapter we're going to look at the what, how, and why of file modification, particularly files that contain machine language or assembly language programs. There will be several lab exercises that give step-by-step instructions on how to make such modifications, including a few that help you create your own machine language programs. The last two exercises (Labs 6.7-1 and 6.7-2) bring all the pieces together in labs that guide you in the modification of CBIOS through the addition of customized I/O drivers.

To provide the background that will help explain why these labs work as they do, Sections 6.1, 6.2, and 6.3 start the chapter off with a brief course in Z80/8080 machine and assembly language programming. If you want to learn more about this topic, the books *Practical Microcomputer Programming: The Intel 8080* [5], and *8080/Z80 Assembly Language* [6] are recommended. Articles about modifying CP/M can be found in magazines like *S-100 Microsystems* [11], *Dr. Dobbs Journal* [7], and *Lifelines* [8]. References [15], [16], and [17] also carry occasional articles on this subject.

It takes a lot of effort to become expert in this area, and the material in this chapter is only a start. For those users of CP/M systems who have neither the time nor inclination to get involved in machine and assembly language programming, an alternate strategy is to buy your software from dealers who are able to work with you on correcting any problems that arise. In that case, a cursory reading of this chapter is still recommended so that you'll be familir with some of the terminology that will be used in discussing whatever changes you and the dealer agree upon.

A Brief Guide to Chapter 6

The content of Chapter 6 is rather complicated, since it deals with both machine language programming and the tools of CP/M that support and use such programming. Here's a brief guide to the content of Chapter 6 that will help clarify which features are covered where.

- Sections 6.1, 6.2, and 6.3 are mostly about programming in Z80/8080 machine language with the help of the CP/M tools ED, ASM, and LOAD. Use of the CP/M BDOS function calls is also introduced. Several complete 8080 programs are presented in the lab exercises.
- Section 6.4 resumes the theme of "what's inside CP/M" begun in Chapters 2 and 3, but this time at the deeper level of the mechanisms it uses for controlling file operations. Additional material on Z80/8080 programming is presented in labs that show how to write machine language programs for manipulating files.
- Section 6.5 revisits the PIP and DDT transient commands, and shows how to use some of the more advanced features of these utility programs.
- Sections 6.6 and 6.7 then show to apply all the information from the preceding sections to the task of modifying CBIOS. A simple patching technique is illustrated in Lab 6.6-1, while the more powerful approach of rewriting and re-assembling an extensively modified CBIOS is illustrated in Lab 6.7-1.

6.1 Z80/8080 Machine Language; An Introduction to ASM

At the heart of every modern microcomputer is a thin slice of silicon called a microprocessor chip (abbreviated either MPU or μp, where μ is the Greek letter mu). The chip is less than 1/4-inch square, but it has engraved on it the equivalent of thousands of transistors (about 4,000 on the 8080 MPU, and over 6,000 on the 8085 MPU). The chip is mounted in what's called a Dual In-Line Package (DIP). This is a plastic or ceramic base about 2 inches long and 5/8 of an inch wide, with 40 pins to which connections can be made (there are 20 in a row on each of the two long

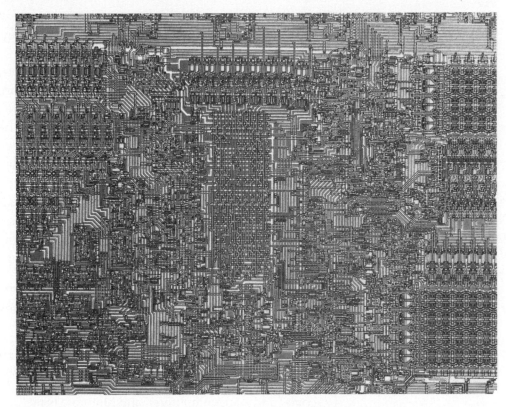

PHOTO 6-1   *This is a photomicrograph of one of the early microprocessor chips. More recent chips have over fifty times as many microscopic components.*

PHOTO 6-2   *The large IC in the upper right of this photo is the Z80 microprocessor. The Large IC to its left is the 8520 ACE UART chip discussed in Section 6.7.*

sides, hence the name "in-line"). Since these packages bring together the equivalent of dozens of complex circuits, they are frequently called integrated circuit packages, or simply ICs.

A microprocessor IC is usually used in conjunction with several others (e. g., with an IC that generates synchronizing "clock" signals) to provide the fundamental logic and arithmetic functions needed to execute computer programs. Taken together, these ICs make up the central processor unit (CPU) of a microcomputer.

Another term you'll see used in describing the technology of IC chips is LSI (large scale integration). LSI technology has also been used for the memory and I/O components that must be added to a CPU before you have a full-fledged computer. In fact, there are now 64K RAM chips (memory ICs with 65,536-bit capacities). The technology they use is called VLSI (very large scale integration) [35].

HISTORICAL NOTE

Complete microcomputer *systems* of the type discussed in this book didn't appear in significant numbers until around 1980. However, the microprocessor chips on which they are based first became available in 1971 when Intel introduced the 4004 (invented by Ted Hoff), followed by the 8008 in 1972 and the 8080 in 1973. Two other popular microprocessors introduced at this time were the MOS Technology 6502 (used in the PET, Apple, and Atari computers), and Motorola 6800 (used in Southwest Technical Products computers). Motorola has since introduced the 6809 used in the TRS-80 Color Computer. The Z80 microprocessor was introduced in 1976 by Zilog Company as an "upward compatible" version of the 8080 (not too surprising since it was designed by former Intel engineers). Intel produced an improved version of the 8080 called the 8085 in 1977. All of these chips (the 8080, 8085, Z80, 6502, 6800, and 6809) use an 8-bit external data bus. They also manipulate data internally in 8-bit chunks called *bytes*. A new generation of microprocessor chips was inaugurated in 1976 when Intel introduced the 8086. This chip uses a 16-bit external data bus. Internally, it has registers (and instruction codes) for manipulating data in 16-bit chunks called *words*. The 8088 (introduced by Intel in 1979) has the same 16-bit internal data manipulating ability as the 8086, but it maintains compatibility with older system architectures by connecting externally to an 8-bit data bus. Zilog introduced the 16-bit Z8000 microprocessor in 1978, while Motorola introduced its 16-bit 68000 microprocessor in 1979. Most of these dates are approximate; in recent years the first announcement of a chip has preceded its actual availability by a year or two. If the microprocessor has a basically new instruction set (as is the case with the 16-bit chips), you also have to figure on a few more years for the software to catch up. This is why it doesn't always pay to be the first one on the block with the latest in microprocessor chips; well-designed, reliable software is far more important.

None of the preceding information is needed by the user of CP/M, even at the machine-language level. IC technology is a fascinating subject, and of great interest to anyone who wishes to work with computer hardware, but from a programmer's point of view, a microprocessor chip is best thought of as a collection of storage locations called *registers*.

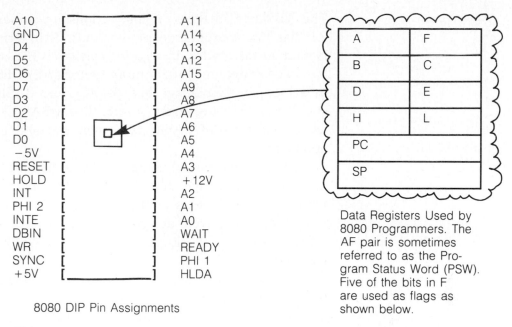

```
A10   [              ]  A11
GND   [              ]  A14
D4    [              ]  A13
D5    [              ]  A12
D6    [              ]  A15
D7    [              ]  A9
D3    [              ]  A8
D2    [              ]  A7
D1    [     □        ]  A6
D0    [              ]  A5
-5V   [              ]  A4
RESET [              ]  A3
HOLD  [              ]  +12V
INT   [              ]  A2
PHI 2 [              ]  A1
INTE  [              ]  A0
DBIN  [              ]  WAIT
WR    [              ]  READY
SYNC  [              ]  PHI 1
+5V   [_____]  HLDA
```

8080 DIP Pin Assignments

A	F
B	C
D	E
H	L
PC	
SP	

Data Registers Used by
8080 Programmers. The
AF pair is sometimes
referred to as the Pro-
gram Status Word (PSW).
Five of the bits in F
are used as flags as
shown below.

FIG. 6-1   A hardware versus software view of the 8080 microprocessor. The hardware representation on the left shows the 40 pin connections used on the 8080 DIP. The pins marked D0, D1, . . . , D7 are data lines, while those marked A0, A1, . . . , A15 are address lines. The 8080 registers occupy a microscopic part of the 8080 chip, but they are at the heart of all its processing. The contents of these registers (shown on the right) are communicated to external memory ICs by way of the 8 data lines, using the 16 address lines to select one of 65,536 possible memory locations. Some of the registers can also send and receive data from up to 256 I/O ports, using the same 8 data lines, and the first 8 of the address lines. Such shared use of lines is called multiplexing.

Fig. 6-1 contrasts the difference between a hardware and a software view of the popular 8080 microprocessor, showing its physical (hardware) appearance as a 40-pin DIP device on the left, and its "software" view as a collection of 10 data registers on the right.

The bits used in F as special "flags" are as follows:

F =	S	Z	0	A	0	P	1	CY

S is the Sign bit, Z is the Zero bit, A is the Aux carry bit, P is the Parity bit, and CY is the normal Carry bit. These bits are used to show the results of certain operations. For example, the Z flag will be set to 1 (True) if a SUB (subtract) operation produces a zero result in the A register (cf. Appendix D).

The Z80/8080 Instruction Set

In addition to the data registers shown in Fig. 6-1, the 8080 (and every other microprocessor) contains circuitry for decoding and executing instructions that say what's to be done with the data in those registers.

The 8080 has 78 types of instructions it "understands," whereas the Z80 has 158. A program expressed entirely in terms of these instructions is said to be written in *machine language*. The structure of a machine language program is much more "nitty gritty" than that of one written in a high level language like BASIC. The BASIC programmer avoids such detail by using an interpreter (like MBASIC) to translate the higher level constructs of BASIC into their detailed expression as machine language.

In this section we're going to learn something about writing programs in machine language directly, using the instruction set of the 8080. Programs written for the 8080 will also run on the 8085 and the Z80 since these chips were designed to include the 8080 instruction set. The other reason for choosing the 8080 is that CP/M is written in its machine language.

The majority of 8080 instructions say something about manipulating the data in its 10 registers (labeled F, A, B, C, D, E, H, L, PC, and SP in Fig. 6-1). For example, the 8080 and Z80 (and most other microprocessors) have an instruction that says, "Move 1 byte of data from a given location of memory into the A register." If you consult the 8080 microcomputer user's manual published by Intel (or look in Appendix E of this book) you'll find that such an instruction can be written in machine language as 7E hex, which is the same as 01111110 binary.

There's no way to tell what this instruction means by looking at it, so a *mnemonic* (memory jogging) form of the same instruction is usually used by programmers. Unfortunately for us, the Intel and Zilog designers couldn't agree on what these mnemonics should be, so in addition to the hex machine code, there are two sets of mnemonics in use. For our example, they are

> MOV A,M   used by 8080 programmers

and

> LD A,(HL)   used by Z80 programmers.

These are both symbolic ways of representing the same instruction, and eventually both have to be changed into the same machine language instruction (7E hex). Appendix E gives a complete listing of the corresponding 8080 and Z80 mnemonics, along with their common hex codes.

When reading the 8080 form of this instruction, you can think of it as meaning, "Move (MOV) the contents of a memory byte (M) into the A register." Actually a better word for "move" would have been "copy," since the contents of the memory byte in question are not erased, but simply reproduced in the A register.

Question:

But there are up to 65,536 bytes of memory in an 8080-based microcomputer. Which one is copied into A?

Answer:

Good question. The answer is that for the 8080 microprocessor, it's always understood that memory references are to the byte at the address stored in the HL *register pair*. Since each register (such as H and L) holds 8 bits, the pair of registers HL can hold 16 bits, and that's what it takes to specify one address.

Now you can guess what the Zilog mnemonic is trying to say. LD A,(HL) means, "Load into the A register a copy of the contents of the byte of memory *pointed to* (addressed by) the contents of the HL register pair." In general, Zilog uses parentheses to mean "contents of memory addressed by this register pair." Notice that for both mnemonic systems, the copying process goes from right to left. Thus the Zilog mnemonic LD A,(HL) means copy from memory into A, whereas LD (HL),A would mean copy A into memory. Similarly, the Intel mnemonic MOV A,M means copy from memory into A, while MOV M,A would mean copy A into memory.

Question:

Now I see what you mean by nitty gritty. Do I have to master 78 instructions of that sort to write an 8080 machine language program?

Answer:

It's worse than that. There are actually 244 separate instruction codes for the 8080 if you count variations (for example the MOV instruction has 63 different forms as shown in Appendix E). There *are* books that teach 8080 programming by explaining all the instructions in Chapter 1, but it's usually a better idea to first look at a small machine language program that does something useful, and concentrate on the dozen or so instructions it uses. If you do this for several applications, you'll eventually find that you've memorized the most useful instructions. It will then be easy enough to look up any new ones that come along, and add those to your repertoire.

Assembly Language Programming; An Introduction to ASM

As mentioned above, when a program is written using the instruction codes understood by a microprocessor—whether in hex or binary form—it's called a *machine language* program. You'll notice in Appendix E that the 8080 instruction codes are made up of two hex characters, which is of course equivalent to 8 bits. Thus each 8080 instruction code will fit in exactly one byte of memory. Each of these bytes has a 16-bit address, so it takes 4 hex digits to represent an address. Here's an actual example of machine language (taken out of a working BIOS) that illustrates this idea. We've also shown the same program (on the right) in mnemonic form. As we'll see in a moment, this form is called an *assembly language* program.

Address	Hex Instruction Code	Mnemonic Form		
EE6B	5F	START	MOV	E,A
EE6C	19		DAD	D
EE6D	7E		MOV	A,M
EE6E	23		INX	H
EE6F	66		MOV	H,M
EE70	6F		MOV	L,A
EE71	E9	CONOUT	PCHL	
EE72	C5		PUSH	B
. . .	. . .		. . .	

Machine Language   Assembly Language

Let's first examine the machine language program on the left. By looking at the addresses, you can tell that this program segment is stored near the top of memory. The instruction code 5F is stored at address EE6B hex (which is $4096*14 + 256*14 + 16*6 + 11 = 61035$ decimal), 19 is at 61036, 73 at 61037, and so on. What does this program do? Right now that's not an easy question to answer. (It has something to do with using the IOBYTE to select the console input driver.) We simply wanted to get across the point that this particular machine language program is nothing more than a sequence of codes stored in memory. In fact if we hadn't told you this was part of a program there would be no way to know if those were instruction codes, data, or perhaps just plain gibberish. *Moral:* It's up to the programmer to make sure instructions are placed in a section of memory where the operating system expects to find them.   .

The mnemonic form of the program (shown on the right) is said to be written in *assembly language*. That's not a very meaningful term, but everyone uses it. Assembly language is very similar to machine language except that it uses mnemonics for the instruction code *operations* (like MOV), together with symbols for the *operands* (like E and A). You should also notice that most addresses are left out of the assembly language form of our example. When addresses are needed (for example when there's a branch to a given instruction), *label* names are used (like START and CONOUT in our example) to represent the addresses of instructions.

Question:

In this example, each instruction took exactly one byte, so the addresses of successive instructions differed by 1. Is that always true?

Answer:

No. The instruction *code* always takes 1 byte, but the total instruction may take 1, 2, or 3 bytes. This happens when an instruction must specify data or an address in addition to the operation. For example, the instruction MVI A,0FFH means "move the hex data FF into the A register." In machine language this instruction would take two bytes: 3E and FF. Therefore the next instruction would be two addresses "up" from this one.

Question:

Up? Which way is up?

Answer:

That *is* confusing. Most books refer to locations with high addresses as being at the top of memory, so a memory map would show a location like EE6D as being above location EE6C. On the other hand, machine language programs are always written down the sheet of paper. Fig. 6-2 illustrates the difference. This shouldn't cause any problems as long as you understand the two conventions (or stand on your head when reading one of them).

Program		*Memory Map*	
. . .		. . .	
EE6B	5F	EE6D	7E
EE6C	19	EE6C	19
EE7E	7E	EE6B	5F

FIG. 6-2   Machine Language vs. Memory Map Conventions.

Most programmers write in assembly language, and then use a system program called an *assembler* to translate what they've written into machine language. The assembler substitutes the correct hex codes, and it also figures out what all the missing addresses should be. The assembler supplied with CP/M is stored as a file called ASM.COM, and we'll discuss its use shortly. Before doing this, let's take a look at another example of a machine language program and its assembly language form.

Note: From now on we'll write all our programs in assembly language, but we'll also show the machine language form. This will be easy to do since ASM.COM produces a handy dandy file called a .PRN file. When typed, this shows the assembly language on the right, and the machine language on the left, complete with all the actual addresses used. For simplicity, we'll refer to either form as an ML (machine language) program.

A Real Live ML Program

In this and the next two sections, we're going to write an 8080 ML (machine language) program that does about the same thing as the following BASIC program.

```
5     REM   NAME200   (PROGRAM TO PRINT YOUR NAME
      200 TIMES)
10    PRINT "PLEASE TYPE YOUR NAME FOLLOWED BY (CR)";
20    INPUT BUF$
30    LET MSG$ = BUF$ + " !!! "
40    LET B = 200
50    PRINT MSG$;
60    LET B = B − 1
70    IF B <> 0 THEN 50
80    END
```

If the name Harry is typed when this program is run, the output will fill the screen by printing "Harry !!! " 200 times.

The main differences we'll notice in writing the program in ML are:

(a) the program is more difficult to write: in fact all we'll do in this section is write the equivalent of line 10 (the rest will be done in Sections 6.2 and 6.3),

(b) getting the program entered, assembled and executed is much more complicated than just saying RUN,

(c) the program executes very rapidly.

The main reason anyone puts up with (a) and (b), is (c). Machine language programs run like greased lightning compared to BASIC programs, but they're tougher to design, write, and debug.

Getting Help from BDOS

Our example program doesn't have any fancy control structures (just one loop) but it's challenging for another reason: it includes interactive I/O. This is a much more complicated business than most people realize. We're going to show you how to manage it by (literally) CALLing for help.

The mnemonic CALL corresponds to an 8080 instruction that's like the GOSUB statement in BASIC. It lets an ML program call upon subroutines stored anywhere in memory, even if they're part of another program. In particular, our program is going to CALL upon I/O subroutines that are already in CP/M—in BDOS and BIOS to be exact. This technique gives CP/M users a real advantage, allowing both beginners and pros alike to avoid the hassle connected with the input and output of data.

Although it's possible to CALL subroutines located in BIOS directly, this is usually not recommended. The reason is that you'd have to know the exact addresses of all the desired subroutines. While it's possible to find out what these are, there's a hazard: if and when you try your ML program on a different CP/M system, it may not work. The reason is that BIOS is the one part of CP/M that is modified ("customized") for each specific computer, so the addresses of its subroutines can vary. A more serious difficulty is that there is no standard way to "pass" data to and from these routines.

The way out of this dilemma is to do all our calls to BDOS which is machine-independent. BDOS will figure out where the needed BIOS subroutines are, and then use them to handle any I/O you requested. More importantly, the registers used for passing data between your program and BDOS have been standardized (see Fig. 6-1).

Version 2.2 of CP/M has provision for 39 different kinds of BDOS calls (which are also called BDOS function calls). No matter what CP/M system you're using, you call for a BDOS function by using the 8080 instruction CALL 05. This means "call upon (goto) the subroutine at location 0005." Why location 5? As we'll see in a moment, this is where the CP/M designers have placed exact information on accessing BDOS in the form of a JMP (jump) instruction.

Before making this call, you have to let BDOS know which one of the 39 subroutines (BDOS functions) you want. There's a chart of all the available BDOS functions at the end of this section, and you'll notice that they each have a number. You tell BDOS which function you want by placing that number in the C register. If the function has something to do with character I/O, the E and A registers are used to "pass" the character to or from BDOS. The chart also shows that for some functions the DE register pair is used, either to give BDOS some extra information about your request (like the location of a string you want to be printed) or to receive back information BDOS generates for you (like the value of the IOBYTE).

Question:

If BDOS is near the top of memory, why do we use CALL 0005 to get to it?

Answer:

True, 0005 is near the bottom of memory, while BDOS is near the top. The problem is that the precise starting address of BDOS varies with systems. CP/M solves this problem by insisting that BDOS's exact starting address be stored in locations 6 and 7. Location 5 contains the 8080 instruction JMP (C3 hex). So CALL 0005 will indirectly mean the same as CALL "starting address of BDOS" on *any* system. (When DDT is running, two JMPs are used as explained in Section 6.5, but CALL 0005 still works).

Let's prepare the way for our program to print a name 200 times by learning how to use BDOS function #9 to handle line 10 of the equivalent BASIC program. This BDOS function does about the same thing as PRINT "string" does in BASIC. Here is a short program segment

that illustrates its use to print the string "MY FIRST ML PROGRAM!"
on the console device.

```
              ORG        0100H
              MVI        C,09
              LXI        D,MSG1
              CALL       05
              JMP        0
MSG1          DB         'MY FIRST ML PROGRAM!$'
              END
```

We'll first explain what each of these assembly language instructions
means, and then go through a lab that shows how to translate the
program into machine language and run it. Before explaining each line,
we should tell you that only *four* of the lines contain mnemonics for
real 8080 instructions (MVI, LXI, CALL, and JMP). The other lines contain
what are called *directives* to the assembler (ORG, DB, END). Directives
are used to give the assembler the additional information it needs to
do such things as figure out which addresses to use for your program,
or how much room to set aside for storing data.

ORG 0100H | This is a directive to the assembler which means "originate" the program at location 0100H, that is, put the first instruction at address 0100H. You usually originate programs at 0100H because this is the start of the TPA. The letter H is appended to numbers to mean hexadecimal. If you leave off the H, or use D, the assembler will interpret the number as decimal. Similarly, the letter B is used to mean binary data, and the letter O or Q to mean octal data.

MVI C,09 | This is an instruction to the 8080 which means "move immediately (directly) the number 9 into the C register." This is being done so BDOS will know that we want function #9 when we call it.

LXI D,MSG1 | This tells the 8080 to load the full 16-bit address that corresponds to the label MSG1 into the DE *pair*. Instructions with X in the mnemonic always refer to pairs of registers. The purpose of this step is to set up DE as a pointer to the start of the string which BDOS function #9 is going to print for us.

CALL 05 | Here's where we tell BDOS "do your stuff," using the function number we just put in C and the string pointer we placed in DE. BDOS obliges by printing the string on the console screen.

JMP 0 | Remember this? It was explained at the end of Section 3.2 where we told you that location 0 contains the instruction JMP (jump to), while locations 1 and 2 contain the address of the warm boot code in BIOS. In general, you should end your ML programs with JMP 0 so that a warm boot occurs, returning you to the system prompt A>.

DB
This is a directive to the assembler that means, "Here come some bytes of data—please store them in memory starting at whatever address you're up to." The DB directive is then followed by the data you want stored. In our case it's a string of 21 characters delineated by *single* quote marks. The reason the last character is a dollar sign is that BDOS function #9 expects this as an "end of string" signal. DE points to the start of the string, but there's no way to tell where the end is unless you mark it, and the official CP/M end-of-string mark for function 9 is a $.

TECHNICAL NOTE 1

Directives are sometimes called "pseudo-ops" because they're instructions to the assembler, not the microprocessor. There are three directives used for data storage. DB (data bytes) reserves space and initializes it with the bytes of data you specify. DW (data words) does the same for 16-bit (two byte) words of data. DS (data storage) reserves as many bytes of storage as you request, but doesn't initialize them. These directives *must* be placed at positions in a program where they cannot possibly be executed as instructions—usually after the last real instruction (JMP 0 in our example), or right after the RET instruction of a subroutine. The other pseudo-ops used by the CP/M assembler are ORG, END, EQU, SET, IF, and ENDIF. We won't discuss IF or ENDIF here. The EQU (equate) directive is used to assign numbers to symbolic names. SET is used in a similar manner, except that it can be used at different points in the program to assign different values to the same name. END is used to tell the assembler "this is the end of the program." Here's an example showing use of ORG, EQU, DB, DS, DW, and END.

```
          ORG    4500H
TPA       EQU    0100H
CR        EQU    0DH
LF        EQU    0AH
NAME      DB     'JOE',CR,LF
AGES      DB     21,43,7+2*19,'X'
SPACE     DS     4
WORDS     DW     'AB',TPA+3250H,65534
          END
```

Even though this "program" does absolutely nothing (it's all directives!), the assembler will accept it and set up data storage as follows. Note that the EQU directives do *not* reserve storage, so the first address (4500H) in the following assembly corresponds to the label NAME.

Hex Address	Hex Contents	ASCII or Decimal Contents
4500	4A	J
4501	4F	O

Hex Address	Hex Contents	ASCII or Decimal Contents
4502	45	E
4503	0D	(CR)
4504	0A	(LF)
4505	15	21D
4506	2B	43D
4507	2D	45D
4508	58	X
4509	--	These are 4 bytes
450A	--	of uninitialized
450B	--	storage space
450C	--	reserved by DS 4.
450D	41	A
450E	42	B
450F	50	= 3350H = 0100H
4510	33	+ 3250H
4511	FE	
4512	FF	= FFFEH = 65534D

Notice that 16-bit numbers are represented with four hex digits, and that this requires two bytes of memory. Also notice that for a 16-bit number (e. g., 3350 hex), the last two hex digits (50) are stored in the first byte (called the low-order byte), while the first two hex digits (33) are stored in the second byte (called the high-order byte). Confusing, but that's how it's done.

TECHNICAL NOTE 2

The 8080 has 78 different *types* of instructions. The word "type" means a general form which may be *realized* in more than one way. For example, the general form

MOV   M,reg

represents one instruction type (move the contents of a register into memory) which has seven different realizations, each with its own 8080 instruction code (also called its "OP" code) as follows:

Mnemonic		8080 OP Code in Hex
MOV	M,B	70
MOV	M,C	71
MOV	M,D	72
MOV	M,E	73
MOV	M,H	74
MOV	M,L	75
MOV	M,A	77

The seven realizations correspond to use of the seven 8080 data registers. (The instruction MOV M,F isn't used because F is not a data register; it's a convenient way to refer to a collection of individual flag bits). The 78 instruction types for the 8080 are summarized in Appendix D, while the 244 possible realizations are shown in Appendix E.

The next lab shows you how to assemble and execute the sample program MYSTRING. Before doing this, it will be worth making the program a bit more elegant. We'll do this by using symbolic names for the BDOS JMP location, and for the function number we're using. This is done with the EQU (equate) directive. For our example, we'll equate the label BDOS with 05, and the label OUTSTR with function #9, so that the program can refer to these numbers by names. In a large program such names may be used several times. Then merely changing one EQU directive would automatically assign a new number to all uses of the name. (Suggestion: Although EQU directives can be placed anywhere in a program, grouping them all at the beginning helps make the program more readable.)

Here's the revised program using two EQU directives. We've also used the semicolon (;) to show how remarks and spaces can be put in a ML program. The ; functions like ' in MBASIC.

```
;   MYSTRING (PROGRAM TO SHOW USE OF BDOS
;           FUNCTION CALL #9 IN A ML PROGRAM)
;
            ORG    0100H
BDOS        EQU    05
OUTSTR      EQU    09
;
            MVI    C,OUTSTR    ;PUT FCN # IN C REGISTER
            LXI    D,MSG1      ;PUT POINTER TO STRING IN DE
            CALL   BDOS        ;CALL BDOS FCN #9
            JMP    0           ;RETURN TO CP/M WITH WARM BOOT
;
MSG1        DB     'MY FIRST ML PROGRAM!$'
            END
```

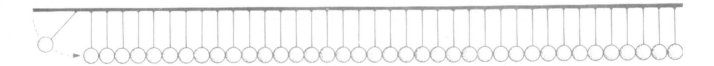

LAB EXERCISE 6.1-1

Writing and Running the Assembly Language Program MYSTRING

Step 1.   Start by typing the program into the computer (using an editor like ED) and saving it as the file MYSTRING.ASM. Before doing this, it would probably be good to re-read Section 3.4 and practice using ED again. You *must* use the extension .ASM, so when you start using ED be sure to type A>ED MYSTRING.ASM.

Fig. 6-3 shows ED being used to enter this program as what's called a *source file*. We deliberately made a mistake in line 7 to show a simple way to use ED to re-do a line. First you type ˆZ to leave insertion mode, then 7: (CR) to go to line 7, and K (CR) to kill it. Now type I (CR) to enter insert mode again, and then type in the corrected line including a CR. Finally type ˆZ again to leave insertion mode, and type B#T to ask ED to go to the beginning of the file and type it all out for proofreading.

```
A>DIR
A: PIP       COM : STAT      COM : GO       COM : ED        COM
A: MYPOEM    TXT

A>ED MYSTRING.ASM

NEW FILE
     : *I
   1: ; MYSTRING (PROGRAM TO SHOW USE OF BDOS FCN #9)
   2: ;
   3:         ORG       0100H                     THIS LINE HAS AN ERROR
   4: BDOS    EQU       05                        (G INSTEAD OF C).
   5: OUTSTR  EQU       09
   6: ;
   7:         MVI       G,OUTSTR
   8:         LXI       D,MSG1  ; PUT POINTER TO STRING IN DE
   9:         CALL      BDOS    ; CALL BDOS FCN #9
  10:         JMP       0       ; RETURN TO CP/M WITH WARM BOOT
  11: ;
  12: MSG1    DB        ´MY FIRST ML PROGRAM!$´
  13:         END
  14:                   ↑Z                                   THE OLD
     : *7:                                                   LINE 7 IS
   7: *K                                                     KILLED AND
   7: *I                                                     A NEW LINE 7
   7:         MVI       C,OUTSTR; PUT FCN # IN C REGISTER     IS INSERTED
   8:                                                        HERE.
   8: *B#T              ↑Z
   1: ; MYSTRING (PROGRAM TO SHOW USE OF BDOS FCN #9)        THE
   2: ;                                                      CORRECTED
   3:         ORG       0100H                                PROGRAM
   4: BDOS    EQU       05                                   IS THEN
   5: OUTSTR  EQU       09                                   TYPED TO
   6: ;                                                      MAKE SURE IT'S
   7:         MVI       C,OUTSTR; PUT FCN # IN C REGISTER    O.K.
   8:         LXI       D,MSG1  ; PUT POINTER TO STRING IN DE
   9:         CALL      BDOS    ; CALL BDOS FCN #9
  10:         JMP       0       ; RETURN TO CP/M WITH WARM BOOT
  11: ;
  12: MSG1    DB        ´MY FIRST ML PROGRAM!$´
  13:         END
   1: *E

A>DIR
A: PIP       COM : STAT      COM : GO       COM : MYSTRING BAK
A: ED        COM : MYPOEM    TXT : MYSTRING ASM
A>
```

E IS THEN TYPED TO TELL ED TO
SAVE THE CORRECTED PROGRAM AS
MYSTRING.ASM WHICH IT DOES.

FIG. 6-3 Example showing how to use ED to create the source program
MYSTRING.ASM.

Incidentally, you can also use a word processor to enter assembly
language programs provided it has a "non-document" mode which gives
you control of all carriage return placements and line length. In other
words, you don't want what's called the "fill" or "wraparound" feature
to be on.

Notice from Fig. 6-3 that assembly language programs are written
in three columns that correspond to *labels*, *operators*, and *operands*. Comments can be placed on any line (usually in column four) provided they
begin with a semicolon. It's best to use the TAB key for moving from

one column to another. This has the same effect as striking the space bar enough times to put a total of 8 characters in each column. Thus labels for assembly language programs start in column 1, operator mnemonics start in column 9, operands start in column 17, and comments (if any) start in column 25. There also can be comments that take up an entire line. These usually start in column 1 and can be spotted by the semicolon.

Before leaving ED, proofread your program one more time by typing ˆZ to leave insertion mode, and then typing B#T to mean "go to the beginning and type everything." If the program looks OK, type E (CR) to end the editing session and save the file.

Instant Quiz

Suppose you forgot the label MSG1 in line 12. What error code would ASM produce? (See Note 1 of Appendix F for ASM error codes.) How could the error be corrected?

Answer

The error code U (undefined label) would be given at step 3 of this lab. To fix this error, use ED as follows:

    A>ED   MYSTRING.ASM
    *#A#T

Then use 12: to go to line 12, K to erase it, and I to insert the correct line. Then use ↑Z and E to exit from ED. This will save the corrected program as MYSTRING.ASM.

Step 2.   Press ˆC to leave ED, and then do a DIR. You'll see your new file there as MYSTRING.ASM plus a backup file called MYSTRING.BAK. This is for safety purposes only, and would not be used unless the .ASM file was destroyed (in which case you'd rename the .BAK file to an .ASM file).

Step 3.   Now assemble the file by typing

        A>ASM MYSTRING

Warning: Do *not* type ASM MYSTRING.ASM. This would be the logical thing to do, but the designers of ASM decided to have the assembler automatically add the extension .ASM to the file name. They then decided to allow a different use of the "extension" characters to designate disk drives. For example, if you type A>ASM MYSTRING.ABC, then A means the disk drive containing the source file, while B and C mean the destination drives for the .HEX and .PRN files produced by the assembler. If you leave off .ABC it's the same as saying "use the logged-in disk for all files." The letter Z in position 2 or 3 means "don't generate this file," while X in position 3 means "send the PRN file to the console."

For a start, the best bet is to leave off the extension, in which case .AAA is used as the default value.

Step 4. Do another directory. You should now see two more files called MYSTRING.HEX and MYSTRING.PRN. This tells you two things: (a) The program ASM has translated your source MYSTRING.ASM into machine language, but in a form called Intel Hex Format (yours is not to reason why right now), and (b) It has also produced a .PRN file which contains both machine language and assembly language. You can look at the .PRN file by typing A>TYPE MYSTRING.PRN.

Step 5. Next you have to translate the .HEX machine language file into a command file. A command file is a binary machine language file that will execute when its name is typed after A>. It's created by using the LOAD transient command as follows:

A>LOAD MYSTRING

Again, do *not* type the extension .HEX—the LOAD program will "know" it's supposed to translate the file MYSTRING.HEX into MYSTRING.COM.

Note: LOAD can be used only with HEX files in which the first instruction is at location 0100H (that is, the ML program used ORG 0100H). DDT can be used to get around this limitation, as discussed in Section 6.5.

Step 6. To see what's just happened, do another directory. At long last you should see a file called MYSTRING.COM—your own, genuine command file.

Step 7. To run your command file just type its name

A>MYSTRING

This will place the file MYSTRING.COM into the TPA, and start it running. If there were no mistakes in your original program, you should see the fruits of your labor print on the screen as follows:

MY FIRST ML PROGRAM!
A>

Fig. 6-4 summarizes the three-stage dialogue used at the console when a program is assembled, loaded, and run under CP/M. The example shown assumes that a source file called MYSTRING.ASM has been created with ED as in step 1. The same three steps would be used for assembling and running any other file which contains an assembly language program and has a secondary file name of .ASM. The example also assumes that there were no syntactic errors in the .ASM program. If there were, the offending lines would have been printed out with an error code in front of them as explained in the CP/M manuals and in Appendix F.

```
A>ASM MYSTRING
CP/M ASSEMBLER - VER 2.0
0120
000H USE FACTOR
END OF ASSEMBLY

A>LOAD MYSTRING

FIRST ADDRESS 0100
LAST  ADDRESS 011F
BYTES READ    0020
RECORDS WRITTEN 01


A>MYSTRING
MY FIRST ML PROGRAM!
A>
```

FIG. 6-4 This is an example of the three steps used in order to assemble, load (which means translate from hex to binary form), and execute an assembly language program.

Step 8.   If your program didn't work (or even if it did) take a look at the .PRN file to see what was wrong (or right!) by using the TYPE command as follows:

A>TYPE MYSTRING.PRN

The .PRN file is produced by the assembler, and it shows both the source program you entered and the machine language translation of this program which was produced by ASM. Fig. 6-5 shows what the MYSTRING.PRN file looks like.

If you have a printer, type a control-P and then repeat the command TYPE MYSTRING.PRN to get a hard copy for study. If you spot errors, go back to step 1 and use ED to correct them. To use ED again, type

```
A>TYPE MYSTRING.PRN


                 ; MYSTRING (PROGRAM TO SHOW USE OF BDOS FCN #9)
                 ;
   0100                    ORG     0100H
   0005 =        BDOS      EQU     05
   0009 =        OUTSTR    EQU     09
                 ;
   0100 0E09            /  MVI     C,OUTSTR; PUT FCN # IN C REGISTER
   0102 110B01          LXI     D,MSG1  ; PUT POINTER TO STRING IN DE
   0105 CD0500          CALL    BDOS    ; CALL BDOS FCN #9
   0108 C30000          JMP     0       ; RETURN TO CP/M WITH WARM BOOT
                 ;
   010B 4D59204649MSG1  DB      'MY FIRST ML PROGRAM!$'
   0120                    END

A>
```

FIG. 6-5 Listing of the file MYSTRING.PRN. The first two columns show the actual addresses used by the program followed by the hex codes for the machine language stored there. The next three columns contain the assembly language version of the program (the one you wrote) which is also called the *source file*.

A>ED MYSTRING.ASM
    *#A#T

Recall that the command #A#T means "append all lines of the file to the text buffer, and type all the lines to verify what's there." Make your changes, and end by typing ^Z followed by E. Now try steps 2–7 again. Have fun!

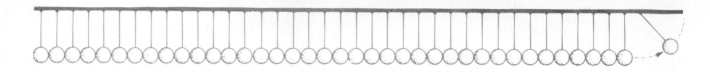

Getting Ready to Finish NAME200

We'll finish writing the program NAME200 in ML in the next two sections. To handle the input of string data in our ML program (the part BASIC does with INPUT BUF$) we'll use BDOS function #10. We'll also want to discuss the use of other BDOS function calls, so we'll end this section by summarizing what all the BDOS functions are, and how the A, C, and DE registers are used with them. The chart of Fig. 6-6 shows the 39 functions described in the version 2.2 CP/M manuals. The notation DE = &Buffer or DE = &FCB means that DE is to be loaded with a pointer (address) to the beginning of the memory buffer or file control block in question (we'll say more about file control blocks in Section 6.4).

6.2 Assembly Language Programming in a Nutshell

It's time to bite the bullet and wade through a blow-by-blow account of what the principal 8080/Z80 instructions do. We'll start off by showing how to do this in terms of five of the compact (but technically complete) explanations found in Appendix D. An instant quiz will then direct you in a study of about twenty additional instructions needed for writing the programs ahead. We'll also show how three additional BDOS function calls work. All of these ideas will then be applied in a lab where we'll explain how to write a program which inputs, concatenates, and prints strings. This program (called CONCAT) will make the writing of NAME200 a lot easier when we finally finish it in Section 6.3. Many of the same instructions will apply to the ML program CHARSORT that will be shown in Section 6.4.

The format we'll use for explaining the 8080/Z80 instructions is similar to that used in Appendix D. The Intel mnemonic form is given first, followed by a symbolic explanation of what the instruction does. Additional information about how many bytes each instruction takes,

BDOS FUNCTION CALLS

FCN #	Function Name	Info. Sent to BDOS	Info. Ret'd. from BDOS
0	System Reset	none	none
1	Console Input	none	A = char
2	Console Output	E = char	none
3	Reader Input	none	A = char
4	Punch Output	E = char	none
5	List Output	E = char	none
6	Direct Console I/O	E = FF or char	A = char,00 = not ready
7	Get I/O Byte	none	A = IOBYTE
8	Set I/O Byte	E = IOBYTE	none
9	Print String	DE = &Buffer	none
10	Read Console Buffer	DE = &Buffer	characters in Buffer
11	Get Console Status	none	A = 00/FF (ready/busy)
12	Return Version Number	none	HL = BA = Version#
13	Reset Disk System	none	none
14	Select Disk	E = Disk Number	none
15	Open File	DE = &FCB	A = Dir Code
16	Close File	DE = &FCB	A = Dir Code
17	Search for First	DE = &FCB	A = Dir Code
18	Search for Next	none	A = Dir Code
19	Delete File	DE = &FCB	A = Dir Code
20	Read Sequential	DE = &FCB	A = Err Code
21	Write Sequential	DE = &FCB	A = Err Code
22	Make File	DE = &FCB	A = Dir Code
23	Rename File	DE = &FCB	A = Dir Code
24	Return Login Vector	none	HL = BA = Login Vector
25	Return Current Disk	none	A = Cur Disk#
26	Set DMA Address	DE = &DMA	none
27	Get Addr(Alloc)	none	HL = &Alloc
28	Write Protect Disk	none	none
29	Get R/O Vector	none	HL = BA = R/O Vector
30	Set File Attributes	DE = &FCB	A = Dir Code
31	Get Addr (disk parms)	none	HL = &DPB
32	Set/Get User Code	E = 0FFH	User Number
33	Read Random	DE = &FCB	A = Rand Code
34	Write Random	DE = &FCB	A = Rand Code
35	Compute File Size	DE = &FCB	r0,r1,r2 of FCB
36	Set Random Record	DE = &FCB	r0,r1,r2 of FCB
37	Reset Drive	DE = drive vector	A = 00
40	Write Random, fill with zeros	DE = &FCB	A = Rand Code

FIG. 6-6 These are the BDOS functions available to a programmer working under CP/M Version 2.2. The notation &Buffer means starting address of Buffer, &FCB means starting address of File Control Block. Dir code = 0, 1, 2, 3, if operation was successful, FF if not. Err code = 00 for successful, non-zero otherwise. Rand codes are: 01 = reading unwritten data, 03 = cannot close current extent, 04 = seek to unwritten extent, 05 = directory overflow in write, 06 = seek past end of disk. Further information about these functions can be found in the CP/M 2.2 Interface Guide. Examples of use are given in Sections 6.1, 6.2, 6.3, and 6.4 of this chapter.

how many machine cycles it takes to operate, and what the actual machine language op code is can be found in Appendices D and E.

To combine the explanations for several instructions into a single symbolic form, several abbreviations will be used as follows:

reg   Stands for the contents of one of the 8-bit registers A, B, C, D, E, H, or L.

rp	Stands for the contents of one of the register pairs BC, DE, HL, or SP.
bp	Stands for the "byte pair" in one of the register pairs BC, DE, HL, or PSW, where PSW means "program status word." PSW is a 16-bit word made up of 8 bits from the A register followed by the 8 bits of the flag register.
addr	Stands for a 16-bit memory address, either in numerical or symbolic form.
data	Stands for data that can be stored in 1 byte (8 bits), represented in either numerical or symbolic form.
data16	Stands for data that can be stored in 2 bytes (16 bits), represented in either numerical or symbolic form.
M	Stands for the contents of the memory byte pointed to by the address in the HL register pair. Another way to abbreviate this is [HL].

The A, B, C, D, E, H, and L registers are called "general purpose" because the data they hold can be interpreted and used in many different ways. On the other hand, the data stored in the F, PC, and SP registers is used for special purposes. In fact F isn't a register at all; it's a handy way to refer to a collection of separate *flag bits* that are turned either on or off (set or reset) depending on what the results of certain operations are. For example, the Z (Zero) flag bit will be set equal to 1 (called the true setting) when operations like SUB (subtract) or DCR (decrement) produce a zero result. Similarly, the CY (carry) flag will be set equal to 1 when operations like ADC (add with carry) or CMP (compare) produce a carry beyond the normal 8-bit register size.

PC stands for *program counter*, and its purpose is to hold the address of the next instruction to be executed. SP means *stack pointer*. It holds an address which points to an area of memory called the *stack*. This is where programmers save register data when the registers need to be used for other purposes. Putting data into the stack area is called *pushing* the stack, while removing data from the stack (using the rule of last-in-first-out) is called *popping* the stack.

Summary of Some Common 8080/Z80 Instructions

ADC M	This means *add with carry*. In symbolic form, this instruction can be expressed as A = A + [HL] + CY. This means replace the contents of the A register with the sum of three things: the present contents of the A register, the contents of memory pointed at by the address in HL, and the contents of CY (the carry bit of F).
ADC reg	This is similar to the preceding instruction except that the contents of one of the registers is added to the present contents of A plus the content of CY. In symbols A = A + reg + CY. When using this

	instruction, "reg" must be replaced with an actual register name (e. g., ADC E or ADC B).
CALL addr	This is used to *call* (go to) the subroutine which starts at the memory address given by "addr". ML programs always get their next instruction from the PC (program counter) register. The CALL instruction works by first saving the address of the normal next instruction by "pushing" the contents of the PC at the top of a special storage area called the *stack*. Then "addr" is placed in PC. This causes the next instruction to be the one at the address of the desired subroutine. At the end of the subroutine a RET instruction is encountered. This causes the saved address to be popped from the stack and be put back in the PC. Thus the program can resume execution at the address it would have used next if it hadn't been for the CALL instruction.
CMP M	This means *compare* the contents of the memory addressed by HL with the contents of register A. Internally, this instruction does a temporary subtraction of A−(HL), using the result to set the Z and CY flags. The Z flag will be set to 1 if A=(HL), and the CY flag will be set to 1 if A<(HL). This instruction is different than SUB (subtract) insofar as the contents of A are not changed.
CMP reg	This works just like CMP M except that the comparison is based on the result of the subtraction A − reg.
DAD rp	This means "double add." The 16-bit contents of the two registers indicated by rp are added to the 16-bit contents of HL, and then stored back in HL. In symbols, HL = HL + rp.

At this point it would be good to pause, and see if you can relate each of the above explanations to the compact form given in Appendix D. You can? Good. You're ready to master machine language programming by developing your own notes on the additional twenty instructions we'll use in the upcoming labs. Here they are.

Instant Quiz/Project

1. Using the symbolic explanations in Appendix D, write out an English statement of what each of the following twenty instructions do. (These instructions, plus those already explained, will be sufficient for writing all the ML programs of this and the next two sections.)

DCR	M	LXI	rp,data16
DCR	reg	MVI	M,data

DCX	rp		MVI	reg,data
INR	M		MOV	reg,M
INR	reg		MOV	M,reg
INX	rp		MOV	reg,reg
JMP	addr		NOP	
JNZ	addr		RET	
LDA	addr		STA	addr
LDAX	B or D		XRA	reg

2. If you've already decided that ML programming is your cup of tea, write out similar explanations for all the remaining instructions of Appendix D.

Some Partial Answers for Question 1

The instructions with DCR mean "decrement," that is, reduce by 1. DCX also means decrement, but for the 16-bit number held in the register pair given (e. g., DCX D means reduce the contents of DE by 1, making DE = DE − 1).

In general, instructions that contain an X in the mnemonic refer to operations with 16-bit numbers stored in register pairs. Thus INX rp means "increment" (add 1) to the 16-bit contents of rp, while LXI rp, data16 means load the given 16-bit data "immediate" (directly) into the named register pair. Notice that register pairs are referenced by just the first register name, so LXI D,20A4H means set DE = 20A4H. The word "immediate" is a way of saying that the data to be moved is given "immediately," that is, as part of the instruction.

XRA (as well as XRI, ORA, ORI, ANA, and ANI) is a logical operator. Logical operators combine the bits of the data involved according to the laws of Boolean arithmetic, using the logical operators XOR (exclusive OR), OR (inclusive OR), and AND (conjunction). These three operators are defined by the following tables:

OR	0 1		XOR	0 1		AND	0 1
0	0 1		0	0 1		0	0 0
1	1 1		1	1 0		1	0 1

For the 8080, logical operators are always applied between the A register and some other byte. Here's an example of what these operators would do when applied between register A and the byte in register B.

		Register A		*Register A*		*Register B*
ORA	B	(11110011)	=	(10010011)	OR	(11110000)
XRA	B	(01100011)	=	(10010011)	XOR	(11110000)
AND	B	(10010000)	=	(10010011)	ANA	(11110000)

For further information about the use of 8080 instructions, see the technical note at the end of this section.

BDOS Functions 1, 2, 9, and 10

We've already seen how to use BDOS function #9 to output a string to the console. Recall that three instructions are needed when using this function.

```
MVI   C,09        ;PUT FUNCTION #9 IN C
LXI   D,MSGPTR   ;PUT STARTING ADDRESS OF STRING IN DE
CALL  05          ;CALL BDOS VIA THE JMP AT 5
```

An even simpler output procedure is available with BDOS function #2. This sends a single character to the console. Instead of loading DE with an address pointing to the character (as with function #9), you go ahead and put the character itself into the E register. If the character is currently in the A register (which is a common place for a main program to put it), here's the code to send the character '?' from A to the console (the ASCII code for '?' is 3F hex = 49 decimal).

```
MVI   A,'?'   ;PUT '?' IN A
MVI   C,02    ;PUT FCN #2 IN C
MOV   E,A     ;MOVE THE '?' TO E
CALL  05      ;CALL BDOS
```

The same thing could be done more directly as follows:

```
MVI   C,02
MVI   E,3FH
CALL  05
```

BDOS function #1 works in a reverse manner. It causes your program to stop, and wait until a character is typed at the console keyboard. This character is then stored in the A register, and the program continues. The character typed is echoed at the console so you can see what you typed. In addition to the normal printing characters, (CR), (LF), tab (CONTROL-I), and backspace (CONTROL-H) are accepted and echoed. CONTROL-P and CONTROL-S are not sent to the A register, but they do have their usual effect as "print toggle" and "scroll toggle" signals. Here's a short test program that uses both BDOS functions 1 and 2.

```
;FCN12 (PROGRAM TO TEST BDOS FCNS 1 & 2)
MVI   C,02    ;USE FUNCTION #2
MVI   E,3FH   ;  TO PRINT A ?
CALL  05      ;  ON THE CONSOLE
MVI   C,01    ;USE FUNCTION #1 TO INPUT A
CALL  05      ;  CHARACTER TO A AND ECHO IT
INR   A       ;INCREMENT THE CHARACTER CODE IN A
```

```
MVI   C,02        ;USE FUNCTION #2 TO
MVI   E,A         ;  PRINT THE INCREMENTED CHAR-
CALL  05          ;   ACTER ON THE CONSOLE
CALL  0           ;RETURN TO CP/M
```

When this program is run, it prints a "?" at the console, and then waits for you to type a character. Suppose you type an "X." Here's what you'll see.

```
A>FCN12
?XY
A>
```

The ? was printed by the first call to BDOS function #2. The X was printed as an automatic echo of the "X" you input to BDOS function #1. The Y was typed by the second call to BDOS function #2. Why Y? Well by that time the ASCII code for the letter X you input had been stored in A by function #1, incremented (increased) to the next ASCII code by INR A, and moved over into the E register by MOV E,A. Thus the last call to function #2 outputs the (ASCII code of X) + 1 which is the code for Y.

The final BDOS function we'll discuss here is #10. This allows the user to input a string of characters at the console. These characters are saved in a memory buffer *you* set aside. This buffer must start with two special bytes. The first one is used to hold MX, a number that indicates the maximum size of the buffer you're going to use. The second byte is used by BDOS to store NC, the actual number of characters the user has input. This number is sometimes called the input byte count; it tells you how many characters were input (not including the final (CR) that a user must type to enter a string). The starting address of the buffer you reserve for input must be passed to function #10 in the DE register. Here's part of a program that uses BDOS function 10 in conjunction with a buffer called INBUF. This buffer is set up in memory by the programmer using the DB and DS directives as shown.

```
        MVI   C,10
        LXI   D,INBUF
        CALL  05
              . . . . . . . . .
              . . . . . . . . .
        JMP   0
INBUF   DB    0FFH        ;SET FIRST BYTE OF INBUF TO MX=255
        DS    256         ;RESERVE STORAGE FOR REST OF INBUF
```

The next lab shows how to use this program segment (along with BDOS functions 2, 9, and 10) in a string manipulation program that will become part of NAME200.

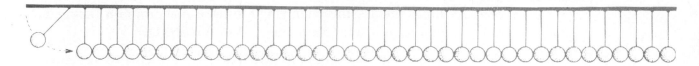

LAB EXERCISE 6.2-1   CONCAT: A Machine Language Program to Input, Concatenate, and Print Strings

Step 1.   Study the ML program shown in Fig. 6-7. This program does about the same thing as the following BASIC program.

10 INPUT A$:B$ = A$ + " !!! " : PRINT B$

```
                    ;CONCAT    PROGRAM TO PRINT A ?, INPUT A STRING, ADD
                    ;A SUFFIX STRING, AND PRINT THE RESULT ON THE CON:
0100                        ORG      0100H
0005 =              BDOS    EQU      05H
000A =              INSTR   EQU      0AH
0009 =              OUTSTR  EQU      09H
0002 =              OUTCHR  EQU      02H
                    ;
                    ;MAIN PROGRAM.  USES SUBROUTINES PUTCHR AND ACCEPT;
                    ;  (ACCEPT USES SUBROUTINE CRLF, CRLF USES PUTCHR)
                    ;
0100 3E3F                   MVI      A,3FH    ;PUT ASCII CODE FOR ? IN A
0102 CD3701                 CALL     PUTCHR   ;PRINT IT AT THE CONSOLE
0105 114901                 LXI      D,INBUF  ;POINT TO LOCAL INPUT BUFFER
0108 CD1601                 CALL     ACCEPT   ;INPUT STRING, ADD SUFFIX + $
010B 0E09                   MVI      C,OUTSTR ;USE BDOS FCN # 9
010D 114B01                 LXI      D,INBUF+2 ;TO ECHO CONTENTS OF INBUF
0110 CD0500                 CALL     BDOS     ;ON THE CONSOLE
0113 C30000                 JMP      0
                    ;
0116 0E0A           ACCEPT  MVI      C,INSTR ;USE BDOS FCN 10 TO INPUT STRING
0118 CD0500                 CALL     BDOS     ;WE ASSUME CALLER HAS LOADED DE
011B 110000                 LXI      D,0      ;ZERO OUT DE PAIR
011E 214A01                 LXI      H,INBUF+1 ;POINT TO CHAR COUNT OF INBUF
0121 5E                     MOV      E,M      ;PUT CHAR COUNT IN E
0122 214B01                 LXI      H,INBUF+2 ;POINT TO START OF INBUF TEXT
0125 19                     DAD      D        ;DISPLACE POINTER TO END OF INBUF
0126 0606                   MVI      B,SUFCNT;NUMBER OF CHARACTERS IN SUFFIX
0128 114A02                 LXI      D,SUFFIX;POINTER TO SUFFIX TEXT
012B 1A             MVBYTE  LDAX     D
012C 77                     MOV      M,A      ;STORE IT AT END OF INBUF
012D 23                     INX      H        ;BUMP INBUF POINTER
012E 13                     INX      D        ;BUMP SUFFIX POINTER
012F 05                     DCR      B        ;DECREMENT SUFFIX COUNT
0130 C22B01                 JNZ      MVBYTE   ;LOOP IF NOT ZERO
0133 CD3E01                 CALL     CRLF     ;SEND CR/LF TO CONSOLE
0136 C9                     RET
                    ;
0137 0E02           PUTCHR  MVI      C,OUTCHR;BDOS FCN # 2
0139 5F                     MOV      E,A      ;MOVE OUR CHAR FROM A TO E
013A CD0500                 CALL     BDOS
013D C9                     RET
                    ;
013E 3E0D           CRLF    MVI      A,0DH    ;ASCII CODE FOR CR
0140 CD3701                 CALL     PUTCHR
0143 3E0A                   MVI      A,0AH    ;ASCII CODE FOR LF
0145 CD3701                 CALL     PUTCHR
0148 C9                     RET
                    ;
0149 FF             INBUF   DB       0FFH     ;FIRST BYTE=MAX BUFFER SIZE
014A                        DS       256      ;SAVE 256 MORE BYTES FOR INBUF
024A 2021212120SUFFIX DB            ' !!! $'
0006 =              SUFCNT  EQU      6        ;COULD BE WRITTEN AS $-SUFFIX
0250                        END
```

FIG. 6-7 This is the PRN file produced after assembling CONCAT.ASM.

Step 2. Enter the assembly language form of the program (using ED), and save it with the name CONCAT.ASM.

Step 3. Assemble the program with ASM. Use TYPE to list the file CONCAT.PRN, and check that it's the same as in Fig. 6-7.

Step 4. Use LOAD to produce a COM file, and then run the program. Here's a sample interaction in which the user typed HAVE A GOOD DAY (CR) after the question mark.

    A>LOAD CONCAT

    A>CONCAT
    ?HAVE A GOOD DAY (CR)
    HAVE A GOOD DAY !!!

    A>

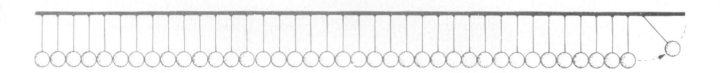

Instant Quiz

1. What does the main program of CONCAT do?
2. What does the subroutine PUTCHR do?
3. What does the subroutine CRLF do?
4. What does the subroutine ACCEPT do? How does it work?

Answers

1. The main program of CONCAT sets up and does three subroutine CALLS. The first is a call to PUTCHR which outputs a question mark (?) on the console. The second is a call to ACCEPT which inputs a string, and then concatenates (adds) the suffix " !!! " to it. The third is a call to BDOS function #9 which prints the concatenated string at the console.

2. PUTCHR is a convenient way of using BDOS function #2 to output whatever character is stored in the A register on the console.

3. CRLF uses PUTCHR twice in a row to send (CR) and (LF) to the console. This is needed to move the cursor to the beginning of a new line.

4. ACCEPT has several parts.

4(a). The first two instructions input a string from the console and store it in memory, starting at the location labelled INBUF (this is location 0149H, placed in the DE pair by LXI D,INBUF just before calling ACCEPT).

4(b). The next three instructions store NC, the number of characters in the input string, in register E.

4(c). The instruction LXI H,INBUF+2 stores the pointer (address) to the start of the input string in HL. The +2 is needed to skip over the MX and NC bytes of the buffer.

4(d). The character count in E (which is the same as DE since DE was zeroed out earlier) is then added to HL with DAD D. This causes HL to point to just after the end of the input string.

4(e). The instruction LXI D,SUFFIX loads the DE register pair with a pointer (address) to SUFFIX (SUFFIX is the label for the string " !!! ").

4(f). The instruction MVI B,SUFCNT is used to store the length of SUFFIX in B. This count is then used in controlling a loop that moves characters, one by one, from the SUFFIX string to the end of INBUF. The loop is made up of the six instructions starting at the label MVBYTE. The instruction JNZ MVBYTE keeps looping back to MVBYTE until the sixth DCR B instruction makes B=0.

Using $ in EQU Directives

The symbol $ can be used in the operand field of assembly language programs to mean the address that the assembler is going to use in assembling its next instruction. Thus if $ is used in anything but an EQU statement, it will mean "starting address for this instruction or pseudo-op." For an EQU directive, the $ will mean "starting address of the next non-EQU operation." This can be useful as shown in the following example.

In CONCAT, the length of SUFFIX was stored as a 6 as follows

```
SUFFIX  DB     ' !!! $'
SUFCNT  EQU    6
        END
```

Instead, we could have let the assembler calculate the 6 by using a $ in SUFCNT as follows (this use of $ is completely different from its use in SUFFIX):

```
SUFFIX  DB     ' !!! $'
SUFCNT  EQU    $-SUFFIX
        END
```

The second form is more general, since it will automatically change SUFCNT for different lengths of SUFFIX strings.

TECHNICAL NOTE

Some Special 8080 Techniques

The 8080/Z80 family of microprocessors has a limited instruction repertoire. In some cases, there simply aren't any instructions for common operations (e. g., multiply and divide). In other cases, the instructions don't match the way higher level programs express ideas (e. g., in comparisons based on the relations "less than," "greater than," or "equal to"). A third problem is that these and many other microprocessors handle data in 8-bit chunks (called bytes) much more readily than they handle larger data types (e. g., the 16-bit chunks called *words* which are used extensively whenever integer arithmetic is done in BASIC or C).

A number of techniques have been developed over the years to overcome these difficulties. Here are a few that programmers have found useful (others can be found by studying Fig. 6-15 and references [5] and [6]).

Division or Multiplication by Powers of Two

Since numbers are represented in binary form in the registers of a microprocessor, division by 2^N can be accomplished by shifting all the bits right N places, while multiplication by 2^N is accomplished with a shift left of N places. There are four shift operations available on the 8080. Two of them act as 8-bit shift/rotations with the mnemonics RLC and RRC, while two act as 9-bit shift/rotations with the mnemonics RAL and RAR. The effect of these instructions can be pictured as follows:

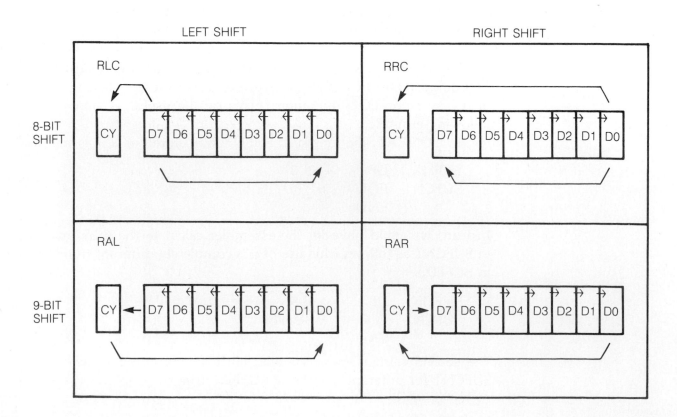

These shift/rotations all act on the A register, moving the 8 data bits D7, D6, . . ., D0 one position to the left or right as shown. The symbol CY stands for the carry bit, and as can be seen, it serves as an extra bit that "catches" the bit shifted out of the A register in four different ways. Here are two program segments that use these instructions for division by 2. To divide by 2^N, the program segments would be placed in a loop that is executed N times.

```
        ;DIVISION OF AN 8-BIT NUMBER X BY 2
DIV2    LDA    X      ;A = X
        ANA    A      ;CY = 0
        RAR           ;DIVIDE BY 2
        STA    X      ;X = X/2

        ;DIVISION OF THE 16-BIT NUMBER IN BC BY 2
DIVWORD ANA    A      ;CY = 0
        MOV    A,B    ;HIGH ORDER BYTE TO A
        RAR           ;DIVIDE BY TWO
        MOV    B,A    ;SAVE HIGH ORDER BYTE
        MOV    A,C    ;LOW ORDER BYTE TO A
        RAR           ;DIVIDE BY 2
        MOV    C,A    ;BC = BC/2
```

Multiplication can be done in an analogous way using shift rotates to the left. Addition and subtraction of 16-bit numbers can be accomplished as follows, using the BC register pair to hold the result (or by using SUM or DIFF for the result).

```
        ;16-BIT ADDITION    BC = COST + OVRHD
ADDWORD LXI    H,COST
        LDA    OVRHD
        ADD    M
        MOV    C,A            ;(OR STA SUM)
        INX    H
        ADC    M
        MOV    B,A            ;(OR STA SUM + 1)
        RET
COST    DW     2500
OVRHD   DW     495

        ;16-BIT SUBTRACTION    BC = GROSS − EXPENSE
SUBWORD LXI    H,EXPENSE
        LDA    GROSS
        SUB    M
        MOV    C,A            ;(OR STA DIFF)
        INX    H
        LDA    GROSS + 1
        SBB    M
        MOV    B,A            ;(OR STA DIFF + 1)
        RET
GROSS    DW     28465
EXPENSE  DW     9842
```

The double add instruction can also be used for adding 16-bit quantities stored in the HL and BC or DE register pairs.

```
DAD    B      ;HL = HL + BC
DAD    D      ;HL = HL + DE
DAD    H      ;HL = 2*HL
```

To move a 16-bit number from memory into the HL pair, use LHLD. Use XCHG to move the contents of HL to DE. Use SHLD to store the contents of HL back in memory. Examples showing how to use these instructions are found in Fig. 6-15 which also shows how to access the elements of an array of 16-bit numbers.

To specify conditional relations, the CMP instruction can be used as follows to test the contents of the A register against one of the other registers. For example, to test A against the D register, use the following:

For unsigned data (0 to 255)			For signed data (−128 to 127)		
CMP	D		CMP	D	
JZ	address	;A=D	JZ	address	;A=D
. . . . .		;A<>D	. . . . .		;A<>D
CMP	D		CMP	D	
JC	address	;A<D	JM	address	;A<D
. . . . .		;A>=D	. . . . .		;A>=D

To compare with a constant, the CPI instruction can be used in a similar manner. For example, CPI 53 means, "Compare A with 53." It has the same effect as MVI D,53, followed by CMP D. To reverse the branching in any of these examples, use the complementary jump instruction (e. g., JNZ instead of JZ, JP instead of JM, JNC instead of JC). To compare 16-bit words for equality, use the 16-bit subtraction routine SUBWORD and test the result for zero as follows

```
CALL    SUBWORD      ;DIFFERENCE IS IN BC
MOV     A,B          ;MOVE LOW ORDER BYTE TO A
ORA     C            ;'OR' B WITH C
JZ      EQUAL        ;GOTO EQUAL ONLY IF B=C=0
```

To gain further insight into how some of these instructions can be used, try your hand at the next lab and the first five exercises of Section 6.9.

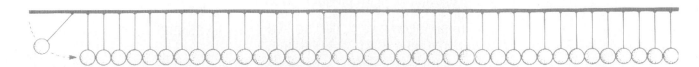

LAB EXERCISE 6.2-2

CHARSORT: A Machine Language Sorting Program

Step 1. Design a machine language program that accepts a string of characters as input, and outputs the string with the characters sorted in alphabetical order. For example, if the string input is WHAMO!, the output string should be !AHMOW.

Step 2. Translate your design into assembly language form using the bubble sort algorithm discussed in Section 6.3 and reference [1].

Step 3. Assemble the program with ASM, and then use LOAD to produce a .COM machine language file.

Step 4. Test the program by running it for several input strings. If you have difficulties, compare your solution to that shown in Fig. 6-8.

```
                    ;CHARSORT      USES BUBBLE SORT ALGORITHM TO PUT CHARACTERS
                    ;              OF ARRAY IN ALPHABETICAL ORDER.
                    ;
0100                        ORG    0100H
0005 =              BDOS    EQU    0005H
0009 =              OUTSTR  EQU    09
0002 =              OUTCHR  EQU    02
                    ;
                    ;MAIN PROGRAM - CONSISTS ENTIRELY OF CALLS TO SUBROUTINES
0100 CD1501                 CALL   MSG1     ;PRINT MESSAGE 1
0103 CD2401                 CALL   DISPLA   ;PRINT UNSORTED ARRAY
0106 CD3601                 CALL   BUBSRT   ;SORT THE CHARACTERS IN ARRAY
0109 CD6C01                 CALL   MSG2     ;PRINT MESSAGE 2
010C CD2401                 CALL   DISPLA   ;PRINT THE SORTED ARRAY
010F CD7B01                 CALL   MSG3     ;PRINT MESSAGE 3
0112 C30000                 JMP    0
                    ;
0115 0E09           MSG1    MVI    C,OUTSTR
0117 119B01                 LXI    D,M1
011A CD0500                 CALL   BDOS
011D CD8A01                 CALL   CRLF
0120 CD8A01                 CALL   CRLF
0123 C9                     RET
                    ;
0124 0E09           DISPLA  MVI    C,OUTSTR
0126 11D401                 LXI    D,ARRAY
0129 CD0500                 CALL   BDOS
012C CD8A01                 CALL   CRLF
012F CD8A01                 CALL   CRLF
0132 CD8A01                 CALL   CRLF
0135 C9                     RET
                    ;
0136 3A1602         BUBSRT  LDA    NUMBER
0139 3D             START   DCR    A
013A CA6B01                 JZ     FINISH
013D 329901                 STA    ITEMS
0140 57                     MOV    D,A
0141 AF                     XRA    A
0142 329A01                 STA    FLAG
0145 01D501                 LXI    B,ARRAY+1
0148 21D401                 LXI    H,ARRAY
014B 0A             LOOP1   LDAX   B
014C BE                     CMP    M
014D D25B01                 JNC    NOSWAP
0150 5E                     MOV    E,M
0151 77                     MOV    M,A
0152 7B                     MOV    A,E
0153 02                     STAX   B
0154 3A9A01                 LDA    FLAG
0157 3C                     INR    A
0158 329A01                 STA    FLAG
015B 23             NOSWAP  INX    H
015C 03                     INX    B
015D 15                     DCR    D
015E C24B01                 JNZ    LOOP1
0161 3A9A01                 LDA    FLAG
0164 B7                     ORA    A
0165 3A9901                 LDA    ITEMS
0168 C23901                 JNZ    START
016B C9             FINISH  RET
                    ;
016C 0E09           MSG2    MVI    C,OUTSTR
016E 11AF01                 LXI    D,M2
0171 CD0500                 CALL   BDOS
0174 CD8A01                 CALL   CRLF
0177 CD8A01                 CALL   CRLF
017A C9                     RET
                    ;
017B 0E09           MSG3    MVI    C,OUTSTR
017D 11C301                 LXI    D,M3
```

FIG. 6-8   This is a machine language program that uses Bubble sort to put the characters of a string in ASCII order.

```
0180 CD0500              CALL    BDOS
0183 CD8A01              CALL    CRLF
0186 CD8A01              CALL    CRLF
0189 C9                  RET
                 ;
018A 1E0D        CRLF    MVI     E,0DH
018C 0E02                MVI     C,OUTCHR
018E CD0500              CALL    BDOS
0191 1E0A                MVI     E,0AH
0193 0E02                MVI     C,OUTCHR
0195 CD0500              CALL    BDOS
0198 C9                  RET
                 ;
0199         ITEMS       DS      1
019A         FLAG        DS      1
019B 3E3E3E2055M1        DB      '>>> UNSORTED ARRAY:$'
01AF 3E3E3E3E3EM2        DB      '>>>>> SORTED ARRAY:$'
01C3 2A2A2A2020M3        DB      '*** DONE ***$'
01D4 5448495320ARRAY     DB      'THIS STRING WILL BE SORTED IN '
01F2 4153434949          DB      'ASCII ORDER STARTING WITH " " (32D)$'
0216 41      NUMBER      DB      $-ARRAY-1
0217                     END
```

```
A>CHARSORT
>>> UNSORTED ARRAY:

THIS STRING WILL BE SORTED IN ASCII ORDER STARTING WITH " " (32D)


>>>>> SORTED ARRAY:

        "" () 23AABCDDDEEEGGHHIIIIIIIIIILLNNNOORRRRRRSSSSSTTTTTWW


***    DONE    ***
```

FIG. 6-8 (*continued*)

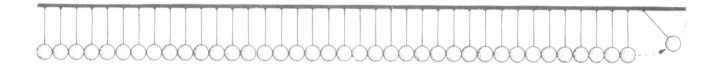

Instant Exercise

Add comments to all the lines of CHARSORT.

6.3 Writing Longer ML Programs; Calling ML from BASIC

The assembly language/ML programs we've seen so far have been modest in length, but even so, it's clear that assembly language does not have "readability" as one of its virtues. The conscientious ML programmer will have to bend over backwards to write assembler code that's at least as digestible for a human reader as it is for ASM.

The principal technique available for making assembler code more intelligible to both yourself and others is *program modularization*. This is the technique of breaking up a large program into bite-sized chunks, but subject to an important restriction: the chunks should always reflect a top-down approach to the overall program design.

The concept of structured, top-down program design was discussed in step 0 of Lab 5.2-1 in connection with BASIC programming. The same ideas are just as valid (if not more so) for assembler/ML programming. In this section we'll put them to work in a rather unique way. We'll do this by asking (and answering) the following question: Can the program NAME200 (introduced in Section 6.1) be written as an extension of the program CONCAT without changing more than one instruction in CONCAT's main program?

As you may suspect, the answer is, "Yes" (why else would we have asked!). The reasoning that shows how to arrive at this answer is the following.

CONCAT already solves the toughest part of NAME200. It inputs a string, concatenates a suffix, and outputs the result. If somehow or other we could just add a word like "etcetera" meaning "do it again" to CONCAT, and then arrange that the process be repeated 200 times, we'll have written NAME200. (Recall that NAME200 is supposed to input a string, concatenate a suffix, and print the result 200 times).

The heart of the high-level idea, then, is to invent a new ML feature called "etcetera", and make sure it has a built-in counter (up to 200 for our example). We'll also want to be cautious about adding this feature, having the suspicion that such a simple fix may be too good to be true. In particular, we'll want to be ready to add some "defensive" code, that is, code which preserves the integrity of those parts of CONCAT that already work.

If you look at CONCAT again (see Fig. 6-7), you'll recall that the "outputting" gets done in the seventh line of the main program with the instruction CALL BDOS. Our high-level idea suggests that we try changing this to CALL ETCETERA, where ETCETERA will be a routine that uses BDOS function #9 200 times. As to the details of this routine, the top-down spirit suggests saying "that's enough work for one day—we can take care of the details tomorrow morning."

(Scene two, The Next Day, 5 AM) The catch to top-down design is that if you don't have a staff to handle details, you must eventually take care of them yourself. So it's time to wear a low-level hat and write the subroutine ETCETERA. Here's what a first attempt might look like, using the B register as a counter for looping through the desired process 200 times.

```
ETCETERA          MVI     B,200
LOOP              CALL    BDOS
                  DCR     B
                  JNZ     LOOP
                  RET
```

That's actually not a bad start. The routine stores the number 200 decimal in the B register, and then calls BDOS (remembering that just before ETCETERA is called, the main program will load the C register with BDOS function #9, and put a pointer to the concatenated string in DE). Thus CALL BDOS should print the same string that CONCAT did. Then DCR will decrement B from 200 to 199. Since 199 is not zero, the JNZ will take execution back to LOOP for another printing of the concatenated string. The process should repeat over and over, eventually using CALL BDOS to produce output 200 times before B equals zero. At that time the program should fall through to RET, and return to the main program where it finds a CALL 0, causing the usual termination with a warm boot.

There's just one problem that arises when you try modifying CONCAT in this way. It doesn't work.

Instant Quiz

1. What's wrong with the modification of CONCAT just suggested?
2. How can the problem be fixed?

Before reading the answers, think about some possible explanations of what could go wrong. If you hit on the right one, you are definitely a prospective ML hacker-cum-laude.

Answers

1. What's wrong is that our solution forgot the advice about defensive coding. Our changes did not preserve the integrity of CONCAT. The villain is the first CALL BDOS in ETCETERA. This works OK, *but* the subroutine being called (#9) will wreak havoc with the contents of the registers we must count on when we call BDOS again, most notably, C and DE. So the next time we CALL BDOS in our loop, it won't have the correct input parameters. Further, the B register will have lost the correct value for counting the number of times around the loop.

   Moral: Always assume that a subroutine *you* didn't write will use all the registers, and mess up any data you thought they contained.

2. The solution to our problem is to preserve all important register contents before calling BDOS function #9 (or any other one for that matter) in a loop. You can do this with the PUSH operation, once for each pair of registers to be saved. PUSH B saves B *and* C on the stack, PUSH D saves D *and* E on the stack, PUSH H saves H *and* L on the stack, and PUSH PSW saves both A *and* F on the stack. To retrieve this information later on, you use corresponding POP operations, but in *reverse* order (this is because POP uses the rule of "last in first out.")

Here's a revised version of ETCETERA (called ETCET) in which all register values are saved just before calling BDOS function #9 in the loop. These values are then retrieved right after the call. Saving *all* the registers is usually overkill, but it's better to be safe than sorry.

```
ETCET    MVI     B,200
LOOP     PUSH    H
         PUSH    D
         PUSH    B
         PUSH    PSW
         CALL    BDOS
         POP     PSW
         POP     B
         POP     D
         POP     H
         DCR     B
         JNZ     LOOP
         RET
```

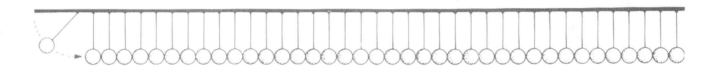

LAB EXERCISE 6.3-1

NAME200: Loop Structures in Machine Language Programs

Step 1.   Modify CONCAT by adding the subroutine ETCET. Also change line 7 of the main program CALL BDOS to CALL ETCET. Fig. 6-9 shows what the modified program should look like.

```
TYPE NAME1.PRN

                ;NAME200    PROGRAM TO PRINT A ?, INPUT A STRING, ADD
                ;A SUFFIX STRING, AND PRINT THE RESULT 200 TIMES.
0100                    ORG     0100H
0005 =          BDOS    EQU     05H
000A =          INSTR   EQU     0AH
0009 =          OUTSTR  EQU     09H
0002 =          OUTCHR  EQU     02H
                ;
                ;MAIN PROGRAM.  USES SUBROUTINES PUTCHR, ACCEPT, AND ETCET.
                ;  (ACCEPT USES SUBROUTINE CRLF, CRLF USES PUTCHR)
                ;
0100 3E3F               MVI     A,3FH    ;PUT ASCII CODE FOR ? IN A
0102 CD3701             CALL    PUTCHR   ;PRINT IT AT THE CONSOLE
0105 115B01             LXI     D,INBUF  ;POINT TO LOCAL INPUT BUFFER
0108 CD1601             CALL    ACCEPT   ;INPUT STRING, ADD SUFFIX + $
010B 0E09               MVI     C,OUTSTR ;USE BDOS FCN # 9
010D 115D01             LXI     D,INBUF+2 ;TO ECHO CONTENTS OF INBUF
0110 CD4901             CALL    ETCET    ;ON THE CONSOLE 200 TIMES
0113 C30000             JMP     0
                ;
0116 0E0A       ACCEPT  MVI     C,INSTR ;USE BDOS FCN 10 TO INPUT STRING
0118 CD0500             CALL    BDOS    ;WE ASSUME CALLER HAS LOADED DE
011B 110000             LXI     D,0     ;ZERO OUT DE PAIR
011E 215C01             LXI     H,INBUF+1 ;POINT TO CHAR COUNT OF INBUF
0121 5E                 MOV     E,M      ;PUT CHAR COUNT IN E
0122 215D01             LXI     H,INBUF+2 ;POINT TO START OF INBUF TEXT
0125 19                 DAD     D        ;DISPLACE POINTER TO END OF INBUF
0126 0606               MVI     B,SUFCNT;NUMBER OF CHARACTERS IN SUFFIX
0128 115C02             LXI     D,SUFFIX;POINTER TO SUFFIX TEXT
012B 1A         MVBYTE  LDAX    D
```

FIG. 6-9   This is the PRN listing of NAME200 after assembly.

```
012C 77                      MOV    M,A      ;STORE IT AT END OF INBUF
012D 23                      INX    H        ;BUMP INBUF POINTER
012E 13                      INX    D        ;BUMP SUFFIX POINTER
012F 05                      DCR    B        ;DECREMENT SUFFIX COUNT
0130 C22B01                  JNZ    MVBYTE   ;LOOP IF NOT ZERO
0133 CD3E01                  CALL   CRLF     ;SEND CR/LF TO CONSOLE
0136 C9                      RET
                  ;
0137 0E02        PUTCHR      MVI    C,OUTCHR ;BDOS FCN # 2
0139 5F                      MOV    E,A      ;MOVE OUR CHAR FROM A TO E
013A CD0500                  CALL   BDOS
013D C9                      RET
                  ;
013E 3E0D        CRLF        MVI    A,0DH    ;ASCII CODE FOR CR
0140 CD3701                  CALL   PUTCHR
0143 3E0A                    MVI    A,0AH    ;ASCII CODE FOR LF
0145 CD3701                  CALL   PUTCHR
0148 C9                      RET
                  ;
0149 06C8        ETCET       MVI    B,200
014B E5          LOOP        PUSH   H
014C D5                      PUSH   D
014D C5                      PUSH   B
014E F5                      PUSH   PSW
014F CD0500                  CALL   BDOS
0152 F1                      POP    PSW
0153 C1                      POP    B
0154 D1                      POP    D
0155 E1                      POP    H
0156 05                      DCR    B
0157 C24B01                  JNZ    LOOP
015A C9                      RET
                  ;
015B FF          INBUF       DB     0FFH     ;FIRST BYTE=MAX BUFFER SIZE
015C                         DS     256      ;SAVE 256 MORE BYTES FOR INBUF
025C 2021212120SUFFIX        DB     ´ !!! $´
0006 =           SUFCNT      EQU    $-SUFFIX
0262                         END

A>
```

FIG. 6-9 *(continued)*

PHOTO 6-3 *This is the output of NAME200 on an 80-column Z19 video terminal. This output will not work on a printer since no (CR) (LF) characters are sent by NAME200.*

Step 2.   Assemble, load, and test run the new version.

Step 3.   Make any additional changes for which you get ideas after seeing the output. Photo 6-3 shows the output on an 80-column video display as a result of typing JUNIPER for the input.

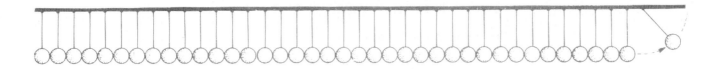

Instant Quiz (somewhat esoteric; OK to skip)

1. In a longer program, there may be a need to save registers at several points in the program. This suggests putting the four PUSH instructions in a subroutine called something like SAVEREG, and putting the four POP instructions in a subroutine called GETREG. Then you could save and restore registers with CALL SAVEREG and CALL GETREG. Will this work?

2. If the answer to 1 is No, is there another way to save registers?

Answers

1. No, it won't work because the CALL instructions also use the stack, placing the address of the next instruction to be executed on it. If you then do a bunch of PUSH instructions, you'll be burying that return address down in the stack where RET can't find it.

2. There's nothing sacred about the stack. It's just ordinary memory that the SP points to. This suggests changing SP to point to your own private stack just before doing all those PUSH instructions (or POP instructions), and then switching back to the regular stack pointer value (which is assigned by CP/M) just before the RET. This is fairly easy to do on the Z80 since this processor has two instructions just made for this purpose, one for storing the SP in memory, and the other for retrieving it. However if you stick to 8080 code, these instructions have to be replaced with several 8080 instructions, and the extra fuss is hardly worth it. You'll also have to save and retrieve HL separately (using SHLD and LHLD) since the HL register pair is needed to point to the part of memory where you put your private stack. Fig. 6-10 shows 8080 versions of two subroutines SAVEREG and GETREG that use a private stack.

Calling ML Programs from BASIC

BASIC-80 includes a facility for calling ML programs when needed. The idea is to first write a BASIC program that uses the high-level syntax of BASIC-80. Those parts of the program that are not critical at execution

```
TYPE SNAME.ASM

ETCET    MVI      B,200
LOOP     CALL     SAVEREG
         CALL     BDOS
         CALL     GETREG
         DCR      B
         JNZ      LOOP
         RET
;
SAVEREG  LXI      H,0
         DAD      SP
         SHLD     SYSTSP
         LHLD     MYSP
         SPHL
         PUSH     D
         PUSH     B
         PUSH     PSW
         LXI      H,0
         DAD      SP
         SHLD     MYSP
         LHLD     SYSTSP
         SPHL
         RET
SYSTSP   DS       2
MYSTK    DS       20H
MYSP     EQU      $
;
GETREG   LXI      H,0
         DAD      SP
         SHLD     SYSTSP
         LHLD     MYSP
         SPHL
         POP      PSW
         POP      B
         POP      D
         LXI      H,0
         DAD      SP
         SHLD     MYSP
         LHLD     SYSTSP
         SPHL
         RET
```

FIG. 6-10 This is how the subroutines SAVEREG, and GETREG would be written so as to use their own private stack (called MYSTK). The pointer to MYSTK is stored in MYSP, while the pointer to the system stack is stored in SYSTSP. On a Z80, the instructions LD (addr), SP and LD SP, (addr) could be used to shorten these routines considerably.

time (for example, input and output operations) can be left intact, while those parts which slow down execution (e. g., the loops in a sorting routine) can then be replaced with calls to equivalent ML code. This way, the overall program will retain its structure and readability.

The two new BASIC statements used for calling ML subroutines are DEF USRn and X=USERn(). DEF USRn tells the BASIC program where in memory the ML program to be used is actually stored, while USERn() is a function that, when called upon, starts execution of this ML program. For example,

200 DEF USR2 = &HC000

says that ML program #2 is stored at location C000 hex, while the statement

800 HL = USER2(X)

starts execution of this program, acting like the instruction

CALL   C000H

in assembly language. As a matter of fact, more recent versions of MBASIC allow you to write this line as

800 CALL FCN2

provided that the assignment statement

200 FCN2 = &HC000

has previously been made.

Of course none of this will work unless an ML program doing something sensible is located at the defined location (C000H in our example). This ML program must first be written as an 8080 assembly language subroutine (using ED), assembled into machine language and then loaded into memory starting at C000H. The neatest way to actually load the ML program is to let BASIC do it by using the READ and POKE statements. However READ requires decimal data so you also have the job of translating the ML file produced by ASM into decimal form. We'll come back to the question of how to do this later, showing how to write a small utility BASIC program that does the translation for you.

Assuming that you finally get your ML program translated into decimal form, you'll want to store this decimal version where POKE can get at it. The easiest approach is to incorporate it as data in the main BASIC program, and then use READ and POKE statements to move the ML program from the DATA statements into memory.

That all sounds pretty complicated (and in many ways it is), but an example done as a lab exercise should help clear up the procedure.

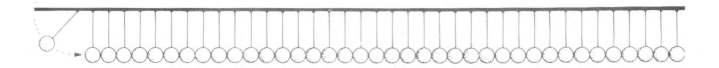

LAB EXERCISE Writing and Running a BASIC Program That Calls an ML Subroutine

6.3-2 *Step 1.* Write a sorting program in BASIC-80, isolating the part which you'll want to later turn into ML as a subroutine. As an example, Fig. 6-11 shows a BASIC program that uses the Bubble sort to sort the integers stored in the array A( ). Since the array is dimensioned as A(800), up to 800 integers can be sorted. (Further information about Bubble sort can be found in reference [1]).

```
LIST
100 '*****************************************************************
110 '*         BUBSORT   (BUBBLE SORT OF POSITIVE INTEGERS)        *
120 '*****************************************************************
130 DEFINT A-Z: DIM A(800)
140 INPUT "HOW MANY INTEGERS TO BE SORTED (MAX=800)"; N
150 IF N<1 OR N>800 THEN 140
160 FOR I=1 TO N: A(I)=INT(256*RND): NEXT I :PRINT
170 PRINT ">>>>>>>>>>>     UNSORTED INTEGERS ARE     <<<<<<<<<<<"
180 GOSUB 430 ' PRINT ROUTINE
190 INPUT "GET STOPWATCH READY & PRESS ENTER TO SORT -- READY";D$
200 ITEMS=N
210 PRINT "********* START TIMING *********"
220 GOSUB 300  'GO TO BUBBLE SORT SUBROUTINE
230 PRINT "*********  STOP TIMING *********"
240 INPUT "TO SEE SORTED DATA PRESS RETURN -- READY"; D$: PRINT
250 PRINT ">>>>>>>>>>>      SORTED INTEGERS ARE     <<<<<<<<<<<<"
260 GOSUB 430 ' PRINT ROUTINE
270 END
280 '=========================================================
290 '        SUBROUTINE TO USE BUBBLE SORT ON A()
300 ITEMS=ITEMS-1: IF ITEMS=0 THEN 410
310 FLAG=0
320 K=1
330 IF A(K+1)>=A(K) THEN 380
340   TEMP=A(K+1)
350   A(K+1)=A(K)
360   A(K)=TEMP
370   FLAG=1
380 K=K+1
390 IF K<=ITEMS THEN 330
400 IF FLAG<>0 THEN 300
410 RETURN
420 '=========================================================
430 'SUBROUTINE TO PRINT N ITEMS, 11 ITEMS/LINE, 6 COLS/ITEM
440 K=0: PRINT
450   FOR J=1 TO 11
455     K=K+1: IF K>N THEN 500
460       PRINT USING "######";A(K);
470   NEXT J
480   PRINT: GOTO 450
500 PRINT:PRINT:RETURN
510 '=========================================================
Ok
RUN
HOW MANY INTEGERS TO BE SORTED (MAX=800)? 22

>>>>>>>>>>>     UNSORTED INTEGERS ARE     <<<<<<<<<<<

    62    78    79   131    14   201   127    93   252   230   186
     1   248     0   244    10   229   169   141   209   232   219


GET STOPWATCH READY & PRESS ENTER TO SORT -- READY?
********* START TIMING *********
*********  STOP TIMING *********
TO SEE SORTED DATA PRESS RETURN -- READY?

>>>>>>>>>>>      SORTED INTEGERS ARE     <<<<<<<<<<<<

     0     1    10    14    62    78    79    93   127   131   141
   169   186   201   209   219   229   230   232   244   248   252
```

FIG. 6-11 This shows a program that sorts up to 800 randomly generated integers. The loop from line 330 to line 390 controls one pass through the data, swapping adjacent items if they are out of order. The loop from 300 to 400 causes repeated passes to be made until no more swaps are detected, that is, until FLAG = 0 in line 400.

Step 2. To see where the bottleneck in this program is, run it for values of N that double each time, e. g., for N = 50, 100, 200, 400, and 800. Time how long the sort takes in each case. Do not include the time for printing either the unsorted or sorted integers—just the time for the sort itself. You should find that for randomly generated data, bubble sort is "of order N-squared." That is, each doubling of N will approximately quadruple the sorting time. On a 4 MHz Z80, the times will be something like 15, 60, 240, 960, and 3840 seconds for N = 50, 100, 200, 400, and 800. In other words, sorting 800 items will take over an hour when using a Bubble sort running under MBASIC.

Step 3. The next step is to rewrite BUBSORT, replacing the subroutine that starts at line 300 with a call to an ML program. This is easier said than done, so expect that you'll be doing much of this lab "by rote"—at least the first time around. Fig. 6-13 shows the rewritten program which is now named BUBML.BAS.

The principal features to notice in the new subroutine (lines 300 to 390) of Fig. 6-13 are as follows:

(a) Line 300, together with line 330, says that the ML routine will be loaded at starting address START = C000 hex. The highest address to be used is assigned as FINISH = C0C5 hex. This information is needed for the loop in line 310.

(b) The decimal codes for the ML routine are found in the DATA statements starting at line 65010. How all this data got there, and what it means is the big question, of course. We'll explain the "how" and some of the "what" shortly.

(c) Line 310 takes all this data and pokes it into memory starting at C000 hex. Here's a map showing what's in memory after line 310 is executed in a 62K system.

EF80	= Top of User RAM
EB00	= Start of CP/M
. . . . . . C0D0 to EAFF not used	
C0CF	= End of DS Area for ML Routine
C0C6	= Start of DS Area for ML Routine
C0C5	= End of ML Sort Routine
C000	= Start of ML Sort Routine
BFFF	= End of RAM Available to BASIC
7000 (more or less)	= Start of A( ) Array
6000 (more or less)	= Start of BUBML.BAS
0100	= Start of MBASIC Interpreter
00FF	= End of CP/M Reserved Area
0000	= Start of RAM & CP/M Reserved Area

(d)   Lines 320, 340, and 350 show one possible technique for *passing* data to an ML routine, namely the use of POKE into a reserved DS (data storage) area. In this example, we are passing the value of N to the DS area labelled ITEMS in the assembly listing of Fig. 6-15. To get the value of N, we first use the BASIC-80 function VARPTR(N) which returns the address of N. We then use PEEK to find its actual value. PEEK must be used twice since MBASIC stores integers like N in two successive bytes.

(e)   Line 360 is where the ML subroutine is actually called, using the MBASIC function USR0(arg). In our example, we let the argument of USR0 be a pointer to the element A(1) in the array A( ). This is how we pass the location of A( ) to the ML routine. The BASIC Manual tells us that this argument will end up in the HL register pair *provided* that our ML program first does a call to the address stored in location 0103. Why there? That's where MBASIC handles the business of converting an argument into a 16-bit integer (which is what we want), and then loading it into the HL register pair. The exact code for making this indirect call is given in lines 4, 5, 6, and 7 of Fig. 6-15. A similar technique is needed to return an integer from HL to X in line 360. For further information, see Appendix C of the BASIC-80 manual.

Note 1:   When typing in the program BUBML.BAS of Fig. 6-13, you only have to type lines 100 to 500. You don't have to type in lines 65010 to 65130 (unless you want to). The reason is that we'll present a program (called DECML) that does this job for you. When finished typing in BUBML, be sure to save your work with

SAVE "BUBML.BAS"

Note 2:   Although it won't be needed until step 8, this would be a good time to enter *and save* the program DECML as shown in Fig. 6-12. Don't forget to first type NEW.

```
100 'DECML    PROGRAM TO CONVERT ML CODES LOADED IN CORE
110 'TO BASIC DATA STATEMENTS & SAVE AS FILE MLDATA.ASC
130 LIN=65010!: L$=MID$(STR$(LIN),2)+" DATA "
140 START=&HC000: FINISH=&HC0C5
150 OPEN "O",1,"MLDATA.ASC"
170 FOR I=START TO FINISH
180    L$=L$+MID$(STR$(PEEK(I)),2)
190    IF (I AND 15) <> 15 THEN L$=L$+",": GOTO 220
200    PRINT #1,L$
210    LIN=LIN+10: L$=MID$(STR$(LIN),2)+" DATA "
220 NEXT I
230 IF LEN(L$)>9 THEN PRINT #1, LEFT$(L$,LEN(L$)-1)
240 CLOSE: END
```

FIG. 6-12   DECML is a program that automatically generates a file of DATA statements corresponding to ML code previously placed in memory by DDT.

The big job now is to get all those data statements added to BUBML. There are two ways to go about this. One is to type lines 65010 to 65130 in as shown, and do another SAVE. In this case, you're all set to try running the program, so go to step 10.

If however you expect to add ML routines to other BASIC programs, you'll want to continue with steps 4, 5, 6, 7, 8, and 9.

```
100 '*************************************************************
110 '*        BUBML    (ML BUBBLE SORT OF POSITIVE INTEGERS)      *
120 '*************************************************************
130 DEFINT A-Z: DIM A(800)
140 INPUT "HOW MANY INTEGERS TO BE SORTED (MAX=800)"; N
150 IF N<1 OR N>800 THEN 140
160 FOR I=1 TO N: A(I)=INT(32000!*RND): NEXT I :PRINT
170 PRINT ">>>>>>>>>>>    UNSORTED INTEGERS ARE    <<<<<<<<<<<"
180 GOSUB 430 '  PRINT ROUTINE
190 INPUT "GET STOPWATCH READY & PRESS ENTER TO SORT -- READY";D$
210 PRINT "********* START TIMING *********"
220 GOSUB 300  'GO TO BUBBLE SORT SUBROUTINE
230 PRINT "*********  STOP TIMING *********"
240 INPUT "TO SEE SORTED DATA PRESS RETURN -- READY"; D$: PRINT
250 PRINT ">>>>>>>>>>>    SORTED INTEGERS ARE    <<<<<<<<<<<"
260 GOSUB 430 ' PRINT ROUTINE
270 END
280 '============================================================
290 '      SUBROUTINE TO USE BUBBLE SORT ON A()
300 START=&HC000: FINISH=&HC0C5
310 FOR K=START TO FINISH: READ D: POKE K,D: NEXT K
320 NADDR=VARPTR(N)
330 DEF USR0=START
340 POKE START+3, PEEK(NADDR)        'ITEMS=N, LO BYTE
350 POKE START+4, PEEK(NADDR+1)      'ITEMS=N, HI BYTE
360 X=USR0(VARPTR(A(1)))
390 RETURN
420 '============================================================
430 'SUBROUTINE TO PRINT N ITEMS, 9 ITEMS/LINE, 7 COLS/ITEM
440 K=0: PRINT
450    FOR J=1 TO 9
455      K=K+1: IF K>N THEN 500
460      PRINT USING "#######";A(K);
470    NEXT J
480    PRINT: GOTO 450
500 PRINT:PRINT:RETURN
65000 '============================================================
65001 '    DECIMAL CODES FOR ML SUBROUTINE
65010 DATA 195,5,192,3,0,33,13,192,229,42,3,1,233,34,201,192
65020 DATA 42,3,192,43,34,3,192,124,181,202,181,192,175,50,198,192
65030 DATA 33,1,0,34,199,192,42,199,192,41,229,205,182,192,25,94
65040 DATA 35,86,235,34,205,192,225,205,189,192,25,94,35,86,213,42
65050 DATA 205,192,235,225,122,172,122,250,78,192,123,149,122,156,23,210
65060 DATA 149,192,42,199,192,41,205,182,192,25,94,35,86,235,34,203
65070 DATA 192,42,199,192,41,229,205,189,192,25,94,35,86,235,34,205
65080 DATA 192,225,205,182,192,25,229,42,205,192,235,225,115,35,114,42
65090 DATA 199,192,41,205,189,192,25,229,42,203,192,235,225,115,35,114
65100 DATA 62,1,50,198,192,42,199,192,35,34,199,192,235,42,3,192
65110 DATA 122,172,124,250,170,192,125,147,124,154,23,210,38,192,58,198
65120 DATA 192,183,194,16,192,201,229,42,201,192,235,225,201,229,42,201
65130 DATA 192,43,43,235,225,201
Ok
```

FIG. 6-13 The program BUBML.BAS shown here is similar to BUBSORT.BAS of Fig. 6-11. The difference is that in BUBML a machine language routine is called upon to do the actual sorting. The ML is stored in decimal form as DATA statements, but poked into memory (starting at location C000 hex) for actual use.

Step 4.   The more general approach to creating the needed data statements is first to write the ML routine in assembly language. The question of how to design such a routine won't be discussed at this point—it would be too distracting and complicated. For now, just copy the assembly language part of Fig. 6-15 (the last three columns only), using ED as follows.

> A>ED BUBML.ASM
> . . . etc. . . .

When finished, type E, telling ED to save your work as the file BUBML.ASM. Use TYPE BUBML.ASM to proofread the file carefully—it must be exactly as shown.

Step 5.   Assemble BUBML.ASM by typing ASM BUBML. This will produce the files BUBML.PRN and BUBML.HEX. If there are errors, go back to step 4, correct BUBML.ASM with ED, and repeat step 5.

Step 6.   Next use DDT to load the ML code you just assembled into memory by typing

> A>DDT BUBML.HEX

DDT will translate the hex file into binary machine language, and load the binary code into RAM from locations C000 to C0C5. It knows about these addresses because they are saved as part of the file BUBML.HEX.

Step 7.   Go into MBASIC, being sure to tell MBASIC that it can't use memory from C000 on up (i. e., above BFFF). You do this by including the /M "switch" in the command line as follows:

> A>MBASIC /M:&HBFFF

Step 8.   We now need to use the program DECML.BAS. If you didn't type it in and save it previously, do so now, copying Fig. 6-12 and using SAVE with the filename "DECML.BAS". If you've already typed and saved DECML.BAS, then load it into memory. In either case, the important thing is to now run this program.

> OK
> LOAD "DECML.BAS"
> RUN
> OK

When run, the program DECML will peek into all those locations of memory where you stored the ML routine (using DDT in step 6), and create an ASCII sequential file called MLDATA.ASC. This file will contain DATA statements numbered from 65010 on up, and the data will correspond to the decimal equivalents of the ML code in BUBML.HEX.

```
RUN
HOW MANY INTEGERS TO BE SORTED (MAX=800)? 50

>>>>>>>>>>>>       UNSORTED INTEGERS ARE       <<<<<<<<<<<<

    7843    9760    9979   16485    1866   25244   15907   11640   31505
   28850   23274     218   31021      56   30599    1304   28691   21126
   17743   26197   29031   27456   27802   16219   18685   14341   27767
    1059   19317   24924    9169   25107    4387    7249    6888   28056
   27436   18174   11669    1067   28047   24425    6443   19474   11956
    7218   23857    8227   29762   14503


GET STOPWATCH READY & PRESS ENTER TO SORT -- READY?
********* START TIMING *********
*********  STOP TIMING *********
TO SEE SORTED DATA PRESS RETURN -- READY?

>>>>>>>>>>>>       SORTED INTEGERS ARE       <<<<<<<<<<<<

      56     218    1059    1067    1304    1866    4387    6443    6888
    7218    7249    7843    8227    9169    9760    9979   11640   11669
   11956   14341   14503   15907   16219   16485   17743   18174   18685
   19317   19474   21126   23274   23857   24425   24924   25107   25244
   26197   27436   27456   27767   27802   28047   28056   28691   28850
   29031   29762   30599   31021   31505
```

FIG. 6-14 This is a run of the program BUBML. It should be timed for values of N up to 800, and compared with the BUBSORT program of Fig. 6-11.

Step 9.   Merge the DATA statements with BUBML as follows:

>LOAD "BUBML.BAS"
>MERGE "MLDATA.ASC"
>SAVE "BUBML.BAS"

If you LIST this last program, you should see all the DATA statements added as in Fig. 6-13.

Step 10.   At long last you're ready to run the program BUBML.BAS, responding as shown in Fig. 6-14. Try values of N = 50, 100, 200, 400, and 800. For N = 800, the time should now be about 60 seconds, as compared to 3800 seconds for BUBSORT.

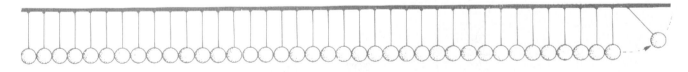

Epilogue

This is a complicated example, and it will take quite some time and experience to fully understand all of it. In particular, it calls upon the 16-bit ML sorting routine shown in both ML and assembly form in Fig. 6-15. This listing doesn't have any comments, so it won't make much sense by itself. However, it corresponds closely to the original BASIC subroutine of Fig. 6-11. If you match the labels of Fig. 6-15 to line numbers in Fig. 6-11 (e. g., match label L320 to line 320), you'll have

```
A>TYPE BUBML.PRN


C000                            ORG      0C000H
C000 C305C0                     JMP      INIT
C003                   ITEMS    DS       2
C005 210DC0            INIT     LXI      H,START
C008 E5                         PUSH     H
C009 2A0301                     LHLD     0103H
C00C E9                         PCHL
                       ;HL NOW HOLDS PTR TO A() = [ATOP]
C00D 22C9C0            START    SHLD     ATOP
C010 2A03C0            L300     LHLD     ITEMS
C013 2B                         DCX      H
C014 2203C0                     SHLD     ITEMS
C017 7C                         MOV      A,H
C018 B5                         ORA      L
C019 CAB5C0                     JZ       L410
C01C AF                L310     XRA      A
C01D 32C6C0                     STA      FLAG
C020 210100            L320     LXI      H,1
C023 22C7C0                     SHLD     K
C026 2AC7C0            L330     LHLD     K
C029 29                         DAD      H
C02A E5                         PUSH     H
C02B CDB6C0                     CALL     AT2
C02E 19                         DAD      D
C02F 5E                         MOV      E,M
C030 23                         INX      H
C031 56                         MOV      D,M
C032 EB                         XCHG
C033 22CDC0                     SHLD     T1
C036 E1                         POP      H
C037 CDBDC0                     CALL     AT1
C03A 19                         DAD      D
C03B 5E                         MOV      E,M
C03C 23                         INX      H
C03D 56                         MOV      D,M
C03E D5                         PUSH     D
C03F 2ACDC0                     LHLD     T1
C042 EB                         XCHG
C043 E1                         POP      H
C044 7A                         MOV      A,D
C045 AC                         XRA      H
C046 7A                         MOV      A,D
C047 FA4EC0                     JM       BOT
C04A 7B                         MOV      A,E
C04B 95                         SUB      L
C04C 7A                         MOV      A,D
C04D 9C                         SBB      H
C04E 17                BOT      RAL
C04F D295C0                     JNC      L380
C052 2AC7C0            L340     LHLD     K
C055 29                         DAD      H
C056 CDB6C0                     CALL     AT2
C059 19                         DAD      D
C05A 5E                         MOV      E,M
C05B 23                         INX      H
C05C 56                         MOV      D,M
```

FIG. 6-15 This is a listing of BUBML.PRN, the ML subroutine called by BUBML.BAS. The labels used (such as L360) correspond to line numbers in the corresponding BASIC subroutine used in BUBSORT. The code in lines 4, 5, 6, and 7 is an indirect call to an argument passing routine of MBASIC whose address is at 0103H.

```
C05D  EB              XCHG
C05E  22CBC0          SHLD    TEMP
C061  2AC7C0    L350  LHLD    K
C064  29              DAD     H
C065  E5              PUSH    H
C066  CDBDC0          CALL    AT1
C069  19              DAD     D
C06A  5E              MOV     E,M
C06B  23              INX     H
C06C  56              MOV     D,M
C06D  EB              XCHG
C06E  22CDC0          SHLD    T1
C071  E1              POP     H
C072  CDB6C0          CALL    AT2
C075  19              DAD     D
C076  E5              PUSH    H
C077  2ACDC0          LHLD    T1
C07A  EB              XCHG
C07B  E1              POP     H
C07C  73              MOV     M,E
C07D  23              INX     H
C07E  72              MOV     M,D
C07F  2AC7C0    L360  LHLD    K
C082  29              DAD     H
C083  CDBDC0          CALL    AT1
C086  19              DAD     D
C087  E5              PUSH    H
C088  2ACBC0          LHLD    TEMP
C08B  EB              XCHG
C08C  E1              POP     H
C08D  73              MOV     M,E
C08E  23              INX     H
C08F  72              MOV     M,D
C090  3E01      L370  MVI     A,1
C092  32C6C0          STA     FLAG
C095  2AC7C0    L380  LHLD    K
C098  23              INX     H
C099  22C7C0          SHLD    K
C09C  EB              XCHG
C09D  2A03C0          LHLD    ITEMS
C0A0  7A              MOV     A,D
C0A1  AC              XRA     H
C0A2  7C              MOV     A,H
C0A3  FAAAC0          JM      NEXT
C0A6  7D              MOV     A,L
C0A7  93              SUB     E
C0A8  7C              MOV     A,H
C0A9  9A              SBB     D
C0AA  17        NEXT  RAL
C0AB  D226C0          JNC     L330
C0AE  3AC6C0    L400  LDA     FLAG
C0B1  B7              ORA     A
C0B2  C210C0          JNZ     L300
C0B5  C9        L410  RET
C0B6  E5        AT2   PUSH    H
C0B7  2AC9C0          LHLD    ATOP
C0BA  EB              XCHG
C0BB  E1              POP     H
C0BC  C9              RET
C0BD  E5        AT1   PUSH    H
C0BE  2AC9C0          LHLD    ATOP
C0C1  2B              DCX     H
C0C2  2B              DCX     H
```

FIG. 6-15 (*continued*)

```
C0C3 EB                    XCHG
C0C4 E1                    POP      H
C0C5 C9                    RET
C0C6            FLAG       DS       1
C0C7            K          DS       2
C0C9            ATOP       DS       2
C0CB            TEMP       DS       2
C0CD            T1         DS       2
                          END
```

FIG. 6-15 (*continued*)

an indication of what each section of the ML code does (e. g., LXI H,1 and SHLD K does the same as LET K=1). A better idea is to restudy the simpler 8-bit Bubble sorting program CONCAT shown in Section 6.2-4, and then re-attack the present 16-bit sort by trying to write it yourself, possibly by extending the 8-bit version.

Epilogue to the Epilogue

We used Bubble sort in the above example to illustrate that even though Bubble is a poor sort for large values of N, translating the sort into ML works as a "brute-force" method for shortening the sorting time. A much more intelligent (and we might add, much cheaper) solution to the problem of reducing sorting time is to use a better algorithm. The Shell sort discussed in Sections 5.5 and 5.7 is such an algorithm. Exercise 5 of Section 6.9 suggests using it (instead of Bubble sort) in Lab 6.3-2, thereby combining the advantages of a superior algorithm and machine language.

6.4 CP/M File Structures

It was back in Chapter 2 that we first mentioned the value of using disk and memory maps to help understand what CP/M does, and how the various tasks managed by CP/M relate to memory usage. Most of our references to maps since then have concentrated on the TPA—on "what" goes "where" in this part of RAM at a given time, and how this picture changes as new CP/M facilities are called upon.

In this section we're going to dig into the subject of memory maps a little further, giving particular attention to two special parts of memory related to files: the BDOS area just above the CCP, and the "private" part of RAM that CP/M sets aside for itself just below the TPA (in locations 0000H through 00FFH). We'll find that a lot of what goes on in both of these areas is related to disk file management, and that a more detailed study of the corresponding memory maps will help complete this part of the CP/M jigsaw puzzle.

Although this is a somewhat exotic area of study, and it can be by-passed by most users of CP/M, it's also a fascinating one. As we'll see, some of the most impressive design features of CP/M lurk in the inner recesses of its disk file management system. If you'd like to gain an insider's appreciation of CP/M, and at the same time try something off the beaten path, grab your base-16 abacus, and join us in our journey from the mountainous passes of BDOS, to the caverns of 00FF hex and below.

How CP/M Organizes and Manages Disk Files

The basic idea behind using disk files is a simple one to state, but an incredibly complex one to realize. From one point of view, a disk system is just a fancy I/O device. Commands like SAVE, SYSGEN, and certain forms of PIP *output* data to the disk device, while other forms of PIP and commands like LOAD, TYPE, and DUMP *input* data from it.

There are two levels of difficulty involved in making the seemingly simple idea of disk I/O actually work. One is at the hardware level, and it includes accomplishing the demanding feat of recording millions (or even billions) of bits on the surface of a fragile, magnetically coated sheet of plastic, followed by the even more amazing feat of finding and reading back the information encoded in those bits. And all of this must be accomplished with close to 100% accuracy. Most computer users don't have to be concerned with knowing how these hardware feats are accomplished, so we'll move on to the equally complex software challenges— but not without first gratefully tipping our hats to the engineers who've made modern disk technology seem so "obvious."

The software level of difficulty is connected with the problem of organizing and managing the flow of data to/from disks in a way that makes the whole process easy to master by moderately experienced users. To say this another way, the average user should be able to ship data back and forth between computer files with all the ease enjoyed by the user of a first-rate library system, oblivious to the behind-the-scenes contributions of its professional staff.

What one can expect of such a staff depends of course on how well organized they are. This is equally true of disk operating systems; not all of them handle the challenges of disk data management and organization equally well. It turns out that CP/M is one of the best in this area. When you add the fact that CP/M was essentially a one-person design (initiated by Dr. Gary Kildall in the early 1970s, long before names like Apple, TRS-80, PET, VIC, Atari, Xerox, or IBM PC even existed), there's little doubt that the disk file management design of CP/M belongs in some kind of hall of fame.

To see what some of the problems are, and how ingeniously CP/M solves them, consider the following list of requirements on a good disk file management system.

1. Even though disk files are stored on a physical medium that is organized in terms of sector and track numbers, users of disk files should be able to refer to their files by meaningful names. Users should also be able to change these names with ease. (There was at least one DOS designed later than CP/M that required users to specify track/sector numbers when using files.)

2. The system should adapt to the dynamic nature of files, and allocate space on the disk in a way that allows files to grow and shrink (or even disappear) without wasting overall disk space. Such a process is called *dynamic file allocation*.

The problem here might be compared to that of a large hotel which allocates blocks of rooms for a variety of convention groups. When one group checks out, a new group should be able to move right in. The difficulty is that the number of rooms required by the incoming group will undoubtedly be different than that vacated by the outgoing group. The challenge is to make the new assignment in a way that uses the available space efficiently, but without disturbing any of the current guests. An example of a poor solution to this problem would be to use a rule something like the following: Always put new groups of guests on floors above those already assigned; when the top floor is reached, post a no-vacancy sign; when a group moves out, blow a whistle and announce, "OK—everybody, shift down toward the ground floor so we'll have more room at the top." Ridiculous, you say? Don't laugh— there's one "modern" DOS that works in exactly that way. As we'll see shortly, CP/M is much smarter (and more thoughtful of its guests) than that.

3. A good DOS must be conscientious about security; its read and write operations should be carefully controlled.

Read operations need only be controlled on a system where it's important that unauthorized users not see the files of others. This is normally not a concern on CP/M systems since different users usually own and control their own floppy disks. If disks are shared, CP/M provides the USER facility, but it's basically an honor system. Serious password protection schemes are reserved for the multi-user version of CP/M called MP/M.

The problem of *write control* is a more serious one, however; it's of concern to both single and multi-user systems alike. The dynamic allocation scheme used by CP/M calls for a particularly sophisticated write-control system. It's analogous to the tricky problem of room control in a hotel where vacated rooms are re-assigned to new guests as soon as possible, yet with the assurance that new guests never move in until the old ones are gone. We'll see that CP/M handles this problem by maintaining a very precise "room-chart" called a *disk allocation bit map*. This map is in RAM, so it can be accessed almost instantaneously (which is not true of systems that keep all the allocation information on disk as part of the file directory).

Another write-protect security feature of CP/M is that it "knows" when a disk has been changed, and is therefore able to prohibit writing of files until a new disk allocation map has been generated. (This is like assuring that a central reservations clerk doesn't use the room allocation chart for the wrong hotel). CP/M handles the disk-change problem by insisting that a warm boot be performed after every disk change (RESET does this from MBASIC). Until the warm boot is performed, writing on the new disk won't be permitted (the ubiquitous "BDOS ERROR" message will appear). What the warm boot does is create a new disk allocation map in RAM, using the information encoded on the new disk directory. This new map knows all about the free space on the new disk, so now writing can proceed safely. This is an important protection facility, one not found on all systems. There's at least one newer (and more expensive) DOS where users can clobber their files if they forget to restart the system when changing disks.

Incidentally, the apparent difficulty of losing the current TPA program when changing disks (because of the required warm boot) is easy to overcome. Just type GO, using the GO.COM file explained at the end of this section. If GO.COM isn't on the disk in question, you can add it at any time with A>SAVE 0 GO.COM.

The File-Related Components of CP/M

There are several specialized parts of CP/M used to implement the file management features just described. These are shown in Fig. 6-16 in relation to a total CP/M system. They include the *file directory* on disk, and seven special memory areas that contain the *disk allocation bit map*, the *disk driver routines* (usually used in conjunction with something called a *skew table*), a collection of 26 disk-related *BDOS functions*, a *disk data buffer*, a disk *file control block*, and a random file *record pointer*.

Before explaining how each of these areas is used, three terms used by CP/M in describing how it structures files need to be defined. These are *record*, *extent*, and *allocation unit* (which is also called an *allocation group* or *cluster*).

In general, a *file* is a large collection of smaller groupings of information. Each smaller grouping is called a *record*. In manual filing systems, records are often stored on cards or sheets of paper. The cards in a library file, or the sheets of paper in a correspondence file are familiar examples of such paper "records."

CP/M computer files are also defined as collections of smaller groupings of information called records. However, the records are always defined as 128 consecutive bytes, irrespective of what the information in these bytes represents. Thus CP/M records may or may not correspond to the groupings of data that a programmer defines to be a record, but that doesn't matter. For example, the data file that was created by the program FILEBOXM in Lab 5.2-1 used groupings of 64 bytes for each record. Internally, CP/M still dealt with that data file in terms of 128 bytes at a time. It simply equated two of the user's records with one of its own.

For large files (e. g., MBASIC.COM or INSTALL.COM) it's also convenient to define "super chunks" of data. CP/M calls these *extents*. An extent is defined as 128 records, so it is equivalent to $128 * 128 = 16,384$ bytes. The main reason for defining the term extent is that it helps set a reasonable size limit on file directory entries, with one directory entry used for each extent. Very large files are handled by using several directory entries, one per extent.

The third term used by CP/M is allocation unit. This unit was invented to deal with the problem of how to efficiently store large files on disk when using the "dynamic allocation" scheme we described earlier. The need for defining a term like allocation unit can be explained

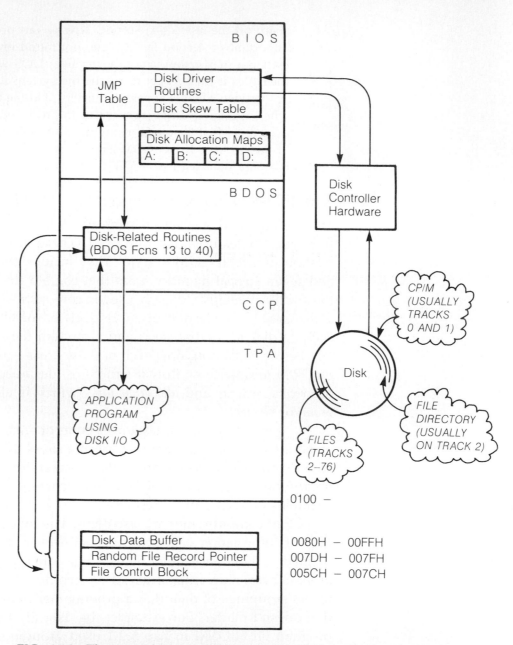

FIG. 6-16 The special areas of RAM shown on this diagram are used in conjunction with the file directory of a disk to manage the disk file operations of programs that run under CP/M. Both application and system programs may use these facilities, assuring a high degree of transportability in disk based programs.

in terms of our earlier example of the room clerk at a hotel which books large conventions.

One question faced by the reservation clerk in such a hotel is this: "What's a good choice for some 'standard' size of blocks of rooms to be used in allocating space for a variety of convention groups?" The same question is relevant to file allocation, where file size corresponds to convention size, and each record is like a room. If the standard block size is small (say, 10 records), then a 5000-record file would be split up into 500 blocks. It could easily happen that these blocks would be scattered all over the disk during a SAVE operation. This is because the dynamic allocation scheme would try to use all the old "standard" blocks from erased files before allocating new ones. Keeping track of such a scattered allocation would force a DOS to spend most of its time on nonproductive managerial tasks. On the other hand, if the standard block size is too large, then the blocks allocated to smaller files will more than likely contain lots of unused records.

The compromise "standard" size used by CP/M is called one *allocation unit*. It's also called a *block* or *cluster*, but in all cases it's defined to be eight disk sectors. Thus one allocation unit is equivalent to 1024 bytes on a standard single-density 8-inch disk (128 bytes per sector), or 2048 bytes on the same disk if double-density recording is used. The allocation unit is the minimum block of disk space allocated by CP/M. This is why doing a STAT *.* shows that even small files (one to seven records) occupy 1K bytes on a single-density disk (or 2K on a double-density disk).

The way these terms relate to each other can be pictured as follows, using a fairly large file (20K bytes) called DEMO.FIL as our example, and assuming an 8-inch single-density disk.

DEMO.FIL = 20K = 20,048 bytes total size
= 160 records of 128 bytes each
= 20 disk allocation units of 1024 bytes each

Each $\boxed{R}$ in this diagram represents one record = 128 bytes.

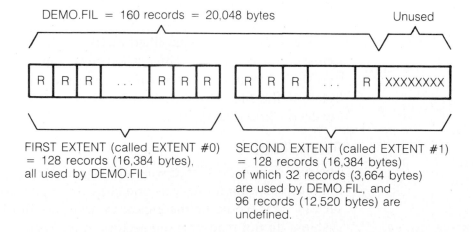

FIRST EXTENT (called EXTENT #0)
= 128 records (16,384 bytes),
all used by DEMO.FIL

SECOND EXTENT (called EXTENT #1)
= 128 records (16,384 bytes)
of which 32 records (3,664 bytes)
are used by DEMO.FIL, and
96 records (12,520 bytes) are
undefined.

When stored on disk, this file would be allocated twenty units of 1024 bytes each. This happens to be a perfect fit, so in this example no disk space will be wasted. A diagram of such a storage would show the file distributed over twenty circular segments of 1024 bytes each. The exact locations on disk where these segments are stored will depend on what allocation units were available on the particular disk that was used when the file was saved, and on something called a *skew table* (explained shortly).

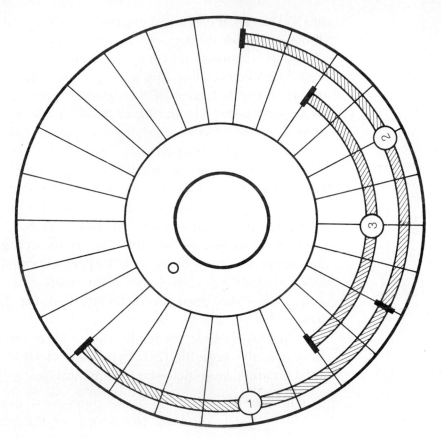

FIG. 6-17   This diagram illustrates how a file with 3,000 bytes would conceptually be stored in three allocation units of 1024 bytes each on a single-density disk. The actual storage arrangement will differ from this because of the way the eight sectors in each unit are "skewed" on the disk.

Fig. 6-17 shows a simplified picture of how a smaller file with 3,000 bytes might be stored. Three allocation units were required. The first two store 2 * 1024 = 2,048 bytes, while the third one holds the last 952 bytes of the file. The remaining 72 bytes of this seventh unit will be "wasted" in the sense that they can't be allocated to any other file.

Skew Tables

The picture just presented was called a simplified one because it implied that each allocation unit was one large arc made up of eight consecutive sectors. This would be the logical thing to do, but in practice, most disk systems do not read or write sectors in consecutive physical order, that is, the second sector written is not placed right next to the first sector. The physical order in which the sectors on a standard 26-sector IBM disk are read (or written) is 1, 7, 13, 19, 25, 05, 11, 17, 23, 3, 9, 15, 21, 2, 8, 14, 20, 26, 6, 12, 18, 24, 4, 10, 16, 22. In other words, the logical sequence 1, 2, 3, 4, . . . , etc. is changed (or "mapped") into the physical sequence 1, 7, 13, 19, . . . , etc. In this case one says that the sectors are skewed by a factor of six.

The reason this is done is that it gives the computer time to "digest" some of the information it has read from one sector before reading the next sector. For example, after reading each sector, PIP will check to see if one of the numbers read (something called the CRC or *cyclic redundancy check*) jibes with a calculation done on the actual data read. If there's a match, you have a pretty good assurance that no read errors took place. The problem is that there is no way that the CRC calculation can be made in the short time that elapses between reading the end of one sector and reading the beginning of the next. The solution is to let a few sectors go by the read head while doing the calculation for sector n, and to define the next logical sector as a physical sector further down the track. The usual choice of the next sector to be read is sector $n+6$ modulo 26. (There's one exception where $n+7$ is used—can you find it in the skew numbers given above?)

The data that shows the sequence of physical sectors to be used on each system is stored either in BDOS or in BIOS as what is called a skew translation table. Users really don't have to be concerned about this table. The translation it does is performed automatically, so it's OK for a programmer to think that the sectors are in the "logical" order 1, 2, 3, . . . , etc., that is, in the order one would logically assume is being used. One warning: If your system has the skew table stored in BDOS rather than BIOS, there will be a mixup if you try to directly call disk driver routines in BIOS; this is why it's better to go through the BDOS disk function calls when writing machine language programs that read or write data on disks.

The Disk File Directory

A directory is a collection of information about the files on a given disk. It is recorded right on the disk itself (in sectors 1 through 16 of track 2 on a standard 8-inch single-density disk). Unfortunately, the position of the directory on nonstandard disk formats varies, so in general, nonstandard systems aren't able to access the directories of each other. (In such situations, the file-transfer techniques of Section 6.5 can be used as illustrated in Labs 6.5-1 and 6.5-2.)

On standard disks, the directory consists of 64 entries, with each entry 32 bytes long, although some CP/M systems have increased the number of entries from 64 to 255. The 32 bytes of each entry contain the following information.

Byte 0	This will contain the value n if the command USER n has been given; otherwise it will be 00H.
Bytes 1–11	hold the file name (8 bytes for the primary name followed by 3 bytes for the secondary name).
Byte 12	holds the *extent number*; this is 00 for the first 16,384 bytes, 01 for the second 16,384 bytes and so on.
Bytes 13–14	are not used; set to zeros.
Byte 15	holds a record count for the file, that is, the number of 128-byte records in the file.
Bytes 16–32	hold numbers that indicate where each of the 16 possible allocation units for this file are located on

the disk. These numbers are also called "block numbers", "group numbers" or "cluster numbers". The numbers 00 and 01 correspond to the two 8-sector blocks reserved for the file directory itself (which therefore occupies sectors 1–8 and 9–16 on track 2 of a standard 8-inch disk). More information on how CP/M assigns these unit allocation numbers is given in the description of the Disk Allocation Bit Map below.

The File Control Block (FCB)

Before a disk file can be used under CP/M, the system must be given precise information on where to find the file. For example, when a BASIC programmer types LOAD "PROG.BAS", CP/M must first do some work behind the scenes to find out which allocation units PROG.BAS has. The information it gathers, along with the name of the file and some other data is stored in RAM in the form of a little table called the FCB (file control block). Machine language programmers do the same thing, creating the FCB with a call to BDOS function #15 (OPEN FILE). In either case the needed information is taken from the directory on the disk, and copied into the FCB. If a write operation is involved, another table called the Disk Allocation Bit Map must also be consulted to see where on the disk new data can be written. At the end of the file write operation, this information is also placed in the FCB, right next to the information on where the previous file data was stored. When the file is finally closed, all of this updated FCB information is written back onto the file directory. Thus the file directory always contains a permanent record of where all the data for each file on the disk is stored.

A file control block can be placed anywhere in RAM. The default location assigned by CP/M is at locations 005CH to 007CH. The layout of the FCB is similar to that of the file directory except that it can have from 33 to 36 bytes organized as follows:

DR	P1	P2	...	P8	S1	S2	S3	EX	S1	S2	RC	A1	A2	...	A16	CR	R0	R1	R2

Byte 00	DR is the drive code. DR=0 means the file is on the currently logged-in disk, while DR=1, 2, . . . , 16 are used to indicate one of the drives A, B, . . . , P.
Bytes 01–08	P1 to P8 hold the primary file name in ASCII upper case, padded with blanks.
Bytes 09–11	S1 to S3 hold the secondary file name in ASCII upper case, padded with blanks.
Byte 12	EX holds the extent number for this FCB.
Bytes 13–14	are reserved for system use; initialized as 0.
Byte 15	RC holds the record count (number of records in this extent).

Bytes 16–31   A1 to A16 hold the allocation numbers (explained below) used for this file. These same bytes are also used to temporarily hold the second filename (F2) in a command like A>MYPROG F1 F2.

Byte 32   CR is the current record, that is, the record number to read or write in a sequential file operation.

Bytes 33–34   hold a 16-bit record number for random access files; R0 = low order byte, R1 = high order byte.

Byte 35   R2 = overflow from R1; if not zero, an error is indicated.

The Disk Allocation Bit Map

As just mentioned, application programs that use disk files must set up a FCB in memory for each such file. In addition, BDOS uses information from the directories of active disks to create tables in CBIOS called *disk allocation bit maps,* or *allocation vectors.* There is one such map for each logged-in disk. If a new disk is logged in (say with a warm boot), a new map is created for that disk, replacing the map for the disk that was removed. Each of these maps is a binary coded table that shows which allocation units (groups of eight logically consecutive sectors) have been assigned to all the files on tracks 2 through 76 of the disk involved.

For an 8-inch single-density disk, the table is basically a string of 243 bits representing each of the (75*26)/8 possible allocation units. The table is called a map because it associates each bit with an *allocation number* (from 00 to F2 hex) that pinpoints the actual position on the disk where the allocation unit starts. Allocation numbers can then be translated into track and sector numbers with formulas based on the number of sectors per track.

When a disk is first formatted and the directory is empty, all the bits in the map are set to 0 (zero) except the first two which are associated with allocation numbers 00 and 01. These bits are set to 1 to indicate that the first two units (first sixteen sectors) are allocated to the disk file directory itself. Whenever a file is about to be written on this disk, BDOS searches through the map for the next available zero bit, and sets it to 1. It then puts the corresponding allocation number in the FCB, using the first free byte within positions 16 to 32 of the FCB. This procedure is repeated every time eight more sectors are needed for the file, so that the FCB eventually holds all the allocation numbers for the new file. If more than sixteen numbers are needed, a new FCB is created for the next extent to the file. Whenever a new extent is required, or whenever a file is closed, the information from the FCB is written onto disk as an entry in the file directory. Thus there will be one file directory entry per extent.

Conversely, when a file is erased, the bits corresponding to the allocation units it used are set back to zero, freeing up this space for future write operations. This is why large files written on a disk that has been in use for sometime may be scattered over different tracks;

SAMPLE FILE DIRECTORY

	FILENAME	EX RC	ALLOCATION NUMBERS (IN HEX)
00	BIGPROG BAS	00000080	02030405060708090A0B0C0D0E0F1011
00	BIGPROG BAS	01000025	12131415160000000000000000000000
E5	TESTPROG	0000007B	171819A1B1C1D1E1F20212223242500
00	MYSTRINGCOM	0000001A	26272829000000000000000000000000

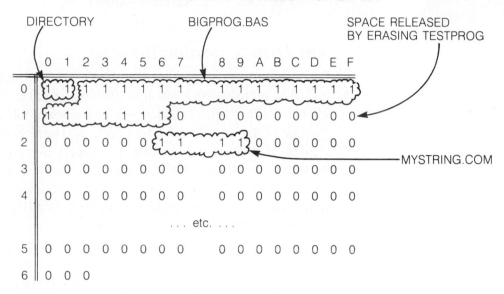

CORRESPONDING ALLOCATION BIT MAP

FIG. 6-18 This figure illustrates the relationship between the file directory stored on a CP/M disk, and the allocation bit map created in RAM when the disk is logged in. When a file is erased, both the directory entry and the actual file data remain intact, so unless a new file has been written since the erasure, "disk fix" utility programs can often be used to recover the file.

the dynamic allocation scheme has simply done its "scavenger" job well in using up all the free allocation units. Note, however, that PIP can be used to regroup the units of a scattered file into closer proximity by copying it onto a new (or almost-new) disk. It's like moving a convention group that was scattered all over one hotel into a nice new empty one; members of the group can then be reassigned rooms that are much closer together.

The directory entries for erased files are not actually erased from the disk. Instead, the code E5 hex is put in the first byte of the directory entry to mean "available for future use." This fact, plus the fact that the original data for a file remains on the disk until overwritten by a new write operation, explains why "lost" files can sometimes be recovered, using one of the disk utility programs mentioned in Section 4.5.

An example showing the file directory and corresponding allocation bit map for a single-density 8-inch disk with three active files is shown in Fig. 6-18. When first created, the directory of this disk was empty, so the allocation map contained all zeros except for the first two bits. These were set to 1 to allocate space for the disk directory. By examining the row and column positions of these bits, you can see that the corresponding allocation numbers are 00 and 01. (CP/M will interpret these to mean logical sectors 1 through 16 on track 2 of the disk.)

The first program stored on this disk was BIGPROG.BAS. It had a total of 165 (A5 hex) records, so it required two extents. There are therefore two directory entries, one for the first 128 (80 hex) records, and one for the remaining 37 (25 hex) records. The allocation numbers for BIGPROG.BAS are 02, 03, . . . , 11, for the first extent, and 12, 13, . . . , 16 for the second. The actual positions on disk corresponding to these numbers are determined by CP/M, using the next eight logical sectors for each allocation number, and moving to the next inner track each time twenty-six sectors are assigned.

The third file written to this disk was TESTPROG, and it was given allocation numbers 17, 18, . . . , 25. However it was later erased, so an E5 was recorded in the first byte of the directory, and the corresponding 1 bits were set back to 0 (zero). The fourth file is MYSTRING.COM with allocation numbers 26, 27, 28, and 29.

How Disk Files Are Written and Read

The actual transfer of data from RAM to a CP/M disk file is done by the *disk driver routines* in BIOS. These can be called directly, but where possible, it's preferable to let BDOS do the job since this part of CP/M is machine-independent. The machine language programmer can call BDOS disk-related functions with the familiar CALL 05 instruction, asking for one of the BDOS functions numbered 13 to 40. The purpose of each of these functions is explained in the *CP/M 2.2 Interface Guide*, and summarized in Fig. 6-6.

Most of the BDOS disk functions perform housekeeping functions (like OPEN FILE). A few move data from RAM to disk (WRITE), or from disk to RAM (READ). In these cases, the "logical" data movement is done one record at a time. (The actual amount of data transferred by a physical read or write is one sector; this could equal several records on nonstandard disks.) The record being transferred is stored in a RAM buffer which is given the default addresses 0080H to 00FFH by CP/M. However the programmer can set up other buffer locations by using BDOS function 26. The size of the new buffer is up to the programmer; it's usually given with a DS directive. The starting address of the buffer is called the DMA address, and it's passed to BDOS in the DE pair. (The term DMA usually refers to special "direct memory access" circuitry that moves data in and out of RAM without going through the CPU, but in the CP/M literature it is used as part of the phrase "DMA address" to simply mean "starting address of the disk data buffer.")

The next lab illustrates use of some of the BDOS functions to write a useful ML program called FILTER.COM. Two other examples worth studying can be found in the *CP/M 2.2 Interface Guide*. There was also an excellent disk-related printing program presented by Chris Terry in Volume 2, No. 3 of *S-100 Microsystems* [11].

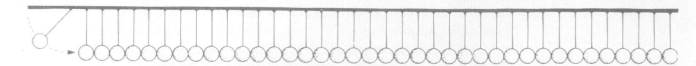

LAB EXERCISE
6.4-1

An ML Program to Filter Control Codes from an ASCII File

Step 0. The idea behind this program is to take a text file created by one word processor, and make it useful for another one by removing (filtering out) any undesired control codes. We'll also "strip off" any high-order bits that have been set, that is, make sure that the ASCII codes for the text all have 0 for their leftmost bit, not 1. We'll call the original file ORIG.TXT and the filtered file FILT.TXT.

Step 1. Design the program in terms of the higher-level functions it will perform. Here's how this might be done on a first pass:

1a. Define useful names using EQU directives (e. g., STDBUF EQU 0080H); set up data storage areas.

1b. Set up FCBs for the files ORIG.TXT and FILT.TXT; Open Files; zero FCB entries as needed.

1c. Read a record from ORIG.TXT into STDBUF. If at EOF go to step 1f.

1d. Filter out the unwanted characters from the text by copying only the desired characters to a buffer called FILTBUF.

1e. When 128 characters accumulate in FILTBUF, write the filtered record onto FILT.TXT; go back to step 1c.

1f. Write any characters still in FILTBUF to disk; close files; print final message.

Step 2. Translate your high-level design into blocks of assembly language code. Then use ED to enter the program using the file name FILTER.ASM. Assemble the program with ASM.COM, and use LOAD to create the file FILTER.COM. Fig. 6-19 shows a sample solution in the form of a PRN listing.

Step 3. Test the program by first generating a file called ORIG.TXT in which there are lots of control characters. The simplest way to do this is to create a text file with a word processor like WordStar, using boldface, underline, and other special features. Run FILTER.COM, by typing

A>FILTER A:ORIG.TXT A:FILT.TXT

The reason this works is that the CCP is smart enough to pick up the two file names we have added to the command line, and put them in

```
                        ;FILTER.ASM  Program to remove high order bits and
                        ;control codes from origfile and save as filtfile.
                        ;To use type:        FILTER origfile filtfile (CR)
                        ;
0000 =                  warmbt   equ     0000h
0005 =                  bdos     equ     0005h
005C =                  origfcb  equ     005ch
005C =                  fname1   equ     origfcb
006C =                  fname2   equ     origfcb+16
0080 =                  stdbuf   equ     0080h
0100 =                  tpa      equ     0100h
                        ;
                        ;NOTE:  Reads are to stdbuf, writes are from filtbuf.
                        ;The next equates define BDOS fcns which do the following:
0009 =                  strout   equ     9        ;    output string to console
000F =                  openf    equ     15       ;    open an old file
0010 =                  closef   equ     16       ;    close a file
0013 =                  deletef  equ     19       ;    delete a file
0014 =                  readseq  equ     20       ;    read from a sequential file
0015 =                  writseq  equ     21       ;    write on a sequential file
0016 =                  makef    equ     22       ;    create and open a new file
001A =                  setdma   equ     26       ;    set address of disk buffer
                        ;
0100                             org     tpa
0100 310903                      lxi     sp,mystptr   ;point to private stack
                        ;-------------------------------------------------------
                        ;      Move second filename from 006c to filtfcb
                        ;-------------------------------------------------------
0103 0E10                        mvi     c,16         ;get set to move 16 bytes
0105 116C00                      lxi     d,fname2     ;from 2nd half of origfcb
0108 214602                      lxi     h,filtfcb    ;to filtfcb
010B 1A         movname ldax    d            ;load first byte into A
010C 13                          inx     d            ;increment source pointer
010D 77                          mov     m,a          ;move byte into filtfcb
010E 23                          inx     h            ;increment destination pointer
010F 0D                          dcr     c            ;decrease counter
0110 C20B01                      jnz     movname      ;repeat 16 times
                        ;
0113 AF                          xra     a            ;set current record = 0
0114 326602                      sta     filtcr       ;in byte 33 of filtfcb
                        ;-------------------------------------------------------
                        ;      Open ORIGIN for read
                        ;-------------------------------------------------------
0117 115C00                      lxi     d,fname1     ;point to ORIG filename
011A CDC501                      call    open         ;open ORIG, A=255 if no file
011D 11E801                      lxi     d,nofile     ;point to no-file message
0120 3C                          inr     a            ;if A=255, A+1 will = 0
0121 CCBD01                      cz      finis        ;quit with error message
                        ;-------------------------------------------------------
                        ;      Open FILT for write
                        ;-------------------------------------------------------
0124 114602                      lxi     d,filtfcb    ;else point to FILT fcb
0127 CDCF01                      call    delete       ;delete name if already in dir
012A 114602                      lxi     d,filtfcb    ;reload DE (delete changed it)
012D CDDE01                      call    make         ;create and open new file
0130 11F501                      lxi     d,nodir      ;if A=255, no room in dir.
0133 3C                          inr     a            ;if A=255, A+1 will = 0
0134 CCBD01                      cz      finis        ;quit with error message
                        ;=======================================================
                        ;      Main program processes one record at a time
                        ;
0137 118000     process lxi     d,stdbuf     ;else start filtering process
013A CDE301                      call    dma          ;using stdbuf at 80h for read
013D 115C00                      lxi     d,origfcb    ;point to source fcb
0140 CDD401                      call    read         ;read 1 record into stdbuf
0143 B7                          ora     a            ;zero in A means read was o.k.
0144 C2AA01                      jnz     eofile       ;else eof occurred
0147 CD4D01                      call    rcdfilt      ;o.k. so filter this record
014A C33701                      jmp     process      ;do it again
                        ;=======================================================
                        ;      The following subroutines are used by main
                        ;
014D 0E80        rcdfilt mvi     c,128        ;initialize stdbuf counter
014F 118000                      lxi     d,stdbuf     ;point to stdbuf
0152 1A         loop1   ldax    d            ;load A with char from stdbuf
0153 C5                          push    b            ;save count in c
0154 D5                          push    d            ;save pointer to stdbuf
```

FIG. 6-19 This is an example of a program that uses BDOS function calls to read a file from disk, and write it back under a new name after filtering out selected control characters. After running the program, DDT was used to verify the filtering.

```
0155 CD6001           call    chrfilt         ;process it
0158 D1               pop     d               ;retrieve pointer
0159 C1               pop     b               ;retrieve count
015A 13               inx     d               ;bump stdbuf ptr
015B 0D               dcr     c               ;decrease counter
015C C25201           jnz     loop1           ;loop 128 times
015F C9               ret
                ;
0160 214502   chrfilt lxi     h,fbufcnt       ;get counter for filtbuf
0163 46               mov     b,m             ;into B register
0164 E67F             ani     07fh            ;strip hi bit from char in A
0166 FE0A             cpi     0ah
0168 CA7D01           jz      keep            ;keep line feeds
016B FE0D             cpi     0dh
016D CA7D01           jz      keep            ;keep carriage returns
0170 FE1A             cpi     01ah
0172 CA7D01           jz      keep            ;keep CP/M EOF (^z)
0175 FE20             cpi     20h
0177 D27D01           jnc     keep            ;keep codes >= 20hex
017A C38901   reject  jmp     next            ;reject all other codes
017D 2AE702   keep    lhld    fbufptr         ;point to filtbuf
0180 77               mov     m,a             ;copy char to filtbuf
0181 23               inx     h               ;bump filtbuf ptr
0182 22E702           shld    fbufptr         ;save pointer for next copy
0185 05               dcr     b               ;decrease filtbuf counter
0186 CC8E01           cz      flush           ;time to write filtbuf to disk
0189 214502   next    lxi     h,fbufcnt       ;get address of fbufcnt
018C 70               mov     m,b             ;save counter there
018D C9               ret
                ;
018E 116702   flush   lxi     d,filtbuf       ;point to start of filtbuf
0191 CDE301           call    dma             ;use filtbuf for write
0194 114602           lxi     d,filtfcb       ;point to fcb for FILT
0197 CDD901           call    write           ;on file named in filtfcb
019A 110A02           lxi     d,nospace       ;anticipate full disk (A<>00H)
019D B7               ora     a               ;set flags to see if A=0
019E C4BD01           cnz     finis           ;no so quit with error message
01A1 0680             mvi     b,128           ;else re-initialize fbufcnt &
01A3 216702           lxi     h,filtbuf       ;use start address of filtbuf
01A6 22E702           shld    fbufptr         ;to reinitialize fbufptr
01A9 C9               ret
                ;
                ;end of ORIG file, so flush one more time and close FILT
01AA CD8E01   eofile  call    flush           ;clean out filtbuf
01AD 114602           lxi     d,filtfcb       ;point to fname 2
01B0 CDCA01           call    close           ;A=255 means can't find
01B3 211C02           lxi     h,wrprot        ;anticipate problem
01B6 3C               inr     a               ;change A=0
01B7 CCBD01           cz      finis           ;quit with error message
01BA 113202           lxi     d,doneok        ;else load success message
                ;
                ;finish routine to print DE message and return to CP/M
                ;
01BD 0E09     finis   mvi     c,strout
01BF CD0500           call    bdos
01C2 C30000           jmp     warmbt
                ;
                ;routines to execute BDOS function and then RET
                ;
01C5 0E0F     open    mvi     c,openf
01C7 C30500           jmp     bdos
01CA 0E10     close   mvi     c,closef
01CC C30500           jmp     bdos
01CF 0E13     delete  mvi     c,deletef
01D1 C30500           jmp     bdos
01D4 0E14     read    mvi     c,readseq
01D6 C30500           jmp     bdos
01D9 0E15     write   mvi     c,writseq
01DB C30500           jmp     bdos
01DE 0E16     make    mvi     c,makef
01E0 C30500           jmp     bdos
01E3 0E1A     dma     mvi     c,setdma
01E5 C30500           jmp     bdos
                ;
01E8 4E4F204F52 nofile  db    'NO ORIG FILES$'
01F5 4E4F20524F nodir   db    'NO ROOM IN DIRECTORY$'
020A 4F5554204F nospace db    'OUT OF DISK SPACE$'
021C 46494C4520 wrprot  db    'FILE WRITE PROTECTED?$'
0232 46494C4545 doneok  db    'FILTERING COMPLETE$'
0245 80           fbufcnt db   128
0246              filtfcb ds   33
0266 =            filtcr  equ  filtfcb+32
0267              filtbuf ds   128
02E7 6702         fbufptr dw   filtbuf
```

FIG. 6-19 (continued)

```
02E9              mystack ds      32
0309 =            mystptr equ     $
0309                      end
```

```
A>FILTER ORIG.TXT NEW.TXT
FILTERING COMPLETE

A>DDT ORIG.TXT
DDT VERS 2.0
NEXT  PC
0280 0100
-D0100,020F
0100 54 65 73 74 20 46 69 6C 65 20 63 72 65 61 74 65 Test File create
0110 64 20 69 6E 20 57 6F 72 64 53 74 61 72 0D 0A 13 d in WordStar...
0120 74 68 69 73 20 69 73 20 75 6E 64 65 72 6C 69 6E this is underlin
0130 65 64 13 0D 0A 74 68 69 73 20 69 73 20 70 6C 61 ed...this is pla
0140 69 6E 0D 0A 02 74 68 69 73 20 69 73 20 62 6F 6C in...this is bol
0150 64 66 61 63 65 02 0D 0A 0D 0A 20 20 20 20 20 48 dface.....     H
0160 65 72 E5 A0 20 69 F3 A0 20 73 6F 6D E5 20 74 65 er.. i.. som. te
0170 78 F4 20 63 72 65 61 74 65 E4 20 77 69 74 E8 20 x. create. wit.
0180 77 6F 72 E4 20 77 72 61 F0 20 70 75 74 74 69 6E wor. wra. puttin
0190 E7 A0 20 69 EE A0 20 73 6F 66 F4 20 8D 0A 63 61 .. i.. sof. ..ca
01A0 72 72 69 61 67 E5 20 72 65 74 75 72 6E F3 20 61 rriag. return. a
01B0 F3 20 38 44 AC A0 20 74 65 6D F0 20 73 70 61 63 . 8D.. tem. spac
01C0 65 F3 20 61 F3 20 41 30 AC A0 20 61 6E E4 20 73 e. a. A0.. an. s
01D0 65 74 74 69 6E E7 20 68 E9 20 6F 72 64 65 F2 20 ettin. h. orde.
01E0 8D 0A 62 69 74 F3 20 61 F4 20 65 6E 64 F3 20 6F ..bit. a. end. o
01F0 E6 20 77 6F 72 64 73 AE 20 20 45 6E E4 20 6F E6 . words. En. o.
0200 20 74 65 73 74 21 0D 0A 1A 1A 1A 1A 1A 1A 1A 1A  test!..........
-^C


A>DDT NEW.TXT
DDT VERS 2.0
NEXT  PC
0280 0100
-D0100,020F
0100 54 65 73 74 20 46 69 6C 65 20 63 72 65 61 74 65 Test File create
0110 64 20 69 6E 20 57 6F 72 64 53 74 61 72 0D 0A 74 d in WordStar..t
0120 68 69 73 20 69 73 20 75 6E 64 65 72 6C 69 6E 65 his is underline
0130 64 0D 0A 74 68 69 73 20 69 73 20 70 6C 61 69 6E d..this is plain
0140 0D 0A 74 68 69 73 20 69 73 20 62 6F 6C 64 66 61 ..this is boldfa
0150 63 65 0D 0A 0D 0A 20 20 20 20 20 48 65 72 65 20 ce....     Here
0160 20 69 73 20 20 73 6F 6D 65 20 74 65 78 74 20 63  is  some text c
0170 72 65 61 74 65 64 20 77 69 74 68 20 77 6F 72 64 reated with word
0180 20 77 72 61 70 20 70 75 74 74 69 6E 67 20 20 69  wrap putting  i
0190 6E 20 20 73 6F 66 74 20 0D 0A 63 61 72 72 69 61 n  soft ..carria
01A0 67 65 20 72 65 74 75 72 6E 73 20 61 73 20 38 44 ge returns as 8D
01B0 2C 20 20 74 65 6D 70 20 73 70 61 63 65 73 20 61 ,  temp spaces a
01C0 73 20 41 30 2C 20 20 61 6E 64 20 73 65 74 74 69 s A0,  and setti
01D0 6E 67 20 68 69 20 6F 72 64 65 72 20 0D 0A 62 69 ng hi order ..bi
01E0 74 73 20 61 74 20 65 6E 64 73 20 6F 66 20 77 6F ts at ends of wo
01F0 72 64 73 2E 20 20 45 6E 64 20 6F 66 20 74 65 73 rds.  End of tes
0200 74 21 0D 0A 1A 1A 1A 1A 1A 1A 1A 1A 1A 1A 1A 1A t!..............
-^C
```

FIG. 6-19 (*continued*)

memory. It puts the first one at the beginning of the default FCB at 005C hex in the proper 11-byte positions for a file name. The second name is put in a temporary area starting at 006C hex. That's why the first thing our program must do is to move this name to its proper place in a second FCB of our own choosing. This second FCB was set up in our program at the address labelled FILTFCB by using the data storage directives

```
FILTFCB DS      33
FILTCR  EQU     FILTFCB+32
```

The second directive is a simple way to give a label to the "current record" byte of FILTFCB. This label can be used for setting the current record to zero during initialization. You don't have to zero the current record byte at 007C hex in the default FCB at 005C hex since CCP does this for you.

The last part of Fig. 6-19 shows a run of the program followed by use of DDT to verify that the filtering has worked properly.

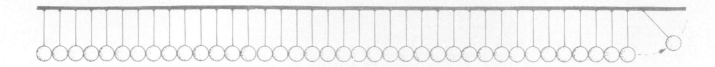

Using the Disk Driver Routines of CBIOS Directly

Some disk operations can't be called from BDOS, in which case direct calls to CBIOS must be used. There are two ways to do this. The first is to call the appropriate locations in the jump table found at the beginning of every CBIOS, and let the jump table find the corresponding drivers for you. The second is to call the drivers in CBIOS directly, using the addresses you find by studying a PRN listing of CBIOS. We'll illustrate the second technique in the following lab.

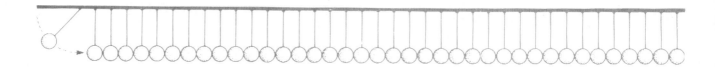

LAB EXERCISE 6.4-2

Using Direct BIOS Calls for Disk Operations under CP/M

Step 1. Study the PRN listing of the CBIOS for your system and identify the areas that do I/O to the disk controller. You can do this by first examining the JMP table at the beginning of CBIOS. You should also study the EQU directives your CBIOS uses to become familiar with the addresses that correspond to certain disk-related labels.

Step 2. Write a program that "exercises" your disk drive by having the read/write head alternately *seek* tracks 0 and 76. Such a program might be useful if you wanted to clean the lead screw in the disk mechanism of your disk drive. This can be done by carefully brushing alcohol on the exposed surfaces of the lead screw while the program forces it to turn between its extremes. (Warning: Don't try this unless you are qualified to do mechanical work of this sort. You could easily do more harm than good.)

A simplified solution to writing such a program is shown in Fig. 6-20. This program was written by Bob Hoffman of Project Solo. It goes to track 76, reads the data from sector 1 into a local DMA buffer (but does nothing with it), and then goes back to track zero (home). The process repeats in an infinite loop until a warm boot is used to stop it.

```
A>pip
*lst:=seek.prn[UT8]


F809 =              TKZERO  EQU     0F809H
F80C =              TRKSET  EQU     0F80CH
F80F =              SETSEC  EQU     0F80FH
F812 =              SETDMA  EQU     0F812H
F815 =              DREAD   EQU     0F815H

0100                        ORG     100H
0100 0E4C           START:  MVI     C,4CH   ;TRACK 76
0102 CD0CF8                 CALL    TRKSET
0105 0E01                   MVI     C,1     ;SECTOR 1
0107 CD0FF8                 CALL    SETSEC
010A 010002                 LXI     B,200H  ;WHERE TO DMA
010D CD12F8                 CALL    SETDMA
0110 CD15F8                 CALL    DREAD   ;SEEK AND READ TRACK 76
0113 CD09F8                 CALL    TKZERO  ;HOME TO ZERO
0116 C30001                 JMP     START   ;DO IT AGAIN
0119                        END     START
*
```

FIG. 6-20   This program uses the addresses of some of the disk driver routines in the special ROM section of the Morrow DJ CBIOS to exercise the track seeking mechanism of the disk drive. The addresses will be different for the CBIOS disk routines of other systems.

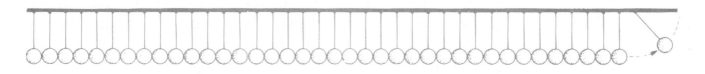

More about ERA, REN, and SAVE

With the background we now have, it's relatively easy to explain how some of the CP/M file-related features we've previously used actually work.

The "ERA ufn" command does two things. It writes the code E5 hex in the first byte of the directory entry (or entries) associated with that file on disk to mean "this entry erased." It also changes all the bits that correspond to that file in the allocation bit map from ones back to zeros, thus releasing that space for other files.

The command REN NEW = OLD simply changes the filename recorded in the disk directory entry from OLD to NEW, padding unused locations with blanks as needed.

The word *page* is used in the CP/M literature to mean a block of 256 bytes of memory. Page zero occupies the bytes with addresses 0000 to 00FF hex, page 1 uses addresses 0100 to 01FF hex, page 2 addresses 0200 to 02FF, and so on. The command

SAVE nn FILE.EXT

means save the contents of nn pages of data from the TPA, *starting with page one*. The data is written to disk, and the filename is recorded in the directory. When using this command, nn must be given as a decimal number. For example, the command

SAVE 12 MYFILE.COM

will save 12 ∗ 256 = 3072 bytes from the TPA as MYFILE.COM, using all the data found in locations of memory as follows:

0100 to 01FF	page 1
0200 to 02FF	page 2
0300 to 03FF	page 3
. . . .	
0C00 to 0CFF	page 12

The number of pages used in the SAVE command is up to the programmer who must know the highest address of the data being saved. In the example just given, the highest address could be anywhere from 0C00 to 0CFF hex since all these addresses are in page 12. If even one more byte of data had to be saved (e. g., at 0D00), then 13 pages would have had to be saved.

SAVE is often used after "patching" a program with DDT. In this case, nn can be determined from the NEXT free byte message displayed by DDT. Subtract one from this number to determine the highest address actually used, and then determine nn from the first two hex digits of this address. Examples:

NEXT (from DDT)	HIGHEST ADDRESS USED	SAVE WITH
02A4	02A3	SAVE 2 MYFILE
2B00	2AFF	SAVE 42 MYFILE
2B01	2B00	SAVE 43 MYFILE

Note 1: The number of pages to be saved is found by changing the first two hex digits of "highest address used" to decimal (e. g., 2A into 42).

Note 2: Each page saved is equal to two CP/M records.

Note 3: SAVE doesn't know where the end-of-file (EOF) is—that's up to you. For your information, EOF is defined as the end of the last record containing data, for non-ASCII files. For ASCII files, the hex code 1A (CONTROL-Z) is used by CP/M to mean EOF (as illustrated in Lab 3.5-1 by the DUMP of the file TEST). The CONTROL-Z is added automatically by ED and (where appropriate) by PIP, but not by SAVE.

The GO.COM Trick Revisited

The command A>SAVE 0 GO.COM will save zero pages of data, storing the file name GO.COM in the disk file directory. The file directory will also have the information that the file has a length of zero records recorded in byte 15. When you give the command A>GO, CP/M does three things: (1) it sets up a FCB with the name GO.COM and a record count CR of zero, (2) it reads CR records of this file into the TPA, and (3) it starts execution of the file at the standard starting address 0100 hex used by all COM files. For GO.COM, step (2) amounts to reading zero records into the TPA, so step (3) will start executing whatever program may have already been in the TPA. This could be PIP, MBASIC, or one of your ML programs—it doesn't matter. The net effect is to restart whatever program was already in the TPA before a "TPA preserving" interruption took place (e. g., a warm boot). It's also OK to use any of CP/M's built-in commands (e. g., DIR or TYPE) before giving the GO command, since these commands do *not* use the TPA. An example of a valuable use of GO in this way is to copy files between disks that do not contain PIP. Here's how to do this.

1. Insert a disk that contains PIP into drive A, and run PIP

    A>PIP
    *

    Remove the disk.

2. Insert the disks that do not contain PIP into the A and B drives and do a warm boot by pressing CONTROL-C. This will load the program allocation bit maps for these disks into RAM, thus allowing them to be written on. After doing the warm boot, it's OK to use any of the CP/M built-in commands (before using GO) since these do *not* use the TPA and therefore do not disturb the PIP loaded in step 1. For example, you could do the following:

    *^C
    A>DIR
    . . .
    A>DIR B:
    . . .
    A>TYPE FILE.ASC
    . . .
    A>TYPE PROG.C
    . . .

3. When ready to use PIP, just type GO:

    A>GO
    *A: = B:MYFILE1
    *A: = B:MYFILE2
    . . . etc. . . . .

    the * means that PIP was still in the TPA and is running again, so as many PIP commands as you wish can be given. When finished, if you want to switch disks again for copying files between other disks, just go back to step 2.

The CP/M Reserved Locations in Page Zero

Whenever CP/M does any disk-related operations, page zero (which is the area just below the TPA) is used for the FCB and disk buffer. A number of other locations of page zero are reserved for system use as follows:

0000H to 0002H	Holds the 3-byte instruction JMP (C3), LOADDR, HIADDR where the 16-bit address HIADDR * 256 + LOADDR points to the warm boot entry point in the BIOS jump table.
0003H	Holds the IOBYTE.
0004H	Holds the default (logged-in) drive number in the low order nibble, with 0 = A, 1 = B, . . . , 15 = P. The high order nibble holds the USER number.
0005H to 0007H	Holds the 3-byte instruction JMP(C3), LOADDR, HIADDR where the 16-bit address 256 * HIADDR + LOADDR points to the start of BDOS.
0008H to 002FH	Not used by CP/M since the 8080 instruction RST n needs these addresses for n = 1, 2, 3, 4, 5.
0030H to 0037H	Used by the RST 6 instruction which has been reserved for future use by CP/M.
0038H to 003AH	Reserved for the RST 7 instruction which is used by CP/M to jump to the "break" routine in DDT.
003BH to 003FH	Reserved for future use by CP/M.
0040H to 004FH	Reserved as a "scratch pad" area; used by some versions of CBIOS.
0050H to 005BH	Reserved for future use by CP/M.
005CH to 007CH	Used as the default FCB for the first filename given in a command to the CCP. *Note:* Locations 006CH to 007B are used as part of a temporary FCB for the second filename (if any) in a command to the CCP. These bytes must be moved to a permanent FCB by the programmer.
007DH to 007FH	Default location for holding the position of a record on a random file.
0080H to 00FFH	Default "DMA" buffer used for read and write operations; holds one record (128 bytes) of data. The same locations are used by the CCP as a temporary place to store the command line for transient commands.

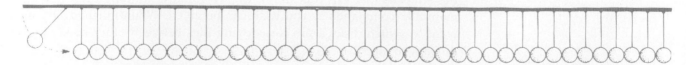

LAB EXERCISE 6.4-3

Experimenting with the CP/M Autoload Feature

There is a way to "fool" the CCP into thinking that a command has been given right after a cold boot. Suppose, for example, you want the command MBASIC GAMEMENU to be loaded automatically after cold booting a special "game demo" disk. Noting that this command has 15 characters, the trick is to use DDT to patch these 15 characters into the CCP module of the CP/M on the game demo disk. You can do this by applying the techniques explained in Section 6.6 as follows:

Step 0. Read Section 6.6. Then prepare a disk that contains SYS-GEN.COM, DDT.COM, MBASIC.COM and GAMEMENU.BAS (as well as a CP/M system). Put it in drive A and boot the system.

Step 1. Use SYSGEN to put a "clone" of CP/M into the TPA; then SAVE it as the file AUTOSYS.COM using the commands

> A>SYSGEN
> (Answer A for SOURCE, and <cr> for DESTINATION.)
> A>SAVE nn AUTOSYS.COM

To calculate nn, you'll need to know the highest address in the TPA used by the cloned BIOS. Then convert the first two hex digits of this address to decimal. For example, if the highest address of the cloned BIOS is 227F hex, then nn is 2 * 16 + 2 = 34. Thus you would use SAVE 34 AUTOSYS.COM.

Note: The highest address of the cloned BIOS is the highest address of the live BIOS plus the OFFSET explained in Section 6.6. For example, on the 62K Morrow system, this would be F7FF + 3C00 = 33FF hex. This gives a value of nn = 3 * 16 + 3 = 51. However pages 45 to 51 are used only for data storage, so in practice nn = 44 usually works OK for this system.

Step 2. Use DDT to bring AUTOSYS.COM back into the TPA, and then find the Digital Research copyright notice. To do this, type

> A>DDT AUTOSYS.COM

and then start your snooping at location 980H, using the D subcommand. Keep pressing D until you see "COPYRIGHT" on the right side of the screen. For standard systems the word copyright usually starts at 0998. For the Morrow system we found it at 1118.

Step 3. Look at the code in front of this copyright for the nearest address ending in 00 or 80 (e. g., 0980 or 0A00). This is the start of CCP. (On the Morrow system, this address was 1100.)

Step 4. Count 8 bytes in from the start of the CCP, and use the S command to set the zero byte there to the number of characters in the desired command line (for our example, you would set location 0987H or 0A07H or 1107 to 0FH to mean "15 characters").

Step 5. Starting at the next byte (e. g., 0988H or 0A08H or 1108) use S to set successive bytes to the ASCII hex codes for the desired command (for "MBASIC GAMEMENU" the codes would be

4D, 42, 41, 53, 49, 43, 20, 47, 41, 4D, 45, 4D, 45, 4E, 55). Then put 00H in the next byte to mean "end of command line."

Warning: Some versions of CP/M (e. g., Morrow) have the ability to defeat the AUTOLOAD feature built into CBIOS. If this is the case, you'll also have to use DDT to remove the defeat mechanism. The code to change on the Morrow system is found near the beginning of CBIOS. It looks like this when viewed with the L command of DDT (except that the addresses D507 and EE4B may differ).

STA	D507	(32, 07, D5 in machine language)
MOV	B,A	(47 in machine language)
CALL	EE4B	(CD, 4B, EE in machine language)
. . . .		
RAR		
RAR		
JC	D500	(DA, 00, D5 in machine language)
. . . .		

The addresses of this code will vary with the size of the system. For a 62K system, use the L command to look for it in the neighborhood of 27F0 to 2810. To undo this code, use S to change the ML as follows:

To replace:	You type in:
32	00<cr>
07	00<cr>
D5	00<cr>
47	<cr>
CD	00<cr>
4B	00<cr>
EE	00<cr>
. . .	<cr>. . .
DA	C3<cr>
00	<cr>
D5	.<cr> (to leave the S command)

Step 6.   Leave DDT with a control-C, and then use SAVE to write the patched system back onto disk (i. e., by typing A>SAVE nn AUTOSYS.COM).

Step 7.   Use SYSGEN to move the patched version onto your autoload disk, answering <cr> for SOURCE and A for DESTINATION. (This is the disk containing GAMEMENU and MBASIC.) If all worked well, this will now be a disk that automatically runs the BASIC program GAMEMENU whenever it's booted. Unfortunately, that's all this disk will do unless you include code at the end of GAMEMENU which writes the original system back on disk!!! A more flexible scheme for producing an autoload-type disk was described in step 6 of Lab 5.4-2.

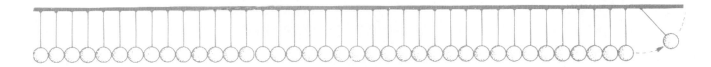

6.5 More about PIP and DDT

Both PIP and DDT have dual personalities. At one level, they are two of the most down-to-earth, hard-working utilities of CP/M. This is the level where you use PIP in the familiar form

A>PIP A:FILENAME = B:FILENAME

The corresponding work-a-day use of DDT is the one in which files are examined by typing DDT FILENAME, followed by successively issuing the D (display) command. All in all, these two usages account for the majority of PIP and DDT activity on most CP/M systems.

But like Clark Kent, both utilities lead other lives, with powers and capabilities known to only a few. In this section we'll see what some of these hidden capabilities are, and how to use them in interesting ways. The extra information about PIP will prove most useful to users interested in transmitting (or receiving) information to/from the world outside their own disk system. The additional features of DDT, on the other hand, will be of greatest use in going in the other direction, delving into the innermost recesses of system, application, and data files.

The General Form of PIP

Although the PIP (Peripheral Interchange Program) can be used in many ways, there is really only one form to the command. This general form may be typed after PIP, or after the PIP asterisk (*) prompt symbol. It can be expressed as

A>PIP data destination = data source(s) [parameters]

or as

A>PIP
*data destination = data source(s) [parameters]

In both cases, the command means *copy* data from the source(s) given on the right, to the destination given on the left, using the parameters (if any) to cause special actions during the copying process. The first form returns you to CP/M after finishing the copy, whereas the second stays in PIP ready for another PIP command.

The word "source(s)" is written with the (s) to indicate that you can specify several data sources separated by commas. In this case, the "concatenation" (sum) of these data sources is copied to the destination. For example,

A>PIP MASTER = B:HEAD,B:MIDDLE,FOOT

will create a file on the disk in drive A called MASTER, and it will contain all the data from the files B:HEAD, B:MIDDLE, and A:FOOT, stored in that order.

To convert the general form of PIP into specific useful forms, the principal thing to know is that the terms "data destination" and "data source" can be replaced with one of three names: the name of a *file*, the name of a *disk drive*, or the name of a *device*, subject to the following rules:

1. The names of files must be given as ufn (unambiguous file names) with one exception. This is when the left side (destination) is given as a disk drive name. In this case, it's OK for the right side to be an afn (ambiguous file name).

   CORRECT: PIP A: = B:*.BAS
   WRONG: PIP *.BAS = PROG.BAS

2. The name of a disk drive can be used as the destination or source, but not both. This is so the system can assign file names by using the rule, "When a disk drive name is used on one side of the = sign, use the same names for both source and destination files."

   CORRECT: PIP A: = FILE
                        PIP A: = B:*.*
                        PIP FILE = B:

   WRONG: PIP A: = B:

3. Device names include all the logical and physical device names used by CP/M except BAT:, that is, CON:, LST:, PUN:, RDR:, LPT:, UL1:, PTP:, UP1:, UP2:, PTR:, UR1:, UR2:, TTY:, CRT:, and UC1:. In addition, there are five special "PIP only" device names that can be used. These are as follows:

NUL: This can be used as a *source* device which sends 40 null characters (ASCII 00 hex) to the destination. NUL: is a handy way to punch leader and trailer sections on a paper tape.

Example: PIP PUN: = NUL:,MYSTRING.HEX,EOF:,NULL:

EOF: This can be used as a *source* device which sends a CONTROL-Z to the destination. CONTROL-Z (ASCII 1A hex) is the official CP/M "end-of-file" character for ASCII files. PIP always adds 1A hex to ASCII disk files, so EOF: is seldom used.

Example: (see above, also compare to step 4f of Lab 6.5-1)

INP: These are "device" names that can be used for private source and
OUT: destination device-driver subroutines. *You* have to write the driver
subroutines, and then tell PIP where they are by putting the
instruction JMP INADDR in locations 103, 104, and 105 hex, and
the instruction JMP OUTADDR in 106, 107, and 108 hex, where
INADDR is the address of your source driver (INP:), and OUTADDR
is the address of your destination driver (OUT:). You must also
use location 109 hex to pass data from your INP: source device
to PIP, and you must use the C register as the location from which
your destination OUT: device gets data from PIP. A convenient
place to put your private device drivers is in locations 109H to
1FFH since PIP doesn't use these. One way to do this is to use
DDT to load PIP, and then patch the new code in, using techniques
similar to those shown in Lab 6.5-2 and Sections 6.6 and 6.7. The
patched version can then be preserved (preferably under a new
name like XPIP) with the SAVE command.

PRN: This is shorthand for LST:=source[T8NP60], where the parameters
in square brackets (explained below) mean "tab 8 spaces, number
all lines, and start a new page every 60 lines".

Example: PIP PRN:=MYPOEM.TXT

Instant Quiz

What do each of the following PIP commands do? Why might one
use them as shown?

   (1) PIP LST:=CON: (5) PIP UL1:=STENO.PAD
   (2) PIP STENO.PAD=CON: (6) PIP PRN:=STENO.PAD
   (3) PIP LST:=STENO.PAD   (7) PIP BASPROG.ASC=RDR:
   (4) PIP LPT:=STENO.PAD   (8) PIP UL1:=CON:[N]

The answers to this quiz can be found in Lab 6.5-1. However,
you'll find that it will be instructive to "guess" at the answers
before reading through the lab.

The PIP Parameters

There are nineteen special actions that can be requested of PIP by adding
selected *parameters* at the end of a PIP command line, enclosing them
in square brackets. For example, you can add the V (verify) and E (echo)
parameters to a disk copying command as follows:

    A>PIP B:=GOODPROG.BAS[VE]

Notice that no spaces are used between parameters. The V means that when the file GOODPROG.BAS is copied from the disk in drive A to the disk in drive B, you want PIP to *verify* that the copying process was successful by reading and comparing the copy with the original. The E causes all data being copied to be *echoed* at the console where the operator can see it.

The nineteen PIP parameters available are as follows:

B	Read data in blocks, i. e., read data into a buffer until an X-OFF CONTROL-S is received (see Section 6.7), and then save it on disk and go back for another block.
Example:	PIP FILE.DSK = RDR:[B]
Dn	Delete all characters past column n in the transfer of line-oriented data. D80 could be used, for example, to truncate 132 column lines in a file when printing it on an 80-column printer.
Example:	PIP UL1: = BIGRPT[D80]
E	Echo the source data that PIP is transmitting by sending it to the console as well as to the specified destination.
Example:	PIP B:COPY.C = ORIG.C[E]
F	Filter (remove) form feed characters (ASCII code 0C hex) from the source data. (The form feed character is used to tell a printer "go to the top of the next page".)
Example:	PIP LST: = RPT.DOC[F]
Gn	Get source data from a file belonging to user number n. This parameter is needed only if the USER command has been employed to mark files.
Example:	PIP B: = A:*.*[G3]
H	Double-check that data being transmitted is in proper Intel Hex format, and take corrective action if not.
Example:	PIP COPY.HEX = ORIG.HEX[H]
I	Ignore hex file records that begin with :00, and also set the H parameter on.
Example:	PIP COPY.HEX = ORIG.HEX[I]

L   Translate all uppercase alphabetic characters in the source to lowercase before sending them to the destination.

Example: PIP EECUMMIN = MYPOEM[L]

N   Add line numbers in the form "26:" to the data before sending to a listing type destination. Using N2 causes the line numbers to be printed in the form "000026 ".

Example: PIP LPT: = PROG.ASM[N]

O   Treat the file as object (non-ASCII) data. Do *not* treat CONTROL-Z as an end-of-file signal, but send it to the destination (see Section 6.4).

Example: PIP B: = OBJPROG.CRL[O]

Note: The [O] parameter is automatically used when .COM files are transferred by PIP

Pn   Start a fresh page every n lines by sending a form feed character to the listing device. Using P or P1 means the same as P60. To remove conflicting form feed characters from the source, you can use the F parameter with Pn.

Example: PIP LST: = PROG1.C[P]

Qs^Z   Quit copying from the source after the string "s" is encountered (but include "s" in the copy). WARNING: If the string "s" contains lower case letters, you must use this command after the PIP * prompt (not after the word PIP) to preserve the lower case.

Example: PIP
            *START.DOC = WHOLE.DOC[Qeternity.^Z]

R   Read (and copy) system files that don't appear in the directory.

Example: PIP B: = *.*[R]

Ss^Z   Start copying from the source when the string "s" is encountered, including "s" in the copy. S and Q can be combined to copy data from the middle of a file.

Example:	PIP
	*MID = WHOLE[Shere^ZQeternity.^Z]
	*LST: = BASPROG.ASC[S500^ZQGOTO 520^Z]

Tn	Expand tabs to columns n, 2n, 3n, etc.
Example:	PIP LST: = MYSTRING.ASM[T8]

U	Translate all lowercase letters to uppercase.
Example:	PIP LST: = PROG1.C[U]

V	Verify that the data written to a file is the same as that read from the source.
Example:	PIP B:FILE.X = OLDFILE[V]

W	Write on top of files that were set R/O without asking user's OK
Example:	PIP SCRATCH = TEST[W]

Z	Zero the parity bit (the leftmost high-order bit) of each byte on the assumption that it is an ASCII character which does not use this bit.
Example:	PIP PROG.ASC = PROG.C[Z]

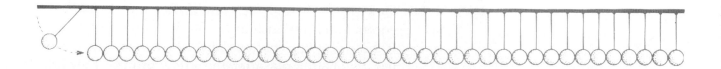

LAB EXERCISE 6.5-1 Exotic Uses of PIP: Electric Typewriter, Electric Steno, Electric Printer, and Electric Courier

This is really four labs in one, with each step a separate experiment that can be tried to explore some of the less familiar aspects of PIP.

Note: The steps which use the LST: device assume that you have a hard-copy printer, and that the IOBYTE is set so that the physical device driver which "talks" to this printer is assigned as the LST: logical device. For most systems, LPT: is assigned as the LST: device. This isn't essential, however, since PIP is "smart" enough to circumvent the default IOBYTE assignment when you give it a physical device name. For example, if your IBOYTE assigns LPT: as the LST: device, but your printer is connected as UL1:, then PIP LST:=TXTFILE won't work. But PIP UL1:=TXTFILE will. Another solution, of course, would be to first modify the IOBYTE with STAT, and then use LST: as follows:

    STAT LST:=UL1
    PIP LST:=TXTFILE

Step 1.   The Electric Typewriter
Suppose you have a CP/M system with a printer that does not have a keyboard (as opposed to a "printing terminal"). There may be times when you want to type a quick note on this printer without the bother of using a word processor program. Here's how to do this with PIP.

        A>PIP LST:=CON:
        DEAR MILKMAN: (CR) (LF)
        PLEASE LEAVE TWO QUARTS OF (CR) (LF)
        REGULAR MILK ON THURSDAY (CR) (LF)
        (^Z)
        A>

Your note will show up on the console, but PIP will also send it to the LST: device (which we assume to be your printer). Notice that you must press both carriage return *and* line feed to start each new line. Also note that you must send PIP a ^Z "end of file" to let it know when you're finished.

Instant Quiz

   1. What would happen if you used a control-P *before* issuing the above PIP command?
   2. What would happen if you used PIP LST:=CON:[N] as the command?
   3. Suppose the IOBYTE assigns LPT: as the listing device on your system, but your printer happens to be connected to the UL1: port driver. What's the easiest way to handle this situation?

Answers

   1. The milkman will think he's seeing double. Each character of your note will be sent to the LST: device twice, once by PIP, and once by the CONTROL-P toggle. The LST: output will be DDEEAARR MMIILLKKMMAANN:: etc.
   2. The milkman would think you worked for a Federal agency since each line of your note would carry a reference number.
   3. Use PIP UL1:=CON:

Step 2.   The Electric Steno
Suppose you want to type a short note and save it on disk for later printing. The best way to do this is with an editor (like

ED) or with a word processor (like MINCE). For a quick and dirty solution, however, you can use PIP as follows:

A>PIP STENO.PAD=CON:

PIP will start by opening a file called STENO.PAD, and then accept everything you type at the console into a buffer. When you type CONTROL-Z, the contents of this buffer will be written onto the file STENO.PAD. You can later print this file by using CONTROL-P followed by TYPE STENO.PAD.

Instant Quiz

1. Name two advantages the method of step 2 has over step 1.

Answers

1(a). In the method of step 2, you can use the backspace key to erase errors on a given line *before* pressing (CR) (LF), and these will not appear on the final printout.

1(b). Since STENO.PAD is a genuine ASCII file, you can later change your mind about "quick and dirty," and use ED or a word processor to expand or change your note.

Step 3. Electric Printer

PIP can be used in a manner similar to TYPE (or LLIST in BASIC) to send ASCII files to a printer. PIP has the advantage that you can use the PIP parameters to make the output more readable, adding such things as larger TAB settings, a specified number of lines per page to create top and bottom margins, and individual line numbers that facilitate references to specific parts of the listing. For example, a long C program could be listed 60 lines per page, with 8-column tabs and individual line numbers by typing

A>PIP LST:=LONGPROG.C[T8P60N]

A shorthand form of this particular use of PIP is allowed as follows:

A>PIP PRN:=LONGPROG.C

A file printed in this way *must* be in ASCII format. Programs written with ED such as C or ASM programs satisfy this criterion. However only BASIC programs that have been saved with the SAVE "PROG.BAS",A option can be listed in this manner.

To make the paging work properly, set the printhead about 1/2 inch below one of the perforation lines used to separate sheets of paper on continuous forms. Then clear the formfeed on your printer (turning the printer off then on usually does this). Next type the required PIP command.

PIP will start by doing one formfeed, so the first sheet of paper will not be used. Printing will then take place 1/2 inch below the top of each succeeding page.

Step 4.   Electric Courier

In this step, we're going to use PIP to send a file from one computer to another over a pair of wires called a *serial line.* This technique will be useful if you want to give a friend a copy of a program you wrote, but the friend's computer isn't able to read your disks, either because they use a different format, or because they are a different size (say 5 1/4-inch instead of 8-inch).

Making such a machine-to-machine file transfer depends on specific hardware connections, so it will not be possible to describe a general technique that works for any pair of computers. We'll therefore describe the technique in terms of two specific systems, and follow this with some general information that will give you some ideas on how to modify the procedure for the hardware you are using.

Our example is based on the following problem: how can we transfer some BASIC files from an "ancient" TRS-80 Model I disk system to a modern CP/M disk system? To solve this problem, we'll let the TRS-80 act as the *data source,* while the CP/M system acts as the *data destination.* From PIP's point of view, however, the data source will actually be the logical device (RDR: in our example) associated with a serial input port on the CP/M system, while the data destination will be the CP/M file onto which we copy the TRS-80 BASIC program. A diagram of the setup used which helps explain this relationship is shown in Fig. 6-21.

The procedure for using the setup shown in Fig. 6-21 is the following:

4a. Connect the hardware as shown (and as explained below), making sure both ports are set at the same baud rate.
4b. Turn the TRS-80 on, and load a serial output driver into high memory (the kind used by the TRS-80 for driving a serial printer).

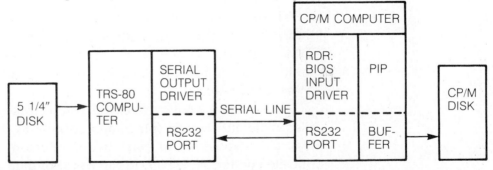

FIG. 6-21   This diagram shows a general setup for sending ASCII formatted BASIC files from a TRS-80 to a CP/M system, using LLIST in the TRS-80, and PIP in the CP/M computer. A similar setup could be used to send ASCII files between two CP/M computers by using PIP at both ends.

4c. Turn the CP/M computer on, and make sure a disk with PIP and adequate storage space is logged in. Use STAT to make sure that the proper physical-device/port-driver is assigned as RDR:.

4d. Load the BASIC program to be transferred by typing the following on the TRS-80:

    BASIC
    LOAD "BASPROG"

4e. Run PIP in the CP/M machine as follows:

    A>PIP PROGCOPY = RDR:[E] (CR)

4f. Send the file from the TRS-80 in ASCII format followed by a CONTROL-Z, as follows (LLIST always sends ASCII format):

    LLIST
    (wait)
    LPRINT CHR$ (26)

4g. Check the transfer by typing the file on the CP/M machine with:

    A>TYPE PROGCOPY

If some lines were messed up in the transfer, use ED or MBASIC to repair them.

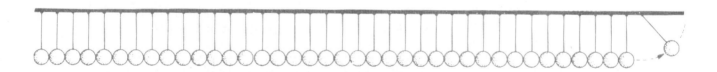

Some Notes on Possible Problems and Solutions

We're assuming that both machines have their serial ports configured as DTE (data terminal equipment) devices, and that a wire from the "transmit" pin (#2) of the TRS-80 goes to the "receive" pin (#3) of the CP/M RDR: port. If one of the machines is set up as DCE (data communications equipment) these pin numbers may have to be changed. To see why, read on.

As everyone knows, electrical connectors come in two "genders" called male and female (plugs and sockets to the uninitiated), and it's physically impossible to mate two connectors unless they are of the opposite gender. However, in the world of data communications there's more than hardware mating to be dealt with. In particular, we have to worry about the fact that what one device calls data *transmission* must be viewed as data *reception* by the device to which this data is being sent (and vice versa).

To establish uniformity in data communication terminology, including such things as signal levels, and which signal goes where, three standards called RS-232C, RS-422, and RS-423 have been established by the EIA (Electrical Industry Association, 2001 I Street NW, Washington, DC 20006).

These standards are complicated, but a very simplified interpretation of the most common one (RS-232C) tells users two things:

1. Signal mating is supposed to be between DTE and DCE devices, where DTE means data "terminal" equipment (computers and peripherals mostly), while DCE means data "communications" equipment (telephone network interfaces and modems mostly).

2. DTE equipment is supposed to transmit data on the wire coming out of pin #2 of the standard DB-25 connector used by most manufacturers for RS-232C, while data reception is on pin #3. The reverse holds for DCE, so DCE and DTE devices mate quite nicely if pin #2 on the DTE goes to a wire that is connected to pin #2 of the DCE, and similarly #3 connects to #3.

However, when two microcomputers are interconnected, it's possible that the I/O ports on both of them are set up as DTE devices. So two computers (like our TRS-80 and CP/M machine) may not mate correctly unless the data transmitting wire (#2) of the data source is connected to the data receiving wire (#3) of the destination and vice versa. It may also be necessary (for reasons we won't discuss here) to add jumpers between pins 4 and 5, between pins 6, 8, 20, and 22, and between pins 1 and 7. Thus to handle DTE to DTE transmission, the following wiring diagram may be needed:

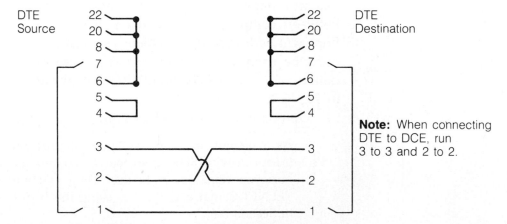

Note: When connecting DTE to DCE, run 3 to 3 and 2 to 2.

You'll know you've got this OK if data transmission takes place, even if it's garbled. To get rid of garbling, check that the *baud rate* used at both ends is the same. Also check that the I/O board option switches such as number of start bits, data bits, stop bits, and parity have been set correctly (usually the right values are start bits = 1, data bits = 8, stop bits = 1, parity = off). One other problem area that can occur with the TRS-80 is that its "clock" messes up data transmission. You can turn the clock off with CMD "T". (CP/M systems don't usually have such a problem.)

Note: PIP can be used with the O parameter to transfer non-ASCII files, but there can be problems since only ASCII files have an EOF mark. If you are interested in doing much data communications work, there are specialized programs available that are more suited to the job than PIP. A good example is Telnet, a program which comes with the BDS C Compiler [12, 20]. The next lab shows how to use Telnet on a CP/M machine to receive data over a telephone line from a remote computer, and store it in the form of a CP/M disk file.

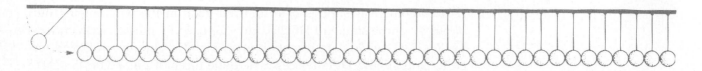

LAB EXERCISE 6.5-2

Data Communication Using Telnet

In order to use Telnet, your computer system should be equipped with an interface (usually RS-232) that is distinct from the I/O interface (and port) used by your console. This is because the console must remain connected to your computer when using Telnet. (The use of a communication program like Telnet is quite different from the simpler arrangement in which a console is disconnected from its computer for use as a terminal to a remote computer.)

When using Telnet, keep in mind that *two computers* are involved: yours and another one we'll call the *remote* computer. If the remote machine happens to be in the same room, a direct wire connection between computers can be used. If not, communication over phone lines will be involved, in which case *modems* (modulator/demodulators) must be used at both ends. Modems are devices that convert digital data to tones that can be handled by telephone lines. The setup is shown in Fig. 6-22.

Here is how to use Telnet with this arrangement:

1. As a preliminary step, you must modify the header file BDSCIO.H (supplied with BDS C) so that it contains data about the I/O modem port you want Telnet to use. Then you must compile the program TELNET.C into a COM file, using the BDS C Compiler as explained in Section 5.6.

2. Boot your CP/M system using a disk that contains the file TELNET.COM. Also make sure that you have a disk with enough space for the file(s) you intend receiving from the remote computer.

3. Run TELNET.COM by typing TELNET (CR). The messages and replies that are generated in a typical file transferring session are shown in Fig. 6-22, along with brief explanations in balloons. In reading this dialogue, notice that your point of view must alternate between two modes: T = Telnet (running in your computer), and R = Remote (the other computer). To enter Telnet mode, you type the *special* character defined in TELNET.C (this is usually ASCII null, which is ˆ@). After

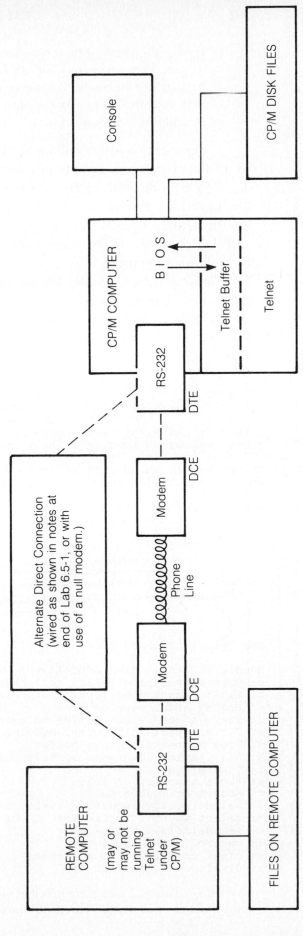

FIG. 6-22 This is the physical arrangement of components and connections needed for using Telnet.

typing ˆ@, you can then type any one of Telnet's 18 single-letter commands. Each command will do whatever its job is, and then put you back in Remote mode. Whenever you're in Remote mode, keep in mind that you are talking to the *other* computer, and must therefore give commands *it* understands.

In our example, we're talking to a large PDP-10 timesharing computer, so all the remote commands you see in the following dialogue (e. g., ˆC, .TTY SYS B, .DIR, .TYPE FWX∗.∗) are given in a form required by this particular system. You'll have to modify this part of the dialogue for the remote system you're using. Incidentally, the fact that .TYPE and .DIR look like CP/M commands is coincidence; they're really PDP-10 system commands.

To keep things simple, we are using Telnet in one machine only. When both computers use Telnet, two-way communication including file exchange is possible. For further information on this subject, study a listing of TELNET.C which contains an explanatory section at the beginning written by Telnet's author, Leor Zolman.

```
A>TELNET
BDS Telnet version 2.3            (July 1980)

Answer ˆyˆ if either your modem is set to half-duplex,
or you expect an echo from the system on the other end
of the line; else answer ˆnˆ:
Do you expect an echo (y/n)? yes
OK; youˆre on line...

Modem is set to 9600 Baud.

  ˆ@

Special:

BDS Telnet commands are:

Double SPECIAL:  send SPECIAL
o: Open output file, start collection
p: Pause (suspend collection or transmission)
r: Resume after pausing
d: Dump (append) text buffer to output file
c: Close output file (after dumping buffer)
v: View contents of text buffer
k: Kill (erase) contents of text buffer
t: Transmit a file to modem
a: Abort transfer of file
n: Accept or ignore Nulls
7: select policy regarding Parity bits
f: select whether to transmit CR-LF as just CR
h: set Half/full duplex mode
l: control CP/M List device
z: clear console terminal screen
s: display Status of Telnet
```

FIG. 6-23.   This is a dialog with Telnet showing how the user can control two computers at once using Telnet commands.

```
q: dump & close output (if open) and Quit to CP/M
b: step through baud rates
```

YOU DECIDE TO CHANGE THE BAUD RATE WITH THE B COMMAND. WHAT TELNET TYPES IS IN REGULAR TYPE; WHAT YOU TYPE IS SHOWN IN BOLDFACE.

`^@`

```
Special: b   Modem is set to 2400 baud.
```

`^@`

```
Special: b   Modem is set to 1200 baud.
```

`T`

```
Special: b   Modem is set to 300 baud.
```

WHEN ANY TELNET COMMAND FINISHES, IT PUTS YOU IN REMOTE MODE UNTIL THE NEXT ^@.

THIS IS THE BAUD RATE YOU WANT, SO YOU STOP. 19,200 AND 9600 BAUD ARE ALSO AVAILABLE.

NOW DIALUP AND LOG ONTO THE REMOTE COMPUTER. A TYPICAL PROCEDURE IS SHOWN FOR THE UNIVERSITY OF PITTSBURGH PDP-10 TIME-SHARING SYSTEM.

`^C`

```
PITT DEC-1099/A 701.22 14:08:45 TTY56 system 1239/1217
Please LOGIN or ATTACH

.TTY SYS B

PITT DEC-1099/B 701.22 14:09:15 TTY56 system 1240/1237
Please LOGIN or ATTACH

.LOG 125521/121641
JOB 38 PITT DEC-1099/B 701.22 TTY56 Wed 28-Apr-82 1409
Password:
Last login: 22-Apr-82 0720
Usage ratio: 0.72   Units used: 3.8  Pages printed: 3

.DIR
```

PASSWORD IS TYPED HERE (NOT ECHOED).

AT THIS POINT YOU ARE COMMUNICATING WITH THE REMOTE COMPUTER. NOTHING 'SPECIAL' WILL HAPPEN WITH YOUR MICROCOMPUTER UNTIL YOU TYPE ^@ AND USE THE COMMANDS OF TELNET.

R = REMOTE MODE

```
(directory of files
on remote computer)
                 .
                 .
                 .
FQ12S9  MAX    5  <057>   22-Apr-82
FQXS10  MAX    5  <057>   22-Apr-82
FQXS11  MAX    5  <057>   22-Apr-82
FQXS17  MAX    5  <057>   22-Apr-82
   Total of 280 blocks in 56 files on USRB: [125521,121641]
```

THESE HAPPEN TO BE ASCII FILES CONTAINING PROGRAMS WRITTEN IN A LANGUAGE CALLED MAXBASIC. SINCE THEY'RE ASCII FORMAT, THEY CAN BE SENT WITH THE 'TYPE' COMMAND OF THIS REMOTE SYSTEM.

`^@`

```
Special: o
Output filename? FQX.MAX
```

BEFORE SENDING THE FILES, SWITCH BACK TO TELNET MODE SO YOU CAN COMMAND IT TO OPEN A CP/M FILE ON YOUR COMPUTER CALLED FQX.MAX. YOU DEFINE IT AS AN OUTPUT FILE BECAUSE DATA (FROM THE REMOTE COMPUTER) WILL BE WRITTEN ON IT.

`T`

```
receiving text (y) or binary data (n)     (y/n)? yes
Stripping parity, ignoring nulls,
   displaying incoming data.
```

YES, THIS FILE WILL BE RECEIVED AS ASCII TEXT DATA, SO IT CAN BE DISPLAYED ON THE CONSOLE.

FIG. 6-23 (*continued*)

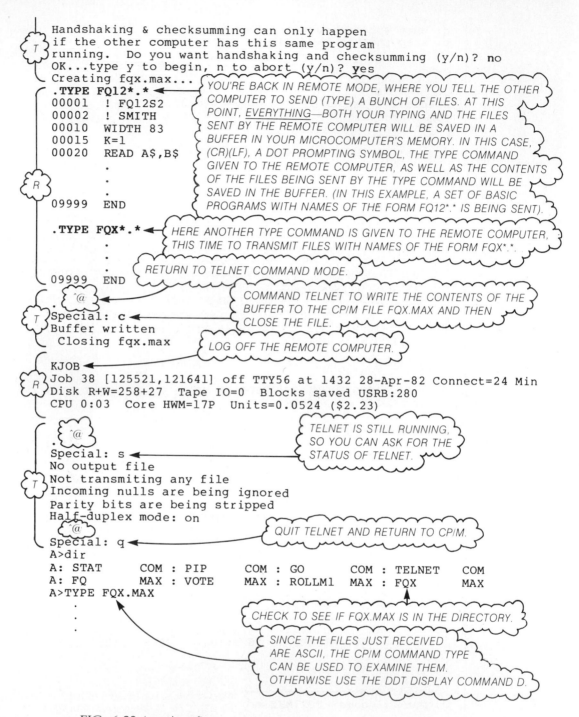

```
   Handshaking & checksumming can only happen
T  if the other computer has this same program
   running.  Do you want handshaking and checksumming (y/n)? no
   OK...type y to begin, n to abort (y/n)? yes
   Creating fqx.max...
   .TYPE FQ12*.*
   00001  ! FQ12S2
   00002  ! SMITH
   00010   WIDTH 83
   00015   K=1
   00020   READ A$,B$
R        .
         .
         .
   09999   END

   .TYPE FQX*.*
         .
         .
         .
   09999   END
   .
      ^@
T  Special: c
   Buffer written
    Closing fqx.max

   KJOB
R  Job 38 [125521,121641] off TTY56 at 1432 28-Apr-82 Connect=24 Min
   Disk R+W=258+27   Tape IO=0  Blocks saved USRB:280
   CPU 0:03  Core HWM=17P  Units=0.0524 ($2.23)

   .  ^@
   Special: s
   No output file
T  Not transmiting any file
   Incoming nulls are being ignored
   Parity bits are being stripped
   Half-duplex mode: on
      ^@
   Special: q
   A>dir
   A: STAT       COM : PIP     COM : GO      COM : TELNET    COM
   A: FQ         MAX : VOTE    MAX : ROLLM1  MAX : FQX       MAX
   A>TYPE FQX.MAX
         .
         .
         .
```

YOU'RE BACK IN REMOTE MODE, WHERE YOU TELL THE OTHER COMPUTER TO SEND (TYPE) A BUNCH OF FILES. AT THIS POINT, EVERYTHING—BOTH YOUR TYPING AND THE FILES SENT BY THE REMOTE COMPUTER WILL BE SAVED IN A BUFFER IN YOUR MICROCOMPUTER'S MEMORY. IN THIS CASE, (CR)(LF), A DOT PROMPTING SYMBOL, THE TYPE COMMAND GIVEN TO THE REMOTE COMPUTER, AS WELL AS THE CONTENTS OF THE FILES BEING SENT BY THE TYPE COMMAND WILL BE SAVED IN THE BUFFER. (IN THIS EXAMPLE, A SET OF BASIC PROGRAMS WITH NAMES OF THE FORM FQ12*.* IS BEING SENT).

HERE ANOTHER TYPE COMMAND IS GIVEN TO THE REMOTE COMPUTER, THIS TIME TO TRANSMIT FILES WITH NAMES OF THE FORM FQX*.*.

RETURN TO TELNET COMMAND MODE.

COMMAND TELNET TO WRITE THE CONTENTS OF THE BUFFER TO THE CP/M FILE FQX.MAX AND THEN CLOSE THE FILE.

LOG OFF THE REMOTE COMPUTER.

TELNET IS STILL RUNNING, SO YOU CAN ASK FOR THE STATUS OF TELNET.

QUIT TELNET AND RETURN TO CP/M.

CHECK TO SEE IF FQX.MAX IS IN THE DIRECTORY.

SINCE THE FILES JUST RECEIVED ARE ASCII, THE CP/M COMMAND TYPE CAN BE USED TO EXAMINE THEM. OTHERWISE USE THE DDT DISPLAY COMMAND D.

FIG. 6-23 (*continued*)

The Many Faces of DDT

The letters DDT mean "dynamic debugging tool." It might be more accurate to refer to this utility as the "duo-decimal toolkit," since DDT is actually an arsenal of 12 different software tools.* Each tool can be used (sometimes in conjunction with the others) to explore and/or manipulate the contents of memory, CPU registers, and files. This means that DDT can be used to examine, test, and alter both programs and data right on down to the level of the individual instruction or byte of data that is being processed by the CPU at any particular point in a program.

The tricky thing about DDT is that both it and the "patient" on which it operates must reside in the TPA at the same time. To see how this two-in-one memory occupation is accomplished (and thereby get a better feel for how DDT and each of its twelve subcommands works) let's look at the memory maps associated with use of the DDT.COM command file.

Case 1. Suppose you decide to use DDT to "work on" the program MYSTRING.COM. The easiest way to do this is with the command

    A>DDT MYSTRING.COM

When you give this command, the memory map goes through two changes as follows:

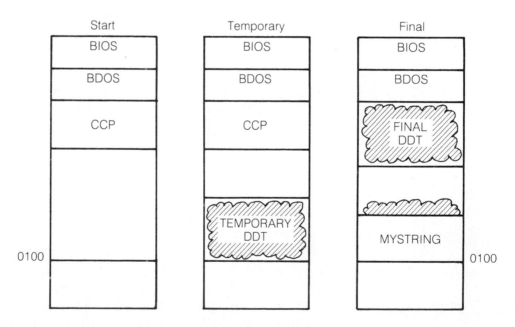

The temporary map shows that DDT, like any other COM file, must first be loaded into the bottom of the TPA and executed. But DDT "knows" it's going to work on another program, so the first thing it does is relocate itself up near the top of the TPA. MYSTRING.COM is

*The CP/M manuals say there are twelve. There are really thirteen if you count the H (hex arithmetic) command illustrated in Fig. 6-26.

then loaded at the start of the TPA right on top of the temporary DDT. Notice that the final DDT overlaps the CCP. This is OK since the CCP (and BDOS) will be reloaded when DDT is exited by doing a warm boot.

A more detailed picture of the final DDT program would show that it consists of two parts: a *nucleus* which handles eight of the DDT sub-commands (D, F, G, I, M, R, S, U), and the assembler/disassembler module (A/L) which handles four subcommands (A, L, T, X). This sep-aration into two parts is made so that users who don't intend using the A, L, T, or X commands can use more of the TPA as seen in the following memory map. The starting address for the DDT nucleus is shown as YYYY, which is about 1300 bytes higher than the start of the A/L module at XXXX.

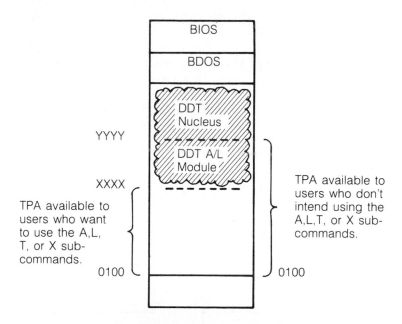

Warning: Once DDT is loaded, you can no longer look at the contents of locations 6 and 7 to find out where BDOS begins. BDOS is still where it's always been, but DDT modifies the contents of locations 6 and 7 to hold either the base address of the DDT Nucleus (YYYY), or the base address of the A/L Module (XXXX). Having this number is useful to programmers who want to know where the top of the reduced TPA is (it will be either at XXXX-1 or at YYYY-1 on our map). However you can still use the BDOS functions with a CALL 05 since this will take you to locations XXXX (or YYYY), and it's *this* location that will contain the needed "JMP to BDOS" instruction.

Case 2.   If you simply type

    A>DDT

then the memory map looks like this:

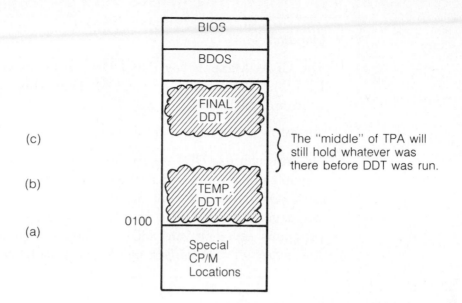

(c)

(b)

(a)

0100

The "middle" of TPA will still hold whatever was there before DDT was run.

In this case all the subcommands of DDT can be used, but no particular file (like MYSTRING) has been loaded into the TPA on which DDT can work. Why would one want to use DDT this way? The map shows that there are three possible reasons:

(a) To examine or modify the "special locations" area of CP/M (e. g., the IOBYTE), or to examine BIOS and/or BDOS.

(b) To examine DDT itself, using the temporary copy of DDT at the bottom of the TPA as the patient. Of course you could also do this with A>DDT DDT.COM.

(c) You could also use DDT to examine whatever is still in the middle of the TPA from a previous operation. For example, you could examine the "clone" BIOS placed there by SYSGEN or MOVCPM (*Warning:* The *loader* part of CP/M placed into the TPA by SYSGEN or MOVCPM will be clobbered by the temporary DDT. See Section 6.6 for a better approach to using DDT on parts of CP/M).

Case 3. You can convert from Case 2 to Case 1 by *reading* a file into the TPA (on top of the temporary DDT). This is done with two of the DDT commands. First you use I (followed by an ufn) to *insert* the file name of your choice into the default FCB (file control block) at location 005CH (the FCB was explained in Section 6.4). Then you use R to *read* the contents of this file (the one whose name you just inserted into the FCB) into the TPA. Thus, for example, you can get the file MYSTRING.COM into the TPA with the sequence of commands

```
A>DDT                (Load and re-locate DDT)
– IMYSTRING.COM      (Insert MYSTRING.COM into the FCB)
– R                  (Read the contents of MYSTRING.COM
                      into the TPA)
```

Issuing these three commands has exactly the same effect as using the one-line command of Case 1.

```
A>DDT MYSTRING.COM
```

Question:

The CP/M Manuals say that DDT can be used in the two forms DDT file.HEX and DDT file.COM. Does this mean DDT can't be used on ASCII files?

Answer:

No. You can use DDT on any file. However, as you'll see shortly, it won't make sense to use the DDT subcommands A, L, G, T, U, or X on anything except binary files that contain 8080 machine language. All COM files fit into this category. Machine language programs saved in Intel HEX format also qualify, since they are *automatically translated back into binary form* when loaded by DDT.

The DDT Subcommands

Here's a brief summary of the twelve DDT subcommands listed in alphabetical order (thirteen if you count H).

A (Assemble)
Forms allowed:
− Axxxx

This command allows you to type 8080 assembly language instructions directly at the console starting at address xxxx. The assembly language instructions are then translated into machine language, and inserted into the address(es) shown, starting at xxxx hex.
Example:

```
   − A013A
  013A   JMP   014F
  013D   MVI   A,FF
  013F   (CR)
   − D013A,013E
  013A C3 4F 01 3E FF
   − L013A,013E
  013A   JMP   014F
  013D   MVI   A,FF
  013F
```

In this example, the instructions JMP 014F and MVI A,0FFH were typed in by the user. They were then translated into machine code and stored in locations 013A and 013D respectively by DDT. To double-check the machine code, the D command was then used. To double-check the assembly language instructions, the L command was used.

D (Display)
Forms allowed:
−D
−Dxxxx
−Dxxxx,yyyy

D shows contents of selected memory in hex digits on the left, and (where possible) as ASCII characters on the right. The first form displays 192 bytes of memory starting at address 0100H. Each successive use of D displays the next 192 bytes of memory. On 80-column terminals, the 192 bytes are displayed as 12 lines of 16 bytes each. The second form is similar to the first except that the display starts at address xxxx. The third form displays all the bytes between the starting address xxxx, and the final address yyyy. Examples of use are shown in Sections 3.5, 6.6, and Lab 6.5-2.

F (Fill)
Forms allowed:
−Fxxxx,yyyy,hh

This command fills memory with the hex constant hh, starting at address xxxx up to and including address yyyy. Thus −F0310,03A0,1A would fill locations 0310 hex to 03A0 hex with 1A hex (which is the ASCII code for CONTROL-Z, and used by CP/M to denote the end of a file). An example of using F was given in Lab 3.5-1.

G (Go)
Forms allowed:
−G
−G,bbbb
−G,bbbb,cccc
−Gxxxx
−Gxxxx,bbbb
−Gxxxx,bbbb,cccc

G means go to some starting address, and begin executing the program found there. The starting address is specified as xxxx in the last three forms. If xxxx is omitted (first form), of if G is followed by a comma (second and third form), the starting address is taken as whatever is contained in the program counter (the normal "next" address). The notations bbbb and cccc both mean "breakpoint." They specify addresses at which execution is stopped, and control is returned to DDT *without* actually executing the instruction addressed by the breakpoint. When two breakpoints are specified, the first one encountered causes the break. In all cases, once a break takes place, the breakpoints are "cleared," and a new G command is needed (see Fig. 6-26).

H (Do Hex Arithmetic)
Forms allowed:
− Hxxxx,yyyy

Gives the hex sum and difference of xxxx and yyyy.

I (Insert or Input)
Forms Allowed:
− Iufn

All that I does is to insert the filename ufn into the default FCB at location 005C hex. To actually bring the contents of the named file into the TPA, a subsequent R (read) command is needed. Note: "DDT filename" is a fast way of giving the following three commands:

    A>DDT
    − Ifilename
    − R

An example of this use is shown in step 7 of Lab Exercise 6.7-1.

L (Disassemble and List)
Forms allowed:
− L
− Lxxxx
− Lxxxx,yyyy

This command causes a "disassembled" form of the contents of memory to be listed at the console (plus printer if a previous CONTROL-P has been typed). The first form starts at address 0100 hex; the second and third start at address xxxx hex. The "disassembling" process is one that converts machine language instructions to mnemonic form (e. g., C3 to JMP). It also puts the addresses or data used by such instructions next to them on the same line. In the third form, the disassembly stops at address yyyy. If yyyy is omitted, 11 instructions are disassembled. An additional 11 instructions are then disassembled for each subsequent use of L. Examples are shown in Fig. 6-28. *Warning:* L will always try to disassemble what's in memory, so its output will be a "lie" if there isn't really ML at the specified locations to begin with. Users must use common sense when interpreting output produced by L.

M (Move)
Forms allowed:
− Mxxxx,yyyy,zzzz

This moves the block of data that resides at locations xxxx to yyyy to a new location starting at address zzzz.

R (Read)
forms allowed:
- R
- Rffff

The R command reads the contents of the file named in the FCB into the TPA, starting at location 0100 hex for COM and ASCII files, or at the addresses specified at the beginning of each record for HEX files. HEX files are automatically translated back to the original binary form. The form Rffff adds the OFFSET ffff to all addresses before loading. The definition of OFFSET, and examples of its use, are given in Section 6.6.

S (Set)
Forms allowed:
- Sxxxx

This command displays the contents of address xxxx, and then allows you to do one of two things: press (CR) if you *don't* want to change the contents, or type in the new contents (in hex) if you wish to make a change. Successive locations are displayed until you type a period (.) to leave Set, or a CONTROL-C to leave DDT. Examples of using Set are given in Labs 3.5-1 and 6.6-1.

T (Trace)
Forms allowed:
- T
- Tn

The first form, T, displays the CPU state, executes 1 step, and displays the next address as *xxxx. The second form, Tn, does T for n steps, where n is a hexadecimal number, but *xxxx is displayed for only the last step. If D is used after T, the default display address is [HL]; if L is used after T, the default list address is [PC]. To return to DDT during Tn, use DELETE (also called RUBOUT). For more information on the CPU state, see the X command. For examples of T, G, X, and U, see Lab 6.5-3.

U (Untrace)
Forms allowed:
- U
- Un

These commands act in the same way as T and Tn, except that the CPU state and next address are displayed only once, showing what they were before the first step (thus U and T do exactly the same thing). To see the CPU state after running through n steps with U, use X or T.

X (Examine the CPU state)

Forms allowed:

−X

−Xr, where r = C,Z,M,E,I,A,B,D,H,S, or P

The letters C, Z, M, E, and I stand for the carry, zero, sign (minus), parity (even), and (intermediate) carry flags. A means A register, while B, D, H, S, and P mean the BC, DE, HL, SP, and PC register pairs.

When the command X is used, the CPU state is displayed as follows:

CfZfMfEfIf A = hh B = hhhh D = hhhh H = hhhh Shhhh Phhhh INST

where f = 0 or 1, hh = byte, hhhh = byte pair, and INST is the next instruction addressed by the PC.

When the command Xr is used, only one of these quantities is displayed, but then the user has two options: to leave it unchanged by pressing (CR), or to make a change by typing in a new value.

The next lab shows how some of the preceding DDT subcommands can be used to trace the execution of a program. Other uses of DDT are shown in sections 6.6 and 6.7. Part 4 of the CP/M DDT User's Guide should also be consulted for an example showing DDT being used to debug an ML program.

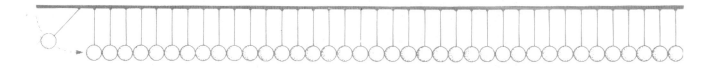

LAB EXERCISE 6.5-3

Using DDT to Trace the Execution of a Program

Step 0.   In this lab we'll use DDT to examine the execution of a small ML program. One normally uses DDT in this fashion to find bugs in a program, but we won't do that. The reason is that the commands of DDT are rather cryptic, and combining the mysteries of DDT with the mysteries of a "buggy" program is not a good way to start. So for this lab we'll use a program that works, and concentrate on the equally important use of DDT as a learning tool, illustrating its use as a system that lets one literally take snapshots of a high-speed program in action.

Step 1.   Type the program of Fig. 6-24 into ED as ALPHABET.ASM, and then assemble the program. Note that a NOP (No Operation) instruction has been placed in the program to reserve space for inserting the "breakpoint" used in step 3. When run, this program will print the first ten letters of the alphabet at the console as the string ABCDEFGHIJ.

Step 2.   Run the program "under DDT" by using XP to change the program counter to 0100, and then typing G as follows:

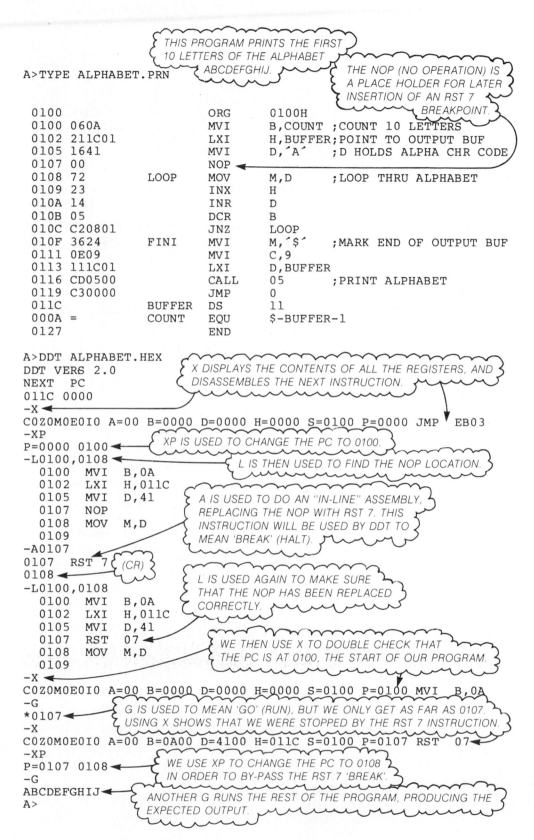

```
A>TYPE ALPHABET.PRN

0100                      ORG      0100H
0100 060A                 MVI      B,COUNT   ;COUNT 10 LETTERS
0102 211C01               LXI      H,BUFFER  ;POINT TO OUTPUT BUF
0105 1641                 MVI      D,'A'     ;D HOLDS ALPHA CHR CODE
0107 00                   NOP
0108 72          LOOP     MOV      M,D       ;LOOP THRU ALPHABET
0109 23                   INX      H
010A 14                   INR      D
010B 05                   DCR      B
010C C20801               JNZ      LOOP
010F 3624       FINI      MVI      M,'$'     ;MARK END OF OUTPUT BUF
0111 0E09                 MVI      C,9
0113 111C01               LXI      D,BUFFER
0116 CD0500               CALL     05        ;PRINT ALPHABET
0119 C30000               JMP      0
011C            BUFFER    DS       11
000A =         COUNT      EQU      $-BUFFER-1
0127                      END
```

```
A>DDT ALPHABET.HEX
DDT VERS 2.0
NEXT   PC
011C   0000
-X
C0Z0M0E0I0 A=00 B=0000 D=0000 H=0000 S=0100 P=0000 JMP  EB03
-XP
P=0000 0100
-L0100,0108
  0100   MVI   B,0A
  0102   LXI   H,011C
  0105   MVI   D,41
  0107   NOP
  0108   MOV   M,D
  0109
-A0107
0107   RST 7   (CR)
0108
-L0100,0108
  0100   MVI   B,0A
  0102   LXI   H,011C
  0105   MVI   D,41
  0107   RST   07
  0108   MOV   M,D
  0109
-X
C0Z0M0E0I0 A=00 B=0000 D=0000 H=0000 S=0100 P=0100 MVI  B,0A
-G
*0107
-X
C0Z0M0E0I0 A=00 B=0A00 D=4100 H=011C S=0100 P=0107 RST  07
-XP
P=0107 0108
-G
ABCDEFGHIJ
A>
```

THIS PROGRAM PRINTS THE FIRST 10 LETTERS OF THE ALPHABET ABCDEFGHIJ.

THE NOP (NO OPERATION) IS A PLACE HOLDER FOR LATER INSERTION OF AN RST 7 BREAKPOINT.

X DISPLAYS THE CONTENTS OF ALL THE REGISTERS, AND DISASSEMBLES THE NEXT INSTRUCTION.

XP IS USED TO CHANGE THE PC TO 0100.

L IS THEN USED TO FIND THE NOP LOCATION.

A IS USED TO DO AN "IN-LINE" ASSEMBLY, REPLACING THE NOP WITH RST 7. THIS INSTRUCTION WILL BE USED BY DDT TO MEAN 'BREAK' (HALT).

L IS USED AGAIN TO MAKE SURE THAT THE NOP HAS BEEN REPLACED CORRECTLY.

WE THEN USE X TO DOUBLE CHECK THAT THE PC IS AT 0100, THE START OF OUR PROGRAM.

G IS USED TO MEAN 'GO' (RUN), BUT WE ONLY GET AS FAR AS 0107. USING X SHOWS THAT WE WERE STOPPED BY THE RST 7 INSTRUCTION.

WE USE XP TO CHANGE THE PC TO 0108 IN ORDER TO BY-PASS THE RST 7 'BREAK'.

ANOTHER G RUNS THE REST OF THE PROGRAM, PRODUCING THE EXPECTED OUTPUT.

FIG. 6-24   Here is how to insert a breakpoint in an ML program, and then run it under DDT.

```
A>DDT ALPHABET.HEX
DDT VERS 2.0
NEXT PC
011C 0000
 -XP
P=0000 0100          These 3 steps can be replaced
 -G                  with G0100.
ABCDEFGHIJ
A>
```

Notice that we never used LOAD to produce a COM file. This wasn't necessary because DDT changes the HEX file to binary form (in the same way that LOAD does). However it leaves the program counter at 0000. So *we* have to change the PC to 0100, which is the origin (first instruction) of our program. An alternate approach would have been simply to type G0100.

Step 3. Now experiment with using a breakpoint to stop the program at location 0107. You insert the breakpoint by replacing the NOP instruction with the RST 7 (restart) instruction. Follow Fig. 6-24 to see how to do this, using the L and A commands of DDT. (A simpler approach to breakpoints will be shown in step 7.)

Step 4. Run the modified program, using Fig. 6-24 as your guide. Notice that you'll have to run the program in two parts, using XP to set the PC to 0108 for the second part of the run. This is necessary in order to jump around the breakpoint which stopped the first part of the program at address 0107 hex.

Step 5. Leave DDT with a CONTROL-C. Since we didn't save the patched program, the RST 7 just inserted will "disappear." (To save the patched program, SAVE 1 ALPHABET.COM could have been used, since our program resides entirely in page 1. We know this since DDT ALPHABET.HEX told us that the highest address used by our program was 011B—one less than the *next* address of 011C.)

Step 6. Now run the program in slow motion, using DDT with the T (trace) and U (untrace) commands. Also experiment with the X command for examining the registers. Use Fig. 6-25 as a guide for this step, but feel free to try other commands as well. You can't hurt anything; if you get lost just reboot and start over.

Instant Quiz

Fig. 6-25 has several "balloons" marked Q1, Q2, Q3, etc., which correspond to the following questions.

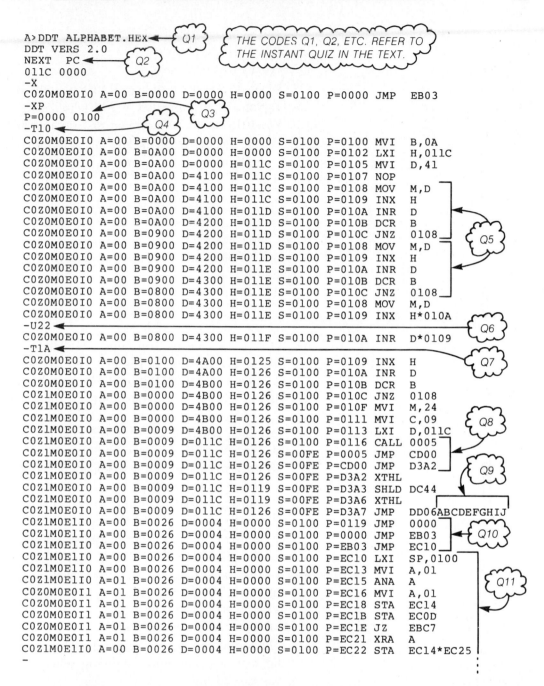

```
A>DDT ALPHABET.HEX ◄─── Q1        THE CODES Q1, Q2, ETC. REFER TO
DDT VERS 2.0                      THE INSTANT QUIZ IN THE TEXT.
NEXT  PC ◄─────── Q2
011C 0000
-X
C0Z0M0E0I0 A=00 B=0000 D=0000 H=0000 S=0100 P=0000 JMP   EB03
-XP
P=0000 0100                       Q3
-T10 ◄─────────────── Q4
C0Z0M0E0I0 A=00 B=0000 D=0000 H=0000 S=0100 P=0100 MVI   B,0A
C0Z0M0E0I0 A=00 B=0A00 D=0000 H=0000 S=0100 P=0102 LXI   H,011C
C0Z0M0E0I0 A=00 B=0A00 D=0000 H=011C S=0100 P=0105 MVI   D,41
C0Z0M0E0I0 A=00 B=0A00 D=4100 H=011C S=0100 P=0107 NOP
C0Z0M0E0I0 A=00 B=0A00 D=4100 H=011C S=0100 P=0108 MOV   M,D ┐
C0Z0M0E0I0 A=00 B=0A00 D=4100 H=011C S=0100 P=0109 INX   H   │
C0Z0M0E0I0 A=00 B=0A00 D=4100 H=011D S=0100 P=010A INR   D   ◄──┐
C0Z0M0E0I0 A=00 B=0A00 D=4200 H=011D S=0100 P=010B DCR   B   │  │
C0Z0M0E0I0 A=00 B=0900 D=4200 H=011D S=0100 P=010C JNZ   0108┘  Q5
C0Z0M0E0I0 A=00 B=0900 D=4200 H=011D S=0100 P=0108 MOV   M,D ┐
C0Z0M0E0I0 A=00 B=0900 D=4200 H=011D S=0100 P=0109 INX   H   │
C0Z0M0E0I0 A=00 B=0900 D=4200 H=011E S=0100 P=010A INR   D   ◄──┘
C0Z0M0E0I0 A=00 B=0900 D=4300 H=011E S=0100 P=010B DCR   B
C0Z0M0E0I0 A=00 B=0800 D=4300 H=011E S=0100 P=010C JNZ   0108┘
C0Z0M0E0I0 A=00 B=0800 D=4300 H=011E S=0100 P=0108 MOV   M,D
C0Z0M0E0I0 A=00 B=0800 D=4300 H=011E S=0100 P=0109 INX   H*010A
-U22 ◄                                               Q6
C0Z0M0E0I0 A=00 B=0800 D=4300 H=011F S=0100 P=010A INR   D*0109
-T1A ◄                                               Q7
C0Z0M0E0I0 A=00 B=0100 D=4A00 H=0125 S=0100 P=0109 INX   H
C0Z0M0E0I0 A=00 B=0100 D=4A00 H=0126 S=0100 P=010A INR   D
C0Z0M0E0I0 A=00 B=0100 D=4B00 H=0126 S=0100 P=010B DCR   B
C0Z1M0E0I0 A=00 B=0000 D=4B00 H=0126 S=0100 P=010C JNZ   0108
C0Z1M0E0I0 A=00 B=0000 D=4B00 H=0126 S=0100 P=010F MVI   M,24
C0Z1M0E0I0 A=00 B=0000 D=4B00 H=0126 S=0100 P=0111 MVI   C,09   Q8
C0Z1M0E0I0 A=00 B=0009 D=4B00 H=0126 S=0100 P=0113 LXI   D,011C
C0Z1M0E0I0 A=00 B=0009 D=011C H=0126 S=0100 P=0116 CALL  0005 ┐
C0Z1M0E0I0 A=00 B=0009 D=011C H=0126 S=00FE P=0005 JMP   CD00 │
C0Z1M0E0I0 A=00 B=0009 D=011C H=0126 S=00FE P=CD00 JMP   D3A2 ┘  Q9
C0Z1M0E0I0 A=00 B=0009 D=011C H=0126 S=00FE P=D3A2 XTHL
C0Z1M0E0I0 A=00 B=0009 D=011C H=0119 S=00FE P=D3A3 SHLD  DC44
C0Z1M0E0I0 A=00 B=0009 D=011C H=0119 S=00FE P=D3A6 XTHL
C0Z1M0E0I0 A=00 B=0009 D=011C H=0126 S=00FE P=D3A7 JMP   DD06ABCDEFGHIJ
C0Z1M0E1I0 A=00 B=0026 D=0004 H=0000 S=0100 P=0119 JMP   0000
C0Z1M0E1I0 A=00 B=0026 D=0004 H=0000 S=0100 P=0000 JMP   EB03 ◄─ Q10
C0Z1M0E1I0 A=00 B=0026 D=0004 H=0000 S=0100 P=EB03 JMP   EC10┘
C0Z1M0E1I0 A=00 B=0026 D=0004 H=0000 S=0100 P=EC10 LXI   SP,0100
C0Z1M0E1I0 A=00 B=0026 D=0004 H=0000 S=0100 P=EC13 MVI   A,01
C0Z1M0E1I0 A=01 B=0026 D=0004 H=0000 S=0100 P=EC15 ANA   A      Q11
C0Z0M0E0I1 A=01 B=0026 D=0004 H=0000 S=0100 P=EC16 MVI   A,01
C0Z0M0E0I1 A=01 B=0026 D=0004 H=0000 S=0100 P=EC18 STA   EC14
C0Z0M0E0I1 A=01 B=0026 D=0004 H=0000 S=0100 P=EC1B STA   EC0D
C0Z0M0E0I1 A=01 B=0026 D=0004 H=0000 S=0100 P=EC1E JZ    EBC7
C0Z0M0E0I1 A=01 B=0026 D=0004 H=0000 S=0100 P=EC21 XRA   A
C0Z1M0E1I0 A=00 B=0026 D=0004 H=0000 S=0100 P=EC22 STA   EC14*EC25
-
```

FIG. 6-25   This is an example of how the T and U commands of DDT can be used to trace the operation of a program. The references Q1, Q2, Q3, etc., are for use with the Instant Quiz in the text.

Q1. Why use a HEX file with DDT rather than a COM file?

Q2. What does NEXT = 011C mean, and what does PC = 0000 mean?

Q3. Did the computer type P = 0000 0100?

Q4. What does T10 do?

Q5. Why does the Program Counter (called P by the Trace) go up to 010C and then reset to 0108 several times?

Q6. What does U22 do?

Q7. What does T1A mean?

Q8. What do the three indicated instructions at P = 0116 do?

Q9. Explain what happened at ABCDEFGHIJ.

Q10. What do the three indicated instructions at P = 0119 do?

Q11. Where did the code starting at P = EC10 come from?

Answers

A1. DDT will actually translate a HEX file into the same binary form used by COM files, but it will make sure to load all instructions at their proper addresses. On the other hand, using DDT with a COM file will always load it starting at 0100, no matter what the ORG of the program was. Another advantage to using a HEX file is that it contains information on the highest address used by the program, so DDT can display an accurate value for the NEXT free address.

A2. NEXT = 011C means that the file ALPHABET.HEX uses locations 0100 to 011B inclusive. The PC is at 0000 simply because it was initialized that way. It must be changed (with XP or as part of G) before executing the program in the TPA.

A3. No. The computer typed P = 0000 after the command XP. The user then typed 0100(CR) which changes the program counter to this value. If the user had typed just (CR), then the PC would have stayed set at 0000, in which case G would cause a warm boot.

A4. T10 causes 16 steps (10 hex) to be traced (executed), with the X command automatically given before each step to display the contents of all the registers, and to show the instruction that will be executed next.

A5. Because as you can see from the trace, the program is executing the loop controlled by JNZ 0108, and the Z flag is still off (Z = 0). When the B register becomes 0, then Z will be set (Z = 1), and the loop will be exited.

A6. U22 does the same as T22 (run through 34 steps), but it displays the registers only once, showing what they were before U22 was carried out.

A7. T1A resumes normal tracing for 26 steps.

A8. The three instructions starting at P = 0116 do an indirect call to BDOS at D3A2, using the intermediate JMP instruction stored in DDT at CD00.

A9. The ABCDEFGHIJ is the actual output produced by our program. However you do not see the instructions of BIOS that produced this output, since DDT suspends the Trace mode during I/O. This is because the slow-motion of Trace would mess up the critical timing and interrupt assumptions of some of the I/O drivers.

A10. The instructions starting at P=0119 cause a warm boot, first by going to EB03 in the BIOS Jump Table, and then by going to the actual warm boot code at EC10. These addresses will vary with your system, but the idea will be the same.

A11. This is part of the actual warm boot code being executed. The code is in BIOS, so it will differ slightly for each system.

Meanwhile, back at the lab.

Step 7. We've saved the best for last. There's a simpler (but in many ways superior) approach to using breakpoints to assist in tracing through a program. It's to use the G command in the form Gxxxx,bbbb (or G,bbbb), where bbbb specifies the address at which we want a break to occur. For example, to trace through

```
A>DDT ALPHABET.HEX
DDT VERS 2.0
NEXT  PC
011C 0000
-G0100,0108
*0108
-T
C0Z0M0E0I0 A=00 B=0A00 D=4100 H=011C S=0100 P=0108 MOV  M,D*0109
-G,0108
*0108
-T
C0Z0M0E0I0 A=00 B=0900 D=4200 H=011D S=0100 P=0108 MOV  M,D*0109
-G,0108
*0108
-T
C0Z0M0E0I0 A=00 B=0800 D=4300 H=011E S=0100 P=0108 MOV  M,D*0109
-G,0108
*0108
-T
C0Z0M0E0I0 A=00 B=0700 D=4400 H=011F S=0100 P=0108 MOV  M,D*0109
-G,0108
*0108
-T
C0Z0M0E0I0 A=00 B=0600 D=4500 H=0120 S=0100 P=0108 MOV  M,D*0109
-G,0108
*0108
-T
C0Z0M0E0I0 A=00 B=0500 D=4600 H=0121 S=0100 P=0108 MOV  M,D*0109
-U10
C0Z0M0E0I0 A=00 B=0500 D=4600 H=0121 S=0100 P=0109 INX  H*010A
-X
C0Z0M0E0I0 A=00 B=0200 D=4900 H=0125 S=0100 P=010A INR  D
-G,0108
*0108
-T
C0Z0M0E0I0 A=00 B=0100 D=4A00 H=0125 S=0100 P=0108 MOV  M,D*0109
-G,0108
ABCDEFGHIJ
A>
```

FIG. 6-26 This figure shows how easy it is to trace a loop in a program by alternately using the G,bbbb and T commands, combined with the use of U to speed up the process when desired.

the loop in the program ALPHABET.HEX, the following sequence of commands can be used:

```
G0100,0108
T
G,0108
T
G,0108
. . . etc. . . .
```

The address 0108 was selected as a breakpoint because we know it's inside the loop. The first G starts the program at location 0100, and runs it up to location 0108. Then a single T (Trace) is used to examine what's in the CPU, and *also* to advance the PC so that another "run around the loop" can be executed by a G,0108.

Try this idea out, using Fig. 6-26 as a guide. Notice how you can see the B register being decremented each time around the loop, while the D register and the HL buffer pointer are incremented. Despite its simplicity, this "breakpoint" form of G, combined with alternate use of T, is recommended as one of the best DDT debugging techniques around.

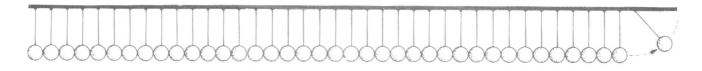

6.6 Modifying BIOS; Using MOVCPM with SAVE and SYSGEN

We're now ready to explore one of the most fascinating aspects of CP/M, a feature one might call its "user-modifiable architecture." Actually, the only part of CP/M anyone is supposed to modify is BIOS (or CBIOS), but that's the section where changes are most desirable. (The cold start loader program can also be modified, but that's not recommended—or needed—for most users.) Being able to fiddle with BIOS means being able to control how CP/M interfaces with *your* computer hardware, whether it be the new dot-matrix printer you found under the Christmas tree, or the telephone modem you have planned for next year. This flexibility is undoubtedly one of the most compelling reasons one could have for choosing CP/M over other disk operating systems.

Before getting started on our explanation of how to make changes in BIOS, two caveats are needed. The first is that this is *not* the sort of thing a beginning user of CP/M can expect to do with immediate success. It takes lot's of know-how, and there are more variables than you can shake an IC at. This doesn't mean that if you're a beginner you shouldn't give it a try. Just don't expect instant success. Also be sure to do all of your experimentation with disks that have copies of CP/M you can afford to mess up (at which time you can go back to Chapter 2 and repeat the backup procedures for re-making the disk).

The second caveat is that some "adaptations" of CP/M have departed from the user-modifiable philosophy of design. For example, the SoftCard version of CP/M for the Apple II doesn't supply an assembly listing of BIOS (they also don't supply the tools MOVCPM or SYSGEN), so users of this system are out of luck when it comes to BIOS customization. On the other hand, Apple users *can* add new interfaces by buying plug-in adapter cards. This had the virtue of convenience, and the vice of adding extra cost. It's also not possible to make more subtle changes (e. g., adding a "print toggle" or "screen dump toggle" to BIOS).

Most 8-inch disk CP/M systems are more open to user-modification. The examples in this and the next section were done on the Intecolor and the Morrow S-100 systems. Both of these supply well-documented CBIOS.ASM programs as well as the MOVCPM and SYSGEN utilities needed for making changes. The Heath/Zenith, Tarbell, California Computer Systems, Godbout/CompuPro, and Ithaca Intersystems versions of CP/M also supply user modifiable versions of CBIOS, as do several others.

Getting Ready for CBIOS Surgery

There are three major steps involved in modifying BIOS (or as we will also call it in this section, CBIOS).

1. First you have to decide what you want to do, how to code it, and where in CBIOS to add the new code. Knowing what to do at this step takes lots of experience, and the best bet for a beginner is to study as many examples as possible.

2. Next you make the desired changes, using one of two techniques.
   (a) If the changes are minor, they can be made with DDT's S (set) command. This process is called *patching* CBIOS. For testing purposes, you can try patching the "live" working CBIOS at the top of memory. However, this will only be a temporary fix (and it *could* crash the system), so it's a better idea to make the patches in the CBIOS placed in the TPA by either SYSGEN or MOVCPM.
   (b) If the changes are going to be substantial, you'll have to go more slowly, first creating a file that contains all of the current CBIOS, plus your new code. This new, improved CBIOS will be created as an assembly language program (using ED), so you'll want to give it a name something like MYBIOS.ASM. This program is then run through ASM, producing the files MYBIOS.PRN and MYBIOS.HEX. It's the HEX version that will be used in step 3.

3. Finally, you'll need to incorporate the new BIOS (either the patched one from 2(a) or the HEX file from 2(b)) as a permanent part of your working CP/M system. The tools for doing this are SAVE, DDT and SYSGEN. How to use these tools will take some explaining. In fact all

three steps involve a fair amount of detail, so let's go over them again, using specific examples as part of two lab exercises. In the lab of this section we'll use the patch technique of 2(a) for making minor changes. In the lab of the next section we'll use the more general method of 2(b).

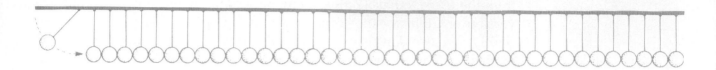

LAB EXERCISE 6.6-1

Modifying CBIOS by Using DDT to Patch Code

In this lab we'll see how to make minor changes in CBIOS, using the DDT patching technique mentioned in 2(a) above. "Minor" changes are those that do not disturb the addresses of the present CBIOS code. They are usually modifications of instruction codes or data already present in CBIOS, subject to the constraint that no bytes may be added or deleted—just changed. You *can* nullify instructions by changing them to NOP codes (do nothing instructions), but the total number of bytes used must remain the same. And of course when you're finished, CBIOS must still work!

Step 0. This is a preliminary (but very important and *very* long) step in which we'll show how to gather the information needed for carrying out the three major BIOS modification steps in this and the next lab. We'll break the step into three parts called (a), (b), and (c).

0a. The first thing to do is obtain a PRN listing of the CBIOS for your system. Start by checking the directory of your CP/M disk, looking for a file called CBIOS.ASM (or something similar). If there is more than one such name, you'll have to check your system documentation to see which one to use. (For example, Morrow CP/M has two files called CBIOS.ASM and CBIOS#.ASM; the file CBIOS#.ASM is the one to use on double density "2D" systems.)

NOTE TO APPLE II USERS

As mentioned earlier, the SoftCard CP/M system does not include a CBIOS.ASM file, nor the programs MOVCPM and SYSGEN, so you won't be able to do this or the next lab. However, there *are* some nonstandard techniques that can be used to add new drivers (but not modify existing ones) to the Microsoft/Apple CP/M. These are explained in Part V of the books that come with the SoftCard System.

Assuming that there's a CBIOS.ASM file on your disk, you obtain a .PRN file listing by running the CBIOS.ASM file through the CP/M assembler as follows:

A>ASM CBIOS   (for Morrow, A>ASM CBIOS#)

(**Warning:** You may get some error messages from ASM. See the next Technical Note for information on what to do if this happens.)

When the assembly is finished, check the directory and make sure you now have a file called CBIOS.PRN (or CBIOS#.PRN). This file can be studied by listing it on the console screen with the TYPE command. However, if at all possible, you should use a system with a printer to obtain a hardcopy listing. In this case use CONTROL-P and the TYPE command as follows:

A>CONTROL-P (CR)
A>TYPE CBIOS.PRN (CR)   (for Morrow, A>TYPE CBIOS#.PRN)

This listing will be valuable for studying how your BIOS works, and finding the best place to install new driver programs. To make the listing more readable, you can force margins at the top and bottom of pages, get expanded tabs, line numbers, and page numbers by using PIP instead of TYPE. There are two ways to do this. The first uses the special PIP "PRN:device" as follows:

A>PIP PRN: = CBIOS.PRN

This is equivalent to using the N, P, and T parameters of PIP as follows:

A>PIP LST: = CBIOS.PRN[NP60T8]

The second form is more flexible, since you can change (or omit) parameters to suit your needs.

> 0b. The next bit of preparation involves some detective work. You'll want to find out exactly where in the TPA copies of CP/M are placed by the programs SYSGEN and MOVCPM. Recall that both programs are able to put copies of CP/M in the TPA where a programmer can work on them, while continuing to use the "live" CP/M located at the top of memory.

The difference is that SYSGEN gets its copy (what we earlier called the "clone" or "export" copy) directly from the system disk (tracks 0 and 1 on a standard 8-inch disk). Thus this copy will be identical to the live CP/M loaded into high memory during a cold boot.

On the other hand, MOVCPM puts a copy of a private "relocatable" version of CP/M in the TPA. This relocatable version is not necessarily the same as the system version stored on tracks 0 and 1. In fact it's stored as part of the file MOVCPM.COM. "Relocatable" means that MOVCPM can modify any code in this private copy that references specific memory locations (e. g., the target addresses of JMP and CALL instructions). The relocation scheme is the simplified one described in *Dr. Dobb's Journal* #22, February 1978. It uses a bit map that pinpoints the code to be changed, but this map applies only to the version of CP/M stored as part of the MOVCPM file. It's usually OK to trust this map when using MOVCPM to relocate your CP/M, and store the relocated version on tracks 0 and 1. But once you decide to make additional changes, it's best to use SYSGEN for placing a clone of the relocated CP/M into the TPA for any additional surgery.

This still leaves the question of finding out exactly *where* in the TPA the CP/M clone will be stored. One way to find out is to examine the TPA after a SYSGEN, looking specifically for the memory locations where SYSGEN has stored CBIOS. You can do this with the DDT L (disassemble) command. The same technique can be used for finding where MOVCPM put BIOS if that's of interest.

Of course it would be very time-consuming to use DDT to disassemble the entire TPA. However you can find out a lot by examining a few "judiciously selected" locations. For example, the Digital Research manuals say that the TPA copy of BIOS should start at location 1F80 hex. Not all versions of CP/M follow this advice, but it's easy to see if they do. The reason is that *all* versions of BIOS, customized or not, start with an easily identified section called a *jump table*. If you look at your listing of CBIOS, you should be able to spot this table near the beginning of the listing. It consists of about seventeen jump instructions in a row that look something like the listing in Fig. 6-27.

```
        ;
        ; I/O JUMP VECTOR
        ; THIS IS WHERE CPM CALLS WHENEVER IT NEEDS
        ; TO DO ANY INPUT/OUTPUT OPERATION.
        ; USER PROGRAMS MAY USE THESE ENTRY POINTS
        ; ALSO, BUT NOTE THAT THE LOCATION OF THIS
        ; VECTOR CHANGES WITH THE MEMORY SIZE.
        ;
        ; NOTE PROGRAMS DIRECTLY ACCESSING THIS TABLE
        ; MAY NOT BE UPWARDLY COMPATIBLE TO MPM
        ;
FA00                    ORG     CPMB+1600H
1600 =          CPML    EQU     $-CPMB
002C =          NSECTS  EQU     CPML/128

FA00 C3CBFA             JMP     BOOT        ;FROM COLD START LOADER.
FA03 C31DFB    WBOOTE:  JMP     WBOOT       ;FROM WARM BOOT.
FA06 C366FB             JMP     CONST       ;CHECK CONSOLE KB STATUS.
FA09 C396FB             JMP     CONIN       ;READ CONSOLE CHARACTER.
FA0C C3AAFB             JMP     CONOT       ;WRITE CONSOLE CHARACTER.
FA0F C3BEFB             JMP     LIST        ;WRITE LISTING CHAR.
FA12 C3D1FB             JMP     PUNCH       ;WRITE PUNCH CHAR.
FA15 C3EDFB             JMP     READER      ;READ READER CHAR.
FA18 C37CFC             JMP     HOM         ;MOVE DISK TO TRACK ZERO.
FA1B C332FC             JMP     SLDSK1      ;SELECT DISK DRIVE.
FA1E C382FC             JMP     STTRK       ;SEEK TO TRACK IN REG A.
FA21 C32CFC             JMP     STSEC       ;SET SECTOR NUMBER.
FA24 C34CFC             JMP     SETDMA      ;SET DISK STARTING ADR.
FA27 C36AFC    READN:   JMP     READA       ;READ SELECTED SECTOR.
FA2A C373FC    WRITEN:  JMP     WRITE1      ;WRITE SELECTED SECTOR.
FA2D C354FC             JMP     LISTST      ;READ PRINTER STATUS
FA30 C326FC             JMP     SECTRAN     ;SECTOR TRANSLATE
```

FIG. 6-27   This is a listing of the jump table found in the ISC CBIOS. Notice that it starts at location FA00 which is near the top of the normal 64K address space. ISC is able to start CBIOS this high (giving users a very large TPA) because it has an additional 40K bank of ROM and RAM memory located above the normal 64K bank. Sophisticated extensions to CBIOS (including full color console drivers) are stored in the second bank, along with a variety of extra printer drivers.

All CP/M BIOS modules (including those cloned into the TPA) have a similar jump table, and they're all supposed to adhere to the order shown. In particular, the first JMP is to CBIOS code that is executed after a cold boot, while the second JMP is to code that gets executed after a warm boot. The address of this second JMP (FA03 in our sample listing) can always be double-checked by examining the contents of locations 0, 1, and 2 (recall that's the official place to go whenever a program is finished and wants to do a warm boot). To examine these locations, you can use the DDT L command as follows:

```
A>DDT
DDT VERS 2.2

-L0000,0002              (You type this with no spaces.)
   0000   JMP   FA03     (Then the disassembler types the instruc-
                          tions in locations 0000,0001, and 0002.)
```

Since JMP instructions take three bytes (the jump code—which is C3—plus two bytes for the target address), and since the warm boot address FA03 is the second entry in the jump table, you can conclude that this CBIOS starts at FA00 (which of course the PRN listing confirms).

But what about the starting location of the CBIOS copied into the TPA by SYSGEN (or MOVCPM)? You can check this out by first using SYSGEN (or MOVCPM), and then using the DDT L command near the suspected location as shown in Figs. 6-28(a) and 6-28(b).

Fig. 6-28(a) shows that in the case of the ISC CBIOS, our guess at 1F80 turned out to be correct. However, for the Morrow CP/M, the guess of 1F80 hex as the start of the SYSGEN clone BIOS is wrong. Fortunately there's a mimeo sheet that comes with the Morrow CP/M that indirectly suggests that they put CBIOS in the TPA at address 2700 hex. As Fig. 6-28(b) shows, this is correct. The jump table we have disassembled starting at 2700 hex matches the jump table in the live CBIOS at the top of memory (which is at location EB00 hex in a system relocated for 62K of RAM).

Question:

How did you know where to find CBIOS in the live CP/M for the Morrow system?

Answer:

The same way you find out for any system—either subtract 3 from the address in locations 1 and 2, or examine the listing of a properly sized CBIOS.PRN (for Morrow, CBIOS#.PRN) and look for the jump table. Another method is to look for the ORG directive in the PRN listing. *Warning:* The actual addresses shown in a listing of CBIOS.PRN (or CBIOS#.PRN) will depend on the ORG put in CBIOS.ASM before it was assembled and these will *not* reflect any changes in location made by MOVCPM. Also note that sometimes

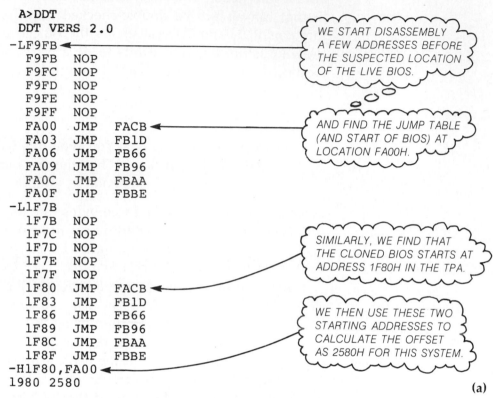

```
A>SYSGEN
SYSGEN VER 2.2
SOURCE DRIVE NAME (OR RETURN TO SKIP) A
SOURCE ON A, THEN TYPE RETURN
FUNCTION COMPLETE
DESTINATION DRIVE NAME (OR RETURN TO REBOOT)

A>DDT
DDT VERS 2.0
-LF9FB
  F9FB   NOP
  F9FC   NOP
  F9FD   NOP
  F9FE   NOP
  F9FF   NOP
  FA00   JMP   FACB
  FA03   JMP   FB1D
  FA06   JMP   FB66
  FA09   JMP   FB96
  FA0C   JMP   FBAA
  FA0F   JMP   FBBE
-L1F7B
  1F7B   NOP
  1F7C   NOP
  1F7D   NOP
  1F7E   NOP
  1F7F   NOP
  1F80   JMP   FACB
  1F83   JMP   FB1D
  1F86   JMP   FB66
  1F89   JMP   FB96
  1F8C   JMP   FBAA
  1F8F   JMP   FBBE
-H1F80,FA00
1980 2580
```

WE START DISASSEMBLY A FEW ADDRESSES BEFORE THE SUSPECTED LOCATION OF THE LIVE BIOS.

AND FIND THE JUMP TABLE (AND START OF BIOS) AT LOCATION FA00H.

SIMILARLY, WE FIND THAT THE CLONED BIOS STARTS AT ADDRESS 1F80H IN THE TPA.

WE THEN USE THESE TWO STARTING ADDRESSES TO CALCULATE THE OFFSET AS 2580H FOR THIS SYSTEM.

(a)

FIG. 6-28 (a) and (b). These listings show DDT being used to verify in which locations the CBIOS jump table is stored. Listing (a) was made on the ISC 8063 computer. The first use of the DDT L command reveals that there's a jump table (and therefore CBIOS) starting at location FA00 hex. This is the "live" CBIOS actually being used by the system. The second use of the L command

ORG is given with an actual address, but more often it is given by a formula that depends on a constant called MSIZE (this is the number of kilobytes of RAM you want your relocated system to occupy). The next two examples show what to look for.

Example 1.   The ISC 8063 64K CP/M System.

```
0040 = MSIZE  EQU  64                ;SIZE IN KB
B000 = CBASE  EQU  (MSIZE–20)*1024   ;BIAS FOR LARGER THAN 20K
E400 = CPMB   EQU  CBASE + 3400H     ;START OF CP/M
EC06 = BDOS   EQU  CPMB + 806H       ;START OF BDOS
FA00 =        ORG  CPMB + 1600H      ;START OF BIOS
```

This system is set for 64K of RAM, so CBASE (the "bias," which means the number of bytes beyond the minimal 20K size recom-

```
A>SYSGEN
SYSGEN VER 2.2
SOURCE DRIVE NAME (OR RETURN TO SKIP)A
SOURCE ON A, THEN TYPE RETURN
FUNCTION COMPLETE
DESTINATION DRIVE NAME (OR RETURN TO REBOOT)

A>DDT
DDT VERS 2.0
-LEAFB
  EAFB  NOP
  EAFC  NOP
  EAFD  NOP
  EAFE  NOP
  EAFF  NOP
  EB00  JMP   EBB1
  EB03  JMP   EC10
  EB06  JMP   EE54
  EB09  JMP   EE60
  EB0C  JMP   EE75
  EB0F  JMP   EE95
-L26FB
  26FB  NOP
  26FC  NOP
  26FD  NOP
  26FE  NOP
  26FF  NOP
  2700  JMP   EBB1
  2703  JMP   EC10
  2706  JMP   EE54
  2709  JMP   EE60
  270C  JMP   EE75
  270F  JMP   EE95
-H2700,EB00
1200 3C00
-G0
```

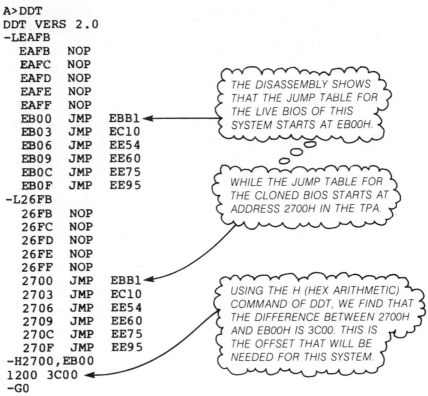

THE DISASSEMBLY SHOWS THAT THE JUMP TABLE FOR THE LIVE BIOS OF THIS SYSTEM STARTS AT EB00H.

WHILE THE JUMP TABLE FOR THE CLONED BIOS STARTS AT ADDRESS 2700H IN THE TPA.

USING THE H (HEX ARITHMETIC) COMMAND OF DDT, WE FIND THAT THE DIFFERENCE BETWEEN 2700H AND EB00H IS 3C00. THIS IS THE OFFSET THAT WILL BE NEEDED FOR THIS SYSTEM.

(b)

shows that SYSGEN has placed a copy of CBIOS in the TPA starting at location 1F80 hex. This is the "clone" version on which we'll later do our patching. Listing (b) is for the Morrow system, and it shows that the live BIOS starts at EB00 hex, while the clone BIOS is at 2700 hex.

mended by Digital Research) is (64-20)*1024 = 45056 bytes. In hex this is B000 (since B is 11 decimal, and 11*4096 = 45056). Thus the live CPM will start at CPMB = CBASE + 3400H which is B000 + 3400 = E400 in hex. BDOS will start 806H bytes higher = E400 + 806 = EC06. The ORG statement of this CBIOS shows that BIOS itself will start at E400 + 1600 = FA00 hex.

Example 2.   The Morrow system is supplied "configured" as a minimal 24K system. If you get a PRN file of the CBIOS#.ASM file supplied on the original disk, you'll see the following equates.

```
0018 = MSIZE  EQU   24
1000 = BIAS   EQU   (MSIZE-20)*1024
3D00 = CCP    EQU   2D00H+BIAS
```

```
4500 = BDOS     EQU     CCP+800H
5300 = BIOS     EQU     CCP+1600H
5300            ORG     BIOS
```

This tells you that for a 24K system, BIOS starts at address 5300H. If you decide to relocate this CP/M (say for a 62K system as we did back in Lab 2.6-1), BIOS will start 38K higher. All the new addresses for this relocated version can be obtained by generating a listing of the 62K version of CBIOS#.PRN for study. To obtain this, what you have to do is change the MSIZE equate from 24 to 62, and then re-assemble the program. The safest approach is to first make a copy of CBIOS#.ASM under a new name—say CBIOS62—as follows:

A>PIP CBIOS62.ASM = CBIOS#.ASM

Next use ED on CBIOS62.ASM to change the MSIZE EQU 24 statement to MSIZE EQU 62, and save the edited file (under the same name) by using the E command of ED. If you now assemble this file by typing

A>ASM CBIOS62

you'll obtain the two files CBIOS62.HEX and CBIOS62.PRN. Using the TYPE command to display the PRN file will show the new equates as follows:

```
003E = MSIZE   EQU     62                      ;MEM SIZE OF CP/M
A800 = BIAS    EQU     (MSIZE–20)*1024         ;MEMORY OFFSET FROM 20K
D500 = CCP     EQU     2D00+BIAS               ;START OF CP/M (CCP)
DD00 = BDOS    EQU     CCP+800H                ;START OF BDOS
EB00 = BIOS    EQU     CCP+1600H               ;START OF BIOS
EB00 =         ORG     BIOS                    ;DIRECTIVE TO ASM TELLING
                                               ;WHERE TO START
```

In other words, for a 62K system, the live BIOS starts at EB00 hex. This is the same result you would have obtained by adding 38K decimal to 5300 hex as follows:

First, 38K = 36*1024 + 2*1024 = 9*4096 + 8*256 = 9800 hex.

And 9800H + 5300H = EB00H.

TECHNICAL NOTE

The files CBIOS#.ASM and CBIOS62.ASM will not completely assemble under ASM since they use some features recognized only by more advanced assemblers. The cheapest fix is to rewrite the offending parts of the program, or if they are not needed, to "comment them out" by putting semicolons in front of the troublesome lines. A more expensive solution is to buy the needed assembler (in this case a program called MAC). In the case of Morrow's CBIOS#.ASM, the only offending section is one that uses the "if-then-else" directive to calculate part of a message about the disk controller origin. This code can all be commented out (starting with the line IF ORIGIN/4096>10 up to but not including the line DB '00H.'). As a quick replacement, the directive DB 'F8' or DB 'E0' (depending on which ROM your disk controller uses) can then be inserted right before the directive DB '00H.'. This data byte is used only for the sign-on message, so nothing will be hurt if you happen to get it wrong or even leave it out. Incidentally, ASM will also squawk about use of the directive TITLE used in CBIOS#.ASM, but no harm will come from ignoring the squawk.

3. For a third example, study the "skeletal" BIOS given in Appendix C of the *CP/M Alteration Guide* received with your system. This is a barebones BIOS with no drivers, but it gives a good feel for the overall structure of BIOS.

4. For a fourth example, there was an improved BIOS for the Tarbell Disk Controller published in *S-100 Microsystems*, Vol. 1, No. 2, p. 49 [11]. It was written by Marty Nichols, and is very well documented. It illustrates a technique for handling a CBIOS that has been enlarged beyond the size originally recommended by Digital Research.

0c. Yes, we're still at the step 0 preparatory stage! If this is the first time you've read about CBIOS detective work, you should be thoroughly confused by now. But forge ahead anyway, planning on a fresh re-reading of all of step 0 in the morning. The picture should be a little less murky by then.

Step 0(c) is pretty straightforward—at least if you've already done steps 0(a) and 0(b) on your system. The idea is to fill in the third column of the following table.

		Morrow 62K	ISC 64K	Your System
(1)	Start of the "clone" CBIOS:	2700H	1F80H	
(2)	Start of the "live" CBIOS:	EB00H	FA00H	
(3)	Difference (negative OFFSET):	3C00H	2580H	
(4)	Number of pages to use in a SAVE of CP/M (as given by the message in MOVCPM * *, or by calculating it from the highest address of the cloned CBIOS as explained in Lab 6.4-3).	44 (decimal) minimum	34 (decimal) minimum	

Items (1) and (2) are found by using DDT's L command to snoop around for the jump table on your system as described in step 0(b). Item (3) is found by subtracting the starting address of the live CBIOS from the starting address of the clone CBIOS, using hex arithmetic. The easiest way to do this subtraction is to use DDT's H (hex arithmetic) command. This gives the sum and difference of any two hex numbers. For our examples, it would work as follows:

```
A>DDT
DDT VERS 2.0
-H2700 EB00
1200 3C00
-H1F80 FA00
1980 2580
```

The hex number that gives the OFFSET in each case is the second one generated by H. It will be needed in this lab to find the addresses of the instructions you wish to patch in the clone CBIOS. It will also be needed in the next section's lab to properly use DDT's R command to "overlay" the clone CP/M with the new CBIOS you've constructed.

TECHNICAL NOTE: BIAS VS. OFFSET

The Digital Research Manuals use the terms *bias* and *offset* in their *CP/M 2.2 Alteration Guide*. Unfortunately the terms are occasionally switched, adding further obfuscation to an already confusing subject. Here's how the terms are used in most of the CP/M 2.2 literature.

Bias means the difference between the starting address of CP/M in a minimal 20K CP/M 2.2 system, and the starting address of CP/M after relocation for the actual memory used. (Recall that a 20K CP/M system means one located at the top of memory in a computer with 20K of RAM, but that most real systems use more than 20K.) Thus for a 20K system, the bias is 20K − 20K = 0. For a 24K system, the bias is 4K, for 28K it's 8K, for 32K it's 12K, and so on up to a 64K system where the bias is 44K. You can think of bias as the number you'd have to add to *any* address in a 20K CP/M system to find out what the corresponding address would be in the relocated system. To convert any of these biases to hex notation, recall that 1000H is the same as 4096 decimal which is 4K. Thus the bias for a 64K system would be 44K decimal which is 11*(4K) = 11*4096 = B000 hex.

On the other hand, *OFFSET* (also called negative offset) is the number you'd have to add to an address in the normal "live" CP/M at the top of memory to find its location down in the TPA as a part of the SYSGEN or MOVCPM "clone" of CP/M. The tricky thing here is that you *add* the OFFSET even though you want to go down. This works because the largest possible address in a 64K system is FFFF hex (65,535 decimal). If you add 1 to FFFF, you get 10000 hex, but since 16-bit addresses can never have more than 4 hex digits, 10000 hex is treated as 0000 hex, i. e., the leftmost digit is thrown away. Thus you can think of OFFSET as a number, which when added to an address, moves that address out of the top of memory and up through the bottom. A better image is to visualize memory as a continuous loop. It's formed by bending the usual rectangular array picture of memory so that the top (location FFFF hex) is brought around to just under the bottom (location 0000 hex). Adding OFFSET simply moves you around this loop.

The numerical value to be used for OFFSET depends on where the live BIOS is located, and where in the TPA the clone BIOS is to be placed. For example, the ISC 64K CP/M system starts its live BIOS code at FA00H, whereas its clone BIOS code starts at 1F80H. So for this system, OFFSET must satisfy the relation

FA00H + OFFSET = 11F80H

where the leftmost 1 in the result will be thrown away for 16-bit addresses. Thus OFFSET = 11F80H − FA00H = 2580H. Don't believe it? To check, add FA00H + 2580H. You get 11F80H which is the same as 1F80H in a 16-bit address scheme. For the 62K Morrow CP/M, the start of the live BIOS is at EB00H, while the clone BIOS starts at 2700H. For this system, OFFSET must satisfy the equation

EB00H + OFFSET = 12700H

Thus OFFSET = 12700H − EB00H = 3C00H. If you find doing the hex arithmetic above difficult (as do most people), you can use the H command in DDT to get the sum and difference of any two hex numbers. For the first example, the interaction with DDT would look like this:

```
A>DDT
−H1F80,FA00
1980 2580
```

This tells you that the sum 1F80 + FA00 = 11980, and the difference 1F80 − FA00 = 2580, with all numbers given in hex.

At long last we're ready to try our hand at modifying CBIOS. The first step is to decide what you want to do, and where in CBIOS to do it. We'll illustrate this step by showing how to make simple changes in our two example CBIOSs. For the Morrow CBIOS, we'll change the value of the IOBYTE used in the cold boot initialization routine. This will be explained as step 1. For the ISC CBIOS, we'll modify the paper tape driver so that it works with a 300 baud serial printer. This will be explained as step 2.

Step 1.   Modifying the IOBYTE initialization in a Morrow 62K CBIOS.

The listing of the file CBIOS#.ASM that comes with the Morrow system shows the following equate and comment:

INIOBY   EQU   80H   ;INITIAL IOBYTE (LST: = LPT:)

One suspects that this means 80H is the value assigned to the IOBYTE during a cold boot. When written in binary, 80H = 10000000, which indicates that the following assignments are made during a cold boot

10	LST: = LPT:
00	PUN: = TTY:
00	RDR: = TTY:
00	CON: = TTY:

We can double check that this is indeed what the assignments are, by doing a STAT DEV: as in Fig. 3-3. Now let's suppose that we want to change this initialization so that LST: = UL1: upon cold boot. The binary code for UL1: is 11, so to make this new assignment (while keeping all the others the same), we'll want an initial IOBYTE of 11000000 = C0 hex = 192 decimal.

There are two ways to make such a change. The first is to change the EQU directive to

INITIOBY   EQU   0C0H

The problem with this approach is that it must be made in the file CBIOS#.ASM, and then this file must be reassembled and integrated into CP/M. Section 6.7 will show how to do this, and as you'll see, it's a pretty complicated procedure.

For a quick fix, a simpler procedure is to find the actual place in CBIOS# where INITIOBY is used, and to replace the machine language code there. Snooping around in the cold boot section of the 62K CBIOS#.PRN, we find the following instruction at address EBB4:

EBB4   CD6DEF   CALL   TINIT   ;INITIALIZE THE TERMINAL

Upon investigating TINIT at addredd EF6D, we find the following code

```
EF6D   3E80      TINIT   MVI A,INITIOBY    ;3E = MVI,80 = INITIAL IOBYTE
EF6F   320300            STA IOBYTE
```

If we change the code at addresses EF6D and EF6E from 3E80 to 3EC0, and save this "patched" version of CBIOS# for later use with SYSGEN, then all disks made with a CP/M that uses the patched code will assign LST: = UL1:.

The exact procedure for doing all this is as follows:

1a. Use SYSGEN to load a clone (copy) of CP/M into the TPA, and then return to CP/M.

1b. Save a copy of the clone as a disk file (we'll call the file DISKCPM.COM) using the command SAVE nn DISKCPM.COM. The nn should be replaced by the number of pages required by your CP/M. For the ISC and most standard versions of CP/M, nn is 34. For the larger Morrow CP/M system nn is 44. You can usually find this number by typing A>MOVCPM * *, and seeing what SAVE command is recommended. Another method is to calculate nn as explained in Lab 6.4-3.

1c. Use DDT to bring the file back into the TPA, check on where the code to be changed is with the H and L (disassemble) commands of DDT, and then patch the code with the S(et) command of DDT. Leave DDT with a CONTROL-C or G0 (go to zero).

1d. If you wish, the patched code can be re-saved as in step 1(b) with another SAVE nn DISKCPM.COM.

1e. Finally, move the patched code from the TPA onto the system tracks of a disk by using SYSGEN, answering with a (CR) to the question about source drive, and with either A or B to the question about destination drive.

Fig. 6-29 shows these steps being carried out for a Morrow 62K system. The trickiest step is 1(c), where we use the OFFSET for this system (3C00) to find the location in the TPA of the code we want to patch. In this example, the initialization code goes from location EF6D

FIG. 6-29 This dialogue shows the procedure for moving CP/M into the TPA, patching some of its code, and re-installing the modified CP/M back on the system tracks of a disk.

to EF71 in the live CP/M, but from 2B6D to 2B71 in the TPA clone CP/M. Once we know this, we can use the S command to modify the TPA code, changing the second byte of the MVI instruction from 80 to C0. The S command is then terminated by typing a period (.).

Step 2.   This step illustrates how the procedure of step 1 can be applied to modifying the code in a driver routine of the ISC BIOS. The original driver code was written for the paper tape punch (PTP:) physical device as follows:

```
FBDE 3E10      PTP     MVI     A, 10H     ;SET BAUD
FBE0 D305              OUT     5          ;RATE = 2400
FBE2 DB03      TXWT    IN      STATUS     ;CHECK STATUS OF THE
FBE4 E610              ANI     10H        ;XMIT BUFFER TXBUF
FBE6 CAE2FB            JZ      TXWT       ;LOOP IF NOT EMPTY
FBE9 79               MOV     A,C        ;EMPTY, SO SEND CHAR.
FBEA D306              OUT     TXBUF      ;IN C TO TXBUF
FBEC C9               RET
```

This driver sends characters out a serial RS-232 port (called TXBUF) at a baud rate of 2400. This baud rate is set on this machine by sending 10H to port 5. We decided to change the baud rate to 300. After some experimentation, we found that sending 04H to port 5 would set the baud rate to 300. We next plugged a 300 baud serial printer into this port. To use this as the LPT: device, one more change was needed. The original BIOS used an LPT: driver in a second bank of RAM. It accessed this bank by the instruction CALL PAGE0. The code was

```
FBCB      CD0B00     LPT     CALL     PAGE0
```

Without even worrying about what went on at PAGE0, we decided to change this instruction to the following:

```
FBCB      C3DEFB     LPT     JMP     PTP
```

Then whenever the LST: device was defined as LPT: (the normal default), CBIOS would jump to our modified PTP driver. Since this "talked" to port 6 at 300 baud, and that's where our printer was installed, all output sent by CP/M to the LST:=LPT: device would then show up on our printer.

The changes were made by patching the TPA clone of CP/M at two places as follows:

	Live CP/M Addr.	*Clone CP/M Addr.*	*8080 Hex Code*		*Mnemonic*	
Before Patch	FBCB	214B	CD0B00	LPT	CALL PAGE0	
After Patch	FBCB	214B	C3DEFB	LPT	JMP PTP	(3 bytes changed)

Before
Patch FBDE   215E   3E10   PTP   MVI   A,10H
After   (1 byte
Patch FBDE   215E   3E04   PTP   MVI   A,04H   changed)

The clone addresses were obtained by using the H command of DDT to add the ISC OFFSET (2580H) to the live addresses as shown in Fig. 6-30. This figure also shows the live addresses of the L command to double check on the code in memory, and use of the S command to

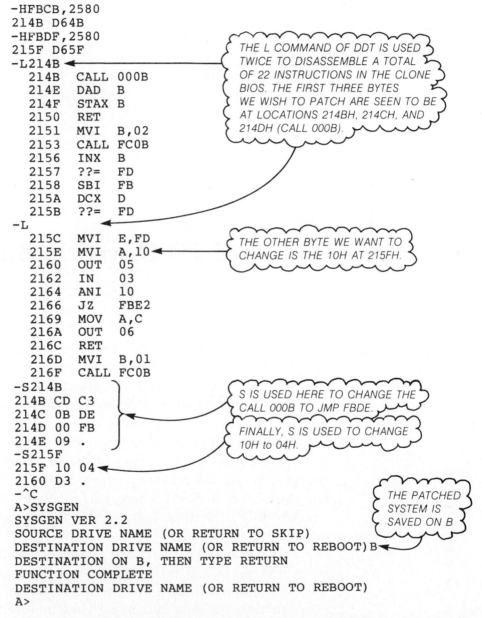

```
-HFBCB,2580
214B D64B
-HFBDF,2580
215F D65F
-L214B
   214B    CALL   000B
   214E    DAD    B
   214F    STAX   B
   2150    RET
   2151    MVI    B,02
   2153    CALL   FC0B
   2156    INX    B
   2157    ??=    FD
   2158    SBI    FB
   215A    DCX    D
   215B    ??=    FD
-L
   215C    MVI    E,FD
   215E    MVI    A,10
   2160    OUT    05
   2162    IN     03
   2164    ANI    10
   2166    JZ     FBE2
   2169    MOV    A,C
   216A    OUT    06
   216C    RET
   216D    MVI    B,01
   216F    CALL   FC0B
-S214B
214B CD C3
214C 0B DE
214D 00 FB
214E 09 .
-S215F
215F 10 04
2160 D3 .
-^C
A>SYSGEN
SYSGEN VER 2.2
SOURCE DRIVE NAME (OR RETURN TO SKIP)
DESTINATION DRIVE NAME (OR RETURN TO REBOOT)B
DESTINATION ON B, THEN TYPE RETURN
FUNCTION COMPLETE
DESTINATION DRIVE NAME (OR RETURN TO REBOOT)
A>
```

THE L COMMAND OF DDT IS USED TWICE TO DISASSEMBLE A TOTAL OF 22 INSTRUCTIONS IN THE CLONE BIOS. THE FIRST THREE BYTES WE WISH TO PATCH ARE SEEN TO BE AT LOCATIONS 214BH, 214CH, AND 214DH (CALL 000B).

THE OTHER BYTE WE WANT TO CHANGE IS THE 10H AT 215FH.

S IS USED HERE TO CHANGE THE CALL 000B TO JMP FBDE.

FINALLY, S IS USED TO CHANGE 10H to 04H.

THE PATCHED SYSTEM IS SAVED ON B

FIG. 6-30 This is part of the dialogue in which DDT is used to patch the CBIOS of the 64K CP/M system used on the ISC color computer. The patches were made so that the first RS-232 serial port on this machine could be connected to a serial printer operating at 300 baud. For higher baud rates, the XON/XOFF protocol described in Section 6.7 would have to be added to the driver.

change the code as needed. Note that in changing the CALL PAGE0 to JMP PTP, 3 bytes were modified with S as follows:

```
    -S214B
    214B        CD  C3      (change)
    214C        0B  DE      (change)
    214D        00  FB      (change)
    214E        09   .      (finished)
```

The change from MVI A,10H to MVI A,04H required patching only one byte at 215F

```
    -S215E
    215E        3E  (CR)    (no change)
    215F        10   04     (change)
    2160        D3   .      (finished)
```

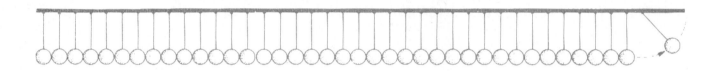

6.7 Adding Customized I/O Drivers to BIOS

This is it—welcome to the big leagues. For our final crash-defying act, we're going to show you how to try your hand at re-writing and re-installing that most fearsome of all beasts—system software. In particular, we'll look at a general method for attacking the problem of re-writing and/or adding new I/O driver programs to CBIOS.

Since such drivers must know about the hardware ports being used, we'll use examples that were developed and tested on specific computer systems. However, we will try to couch our explanations in terms that will make the ideas useful no matter what the machine be on which you do your CP/Ming. There will be no hope, of course, for those systems that do not provide a source listing of BIOS, and/or which do not store BIOS in RAM where you can work on it. (At present, the AppleSoft CP/M and the Osborne I CP/M fall into the first and second categories, respectively.)

To illustrate the general procedure for modifying CBIOS, our first lab will direct you in the installation of a printer driver that uses the XON/XOFF protocol. Let's first see what this is all about, and then show how the ideas translate into an 8080 assembly language driver program that can be added to CBIOS.

Handshaking Protocols for Printers

Computer I/O ports can send (and receive) data much faster than mechanical devices such as printers. To accommodate this incompatibility, the computer output must be slowed down so that the characters it sends to a printer don't get lost. There are several ways to do this, and which one you choose depends on the kind of computer/peripheral interface involved. In general, the procedure used for synchronizing communication between disparate devices is called a *protocol*. A protocol specifies how to exchange certain, "After you my dear Alphonse—No, after you my dear Gaston" type information. The exchange process itself is often called *handshaking*.

There are two kinds of interfaces used between computers and printers, called *parallel* and *serial*. On microcomputers, parallel interfaces usually send their data one byte at a time, with all eight bits leaving the computer simultaneously (in parallel) on eight separate wires. In addition, there is also a common ground wire (plus any additional wires needed for handshaking signals).

Serial interfaces send the individual bits of data in each byte sequentially, that is, one after the other. Thus they only need a single wire for sending data to an external serial device (plus of course a ground wire and any wires needed for handshaking signals). Similarly, a single wire is used for serial reception (from the printer), so a practical minimum serial cable has three wires: send, receive, and ground.

The simplest way to synchronize a serial printer with a serial interface on a computer is to set both devices at the slowest *baud rate* the printer can handle, in which case special handshaking (synchronizing) signals are not usually needed. For example, many printers will work OK without special synchronization at 300 baud, that is, with data signals showing up at the rate of 300 bits per second. How fast is this? Since serial transmission needs extra "start" and "stop" bits to mark the beginning and end of each byte, it takes ten bits to send a byte. One byte can represent one character, so a 300-baud connection can send up to 30 characters per second.

With such an arrangement, the computer serial output circuitry must also be slowed down to 300 baud. To allow higher baud rates, most serial printers include a small amount of RAM memory called a print *buffer*. This can accept characters at a higher rate (say 1200 baud) from the computer, passing the characters on to the printed mechanism at the highest rate it can accept them. Many daisy-wheel printers can print an *average* of about 45 characters per second under such an arrangement. The buffer "smooths" out the variations in timing required for different phases of the print cycle (e. g., printing versus carriage return), pumping characters to the print head at whatever rate it can accept them. Thus the buffer accepts characters at about 120 characters per second, and hands them out to the printer at an *average* of 45 per second.

Of course 120 is still higher than 45, so eventually the buffer will receive more characters from the computer than it can send to the printer, at which time there will be *buffer overflow*. The result of overflow will be lost characters.

To prevent this, when the buffer is almost full, the printer sends a signal back to the computer telling it to stop transmission. This is called the XOFF signal, and it is represented by control-S (ASCII code 13 hex = 19 decimal). Then when the buffer is empty (or almost empty) again, the printer sends the XON signal (control-Q = ASCII code 11 hex = 17 decimal) to the computer, meaning "start transmitting again." Thus these two signals keep things synchronized so that characters are never lost.

The XON/XOFF synchronization must be added to the CBIOS driver program that talks to your printer. Here's an example of a printer driver program *without* the XON/XOFF protocol. It uses port 1 to send signals out to the printer, and one of the bits in port 2 to determine the *status* of port 1. Status checking is necessary because while port 1 is "serializing" one byte of data for transmission (say at 1200 baud), the computer had better not ask port 1 to start work on serializing the next character. In other words, there are really two synchronization problems with serial transmission: an internal one at the computer I/O port, and an external one at the printer. The following driver program handles the internal synchronization problem only.

```
LPTDRVR  IN     2           ;GET OUTPUT STATUS FROM PORT 2
         ANI    80H         ;SEE IF HIGH ORDER BIT ON
         JZ     LPTDRVR     ;IT'S NOT, SO WAIT
         MOV    A,C,        ;IT'S ON, SO MOVE CHAR TO A
         OUT    1           ;SEND IT OUT PORT 1
         RET                ;WHICH IS CONNECTED TO PRINTER
```

This driver assumes that the character to be sent starts out in the C register, and that it is to be sent to the printer via port 1. It also assumes that the "ready for next character" status is signalled by the high order bit of port 2 being on, that is, that the pattern 1xxxxxxx appears in port 2. This will vary with systems, of course, so you'll have to modify the driver for the conventions used in your I/O interface circuitry.

An XON/XOFF Driver Program

The nice thing about the XON/XOFF protocol is that it doesn't require separate wires for handshaking. The synchronization signals are transmitted from the printer to the computer as control characters, arriving on the computer's "data input" line. The following ML subroutine is an extension of the previous driver that shows how such external synchronization using the XON/XOFF protocol is handled. It assumes that the control-S and control-Q (XON/XOFF) characters sent by the printer are *received* by the computer at port 1. In other words, port 1 is used by the computer for both data output and data input.

One small complication arises with the XON/XOFF protocol. To make sure none of the control characters received from the printer are lost, a second kind of internal synchronization is needed. This is a simple test to see whether a character has been received from the printer before even looking at it (it's like looking out your window to see if the "flag" is up on your mailbox before going for the mail). Our driver assumes that the "character received" signal for this system is bit 6 *on* in port 2, that is, that the pattern x1xxxxxx has appeared in port 2. Here's how all these ideas go together.

```
LPT        IN      2           ;CHECK STATUS PORT
           ANI     40H         ;CHARACTER RECEIVED?
           JZ      OUTPUT      ;NO, SO O.K. TO OUTPUT
           IN      1           ;YES, SO GET THE CHARACTER
           ANI     7FH         ;STRIP TO ASCII CODE
           CPI     13H         ;WAS XOFF RECEIVED?
           JNZ     OUTPUT      ;NO, SO O.K. TO OUTPUT
WAIT       IN      2           ;ELSE LOOK FOR NEXT CHARACTER
           ANI     40H         ;CHECK STATUS TO SEE IF CHAR. REC'D.
           JZ      WAIT        ;NO, SO WAIT
           IN      1           ;YES, GET IT
           ANI     7FH         ;STRIP TO ASCII
           CPI     11H         ;WAS IT XON?
           JNZ     WAIT        ;NO, KEEP WAITING
OUTPUT     IN      2           ;YES, O.K. TO PRINT
           ANI     80H         ;FIRST CHECK OUT STATUS
           JZ      LPT         ;NOT READY, START OVER
           MOV     A,C         ;FINALLY!
           OUT     1           ;SEND IT TO PRINTER
           RET
```

Adding the XON/XOFF Driver to CBIOS

To incorporate the preceding driver into your CBIOS, it will be necessary to do the following:

1. Use PIP to make a copy of your CBIOS.ASM file. Let's call this copy DBIOS.ASM. Then use ED to add the XON/XOFF driver to DBIOS.ASM.
2. Use ASM to assemble DBIOS.ASM, creating the file DBIOS.HEX.
3. Use SYSGEN together with DDT and SAVE to "add" DBIOS.HEX to CP/M, creating a new file (we'll call it DPM.COM) that contains a complete modified CP/M system.
4. Use SYSGEN and DDT to put DPM.COM on the system tracks of as many disks as you wish.

The details involved in each of these steps are spelled out in the next lab.

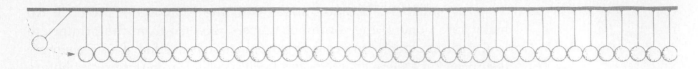

LAB EXERCISE 6.7-1

Adding New Driver Routines to CP/M

Step 1. (Optional) If you have a system where CP/M needs to be relocated to the top of whatever memory you have, do this first on a backup disk that contains MOVCPM and SYSGEN, following any instructions that came with your system. For example, to relocate and save the 24K CP/M that comes with the Morrow disk system for 62K of memory, you'd do the following:

> A>MOVCPM 62 *
> A>SYSGEN (answer <cr> for SOURCE, A for DESTINATION)
> A>SAVE 44 CPM62.COM

The system tracks of this disk now contain a 62K CP/M system, and a spare copy of the system has been saved for future use. We'll assume that 62K is the size being used in the rest of these steps. We'll also assume that the backup disk you're using for this lab contains PIP.COM, ASM.COM, SYSGEN.COM, CBIOS.ASM (or CBIOS#.ASM), and ED.COM.

Step 2. Make a spare copy of your present CBIOS.ASM file using PIP.

> A>PIP DBIOS.ASM = CBIOS.ASM

where CBIOS.ASM is the source file that came with your system. (On the Morrow CP/M disk system use A>PIP DBIOS.ASM = CBIOS#.ASM.)

Step 3. Use ED to insert the XON/XOFF driver into DBIOS.ASM at the place where your CBIOS expects to find a printer driver. This is usually at a label corresponding to the LPT: or UL1: devices. In the Morrow CBIOS the label for the LPT: driver is COLPT, whereas in the ISC CBIOS it's LPT. To deactivate the driver that's already there, but keep it on file for future reference, you can "comment it out." This means put a semicolon (;) or asterisk (*) in front of each of its lines so that ASM will treat the old code as comments. Fig. 6-31 shows part of a session with ED in which new code is added to DBIOS.ASM.

Before leaving ASM, also modify the MSIZE equate directive if necessary (this change will be needed only if you did step 1). For example, to change the Morrow 24K system CBIOS# to a 62K system version, you should change the line

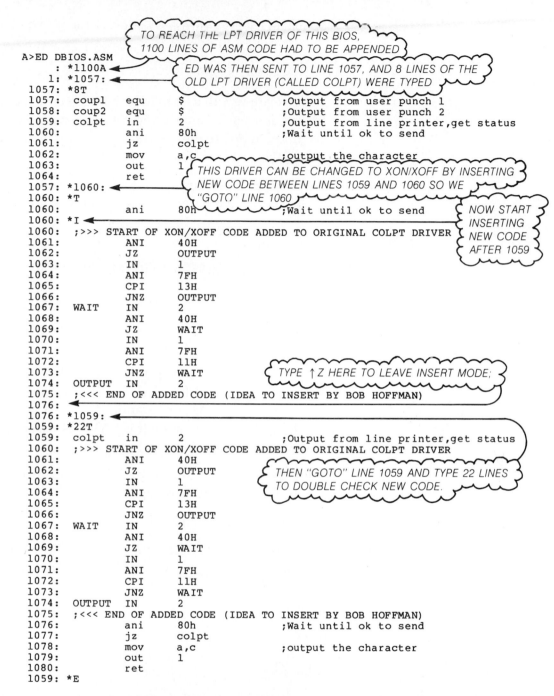

```
A>ED DBIOS.ASM
     : *1100A
   1: *1057:
1057: *8T
1057:   coupl   equ     $                       ;Output from user punch 1
1058:   coup2   equ     $                       ;Output from user punch 2
1059:   colpt   in      2                       ;Output from line printer,get status
1060:           ani     80h                     ;Wait until ok to send
1061:           jz      colpt
1062:           mov     a,c                     ;output the character
1063:           out     1
1064:           ret
1057: *1060:
1060: *T
1060:           ani     80h                     ;Wait until ok to send
1060: *I
1060:   ;>>> START OF XON/XOFF CODE ADDED TO ORIGINAL COLPT DRIVER
1061:           ANI     40H
1062:           JZ      OUTPUT
1063:           IN      1
1064:           ANI     7FH
1065:           CPI     13H
1066:           JNZ     OUTPUT
1067:   WAIT    IN      2
1068:           ANI     40H
1069:           JZ      WAIT
1070:           IN      1
1071:           ANI     7FH
1072:           CPI     11H
1073:           JNZ     WAIT
1074:   OUTPUT  IN      2
1075:   ;<<< END OF ADDED CODE (IDEA TO INSERT BY BOB HOFFMAN)
1076:
1076: *1059:
1059: *22T
1059:   colpt   in      2                       ;Output from line printer,get status
1060:   ;>>> START OF XON/XOFF CODE ADDED TO ORIGINAL COLPT DRIVER
1061:           ANI     40H
1062:           JZ      OUTPUT
1063:           IN      1
1064:           ANI     7FH
1065:           CPI     13H
1066:           JNZ     OUTPUT
1067:   WAIT    IN      2
1068:           ANI     40H
1069:           JZ      WAIT
1070:           IN      1
1071:           ANI     7FH
1072:           CPI     11H
1073:           JNZ     WAIT
1074:   OUTPUT  IN      2
1075:   ;<<< END OF ADDED CODE (IDEA TO INSERT BY BOB HOFFMAN)
1076:           ani     80h                     ;Wait until ok to send
1077:           jz      colpt
1078:           mov     a,c                     ;output the character
1079:           out     1
1080:           ret
1059: *E
```

FIG. 6-31   This is an example of the use of ED to modify DBIOS.ASM. The original LPT driver with label COLPT has been extended by inserting the extra code needed for the XON/XOFF protocol just above line 1060.

                MSIZE   EQU   24

        to

                MSIZE   EQU   62

If your system doesn't use an MSIZE equate, you may have to change the ORG directive (which is rather unusual).

Step 4. Leave ED with control-z followed by E. Then assemble your new CBIOS with

A>ASM DBIOS

If errors are reported, it may be because the original CBIOS.ASM source file used some directives not understood by ASM. A technical note in the preceding section explains what to do about this.

Step 5. Now bring your current CP/M from the system tracks into the TPA, and save a copy of it as a COM file as follows:

A>SYSGEN

. . . .

SOURCE DRIVE NAME (OR RETURN TO SKIP) A

. . . .

DESTINATION DRIVE NAME (OR RETURN TO REBOOT)
    <cr>
A>SAVE nn CPM62.COM

The number nn says how many pages are needed to save the TPA image of CP/M (cf., Lab 6.4-3). The value of nn is usually 44 for Morrow or 34 for "standard" CP/M systems. (Note that you may have *already* done this SAVE as part of step 1, in which case step 5 can be omitted.)

Step 6. Bring DDT into the top of the TPA, and put CPM62.COM into the bottom. You do this with

A>DDT CPM62.COM

Step 7. Now overlay the CBIOS part of CPM62.COM with the DBIOS.HEX file you created in step 4 as follows (you're still in DDT).
    -IDBIOS.HEX
    -Rxxxx

where xxxx is the hex value of OFFSET for your system as explained in Section 6.6. For a 62K Morrow system, xxxx = 3C00; for an ISC 64K system xxxx = 2580.

Step 8. Type control-C to return to the system, and then use SYSGEN to put the modified CP/M on the system tracks of a disk. Also use SAVE to keep a copy of the modified system on file. You do this as follows:

A>SYSGEN

. . . .

SOURCE DRIVE NAME (OR RETURN TO SKIP) <cr>

. . . .

DESTINATION DRIVE (OR RETURN TO REBOOT) A (or
    B if you wish)

. . . .

DESTINATION ON A, THEN TYPE RETURN <cr>

. . . .

DESTINATION DRIVE (OR RETURN TO REBOOT) <cr>

A>SAVE nn NEWCPM.COM

Warning: If very much code has been added to CBIOS, the value of nn will have to be increased by 1 for each 256 bytes added (cf., Lab 6.4-3).

Step 9.   Test your new disk by making sure it's in drive A, and doing a cold boot. If it boots, O.K., try using it with your printer, making sure that all the connections and baud rate settings are correct. Also make sure that your IOBYTE assigns LST: to the correct physical device, that is, the device name that labels your new driver (use STAT DEV: to find out). In our example, we assumed that the IOBYTE assigned LPT: as the LST: (listing) device, so we put our new driver in CBIOS under the label LPT (or COLPT). We could just as well have put the driver under the UL1:, TTY:, or CRT: labels, but then the IOBYTE assignment would have to be changed accordingly.

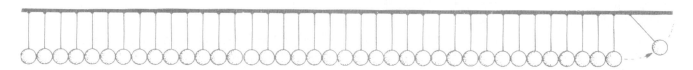

Instant Quiz

1. What's the simplest way additional disks with the new system can be made?
2. What's a second way of putting the new system on disks?
3. How about a third method? A fourth?

Answers

1. Assuming the new system is on the disk in drive A, and a formatted disk is in drive B, use SYSGEN. Answer A for SOURCE DRIVE NAME, and B for DESTINATION DRIVE.
2. Assuming you saved the new system as the file NEWCPM.COM, first use DDT to load it into the TPA.

    A>DDT NEWCPM.COM

    . . . .

    ^C

    A>

    Then use SYSGEN, answering <cr> for SOURCE DRIVE NAME, and answering with the name of the drive where you want the new system copied for DESTINATION DRIVE.

3. There's an undocumented feature of SYSGEN that allows you to do both parts of step 2 at once. All you do is type

    A>SYSGEN NEWCPM.COM

    SYSGEN will *not* ask you for SOURCE DRIVE NAME this time—just for DESTINATION DRIVE. By putting freshly formatted disks in drive B, you can make as many copies of the NEWCPM system as you wish by answering B for each new disk you insert. A fourth approach is to use the "system tracks only" option of certain COPY programs.

Adding UART Initialization Code to CBIOS

As we saw in the previous lab, the I/O drivers you add to CBIOS must make specific reference to the INPUT data port, OUTPUT data port, and any status ports being used. In practice, these ports usually correspond to registers in the circuitry of the UART (Universal Asynchronous Receive and Transmit) chips used for RS-232 serial interfaces.

Modern UART chips are very sophisticated devices, and in addition to data and status registers, they contain registers for setting baud rates, enabling interrupts, and detecting the presence of additional handshaking signals. Moreover, these registers can be "set" and "reset" by software. In both ML and BASIC the setting can be done with an OUT instruction. Thus by sending a sequence of OUT instructions to the proper port numbers, you can reconfigure the UART without ever touching the hardware.

Before using such a programmable UART in a driver, it needs to be initialized. The best place to put the software that gives a UART the commands specifying its initial state (e. g., baud rate), is in the initialization section of CBIOS. This section is usually a set of subroutines that are called by the cold boot code of CBIOS, so resetting a system with a cold boot will automatically reset the UART.

Programming the 8250 ACE I/O Chip

An example of a programmable UART that has become quite popular is the National Semiconductor 8250 which is sometimes called the ACE (Asynchronous Communications Element). The ACE (and most other UARTs used with 8080/Z80 systems) receives and sends its data/commands by way of the special I/O ports available to the 8080/Z80 microprocessor. There are 256 of these ports, and they have addresses 0 through 255 which are completely separate from the 65,536 addresses used for memory.

To perform all of its functions, the ACE has ten programmable registers. However it takes only seven ports to control these registers. The ports are assigned to consecutive addresses starting at any of the following I/O addresses: 00H, 08H, 10H, 18H, . . . , F0H, F8H. Thus there could be up to 32 ACE UARTS on an 8080/Z80 system. You usually specify which of these starting addresses you want by setting switches on the I/O board that contains the ACE. For our examples below, we'll assume these switches have been set for a starting address of F0 hex (which is 240 decimal). Thus we'll be using the seven ports from F0 to F6 for the following register functions:

Address in hex:	Function(s) of Register:
F0	(a) Receiver Buffer Register (data in) or Transmitter Holding Register (data out).
	(b) Least Significant Byte of Baud Rate Divisor.
F1	(a) Interrupt Enable Register.
	(b) Most Significant Byte of Baud Rate Divisor.
F2	Interrupt Identification Register.
F3	Line Control Register.
F4	Modem Control Register.
F5	Line Status Register.
F6	Modem Status Register.

(*Note:*   The address 0F7 is not used; the next address at which the ports for another ACE could be assigned is 0F8.)

The letters (a) and (b) used in the first two functions indicate that the registers at these addresses can do double duty. They will function in the (a) mode if the seventh bit of port 0F3 is off (=0). They'll function in the (b) mode if this bit is on (=1). This bit is called the "Divisor Latch Bit" since the (b) mode is the one in which the contents of the corresponding registers act as baud rate divisors.

A baud rate divisor is a number that determines the baud rate used by the ACE. It is given by four hex digits. The first two give the most significant byte (MSB), while the last two give the least significant byte (LSB) of the divisor. For example,

    For 300 baud, the divisor = 0180.
    For 1200 baud, the divisor = 0060.
    For 4800 baud, the divisor = 0018.
    For 9600 baud, the divisor = 000C.

For 9600 baud the MSB of the divisor is 00, while the LSB is 0C.

We won't discuss use of the interrupt enable or interrupt identification registers. For your information, the individual bits of these registers are used as follows:

	Interrupt Enable Register	Identification Register
Bit 0	Data in Receive Register	Interrupt Pending
Bit 1	Transmit Register Empty	ID Code Bit 1
Bit 2	Receiver Line Status	ID Code Bit 0
Bit 3	Modem Status	Always = 0

The ID codes are 00 = change in RTS, DTR, TXD, or DRS, 01 = Transmit register empty, 10 = Data in Rcvr Buf, 11 = Error condition in line status register.

The Line Status register uses its first seven bits to mean the following for bit ON (=1):

Bit 0   Data available in receiver buffer.
Bit 1   Overrun error.
Bit 2   Parity error.
Bit 3   Framing error.
Bit 4   Break interrupt.
Bit 5   Transmitter holding register empty.
Bit 6   Transmitter shift register idle.

The modem control registers use bit ON as follows:

Bit 0   DSR (data set ready).
Bit 1   CTS (clear to send).
Bit 2   RLSD (received line signal detect).
Bit 3   SQD (signal quality detect).
Bit 4   Loopback of data ON.

The modem status register tests bits in register F6 as follows:

Bit 0   Delta RTS (change in ready to send).
Bit 1   Delta DTR (change in data terminal ready).
Bit 2   Autobaud Edge (change in received data).
Bit 3   Delta DRS (change in data rate select).
Bit 4   RTS (RTS is on).
Bit 5   DTR (DTR is on).
Bit 6   Autobaud (data received).
Bit 7   DRS (state of DRS line).

The Line Control Register uses its bits as follows:

Bit 0   Word length, first bit.
Bit 1   Word length, second bit.
Bit 2   Stop bit select.
Bit 3   Parity enable.
Bit 4   Even parity select.
Bit 5   Stick parity (freezes parity bit).
Bit 6   Set break.
Bit 7   Divisor latch bit (selects (a) or (b)).

Word length codes are 00 = 5 bits, 01 = 6 bits, 10 = 7 bits, 11 = 8 bits. Stop bit codes are 0 = 1 bit, 1 = 2 bits.

Of course most of these terms will be pretty cryptic unless you've done work with I/O communications and interfacing before. Reference [27] contains lots of information on this subject.

Here's an example of an ML subroutine that initializes an ACE addressed at 0F0H to 9600 baud for 8 bit words, 1 stop bit, and no parity.

```
ACEINIT MVI    A,0FH    ;SEND 00001111 TO
        OUT    0F4H     ;MODEM CONTROL REGISTER
        MVI    A,83H    ;SEND 10000011 TO
```

```
        OUT   0F3H   ;LINE CONTROL TO SET LATCH
        MVI   A,00H   ;SEND 00000000 TO
        OUT   0F1H   ;BAUD DIVISOR MSB
        MVI   A,0CH   ;SEND 00001100 TO
        OUT   0F0H   ;BAUD DIVISOR LSB
        MVI   A,3     ;SEND 00000011 TO
        OUT   0F3H   ;SET WORD LENGTH, RESET LATCH
        MVI   A,0     ;SEND 00000000 TO
        OUT   0F1H   ;DISABLE ALL INTERRUPTS
        RET
```

To use this subroutine, it must be added to CBIOS.ASM at any convenient place. Then the instruction CALL ACEINIT must be added to the cold boot part of CBIOS so that the initialization takes place every time the system is cold booted.

A Driver for the Serial MX-80 Printer

Many printers do not support the XON/XOFF protocol described at the beginning of this section. The circuitry needed to send characters like ^S and ^Q from the printer is expensive. Instead, a single bit control signal is used to mean, "OK to print." The protocol is a simple one: When this bit is on, the computer should send data to the printer; when it is off, the computer should stop sending data.

The Epson MX-80 printer uses this protocol with the control bit sent on the RS-232 line called DTR (data terminal ready). Here's a driver for the ACE that tests the DTR line (bit 5 of the modem status register) to see if the printer is ready. It also checks bit 5 of the line status register to see if the transmitter holding register is empty.

```
COUL1   IN    0F6H    ;GET MODEM STATUS
        ANI   20H     ;IS DTR SET?
        JZ    COUL1   ;NO, LOOP HERE
        IN    0F5H    ;YES, GET LINE STATUS
        ANI   20H     ;XMIT HOLDING REGISTER EMPTY?
        JZ    COUL1   ;NO, LOOP SOME MORE
        MOV   A,C     ;YES, GET CHARACTER
        OUT   0F0H    ;SEND IT TO ACE AT 0F0
        RET
```

This routine was written by Bob Hoffman for use in the microcomputer lab at the University of Pittsburgh. You can see that it was decided to install the driver at the label COUL1 (which may be called UL1 in your CBIOS). Thus the Epson printer (which is connected to ACE data output port 0F0H) will become the LST: device if you initialize the first two bits of the IOBYTE to 11, or if you use

A>STAT LST:=UL1

The MX-80 driver would of course have to be added to CBIOS along with the routine ACEINIT, using the techniques explained in Lab 6.7-1.

If all of the drivers as well as the initialization code described in this section are desired, the changes could all be made at once.

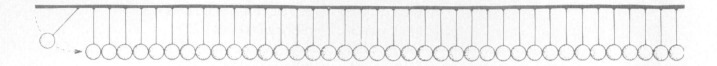

LAB EXERCISE   Making Multiple Changes in CBIOS
6.7-2

Step 1. Reread this section, decide on all the changes you wish to make to CBIOS, and lay out your plan of attack on paper.

Step 2. Gather up all the needed tools, plans, and disks, and follow the general outline of Lab 6.7-1.

Step 3. Go to it. If you've gotten this far, you don't need any more instructions. Have fun.

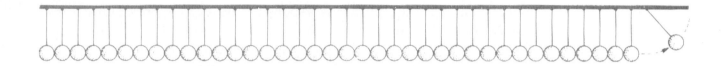

6.8 Other Operating Systems: CP/M Plus, CP/M-86, MP/M, IBM PC-DOS, and UNIX

The operating system discussed in this book is sometimes referred to as CP/M-80 since it runs on the 8080, Z80 and 8085 microprocessors. From a technical point of view, CP/M-80 can be described as a single-user, single-task disk operating system. This means that it is controlled by a single user-console, and that it normally executes only one program (task) at a time. Application software can create multi-tasking (e. g., the "print spooler" in WordStar which prints one file while a second is being edited), but this is independent of CP/M.

For most users of personal computers, the single-user, single-task restrictions are of no consequence. Personal computers work just fine with one console, and where multi-tasking is desired, it can be built into the application program. As a result, there are probably more people using CP/M-80 worldwide than any other operating system in the history of computing.

The most recent versions of CP/M-80 are called versions 2.2 and 3.0. Version 3.0 is also called CP/M Plus. It is "upward compatible" from version 2.2, which means that it has about the same features as 2.2, but with a few extras thrown in. For most current users of CP/M, the extras won't be useable since they require special hardware that allows use of larger amounts of RAM memory. Other differences between versions 3.0 and 2.2 have to do with internal changes that are not visible to the user (e. g., use of "hashing" to locate directory entries).

Version 3.0 actually comes in two sub-versions called "banked" and "non-banked." The banked version allows use of several 64K *banks* of memory (a minimum of 1.5 banks is required). The non-banked version works with the single bank of 64K RAM found in most systems using version 2.2. However, it uses up over 12K of this 64K for CP/M, so it may cause problems with some application programs. Additional information about CP/M Plus can be found in a series of articles that began in the February 1983 issue of *Microsystems* [11].

A new single-user, single-task operating system called CP/M-86 was introduced by Digital Research in 1981. It is quite similar to CP/M-80, but it is written in 8086 machine language (which is the same as 8088 machine language). Both the 8086 and 8088 are 16-bit microprocessors, so some of the utility programs supplied with CP/M-86 (e. g., ASM-86) have been rewritten to allow ML programmers to use the 16-bit instruction set for these new chips. One of the distinctive features of 8086/8088 ML code is that it is relocatable. As a result, the procedure for adding a modified CBIOS to CP/M-86 is much simpler than the procedure required for CP/M-80 as discussed in Sections 6.6 and 6.7. One of the disadvantages of CP/M-86 is that there won't be true 8086/8088 application software available on the same scale as 8080/Z80 software for a number of years. Some of the older 8080 software has been "emulated" for CP/M-86, but it actually runs slower than the original version. This is because the emulation process is a "quick and dirty" translation that ignores the true power of the 16-bit microprocessor chips. Most of this emulated software offers no advantages to the end user. Our advice here is to hold out for true 8086 "native code" systems and application software.

On the positive side, the designers of CP/M-86 have been careful to make CP/M-80 and CP/M-86 files completely compatible. Thus a good solution for those users who don't want to wait, and wish to explore both the 8-bit and 16-bit worlds, is to obtain a computer containing microprocessors that can run either system. A good example of such a machine is the G & G Godbout CompuPro dual-processor system (for further information see the caption for the photograph of this system in the color section of this book). The CompuPro uses a CPU board which contains both the 8085 and 8088 microprocessors. Both CP/M-80 and CP/M-86 are supplied with the system, so users can have the best of both worlds, exchanging files between systems where desired. The Zenith Z100 and DEC "Rainbow" personal computers also use this approach.

Another 16-bit microprocessor chip being used in recent microcomputers is the Motorola MC68000. Digital Research has announced that it will offer a version of CP/M for this chip called CP/M-68K. Other vendors have announced that they will be developing microcomputer versions of an operating system called UNIX for the MC68000. UNIX was originally developed at Bell Laboratories for use on the PDP-11 series of computers. It is a time-sharing system that supports multiple users and multiple tasks. For more information on UNIX, references [25] and [26] can be consulted.

A multi-user version of CP/M called MP/M II is also available from Digital Research. With MP/M, several users sitting at different consoles can access the same computer, and each user can run a different task. There's still only one microprocessor, but its use is shared by means of an *interrupt* scheme. When it's time for one user to take over, an interrupt signal is sent to the CPU, telling it to switch to the new task, suspending all other programs. Two other well-regarded multi-tasking systems are called OASIS [38] and TURBODOS [39], and users interested in such applications would do well to investigate these systems. A review of OASIS appeared in the March 1982 issue of *Microsystems* [11]. A review of TURBODOS appeared in the May 1982 issue of *Lifelines* [8]. As pointed out there, TURBODOS is more than a multi-task system; it is actually a *multi-processor* system, that is, it can manage a network of computers. Since each task can have its own CPU, the power of the overall system is potentially great.

Another version of CP/M called Concurrent CP/M-86 has been announced. Most computer scientists would insist that *concurrent* mean *synchronized* in terms of both program control and data interchange. The idea of Concurrent CP/M is simpler: it allows one user to run several tasks, but the synchronization does not concern itself with the sharing of data between tasks. For example, one user could "simultaneously" enter information into dBASE II, print a WordStar file, and receive electronic mail over a communications system, provided these were independent tasks.

The idea of communicating between computers is a relatively new one. It requires additional system software "on top of" the individual operating systems used by the communicating computers. Digital Research offers such a product called CP/NET. With this or similar network systems, there can be multiple computers, but these won't necessarily be doing cooperative work. Unless other software is added, the processing done in such networks remains essentially unsynchronized. There sometimes *is* a form of interplay between the separate CPUs using such networks by way of access to common data bases. However, even here there are lots of problems to be solved in preserving data integrity. Networking is an exciting area, but it is still in its infancy.

To make life even more complicated, some manufacturers have introduced operating systems unique to their hardware. For example, the IBM Personal Computer uses IBM PC-DOS (also called MSDOS) which has been described as a "CP/M look-alike". As users of the first version (1.0) found out, PC-DOS had some problems; many of these were straightened out with later versions, but the lesson of sticking with software that has had sufficient time to "mature" is a good one to remember. A comparative review of PC-DOS versus CP/M-86 appeared in the November 1982 issue of *Dr. Dobbs Journal* [7].

The future of operating systems is obviously an intriguing one, and the investigation of new products will always be a fun thing to try. Just don't forget that most releases about new operating systems come from PR departments, and that instead of "public relations" the initials PR can mean "promised, not reality" more often than not. In the meantime, if you're using an "ancient" CP/M-80 system, relax, learn, and above all, enjoy. You've got yourself a real classic.

6.9 Problems and Projects

1. Study references [5] and [6], and then write ML subroutines to add and subtract 16-bit numbers.
2. Repeat problem 1 for multiplication and division, allowing 32-bit numbers for products and dividends.
3. Use the results of problem 1 to write an 8080 ML program that accepts two numbers in "string" form as input, converts them to 16-bit binary numbers, and stores them in successive words (two-byte pairs) of memory. The program should then print the sum and difference of these numbers, along with a message to indicate whether overflow occurred.
4. Use the results of problem 2 to modify problem 3 to handle multiplication, but permit products that occupy up to 4 bytes (32 bits) before overflow occurs.
5. Repeat Lab 6.2-2 using the Shell sort Algorithm (instead of Bubble sort). Shell sort is discussed in [1], and use of the algorithm was illustrated in Sections 5.5 and 5.7. When you have this working to sort characters, see if you can extend it to sort 16-bit integers.
6. Using the program datasys.c from section 5.7 as a guide, write an 8080 ML program to (a) input data strings and save them in a string array, (b) retrieve these strings and display them on the console.
7. Using the BDOS file functions wherever possible, extend project 6 to save the string array as a disk file. Also add a feature that reloads this file into the array when the program is run at a later time.
8. Write an ML program that does a Shell sort of data stored as successive elements in a string array. Do not swap the strings when they are out of order, but swap the pointers to the strings. For an example showing how this is done in BASIC, see the program INSERT2 in reference [4].
9. See if you can write a screen-oriented data entry module in ML. The idea is to allow the user to move the cursor of the console to any position on the screen, and then enter text starting at that position. A useful extension to this program would be one that allowed the user to "capture" the screen image as a file for later playback. One approach to solving this problem is to maintain a complete byte-by-byte image of the screen in memory, and save this. Another approach is to save a pair of screen coordinates at the beginning (or end) of

each string. In any case, it's a challenging problem, one that will make you better appreciate the software discussed in Chapter 4.

10. Consider writing an elementary word processor in ML. Some ideas that can be used are found in the program EDIT1000 of reference [2]. This is a tough project, so it would be best to break it up into a number of subprojects. (For example, project 9 above would make a good submodule.)

11. Research the subject of modems available for microcomputer systems, and develop a modem driver program that could be incorporated into CBIOS for use with a modem of your choice. Compare your efforts with the driver software that is supplied with some of the more popular modems. What were the differences and why? Who knows—your product might turn out to be the more sophisticated one.

12. Repeat Lab 6.3-2 using the Shell sort algorithm for the ML part of the program. Then extend the program to one that sorts records, using any field in the record as sorting key. (This project will help you to appreciate the CP/M SuperSort program discussed in Section 4.3.)

APPENDIX A
The ASCII Codes

Binary Form	Key (and Meaning)	Hex Form	Decimal Form	Binary Form	Key (and Meaning)	Hex Form	Decimal Form
00000000	^@ (NULL)	0	0	00100000	\<space\>	20	32
00000001	^A (SOH)	1	1	00100001	!	21	33
00000010	^B (STX)	2	2	00100010	''	22	34
00000011	^C (ETX)	3	3	00100011	#	23	35
00000100	^D (EOT)	4	4	00100100	$	24	36
00000101	^E (ENQ)	5	5	00100101	%	25	37
00000110	^F (ACK)	6	6	00100110	&	26	38
00000111	^G (BELL)	7	7	00100111	' (quote)	27	39
00001000	^H (BS)	8	8	00101000	(	28	40
00001001	^I (HT)	9	9	00101001	)	29	41
00001010	^J (LF)	A	10	00101010	*	2A	42
00001011	^K (VT)	B	11	00101011	+	2B	43
00001100	^L (FF)	C	12	00101100	, (comma)	2C	44
00001101	^M (CR)	D	13	00101101	- (hyphen)	2D	45
00001110	^N (SO)	E	14	00101110	.	2E	46
00001111	^O (SI)	F	15	00101111	/	2F	47
00010000	^P (DLE)	10	16	00110000	0	30	48
00010001	^Q (DC1)	11	17	00110001	1	31	49
00010010	^R (DC2)	12	18	00110010	2	32	50
00010011	^S (DC3)	13	19	00110011	3	33	51
00010100	^T (DC4)	14	20	00110100	4	34	52
00010101	^U (NAK)	15	21	00110101	5	35	53
00010110	^V (SYN)	16	22	00110110	6	36	54
00010111	^W (ETB)	17	23	00110111	7	37	55
00011000	^X (CAN)	18	24	00111000	8	38	56
00011001	^Y (EM)	19	25	00111001	9	39	57
00011010	^Z (SUB)	1A	26	00111010	:	3A	58
00011011	^[(ESC)	1B	27	00111011	;	3B	59
00011100	^\ (FS)	1C	28	00111100	<	3C	60
00011101	^] (GS)	1D	29	00111101	=	3D	61
00011110	^^ (RS)	1E	30	00111110	>	3E	62
00011111	^_ (US)	1F	31	00111111	?	3F	63

Control Codes   The codes from decimal 0 to decimal 31 are non-printing and are used for special purposes. The meanings shown in parentheses date from the original ASCII definitions for communications work (e. g., ETX means End of Text). Some of these meanings still hold for microcomputers. For example, codes 7 to 13 decimal still mean "ring bell or beeper," backspace, horizontal tab, line feed, vertical tab, form feed, and carriage return on most systems. Codes 0 and 27 also mean null and escape, but the meaning of the other codes depends on the

Binary Form	Key (and Meaning)	Hex Form	Decimal Form	Binary Form	Key (and Meaning)	Hex Form	Decimal Form
01000000	@	40	64	01100000		60	96
01000001	A	41	65	01100001	a	61	97
01000010	B	42	66	01100010	b	62	98
01000011	C	43	67	01100011	c	63	99
01000100	D	44	68	01100100	d	64	100
01000101	E	45	69	01100101	e	65	101
01000110	F	46	70	01100110	f	66	102
01000111	G	47	71	01100111	g	67	103
01001000	H	48	72	01101000	h	68	104
01001001	I	49	73	01101001	i	69	105
01001010	J	4A	74	01101010	j	6A	106
01001011	K	4B	75	01101011	k	6B	107
01001100	L	4C	76	01101100	l	6C	108
01001101	M	4D	77	01101101	m	6D	109
01001110	N	4E	78	01101110	n	6E	110
01001111	O	4F	79	01101111	o	6F	111
01010000	P	50	80	01110000	p	70	112
01010001	Q	51	81	01110001	q	71	113
01010010	R	52	82	01110010	r	72	114
01010011	S	53	83	01110011	s	73	115
01010100	T	54	84	01110100	t	74	116
01010101	U	55	85	01110101	u	75	117
01010110	V	56	86	01110110	v	76	118
01010111	W	57	87	01110111	w	77	119
01011000	X	58	88	01111000	x	78	120
01011001	Y	59	89	01111001	y	79	121
01011010	Z	5A	90	01111010	z	7A	122
01011011	[	5B	91	01111011	{	7B	123
01011100	\	5C	92	01111100	|	7C	124
01011101	]	5D	93	01111101	}	7D	125
01011110	^ (up arrow)	5E	94	01111110	~	7E	126
01011111	_ (undrln.)	5F	95	01111111	<delete>	7F	127

application. Examples of special CP/M control code definitions are given in Section 3.3; MBASIC definitions are listed in Appendix B, while some word processor definitions are given in Section 4.1.

Control codes can be sent to the computer in several ways. From the keyboard, you hold down the control key and press the character key indicated. (If you check the ASCII codes for these characters you will notice that they are 01000000 binary higher than the corresponding control codes, that is, the control key subtracts 01000000 from the character code.) When using BASIC-80, you use the CHR$(x) function, where the expression x represents the *decimal* form of the code you wish to send. For example, to have a program ring the bell, a statement like 10 PRINT CHR$(7) would be used in BASIC. In C, you could use putchar(7), while in machine language the code is MVI C,2   MVI E,7   CALL 5.

APPENDIX B
Summary of Microsoft Disk-Extended BASIC (BASIC-80)

Note: This summary is for the interpreted versions of disk-extended BASIC-80 called MBASIC 5.0, 5.1 and 5.3. The same features are acceptable to BASCOM (the Microsoft BASIC compiler) except as follows: AUTO, CLEAR, CLOAD, CSAVE, CONT, DELETE, EDIT, NEW, LIST, LLIST, RENUM, SAVE, LOAD, MERGE, and COMMON. Do *not* use any of these keywords if you expect to later use BASCOM, and use CALL instead of the USR function.

General Information

Character Set

BASIC-80 recognizes the printing ASCII character set and some of the ASCII control characters. The following keys are assigned special meanings (^A means type <control> simultaneously with A):

<rubout>	deletes the last character typed.
<escape>	(see Edit Mode).
<tab>	moves print position to next tab stop (8 column stops).
<line feed>	moves to next physical line (see Line Format).
<cr>	terminates the input of a line.
^A	enters edit mode on the line being typed.
^C	stops execution of a program, returns to command level.
^G	rings the bell at the terminal.
^H	backspace; deletes the last character typed.
^I	tabs (tab stops are every 8 columns).
^O	halts output of a program while execution continues.
^R	retypes the line currently being typed.
^S	suspends program execution.
^Q	resumes program execution after ^S.
^U	deletes the line currently being typed.

Constants

String Constants. Up to 255 alphanumeric characters enclosed in double quotations, e.g., "249 Nowhere St."

Integer Constants. Whole numbers between −32768 and +32767.

Fixed Point Constants. Positive or negative real numbers, e.g., −.5.

Floating Point Constants. Positive or negative real numbers in exponential form:

Single precision (7 digits of precision):
235.988E-7 (= .0000235988)
2359E6 (= 2359000000)

Double precision (16 digits of precision):
    3.141592653589794D3 = 3141.592653589794

Hexadecimal Constants.   Hexadecimal numbers are written with the prefix &H, e.g., &H32F.

Octal Constants.   Octal numbers are written with the prefix &O or &, e.g., &O347, &234.

Note: You may indicate single-precision by using 7 or less digits, using E for exponential notation, or including a trailing (!). You may indicate double-precision by using 8 or more digits, using D for exponential notation, or including a trailing (#).

Initializing BASIC

The procedure for starting BASIC-80 differs with each implementation. Consult the manual for your system. The following is the procedure used under the CP/M operating system. The system prompt is A>, all lines are followed by <cr>. You may type, for example:

1. A>MBASIC
2. A>MBASIC /F:n
3. A>MBASIC /M:m
4. A>MBASIC filename
5. A>MBASIC filename.ext
6. A>MBASIC filename/F:n/M:m

Explanation: 1 starts BASIC-80 executing; 2 also reserves memory for n files to be opened (default is 3); 3 reserves memory locations above m, otherwise BASIC may fill all available non-system memory; 4 causes BASIC to load and run the named file with the extension .BAS.

Note: Return from BASIC to CP/M is via the SYSTEM command.

Line Format

BASIC-80 program lines have the following forms:

    nnnnn BASIC statement<cr>
    nnnnn BASIC statement:BASIC statement: . . . etc. . . . <cr>

where nnnnn is a line number in the range 0 to 65529. Lines may contain a maximum of 255 characters and more than one physical line may be used by pressing <line feed> to continue the line. <carriage return> terminates the line.

Modes of Operation

Direct Mode.   BASIC-80 statements not preceded by a line number will be executed immediately after they are entered, after <cr> is pressed.

Indirect Mode.   BASIC-80 statements preceded by a line number are stored for later execution using the RUN command.

Edit Mode.   Indirect mode statements may be modified with the BASIC-80 line-oriented editor. See the command EDIT.

Operators

The following are listed in the order they will be performed. (Those with equal precedence are performed left to right.)

    ^   exponentiation
    −   negation

*, /	multiplication, division (floating point)
\	integer division
MOD	modulus arithmetic (remainder)
+, −	addition, subtraction
=	equality, assignment (see LET)
<>	inequality
<	less than
>	greater than
<=	less than or equal to
>=	greater than or equal to
NOT	negation
AND	conjunction
OR	disjunction
XOR	exclusive or
IMP	implication
EQV	equivalence

String Operations. Strings are compared using the relational operators =, <>, <, >, <=, >=. The ASCII sequence of codes is used to determine the ordering of strings on a character-by-character basis. The + operator is used to concatenate strings. Parentheses () can be used to change the order in which operations are performed, e.g.,

$$X + Y/Z \quad \text{means} \quad x + \frac{y}{z}, \quad \text{while} \quad (X + Y)/Z \quad \text{means} \quad \frac{x + y}{z}.$$

Note: In case of division by zero or overflow, an error message is printed and execution continues using "machine infinity" for the expression.

Variables

Names may be any length; 40 characters are significant; letters, numbers, and the period (.) are acceptable. The first character *must* be a letter, the last character may be a type declaration character. The variable name may not be a reserved word of BASIC-80, but may contain one. String variable names must be written with $ as the last character unless previously declared (see DEFSTR), numeric variables are assumed to be single-precision real numbers unless declared otherwise (see DEFINT, DEFDBL, DEFSNG). *Note:* Upper- and lowercase are treated the same in BASIC-80 except for string constants and filenames, i.e., TOT and tot become the same variable name, PROG1 and prog1 are different filenames.

Types

N$, CURRENT.WORD$	string variables
X1,Y1,TOTAL	single-precision values
MINIMUM!	single-precision value
COUNTER%	integer value
PI#	double-precision value

Arrays

PRICE(I) means the ith element of an array. SALES(I,J) means the element in the ith row and jth column of a two-dimensional array (or matrix).

Arrays of over 10 elements (11 if you count the zeroth element) per dimension must be dimensioned before use (see DIM). String arrays work similarly to numeric, i.e., each element of a string array is a string, which may be up to 255 characters long. The maximum number of dimensions is 255. The maximum number of elements per dimension is 32767.

BASIC-80 Commands, Keywords, and Functions

Note: Most of these can be used both in immediate mode and as part of a program. Conventions used below are: Uppercase means 'required', lowercase means 'you supply'; v, v1 are numeric variable names; v$, v1$ are string variable names; n, m are numeric constants; x, y are numeric expressions; x$, y$ are string expressions; i, j are integer expressions; exp, exp1 are numeric or string expressions; f is a file number; d is a dummy argument. Functions are shown as part of an assignment statement. However, functions may be used anywhere that the variable to which they are shown assigned (v, v%, v#, v!) could be used.

v = ABS(x)

Returns the absolute value of x.

```
10 A = 10: B = 25: DIFF = ABS(A − B): PRINT DIFF
RUN
 15
```

v = ASC(x$)

Returns the ASCII Code (in decimal) of the first character of x$. (See Appendix A for ASCII Codes.)

```
100 A$ = "BEAR": A = ASC(A$): PRINT A$,A
RUN
BEAR              66
```

v = ATN(x)

Returns the arctangent of x in radians.

```
100 X = 2: Y = ATN(X): PRINT X, Y
RUN
 2            1.10715
```

AUTO

Starts generating line numbers at 10, incrementing by 10.

AUTO n

Starts generating line numbers at n, incrementing by 10.

AUTO n,m

Starts generating line numbers at n, incrementing by m.

```
AUTO 1000
AUTO 1000,20
```

CALL v
CALL v,exp
CALL v,exp1, exp2,
. . . expn

Transfers control to a machine language routine at address v, and passes to it argument(s) exp1, etc. (See USR function.)

```
110 SUBR1 = &HF200
120 CALL SUBR1(A$,B$,X + 2,J)
```

v# = CDBL(x)

Converts x to a double-precision number.

        110 A=1: B=3: PRINT A/B, CDBL(A)/CDBL(B)
        RUN
          .333333   .3333333333333333

CHAIN "filename"	Loads the named program into memory (erasing the current program), passes values to it from the current program, starts executing it.
CHAIN MERGE "file-name"	Loads the named program into memory (does not erase the current program but merges the programs line by line), passes values to it from the current program, starts executing it and leaves files open. The named program must be in ASCII format (see SAVE).
CHAIN "filename",x	As above, but starts executing the new program at line x.
CHAIN "filename",x,ALL	As above, but passes all variable values, not just common (See COMMON.)
CHAIN "filename", x,DELETE m-p	As above, but deletes the chained program after executing, from line number m to p.

        9010 CHAIN "PART2",50,DELETE 5000-7000

v$ = CHR$(x)	Returns the character that corresponds to ASCII Code x.

        110 PRINT CHR$(7)   'RING BELL
        120 PRINT CHR$(27)+"E"   'CLEAR SCREEN OF Z19

v% = CINT(x)	Converts x to an integer; rounds the fraction, if any.

        100 NUM=95.67: A%=CINT(NUM): PRINT NUM, A%
        RUN
          95.67   96

CLEAR	Sets all numeric variables to zero, strings to null, closes all open files.
CLEAR,x1	As above, but sets highest memory location available to BASIC to expression x1.
CLEAR,x1,x2	As above, but sets the stack space available to BASIC to expression x2.
CLEAR,,x2	Clears variables and sets stack space to x2.

        10 CLEAR,32768,2000

CLOAD "filename"	Loads named file from a cassette tape.
CLOAD? "filename"	Verifies tapes by comparing with the program currently in memory.
CLOAD* v	Loads a numeric array from cassette tape.

        CLOAD "INFO4"
        100 CLOAD* A

Note: CLOAD and CSAVE are not implemented in all versions of BASIC-80.

CLOSE	Closes (terminates I/O to) all open disk files.
CLOSE #f	Closes file #f if open.
CLOSE #f1,#f2 . . ., #fn	Closes files f1, f2, etc. if open.

```
CLOSE
1000 CLOSE #1, #2, #3
```

Note: In the file handling statements starting with CLOSE, OPEN, FIELD, PUT, and GET, #f may be replaced with f. In all others (PRINT#, INPUT#, PRINT# USING, LINE INPUT#, and WRITE#, the # is mandatory.

COMMON v1, . . ., vn	Designates those variables whose values are to be passed to a chained program.

```
1000 COMMON J, K, L, M, N(), P$
1010 CHAIN "PART2"
```

CONT	Continues program execution at the point where a break occurred.
v = COS(x)	Returns the cosine of x in radians.

```
100 E = .6: F = 2*COS(E): PRINT E, F
RUN
   .6             1.65067
```

v! = CSNG(x)	Converts x to a single-precision number.

```
100 TS# = 3.141592653589794: PRINT TS#, CSNG(TS#)
RUN
   3.141592653589794        3.14159
```

CSAVE x$	Saves a program currently in memory on a cassette tape, using the first letter of x$ as the filename.
CSAVE* v	Saves the values of a numeric array on cassette tape.

```
10 CSAVE "A"
10 CSAVE* B
```

v# = CVD(8-byte string) v% = CVI(2-byte string) v! = CVS(4-byte string)	Converts string values from a random file buffer to double-precision, integer, or single precision numbers.

```
2010 FIELD #1, 2 AS A$, 4 AS B$, 8 AS C$
2020 GET #1
2030 A% = CVI(A$): B! = CVS(B$): C# = CVD(C$)
```

DATA n1, n2, . . ., nn DATA string1, string2, . . ., stringn DATA string1, n1, string2, n2, . . ., etc.	Stores numeric and string constants to be accessed by READ statements.

```
500 DATA 25, 32, 46, 78, 92, 23
510 DATA APPLE, ORANGE, PEAR, "BEAN SPROUTS"
520 DATA STRUDEL, 1.98, CAKE, 2.25
```

DEF FNname = x DEF FNname (p1, . . ., pn) = x DEF FNname$ = x$ DEF FNname$ (p1, . . ., pn) = x$	Defines and names a function written by the user (where name is a legal variable name). It may have parameters p1, etc. x represents an expression which defines the function. Variables within this expression are local. 500 DEF FNA(P,Q) = P^2/Q^3 :DEF FNE$(x$) = x$ + "!!!" 510 T = FNA(A,B) :Y$ = FNE$(Y$)
DEFDBL letter DEFDBL letter-letter	Declares variables with names beginning with letter(s) in the range as double precision numeric unless redefined by a type declaration character.
DEFINT letter DEFINT letter-letter	As above, but integer.
DEFSNG letter DEFSNG letter-letter	As above, but single-precision numeric.
DEFSTR letter DEFSTR letter-letter	As above, but string. 10 DEFINT A, J − N, X − Z
DEF USRn = i	Specifies the starting address i of a user-defined machine language sub-routine. n can be 0 − 9, if not given, 0 is assumed. 210 DEF USR1 = 24000 220 DEF USR2 = &HC000
DELETE n DELETE n-m DELETE -m	Deletes the indicated program lines; the third form deletes all program lines up to and including the indicated line number. DELETE 10-100 DELETE -100
DIM v1(x1), v2(x2,x3), . . ., etc.	Specifies the maximum number of elements for array variables. If no DIM statement is used, the maximum number is 10. Subscripts start at 0 unless otherwise specified. (See OPTION BASE.) DIM sets all values to 0 or null. 10 DIM X1(100), Y1(100), Z(100,100), A$(100,4)
EDIT n	Enters Edit Mode with the specified line ready to be edited.
EDIT.	Enters Edit Mode with the last line typed ready to be edited.
^A	Enters Edit Mode with the current line ready to be edited. In Edit Mode the following commands are allowed (they are not echoed):

n\<space\>	Moves the cursor to the right n positions.
n\<rubout\>	Moves the cursor to the left n positions.
I	Enters insert mode, typed text will be inserted at the cursor position.
\<esc\>	Leaves insert mode.
X	"Extend" Moves cursor to the end of the line and enters insert mode.
D	Deletes 1 character to the right of the cursor.

nD	Deletes n characters to the right of the cursor.
H	"Hack" Deletes all characters to the right of the cursor and enters insert mode.
Sc	Search for the first occurrence of c.
nSc	Search for the nth occurrence of c.
Kc	Kill all characters up to the first occurrence of c.
nKc	Kill all characters up to the nth occurrence of c.
Cc	Change one character at cursor position to c.
nCx	Change n characters at cursor position to string x.
<cr>	Leaves Edit Mode, saves all changes.
E	Same as <cr> but rest of line is not printed out.
Q	Leaves Edit Mode, no changes will be saved.
L	Lists the line, saves changes, repositions the cursor at the beginning of the line, stays in Edit Mode.
A	Cancels changes, repositions the cursor at the beginning of the line, stays in Edit Mode.

Note: To duplicate line m as line n, use the sequence LIST m, ^A, In, <cr>

END   Terminates program execution. END is optional.

9999 END

EOF(f)   End of file. Returns -1 (true) if the end of a sequential file has been reached. Under CP/M, with random files, if a GET is done past the end of file, EOF will return -1.

310 IF EOF(1) THEN 1000

ERASE v1, v2, . . ., vn   Eliminates arrays from a program. Must be done before re-dimensioning them.

600 ERASE A,B,C
610 DIM A(100),B(50,40),C(40)

ERROR x   If x > 0 and < 255, simulates the occurrence of the error specified by x. Otherwise, allows the user to define an error. For writing error handling routines, special variables ERR and ERL are available. These contain respectively the error code and the line number where it occurred.

ERROR 15
10 A = 15: ERROR A

v = EXP(x)   Returns e to the power of x.

10 X = 6: PRINT X, EXP(X)
RUN
   6   403.429

FIELD #f, n1 AS vl$, n2 AS v2$,. . ., nn AS vn$ Allocates space for variables in a random file buffer. n1 is the width (in bytes) of the first field in the random file buffer, v1$ is a variable which points to the correct place in the buffer, and so on.

2010 FIELD #1, 2 AS A$, 4 AS B$, 8 AS C$

```
2020 GET #1
2030 A% = CVI(A$): B! = CVS(B$): C# = CVD(C$)
```

Note: Field width may also be given as an expression *in parentheses*, e.g.,

```
2040 FIELD #2,(14 + 2*J) AS D$, 4 AS N$
```

FILES	Under CP/M, prints filenames of files on the currently logged in disk drive.
FILES "d:*.*"	Under CP/M, prints filenames of all files on disk drive d:.
v = FIX(x)	Returns the truncated integer part of x.

```
10 X = 45.93: PRINT X, FIX(X)
RUN
  45.93            45
```

FOR v = n1 TO n2
FOR v = n1 TO n2 STEP n3
  Always used with:

NEXT
NEXT v
  or in the case of nested loops:

NEXT v1, v2, . . ., vn

Causes the statements after the FOR and preceding the NEXT to be executed a given number of times. n1 is the initial value of v, n2 is the final value of v, n3 is the increment (if not given, 1 is used). The statements will be executed once for every increment of v until v exceeds n2.

```
10 LET A = 1: B = 10: C = 2
20 FOR X = A TO B STEP C: PRINT X;: NEXT X
30 PRINT: PRINT X
RUN
  1  3  5  7  9
  11
NEW
10 FOR X = 1 TO 1: PRINT X: NEXT X: PRINT "DONE"
RUN
  1
DONE
10 FOR X = 1 TO 0: PRINT X: NEXT X: PRINT "DONE"
RUN
DONE
```

FRE(d)	Returns the number of bytes of memory not being used by BASIC-80.

```
PRINT FRE(0)
31016
```

GET #f
GET #f,r

Reads the next record from a random disk file into the random buffer, or reads the specified record from a random disk file into the random buffer. (See CVD.)

```
1000 GET #1,25
```

GOSUB n

Transfers control to a subroutine at line number n. See RETURN.

```
100 GOSUB 1000
```

GOTO n

Transfers control to line n.

        100 GOTO 200

v$ = HEX$(x)

Returns a string representing the hexadecimal value of x. x is rounded to an integer first.

        10 J=255: PRINT J, HEX$(J)
        RUN
         255   FF

IF exp THEN
clause1
IF exp THEN
clause1
ELSE clause2

Either clause1 or clause 2 may be: (a) a line number (in which case GOTO may replace THEN), (b) a statement, or (c) a compound statement made by joining statements with colons (:). If exp is true, clause1 is executed, if exp is false clause2 is executed. If clause2 is not present, control proceeds to the next higher line number. IF statements may be nested (a clause may contain another IF statement) up to the limit of line length (255 characters).

        100 IF A>B THEN 150
        110   IF   A$="YES"   THEN   F=1:G=0   ELSE   PRINT"WHY
        NOT?":GOTO 10

Note: In case an IF statement forms the body of a FOR loop, the NEXT statement *may not* be included on the same line as the IF:

        WRONG — 100 FOR I=1 TO 10: IF X>Y THEN 999: NEXT I
        OK   — 100 FOR I=1 TO 10: IF X>Y THEN 999
                110 NEXT I
        BETTER
        LOOKING — 100 FOR I=1 TO 10
                110   IF X>Y THEN 999
                120 NEXT I

x$ = INKEY$

Returns the first character typed at the console. Returns a null if no character is pending at the keyboard.

        100 PRINT"O.K. TO PROCEED (Y/N)?"
        110 A$=INKEY$: IF A$="" THEN 110 ELSE PRINT A$

v = INP(i)

Returns the byte read from port i. See also OUT

        100 CHECK=INP(255)

x$ = INPUT$(x)
x$ = INPUT$(x,#f)

Returns a string x characters long read from the terminal, or if f is given, from file f. All characters are passed through except ˆC which interrupts the function.

        100 D$=INPUT$(1,#1)

INPUT v
INPUT;"prompt
string";v
INPUT"prompt

Allows input from the terminal during program execution. Prints a question mark, the prompt string (if present) and waits for input to be typed, followed by <cr>. Assigns the values input to the variable(s) mentioned. <cr> typed alone is stored as a ∅ or null string. Input items

string";v
INPUT v1, v2, v3, . . .
vn

are separated by commas The semicolon after INPUT suppresses the
<cr><lf> sequence echoed after the user's <cr>. A comma may be
used instead of a semicolon after the prompt string to suppress the ?.
See also LINE INPUT.

```
100 INPUT;"SIZE";A: INPUT" STYLE";B
110 PRINT A,B
RUN
SIZE? 14 STYLE? 2345
    14          2345
```

INPUT#f,v
INPUT#f, v1, v2, . . .,
vn

Reads data items from a sequential disk file and assigns them to the
variable(s) mentioned. f is the number used when the file was opened.

```
100 INPUT#1, A$, B$, C$
```

v = INSTR(x$,y$)
v = INSTR(i,x$,y$)

Returns the position at which y$ occurred in x$ (the first occurrence).
The search will start at position i (or 1 if i is not given). If y$ is not
found, 0 will be returned. 0 is also returned if x$ is null or i > the
length of x$. If y$ is null i or 1 is returned.

```
10 A$="ARE YOU READY?": B$="YOU"
20 PRINT INSTR(A$,B$), INSTR(6,A$,B$)
RUN
    5              0
```

v = INT(x)

Returns the largest integer less than or equal to x.

```
10 PRINT INT(79.623), INT(-79.623)
RUN
    79            -80
```

KILL "filename"

Deletes a file from disk.

```
1000 KILL "TEMP"
```

v$ = LEFT$(y$,i)

Returns a substring of y$, i characters long, starting at the left.

```
10 A$="PEACH BUTTER": PRINT LEFT$(A$,5)
RUN
PEACH
```

v = LEN(x$)

Returns the number of characters in x$.

```
10 A$="SESAME BUTTER": PRINT LEN(A$)
RUN
    13
```

LET v = exp
v = exp

Assigns the value of an expression to variable v.

```
10 LET A=25: B=A+10: C=A*B/3: PRINT A,B,C
RUN
    25          35          291.667
```

LINE INPUT v$ LINE INPUT"prompt string";v$ LINE INPUT;"prompt string";v$	Allows the input of an entire line (up to 254 characters) to a string variable v$, including commas and spaces. A question mark is not printed unless it is part of a prompt string. The semicolon after INPUT suppresses the <cr><lf> sequence echoed after the user's <cr>. See also INPUT.

                                 200 LINE INPUT A$

LINE INPUT#f,v$	Reads an entire line (up to 254 characters) from a sequential disk file to a string variable. f is the number used when the file was opened. All characters up to a <cr> will be read into v$.

                                 200 LINE INPUT #1, A$

LIST	Prints out the whole program in memory at the terminal.
LIST n	Prints out line n of the program in memory.
LIST n-m	Prints out the program in memory from line n to line m.
LIST -m	Prints out the program in memory up to line m.
LIST n-	Prints out the program in memory from line n to the end.

                                 LIST 1-100

LLIST	Prints out the whole program in memory at the line printer.
LLIST n	Prints out line n of the program in memory.
LLIST n-m	Prints out the program in memory from line n to line m.
LLIST -m	Prints out the program in memory up to line m.
LLIST n-	Prints out the program in memory from line n to the end.

                                 LLIST 1-300

LOAD "filename" LOAD "filename",R	Loads a file from disk into memory, deleting the program currently in memory. If no extension is mentioned, .BAS is assumed. Unless the R option is used, closes all files and deletes all variables. If R is used the program will be run after loaded.

                                 1000 LOAD "INFO3"

v = LOC(f)	If referring to a random disk file f, returns the record number that the next GET #f or PUT #f will use. If referring to a sequential file f, returns the number of 128 byte blocks read from or written to the file since opening.

                            100 IF LOC(1)>100 THEN STOP

v = LOF(f)	Under CP/M, returns the number of 128 byte records present in the last extent read or written. For files less than one extent (128 records) this is the true length of the file.

                         10 IF LOF(1) > Ø THEN PRINT"OLD FILE—STAND BY FOR READ"
                              ELSE PRINT "NEW FILE—STAND BY FOR INITIALIZATION"

v = LOG(x)	Returns the natural logarithm of x.

     10 L = 45: M = LOG(L): PRINT L,M
     RUN
      45   3.80666

v = LPOS(d)	Returns the position of the line printer head within the line printer buffer. This is not necessarily the physical position of the print head.

     110 IF LPOS(X)>65 THEN LPRINT CHR$(13)

LPRINT exp LPRINT exp1, exp2, . . ., expn	Same as PRINT, except that output goes to the line printer (or LST: device in CP/M).
LPRINT USING x$; exp1, exp2, . . . expn	Same as PRINT USING, except that output goes to the line printer (or LST: device in CP/M).
LSET v$ = x$	Moves data from memory to a random file buffer in preparation for a PUT statement. Left-justifies x$ in buffer variable v$, pads with blanks on right, truncates on right. Can also be used to left-justify regular string variables.

     2010 FIELD #1, 2 AS A$, 4 AS B$, 8 AS C$
     2020 LSET A$ = MKI(A%): LSET B$ = MKS(B!): LSET C$ = MKD(C#)
     2030 PUT #1

MERGE "filename"	Loads the file into memory without erasing a program in memory. Programs are merged line-by-line, with same-numbered lines from the incoming file superceding the ones in memory. The merging file must be in ASCII format.

     1000 MERGE "INFO3"

MID$(x$,i) = y$ MID$(x$,i,j) = y$	Replaces the characters in string expression x$, beginning at position i, with the characters of y$. j can be used to specify how many characters of y$ to use. The length of x$ is not changed.

     10 A$ = "BOOKKEEPER": MID$(A$,5,4) = "WALKING": PRINT A$
     RUN
     BOOKWALKER

v$ = MID$(x$,i) v$ = MID$(x$,i,j)	Returns a substring of x$ starting with the ith character and including the rest of the string to the right. If j is specified, returns a substring starting at i, j characters long.

     10 X$ = MID$("BOOKKEEPER",5,4): PRINT X$
     RUN
     KEEP

v$ = MKD$(x#) v$ = MKI$(x%) v$ = MKS$(x!)	Converts numeric values into strings, in preparation for placing them in a random file buffer.

     2010 FIELD #1, 2 AS A$, 4 AS B$, 8 AS C$
     2020 LSET A$ = MKI(A%): LSET B$ = MKS(B!): LSET C$ = MKD(C#)
     2030 PUT #1

NAME "old filename" AS "new filename"	Changes the name of a disk file.
	NAME "KIPPER1" AS "KIPPER2"
NEW	Deletes the program currently in memory and clears all variables.
NEXT	See FOR . . . NEXT
NULL x	Sets the number of nulls to be printed at the end of each line. Needed on terminals with a slow <cr>.
	NULL 3
v$ = OCT$(x)	Returns a string representing the octal value of x. x is rounded to an integer first.
	10 A=255: PRINT A, OCT$(A) RUN 255 377
ON ERROR GOTO n ON ERROR GOTO 0	When an error is detected, transfers control to a subroutine at line n. If n=0, turns off error trapping and prints an error message for subsequent errors (useful inside the subroutine).
	100 ON ERROR GOTO 1000
ON v GOSUB n1, n2, . . ., nn ON v GOTO n1, n2, . . ., nn	If the value of v is 1, transfers control to line n1, if the value of v is 2, to n2, etc. For ON . . . GOSUB a subroutine should be located at n1, n2, etc. If v < 0 or v > the number of line numbers in the list, control passes to the next line. If v > 255, an error results.
	100 ON X GOTO 110, 120, 130
OPEN "O",#f,"filename" OPEN "I",#f,"filename" OPEN "R",#f,"filename",r	Allocates a buffer to a disk file to allow for I/O, specifies a mode: Sequential Output (O), Sequential Input (I), or Random Input/Output (R). File number f can be 1 to 15, Record length r can be set for random files (the default is 128 bytes which is the maximum allowed). Opening a file for sequential output, "O", destroys its current contents.
	10 OPEN "O",1,"INFO1"
OPTION BASE n	Sets the lowest value for array subscripts to 0 or 1 (default is 0).
	10 OPTION BASE 1
OUT i,j	Sends a byte j, to a machine output port i. i and j must be in the range 0 to 255. See INP(i).
	500 OUT 255, &H1A
v = PEEK(i)	Returns the byte read from memory location i.
	100 PRINT PEEK(65535)
POKE i,j	Writes a byte j, to a memory location i. i must be in the range 0 to 65535, j must be 0 to 255. See PEEK.

100 POKE &H5A00, &HFF

v = POS(d)   Returns the current cursor position in a line. The leftmost position is 0.

100 IF POS(0)>80 THEN PRINT CHR$(13)

PRINT   Prints out at the terminal the values of the expression(s), or a <cr> if
PRINT exp1; exp2;   no expressions are present. Punctuation determines the spacing across
. . .; expn   the line, as follows:
?
? exp1; . . .; expn   Comma causes the next item to be printed in the next print zone 14 columns wide.
                          Semicolon causes the next item to be printed immediately after the preceding item.
                          Repeated commas "push over" the item one print zone each.
                          A semicolon at the end of an expression list will cause the next PRINT statement to begin printing right after the last item of the previous PRINT statement.

                          10 A = 2.98: B = 2344
                          20 PRINT "AGREED PRICE IS:" A "FOR #";
                          30 PRINT B
                          RUN
                          AGREED PRICE IS: 2.98 FOR # 2344

PRINT USING x$;   Prints at the terminal the results of the expression(s) using a format
exp1; exp2; . . .; expn   specified by special characters in the formatting string x$:

!	print only the first character of a string.
\ \	print 3 characters of a string (include more spaces for longer string formats).
&	a variable-length string field.
#	represents 1 digit position in the format.
.	represents the decimal point.
+	print the sign of the number at this position.
−	after a numeric field, print a trailing minus.
**	fill the leading spaces with asterisks.
$$	print $ in front of this numeric field.
**$	combines the two previous signs.
,	before the decimal, print commas every 3rd digit.
^^^^	after the digit position characters, print in exponential format.
_	print next character 'as is'.

                          100 A$ = "EXPENSES": A1 = 1234.5: A2 = 123456: A3 = 12.3
                          100 P$ = "\   \ ####.## ######, $$##.##"
                          120 PRINT USING P$; A$, A1, A2, A3
                          RUN
                          EXPENSES   1234.50 123,456 $12.30

PRINT#f,exp1;exp2; . . .; expn	Writes data to a sequential disk file. 10 PRINT#1, A, A$; ","; B$
PRINT#f, USING x$; exp1;exp2; . . .; expn	Writes data to a sequential disk file using the format specified by the special characters in the formatting string. 10 PRINT#1, USING P$; A, A$, B, B$
PUT #f	Write the next available record from a random buffer to random disk file f.
PUT #f,r	Write record r to file f. 2010 FIELD #1, 2 AS A$, 4 AS B$, 8 AS C$ 2020 LSET A$ = MKI(A%): LSET B$ = MKS(B!): LSET C$ = MKD(C#) 2030 PUT #1,R
RANDOMIZE RANDOMIZE n	Reseeds the random number generator. If n is omitted, a message requesting a number will be printed. Without RANDOMIZE, the RND function generates the same sequence of random numbers each time. 10 RANDOMIZE 10 RANDOMIZE 2
READ v1, v2, . . ., vn	Reads values from data statements and assigns them to variables. 100 READ A, A$, B, C, SALES
REM remark ´remark	Allows explanatory remarks to be included with the program listing. REM statements are not executed. 10 REM PROGRAM TO CALCULATE INTEREST 20 ´ THE FOLLOWING VARIABLES ARE USED: 500 X = 25 ´CHANGE THIS VALUE LATER
RENUM	Renumbers the entire program starting with 10, with increments of 10.
RENUM a RENUM a, b, c RENUM a,,c	Renumbers the program starting with a new line number a. If b and c are present, renumbers starting at current line b with increments of c. RENUM 1000, 500, 20
RESET	Under CP/M, resets the disk allocation vectors in RAM so that data may be written on a changed disk.
RESTORE	Allows all data to be reread from the beginning.
RESTORE n	Allows data to be reread from line n. 1000 RESTORE 8500
RESUME RESUME 0	Continues program execution after an error recovery procedure, at the statement which caused the error.
RESUME NEXT	Continues program execution after an error recovery procedure, at the statement after that which caused the error.

RESUME n

Continues as above, at line n.

> RESUME 1000

RETURN

Transfers control to the statement following the most recently executed GOSUB statement.

> 1090 RETURN

v$ = RIGHT$(x$,i)

Returns a substring of x$, i characters long, starting at the right.

> 10 X$ = RIGHT$("BOOKKEEPER",6): PRINT X$
> RUN
> KEEPER

v = RND
v = RND(x)

Returns a random number between 0 and 1. The same sequence is generated for each run unless RANDOMIZE is used. A value of x>0 has the same effect as if x is omitted. x=0 repeats the last number generated, x<0 restarts the same sequence for any number given.

```
10 FOR I = 1 to 5: PRINT RND;: NEXT I
RUN
 .245121      .305003      .311866      .515163      .0583136
RUN
 .245121      .305003      .311866      .515163      .0583136
10 FOR I=1 TO 5: PRINT RND(1);: NEXT I
RUN
 .245121      .305003      .311866      .515163      .0583136
RUN
 .245121      .305003      .311866      .515163      .0583136
10 Z=RND(-3): FOR I=1 TO 5: PRINT RND;: NEXT: PRINT
20 Z=RND(-4): FOR I=1 TO 5: PRINT RND;: NEXT: PRINT
30 Z=RND(-3): FOR I=1 TO 5: PRINT RND;: NEXT: PRINT
RUN
 .709808    .658938    .639327    .0685806    .104624
 .498871    .670127    .98706     .739354     .783018
 .709808    .658938    .639327    .0685806    .104624
10 FOR I=1 TO 5: PRINT RND;: NEXT: PRINT
20 FOR I=1 TO 5: PRINT RND(0);: NEXT: PRINT
30 FOR I=1 TO 5: PRINT RND;: NEXT: PRINT
RUN
 .245121    .305003    .311866    .515163    .0583136
 .0583136   .0583136   .0583136   .0583136   .0583136
 .788891    .497102    .363751    .984546    .901591
```

RSET v$ = exp$

Moves data from memory to a random file buffer in preparation for a PUT statement. Right-justifies exp$ in buffer variable v$, pads with blanks on left, truncates on right. Can also be used to right-justify regular string variables.

```
2010 FIELD #1, 2 AS A$, 4 AS B$, 8 AS C$
2020 RSET A$ = MKI(A%): RSET B$ = MKS(B!): RSET C$ = MKD(C#)
2030 PUT #1,R
```

RUN	Executes the program currently in memory.
RUN n	Executes the program currently in memory from line n.
RUN "filename" RUN "filename",R	Deletes the file currently in memory, loads a file from disk into memory and runs it. Unless option R is used, closes all open files.

      RUN
      1000 RUN "PART3",R

SAVE "filename" SAVE "filename",A SAVE "filename",P	Saves a file in memory on disk in compressed binary format. With option A, saves the file in ASCII format; with option P, the file is protected by storing in encoded binary format—it cannot be listed or edited.

      SAVE "PROG1"
      SAVE "PROG1.ASC",A
      SAVE "PROGRAM1",P

v = SGN(x)	If x > 0, returns 1. If x = 0, returns 0. If x < 0, returns − 1.

      100 ON SGN(NUM)+2 GOTO 1000, 2000, 3000

v = SIN(x)	Returns the sine of x in radians.

      10 DSINE=SIN(1): PRINT DSINE
      RUN
       .841471

v$ = SPACE$(x)	Returns a string of spaces x long.

      10 FOR S = 1 TO 3: X$=SPACE$(S): PRINT X$"LINE #"S: NEXT
      RUN
       LINE #1
        LINE #2
         LINE # 3

SPC(i)	Prints blanks on the terminal. Used in PRINT statements.

      10 PRINT SPC(3) "SECTION 3.0"

v = SQR(x)	Returns the square root of x.

      10 B=25: ROOT=SQR(B): PRINT B, ROOT
      RUN
      25   5

STOP	Terminates program execution.

      1000 STOP

v$ = STR$(x)	Returns a string representation of the value of x.

      10 NUM=10232: L$=STR$(NUM): L=LEN(L$): PRINT NUM,L,"!"L$"!"

RUN
10232   6   ! 10232!

x$ = STRING$(i,j) x$ = STRING$(i,y$)	Returns a string i long whose characters all have ASCII code j, or which equal the first character of y$.

10 PRINT STRING$(10,65), STRING$(5,"B")
RUN
AAAAAAAAAA   BBBBB

SWAP a,b	Exchanges the values of two variables.

110 A=25: B=3: SWAP A,B: PRINT A;B
RUN
 3   25

SYSTEM	Under CP/M, returns control to the CP/M operating system by performing a warm boot.

TAB(i)	Spaces over to position i on the terminal.

100 PRINT TAB(35)"SUMMARY OF STATISTICS"
100 LPRINT TAB(115)"BUDGET REPORT"

x = TAN(y)	Returns the tangent of y in radians.

10 G=1: S=TAN(G): PRINT S
RUN
   1.55741

TRON	Switches on the trace feature.

TROFF	Switches off the trace feature. When the trace debugging aid is on, each line number of the program is printed as it is executed.

x = USR(y) x = USRn(y)	Calls the user's assembly language subroutine with the argument y. n = 0 to 9 and corresponds to that given in the DEF USRn (if omitted, 0 is assumed).

1010 M = USR5(R)

v = VAL(x$)	Returns the numerical value of string x$.

10 S$="   1025.27": PRINT VAL(S$)
RUN
   1025.27

v1 = VARPTR(v2)	Returns the address of the first byte of data identified with v2.

v1 = VARPTR(#f)	Returns the starting address of the disk I/O buffer (or FIELD buffer for random files) assigned to file f.

1010 A = USR(VARPTR(B))

WAIT p,i
WAIT p,i,j

Suspends execution of a program until port p develops a certain bit pattern. The pattern is XOR'ed with j and AND'ed with i. If the result is 0 the port is read again. j is assumed to be 0 if not present.

> 100 WAIT 250, 2

WHILE exp
  Always used with:

WEND

Executes the statements below WHILE and above WEND as long as (while) the given expression is true. May be nested to any level.

> 90 WHILE A<B
> .
> .
> .
> 290 WEND

WIDTH n
WIDTH LPRINT n

Sets the printed line width in characters for the terminal or line printer.

> 10 WD = 80: WIDTH WD

WRITE
WRITE exp1, exp2,
. . ., expn

Outputs data to the terminal in ASCII form, separated by commas and with strings enclosed in double quotation marks. Outputs a blank line if no expression given.

> 20 WRITE A,B,C$

WRITE#f, exp1, exp2,
. . ., expn

Writes data to a sequential file. Inserts commas between the items and encloses the strings in quotation marks. Strings may contain commas.

> 20 WRITE#1,A,B,C$

APPENDIX C
Summary of C

Programs

A C program consists of a sequence of external definitions ("external" means that one definition cannot appear inside another). Four kinds of definitions can be used in a C program, but three are optional.

1. Compiler-control line definitions (optional).

   Examples: #define MAXSIZE 255
                        #define EVER ;;
                        #include "bdscio.h"

2. Definitions of external variables (optional).

   These are variables that will be global to the program, that is, available to all the functions that come after the definition.

   Examples: int num,max,array[801],table[100][8];
                        char dummy,buf[MAXSIZE],*alloptr;

3. Definition of a main function (required).

   This is usually of the form

   ```
   main()
   {
   --------------------
   --------------------
   }
   ```

   where the dashed lines represent the body of the function.

4. Definitions of user-written functions (optional).

   These have the same form as main except that the user assigns the function name. The type of function arguments must be declared before the body of the function definition.

   Example: myfcn3(m,data)

   ```
   int m,data[];
   {
   --------------------
   }
   ```

Identifiers

(Also called *names*.) These may be up to 8 alphanumeric characters, starting with a letter or the underscore (_). The only special symbol permitted is the underscore (_). Upper- and lowercase are treated as being different. Identifiers are used for variable names, function names, file names, and #DEFINE names.

Keywords

(Also called *reserved words*.) These are words that may not be used as identifiers since their use is reserved as follows:

Used in statements: if, else, while, do, for, switch, case, sizeof, default, break, continue, return, goto, entry

Used in type or storage specifiers: char, int, short, long, unsigned, float, double, struct, union, typedef, auto, static, extern, register

Note: BDS C does not support short, long, float, double, static, or register. Initializers (e.g., int m=5;), static, extern, and sizeof (typename) are also not supported.

Operators Used in C

Operator	Use
()	Parenthesized expressions
[]	Array elements
→	Pointer to structure member
.	Structure member
!	Logical complement
~	Bitwise complement
++	Increment
−−	Decrement
−	Unary negation
(type)	Type cast
*var	Indirection (contents of variable pointed to by "var")
&var	Address of variable "var"
sizeof	Storage space required by variable (in bytes)
*	Multiplication
/	Division
%	Modulus (Remainder after integer division)
+	Addition
−	Subtraction
<<	Left shift
>>	Right shift
<	Logical less-than
<=	Logical less-than-or-equal-to
>	Logical greater-than
>=	Logical greater-than-or-equal-to
==	Logical equality
!=	Logical inequality
&	Bitwise AND
^	Bitwise Exclusive-OR
|	Bitwise OR
&&	Logical AND
||	Logical OR
?:	Conditional expression (ternary)

```
=           Assignment
op=         Assignment operator
'           Multiple-expression operator
```

Precedence of Operators

Operators shown here on the same line have the same precedence. Operators on a given line have higher precedence than all operators on lower lines.

Operator	*Associativity*
() [] → .	left to right
! ˜ ++ −− − (type) ∗ & sizeof	right to left
∗ / %	left to right
+ −	left to right
<< >>	left to right
< <= > >=	left to right
== !=	left to right
&	left to right
^	left to right
|	left to right
&&	left to right
||	left to right
?:	right to left
= += −= etc.	right to left
, between expressions	left to right

Statements in C

In the following the word *statement* may be replaced by *compound statement*, that is, a block of statements surrounded by curly brackets {. . .}. All statements end with a semicolon (;) but you do not put a semicolon after the right bracket of a compound statement.

The simplest kind of statement is an expression followed by a semicolon.

```
Examples:    k++;
             getchar();
             x=15;
```

More complicated statements are constructed with various key words as follows:

1. if (expression) statement

   Example: if (x==0) printf("No data available\n");

2. if (expression) statement else statement

   Example: if ((n%20)==19) {
                   printf("Press any key to continue \n");
                   getchar();

```
}
else {
  printf("%3d",array[n]);
  n++;
}
```

Note: n%20 means "the remainder after dividing n by 20".

3. while (expression) statement

    Example: k=0;
```
                while (k <= 99){
                array[k]=100*k+k;
                k++;
                }
```

4. do statement while (expression)

    Example: do{
```
                printf("how many numbers to be sorted
                (max=800)?");
                scanf("%d",&n);
                putchar(10);
                }while (n < 0 || n > 800);
```

5. switch (expression) statement

   (See example in 7.)

6. case constant-expression : statement

   (See example in 7.)

7. default : statement

   Example: switch, case, and default are usually combined as follows:
```
    switch (c)  {
       case 'a'  :
       case 'A'  : r=append(r,lim); break;
       case 'q'  :
       case 'Q'  : break;
       default   : printf("** Illegal Command **");
    }
```

8. break;

   Note: break causes an early exit from the body of switch, for, while, or do statements.

   Example: (see example in 7.)

9. continue;

   Note: continue causes a skip to the next iteration in a for, while, or do loop.

Example: for (i=0; i<99; i++){
                  if (array[i] < 0) continue; /* skip to next i */
                  array[i] = i+100;
             }

10. return; or return (expression);
    Example: square(n)
                 int n;
                 {
                     return (n*n);
                 }

11. goto identifier;
    Example: start:
                 puts(CLEARS);
                 - - - -
                 if (x < 200) goto start;

Library Functions Available in BDS C

Functions available with BDS C version 1.45 are listed here alphabetically by function name. If a value is returned, its type is indicated by prefacing the function name with int, char, or char *.

int abs(n)	Returns the absolute value of n.
char *alloc(n)	Allocates string space; see BDS Manual.
int atoi(string) char *string;	Converts ASCII string to an integer.
int bdos(c,de)	Calls BDOS function #c; passes de.
char bios(n,c)	Calls BIOS jump table entry #n; passes c.
int call(addr,a,h,b,d)	Calls a ML subroutine at addr; returns HL.
char calla(addr,a,h,b,d)	Like call except it returns A.
int close(fd)	Closes file; does not flush file buffer.
char *codend()	Returns pointer to last code byte +1.
int creat(filename) char *filename;	Creates and opens a file.
char csw()	Returns console switch register.
char *endext()	Returns pointer to byte after data area.

int exec(prog) char *prog;	Loads and executes a prog.com.

int execl
    (prog,arg1,arg2,
    . . ., 0)
    char *prog, *arg1,
    *arg2, . . .
	See BDS Manual.

exit()	Closes open files, reboots CP/M.
char *externs()	Returns pointer to external data area.
int fabort(fd)	Frees up file descriptor fd without close.
char *fcbaddr(fd)	Returns address of fcb for fd.
int fclose(iobuf) struct _buf *iobuf;	Closes buffered I/O file.

int fcreat (filename,
    iobuf)
    char *filename;
    struct _buf *iobuf;
	Creates and opens file for buffered output.

int fflush(iobuf) struct _buf *iobuf;	Flushes iobuf to disk.

char *fgets(str,iobuf)
    char *str;
    structure _buf
    *iobuf;
	Reads line from iobuf to memory at str.

int fopen(filename,
    iobuf)
    char *filename;
    struct _buf *iobuf;
	Opens file for buffered input.

int fprint(iobuf,
    format, arg1,
    arg2, . . .)
    struct _buf *iobuf;
    char *format;
	Like printf using iobuf instead of CON:

int fputs(str,iobuf)
    char *str;
    struct _buf *iobuf;
	Writes the null-terminated string at str into iobuf.

free(allocptr) char *allocptr;	Frees up string space; see BDS Manual.

int fscanf(iobuf,
    format, arg1,
    arg2, . . .)
    struct _buf *iobuf;
    char *format;
	Like scanf using iobuf instead of CON:

int getc(iobuf) struc _buf *iobuf;	Returns the next byte from iobuf.
int getchar()	Returns the next character typed at CON:
char *gets(str) char *str	Like BDOS function #10.
int getval(strptr) char **strptr;	See BDS Manual.
int getw(iobuf) struct _buf *iobuf;	Does two calls to getc.

initb (array,string)
    char *array,
    *string;
	Initializes character array; see BDS Manual.

initw(array,string)
    int *array;
    char *string;
	Initializes an integer array; see BDS Manual.

inp(n)	Returns the value in port n.
int isalpha(c) char c;	Returns true if c alphabetic.
int isdigit(c)	Returns true if c is a decimal digit.
int islower(c)	Returns true if c is lowercase.
int isspace(c)	Returns true if c is blank, tab, newline
int isupper(c)	Returns true if c is uppercase.
int kbhit()	Returns true if any key hit.

movmem(source,
    dest, count)
    char *source,
    *dest
	Moves count bytes from source to dest.

nrand(−1,s1,s2,s3)
    nrand(0,prompt
    _string)
    int nrand(1)
	Another rand; see BDS Manual.

int open   Opens file for I, O, I/O for mode = 0, 1, 2.
  (filename,mode)
  char *filename;

outp(n,b)   Sends b to port n.

pause()   Loops until console input occurs.

char peek(n)   Returns contents of memory location n.

poke(n,b)   Stores b in memory location n.

printf(format, arg1,   Print with format.
  arg2, . . .)
  char *format;

                          Note: Conversion characters used in format are d = decimal, o = octal,
                          x = hex, u = unsigned decimal, c = character, s = string, e = exponential,
                          f = floating point, g = shorter of e or f.

int putc(c,iobuf)   Writes c to iobuf.
  char c;
  struct _buf *iobuf;

putch(c)   Like putchar except ^C is not recognized.

putchar(c)   Prints c on CON:

puts(str)   Prints from str to null on CON:
  char *str

int putw(w,iobuf)   Does two calls to putc.
  struct _buf *iobuf;

qsort (base,nel,   Sorts nel items of width bytes starting at base, where compar is a pointer
  width,compar)   to a function similar to strcmp.
  char *base;
  int (*compar)();

int rand()   Returns 0 < rand < 32768.

int read(fd,buf,nb1)   Reads nb1 records of fd into memory at buf.
  char *buf;

int rename(old,new)   Renames a file.
  char *old,*new

rsvstk(n)   Used with sbrk; see BDS Manual.

char *sbrk(n)   Used by alloc; see BDS Manual.

int scanf (format,   Input with format.
  arg1,arg2, . . .)
  char *format;

Note: Conversion characters used in format are d, o, x, c, s (f, h, and u are not allowed in BDS C).

int seek (fd,offset, code)	See BDS Manual.
int setfcb (fcbaddr, filename) char *filename;	Initializes a CP/M file control block.
setmem(addr, count,byte)	Sets count bytes of memory starting at addr to byte.
sleep(n)	Waits n/10 seconds on the 8080.
sprintf(string, format,arg1, arg2, . . .) char *string, *format	Write with format to memory at string.
srand(n)	Initializes srand; n=seed; n=0 uses CR.
srand1(string) char *string	Like srand(0) with prompt=string.
int sscanf(string, format,arg1, arg2, . . .) char *string,*format;	Input from memory starting at string.
strcat(s1,s2) char *s1,*s2;	Concatenates s2 onto s1
int strcmp(s1,s2) char *s1,*s2;	Returns +, 0, − for s1>s2, s1=s2, s1<s2.
strcpy(s1,s2) char *s1,*s2;	Copies the string at s2 to s1.
int strlen(string) char *string;	Returns the length of string.
int swapin (filename,addr) char *filename;	Loads named file at addr.
int tell(fd)	Returns the value of the pointer to the next sector.
int tolower(c)	Converts c to lowercase.
char *topofmem()	Returns pointer to top of TPA=top of stack.

int toupper(c)   Converts c to uppercase.

ungetc(c,iobuf)   Pushes c back onto iobuf.
   char c;
   struct _buf *iobuf;

char ungetch(c)   See BDS Manual.

int unlink(filename)   Deletes a file.
   char *filename;

int write(fd,buf,nb1)   Writes nb1 records from mem at buf to fd.
   char *buf;

APPENDIX D
Summary of 8080 Instructions with Intel Mnemonics

Mnemonic	Operand	Flags CAZSP	Bytes, Cycles	Explanation (See Notes)
ACI	data	fffff	2,7	A = A + data + CY
ADC	M	fffff	1,7	A = A + [HL] + CY
ADC	reg	fffff	1,4	A = A + reg + CY
ADD	M	fffff	1,7	A = A + [HL]
ADD	reg	fffff	1,4	A = A + reg
ADI	data	fffff	2,7	A = A + data
ANA	M	0ffff	1,7	A = A AND [HL]
ANA	reg	0ffff	1,4	A = A AND reg
ANI	data	00fff	2,7	A = A AND data
CALL	addr		3,17	[SP − 1] = PCHI,[SP − 2] = PCLO,SP = SP − 2, PC = addr
CC	addr		3,11/17	If CY = 1,[SP − 1] = PCHI,[SP − 2] = PCLO, SP = SP − 2,PC = addr
CM	addr		3,11/17	If S = 1,[SP − 1] = PCHI,[SP − 2] = PCLO,SP = SP − 2, PC = addr
CMA			1,4	A = Complement of A
CMC		f	1,4	CY = Complement of CY
CMP	M	fffff	1,7	Compare mem & A;set Z = 1 if A = (HL),CY = 1 if A<(HL)
CMP	reg	fffff	1,4	Compare reg & A;set Z = 1 if A = reg,CY = 1 if A<reg
CNC	addr		3,11/17	If CY = 0,[SP − 1] = PCHI,[SP − 2] = PCLO, SP = SP − 2,PC = addr
CNZ	addr		3,11/17	If Z = 0,[SP − 1] = PCHI,[SP − 2] = PCLO,SP = SP − 2, PC = addr
CP	addr		3,11/17	If S = 0,[SP − 1] = PCHI,[SP − 2] = PCLO,SP = SP − 2, PC = addr
CPE	addr		3,11/17	If P = 1,[SP − 1] = PCHI,[SP − 2] = PCLO,SP = SP − 2, PC = addr
CPI	data	fffff	2,7	Compare data & A;set Z = 1 if A = data,CY = 1 if A<data
CPO	addr		3,11/17	If P = 0,[SP − 1] = PCHI,[SP − 2] = PCLO,SP = SP − 2, PC = addr
CZ	addr		3,11/17	If Z = 1,[SP − 1] = PCHI,[SP − 2] = PCLO,SP = SP − 2, PC = addr

Mnemonic	Operand	Flags CAZSP	Bytes, Cycles	Explanation (See Notes)
DAA		fffff	1,4	Decimal adjust A to two BCD digits
DAD	rp	f	1,10	HL = HL + rp
DCR	M	ffff	1,10	[HL] = [HL] − 1
DCR	reg	ffff	1,5	reg = reg − 1
DCX	rp		1,5	rp = rp − 1
DI			1,4	Disable interrupts
EI			1,4	Enable interrupts
HLT			1,7	Halt
IN	port		2,10	A = [port]
INR	M	ffff	1,10	[HL] = [HL] + 1
INR	reg	ffff	1,5	reg = reg + 1
INX	rp		1,5	rp = rp + 1
JC	addr		3,10	If CY = 1, PC = addr
JM	addr		3,10	If S = 1, PC = addr
JMP	addr		3,10	PC = addr
JNC	addr		3,10	IF CY = 0, PC = addr
JNZ	addr		3,10	If Z = 0, PC = addr
JP	addr		3,10	If S = 0, PC = addr
JPE	addr		3,10	If P = 1, PC = addr
JPO	addr		3,10	If P = 0, PC = addr
JZ	addr		3,10	If Z = 1, PC = addr
LDA	addr		3,13	A = [addr]
LDAX	B or D		1,7	A = [BC] or A = [DE]
LHLD	addr		3,16	L = [addr], H = [addr + 1]
LXI	rp,data16		3,10	rp = data16
MVI	M,data		2,10	[HL] = data
MVI	reg,data		2,7	reg = data
MOV	reg,M		1,7	reg = [HL]
MOV	M,reg		1,7	[HL] = reg
MOV	reg,reg		1,5	reg = reg
NOP			1,4	No operation
ORA	M	0ffff	1,7	A = A OR [HL]
ORA	reg	0ffff	1,4	A = A OR reg
ORI	data	00fff	2,7	A = A OR data
OUT	port		2,10	[port] = A
PCHL			1,5	PC = HL
POP	bp		1,10	bpLO = [SP],bpHI = [SP + 1],SP = SP + 2
PUSH	bp		1,11	[SP − 1] = bpHI,[SP − 2] = bpLO,SP = SP − 2
RAL		f	1,4	Rotate A left;A0 = CY,CY = A7 (9-bit rotate)
RAR		f	1,4	Rotate A right;A7 = CY,CY = A0 (9-bit rotate)
RC			1,10	If CY = 1,PCLO = [SP],PCHI = [SP + 1],SP = SP + 2
RET			1,10	PCLO = [SP],PCHI = [SP + 1],SP = SP + 2
RLC		f	1,4	Rotate A left;A0 = A7,CY = A7 (8-bit rotate)

Mnemonic	Operand	Flags CAZSP	Bytes, Cycles	Explanation (See Notes)
RM			1,5/11	If S = 1, PCLO = [SP],PCHI = [SP + 1],SP = SP + 2
RNC			1,5/11	If CY = 0, PCLO = [SP],PCHI = [SP + 1],SP = SP + 2
RNZ			1,5/11	If Z = 0, PCLO = [SP],PCHI = [SP + 1],SP = SP + 2
RP			1,5/11	If S = 0, PCLO = [SP],PCHI = [SP + 1],SP = SP + 2
RPE			1,5/11	If P = 1, PCLO = [SP],PCHI = [SP + 1],SP = SP + 2
RPO			1,5/11	If P = 0, PCLO = [SP],PCHI = [SP + 1],SP = SP + 2
RRC		f	1,4	Rotate A right;A7 = A0,CY = A0 (8-bit rotate)
RST	n		1,11	Restart: [SP − 1] = PCHI,[SP − 2] = PCLO,SP = SP − 2, PC = 8∗n
RZ			1,5/11	If Z = 1,PCLO = [SP],PCHI = [SP + 1],SP = SP + 2
SBB	M	fffff	1,7	A = A − [HL] − CY
SBB	reg	fffff	1,4	A = A − reg − CY
SBI	data	fffff	2,7	A = A − data − CY
SHLD	addr		3,16	[addr] = L,[addr + 1] = H
SPHL			1,5	Exchange SP with HL
STA	addr		3,13	[addr] = A
STAX	B or D		1,7	[BC] = A or [DE] = A
STC		1	1,4	CY = 1
SUB	M	fffff	1,7	A = A − [HL]
SUB	reg	fffff	1,4	A = A − reg
SUI	data	fffff	2,7	A = A − data
XCHG			1,4	Exchange DE with HL
XRA	M	00fff	1,7	A = A XOR [HL]
XRA	reg	00fff	1,4	A = A XOR reg
XRI	data	00fff	2,7	A = A XOR data
XTHL			1,18	Exchange [SP] with L, [SP + 1] with H

Note: reg = register (A,B,C,D,E,H,L)
addr = 16-bit memory address
data = 8-bit data
data16 = 16-bit data
M = memory byte addressed by HL
n = 0,1,2,3,4,5,6, or 7
rp = register pair symbol (B=BC, D=DE, H=HL, SP=SP)
bp = byte pair symbol (B=BC, D=DE, H=HL, PSW = AF)
f means flag is affected (fffff = CY, A, Z, S, P)

Capital letters in the *explanation* column refer to contents of registers, e.g., B means 'contents of B', SP means 'contents of SP'. Similarly, reg and rp in the explanation column mean 'contents of register' and 'contents of register pair'. Square brackets mean 'contents of memory indexed by the contents of the bracketed expression', e.g., [HL] means 'contents of memory indexed by the address of HL'. HI and LO mean the high order and low order bytes of the register pair referenced, e.g., PCLO = low order byte of PC.

Assembly Language Mnemonics for the 8080 and Z80 with Hexadecimal Codes

8080 Mnemonic	Z80 Mnemonic	Hex Code	8080 Mnemonic	Z80 Mnemonic	Hex Code
ACI data	ADC A,data	CE	CALL addr	CALL addr	CD
ADC B	ADC A,B	88	CC addr	CALL C,addr	DC
ADC C	ADC A,C	89	CM addr	CALL M,addr	FC
ADC D	ADC A,D	8A	CNC addr	CALL NC,addr	D4
ADC E	ADC A,E	8B	CNZ addr	CALL NZ,addr	C4
ADC H	ADC A,H	8C	CP addr	CALL P,addr	F4
ADC L	ADC A,L	8D	CPE addr	CALL PE,addr	EC
ADC M	ADC A,(HL)	8E	CPO addr	CALL PO,addr	E4
ADC A	ADC A,A	8F	CZ addr	CALL Z,addr	CC
ADI data	ADD A,data	C6			
ADD B	ADD A,B	80	CMC	CCF	3F
ADD C	ADD A,C	81			
ADD D	ADD A,D	82	CPI data	CP data	FE
ADD E	ADD A,E	83	CMP B	CP B	B8
ADD H	ADD A,H	84	CMP C	CP C	B9
ADD L	ADD A,L	85	CMP D	CP D	BA
ADD M	ADD A,(HL)	86	CMP E	CP E	BB
ADD A	ADD A,A	87	CMP H	CP H	BC
			CMP L	CP L	BD
DAD B	ADD HL,BC	09	CMP M	CP (HL)	BE
DAD D	ADD HL,DE	19	CMP A	CP A	BF
DAD H	ADD HL,HL	29	CMA	CPL	2F
DAD SP	ADD HL,SP	39			
			DAA	DAA	27
ANI data	AND data	E6			
ANA B	AND B	A0	DCR B	DEC B	05
ANA C	AND C	A1	DCR C	DEC C	0D
ANA D	AND D	A2	DCR D	DEC D	15
ANA E	AND E	A3	DCR E	DEC E	1D
ANA H	AND H	A4	DCR H	DEC H	25
ANA L	AND L	A5	DCR L	DEC L	2D
ANA M	AND (HL)	A6	DCR M	DEC (HL)	35
ANA A	AND A	A7	DCR A	DEC A	3D

8080 Mnemonic	Z80 Mnemonic	Hex Code	8080 Mnemonic	Z80 Mnemonic	Hex Code
DCX B	DEC BC	0B	SHLD addr	LD (addr),HL	22
DCX D	DEC DE	1B	STAX B	LD (BC),A	02
DCX H	DEC HL	2B	STAX D	LD (DE),A	12
DCX SP	DEC SP	3B	LHLD addr	LD HL,(addr)	2A
DI	DI	F3	MOV A,B	LD A,B	78
EI	EI	FB	MOV A,C	LD A,C	79
			MOV A,D	LD A,D	7A
XCHG	EX DE,HL	EB	MOV A,E	LD A,E	7B
XTHL	EX (SP),HL	E3	MOV A,H	LD A,H	7C
			MOV A,L	LD A,L	7D
HLT	HALT	76	MOV A,M	LD A,(HL)	7E
			MOV A,A	LD A,A	7F
IN port	IN A,(port)	DB			
			MOV B,B	LD B,B	40
INR B	INC B	04	MOV B,C	LD B,C	41
INR C	INC C	0C	MOV B,D	LD B,D	42
INR D	INC D	14	MOV B,E	LD B,E	43
INR E	INC E	1C	MOV B,H	LD B,H	44
INR H	INC H	24	MOV B,L	LD B,L	45
INR L	INC L	2C	MOV B,M	LD B,(HL)	46
INR M	INC (HL)	34	MOV B,A	LD B,A	47
INR A	INC A	3C	MOV C,B	LD C,B	48
INX B	INC BC	03	MOV C,C	LD C,C	49
INX D	INC DE	13	MOV C,D	LD C,D	4A
INX H	INC HL	23	MOV C,E	LD C,E	4B
INX SP	INC SP	33	MOV C,H	LD C,H	4C
			MOV C,L	LD C,L	4D
JMP addr	JP addr	C3	MOV C,M	LD C,(HL)	4E
JC addr	JP C,addr	DA	MOV C,A	LD C,A	4F
PCHL	JP (HL)	E9			
JM addr	JP M,addr	FA	MOV D,B	LD D,B	50
JNC addr	JP NC,addr	D2	MOV D,C	LD D,C	51
JNZ addr	JP NZ,addr	C2	MOV D,D	LD D,D	52
JP addr	JP P,addr	F2	MOV D,E	LD D,E	53
JPE addr	JP PE,addr	EA	MOV D,H	LD D,H	54
JPO addr	JP PO,addr	E2	MOV D,L	LD D,L	55
JZ addr	JP Z,addr	CA	MOV D,M	LD D,(HL)	56
			MOV D,A	LD D,A	57
LDA addr	LD A,(addr)	3A			
LDAX B	LD A,(BC)	0A	MOV E,B	LD E,B	58
LDAX D	LD A,(DE)	1A	MOV E,C	LD E,C	59
STA addr	LD (addr),A	32	MOV E,D	LD E,D	5A

8080 Mnemonic	Z80 Mnemonic	Hex Code	8080 Mnemonic	Z80 Mnemonic	Hex Code
MOV E,E	LD E,E	5B	LXI B,data16	LD BC,data16	01
MOV E,H	LD E,H	5C	LXI D,data16	LD DE,data16	11
MOV E,L	LD E,L	5D	LXI H,data16	LD HL,data16	21
MOV E,M	LD E,(HL)	5E	LXI SP,data16	LD SP,data16	31
MOV E,A	LD E,A	5F			
			NOP	NOP	00
MOV H,B	LD H,B	60			
MOV H,C	LD H,C	61	ORA A	OR A	B7
MOV H,D	LD H,D	62	ORA B	OR B	B0
MOV H,E	LD H,E	63	ORA C	OR C	B1
MOV H,H	LD H,H	64			
MOV H,L	LD H,L	65	ORA D	OR D	B2
MOV H,M	LD H,(HL)	66	ORA E	OR E	B3
MOV H,A	LD H,A	67	ORA H	OR H	B4
			ORA L	OR L	B5
MOV L,B	LD L,B	68	ORA M	OR (HL)	B6
MOV L,C	LD L,C	69	ORI data	OR data	F6
MOV L,D	LD L,D	6A	OUT port	OUT (port),A	D3
MOV L,E	LD L,E	6B			
MOV L,H	LD L,H	6C	POP B	POP BC	C1
MOV L,L	LD L,L	6D	POP D	POP DE	D1
MOV L,M	LD L,(HL)	6E	POP H	POP HL	E1
MOV L,A	LD L,A	6F	POP PSW	POP AF	F1
			PUSH B	PUSH BC	C5
MOV M,B	LD (HL),B	70	PUSH D	PUSH DE	D5
MOV M,C	LD (HL),C	71	PUSH H	PUSH HL	E5
MOV M,D	LD (HL),D	72	PUSH PSW	PUSH AF	F5
MOV M,E	LD (HL),E	73			
MOV M,H	LD (HL),H	74	RET	RET	C9
MOV M,L	LD (HL),L	75	RNZ	RET NZ	C0
MOV M,A	LD (HL),A	77	RZ	RET Z	C8
			RNC	RET NC	D0
MVI B,data	LD B,data	06	RC	RET C	D8
MVI C,data	LD C,data	0E	RPO	RET PO	E0
MVI D,data	LD D,data	16	RPE	RET PE	E8
MVI E,data	LD E,data	1E	RP	RET P	F0
MVI H,data	LD H,data	26	RM	RET M	F8
MVI L,data	LD L,data	2E			
MVI M,data	LD (HL),data	36	RLC	RLCA	07
MVI A,data	LD A,data	3E	RRC	RRCA	0F
			RAL	RLA	17
SPHL	LD SP,HL	F9	RAR	RRA	1F

8080 Mnemonic	Z80 Mnemonic	Hex Code	8080 Mnemonic	Z80 Mnemonic	Hex Code
RST 0	RST 0	C7	SUI	SUB data	D6
RST 1	RST 8	CF	SUB B	SUB B	90
RST 2	RST 10H	D7	SUB C	SUB C	91
RST 3	RST 18H	DF	SUB D	SUB D	92
RST 4	RST 20H	E7	SUB E	SUB E	93
RST 5	RST 28H	EF	SUB H	SUB H	94
RST 6	RST 30H	F7	SUB L	SUB L	95
RST 7	RST 38H	FF	SUB M	SUB (HL)	96
			SUB A	SUB A	97
SBI	SBC A,data	DE			
SBB B	SBC A,B	98	XRI	XOR data	EE
SBB C	SBC A,C	99	XRA B	XOR B	A8
SBB D	SBC A,D	9A	XRA C	XOR C	A9
SBB E	SBC A,E	9B	XRA D	XOR D	AA
SBB H	SBC A,H	9C	XRA E	XOR E	AB
SBB L	SBC A,L	9D	XRA H	XOR H	AC
SBB M	SBC A,(HL)	9E	XRA L	XOR L	AD
SBB A	SBC A,A	9F	XRA M	XOR (HL)	AE
			XRA A	XOR A	AF
STC	SCF	37			

APPENDIX F
Summary of CP/M

Abbreviations used in this summary are as follows:

d:	disk drive name, where d is A, B, C, D, . . . , P
[d:]	optional drive name; when omitted, the logged-in drive is understood
[p]	optional parameter, used with PIP
priname	primary name using 1 to 8 characters except < > . , ; : = ? * [ ]
[secname]	optional secondary name using 0 to 3 characters except < > . , ; : = ? * [ ]
filename	the combination [d:]priname[.secname]
ufn	unambiguous filename (e. g., B:GAME.COM, SORTPROG, DATA.1)
afn	ambiguous filename (e. g., TR??.*, B:*.*, T*.BAS, TREK.?)
afn/ufn	either afn or ufn
+/−	either + or −

Built-In Commands and Purpose: — *Examples:*

d:	Change logged-in drive to d:	A>B:
DIR	Display file directory of logged-in drive	A>DIR
DIR d:	Display directory of disk in drive d:	A>DIR B: A>DIR A:
DIR afn/ufn	Display directory of requested file(s)	A>DIR ORD.C A>DIR *.BAS
ERA afn/ufn	Erase filename(s) from directory	A>ERA TEST.ASM A>ERA B:*.BAK
REN ufn2=ufn1	Rename old ufn1 to new ufn2 on specified disk (ufn1 and ufn2 must be on the same disk)	A>REN PROG.C=XPER A>REN B:NEW=OLD
SAVE n ufn	Save n pages of the TPA as ufn (1 page = 256 bytes)	A>SAVE 4 DEMO.COM
TYPE ufn	Type the ASCII file ufn on the console	A>TYPE B:RALLY.C
USER n	Limit all files to user area n	A>USER 2

Transient Commands and Purpose: — *Example:*

Note: The following transient commands are stored as .COM files. If the file you want is on the logged-in disk, you just type its name (e. g., DDT). If it is on a different disk, type the disk drive designator in front of the name (e. g., B:DDT).

ASM priname	Load and run the assembler program ASM.COM. The assembler then loads the file 'priname.ASM' from the logged-in disk, assembles it, and stores the results back on the logged-in disk	A>ASM MYSTRING A>B:ASM MYSTRING

	as 'priname.HEX' and 'priname.PRN' (see Note 1 for more on ASM).	
ASM priname.d1d2d3	Same as above except 'priname.ASM' is loaded from disk d1, while 'priname.HEX' is stored on disk d2, and 'priname.PRN' is stored on disk d3. To skip generation of the HEX and/or PRN files, use Z for d2 and/or d3. To send 'priname.PRN' to the console, use X for d3.	A>ASM MYSTRING.BBB A>ASM MYSTRING.AZX A>ASM MYSTRING.AZZ
DDT	Load and run DDT.COM (the Dynamic Debugging Tool) into high memory (see Note 2 for further details).	A>DDT A>B:DDT
DDT ufn	Load and run DDT.COM as above, and then load the file ufn into the TPA where it can be worked on by DDT.	A>DDT BIOS.HEX A>DDT B:PONG.COM
DUMP ufn	Load and run DUMP.COM which then displays ufn on the console, 16 bytes per line in hex form.	A>DUMP COPY.COM
ED ufn	Load and run ED.COM for use in creating or editing ufn (see Note 3).	A>ED PROG.ASM
LOAD priname	Load and run LOAD.COM which then converts the file 'priname.HEX' into 'priname.COM' and saves it.	A>LOAD MYSTRING
MOVCPM N *	Load and run MOVCPM.COM which then creates an nK byte version of CP/M in the TPA ready for SAVE or SYSGEN.	A>MOVCPM 48 *
MOVCPM n	Same as above but the new CP/M is put into the top of memory and started running.	A>MOVCPM 32
MOVCPM * *	Same as MOVCPM n * except n is made the maximum possible value for the available memory.	A>MOVCPM * *
PIP dest = source[p]	Copies source to dest. (See Note 4 for further details.)	A>NEWFILE = B:OLDFILE[E]
STAT	Give the amount of unused space and R/W status for the logged-in disk.	A>STAT
STAT d:	Same as above for the disk in drive d:.	A>STAT B:
STAT ufn/afn	Give size of requested files in bytes, records, and extents.	A>STAT RPT.DOC A>STAT *.*
STAT ufn/afn $S	Same as above with added information on size.	A>STAT *.COM $S
STAT DEV:	Shows current logical-physical device assignments.	A>STAT DEV:

STAT [d:]DSK:	Shows statistics about the number of records, sectors and bytes on the disk in drive d:.	A>STAT DSK: A>STAT B:DSK:
STAT VAL:	Shows all valid logical-physical device assignments and STAT options.	A>STAT VAL:
STAT USR:	Shows current user number and other users with files on current disk.	A>STAT USR:
STAT ufn/afn $R/O	Places the file(s) in read-only status.	A>STAT *.BAS $R/O
STAT ufn/afn $R/W	Places the file(s) in read-write status.	A>STAT TEXT.BAS $R/W
STAT d: = R/O	Sets drive d: as R/O until next warm or cold boot.	A>STAT B: = R/O
STAT log: = phy:	Assigns the physical device driver 'phy:' to the logical device name 'log:'.	A>STAT CON: = TTY: A>STAT LST: = UL1:
STAT ufn/afn $SYS	Gives the file(s) system status so they don't show in the directory.	A>STAT *.C $SYS
STAT ufn/afn $DIR	Removes system status.	A>STAT SAFE.C $DIR
SYSGEN	Load and run SYSGEN.COM; used to copy or work on CP/M.	A>SYSGEN
SUBMIT priname	Load and run the program SUB-MIT.COM which then uses the file 'priname.SUB' to execute a batch of CP/M commands.	A>SUBMIT AUTO
SUBMIT priname p1 p2	Same as above except parameters p1, p2, etc. are first substituted in the file 'priname.SUB'.	A>SUBMIT AUTO F1 F2
XSUB	If this is placed as the first command in 'priname.SUB' above, the submit file can be used to supply responses normally required from the console during certain program runs (e. g., FORMAT).	See Section 5.4 for examples.

Note 1: More about ASM.

ASM works only on files named 'priname.ASM'. Each line of 'priname.ASM' should be of the form

[LABEL[:]]   INSTRUCTION   OPERAND(S)   ;Comments

Constants: B (Binary), Q or O (Octal), D or nothing (Decimal), H (Hexadecimal), 'abc' (ASCII).

Labels can have up to 16 characters except $ (which acts as a separator). Forbidden labels are 8080 mnemonics & register names, & ASM directives.

Instructions are Intel 8080 mnemonics or pseudo-ops called directives. Mnemonics are given in Appendices D and E. Directives used in ASM are ORG, END, EQU, SET, IF, ENDIF, DB, DW, DS

Operands consist of labels, constants, and register names. These can sometimes be arranged into expressions by using the operators +, −,

*, /, MOD, NOT, AND, OR, XOR, SHL, and SHR. When the symbol $ is used in the operand (but not as part of a label or constant) it refers to the address of the next instruction.

```
                   ;SILLY.ASM (EXAMPLE OF A 'PRINAME.ASM' FILE)
0100              START    ORG   0100H       ;HEX NUMBERS MUST START WITH
0005 =            BDOS     EQU   5H          ;A DIGIT BETWEEN 0 AND 9
0009 =            OUT$STR  EQU   9H          ;THE LABEL OUT$STR IS SAME AS OUTSTR
0100 0E09                  MVI   C,OUTSTR    ;C IS AN 8080 REGISTER NAME
0102 110B01                LXI   D,MSG       ;IN LXI AND SIMILAR 'X' INSTRUCTIONS
0105 CD0500                CALL  BDOS        ;D MEANS DE, B MEANS BC, H MEANS HL
0108 C30000                JMP   0           ;0 IS 0 DECIMAL WHICH = 0 HEX
010B 414E592053MSG         DB    'ANY STRING HERE',CR,LF,'$' ;THE $ IS FOR BDOS
011D 152D41      JUNK      DB    21,2*20+5,'A'  ;MORE DATA INITIALIZATION
0120              SPACE     DS    4              ;AND DATA STORAGE (NOT USED
0124 41420700FEWORDS       DW    'AB',BDOS+2,65534        ;IN THIS PROGRAM)
000D =            CR        EQU   0DH
000A =            LF        EQU   0AH
012A                       END
```

Precedence of Operators

* / MOD SHL SHR	**Note:**
− +	a MOD b = remainder from a/b
NOT	a SHL b = shift a left b bits
AND	a SHR b = shift a right b bits
OR XOR	Both shifts fill with zeros

Error Codes Produced by ASM

D   Data error (bad operand for DB or DW).

E   Expression error (incorrectly formed expression).

L   Label error (possibly duplicate label).

N   Not available (feature available in MAC but not in ASM).

O   Overflow (expression too complicated; simplify it).

P   Phase error (label value changed without use of SET).

R   Register error (register not legal for this operation).

U   Undefined label (label used in operand not found in label column).

V   Value error (operand is improperly formed).

Note 2: DDT has the following 13 subcommands. All arguments are in hex; square brackets indicate optional argument; addr1 means starting address, addr2 means end address; when addr1 is omitted, current address is used.

A addr1	Assemble 11 lines starting at addr1
D [addr1][,addr2]	Display memory in hex and ASCII from addr1 to addr2.
F addr1,addr2,const	Fill memory from addr1 to addr2 with a constant.
G [addr1][,bk1][,bk2]	Execute program from addr1 with breakpoints bk1 and bk2.
H xxxx,yyyy	Give hex sum and difference of xxxx and yyyy.

I filename	Insert filename in FCB at 05CH.
L [addr1][,addr2]	Dissassemble and list from addr1 to addr2.
M addr1,addr2,addr3	Move block addr1 . . . addr2 to addr3.
R [offset]	Read file specified by FCB into memory starting at normal address plus offset.
S addr1	Let user reset contents of memory starting at addr1.
T[n]	(Display CPU state and execute) n instructions.
U[n]	(Display CPU state) and execute n instructions.
X[r]	Display [register r of] CPU state.

Note 3: ED subcommands. In the following, n means a positive *or* negative integer, while m means a positive integer. In the F, S, and J commands, CONTROL-L should be used to represent the (CR)(LF) pair. Directions like right/left correspond to n being $+/-$.

mA	Append m lines to the buffer.
B	Move the CP to the beginning of the buffer.
−B	Move the CP to the end of the buffer.
nC	Move the CP n characters right/left.
nD	Delete n characters to the right/left, starting at the CP.
E	End the edit session, save and rename files.
mFtext(CR)	Find the mth occurrence of 'text' in the buffer and put the CP after it.
H	Do an E and restart ED with the same filename.
I . . . ˆZ (i . . . ˆZ)	Insert text into the buffer. That is, go into insert mode to insert text; leave by typing ˆZ.
mJtext1ˆZnew ˆZtext2(CR)	Juxtapose 'new'. That is, remove everything between 'text1' and 'text2' and insert 'new' in its place, leaving the CP at the end of the 'new'.
nK	Kill n lines after/before the current line plus characters after/before the CP.
nL	Move the CP to the beginning of a line n lines after/before the CP.
mMstring	Repeat a macro (string of commands) m times.
mNtext	Search the entire source file for the mth occurrence of 'text' appending new lines to the buffer as needed.
O	Scratch the results of editing and restart.
nP	Print (and move the CP) n pages; then print one more page (page = 23 lines); 0P means print 1 page.
Q	Quit edit, don't save any work.
Rfilename	Read a library file and insert a copy in the buffer after the CP.
mStext1 ˆZtext2(CR)	Substitute 'text2' for 'text1' up to m times, leaving the CP at the last occurrence of 'text2'.
nT	Type n lines after/before the CP.
U	Turn upper case translation on (−U to turn off).
V	Turn line numbering on (−V to turn off, 0V to print the number of bytes left in the buffer).
mW	Write m lines of the buffer to the temporary file and shift the remaining lines to the top of the buffer.
mX	Part of block move; transfers the next m lines from the buffer to a temporary file; you retrieve them with R; use nK to delete the old block; use 0X to retrieve *and* delete lines from the temporary file.

mZ	Sleep. Suspend the actions of ED for m time units.
n	Move the CP n lines down/up and type the last one.
m:	Go to line m.
m:string	Go to line m and do a string of commands.
string:m	Do a string of commands, from the CL up to line number m.
m::pstring	Do a string of commands, from line m to line p.

Note 4: More about PIP; the PIP parameters.

The command PIP dest=source[p] can be used with either destination or source replaced by (1) a filename, (2) a CP/M logical or physical device such as CON:, LST:, PUN:, RDR:, LPT:, UL1:, PTP:, UP1:, UP2:, PTR:, UR1:, UR2:, TTY:, CRT:, or UC1:, (3) a PIP special device such as PRN:, NUL:, EOF:, INP:, or OUT: or, (4) The name of a disk drive but only on one side of the =. Filenames must be ufn unless dest is a drive name. The optional parameter p may be any sequence of the following:

B	Block read.
Dn	Delete characters past column n.
E	Echo source data to console.
F	Filter out form feeds.
Gn	Get source data from user n.
H	Check that source data is in proper hex form.
I	Ignore hex files that begin at location 00 and turn on H parameter.
L	Translate upper case in source to lower case.
N	Add Line numbers to destination data.
O	Treat file as object (non-ASCII) data.
Pn	Start fresh page every n lines.
Qs^z	Quit copying after string s is found.
R	Read and copy system files *not* in directory.
Ss^z	Start copying from source at string s.
Tn	Expand tabs to n columns.
U	Translate lower case in source to upper case.
V	Verify that data written is same as data read.
W	Write on top of R/O files.
Z	Zero the parity (high order) bit.

Note 5: Control characters used by CP/M

^C	Warm boot.
^E	Start new line.
^H	Backspace and erase.
^I	Tab 8 columns.
^J	Line feed.
^L	Put <lf><cr> in ED source.
^M	Carriage return.
^P	Print toggle.
^R	Retype current line.
^S	Stop display on console.
^U	Delete line and start new line.
^X	Delete line and erase from screen.
^Z	End of string or end of console input.

APPENDIX G
References Cited in the Text

References and addresses cited in the text are listed here in order of reference number.

[1] Dwyer, T., and M. Critchfield, *BASIC and the Personal Computer*, Reading, MA: Addison-Wesley, 1978.

[2] Dwyer, T., and M. Critchfield, *Structured Program Design with TRS-80 BASIC*, New York: McGraw-Hill, 1984.

[3] Myers, R., *Microcomputer Graphics*, Reading, MA: Addison-Wesley, 1982.

[4] Dwyer, T., and M. Critchfield, *A Bit of BASIC*, Reading, MA: Addison-Wesley, 1980.

[5] Weller, W., *Practical Microcomputer Programming: The Intel 8080*, Chicago: Northern Technology Books, 1976.

[6] Miller, A., *8080/Z80 Assembly Language*, New York: John Wiley & Sons, 1981.

[7] *Dr. Dobb's Journal*, 1263 El Camino Real, Menlo Park, CA 94025.

[8] *CPMUG/Lifelines*, 1651 Third Ave., New York 10028

[9] SIG/M, Box 97, Iselin, NJ 08830.

[10] BDS C User's Group, Box 287, Yates Center, KS 66783.

[11] *Microsystems*, Box 1192, Mountainside, NJ 07092.

[12] Mark of the Unicorn, P.O. Box 423, Arlington, MA 02174.

[13] Knuth, D., *The Art of Computer Programming, Vol. 3*, Reading, MA: Addison-Wesley, 1973.

[14] Press, Larry, *Low-Cost Word Processing*, Reading, MA: Addison-Wesley, 1983.

[15] *Interface Age*, 16704 Marquardt Ave., Cerritos, CA 90701.

[16] *Byte*, 70 Main St., Peterborough, NH 03458.

[17] *Kilobaud Microcomputing*, 80 Pine St., Peterborough, NH 03458.

[18] Supersoft, P.O. Box 1628, Champaign, IL 61820.

[19] MicroPro International, 33 San Pablo Avenue, San Rafael, CA 94903.

[20] BD Software, P.O. Box 9, Brighton, MA 02135.

[21] Kernighan and Ritchie, *The C Programming Language*, Prentice-Hall, 1978.

[22] Solo 4, 312 Alumni, Pittsburgh, PA 15260.

[23] Intelligent Systems Corp., Intecolor Drive, 225 Technology Park/Atlanta, Norcross, GA 30092.

[24] Dwyer, T., *C and the Personal Computer*, Reading, MA: Addison-Wesley, 1985.

[25] Yates, *A Business Guide to UNIX*, Reading, MA: Addison-Wesley, 1983.

[26] Yates and Thomas, *Programmer's Guide to UNIX*, Reading, MA: Addison-Wesley, 1983.

[27] Sargent and Shoemaker, *Interfacing Microcomputers to the Real World*, Reading, MA: Addison-Wesley, 1982.

[28] Peachtree Software, 3445 Peachtree Road N. E., Atlanta, GA 30326.

[29] Ashton-Tate, 10150 West Jefferson Blvd., Culver City, CA 90230.

[30] Sorcim Corporation, 2310 Lundy Avenue, San Jose, CA 95131.

[31] Critchfield, M., and T. Dwyer, *A Pocket Guide to Microsoft BASIC*, Reading, MA: Addison-Wesley, 1983.

[32] Dwyer, T., and M. Critchfield, *A Pocket Guide to CP/M*, Reading, MA: Addison-Wesley, 1983.

[33] Digital Research Inc., P.O. Box 579, Pacific Grove, CA 93950.

[34] Cortesi, D., *Utilities for CP/M-80*, Reston, VA: Reston Publishing, 1983.

[35] Mead, C., and L. Conway, *Introduction to VLSI Systems*, Reading, MA: Addison-Wesley, 1980.

[36] Date, Chris, *A User's Guide to Database Systems*, Reading, MA: Addison-Wesley, 1983.

[37] Sargent, M., and R. Shoemaker, *Interfacing Microcomputers to the Real World*, Reading, MA: Addison-Wesley, 1981.

[38] OASIS is distributed by Phase One Systems, 7700 Edgewater Drive, Oakland, CA 94621.

[39] TURBODOS is distributed by MuSys Corp., 1752 Langley, Irvine, CA 92714.

Index

Other books in the Microcomputer Books Series, available from your local computer store or bookstore. For more information write:

General Books Division
Addison-Wesley Publishing Company, Inc.
Reading, Massachusetts 01867
(617) 944-3700